WILHELMUS à BRAKEL, Th. F.
(1635-1711)
Minister of the Gospel in Rotterdam

THE CHRISTIAN'S REASONABLE SERVICE

in which Divine Truths concerning the

COVENANT OF GRACE

are Expounded, Defended against Opposing Parties,
and their Practice Advocated

as well as

The Administration of this Covenant in the Old and New Testaments

by

WILHELMUS à BRAKEL, Th.F.
Minister of the Gospel in Rotterdam

Volume One

Translated by Bartel Elshout
Edited by Joel R. Beeke

REFORMATION HERITAGE BOOKS
Grand Rapids, Michigan

Reformation Heritage Books
2919 Leonard St., NE
Grand Rapids, MI 49525
616-977-0599/Fax 616-977-0889/e-mail jrbeeke@aol.com
website: www.heritagebooks.org

This translation is based on the
third edition of the original Dutch work entitled
Redelijke Godsdienst
published by D. Bolle, Rotterdam, The Netherlands.

The Christian's Reasonable Service, Volume 1
ISBN 1-877611-56-5

Copyright © 1992

First printing 1992
Second printing 1995
Third printing 1999

ΛΟΓΙΚΗ ΛΑΤΡΕΙΑ

DAT IS

REDELIJKE GODSDIENST

IN WELKEN DE GODDELIJKE WAARHEDEN VAN HET

GENADE-VERBOND

WORDEN VERKLAARD, TEGEN PARTIJEN BESCHERMD EN TOT
BEOEFENING AANGEDRONGEN,

ALSMEDE

DE BEDEELING DES VERBONDS IN HET O. EN N. T.

EN

DE ONTMOETING DER KERK IN HET N. T.

VERTOOND IN EENE VERKLARING VAN DE

OPENBARINGEN VAN JOHANNES

DOOR

W. à BRAKEL Th. F.,

IN LEVEN BEDIENAAR DES GODDELIJKEN WOORDS TE ROTTERDAM.

———————

IN DE TEGENWOORDIGE SPELLING,

ONVERANDERD NAAR DE BESTE UITGAVE.

DERDE DRUK

EERSTE DEEL.

ROTTERDAM — D. BOLLE

Title page from the Third Edition published in Rotterdam, The Netherlands.

The Christian's Reasonable Service
General Contents

VOLUME ONE

VOLUME FOUR

Soteriology: *The Doctrine of Salvation* (cont.)

Contents – Volume One

THE CHRISTIAN'S REASONABLE SERVICE

Theology: *The Doctrine of God*

Anthropology: The Doctrine of Man

Christology: *The Doctrine of Christ*

Preface

Those acquainted with Dutch Reformed orthodoxy will know that the name of Wilhelmus à Brakel is among the most venerated of the theologians representing the Dutch Second Reformation (*Nadere Reformatie*) period which is similar to and coincides with English Puritanism. This veneration is largely due to the profound influence of his magnum opus *De Redelijke Godsdienst*, now being made available in English for the first time as *The Christian's Reasonable Service*.

The importance of this work was recognized soon after its publication in 1700. Even though à Brakel had great difficulty finding a publisher for the initial edition (finally finding a Roman Catholic publisher!) his work was in demand within a very short time. New and improved editions soon followed, twenty in the eighteenth century alone. The respect for à Brakel was such that he was commonly referred to as "Father Brakel," a title not only expressive of high esteem but also of the authority he commanded and the influence he exerted. He is still known today in the Netherlands by this honorary title. It ought therefore to be self-evident that Father Brakel is considered one of the fathers of the Reformed tradition to be found in present day orthodox Reformed circles in the Netherlands.

One of à Brakel's contemporaries, Abraham Hellenbroek, who spoke of his friend as being a man of tender and intimate piety,[1] recognized the importance of this work when he stated in almost prophetical terms that this work was so valuable that it would transcend the passage of time.[2] We trust that the very fact that this work is now being made available to the English-speaking world will assist in validating these words.

To provide one practical illustration of the influence of this work in the Netherlands which now spans nearly three centuries, we wish to relate an incident from the life of the Rev. G. H. Kersten, the founder of the denomination (the *Gereformeerde Gemeenten* — the Netherlands Reformed Congregations) which has initiated and undertaken the translation and publication of this classic. When Rev. Kersten was approximately twelve years old, his parents discovered that their young son, in whose heart the Lord had begun a saving work, was reading regularly far beyond midnight. In order to keep himself awake, he placed his feet in a basin filled with cold water. What book was it that so captivated the mind and heart of this young seeker after God? à Brakel's *Redelijke Godsdienst.* When asked by his parents why he sacrificed his sleep to read this weighty book which was well beyond the level of twelve-year-olds, he responded, "I must know how the Lord converts His people." The reading of these volumes clearly placed a stamp upon the writings and entire ministry of Rev. Kersten.

Why is it that à Brakel's work is one of the true classics of the Dutch Second Reformation? Why has this work been so influential? Why do we trust that *The Christian's Reasonable Service* will be a valuable addition to the rich heritage of post-Reformation orthodoxy?

The uniqueness of à Brakel's work lies in the fact that it is more than a systematic theology. His selection of the title is already an indication that it was not merely his intention to present a systematic explanation of Christian dogma to the public. In selecting the words of Romans 12:1 as the basis for his title, à Brakel not only wished to indicate that it is an entirely reasonable matter for man to serve His Creator who has so graciously revealed Himself in His Son Jesus Christ by means of His Word, but he primarily wished to convey that God demands from man that he serve Him in spirit and in truth, doing so in an intelligent, reasonable, and godly manner.[3]

This brings us at once to the heart of the matter. à Brakel wrote this work for church members — not for theologians, though it was his wish that they benefit from it as well. This explains why this work is permeated with practical application of the doctrines he so thoroughly explains. à Brakel's intent in writing is inescapable: He intensely wished that the truths expounded may become an experiential reality in the hearts of those who read. In a masterful way he establishes the crucial relationship between objective truth and the subjective experience of that truth. He first establishes a solid biblical foundation for each doctrine with which he deals, by quoting profusely from the Scriptures. You will find his selection of quotes to be a most impressive feature of this work, proving he had a profound grasp of the Scriptures and their comprehensive context. This scripturalness is rationally reenforced by his frequent resorting to the scholastic method to validate his positions.

As a man taught of God, he very ably defined and described Christian experience in biblical terms. The undeniably mystical flavor of this work represents biblical mysticism at its best — a Spirit-wrought mysticism that fully harmonizes with the Spirit-inspired Scriptures. This explains at once why Jesus Christ truly has the preeminence in this work. It is the Logos, Jesus Christ, who is the very marrow of God's Word and every doctrine contained in it. It is therefore self-evident that in the subjective experience of this Word, Jesus Christ also has the preeminence. No wonder then that this work brims with references to Him whom the Father has given a name above every name. For à Brakel the name of Jesus is sweeter than honey; you can almost sense the inner stirrings of His soul when He exalts Jesus as the Father's unspeakable gift to fallen sons and daughters of Adam.

These rich experiential applications found at the conclusion of each doctrinal chapter in the first two volumes make this work invaluable and pastoral. à Brakel was first and foremost a pastor who made his astute theological acumen entirely subservient to the glory of God and the spiritual welfare of His church. In writing this work, à Brakel practiced what he advised all ministers to do. In chapter 28 he writes: "He [the minister] ought to use all his scholarship to formulate the matters to be presented, in order that he might express them in the clearest and most powerful manner. While using his scholarship, however, he must conceal his scholarship in the pulpit." When necessary, however, he will cause his scholarship to bear on an argument, thereby proving himself to be a theologian par excellence.

In reading this work, one cannot but be struck by its kinship with English Puritan literature. This is particularly evident in the third and fourth volumes which are devoted almost entirely to the life of sanctification. As is true for the Puritans, à Brakel was a most able physician of souls. How ably he proves himself to be a divine intimately acquainted with spiritual life and all its vicissitudes! The chapters pertaining to sanctification particularly validate Hellenbroek's observation that à Brakel was a man of tender, intimate piety. Like the Puritans, he makes it unmistakably clear that godliness is a scriptural vindication that we have experienced the truth in our souls. Inward experience manifests itself outwardly in true piety. à Brakel does not leave us in the dark as to what he understands the Christian life to be. We believe it will be difficult to find a work in English devotional literature which spells out the nature of true holiness as specifically and meticulously as à Brakel does.

The obvious similarity between à Brakel's writings, which represent the cream of Dutch Second Reformation literature, and Puritan literature is highly significant. It proves that the Puritans and the Dutch Second Reformation divines (sometimes referred to as the Dutch Puritans) were essentially cut from the same cloth. It will be difficult to find essential differences in Christian experience between à Brakel and such English Puritans as John Owen, Thomas Goodwin, and John Bunyan. The divines of the Dutch Second Reformation have translated literally hundreds of English Puritans into Dutch, recommending them warmly to their congregations. The Dutch Second Reformation was greatly indebted to English Puritanism for a wealth of sound experiential material. On the other hand, few writings of Dutch Second Reformation divines were translated into English. The translation of à Brakel's *The Christian's Reasonable Service* is an initial attempt to redress an imbalance of several centuries.

To acquaint the English reader somewhat with à Brakel's life and times, as well as provide him with an overview of the Dutch Second Reformation, we have included the following in this volume:

(1) A translation of the applicable portion of *Theodorus à Brakel, Wilhelmus à Brakel, en Sara Nevius* (Houten: Den Hertog, 1988), authored by Dr. W. Fieret and A. Ros. Dr. Fieret is the author of the Wilhelmus à Brakel biography;

(2) A slightly revised appendix to *Assurance of Faith: Calvin, English Puritanism, and the Dutch Second Reformation,* by Joel R. Beeke (New York: Peter Lang, 1991), entitled: *The Dutch Second Reformation (De Nadere Reformatie).*

Hopefully, the translation of à Brakel's work in four volumes (volumes 2, 3, and 4 should be available within a year, D.V.) will initiate in some small measure the merger of the rich heritages of the two premier experiential movements of the post-Reformation period: English Puritanism and the Dutch Second Reformation. Orthodox Reformed circles in the Netherlands have enjoyed this privilege already for centuries and have witnessed divine approbation upon these writings.

May God grant that the publication of this work will enhance the ongoing proliferation of Reformed experiential writings throughout the world. May this phenomenon prove to be preliminary to a Spirit-worked revival of lukewarm, famished Christianity. Then the vital Christianity à Brakel promotes throughout this work will again flourish and adorn the church of Jesus Christ. May David's cry therefore be ours, "O God, Thou art my God; early will I seek Thee: my soul thirsteth for Thee, my flesh longeth for Thee in a dry and thirsty land, where no water is; to see Thy power and Thy glory, so as I have seen Thee in the sanctuary" (Psa. 63:1-2). To that end may we pray without ceasing to the God of the covenant of grace — a covenant that has such a central place in this work —

crying out with the bride, "Awake, O north wind; and come, thou south; blow upon my garden, that the spices thereof may flow out. Let my Beloved come into His garden, and eat His pleasant fruits" (Song of Sol. 4:16).

—Joel R. Beeke
Bartel Elshout

---

[1]J. van Genderen, *De Nadere Reformatie: Beschrijving van haar voornaamste vertegen-woordigers* ('s Gravenhage: Boekencentrum, 1986), p. 165.

[2]Ibid., p. 166.

[3]Ibid., pp. 170-171.

Acknowledgments

We are indebted to the following persons for rendering us valuable assistance in preparing this translation for print:

Garret J. Moerdyk, elder of the Netherlands Reformed Congregation of Kalamazoo, Michigan. Mr. Moerdyk, who is proficient in both Dutch and English, carefully compared the entire translation with the original and forwarded numerous valuable suggestions.

John C. Wesdyk, member of the Ebenezer Netherlands Reformed Congregation of Franklin Lakes, New Jersey. Mr. Wesdyk's thorough grasp of English style and grammar uniquely qualified him for a thorough proofreading of the manuscript. Due to his probing and meticulous analysis of every sentence and paragraph, he has made a significant contribution to the linguistic quality of this translation.

Rev. Cornelis Vogelaar, pastor of the Ebenezer Netherlands Reformed Congregation of Franklin Lakes, New Jersey. Rev. Vogelaar's knowledge of seventeenth century Dutch proved to be most helpful in arriving at the correct translation of difficult passages and phrases.

Nicholas L. Greendyk, elder of the Ebenezer Netherlands Reformed Congregation of Franklin Lakes, New Jersey. Mr. Greendyk, who is well-versed in the writings of English divines and has an extensive knowledge of Reformed doctrine, carefully read the entire translation to assure doctrinal and semantic accuracy.

Dr. Joel R. Beeke, pastor of the First Netherlands Reformed Congregation of Grand Rapids, Michigan, and *Mrs. Laurena Quist,* his personal secretary and member of the same congregation. After implementation of the suggestions and/or corrections forwarded by all individuals involved, both Dr. Beeke and Mrs. Quist very ably proofread the manuscript prior to being typeset.

Dr. Willem Fieret and *Den Hertog, B.V., Publishers,* for their permission to translate and include Dr. Fieret's biography of à Brakel in this work.

Gary and *Linda den Hollander,* the typesetters of these volumes and members of the Ebenezer Netherlands Reformed Congregation of Franklin Lakes, New Jersey. Mr. den Hollander, in assisting his wife in her typesetting duties, did a final and thorough proofreading of the manuscript in type-set form.

William D. Berkenbush, member of the Ebenezer Netherlands Reformed Congregation of Franklin Lakes, New Jersey. Mr. Berkenbush, who frequently contributes his time and talent to NRC publications, provided the excellent negatives for the photography found in this work.

Robert Fletcher and *Samuel Van Grouw, Jr.,* members of the Ebenezer Netherlands Reformed Congregation of Franklin Lakes, New Jersey. Mr. Fletcher did the artistic design work, and Mr. Van Grouw did the final layout and design of the cover.

I assume full responsibility for any remaining improprieties in this translation.

Among those who have contributed directly or indirectly to the translation and publication of this work, also my dear wife, Joan, deserves special mention. In having been directed providentially to do the translation of this work, it has been confirmed for us in a most personal way that God's ways are higher than our ways and His thoughts than our thoughts. As my faithful helpmeet, her support behind the scenes has been invaluable in my pursuance of this task.

Furthermore, I wish to pay tribute to my beloved natural and spiritual father, the late Rev. Arie Elshout, pastor of the Netherlands Reformed Congregations from 1955-1991 — seven years in the United States and twenty-nine in the Netherlands. At the age of eighteen, shortly after the Lord had begun His saving work in him, he received, upon personal request, the *Redelijke Godsdienst* as a birthday present from his parents. He immediately began to read these volumes with great diligence — the first religious works he had ever read. à Brakel's work had a profound and lifelong influence upon him and clearly was used by the Lord to mold him for the ministry to which He would call him. He rejoiced in the fact that the Lord led me to translate this unique work into English. He, together with my beloved mother, often encouraged me to persevere in this task, being convinced that the Lord would also cause the English version of this work to bear fruit — as has abundantly been true in the Netherlands.

Finally, it is my foremost desire to acknowledge the Lord humbly for having enabled me to complete this rewarding and edifying task. I have truly experienced that the Lord makes His strength perfect in weakness. To Him alone be all the glory for what has been accomplished.

May it please the Lord, who sovereignly has caused this valuable work to become available to the English-speaking world, to bless the writings of this beloved servant of God. May this work also contribute to stimulate the growing interest in the writings of the divines of the *Nadere Reformatie* (the Second Reformation) as well as an ever-deepening appreciation for the rich Puritan heritage the Lord has preserved for us.

Above all, may God's kingdom come — also as a result of this work. If it may please the Lord Jesus Christ to use this work to build up His people in their most holy faith and add fallen sinners as jewels to His mediatorial crown, my labors will have been richly rewarded and the deep wish of "Father Brakel" will have been fulfilled — a wish expressed in his preface: "May the almighty and good God, who repeatedly encouraged me when I had intentions of discontinuing this task and who is the Author of whatever good is to be found in this work, pour out His Holy Spirit upon all who will either read or hear this book read."

The Translator

Second Printing

We are grateful that a second printing is being called for of volume 1 of Wilhelmus à Brakel's classic, *The Christian's Reasonable Service,* and pray that it may continue to be a blessing for many. This printing is identical to the first with the exception of the correction of some Hebrew and Greek spellings and transliterations, and the correction of a few typographical errors, for which we thank Rev. Charles Krahe and Raymond Van Grouw respectively.

The entire four-volume set of à Brakel's *The Christian's Reasonable Service* is now available; volume 4 contains detailed indexes.

— BE/JRB

August 1995

Wilhelmus à Brakel

- Youth and Education
- Views Concerning the Office
  of the Ministry
- Sermons
- Pastorates in Friesland
- Pastorate in Rotterdam

Wilhelmus à Brakel

by Dr. W. Fieret[1]

His Youth and Education

Wilhelmus à Brakel was born on January 2, 1635, in Leeuwarden, the Netherlands. He was the only son born to Theodorus à Brakel and Margaretha Homma — a marriage blessed with six children.

To the great joy, wonder, and gratitude of both parents, it became evident at a very early age that the fear of the Lord was to be found in the young Wilhelmus. At a later date he was at times compared

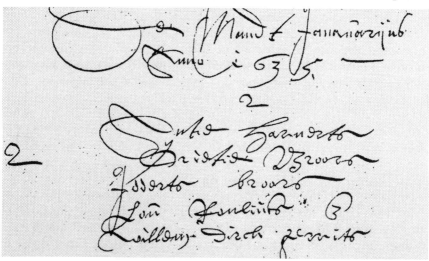

An excerpt from the baptismal records of the congregation of Leeuwarden. The last name is: *Willem Dick Gerrits*. This baptismal record is attributed to Wilhelmus à Brakel.

---

[1] Dr. Fieret teaches history and sociology at the Van Lodenstein College in Amersfoort, the Netherlands — a school of orthodox Reformed persuasion. He received his doctorate in history from the Rijksuniversiteit (State University) of Utrecht, the Netherlands. He is a professing member of the *Oud Gereformeerde Gemeente* (Old Reformed Congregation) of Woudenberg, the Netherlands.

with Obadiah who, by grace, was able and privileged to say, "I thy servant fear the LORD from my youth." Later in his life à Brakel said he knew of no change in his life. From his earliest years he remembers having had a great love for His Savior Jesus Christ.

A Christmas sermon by his father, Theodorus à Brakel, made a deep impression upon the young Wilhelmus. The commemoration of the fact that Jesus came into the world to save sinners had so affected him that he asked more than once, "Father, when will it be Christmas again?"

He spoke to his mother about spiritual life on numerous occasions. Once it happened that he asked her a very profound question about the life of grace. She did not respond to that question, but replied: "Child, that is beyond your understanding." This reaction caused him to become somewhat inhibited; no longer did he have the courage to speak as freely about deep spiritual matters. This was no indication, however, that his mother was indifferent toward her child. On the contrary, more than once she would tell him that she prayed so intensely for him that she would forget herself.

As Monica, the mother of Augustine, prayed incessantly for the salvation of her son, so did Margaretha Homma. She would earnestly warn him, "Child, how much you will have to answer for if you do not fear God!" In spite of his longing for Christmas and his profound questions which gave evidence of spiritual life, she continued to admonish her son in love. She wanted to impress deeply upon him what it means to "lose life in order to find life," as well as the necessity of the mortification of the old man and the quickening of the new man.

Following his childhood, Wilhelmus attended the Latin school in Leeuwarden. At that time his father pastored in the village of Beers, southwest of Leeuwarden. Distance made it impossible to travel back and forth each day. Wilhelmus would come home on Saturday and return to school on Monday. His father would accompany him for some distance. As long as possible he would watch his son in the distance while quietly beseeching the Lord to protect him. This concern and dependency upon God made such a deep impression upon Wilhelmus that he would frequently be in prayer himself as he continued his walk to Leeuwarden.

At the age of nineteen, in 1654, Wilhelmus matriculated at the academy of Franeker. His education was thorough and comprehensive. He studied languages, philosophy, history, was in some measure acquainted with the study of medicine, and naturally studied his main subject, theology. Later he would write that a minister needs a thorough education. Through philosophy and natural scholarship the intellect and ability to think need to be exercised.

Upon completion of his education the twenty-four-year-old à Brakel

The Academy of Franeker where Wilhelmus studied theology from 1654-1659.

was examined by Classis Leeuwarden (the equivalent of a presbytery). This examination included the preaching of a trial sermon. He spoke on Revelation 21:11: "Having the glory of God: and her light was like unto a stone most precious, even like a jasper stone, clear as crystal." The measure of satisfaction with the sermon as well as the answers given (which evidenced thorough study) were such that the brothers decided unanimously to admit him to the sacred ministry.

He was promoted to be a candidate for the ministry with a "general commission"; in addition to which, as was common in Friesland, he was also authorized to administer the sacraments. This general commission subsequently rendered him much freedom and joy in the exercise of this honorable office. Since this commission was not limited to the congregation to which he was united as minister, he deemed himself to be a sent servant wherever he came.

Views Concerning the Office of the Ministry

Having received his credentials as a candidate for the ministry, Wilhelmus à Brakel was privileged to labor in the Lord's vineyard. He considered his office to be very weighty, for a minister deals with souls created for eternity. He therefore wrote about the office of the ministry with great earnestness and urgency. In his view there is not a "more abominable man than an unregenerate minister, who uses the holy things of God to his own advantage." He sharply condemned those ministers who performed their task only to gain honor and wealth. They would have been much happier had they become shoemakers.

He deemed the knowledge of Greek and Hebrew to be indispensable for every minister since the Bible was originally written in those languages. He spoke of a "wretched congregation" if the minister of that congregation would be satisfied with a limited knowledge of theology — a knowledge limited to what had been committed to memory. The searching of the Scriptures is a necessity: the interrelatedness of passages of Scripture needs to be searched out — such as prophecies and their fulfilment. In short, a minister must daily, while prayerfully looking unto the Lord, engage himself in the study of His Word, as he is the mouth of the Lord to the congregation.

"All this knowledge would be insufficient for a minister, however — à Brakel even used the phrase 'of no avail' — if he himself has neither been illuminated nor converted by the Holy Spirit, for the truths which he reads in God's Word must be found in his own heart. He must know by personal experience what conversion, prayer, believing in Christ, wrestlings of faith, the subtle delusions and assaults of Satan, darkness, the sealing work of the Spirit, self-denial, and mortification of sin, etc., are." In addition to these two important prerequisites — regeneration and learning — a minister ought to be dignified, lest anyone should despise the minister of the Word of God. Such dignity should, however, not degenerate into affectation, pretending to be different from what he really is, doing so solely to make an impression upon men. As examples of such affectation à Brakel mentions the manner in which some people would wear their hat, hold their heads, or walk. "How abominable is such ludicrous affectation, which has self-aggrandizement as its mother!"

Other traits of a good minister, according to à Brakel, are love toward Christ, His cause, and His sheep; denial of one's own honor and possessions — yes, even one's own life; and being diligent and exemplary in all things. If a called servant possessed these "prerequisite qualities," he was permitted to commence his ministry.

à Brakel mentions congregational prayer before God as being the first aspect of a minister's task; while praying he is the mouth of the congregation toward God. He ought to pray with great reverence, realizing that he is addressing the eminent majesty of

God Himself. This obligation to be reverent engenders modesty and orderliness in the manner in which he expresses himself. "It is dreadful to babble some words in an unintelligible fashion, jumping from one matter to the next, and to speak on, without any rhyme or reason." Then the congregation would benefit much more if the minister were to use a form prayer.

Rev. à Brakel did not disapprove at all of a minister quietly contemplating what he would mention in his prayer and lay before the Lord. It could even be beneficial to make some notations for this purpose, as long as one would not always avail himself of them, as this would result in spiritless intercession, since in true prayer the Holy Spirit prays for us with groanings which cannot be uttered.

If a minister is not very healthy, he should not dwell upon his weakness in public prayer before the congregation. Often a minister will elaborate upon his weakness when he did not fare too well during the sermon — for instance, due to lack of study or to solicit admiration for doing so well in view of being so weak. à Brakel evidently had a great measure of common sense.

à Brakel mentions preaching as being the second duty, calling it "a great work." The realization that he is God's ambassador who speaks on God's behalf ought to fill the minister with fear and trembling. The Lord will take careful note of how a minister proclaims His Word. Furthermore, preaching is the means which God uses to translate souls from darkness into light — from the domain of the prince of darkness into the kingdom of Jesus Christ. It is therefore of the greatest importance how a minister explains the Word of God. A continual prayer for a sanctified heart and the presence of the Lord Himself will then precede every sermon. For indeed, the object of every sermon must be the honor of God and the welfare of the souls entrusted to him.

A good minister will not flaunt his scholarship on the pulpit, for then he is seeking to honor himself. Even if someone can preach as an angel, it is nothing more than hypocrisy if personal honor is the objective. Such preaching seeks to solicit the praise of men. Such a minister will be very satisfied if there are many people who appear to be emotionally moved. He prefers to be in the company of those who praise and even idolize him. People ought to be well aware of the fact, however, that the devil can also transform himself into an angel of light. The servants of such angels of light can indeed put on the mantle of either Elijah or John the Baptist, but their exterior deportment will be fundamentally different from their heart.

à Brakel mentions catechizing as being the third task. A minister

Rev. à Brakel regularly conducted religious exercises or public catechism classes pertaining to practical godliness. In this illustration it is to be observed that the minister did not preach during such an exercise, but rather conversed with those present.

ought to give much attention to this task. He deemed it to be the best means to instill the fundamentals of truth and godliness.

Rev. à Brakel distinguished between four types of catechism:

(1) There must be instruction for children. They are baptized and therefore belong to the church. They are, "in a manner agreeable to their level of comprehension," to be instructed in the doctrines of Christ.

(2) There must be instruction for adults who have indicated that they wish to partake of the Lord's Supper. This initial instruction is insufficient for the partaking of this sacrament. For indeed, such must make confession of their faith and give an account of the hope that is in them. This instruction and examination must be very thorough, for — thus warns à Brakel — the well-being of the church is contingent upon granting permission to partake of the Lord's Supper.

(3) There must be instruction for younger and older men who are called upon to defend the truth against assaults from without and within. From this third group some could be trained to function as "assistants" to visit the sick and read in church. The most capable among them could be trained for the ministry.

(4) The subject for the final catechism class was the practice of godliness. Among the subjects which were dealt with, à Brakel mentions the following: analysis of God's dealings with souls in conversion; discussion of the present state of the soul; and giving guidance so that believers may steadfastly walk upon the way of godliness. This type of catechism does not so much consist in an address by the minister, as in having open discussions by means of questions and answers.

All these catechetical labors ought to be performed painstakingly and zealously. à Brakel was well aware of this. He wrote: "I cannot see how a minister who does not engage in the task of catechizing can live and die with a good conscience."

The fourth aspect of the work of a minister consists in the visitation of the members of the congregation. Family visitation must not only be conducted prior to the administration of the Lord's Supper, but the minister ought to visit members of his congregation on a daily basis. These visits, according to à Brakel, require thorough preparation. The minister must be fully aware for what reason he makes the visit, as this will keep him from engaging in frivolous and "worldly" conversation. Fundamental matters concerning eternity ought to be discussed.

Undoubtedly the issue of family worship will then have been raised to ascertain whether this was indeed practiced — as ought to be the case in every Christian family. Twice a day — morning and evening, and if possible also at noon — the father as head of the family ought to read a chapter from the Bible, explain what has been read, provide instruction for the children and the servants, and then conclude this exercise with the singing of a psalm and by offering prayer. Such exercises would bear much fruit: "The Lord will then bless the home; the children and the servants will learn to fear the Lord and thus attain salvation; it will beget mutual love and respect; and this will cause everyone to refrain from sinning. People will thus exemplify godliness to each other and emulate it."

If the father was absent for some reason, or if he was incapable of either reading or explaining, it would be the mother's obligation to assume this task. The actual goal which à Brakel pursued, and with him all the representatives of the Dutch Second Reformation, was that the family be a small church. Family visitations were therefore highly important, for ministers were obligated to stimulate people to an understanding of what their task consists.

Every member, whether poor or rich, had to be visited. It would often happen that a minister would tarry long in the residences of the rich where a glass of wine would be offered to him. Consequently, there would hardly be any time left for others. à Brakel lamented, "How wretched are such ministers and how wretched are family visitations which are thus conducted!"

The minister ought to administer the sacraments with reverence for the Lord, doing so as an ambassador of Christ. By means of this sacred administration he seals the promise of the gospel: he who believes in the Son has eternal life. This fifth aspect of the ministry would be "a dreadful desecration of the holy things" if it were to be performed in a careless manner.

à Brakel identified the use of the keys of the Kingdom of Heaven as the last aspect of the work of a minister. This task is performed while delivering the sermon, whereby the forgiveness of sins by virtue of the merits of Christ is proclaimed to believers, whereas unbelievers are admonished to repent since they continue to live under the wrath of God. Eternal damnation is imminent for them if they remain unconverted. With care and a sense of responsibility the minister ought to make use of the authority entrusted to him. The use of the second key, Christian discipline, is not the jurisdiction of the minister alone, but rests with the entire consistory (i.e. session).

In order to stimulate himself and others, à Brakel concludes his description of the office of the ministry with a word of warning concerning the account that will once have to be given before God. The Lord will ask how the congregation has been dealt with: "How

A portrayal of a church service in the seventeenth century.

did you deal with souls? Are you to be blamed for any of them going lost? Did you tenderly give attention to My lambs and sucklings? Or did you unjustly grieve them, slay them, and take their veil away from them? Where are the souls which by means of your service have been converted, comforted, and built up?"

à Brakel writes that for many ministers this will be a grievous examination. They will wish to have never occupied that office — yes, never to have been born. How dreadful it will be if you must perish due to your own sin and guilt! It will be a dreadful burden to hear the accusations of misled and neglected souls: "You knew very well that I was ignorant and lived in sin. If you had looked after me, had warned and rebuked me, and instructed and directed me in the way of salvation, I would have been saved. Look, however, you unfaithful minister, you unfaithful elder — I am now going lost! Let God require my blood from your hand, and deal with you as a wicked and lazy servant."

On the other hand, many faithful ministers will also be found. The Lord will bring their work, prayers, comforts, and admonitions to the foreground and say to them, "Well done, thou good and faithful servant: thou hast been faithful over a few things, I will make thee ruler over many things: enter thou into the joy of thy Lord."

Someone who writes so solemnly about the ministerial office which he himself held, will have engaged himself in this task with all his energy — in spite of the realization of imperfection and sinfulness. This was indeed true for Wilhelmus à Brakel. Also in his *magnum opus, De Redelijke Godsdienst [The Christian's Reasonable Service]* — which occasionally is referred to as the most popular Dutch dogmatics of the eighteenth century — he continually pointed to the one thing needful, and instructed believers. In his exposition of doctrinal tenets he did not restrict himself to a dry and logical discourse.

For example, when dealing with the prophetical office of Christ, after a clear explanation of what this office entails, he addresses the unconverted as follows: "You who are unconverted, reflect upon your case for a moment! How long has this Prophet already been engaged in instructing you? How many servants has He already sent to you? How often has He convinced you of sin, of your unconverted state, and of eternal condemnation? How frequently has He persuaded you to become a Christian, to repent, and to enter into a covenant with Him?... Tell me, would it not be just if this Prophet were to turn away from you, and let you go your own way, since you do not desire to hear Him anyway? Has He not stretched out His hands long enough to you? If He were to cease doing so at this moment, would not your condemnation be just?"

He reminds the regenerate that they were no better. Instead, the Lord in His great mercy persevered and by His almighty power opened their hard heart. It therefore behooved them to be grateful and astonished, for it was the work of the Lord alone. These words are followed, however, by an admonition and exhortation: "Consider, however, at the same time how disobediently you behave yourself concerning this Prophet. You have but a glimmer of light, and should you be satisfied with that?"

Sermons

In the few sermons of à Brakel which have been preserved, we again encounter him as a serious minister. In every sermon he addressed all who were present; no one left the church without being warned. He addressed words of comfort to believers. They are united to Christ and are His property for time and eternity. In this context à Brakel stated, "Only he who is in Christ is a new creature." The state of the regenerate is much more glorious than that of Adam in the state of rectitude, for their union with Christ is unbreakable. All blessings and benefits issue forth from this gracious gift. That this is indeed a gift of God Himself is continually stressed by à Brakel: "God alone is the One who conceives, begins, and accomplishes salvation. Paul therefore states in Philippians 1 that He who has begun this good work shall also finish it. Therefore, the work of salvation must neither be initiated by nor derived from our own strength, but from God alone." Elsewhere in his sermons he states, "The Lord is the cause of our new nature, and not man — not in the least measure."

Regardless of the grace the regenerate had received, à Brakel considered it to be his task to give them further instruction; for indeed, there are children, young men, men, and fathers in grace. "Do whatever you can to please Him and render Him pleasure by always giving heed to and improving His stirrings within; by always being submissive to His leadings; and being opposed to sin and committed to virtue — so that He may seal you more and more and strengthen your soul."

Converted people can so easily grieve the Spirit of God when, for example, there is no special comfort subsequent to the administration of the Lord's Supper. Dissatisfaction with that is an expression of being at odds with God's leading. "Even though you may have prepared yourself well, He is not obligated to give you your wish." Others were warned against being excessively concerned about committed sins. Such a concern is not good; he called it "an unprofitable concern." Isaiah's words, "in quietness and in confidence shall be your strength," ought to be observed more. In this manner à Brakel directed the converted to Paul's example of the spiritual race: "I press toward the mark for the prize of the high calling of God in Christ Jesus" (Phil. 3:14).

The contrast between those who may possess this "most eminent life of grace" and those who still live for their own account is great. They live "a most wretched life." Unregenerate men are dead in spiritual matters. à Brakel, in one of his sermons, made a comparison between a naturally and spiritually dead person. As a person who is dead in a natural sense is stiff and cold, likewise a spiritually dead person is cold in spiritual matters. In a profound sense he is also insensitive to the Word of God. Even if an unconverted person exerts himself to please God, he finds no delight in it. "O wretched condition — yes, thrice wretched men! Give ear, you who are spiritually dead; that is, if you are able to hear. Do you not know that you are dead before God, and thus also in all your works? As long as you remain thus, death will be stamped upon all that you do."

After having addressed the unconverted in such an earnest manner, he calls them to repentance. There are three examples in the Bible of people who have been resurrected: the daughter of Jairus, the young man of Nain, and Lazarus. Therefore, "do not despair, but rather look unto this living Jesus and listen to His Word. For, when He called Lazarus, He also gave him the ability to hear. This Jesus is mighty to make you alive, for He is the

resurrection and life itself." When someone is sick, he will drink a
potion, causing him to expel all the corruption in his body in order
to regain his health. Thus, the sinner must remove the evil from
his soul by means of a true confession of guilt before God. It is
essential for every unconverted person to examine his entire life in
the light of the law — from commandment to commandment.
Then it will be evident that the entire law has been transgressed.
The Lord pronounces judgment — the curse of the law — upon
everyone who transgresses His commandments. In one's own strength
there is no expectation of deliverance; despair therefore of your
own ability. This will be followed by deep humiliation before the
Lord, an earnest confession of guilt, and a supplicating for grace.
"Persevere in this until you receive it. You will experience that He
who has never said to the seed of Jacob 'seek Me in vain,' will
manifest Himself while you are inquiring after Him.... Even if you
had committed the sins of all men in a most dreadful manner,
there is a sufficient fullness in Jesus."

The third group addressed by à Brakel were the hypocrites.[2]
Some are conscious of the fact that they are deceiving themselves
for eternity. Consciously they convince themselves that they possess true faith. Such blatant hypocrites, as à Brakel called them, are
not so dangerous for the church. The sophisticated hypocrites,
however, have much in common with true believers. It can be that
they have such exceptional insight into the fundamentals of religion that they can even instruct others with profit. This can be
accompanied by an aversion for sin, so that they see themselves as
sinners who have made themselves worthy of God's eternal judgments. They confess God to be just in all His punishments. This
does not lead them to despair, for by the so-called common
operations of the Spirit — in contrast with the special, saving
operations of God the Holy Spirit — they see the all-sufficiency of
Christ as having merited salvation.

With urgency, Rev. à Brakel pointed the members of his congregation to the warning examples which are given in the Bible:
Herod was pleased to hear John the Baptist; Simon the Sorcerer
was a member of the congregation of Samaria, having been baptized and of whom the Christians said that he was a great power of
God; Judas Iscariot, in the presence of the Lord Jesus Himself and
the other eleven disciples, partook of the Lord's Supper; and, in
the parable, the ten virgins all went to meet the bridegroom —

---

[2] The author uses "geveinsden," "huichelaars," and "hypocrieten," all of which are
translated as "hypocrites" in English.

Wilhelmus à Brakel dressed in bands and gown.

being similar in so many respects, whereas five of them were nevertheless foolish.

In one of his sermons à Brakel made a distinction between the sorrow for sin which many have whose conversion is but counterfeit, and the sorrow which true believers have. The sorrow of the first issues forth from a fear for punishment, whereas with the latter there is a sorrow for sin itself, God's goodness and justice having been offended thereby. Hypocrites can also hate sin and be desirous to live a holy life. They deem such a life to be a bitter potion, however — which, alas, is a prerequisite unto salvation. The true believer, even if he could be saved without living a godly life, would not desire this, for it is his wish to live a life acceptable to God and pleasing to Him.

à Brakel identified self-examination as one of the preeminent activities a listener must engage in. He quotes Hebrews 6, where mention is made of people who have been enlightened, have tasted the heavenly gift, have been made partakers of the Holy Ghost, and have tasted the good word of God and the powers of the world to come (that is, of life after this life), who nevertheless became apostate and thus did not possess true saving faith. "A hypocrite can be a partaker of God in some measure, at least as far as His ordinances and gracious gifts are concerned, being a partaker of some remote operations of the Spirit. They are not — which, however, is true for every believer — of one spirit with the Lord."

In his sermons, à Brakel regularly addressed the government and exhorted it to carry out its task properly. Rulers ought to give a good example in all areas — especially in the realm of justice. By exercising justice indiscriminately toward all men, the government will grow stronger. Moreover, God Himself requires this: "He that ruleth over men must be just, ruling in the fear of God" (2 Sam. 23:3). à Brakel mentions the example of two Roman government officials of whom it was said that it would be easier to pluck the sun from the firmament than to accuse them of injustice. Such was the measure of moral fortitude issuing forth from Roman philosophy. Would then grace not exert a much greater influence? "Oh, that governments and those who govern would find their delight primarily in the exercise of justice." Regretfully, à Brakel had to conclude that there were many judges in the Republic who were blind to justice. Ungodly lawyers were representing cases which they knew were indefensible. These matters were the cause of God's displeasure toward the Netherlands.

He denounced other sins, such as frequenting fairs, desecrating God's Name and day, drunkenness, excess, and proud dress. Even on days of penitence there were people who would come to church dressed according to French fashion — a nation which suppressed the Netherlands for such a long period. He reminded them of the cruelties which the French committed in 1672 — a year of great calamity.[3]

---

[3] In Dutch history this year is referred to as "het rampjaar"— the year of disaster.

Rather than excess — also as far as eating and drinking are concerned — moderation ought to be practiced. Besides a Christian's duty to be moderate in light of being a stranger in this world — "there is but a very minimal partition which separates them from heaven" — moderation also yields advantages for man's intellect and memory. à Brakel advised that one should eat "a sober diet, for too much food and drink is harmful to the brain, and this in turn renders the memory weak." The weakening of the memory would be detrimental to the retention of spiritual knowledge, for the truths of the gospel must be hid and stored in the heart. Indeed, it is the gospel which directs the sinner in the way which he must go to attain eternal life. By nature man has, however, but little room for the things of God's kingdom. Instead, old songs which one learned at an earlier time, as well as former suffering and sinful deeds, are remembered for many years, whereas a sermon is forgotten after a few hours. Thus, evil is continually retained in man's thoughts.

Rev. à Brakel, in one of his sermons, compared the memory of a fallen man to a sieve: that which is good falls through it and disappears, and that which is sinful remains. Thus, man forgets what he should primarily be thinking about: God, our Creator and Preserver; His Son Jesus Christ who gave Himself for the sins of His people; religious truths (are there not many people who have heard God's Word preached and yet are unable to describe faith as it functions in the soul?); the duties prescribed by Christian doctrine, such as visiting prisoners and the observance of the Lord's Day; hospitality; our committed sins which we ought to hate; our vows which we made in times of danger or during a serious illness ("Do not be deceived; God will not permit Himself to be mocked. He has various ways whereby He will cause you to remember them"); the church of God throughout the entire world; and the end of our life.

Pray for renewal of heart, for in conversion all the faculties of the soul are renewed, and thus also our corrupt memory. "Grace fills the gap (in the memory) which sin has made." Believers must see to it that their memories are not excessively filled with worldly things, for then there will no longer be room for spiritual matters. Especially young people whose "memories are still vigorous," must frequently think upon their Creator. Later in life this faculty will be weakened due to sorrow and grief. "Therefore, obtain a Bible, books, a catechism, and a collection of beautiful texts and good instructions. They will not occupy much space." Parents, for example, ought to stimulate their children in this respect by asking them questions about the sermons they hear. Children must have the doctrine according to godliness impressed upon them from their youth. They so easily depart from the way, often causing their parents great sorrow. "Parents, how grievous it would be to bring forth children who will tear down God's temple. Therefore, be diligent in giving them a godly education and pray for them."

à Brakel gave some advice concerning training one's memory. First of all both temperature and humidity need to be comfortable. "Cold brains engender forgetfulness." As a second help he mentions a peaceful conscience; then one's memory is receptive for everything. A third help is repetition. To that end à Brakel advanced the idea that it was useful to take notes of what one heard during the sermon. He called this a good means "to keep you wakeful during the administration of God's ordinances. One will then neither sleep nor look around, which would be detrimental to our mind, causing our thoughts to wander elsewhere." It ought to be recognized, however, that the Spirit's teaching excels this. The truth of the gospel ought to be engraved in our hearts to such an extent that with the Roman, Cassius Severus — when the Senate ordered that his book be burned — one could say: "You may as well burn me also, for it is written in my heart." Forgetfulness can be an impediment to our conversion. "How can we be repentant of or grieve over what we have so readily forgotten?" We must not think that God will forget sin. "Verily, I shall never forget their works."

Those who were of the opinion, however, that salvation was to be obtained via a good memory and much knowledge, were corrected by à Brakel with the remark that there are indeed people who can repeat everything; however, when it comes to the practice of godliness they are but midgets. Knowledge without love will puff a person up, and will engender high thoughts of self and a looking down upon others. Therefore, strive to obtain that knowledge which is associated with love, for "it has its origin in God."

Pastorates in Friesland[4]

For more than forty-nine years, Wilhelmus à Brakel served various congregations in the national church of the Netherlands. After having completed his studies in Franeker in 1659, he did not immediately receive a call. There were scarcely any vacancies in Friesland at that time. à Brakel, who then was twenty-four years of age, went to

---

[4] Friesland is one of the twelve provinces of the Netherlands.

Utrecht where, until 1662, he received instruction from the well-known theologians Gisbertus Voetius and Andreas Essenius.

1662 - 1665: Exmorra

In 1662 he received a call from the congregation of Exmorra. This village is located in the province of Friesland, southwest of Leeuwarden[5] and a short distance from Makkum where his father, Theodorus à Brakel, had been pastor for a period of time. The vacancy in Exmorra was only the third in Friesland since 1659, there evidently being no shortage of ministers. Yet they called a young and inexperienced candidate for the ministry. The reason for this was, according to one of à Brakel's contemporaries, that his preaching gifts had become known. During the period between 1659 and 1662 he had preached fairly regularly in addition to his studies.

Exmorra was not an easy congregation, as he had to cope with much indifference among its population. He nevertheless labored with great zeal in his congregation and utilized all his talents as he endeavored to cause God's Word to find entrance. His attention was so strongly focused upon his congregation that he was hardly known outside Exmorra. A contemporary said of him that he buried himself as it were within this village. Approximately a year and one half after his installation in Exmorra, the young minister married Sara Nevius.

A picture, dating from the eighteenth century, of the rural community of Exmorra — the first congregation of Wilhelmus à Brakel.

---

[5] Leeuwarden is the capital of the province of Friesland.

His tenure in Exmorra would not last long; after three years he received a call from the much larger congregation of Stavoren, a port city at the Zuiderzee.[6] Rev. Abraham Hellenbroek, who delivered the funeral sermon upon à Brakel's decease in 1711, commented: "The Lord wanted to use him for a greater task." His departure must have been to the regret of the congregation of Exmorra, there being evidence of a "noticeable stirring and blessing" during his tenure. He nevertheless believed that he had to depart. He considered the call for help from Stavoren, which was without a minister at that time, to be a divine mandate.

1665 - 1670: Stavoren

Shortly after his installation on December 3, 1665, it became evident that the congregation was too large for one minister. The ministers who had served this congregation prior to à Brakel were evidently not of that opinion; however, the new minister wanted to serve this much larger congregation with the same zeal and faithfulness as he had served the significantly smaller congregation of Exmorra. The congregation of Stavoren, due to the costs involved, was not able — or perhaps not willing — to call a second minister.

The "Zuiderzee" city, Stavoren — the second congregation served by Wilhelmus à Brakel.

Rev. à Brakel then turned to princess Albertina Agnes of Orange, a daughter of governor Frederik Hendrik, born to him in 1634. She was governor on behalf of her son — the Frisian governor Hendrik Casimir II — who was under age. The request for a contribution towards filling the vacancy for a second ministerial position was honored by her; she gave fl. 800.00 from her own means. This was a considerable amount for that time — an amount to be paid each year. à Brakel decided to forego his own guaranteed salary from the city and receive the much less secure salary

---

[6] During the days of à Brakel the Zuiderzee was an extension of the North Sea reaching into the very heart of the Netherlands. This sea which has now been severed from the North Sea via a large dam (the "Afsluitdijk") is presently known as "Het IJselmeer" (the IJsel lake).

from the governor's mansion. He made this decision to remove all objections for calling a second minister.

Rev. à Brakel was most grateful toward the princess. When the book *De trappen des Geestelijken Levens* [The Steps of Spiritual Life] by his late father, Theodorus à Brakel, was published in 1670, Wilhelmus dedicated it to her. He wished her God's blessing in temporal things, but above all with regard to spiritual life. She was evidently a good example for other government officials — as evidenced by her care for the congregation of Stavoren.

During his tenure in Stavoren, à Brakel came into contact with the French revival preacher, Jean de Labadie. From a letter written at a later date — à Brakel already resided in Rotterdam — it is evident that he initially did not reject this gifted minister and his objectives. (In the section, "Pastorate in Rotterdam," more attention will be given to the relationship between à Brakel and the Labadists.)

Not much is known about à Brakel's work in Stavoren since both consistorial minutes and records of city resolutions (ordinances of the city government) are lacking. In the previously mentioned funeral sermon, Rev. Hellenbroek said, "The extraordinary fruit which he enjoyed in Stavoren has been very significant and widely recognized." Thus, also in this city his labors were not in vain in the Lord.

1670 -1673: Harlingen

After having labored in Stavoren as a minister of God's Word for five years, a call was extended to à Brakel by Harlingen which, after Leeuwarden, was the largest and wealthiest city of Friesland. Business flourished in Harlingen, an old fortified city. Due to its favorable location, being a port city at the Zuiderzee, there was intense shipping traffic. The increased prominence of the city was evident, among other things, from the transfer of the naval headquarters of Friesland and Groningen[7] from Dokkum to Harlingen in 1645.

Rev. à Brakel accepted the call which had been extended to him in January, 1670 after the death of one of the four ministers in the city, Rev. M. B. Brugbon. He labored in Harlingen for three years with much blessing. Rev. Hellenbroek testified, "The shining forth of the countenance of God upon his ministry was also so evident for him there, that the blessing which he enjoyed and the love of the congregation for him can hardly be expressed. A wondrous change took place under his ministry. He has begotten a multitude of spiritual children there." In *The Christian's Reasonable Service* à

---

[7] Groningen is the province adjacent to the province of Friesland.

Brakel himself makes mention of the extraordinary blessing he experienced in Harlingen. When dealing with the prophetical office of the Lord Jesus and the duty of believers to conduct themselves as prophets toward their fellowmen in explaining the hidden matters of Scripture, he writes that there were six or eight young women in Harlingen who "gave themselves to be prophetesses in the service of the Lord." They traversed the congregation and stirred people up to acquire knowledge and to repent. The Lord richly blessed those labors and many people were converted.

After à Brakel had resided in Harlingen for more than a year, there was much unrest in the Republic of the Netherlands. The events which took place at that time (1672) were of such a far-

Wilhelmus à Brakel served the port city Harlingen, the second most important city of Friesland, from 1670-1673.

reaching nature that this year is referred to as the year of disaster. Much also transpired in Friesland. Although there was not much fighting in this region, tensions were high. The aristocratic "grietmannen" who on the basis of old charters had great influence, formed a clique of regents and gradually gained power in the Frisian states. There was dissatisfaction concerning this among the population, which was further aggravated by the heavy tax burden. There was even the threat of rebellion. Added to this were the panic and fright caused by the unexpected attack upon the Republic from four sides: France, England, Munster, and Cologne.

Stirred by the threatening danger, the ministers of Classis Franeker (to which also Harlingen belonged) resolved "that they would unitedly join hands before God's countenance, and not without tears" exert themselves with new zeal for the interests of the church. They confessed that due to numerous offenses they had become "largely abhorrent and unprofitable." At the same time, probably at the request of the government, the resolution was made to convene all the ministers from the region of Friesland in Leeuwarden. From all the classes of Friesland the ministers traveled to the capital. Most of them probably arrived by canal barge. This assembly of 156 ministers took place in July, 1672. It appointed a committee, consisting of six ministers from its midst, to address the parliament of the commonwealth of Friesland, requesting that the proposals for the liberation of this region and the removal of dissatisfaction be implemented. The most significant request — the promotion of Hendrik Casimir II, who was but fifteen years old, as governor and commander-in-chief of Friesland — was already granted a day later.

A short time later the ministers again visited the state parliament to "admonish the honorable gentlemen, yes, to beseech them in Christ's Name that they be inclined to investigate and purify all those unhealthy conditions which had also polluted them and brought disarray among them." By taking measures it was hoped that God would be merciful and that thus the land be spared and the church be blessed more abundantly.

It seems that the forceful action of the ministers encouraged the Frisian commonwealth which, due to the rapid succession of both war and dissatisfaction, was in a state of despair. The bishop of Munster met with resistance when he invaded the southeastern part of Friesland. In addition to this, several dikes in this region had been slashed. The Frisians were safe behind their water barrier and the advance of the army from Munster stagnated. Later this army withdrew itself from southeastern Friesland and the siege of Groningen had to be discontinued as well. Bishop Barend van Galen attributed the valiant stance of Friesland to the ministers, whom he furiously cursed with the words: "der Teufel hole die Pfaffen" (May the devil get those popes). The action of the ministers probably prevented excessive manifestations of popular wrath as occurred in the province of Holland. There Johan and Cornelis de Witt were murdered in a most abominable manner in August, 1672.

After stability had in some measure returned, a general Frisian Synod was held. This assembly decided to proceed with the work of reformation. All ministers were under obligation to preach from the Heidelberg Catechism on Sunday afternoon. Those who failed to do so were resolutely excluded from all synodical and classical assemblies. More attention also had to be given to the exercise of ecclesiastical discipline. In short, some measures needed to be taken, the objective being to promote a further reformation of society at large.

These and other measures undoubtedly met with Wilhelmus à Brakel's approval. The fact that the government also exerted pressure to have these resolutions implemented must have caused him and others to rejoice. To have the government function as a wall surrounding the church was an ideal which many espoused as far as the relationship between church and state was concerned.

1673 -1683: Leeuwarden

Shortly after this turbulent period, à Brakel received a fourth call — this time from the Frisian capital, Leeuwarden. In the case of Leeuwarden we are well-informed as to the manner in which a call was extended. It was the consistory rather than the congregation which cast the deciding vote as far as selecting a minister to be called. It was not true, however, that the consistory could act entirely on its own in extending a call. The government also had some jurisdiction in this matter.

The first thing a consistory was obligated to do was to ask the local government (i.e., the magistrate) for permission to extend a call. When this was granted, the consistory would establish a list of twelve candidates. During a subsequent meeting, six would be selected from this list, from which in turn three would be selected. After this a delegation of the consistory would go to the magistrate to inform him about the names of the three remaining candidates. The commissioners would then decide whether a minister could be called from this trio.

After the consistory had made its final decision, the magistrate would be informed of this as well. Concurrently, the call letter would be delivered to the minister — usually by the caretaker of the church. A consistory committee would then visit the consistory of the congregation which the called minister was presently serving, as well as the Classis to which that congregation belonged. In taking all these steps they would beseech the Lord that the decisions about to be made, and those already made, would be in His favor.

The calling procedure was not the same in all congregations. In some cases the government would make up a gross list from which the consistory could make a choice. In rural areas it was frequently a requirement to obtain permission from gentlemen or ladies belonging to the nobility, based on ancient privileges. The government's involvement was logical since it paid the salaries. There was the danger, however, that the civil government would involve itself in matters which were purely ecclesiastical in nature. We shall observe subsequently that it was particularly à Brakel who recognized this

Wilhelmus à Brakel served the congregation of Leeuwarden, the capital city of the province Friesland, for ten years.

danger and would resolutely correct the government when it would overstep its boundaries.

After the foregoing procedure had been followed, Rev. Wilhelmus à Brakel could be installed in the city of his birth in 1673, it being the largest city of Friesland with a population fluctuating between 15,000 and 20,000. The provincial government was located in this city, and it was especially the presence of the governor's residence, along with its resident nobility, which gave Leeuwarden the appearance of a distinguished city.

There was much work for the six ministers who resided in Leeuwarden. Three services were conducted on Sunday in the "Groote" or "Jacobijnerkerk," two in the "Galileerkerk," and also two in the "Westerkerk." On Monday, catechism instruction for the public was provided in the "Groote Kerk," and there was a morning service on Wednesday. In the "Westerkerk" there was a morning service on Friday, and "kapittelpreken" (literally, chapter sermons) were delivered on Thursday in the "Galileerkerk." There was a temporary intermission in this sequence during the passion weeks, since attention was then given to passion material. In addition to these services, there were also the various catechism classes and family visitations. Every minister was obligated to visit every family in his parish at least prior to the administration of the

Lord's Supper. This sacrament was administered five times annually. The other pastoral labors — such as visitation of the sick and attendance at consistory, classical, and synodical meetings — must have also demanded much time.

Discord Concerning the "Conventicles"

Rev. à Brakel was even busier than that, for in addition to his official labors, he organized church gatherings for godly persons who desired more depth in their spiritual life. These house services or "conventicles" were referred to earlier already when mention was made of the various catechism classes (p. xxxvii). In his previous congregations, Stavoren and Harlingen, à Brakel had also led similar services. In addition to hearing expositions about portions of the Bible and the explanation of doctrine, there was a desire among members of the congregation to speak about the inner, experiential life of faith — the practice of godliness. These services were held in private homes.

à Brakel saw many advantages in these services. They could result in the revival of the life of faith as well as of the entire church; and thus they most suitably complemented his endeavor to bring about a further reformation. The consistory was not in favor of this, however, being fearful that this would give rise to a church within a church as well as the possible danger of schism.

Precisely during that time the Labadists had returned from

The *Westerkerk* in Leeuwarden.

The *Grote Kerk* in Leeuwarden.

Altona, Germany, and settled in Wiewerd, Friesland. These followers of Jean de Labadie had separated themselves from the church and formed an exclusive group to which only believers could join themselves. From his later writings it is evident, that à Brakel was vehemently opposed to the Labadists.

The consistory decided that it would take measures to forbid the conducting of private services. In October, 1676, à Brakel was accused by Classis Leeuwarden of continuing to conduct "his inappropriate and unauthorized catechism classes which were held in secret" in spite of the resolution made by the parliament of Friesland that "coventicles" could only be held with the knowledge and approbation of the consistory. This ordinance of the Frisian government was probably intended for the Labadists, but was now used by the opponents of à Brakel. After Classis Sneek also had issued a prohibition concerning "conventicles," the consistory of Leeuwarden drafted a resolution which determined that every minister could instruct individuals in his own parish who were not sufficiently educated but who had expressed their desire to partake of the Lord's Supper. For those who were more advanced, a public catechism class would be held, which would be conducted by all the ministers, each taking his turn. à Brakel acquiesced in this decision, but not with his whole heart. It must seriously be asked whether this decision of the consistory issued from a true concern for the welfare of the church or whether it was motivated by envy.

The Koelman Controversy

There was another issue which brought à Brakel into conflict with the consistory — the fact that he allowed Rev. Jacobus Koelman to preach. This forthright minister, who in addition to his theological study also received a doctorate in philosophy, had particularly become renowned for his serious endeavor to bring about a further reformation. He, along with à Brakel, detected serious spiritual lukewarmness, aggravated by the laxness of many ministers in preaching and of consistories in exercising ecclesiastical discipline. A variety of sins, such as frequenting fairs, public drunkenness, desecration of the Sunday, abuse of the sacraments, etc., were committed by many members of the church. The government, whose duty it was to make ordinances to restrain the sins of its subjects, was also lax in opposing public sin.

When Koelman was installed in Sluis, Zeeuwsvlaanderen,[8] in 1662, he made it his objective to warn the population incessantly against sin and to exercise discipline vigorously if necessary. That he did this without having respect of persons was evident in his action taken against two government officials, Commissioner Brienen and Mayor Sluymer. Both men were guilty of drunkenness, and Sluymer had even fought in public. The fact that he did not spare these men earned him their wrath as well as that of a number of magistrates. The government hardly cooperated in carrying out those resolutions which called for reformation. Nevertheless, a certain measure of spiritual prosperity became evident in the congregation — especially due to impressions left by the plague in 1666 and the events in 1672, "the year of disaster."

In striving for spiritual revival, Koelman also objected to the forms read at the administration of Baptism and the celebration of the Lord's Supper, as well as all form prayers. It was his view that these forms caused deadness and a lack of zeal whereby "godliness is greatly inhibited; they greatly suppress, limit, and quench the Spirit. They greatly increase a lack of self-knowledge and it entrenches people in laziness, carnal sloth, and ignorance." In opposition to this "routine religion"[9] engendered by forms and form prayers, he proposed that speaking and praying should occur extemporaneously.

---

[8] This is the southern portion of the province Zeeland.

[9] The Dutch reads: "Sleur- en slenterdienst."

One would then be in need of and ask for God's help, and it would be beneficial for spiritual life. He also condemned ecclesiastical feast days. Their institution was not commanded in the Bible and was a human invention reminiscent of the Roman Catholic Church with all her anniversaries and holy days. The Lord instituted the Sabbath so that the salvific events of Jesus' birth, passion, death, resurrection, and ascension could repeatedly be commemorated.

Due to his consistent stand — he refused to read the forms and preach about the salvific event related to a given Christian feast day — charges were filed against Koelman by his opponents. The parliament of Zeeland (the civil government) involved itself and gave Koelman a choice: yield or leave Sluis. He neither could nor

Rev. Jacobus Koelman (1633-1695). Wilhelmus à Brakel permitted the deposed Koelman to preach and thereby brought himself into great difficulty.

was willing to subject himself, and while a mourning congregation bade him farewell, the minister departed from Sluis on June 17, 1675. After sometime he arrived in Amsterdam. Wherever he came he was informed that he could not preach. Nevertheless, he deemed it to be his calling and therefore organized "house services."

Rev. à Brakel made the situation of Koelman his concern. When the exiled minister came to Leeuwarden — the two men evidently knew each other — à Brakel permitted him to preach in his place. During the classical meetings of 1676 and 1677 it was pointed out to à Brakel that he was not permitted to allow Koelman to preach. The Classis did not wish to impose a prohibition upon him, but he was advised to conduct himself with caution. At the Synod of Friesland, over which à Brakel presided, the proposal was made by a delegate from Zuid-Holland[10] to impose upon Koelman a general prohibition to preach. à Brakel vehemently opposed this. The most significant argument he advanced was that Koelman had never been subjected to ecclesiastical discipline, nor had been deposed as a minister, but rather that this had been initiated by the government. He was of the opinion that "no political body had the authority to depose a minister."

The delegates of the parliament of Friesland, who were always present at such meetings, were offended since in their opinion à Brakel had spoken of the government in an insulting manner. At this meeting they announced that they would inform the parliament of this discourse. In July of that year à Brakel received an invitation to appear before the parliament of Friesland. Before the "offended" government officials he stated that the accusation of insult was unfounded. Furthermore, there was no need for him to be present, for a minister is not accountable to the civil government about ecclesiastical matters. The fact that Koelman was no longer permitted to preach was unlawful, for he had not been deposed by an ecclesiastical assembly. He expressed his view in two "remonstrances" (grievances) which he forwarded to the parliament. However, the parliament was not convinced. Retribution had to be meted out for having offended "his majesty." The penalty was a four-week suspension of ministerial duties. Both the consistory and the Classis would be informed about this decision.

Rev. à Brakel declared boldly before the parliament that he would not subject himself to this penalty, "and that he would be obliged to continue preaching, even if he would shortly have to lay down his life." On Friday, July 21, it was à Brakel's turn to preach again. Tension was mounting. From various quarters he received advice to let someone else take his turn, and a delegation of the consistory would then go to the parliament with the request that any penalty to be meted out to à Brakel be imposed by ecclesiastical assemblies. Thus they were of the opinion that the government had overstepped its bounds; however, many delegates thought it too precarious to oppose them directly in this matter.

Rev. à Brakel, however, ignored this well-intended advice. On Thursday, July 20, late in the evening, a sheriff's officer arrived to inform him that he had received written orders from the parliament to prevent the suspended minister from preaching. He asked à Brakel not to go to church for the purpose of administering the Word. à Brakel replied that he would not oppose the use of force,

---

[10]One of the coastal provinces of the Netherlands.

Waarachtich Verhaal

Van de

R E K E N S C H A P,

Gegeben ban

D. WILHELMUS à BRAKEL,

Wegens zijn E. verdediging van 't Recht
der KERKE.

Waar upt blijckt /

Hoe zijn Eerw : de *usurpeerende Macht der Hooge Ove-
righeidt*, in het Sufpendeeren, en Deporteeren van een Predikant om
Kerckelijke zaaken, met woorden en daaden, in het *Synodus*, laaft in
Vrieflandt gehouden, en by de *Ed : Mog :* *Gedeputeerde Staaten* van die
Provincie, *kloeckmoedelijk* en *onbeweeglyk* heeft tegen geftaan.

Uitgegeven /

Tot *Overtuiging* van vleyende, en tot *Aanmoediging* van
vreefachtige Leeraars in Neerlandt.

t'U T R E C H T.

Gedruckt by W I L L E M C L E R C K, boeckdruc-
ker, woonende op de Neude, Anno 1681.

Title page of the pamphlet containing a detailed description of
the conflict between Wilhelmus à
Brakel and the Frisian Parliament.

but he was neither desirous nor able to stay away voluntarily. The
following day à Brakel went to church at the usual time. There
must undoubtedly have been more churchgoers than would normally have been the case. Those who were anticipating a riot were
disappointed, however, for there was neither a sheriff's officer nor
anyone else who prevented him from preaching. Without any
disturbance he was privileged to proclaim the Word of his Master.
He perceived this to be an answer to prayer.

After the service several consistory members visited him to ask on
behalf of the parliament whether he would be willing to make
confession of guilt for those expressions which were difficult to
accept. They would then leave the matter of discipline to the church.
This was precisely à Brakel's objective and he was certainly prepared
to offer his apologies if he had unintentionally offended the government. A statement was drafted in which he promised to render the
government the respect to which it was entitled and to exhort others
to do likewise. Hereby the matter became a closed case.

The government had acknowledged that in this matter of principle
the church had the right to govern its own territory. The government

indeed had a task in support of the church, but not a task within the church. By virtue of this courageous conduct, à Brakel became known everywhere. Particularly after the publication of *Waarachtig Verhaal van de rekenschap gegeven van D. Wilhelmus à Brakel wegens zijn E. verdediging van 't Recht der kerke* [True Account of the Explanation given by Rev. Wilhelmus à Brakel in Defense of the Rights of the Church] — in which in all probability a colleague of à Brakel gives an accurate account of the events — this controversy and its outcome became known everywhere. It is made clear in this publication that à Brakel could not have conducted himself differently. On the title page it is stated that it was published "to the conviction of ministers given to flattery and to the encouragement of fearful ministers in the Netherlands." The Frisian government will probably have regretted this publication even more than being forced to yield in the à Brakel controversy.

The Van Giffen Controversy

The first book authored by Wilhelmus à Brakel was published during these years. The reason for writing was a difference of opinion with Cocceian minister, David Flud van Giffen. A characteristic of the followers of Cocceius was that they believed that prophetical types of the Lord Jesus could be found throughout the Old Testament. If a given prophecy was not that clear, the text would be exegeted in an unnatural manner. One would then read things into the text which were not to be found in it. One of the ministers of Leeuwarden, during the winter of 1679-1680, had denounced the prophetical exposition of Psalm 8. He viewed this psalm as a doxology of the majesty of God and His government in nature over all men. "O LORD our Lord, how excellent is Thy Name in all the earth! who hast set Thy glory above the heavens.... When I consider Thy heavens, the work of Thy fingers, the moon and the stars, which Thou hast ordained; what is man, that Thou art mindful of him? and the son of man, that Thou visitest him?" (Psa. 8:1-4).

When Rev. van Giffen, who served the neighboring village of De Knijp, led a service for one of à Brakel's colleagues, he preached about the same psalm and stated with great emphasis that this psalm was a prophecy about the anticipated advent of Christ. It was so obvious that the sermon was a defense of the Cocceian position, that it engendered dissatisfaction among churchgoers and consistory members.

That same day Rev. van Giffen was informed that "the correct exposition" would be given on the next Sunday. Rev. à Brakel took this task upon himself. He explained clearly that one could not explain this psalm to be a prophecy about the condition of the church in the time of the New Testament. Rather, this psalm expresses the holy amazement of a child of God about the glory of God as revealed in the preservation and government of the entire earth — and particularly in God's care for His children.

This sermon was published under the title *Davids Hallelu-Jah, ofte lof des Heeren in den achste Psalm, verklaert, tot navolginge voorgestelt, en de verdedicht* [David's Hallelujah, or the Praises of the Lord in the Eighth Psalm Expounded, the Practice Thereof Advocated and Defended]. It was soon sold out. Since reconciliation between the two ministers fortunately came about afterwards, à Brakel rightfully deemed it incorrect to republish this sermon in unaltered form. Instead of that portion in which the Cocceian view was denounced, à Brakel wrote an extensive treatise on the covenant of grace. The title of this new book (reprinted as recently as 1979) was: *Halleluja of Lof des Heeren over het genadeverbond opgesteld naar aanleiding van de verklaring van Psalm 8* [Hallelujah, or the Praises of the Lord Relative to the Covenant of Grace, Composed as a Result of the Exposition of Psalm 8].

In spite of all the stir surrounding these three controversies — the "conventicles," giving Koelman permission to preach, and the discord with Rev. van Giffen — à Brakel's primary task remained caring for the congregation. As in his three previous pastorates, he pastored painstakingly. His great gifts as a preacher and his forthright conduct caused him to be highly respected in Leeuwarden. It has been suggested that the parliament did not dare to force the issue with à Brakel in view of the love he enjoyed from the population.

Wilhelmus à Brakel opposed Rev. David Flud van Giffen's Cocceian views concerning Psalm 8.

It is not surprising that à Brakel received several calls. In 1678 the congregation of Middelburg extended a call to him, which he declined. In 1683, a call from Rotterdam followed, one of the largest cities in the republic with a population of approximately 55,000. In January of that year a minister of Rotterdam, Franciscus Ridderus, had died. The consistory regretted the departure of this renowned minister and was

HALLELU-JAH,

Ofte

LOF des HEEREN,

OVER HET
GENADEN-VERBONDT,

Ende des felfs Bedieninge in het Oude
en N. Teftament.

Bp occafie ban de Berklaringe ban den
VIII. PSALM,

Vertoont door
WILHELMUS à BRAKEL,

Bedienaer des H. Euangeliums tot
Rotterdam.

Den bijfden Druk.

TOT ROTTERDAM,

By REINIER VAN DOESBURG, Boek-berkoo-
per op de Bifchmakt in de Waerheyt. 1696.
Met Privilegie voor 15 Iaren.

Title page of Wilhelmus à Brakel's first book in which he refuted the view of Rev. van Giffen.

desirous to have an equally capable minister as a replacement. Rev. Hellenbroek noted, "No one was more qualified than à Brakel, the great light of the Frisians. It had shone long enough in Friesland and now the time had come that Holland was to share in this light." After à Brakel had served Leeuwarden for ten years, the call from Rotterdam arrived in July or August, 1683. He declined this call. The consistory of Leeuwarden had acquiesced in a wish which à Brakel had cherished for some time, that is, to be the only one to catechize in the "Westerkerk" on Sunday and Wednesday, and thus not have to share this assignment with others. This wish was undoubtedly related to the "conventicles" in and around Leeuwarden. The fact that the consistory acquiesced in this wish (the opinions as to why vary) indicates that they were desirous to keep à Brakel as a minister.

There was disappointment in Rotterdam about à Brakel's decision, and it was decided to extend a second call to him. A special emissary, carrying with him letters of the magistrate and consistory of Rotterdam for à Brakel himself and the consistory and government of Leeuwarden, traveled to the north. On this journey he was accompanied by "many prayers of the godly." à Brakel had no freedom to decline this second call, and to the disappointment of the consistory of Leeuwarden he bade them farewell. For twenty-one years à Brakel had administered the Word of His Master in Friesland.

Pastorate in Rotterdam

The journey from Leeuwarden to Rotterdam was made by ship — from Harlingen they sailed onto the "Zuiderzee." During this journey a fierce windstorm arose accompanied by a thunderstorm.

The crew members and the passengers feared the worst and prepared themselves for the approaching end. During this storm à Brakel must undoubtedly have asked himself whether the acceptance of this call was indeed in God's favor. Did the Lord perhaps cause this fierce storm to arise to send him back as it were, or to chastise him? It is true, is it not, that nothing happens by chance? It became evident, however, that à Brakel's work in the vineyard of His Master had not been completed. The Lord spared the ship and all its passengers. After the storm had subsided, it became evident that the ship was considerably off course. This caused the journey to be prolonged, and the sorrowful news already spread through Rotterdam that the ship had perished. The alarm and consternation which this news triggered in the city were great. When the minister who had been presumed dead finally appeared, joy and astonishment were that much greater.

à Brakel was installed on November 21 by his local fellow servant, Petrus Tilenus, from Isaiah 52:7, "How beautiful upon the mountains are the feet of him that bringeth good tidings, that publisheth peace; that bringeth good tidings of good, that publisheth salvation; that saith unto Zion, Thy God reigneth!" A week later he preached his first sermon in Rotterdam. His text was 2 Corinthians 5:20, "Now then we are ambassadors for Christ, as though God did beseech you by us: we pray you in Christ's stead,

This picture of Wilhelmus à Brakel reveals that ministers during that period wore a jacket with buttons. Over this they wore a gown. The collar was replaced by a bib.

The flourishing merchant city Rotterdam. Wilhelmus à Brakel served here from 1683 until his decease in 1711.

be ye reconciled to God." With these penetrating words à Brakel began his ministry in Holland. In this sermon he only allowed God's Word to speak for itself; he shared nothing concerning himself. He did not mention where he came from, where he had served, what he had done, and what labors he anticipated to perform, etc. He stood as one who had been commissioned to pass on the words of His Master, or as he himself wrote later: to be the mouth of God to the congregation. This certainly is indicative of the seriousness with which he commenced this new episode in his life.

The Struggle against the Labadists

During his tenure in Friesland, only one book authored by à Brakel was published; however, during his tenure in Rotterdam many would follow. A year and one half after his installation in Rotterdam, à Brakel "went to battle" against the Labadists. In two elaborate letters to a circle of friends in Harlingen he delineated his objections against this sect. It is probable that these friends had asked him for advice. In all honesty he wrote that during his tenure in Stavoren he had been sympathetic towards the Labadists and had seriously considered joining them. Yet he had wanted to know more of de Labadie and his views and therefore had traveled to Amsterdam where the Labadists had settled at that time.

He had various conversations with Anna Maria van Schurman, a very gifted woman who prior to her transfer to the Labadists had many contacts with the ministers of the Second Reformation — among others with Voetius. à Brakel also had extensive conversations with de Labadie himself. In spite of the attractive things he had heard, he was not convinced. De Labadie then gave him the advice to lay this matter before the Lord Himself and to pray for wisdom, doing so in the greatest possible solitude. à Brakel, according to this letter, had followed his advice. "Very early in the morning I went into my garden and remained there all day until late in the evening. I fasted, prayed, and supplicated to understand the will of God. I also read, and after considerable time had passed, the Lord showed me very clearly from His Word and gave a clear impression in my heart that I was in the right way, and that their way (that is, of the Labadists) was a departure from the truth." Nevertheless, it so much appealed to à Brakel that he continually prayed, asking the Lord as it were for permission to join this group. The result was that the Lord showed him with increasing clarity the error of the Labadists while rebuking à Brakel at the same time. It was as if the Lord said: "Did I not reveal this to you? Why then do you persevere?" Subsequent to this à Brakel firmly resolved to remain in the Reformed Church. He continued to thank the Lord for having prevented him from taking a wrong step.

In what did the attraction of Jean de Labadie and his followers consist, so that even a staunch Reformed man as Wilhelmus à Brakel was strongly attracted by it? If he, as he said himself, vacillated to such a degree, people with much less education and experience must have had strife to a far greater degree. In his second letter à Brakel primarily addressed the regenerate and advised them in the strongest possible terms not to join the Labadists. It must indeed be evident that the conduct of Jean de Labadie and his followers caused much agitation in the church. However, à Brakel was not the only minister who felt attracted toward this revivalist.

Who was de Labadie and what did he teach? This Frenchman, who had been trained as a Jesuit, left the monastery in 1639; he was twenty-nine years old at that time and until 1650 traveled around as an itinerant preacher. In that year he joined the Reformed Church of Montauban, one of the Huguenot cities. He became the minister of this church and also taught at the Academy. From 1659 to 1666 Geneva was his residence. With great zeal he preached for hours about the great ideal that had to be transformed into reality: a pure church in which the Christian religion would be practiced as strictly as possible. This engendered the idea that only true believers, that is, only those who were partakers of the Spirit of Christ, constituted the pure church. Thus, within the confines of the visible church as institution, a church of the regenerate came into existence. De Labadie organized "conventicles" of true believers and thus attempted to lead the church back to the original manifestation of the Christian church in the first century — that is, as he perceived it to be.

The ideas which de Labadie proclaimed in a captivating and convincing manner — he could preach for four hours at a stretch without his hearers losing interest — met with both approbation and resistance. The proponents of these ideas were so convinced of their correctness that many could no longer be convinced to change their minds. Opponents, however, saw so much danger in these ideas that they opposed them with all their might. Therefore, there came unrest wherever de Labadie resided for some time. De Labadie's acceptance of a call to the French congregation in Middelburg signalled the termination of a period of great agitation for the Reformed Church in Geneva.

When he came to the Republic in 1666, he traveled on to Utrecht. The *Friends of Utrecht* — to which belonged, among others, Voetius and van Lodenstein — gave him a friendly reception. After having been installed in Middelburg, Koelman from Sluis went to hear him. de Labadie had a tremendous reputation. The same matters which the representatives of the Second Reformation were pursuing were also his objectives. He warned strongly against the laxness of many Christians, the desecration of the Sabbath, the lack of spirituality and morality displayed by many ministers, the non-Reformed and often coarse lifestyle of many church members, etc. His calls to prayer and fasting had effect; and especially due to his many family visitations the results of his activity were noticeable everywhere. Nevertheless, there came discord also in Middelburg, and after many difficulties de Labadie, with a group of followers, moved to nearby Veere. Many supporters from Middelburg went to hear the deposed minister. The parliament of Zeeland intervened at last and expelled de Labadie. When the use of force was imminent, the exiled minister took refuge in Amsterdam.

In the meantime, sympathy for him among the Reformed had waned, for he had severed himself from the Reformed Church. He viewed the circle of his followers as a community of the regenerate who had left the worldly national church and had joined the new "house church" of de Labadie. Elsewhere in the Republic similar house churches came into existence as well. Amsterdam evidently was not the terminus for this group; they crossed the border into Germany, and, after roaming about, settled in Wiewerd, a village south of Leeuwarden. The influential Cornelis van Aerssen had made the castle "Walta Estate" available. De Labadie himself had died in the meantime. Peter Yvon, due to his organizational talent, had succeeded in giving the congregation a solid footing. Around 1680 his following in Wiewerd consisted of about three hundred people.

The Labadists were all dressed in the same handmade, modest

Jean de Labadie (1610-1674). He vied for a church consisting of believers only.

Title page of the book in which Wilhelmus à Brakel opposed Labadistic views.

LEERE ᴇɴ LEYDINGE
DER
LABADISTEN
Ontdekt en wederlegt in een Antwoord
*Op Yvons Examen over onfe Trouw-
hertige Waarfchouwinge*, ᴅᴏᴏʀ
WILHELMUS à BRAKEL
*In zyn Ed. Leven Bedienaar des H. Euangeliums
tot* Rᴏᴛᴛᴇʀᴅᴀᴍ.
Den Tweeden Druk
Met een Voorrede, behelfende een
REDENEREND
ONDERRECHT,
Aangaande zeker Boek, genaamt
NUTTIGE t'SAMENSPRAAK, OFTE
ZIELS EENZAME MEDITATIEN,
t'Saamgeftelt door J. E. *en ten twede en derde
maal uitgegeven door* J B.
Waar in het fchadelyke en verdervelyke, in het zelve
vervat, ontdekt word, tot waarfchuwinge tegen
de verleidinge en archliflige bedriegeryen der
menfchen, op dat en Waarheft en Godzalig-
heit onkreukbaar gehandhaavt werde , en
onaffcheidbaar hand aan hand gepaart gaan.
ᴅᴏᴏʀ
JOHANNES ᴅᴜ VIGNON
Leeraar in Jefus Gemeinte te Rᴏᴛᴛᴇʀᴅᴀᴍ.

TE ROTTERDAM,
By NIKOLAAS TOPYN, Boekverkoo-
per in den Houttuin, 1738.

clothing. As a community they farmed the soil surrounding the castle. Dairy farming was also a means whereby they supported themselves. During meals there was singing and prayer and one or more persons would speak a word. Worldly conversation was held to a minimum; they preferred to share their spiritual experiences. These experiences, according to the Labadists, could occur outside the context of the Word of God. Especially during and after communion services members of the congregation would come into a state of ecstasy, believing the Holy Spirit to be working in them. They would embrace each other, skip and dance, and mutually entertain themselves in spiritual Christian love.

After Voetius and Koelman had recognized the dangers of Labadism, they warned the Reformed against this error. Koelman did this in his work *Historisch verhaal der Labadisten* [Historical Account of the Labadists]. At the end of this work he printed the two letters of à Brakel. Yvon reacted to the contents of these letters by way of a brochure. In this manner à Brakel also became involved in the battle against the Labadists. His best known work, in which these letters were included again, was *Leer en Leydinge der Labadisten* [Doctrine and Government of the Labadists].

Rev. à Brakel, with the Labadists, confessed the corruption ("de verdorvenheyt") of the church; she was corrupt from the head to the sole of the foot. The field of the Lord was filled with weeds and His threshing floor was filled with chaff. The vineyard of the Lord had become a wilderness; thorns and thistles were growing in it. After having enumerated a variety of sins which were committed by members of the church, giving a description of the government as not manifesting itself as the guardian of the church, and deploring the fact that so many ministers proved to be unfaithful shepherds, à Brakel writes: "Who would not weep when he thinks upon Zion and perceives that the Lord is departing from her?" Yet, departure from a church which is that corrupt is not permitted! "May we say that she is no longer the church of Christ due to her corruption? Shall we despise her? Shall we walk away from her? No, that is foolishness. It is certain that a corrupt church is nevertheless a church and that from the beginning until the present God has always permitted His church to be filled with many corruptions. Therefore, he who despises a church for its corruption acts contrary to God's Word and all experience, thereby denying her to be a church."

Using examples from the Bible, à Brakel demonstrated that sin, corruption, and a lack of spirituality were to be found in many congregations. Consider the confusion in the congregation of Corinth and the exhortations of John to the congregations in Asia Minor. How could someone have the courage to sever himself from her and thereby despise God and Christ Himself? Thus, à Brakel was strongly opposed to the Labadistic spirit of separatism (or schismatic spirit).

In addition to this objection, he identifies three theological differences. The first concerned the doctrine of justification, particularly as it relates to the leading of souls unto Christ. Yvon detained the souls of penitent persons too long. First the soul had to see clearly the sins of the old man and diligently strive against sin, the devil, and one's own flesh and thus in an alternate way seek to escape the dominion of sin. This would then be followed by a holy life, and a life in which one would quietly wait upon the Holy Ghost. This quiet separation would have to go sufficiently far that there would no longer be any striving between the flesh and the spirit — so much so that one would no longer pray for a new life. All this, according to Yvon, "precedes faith in Christ; God unites the soul to Christ subsequent to that."

Rev. à Brakel taught something different. It seemed as if Yvon established conditions which the sinner would first have to meet. This is incorrect, for the sinner may "at once . . . as sinful as he is, receive Jesus by a true, justifying faith." Having received the satisfaction and righteousness of Christ, the sinner can and may go to God, "in order to be reconciled with God and be justified by Him."

It seems that, relative to this point, à Brakel and Yvon have parted ways more than was necessary. Yvon made no difference between fathers and children in grace, whereas à Brakel seemed to reject the idea that convicted souls must see themselves so worthy of punishment that they will be prepared to accept God's eternal judgment. However, reference is made to this also in Leviticus 26: "If then their uncircumcised hearts be humbled, and they then accept of the punishment of their iniquity: then will I remember My covenant."

The second point related to pure and impure love. Yvon called fear for damnation a love for the preservation of self and thus impure since it did not proceed from love toward God. Therefore, this love — this concern for one's own salvation — could not be the immediate cause of regeneration. In contrast to this, à Brakel affirms pointedly that no one would then be converted, for no one possesses this eminent love for God prior to conversion. The Lord Himself has caused promises and threatenings to be recorded in His Word in order to induce people to seek their own salvation. Fear for punishment and death are innate and this cannot be designated as impure love. The Lord Jesus Himself was also fearful of death.

à Brakel perceived a different and more dangerous error in
Yvon's proposition. This pure love would already be a work of
God, and thus spiritual life would already be present prior to one's
believing in Christ. "How can anyone be a child in Christ and yet
neither be born again, believe in Christ, nor be in Him? What
strange error is this? We posit as an irrefutable fact that man
neither has life nor can do anything that is pleasing before God
prior to believing in Christ."

Finally, à Brakel opposed Yvon's notion that people can have an
absolute knowledge about the regeneration of their neighbor. The
Labadists would only admit someone to their fellowship when they
were certain that he or she was regenerate. à Brakel taught that
only God knows the heart, whereas man only sees what is before
his eyes. Furthermore, there are great similarities between true
believers on the one hand and hypocrites and temporal believers
on the other hand. A minister neither may nor is capable of saying
to someone in God's Name and with absolute certainty that he is
regenerate. That judgment is reserved for the Lord alone. The
conditions upon which persons are to be admitted as members of
the congregation are knowledge and confession of the truth. The
apostles baptized upon confession of sin. This also included people of whom it later became known that they were not regenerate.
Think of Ananias and Sapphira, Hymeneus, Alexander, and Simon
the Sorcerer. Confession was the basis upon which the apostles
baptized — not being cognizant of someone's regeneration.

à Brakel earnestly warned Yvon and those who sympathized with
him against Labadism. When Yvon subsequently reacted to à Brakel's
book, he used rather radical statements. à Brakel, who defended
himself, wrote in the introduction that he had besought the Lord
not to hold Yvon accountable for this. Also elsewhere it was
evident that à Brakel did not fight for the sake of fighting itself. He
wrote that Yvon had said to him during a conversation that he
(Yvon) would testify against him in the day of judgment. This
statement had such an impact upon à Brakel that he was obligated
to respond in love to Yvon with a subdued and solemn voice: ". . .
or I against you."

A matter closely related to the generally perceived decay of the
church was the celebration of the Lord's Supper. In 1690 à Brakel
published a brochure in which he contested the idea that believers,
due to the corruption of the church, ought not to partake. The fact
that many attended without having a right to do so did not mean
that believers should therefore remain seated. The Lord Jesus said:
"Do this in remembrance of Me." Who would dare to ignore such

an express command of Christ? For true believers the Lord's Supper is a means to make their calling and election sure. Many blessings may be enjoyed prior, during, and subsequent to partaking of the Lord's Supper. It is the duty of every true Christian to confess his Savior by means of the sacrament. In à Brakel's view the communicant makes the following confession: "I deem and confess the Lord Jesus to be the only true Savior. In Him I seek my salvation and with Him I enter into a covenant. He is my reliance and for Him I wish to live and die." Such a confession cannot be made by church attendance only. Therefore, true believers, do not abstain, for by your abstinence unrest and confusion will only increase in the church. Consider that your own advantage, honor, and opinion may not have precedence over the honor of Christ and the welfare of the church. God will secretly send judgment upon those who are absent. They frequently will fall into error and become ensnared. Sometimes they will return embracing a different doctrine and will then be as loose as they were strict before. à Brakel exhorted believers who did not attend anymore to humble themselves before God, beseeching Him for forgiveness.

A Proponent of the Independence of the Church

à Brakel's conflict with the government in 1688 was a noteworthy experience during his tenure in Rotterdam. In describing the calling procedure in Leeuwarden, it already became evident that the government was capable of exercising great influence in ecclesiastical matters. This was also the case in Rotterdam. This great influence became very evident after the death of a minister of Rotterdam, Johannes Ursinus. The consistory followed the usual procedure in calling a successor. The final choice was David Combrugge, a minister from Utrecht and a man whose walk was beyond reproach. A delegation of the consistory informed the government of this decision and did not expect anything but approbation from city hall. To the amazement and indignation of the brothers this was not granted. The magistrate had decided to disapprove of the call without giving any reason for doing so. Rev. à Brakel, who at that time was president of the consistory — together with a fellow minister, an elder, and a deacon — was delegated to visit city hall to request that the call still be extended. The consistory minutes convey, however, that this committee, for reasons not given, did not carry out its task. It is not mere conjecture to think that the consistory upon further consideration decided not to pursue this matter which displeased the government.

By renewal, the calling procedure was implemented. The consistory again composed a list of twelve candidates and it seems as if the consistory would yield to the government having gone beyond the bounds of its authority. However, à Brakel would not acquiesce in this. Several Sundays later he preached in the "Grote Kerk" from Psalm 2:6: "Yet have I set My King upon My holy hill of Zion." In this sermon he dealt with the question of whether the government has the authority to rescind the call of a lawfully called minister and to compel the church to call someone else. In an elaborate exposition he based his negative answer upon the Bible, the Belgic Confession of Faith, and the opinions of the best known theologians of that time. The Arminians had also been proponents of the government's involvement in ecclesiastical matters, this being one of the additional reasons why they had been condemned at the Synod of Dordt.

This sermon caused the magistrate to be agitated. à Brakel was asked to deliver the sermon in written form at city hall. He did this and seemed to be rather at ease as to the outcome of this matter. The consistory, however, was less at ease. It appointed a committee consisting of four ministers to discuss the difficulties that had arisen with the government. The members of city hall had observed in the meantime that à Brakel had turned against the government, and in their view he had, in doing so, undermined the respect and authority of the magistrates. They took strong measures: à Brakel was tempo-

De Heere
JESUS CHRISTUS
Voor de Alleene ende Souveraine
KONING
Over zyne KERKE
Uytgeroepen in een verhandelinge over
PSALM II. vers 6.
Ik doch hebbe mynen Koning gefalft over Zion, den bergh myner Heyligheyt.
Door
WILHELMUS à BRAKEL,
Bedienaar des H. Euangeliums tot Rotterdam.

TOT AMSTERDAM,
By Johannes Boekholt, Boekverkoper. Anno 1688.

Title page of a recorded sermon in which Wilhelmus à Brakel declared the government to lack the right to intervene in internal ecclesiastical matters.

rarily prohibited from preaching and his salary from the city was withheld. In spite of the mediation efforts of the consistory which agreed with the tenor of à Brakel's sermon, the government upheld the penalty which had been levied. On Wednesday, July 28, à Brakel simply continued — not due to stubbornness, as he said, but in obedience to the commandment of his King.

Upon the urgent advice of friends, à Brakel decided to make a house outside of the city his temporary residence. He continued, however, to fulfil his preaching engagement. Three weeks later à Brakel visited the mayor of the city to discuss how the conflict might be resolved. One of the demands which the government made was that à Brakel would make amends. Understandably, à Brakel wanted to know what the city fathers meant by this. They did not give a satisfactory answer; however, they did request him emphatically not to preach any longer. With strong determination he indicated that he would not comply with this request. He would rather be exiled, yes, lose his life than not preach. The two positions were diametrically opposed to each other.

The government asked the consistory to mediate and it made an urgent request to à Brakel "to be silent tomorrow, and to allow someone else to take his turn this time." à Brakel did not ignore this request but complied with it, for it originated with the church. As negotiations continued, the consistory advanced this proof as fact that à Brakel was not a revolutionary, but as minister was willing to submit himself to ecclesiastical institutions. After the government had twice declared the explanation of à Brakel to be unsatisfactory, a peace accord was signed at last. In reality à Brakel was able to maintain his position that the government has no right to forbid the extension of a call.

Nevertheless, this controversy had additional consequences. The sermon in question had been recorded during the church service and had been published in such a mutilated fashion that à Brakel, in order to remove all defamation and slander, published the actual sermon. He added an extensive description of his contacts with the government. The title was pregnant with meaning: *De Heere Jezus Christus Voor de Alleene ende Souveraine Koninck Over sijne Kercke uytgeroepen* [The Lord Jesus Declared to be the Only Sovereign King of His Church]. This title and the appendix to the sermon, in which à Brakel made known that he neither could nor was permitted to abandon his position, engendered the wrath of the magistrate. à Brakel had to be punished to set an example. His exile appeared to be imminent.

It was then that an influential protector acted on his behalf:

Governor William III requested the mayor of the city by letter to allow the matter concerning à Brakel to rest until he had discussed it with the magistrate himself. Shortly afterwards, however, the prince departed for England, where, after a change of government, he was crowned king. The magistrate decided at last to let the matter rest. In this final conflict the consistory had unquestionably chosen sides with à Brakel. It is possible that the magistrate yielded due to this position. When another magistrate came into office, the city salary was paid again. The relationship between church and government had become so poor, however, that several times subsequent to this the government rejected a call, even giving the consistory orders to cease with the work of calling temporarily. Not until January, 1690 could the vacancy of Ursinus be filled.

"De Redelijke Godsdienst" — *The Christian's Reasonable Service*

After this tumultuous period — the battle with the Labadists and his conflict with the government — circumstances surrounding à Brakel became more tranquil. He was now able to devote himself to the book which would become his main work: *De Redelijke Godsdienst* [The Christian's Reasonable Service]. à Brakel derived this title from Romans 12:1: "I beseech you therefore, brethren, by the mercies of God, that ye present your bodies a living sacrifice, holy, acceptable unto God, which is your *reasonable service*."

This book was not, as was customary at that time, dedicated to people who had a high position in church or state. à Brakel dedicated it to "the Congregation of God in the Netherlands,"[11] thereby having particularly in view his congregation of Rotterdam, his former congregation of Leeuwarden, and Middelburg (where he had been called twice). He exhorted readers to form small groups of acquaintances to read this work chapter by chapter and then have discussions about what had been read. Its contents could perhaps also be useful to instruct theological students, candidates for the ministry, and young ministers — to "enable them to comprehend the unique, distinct nature of divine truths so that they might safeguard and practice these truths in deed, presenting them to the congregation in such a manner that it results in the conversion and strengthening of souls and the edification of the church of our Lord Jesus Christ."

The first edition was sold out after a year, and the second edition was published in 1701. The third edition was enlarged

---

[11]In the subsequent translation of à Brakel's preface (p. cxiii) all references to the Netherlands have been dropped, this translation being intended for the English-speaking world.

ΛΟΓΙΚΗ ΛΑΤΡΕΙΑ,

DAT IS

REDELYKE

GODTSDIENST,

In welken de Goddelyke Waerheden des

GENADE-VERBONDTS

worden verklaert, tegen partyen befchermt, en tot de practyke aengedrongen.

ALS MEDE

De Bedeelingen des Verbondts in het O. C./ende in het N. C. Ende de Ontmoetingen der Kerke in het N. C./ vertoont in eene Verklaringe der

OPENBARINGE van JOHANNES,

DOOR

WILHELMUS à BRAKEL Th: F.

In fyn leven Bedienaar des Goddelyken Woordts te ROTTERDAM.

EERSTE DEEL.

De Twintigfte Druk.

TE DORDRECHT,

By ABRAHAM BLUSSÉ en ZOON, Boekverkoopers op de Voorftraet, over de Beurs. *Met Privilegie.*

The primary work of Wilhelmus à Brakel: *De Redelijke Godsdienst* (The Christian's Reasonable Service). This is the title page of the twentieth (!) edition.

significantly by à Brakel, as various portions were added to his work. In his foreword he told those who possessed a first and second edition that they ought not to be dissatisfied. Instead, he advised them to give their book to someone who could not pay for a book, and to purchase a third edition themselves!

He considered it to be a miracle that the art of printing had been invented shortly before the Reformation. Prior to this a preacher could only reach a small number of hearers during his lifetime. By virtue of the art of printing, however, he could preach throughout the land, even throughout the entire world — also after his death. "With joyful readiness I avail myself of this opportunity to preach to the Netherlands[12] long after my death, according to the measure of the gifts the Lord has bestowed upon me — whatever they may be."

This work, which has more than two thousand pages, is divided into three volumes. The first volume is a dogmatic exposition. In forty-two chapters the doctrines of faith are discussed in a practical, experiential manner. In the second volume a description is given of how believers are to live a holy life before God. The ten command- ments, prayer, patience, sincerity, and other important subjects are dealt with here. The third volume contains, among other things, an exposition of the Revelation of John.[13] At the same time à Brakel gives here an elaborate explanation of his view concerning the

The conclusion of Wilhelmus à Brakel's will. His signature is beneath the text most likely written by a legal clerk.

---

[12]See previous footnote.

[13]This division of volumes does not coincide with the division of volumes of this translation, which consists of four volumes.

Abraham Hellenbroek (1658-1731), one of Wilhelmus à Brakel's fellow ministers in Rotterdam.

Jews. It was his view that, relative to the Jews, there are as yet many promises which need to be fulfilled. He believed firmly that the Jews would return from all parts of the world to the land of Canaan and establish a new Jewish state there, which of course occurred in 1948.

à Brakel's views concerning the Jews are related to his views concerning the millenium as described in Revelation 20. He views this as relating entirely to the future. During this kingdom of peace in which the antichrist will have been annihilated and the devil will have been bound, "the entire Jewish nation will acknowledge our Lord Jesus to be the only and promised Messiah, will turn to Him in repentance, will love Him in an extraordinary manner, and honor and glorify Him." Not all Reformed theologians are of this opinion. Therefore, this third volume — only 350 pages of the more than two thousand pages — is the most controversial volume.

Nevertheless, *De Redelijke Godsdienst* has become a standard reference work for the heirs of the Second Reformation. There have been more than twenty editions, and it was also translated into German.

Death

As à Brakel advanced in years, bodily ailments and weakness increased. He had difficulty in walking and also his memory decreased. Nevertheless, he continued to preach and exhort as long as he was able. Particularly his exhortations in a chapel in Rotterdam had considerable attendance. Many people from the city itself, but also from Bleiswijk and Zevenhuizen, attended these services. Upon conclusion of the service, the people would gather

The two ministers Le Roy and Hellenbroek preached funeral sermons at the occasion of the decease of Wilhelmus à Brakel. The sermon of Hellenbroek has also been printed in later editions of the *De Redelijke Godsdienst* (The Christian's Reasonable Service).

near the exit of the chapel and wait until "Father Brakel" would come outside. He would address them and pronounce a benediction upon them as they embarked on their homeward journey. Thus, through the dark night, they would "go on their way rejoicing."

On Sunday, August 30, 1711, à Brakel preached for the last time. In the afternoon he had been driven to the church with a coach and the custodian assisted him in ascending the pulpit. During his sickness, which lasted two months, he suffered much — especially due to chest congestion. He prayed continually for the welfare of the church, particularly for the congregation of Rotterdam. It was his prayer that the Lord would preserve her in the truth. During the night prior to his death, one of the bystanders asked him how his condition was. "Very well," was his response, "I may rest in my Jesus. I am united to Him and I am awaiting His coming for me; however, I submit myself in all quietness." Shortly after this he died peacefully and with full assurance at the age of seventy-six. His industrious life had come to an end. He departed to inherit eternal life — not due to his merit, but by virtue of the finished work of His Master, the Lord Jesus Christ. The epitaph reads as follows:

Hier rust hij, die niet rusten kon,
Voor hij aan Jezus zielen won.
Een bidder voor zijn vaderland,
Maar nu is hij aan d' anderen kant:
In 't vaderland van Abraham,
Alwaar hij volgt het zalig Lam.
Volgt dan zijn leer en leven na,
Zoo zingt g'ook eens Halleluja!

Here rests one who could not rest,
Ere to winning souls for Jesus he could attest.
A supplicant for the land of his nativity,
Who on the other side now may be:
In the native land of Abraham,
Where he may follow that blessed Lamb.
May your doctrine and life be like his,
Then Hallelujah will be your song in
  eternal bliss.

BIBLIOGRAPHY

For this biography the following sources were consulted:

The Works of Wilhelmus à Brakel

De Redelijke Godsdienst. Utrecht, 1985.

De scrupuleuse omtrent de Commissie des Heilg Avondmaal in een verdorvene Kerke onderrechtet. Rotterdam, 1690.

De ware christen of opregte geloovige hebbende deel aan God in Christus. Rotterdam, n.d.

Een godvruchtige brief tot raadgeving en besturing aan kinderen in Jezus Christus. Middelburg, n.d.

Hallelujah of Lof des Heeren over het genade verbond opgesteld naar aanleiding van de verklaring van Psalm 8. Utrecht, 1979.

Het afsterven of laatste uren van Theodorus à Brakel in leven predikant te Mackum. Volgens zijn bevel na zijnen dood aan het ligt gebragt. Rotterdam, n.d.

Leere en Leydinge der Labadisten, ontdeckt en wederleyt in een Antwoort op P. Yvons Examens over onse Trouwhertige Waerschouwige. Rotterdam, 1685.

Stichtelijke oefeningen over de voorbereiding, betrachting en nabetrachting van het sacrament van het Heilig Avondmaal. Houten, 1985.

Waerachtich Verhaal van de rekenschap gegeven van D. Wilhelmus à Brakel Wegens zijn E. verdediging van 't Recht der Kerke. Utrecht, 1682.

Other Sources

Aa, A.J. van der, "Brakel, Dirk Gerrits of Theodorus Gerardi à" en "Brakel, Willem à." In *Biographisch Woordenboek der Nederlanden,* vol. 1. Haarlem, 1852.

Biographisch Woordenboek van Protestantse Godgeleerden in Nederland, J.P. de Bie, J. Loosjes, et al., editors, vol. 1, "Brakel, Dirk Gerryts of Theodori à" en "Brakel, Wilhelmus à," vol. 1, pp. 560-571. 's-Gravenhage, 1903.

Boot, I., *De allegorische uitlegging van het Hooglied, voornamelijk in Nederland,* pp. 163-172. Woerden, 1971.

Brienen, T., *De prediking van de Nadere Reformatie.* Amsterdam, 1974.

Dijk, D. van, "Van een oude Makkumer dominee, Dirck Gerrits of Theodorus à Brakel." In *Makkum, sier en sied fan Wunseradiel.* Boalsert, n.d.

Evenhuis, R.B., *Ook dat was Amsterdam III. De kerk der Hervorming in de tweede helft van de zeventiende eeuw: nabloei en inzinking.* Amsterdam, 1971.

Genderen, J. van, *Herman Witsius. Bijdrage tot de kennis der gereformeerde theologie.* 's-Gravenhage, 1953.

Groenhuis, G., *De predikanten. De sociale positie van de gereformeerde predikanten in de Republiek der Verenigde Nederlanden voor ±1700.* Groningen, 1977.

Haar, J. van der, "Theodorus à Brakel." In *Het blijvende Woord. Plaatsen waar en predikanten door wie dit woord verkondigd is,* pp. 39-41. Dordrecht, 1985.

Hellenbroek, Abr., *Algemeene rouklagt in de straaten van Rotterdam over den zeer eerwaarden, godvrugtigen en geleerden heere Wilhelmus à Brakel,* Seventh Edition, pp. 135-174. Amsterdam, 1737.

Hollandse Geloofshelden. Levensbeschrijvingen van tien bekende Nederlandse oudvaders door henzelf of door hun tijdgenoten geschreven. Compiled and amplified by H. Florijn. Houten, 1981. Selections used: Theodorus à Brakel, pp. 9-33, and Wilhelmus à Brakel, pp. 135-174.

Kalma, J.J., *Mensen in en om de Grote Kerk. Beelden uit de Leeuwarder kerkgeschiedenis.* Drachten/Leeuwarden, 1987.

Krull, J.J., *Jacobus Koelman.* Amsterdam, 1972.

Leurdijk, G.H., "Theodorus à Brakel." In T. Brienen, et al., *Figuren en thema's van de Nadere Reformatie I,* pp. 52-63. Kampen, 1987.

Los, F.J., *Wilhelmus à Brakel.* Leiden, 1892.

Los, F.J., "Theodorus à Brakel." In *Troffel en zwaard VII,* pp. 16-39. 1904. Nauta, D., "Jean de Labadie," from: *Biographisch Lexicon voor de geschiedenis van het Nederlandse Protestantisme,* vol. 2, pp. 396-399. Kampen, 1983.

Schurman, Anna Maria van, *Eukleria of uitkiezing van het Beste Deel,* with an introduction by S. van der Linde. Leeuwarden, 1978.

Smit, G., *De Makkumer kerk van 1660 tot 1910. De stichting en bijzonderheden,* pp. 4-10. Bolsward(?), n.d.

Steenbeek, B.W., "Theodorus (of Dirck Gerrits) à Brakel." In *Biographisch Lexicon voor de geschiedenis van het Nederlands Protestantisme,* vol. 1, pp. 55-56. Kampen, 1978.

Witteveen, K.M., "Anna Maria van Schurman." In *Biographisch Lexicon voor de geschiedenis van het Nederlands Protestantisme,* vol. 2, pp. 396-399. Kampen, 1983.

Ysseling, P.C., "Een gereformeerd mysticus." In *Troffel en Zwaard II,* pp. 249-288. 1908.

The Dutch Second Reformation
("*Nadere Reformatie*")

- The Term "Nadere Reformatie"
- The Essence of the Dutch Second Reformation
- Assessment in Secondary Sources

The Dutch Second Reformation
("Nadere Reformatie")

by Dr. J.R. Beeke*

The Dutch Reformation proper may be divided into four periods: the *Lutheran* period (1517-26), the *Sacramentarian* phase (1526-31), the *Anabaptist* movement (1531-45),[1] and the most influential — the *Calvinist* infiltration.[2] From the outset of the Calvinist penetration into the Netherlands (southern Netherlands, c. 1545; northern, c. 1560), the movement showed greater strength than its persistent numerical inferiority might suggest. Nevertheless, the buds of Dutch Calvinism did not flower profusely until the seventeenth century, initiated by the Synod of Dort in particular (1618-19), and intensified by the Dutch Second Reformation (*Nadere Reformatie*), a primarily seventeenth- and early eighteenth-century movement, which may be dated from such early representatives as Jean Taffin (1528-1602)[3] and Willem Teellinck (1579-1629),[4] to its last brilliant lights, Alexander Comrie (1706-74)[5] and Theodorus van der Groe (1705-84).[6]

The Term "Nadere Reformatie"

The term *Nadere Reformatie* poses a problem.[7] There is no standard English translation of "nadere," no doubt partly due to its inexactness, and perhaps also because the movement has been unaccountably ignored in English-speaking scholarship. Literally, "Nadere Reformatie" means a "nearer," "more intimate," or "more precise Reformation." The intended emphasis lies on working out the

---

*Dr. Beeke is pastor of the First Netherlands Reformed Congregation of Grand Rapids, Michigan, and editor of two denominational publications: *The Banner of Truth* and *Paul*. He received his Ph.D. from Westminster Theological Seminary. This chapter is a slightly revised appendix from his doctoral dissertation, *Assurance of Faith: Calvin, English Puritanism, and the Dutch Second Reformation*. In addition to editing and translating a number of works, he has authored *Jehovah Shepherding His Sheep, Backsliding: Disease and Cure, Bible Doctrine Student Workbook, Student Workbook of the Reformed Faith,* and several hundred articles.

initial Reformation more intimately in personal lives, in the church's worship, and in society as a whole.

Translations of *Nadere Reformatie* inevitably express judgments of its significance. Consequently, it has been translated on occasion as "Further Reformation." This is not altogether accurate, since "further" implies that the first Reformation did not proceed far enough. This was not the contention of the *Nadere Reformatie*. Rather, it sought to *apply* Reformation truths to daily life and "heart" experience. To avoid this false implication, Cornelis Graafland has suggested the terms "Continuing Reformation" or "Second Reformation." But the term "continuing" has three disadvantages: It does not sufficiently distinguish the *Nadere Reformatie* from the Reformation proper; it is of recent usage in English;[8] furthermore, it sounds awkward.

We prefer to use "Dutch Second Reformation" or "Second Reformation." While this is a weak translation and "misses the Dutch term's emphasis on continuity,"[9] it has a long pedigree and appears to be gaining acceptance among scholars, albeit partially by default.[10] Moreover, "Second Reformation" was a term used by some of the Dutch divines of that era. For example, Jacobus Koelman (1632-1695), who had much contact with Scotland's Second Reformation, spoke of the Dutch movement as a "second reformation" and a "second purging."[11]

Others have dubbed the *Nadere Reformatie* descriptively as "Dutch Precisianism," "Dutch Puritanism," or "Dutch Pietism." There are objections to each of these designations.

First, "Dutch Precisianism" is a pejorative rather than a constructive expression. It is the least acceptable representation of the *Nadere Reformatie*, since it attributes to the movement a legalistic (*wettisch*) tone which caricatures the whole. It is true that most Second Reformation divines promoted a strong negative ethic. Voetius, for example, forbade "such practices as visiting public houses, playing with dice, the wearing of luxurious clothes, dancing, drunkenness, revelry, smoking and the wearing of wigs." Nevertheless, such "precisianism" was not an end in itself. Rather, it was cultivated "in the face of the alleged worldliness then prevailing" and "as a means of sustaining and developing individual faith and conduct against spiritual shallowness."[12]

Secondly, the *Nadere Reformatie* is in fact the Dutch counterpart to English Puritanism (and in some senses, to the Scottish Covenanters). The link between these movements is strong, historically and especially theologically.[13] Keith Sprunger has documented that during the seventeenth century there was an English-Scottish community of Puritan persuasion numbering tens of thousands in the

Netherlands, at one point consisting of more than forty congregations and 350 ministers. The Dutch government allowed them to organize churches and form an English Classis within the Dutch Reformed church. Cornelis Pronk rightly notes:

> The presence of so many English and Scottish Puritans was bound to have some influence upon the Dutch churches. Many Dutch Reformed ministers were impressed by the practical divinity of the English Puritans. They saw it as a healthy corrective to the dry intellectualistic sermonizing that was becoming the trend in their churches.[14]

And Douglas MacMillan summarizes:

> Both Puritans and Covenanters were to interact very intimately with religious life in the Netherlands. This linking...helps identify the point at which British and Dutch Calvinism had their closest contact. Both these great spiritual movements were concerned with Second Reformation issues and that concern was to shape the course of the 17th century in England and Scotland. Events there were, in turn, to reach deeply into the Netherlands, influencing its theology, deepening its spirituality, and linking it closely into the traumatic experiences of the British Church. We have to learn to look at the Second Reformation, not as a small, localised, Scottish, or even British, phenomenon but as a movement of international significance.[15]

The divines of these groups held each other in high esteem. They influenced and enriched each other through personal contact and especially a vast array of translated writings, particularly from English into Dutch.[16] More Reformed theological books were printed in seventeenth-century Netherlands than in all other countries combined.[17] These movements embraced similar ideals and bore similar roles: to foster biblical and God-glorifying experiential piety and ethical precision in the life of individuals, churches, and the entire nation. Only England, however, had an opportunity to work out these ideals in full, during the Cromwellian years.

Thus, despite similar outlooks, these parallel movements did have and would develop historically and theologically distinctive identities. To call the *Nadere Reformatie* "Dutch Puritanism" denies the endemic nature of the Dutch movement. Hendrikus Berkhof provides too simplistic an analysis when he states that the Second Reformation resulted merely from "the practical piety of the English Calvinists blowing over to the Netherlands."[18] Though English Puritanism was of *primary* influence on the *Nadere Reformatie*, as Willem Jan op 't Hof has ably and perhaps exaggeratingly emphasized (particularly in stressing the need for a personal, domestic, and congregational lifestyle of experimental and practical godliness),[19] it was not an *exclusive* influence, for the Dutch movement was coupled with other non-English factors.[20] In fact, in some respects the Dutch movement was more Puritan-Reformed than English Puritanism itself:

> In England from an orthodox Reformed perspective, for all but a short period under Cromwell, there were always grossly unbiblical things to fight: the presence of bishops, superstitious rites in the Book of Common Prayer, vestments, etc. In the Netherlands none of these were present, and the task was all the more subtle. Defenders of the *status quo* were not so clearly unreformed as in England. In this context the true spirit of Puritanism came to the fore.[21]

Despite similar emphases, English Puritanism and the *Nadere Reformatie* differed from each other in significant ways. Generally speaking, Dutch Second Reformation divines were less interested in reforming the government and organization of the church (as long as the church was not controlled by the state) than were their English brethren. Theological emphases also varied at times; this work has shown that variations existed between these groups on the doctrine of assurance.[22] The Dutch were more inclined to emphasize theology as a science, whereas the English emphasized the practical aspects of theology.[23] These variations are not respected sufficiently when the Dutch movement is collapsed too fully into the English by the use of "Dutch Puritanism."[24] As Jonathan Neil Gerstner concludes:

> To notice a similar role between two movements does not imply that one is dependent on the other. Even if English thought had given the initial impetus to the Continuing Reformation, it does not follow that its success was not due to similar ideas present in the Netherlands.[25]

"Dutch Pietism" might appear at first to be an acceptable alternative to represent the *Nadere Reformatie*. Its usage has been the most widespread,[26] underscoring that the *Nadere Reformatie* was pietistic in many respects. Problems with this term, however, also exist. (1) Calling the Dutch movement Pietism suggests too strongly an intimate German connection.[27] Moreover, the *Nadere Reformatie* predates Spener's initial appeal for reform by nearly half a century and became a more extensive movement than German Pietism. (2) Pietism in German Lutheranism came to be regarded as being largely concerned with the believer's inner life rather than with transforming society, whereas most *Nadere Reformatie* divines were dedicated also to the latter.[28] (3) Pietism is usually regarded as a protest against rational Protestant scholastic theology and doctrinal precision, whereas many *Nadere Reformatie* divines were formulators of Reformed orthodoxy and meticulous doctrinal analysts:

> Gisbertus Voetius is generally acknowledged as both the greatest Dutch Reformed scholastic theologian and one of the greatest representatives of the Continuing Reformation. Pietism as it would later de-

velop would more and more show marked antipathy for all but the most simple doctrinal concepts.... Pietism was ready to embrace and work with all other believers who strove after a godly life, regardless of their confession. Zinzendorf tried to bring all churches together ignoring theological differences. The Continuing Reformation, on the contrary, was on the polemical forefront against theological errors, seeing the divisions within Protestantism as far from irrelevant. William Ames, one of the direct links between English Puritanism and the Dutch Continuing Reformation called Lutherans heretics. When Pietism appeared on the continent, leaders of Dutch Continuing Reformation like Wilhelmus à Brakel attacked the movement.[29]

Confusing misconceptions arise when the term "Pietism" is used to describe the Second Reformation, for these terms represent distinct movements which vary in a number of important senses.[30] German Pietism, English Puritanism, and the Dutch Second Reformation had much in common. Each was rooted deeply in the sixteenth-century Reformation and longed for more thorough reform; yet each movement retained a distinct historical, theological, and spiritual character.[31]

The Essence of the Dutch Second Reformation

Several additional factors also served to promote the emergence of the Dutch Second Reformation. After the Reformation in the Netherlands, strenuous efforts were made to replace the Roman Catholic Church with the Reformed Church as an inclusive people's church (*volkskerk*). During the Reformation, one-tenth of the population held membership in the Reformed church. By the end of the seventeenth century more than sixty percent of the Dutch population were members of the Reformed Church which possessed a "preferred status" (*bevoorrechte*) with the government.[32] The church's success in acquiring external growth, however, had dire consequences for spiritual life. Abraham Kuyper claimed that this additional fifty percent of the population which flooded into the church ruined its Reformed distinctiveness: "From that moment on it was impossible to maintain church discipline."[33] It became easy to confuse being anti-Catholic with being Reformed. Nominal church membership and loose living became fashionably acceptable. Spiritual and ethical sterility grew rampantly, particularly when combined with newfound prosperity. The United East-India Company, formed in 1602, and other Dutch industry ushered in a period of unparalleled affluence. The majority were inclined to live for this life rather than for the world to come. Moreover, the state increasingly interfered in church matters and church discipline.[34] The state controlled the universities where Reformed ministers were

xc   **The Dutch Second Reformation**

being trained under the increasing influence of Rationalism, particularly the philosophy of Descartes and Spinoza.

These spiritual, social, and intellectual conditions existed in sharp tension with historic Dutch Calvinism which was intrinsically oriented toward sound doctrine and piety. The Calvinism of the Canons of Dort stood in marked contrast to the spirit of the age. Moreover, the stipulations the Synod of Dort had laid down with regard to the supervision of pastors, professors, and theological writings were not being followed. All of these circumstances, combined with the influence of English Puritanism, German Pietism, the Genevan reform,[35] and native Dutch influences (e.g., medieval mysticism,[36] the *Devotio Moderna*, and Anabaptism[37]— each of which emphasized sanctification), gave rise to the Dutch Second Reformation and its protest against the laxity of the age. Reflecting the concern of the Second Reformation, P. de Witte wrote, "Oh times, oh morals! What do parents do but bring up their children to become the prey of all kinds of seductive spirits, such as the papists, anabaptists, Arminians, and libertines? Yes, even to become the booty of the devil, to be the heirs of eternal damnation and the firewood of hell."[38]

The Dutch Second Reformation was a movement that arose out of the ashes of the burning expectation which had moved the early Reformers. Also the early Second Reformation divines envisioned a theocratic society and an ideal church in which the bulk of the population would be involved in personal and communal renewal. Reference was frequently made to the unbreakableness of a "threefold cord," consisting of God, the Netherlands, and the House of Orange. But the vision that the Netherlands would yet become "the New Israel of the West" in society and church life proved to be an unattainable ideal. The post-Reformers lived to view the failure of that dream. They faced the painful reality that the majority of parishioners had not become more spiritual as a result of the Reformation. To their followers, many of whom found conventicles (*gezelschappen*)[39] more spiritually edifying than formal worship, the church was no longer the communion of saints, but at best a very mixed multitude and at worst a "Babylon" or an "Egypt." Jodocus van Lodenstein's assessment of the Reformed church in his day is typical of that of later Second Reformation divines: "Babylon of Babylons, a thousand times worse than that of the Papacy because of the light that she had but did not rightly use."[40] The church seems "more deformed than reformed," he lamented. "There is no practicing of the truth, but a parroting of the words of the catechism is all that one finds among Reformed people."[41]

Another prominent Second Reformation divine, Bernardus Smytegelt complained:

> There are few converted preachers. Many of them are lazy idlers, vain fops. . . . Among external professors you will find much chaff and hardly a grain of wheat. There are heaps of external professors, and are they not indifferent and ungodly? What are they like in the families? Dear man! Do you not know how scarce pious parents are? How rare it is to find a godly mother or grandmother! How unusual to find a pious servant or maid! How unusual to find godliness among children as with Timothy! . . . How few are acquainted with the Bible! How few use the Bible regularly in the home! How few pray with each other, teach each other, and seek to lead each other toward heaven![42]

Consequently, in opposition to sin and complacency, an urgent, zealous call went out for fresh personal, church,[43] and societal reform: *The scriptural appeal for sanctification must be zealously pursued; Reformation doctrine must be lived.*

S. van der Linde, a leading Dutch scholar on the Second Reformation, rightly affirms that the movement must not be equated with "non-dogmatical" (*ondogmatisch*) Christendom; rather, its goal was to join doctrine (*leer*) to the whole of daily life (*leven*):

> The Second Reformation . . . is not at all a-dogmatic or anti-dogmatic. It only desires that dogma be experienced as spirit and life. . . .[44]
>
> The protest of the Second Reformation is not primarily against dogmatism as engendering a quenching of the Spirit, but much more against a certain *vitalism* as well as *secularism* whereby one observes the Spirit as being grieved.[45]

Elsewhere van der Linde expands these concerns and notes:

> The Second Reformation sides entirely with the Reformation and levels criticism not so much against the *reformata* (the church which is reformed), but rather against the *reformanda* (the church which needs to be reformed).[46]

Moreover, though the Second Reformation is preeminently concerned with spiritual life (*geestelijk leven*) and experience (*bevindelijk*), so that a heavy accent falls on the practice of piety (*praxis pietatis; praktijk der godzaligheid*) and even on precision (*preciesheid*), there is notwithstanding an array of emphases:

> In Voetius we have the church-organizer, in Ames a very original theologian, in Teellinck and Brakel, divines of practical religion, and in Lodensteyn and Saldenus, the men of "mysticism," cross-bearing, and meditation upon the life to come.[47]

Despite diversity, however, van der Linde concludes that there is an underlying element of "precision" in the Second Reformation which is inseparable from a fervent desire to counteract prevailing impiety with a piety which "consciously consecrates all of life to God."[48]

Several attempts have been made to define the core of the Dutch Second Reformation as a logical development from and application of the Reformation proper.[49] Herman Witsius emphasized that the motto, "the Reformed church needs to be ever reforming" (*ecclesia reformata, semper reformanda*) applies only to the church's life and not to doctrine since Reformation doctrine was established as foundational truth. Every Second Reformation divine was convinced he was following his Reformed forebears and upholding Reformed orthodoxy, although some pointed out defects in the Reformation era, usually centering around the fact that the Reformation divines were also sons of their time. For example, Teellinck gently chides the Reformers for being more concerned with the reformation of doctrine than of life, with justification than sanctification.[50]

Consequently, Heinrich Heppe defines the Second Reformation as "a striving for the completion of the church reformation of the sixteenth century (as being a mere reform of doctrine) by way of a revival of piety or by a reformation of life."[51] Johannes Hofmeyr concludes:

> Although this movement also had other spiritual fathers, it can be contended that the central thrust of the Second Reformation (which involves a personal spiritual piety, an articulated ecclesiology and a theocratic outlook on society) is broadly derived from Calvin. It should therefore be regarded not as a correction but as a development of the Reformation.[52]

J. van Genderen enlarges these concepts:

> By this term, *Nadere Reformatie*, we mean a movement in the 17th century which was a reaction against dead orthodoxy and [the] secularisation of Christianity in the Church of the Reformation and which insisted on the practise of faith. This may also be called a special form of Pietism, because the central idea is the "praxis pietatis." The origin of the pietistic trend lies in England and the father of Puritan Pietism [who] was William Perkins. Via Willem Teellinck and Guilielmus Amesius a direct influence on a kindred movement in Holland ensued. To this movement belong the Teellincks, Voetius, Van Lodenstein, Saldenus, the two Brakels, and especially also Witsius. This movement is not meant as a correction of the Reformation but as the consequence of it. The background of the conspicuous preciseness is the desire to serve God fully according to His will.[53]

Cornelis Graafland, another leading Dutch scholar on the Second Reformation, refers to it as a movement "which turned against the generally poor conditions prevailing in the Reformed church...to achieve a radical and complete sanctification of all facets of life."

Graafland describes the movement as a "deepening and broadening of the sixteenth-century Reformation."[54]

Another attempt to express the heart of the Second Reformation is that of P. B. van der Watt,[55] which is paraphrased by Hofmeyr as follows:

> [The Second Reformation] revolted against the unspiritual state of the nation, ministers, and congregations. They plead also for a personal commitment to Christ. The experienced and tested religion is to them of central importance. Although nothing is done to undermine the church, the office, the sacrament, and the covenant, they regard rebirth as the priority. They also assume a reasonably strong Puritan point of view. They plead for the observance of the Sabbath and the carrying out of the demands of the Lord. The church must be pure and should be cleansed of all that is unholy. Finally, they had a high regard for the Scriptures and for the Heidelberg Catechism.[56]

Finally, a definition of the Second Reformation was formulated in 1983 by the group of scholars responsible for *Documentatieblad Nadere Reformatie*:

> This movement within the "Nederduits Gereformeerde Kerk," while opposing generally prevailing abuses and misconceptions and pursuing the broadening and progressive advancement of the sixteenth-century Reformation, urges and strives with prophetic zeal for both the inner experience of Reformed doctrine and personal sanctification, as well as the radical and total sanctification of all spheres of life.[57]

Despite these somewhat oversimplified generalizations of the versatile Dutch Second Reformation, its complexity is not to be underestimated. Graafland points out that the Second Reformation had no organizational structure beyond a strong feeling of spiritual kinship existing among its divines. At times this led to small organized circles such as the so-called "Utrecht Circle" under the leadership of Voetius or to programs for action such as those promoted by Willem Teellinck and Jacobus Koelman. For the most part, however, each Second Reformation divine brought the message of the necessity of reform to his own parishioners. The contours of this call to reform naturally took on distinctive shapes in each locality and generation.[58]

Due to this lack of organization and an increasing emphasis on internal, experiential life, the Second Reformation's initial call to action in every sphere of life diminished rapidly.[59] For example, in its earlier, so-called *classical* period, the Second Reformation strongly opposed a state-dominated church and worked strenuously for the church's independence. Due to opposition from both the government and citizens, however, the classical Second Reformation could not retain this position. Anabaptist tendencies towards isolation increased with time. Various sub-movements, such as the Labadists, tended to withdraw from civil and church affairs, and became separatists, but continued to bear substantial influence on the larger movement.[60] Though few Second Reformation pietists condoned separatism,[61] numerous conventicles (*gezelschappen*) were formed for the nourishing of spiritual life. Gradually the Second Reformation became increasingly reminiscent of the *Devotio Moderna* in its emphasis on thorough separation from the unredeemed world. This is exemplified in a comparison of Willem Teellinck and Wilhelmus Schortinghuis (1700-1750; renowned for his *Het Innige Christendom [Inner Christianity]*) as typical early and late representatives of the movement:

> For Teellinck the experience of the heart remained central, but then as a center which penetrated a wide area, including not only the family and the congregation, but also the entire church and nation, politics inclusive. For Schortinghuis subjective experience is the fort to which the believer withdraws himself from the world and even from the congregation around him.[62]

These differences must not be exaggerated, however, for Teellinck also displayed elements of internal withdrawal, as did other early Second Reformation proponents such as Koelman and Lodenstein,[63] whereas van der Groe, often considered the last representative of the movement, strongly emphasized church and social life as a whole, including the political context.[64] Van der Linde concludes:

> Most of those who can be considered representative of the Second Reformation, being promoters of a theocratic structure as far as the relationship between church and state are concerned, are open for that which is not so purely spiritual, such as the political state.[65]

Generally speaking, the complex Dutch Second Reformation focused on a variety of major themes. In summarizing the movement, Graafland addresses the following contours: election, regeneration, sanctification, the family and the congregation, the church, creation and natural theology, eschatology, and theocracy.[66] Through promoting a pious lifestyle and a theocratic concept of all social relationships based on family worship, the parish, and the church as a whole, the Second Reformation aimed to establish and enforce moral and spiritual discipline in all spheres of life. Second Reformation sermons addressed all of these mostly active themes, but simultaneously stressed the fall of Adam, the natural man's inability to aspire to good, the absolute sovereignty of divine predestination and grace, dependence upon God, the necessity of adequate conviction of sin, the experience of conversion, and the simplicity of true worship.[67] C. Vogelaar's summaries of the content of the preaching of Bernardus

Smytegelt (1665-1739) and Johannes Beukelman (1704-1757), are typical particularly of the later period of the Second Reformation:

> In [Smytegelt's] sermons much emphasis was laid on the practice of godliness, on the holy duties of Christians, on the life of God's people and on the frames of their hearts, as well as their experiences of light and darkness, the leading and operation of the Holy Spirit, and giving instructions and directions to the godly.[68]
>
> In his sermons [Beukelman] applied the message to his hearers: revealing clearly the false, sandy foundations of the nominal Christians, proclaiming plainly our misery and total depravity, recommending especially the way of reconciliation with God in Christ, bringing the sincere invitations and callings of the gospel, encouraging the concerned souls of true seekers of God, showing unto the godly ones the causes for their little progress in faith and sanctification, and also giving the right means to make their calling and election sure — and to live in true sanctification in the fear of God's Name and to His honor.[69]

Thus, the preaching of the Second Reformation emphasized *experiential theology*, which M. Eugene Osterhaven has defined as "that broad stream of Reformed teaching which, accepting the creeds of the church, emphasized the new birth, the conversion, and the sanctification of the believer so that he might acquire an experiential or personal knowledge of Christ's saving grace."[70] External religion, orthodox doctrine, sound theological propositions are all insufficient for salvation; feeling, experience, spiritual warfare, and genuine prayer are essential for faith and practice. The "head" knowledge of doctrine, albeit necessary, must be accompanied by the "heart" knowledge of scriptural experience:

> There were some, of course, who carried the emphasis on feeling, on intense religious experience of an emotional nature, to dangerous lengths, but most Reformed pietists stopped far short of making that the norm. The norm is Scripture alone but, they held, as the Frisian Catechism put it, that "true faith demands an experiential knowledge, emerging from a conviction and an experiencing of God's Spirit, and conforming to the word of truth."[71]

For Second Reformation adherents, "formal Christianity, by which they meant a Christianity exhausting itself in externals, was only slightly better than none at all. For that reason they, like the mystics before them, emphasized the primacy of the inward response to God."[72] Hence struggles of faith held a central place.[73]

With regard to assurance of faith, the Second Reformation as a whole not only emphasized the promises of God and the witness of the Spirit, but also increasingly accentuated the syllogisms, making a transition from the *syllogismus practicus* in the classical period to the *syllogismus mysticus* in the later period.[74] Graafland

and van der Linde are sharply critical of this transition, but the latter fails to note that also the mystical syllogism is inseparable from the enlightening of the Spirit:

> Rather than seeking assurance in the Spirit, i.e., in the promise of the gospel and thus not in ourselves, the "marks of grace" have come upon the scene. It is difficult to view them with anything but pity since they yield so much melancholy and uncertainty. It is thus obvious that one believes to honor the Spirit the most by seeking assurance of faith and salvation primarily in the so-called mystical syllogism, i.e., that one endeavors to draw the conclusion that he is indeed a true Christian due to being acquainted with mystical, inner stirrings and emotions of which a worldly person has no knowledge.... Our Heidelberg Catechism does as yet have the courage to state that we can be assured of our sonship by our good works as being fruits of faith. In the course of Reformed tradition this practical syllogism has increasingly fallen into abeyance. This did not only occur in conjunction with a turning away from all that is external in order only to deem "internal" matters as being spiritual and valid (incorrectly in our opinion), but also due to a fear for hypocrisy when considering how our "pious flesh" is capable of adorning itself....
>
> We are without expectation as far as the *syllogismus mysticus* is concerned. If this is not conjoined to the external practice of faith, there will be nothing to hold on to for the man who is genuinely in need.... His only certainty is definitely not a syllogism, for it is not logic which reigns in the grace of God, but only the witness of the Holy Spirit in and through the gospel.[75]

Assessment in Secondary Sources

The complexity of the Dutch Second Reformation is compounded by its assessment in secondary sources. The nineteenth-century theologians at Groningen were the first to make an effort to view the Second Reformation as a movement from a historical perspective. W. van 't Spijker shows, however, that these divines, such as P. Hofstede de Groot, differed little from the view of Ypeij and Dermout in their *Geschiedenis der Nederlandsche Hervormde Kerk (History of the Reformed Church of the Netherlands)*. Neither Ypeij and Dermout nor the Groningen professors researched the movement from its primary sources, but tended to model the movement after their own ideals. In particular, the Groningen theologians viewed Thomas à Kempis, Wessel Gansfort, Willem Teellinck, Jodocus van Lodenstein, and others as their ideal.[76]

Later in the nineteenth century (1879), Heinrich Heppe published *Geschichte des Pietismus und der Mystik in der reformirten Kirche, namentlich der Niederlande (The History of Pietism and Mysticism in the Reformed Church, particularly in the Netherlands)*. The following decade

Albrecht Ritschl's three-volume history of Pietism was published (*Geschichte des Pietismus,* 1880-86). These works helped to establish the seminal issues involved in the Second Reformation and are still being discussed by scholars of the movement. Heppe concludes that the roots of Pietism are found in Puritanism, for he posits that the "second reformation" moved from English Puritanism to the Dutch Second Reformation to German Pietism. Ritschl placed Pietism in a broader framework of movements of reform present in the Western church since the Middle Ages, pointing particularly to Franciscan observances, the mystical theology of Bernard de Clairveaux, and the Anabaptists with regard to the Dutch Second Reformation.[77]

Van 't Spijker views the 1911 work of W. Goeters (*Die Vorbereitung des Pietismus in der reformierten Kirche der Niederlande bis zur labadistischen Krisis 1670; The Groundwork for Pietism in the Netherlands until the Labadistic Crisis in 1670*) as a significant step forward in research on the Dutch Second Reformation in that he emphasized the need to study the divines of the movement on an individual basis. Goeters detected various streams of thought in the Second Reformation and avoided simplistic assessments as to their origins. Moreover, in addition to theological and practical issues, he pointed to social and historical roots which paved the way for the movement. He also highlighted some important themes of the Second Reformation, such as the striving for an ideal church. In fact, he defined "the essence of this movement to be a striving of the visible church to approximate her essence (which is found in the invisible church) as much as possible."[78]

Much negative reaction against the Second Reformation can be traced to Abraham Kuyper and his emphasis on the church's cultural mandate. Early in his ministry Kuyper was profoundly influenced by a simple, God-fearing woman of Second Reformation persuasion, Pietje Baltus, who emphasized the necessity of experimental conversion. Subsequently, however, he became troubled that the Christians among whom he labored had become too pietistic and sheltered due in part to a constant diet of reading the "old writers" (*oude schrijvers*), as experimentally oriented laymen were fond of calling Second Reformation authors. At times Kuyper disparagingly called the pietistic elements in the Dutch church, "Methodists,"[79] though he retained a strong element of piety in his devotional writings as well as respect for the Second Reformation divines.[80] Kuyper's attempts to teach laymen to apply Christianity to all spheres of life led to a revival of Calvinism in the Netherlands. His followers, however, frequently called neo-Calvinists, went far beyond Kuyper by rejecting nearly all semblances of piety and by "externalizing the gospel" in a flurry of kingdom-activity. Still today "the neo-Calvinists in The Netherlands on the whole are quite antagonistic toward the Second Reformation. They see it as an other-worldly, anti-cultural and scholastic movement which has done the church more harm than good."[81]

Also reacting negatively to the Second Reformation are Otto Ritschl who views the Second Reformation as a falsification of the Reformation;[82] Theodorus L. Haitjema who regards it as degeneration (*ontaarding*);[83] and Aart A. van Schelven who esteems it to be overly baptistic, spiritualistic, and influenced by Semi-Pelagianism.[84] E. D. Kraan considers the Second Reformation to be too steeped in subjectivism,[85] while Rudolf Boon states that it "inclines to Anabaptism."[86] Teunis Brienen sets Reformation gospel preaching over against Second Reformation preaching which speaks to various "soul conditions" among the hearers.[87]

Positively, Hans Emil Weber,[88] Arie Vergunst,[89] James Tanis,[90] J. H. R. Verboom,[91] Jonathan Gerstner,[92] Willem Jan op 't Hof[93] and others view it largely as a profitable outgrowth of Calvinism. Also Stoeffler's assessment is largely positive and a most helpful, needed corrective:

> [The Second Reformation] was by and large a thoroughly responsible, evangelical movement. On the personal level it emphasized love for God and man and a type of daily conduct based on what it regarded as the New Testament ethic. Its larger aim was the reformation of the visible Church according to the pattern of apostolic Christianity. Intellectually it was highly respectable in so far as practically all of its leaders had enjoyed the opportunity of excellent theological training. For that reason it had the support of the best minds of the day. Voetius, Essenius, Hoornbeeck, and later such Coccejans as Witsius endorsed it enthusiastically. . . . [It] constituted a significant and influential party with the Reformed churches. . . .
>
> The coming of Pietism [i.e., the Second Reformation], like the rise of any reform movement which tends to challenge the established order of things, caused some strains and difficulties. At the end, . . . however, the Reformed churches were the better for having made the necessary adjustments.[94]

Still others provide mixed assessment, noting the evolving changes within the movement itself. This is particularly true of several Reformed scholars in the Netherlands (such as J. G. Woelderink, Arnold A. van Ruler, S. van der Linde, Cornelis Graafland, Willem Balke,[95] K. Exalto, W. van 't Spijker, J. van Genderen, and others[96]) who have done considerable pioneer work on the Second Reformation. Generally speaking, these Dutch scholars have varying degrees of appreciation for the Dutch Second Reformation (particularly its classical period) though they feel that it was not as theologically rich as the Reformation proper. S. van der Linde and Cornelis Graafland affirm the early Dutch Second Reformation as embracing some positive characteristics, but see decay setting in largely through excessive introspection such that the movement failed in the late seventeenth and early eighteenth centuries "to combine breadth with depth."[97] Similarly, Hofmeyr asserts that "the classical phase of the Second Reformation shows definite links with Calvin, while the distance between Calvin and the stricter pietism of the later phase of the Second Reformation is much greater."[98] In a different vein, Prozesky concludes that "the movement as a whole underwent gradual change with its early precisianism losing ground to devotional and on occasion mystical pursuits, besides also evolving or adapting its own typical institutions, such as conventicles, edificatory sermons and Pietistic literature."[99] Osterhaven discerns two streams in the Second Reformation:

> The one stream emphasized mysticism, inwardness, felicity, prayer, spiritual elation, and joy in the Lord. Overworked words among these folk were *gelukzaligheid* and *godzaligheid*.... Involving the whole person, his intellect, feeling, and will, it is the ultimate blessing that God can give one in this life and the greatest proof that God is a gracious father to his children. The other stream was activistic and laid stress on doing the will of the Lord. Here the law as an expression of God's will was much to the fore and the practice of piety was conceived largely in thinking, saying, and doing what is right before the Lord. This latter emphasis... came to be know as *Preciesen* in Dutch, or, as they were sometimes called by their opponents, *Fijnen*, sanctimonians, we might say.
>
> Whatever the emphasis, all pietists believed heartily in experiential theology and were known as *de ernstige*, the earnest, zealous Christians of their place and time....
>
> In its better representatives, like Wilhelmus à Brakel, the experiential theology sought a healthy balance between mysticism and precisionism.[100]

Van Ruler calls the movement as a whole a "legitimate experiment."[101]

The wide divergence of these opinions calls for further studies in the Dutch Second Reformation as a movement in its own generations. In future studies the Second Reformation should be evaluated in its distinct spiritual, theological, and political milieu. Too often the Second Reformation is judged by the Reformation proper, the latter being regarded as normative. Calvin is presented by A. Ritschl and others as an ideal and all differences from him (even in areas where his thinking is largely embryonic, such as covenant theology)[102] are prone to be considered in a negative light. The unfair conclusion is then reached that the Second Reformation is not a "further reformation" (*nadere reformatie*), but a "further deformation" (*verdere deformatie*).[103] It is our conviction that a more careful, objective study of the Second Reformation will yield the conclusion that these Dutch divines as a whole did not misread Calvin and the Reformers, but simply adapted the teaching of the early Reformers in a practical way to their own day.

Additional work also needs to be done on the influence of Phillipp Jakob Spener, August Hermann Francke, Friedrich Adolph Lampe, Gerhard Tersteegen, and other German Pietists on the Dutch Second Reformation. Monographs need to be written on several important Second Reformation divines who are either the subjects of outdated studies or who, as yet, have not been thoroughly studied.[104] Caricatures against the movement and the influence of Reformed scholastic orthodoxy need to be unveiled for what they are. Particularly needed are both primary[105] and secondary sources published in English on the Dutch Second Reformation.

English and American Puritanism have received considerably more attention from Dutch writers than the Dutch Second Reformation has received from English writers. The Dutch Second Reformation divines deserve to be treated with the same scholarly care devoted to their Puritan counterparts. Such treatment will recognize that the long-term influence of the Second Reformation has been seriously underestimated. An amplification of Stoeffler's reassessment is needed:

> While the [Second Reformation] dream of reforming the Reformed never succeeded it could hardly be doubted that the perfectionistic ideals of this reform party brought about significant changes in the life of the Church. It was responsible for an emphasis upon effective, religiously significant preaching such as is seldom found in territorial churches, together with a similar emphasis upon pastoral work which is equally unusual under such surroundings. Many of the classes and synods began to stress catechization to a degree unknown since the early days of the Genevan reformation. Church discipline, which had been exercised almost solely with regard to faith and order, was oriented to include the daily conduct of church members. A devotional literature was created such as continental Protestantism had never known because its need had not been recognized. Family worship was encouraged and free prayer found a place along with printed prayers. In fact prayer was encouraged as perhaps never before within the Reformed churches. Even conventicles...were authorized by various ecclesiastical bodies. For the first time since the days of Geneva the Reformed churches knew of genuine religious awakenings such as the one at Friesland in 1672, where a group of pastors entered together upon an evangelistic venture with noticeable results. Last but not least the matter of training an effective ministry, interested in piety as well as doctrine and polity, was given serious attention. The result was the later development of theological seminaries.[106]

Further, the influence of Second Reformation devotional writings and sermons in the eighteenth and nineteenth (and even twentieth) centuries remained great among the conservative, experimental Reformed in the Netherlands, South Africa,[107] and North America. Today their writings are being reprinted as rapidly as the Puritans are in the English-speaking world. It is our hope and prayer that the translation of Wilhelmus à Brakel's classic, *De Redelijke Godsdienst*, may serve to arouse interest in the history and theology of the Dutch Second Reformation.

[1]Dutch Anabaptists continued to be martyred, however, until the 1570s in the Netherlands, despite the fact that the movement itself lost impetus by 1545.

[2]Mention should also be made of the followers of Erasmus who precipitated the Dutch Second Reformation in a negative sense. Cf. W. Robert Godfrey, "The Dutch Reformed Response," in *Discord, Dialogue, and Concord*, ed. by Lewis W. Spitz and Wenzel Lohff (Philadelphia: Fortress Press, 1977), pp. 166-67. Godfrey also gives a succinct overview of the Calvinist aspect in "Calvin and Calvinism in the Netherlands," in *John Calvin: His Influence in the Western World*, ed. by W. Stanford Reid, pp. 95-122. Cf. Walter Lagerwey, "The History of Calvinism in the Netherlands," in *The Rise and Development of Calvinism*, ed. by John Bratt, pp. 63-102; Jerry D. van der Veen, "Adoption of Calvinism in the Reformed Church in the Netherlands" (B. S. T. thesis, Biblical Seminary in New York, 1951).

[3]Taffin is often regarded as a precursor of the Dutch Second Reformation, due in part to his being a sixteenth-century Reformer, but S. van der Linde has argued persuasively that he should be regarded as the earliest representative of the Dutch Second Reformation. ("Jean Taffin: eerste pleiter voor 'Nadere Reformatie' in Nederland," *Theologia Reformata* 25 [1982]:6-29; *Jean Taffin. Hofprediker en raadsheer van Willem van Oranje* [Amsterdam: Ton Bolland, 1982]). Cf. C. Vogelaar, "Pioneers of the Second Reformation," *The Banner of Truth* 52 (1986):150-51.

[4]What William Perkins was to English Puritanism, Willem Teellinck was to the Dutch Second Reformation; hence these divines are often denominated as "the fathers" of these movements (Joel R. Beeke, *Assurance of Faith: Calvin, English Puritanism, and the Dutch Second Reformation* [New York: Peter Lang, 1991], pp. 105-138).

[5]Ibid., pp. 281-320.

[6]For a concise introduction to leading Second Reformation divines, see B. Glasius, ed., *Godgeleerd Nederland: Biographisch Woordenboek van Nederlandsche Godgeleerden*, 3 vols. ('s-Hertogenbosch: Gebr. Muller, 1851-56); Sietse Douwes van Veen, *Voor tweehonderd jaren: Schetsen van het leven onzer Gereformeerde Vaderen*, 2nd ed. (Utrecht: Kemink & Zoon, 1905); J. P. de Bie and J. Loosjes, eds., *Biographisch Woordenboek der Protestantsche Godgeleerden in Nederland*, 5 vols. ('s-Gravenhage: Martinus Nijhoff, 1907-1943); *Christelijke Encyclopedie*, 6 vols., 2nd ed. (Kampen: J. H. Kok, 1959); K. Exalto, *Beleefd Geloof: Acht schetsen van gereformeerde theologen uit de 17e Eeuw* (Amsterdam: Ton Bolland, 1974), and *De Kracht der Religie: Tien schetsen van Gereformeerde 'Oude Schrijvers' uit de 17e en 18e Eeuw* (Urk: De Vuurtoren, 1976); H. Florijn, ed., *Hollandse Geloofshelden* (Utrecht: De Banier, 1981); W. van Gorsel, *De IJver voor Zijn Huis: De Nadere Reformatie en haar belangrijkste vertegenwoordigers* (Groede: Pieters, 1981); C. J. Malan, *Die Nadere Reformasie* (Potchefstroom: Potchefstroomse Universiteit vir CHO, 1981); H. Florijn, *100 Portretten van Godgeleerden in Nederland uit de 16e, 17e, 18e Eeuw* (Utrecht: Den Hertog, 1982); D.

Nauta, et al., *Biografisch Lexicon voor de Geschiedenis van het Nederlandse Protestantisme*, 3 vols.(Kampen: Kok, 1978-88); T. Brienen, et al., *De Nadere Reformatie. Beschrijving van haar voornaamste vertegenwoordigers* ('s-Gravenhage: Boekencentrum, 1986); T. Brienen, et al., *De Nadere Reformatie en het Gereformeerd Piëtisme* ('s-Gravenhage: Boekencentrum, 1989); J. R. Beeke, "Biographies of Dutch Second Reformation Divines," *Banner of Truth* 54, 2 (1988) through 56, 3 (1990), a series of twenty-five articles representing the major divines of the movement.

For bibliography of the Dutch Second Reformation, see P. L. Eggermont, "Bibliographie van het Nederlandse Piëtisme in de zeventiende en achttiende eeuw," *Documentatieblad 18e eeuw* 3 (1969):17-31; W. van Gent, *Bibliotheek van oude schrijvers* (Rotterdam: Lindebergs, 1979); J. van der Haar, *Schatkamer van de Gereformeerde Theologie in Nederland (c. 1600-c.1800): Bibliografisch Onderzoek* (Veenendaal: Antiquariaat Kool, 1987).

Cf. F. Ernest Stoeffler, *The Rise of Evangelical Pietism* (Leiden: E.J. Brill, 1971), pp. 109-68, covering twelve Second Reformation divines in varying depth and quality; Cornelis Graafland, *De Zekerheid van het Geloof: Een onderzoek naar de geloofbeschouwing van enige vertegenwoordigers van reformatie en nadere reformatie* (Wageningen: H. Veenman & Zonen, 1961), pp. 138-244, concentrating on the doctrine of faith and assurance in fourteen Second Reformation theologians; Johannes de Boer, *De Verzegeling met de Heilige Geest volgens de opvatting van de Nadere Reformatie* (Rotterdam: Bronder, 1968), which examines the soteriological thought of fourteen Second Reformation divines.

[7]The term was used as early as Jean Taffin (1528-1602). Cf. L. F. Groenendijk, "De Oorsprong van de uitdrukking 'Nadere Reformatie,'" *Documentatieblad Nadere Reformatie* 9 (1985):128-34; S. van der Linde, "Jean Taffin: eerste pleiter voor 'Nadere Reformatie' in Nederland," *Theologia Reformata* 25 (1982):7ff. Cf. W. van 't Spijker, *De Nadere Reformatie en het Gereformeerd Piëtisme*, pp. 5ff..

[8]Jonathan Neil Gerstner, *The Thousand Generation Covenant: Dutch Reformed Covenant Theology and Group Identity in Colonial South Africa, 1652-1814* (Leiden: E. J. Brill, 1991), pp. 75ff.

[9]Ibid., p. 75n.

[10]Cornelis Pronk, "The Dutch Puritans," *The Banner of Truth*, nos. 154-55 (July-August 1976):1-10; J. W. Hofmeyr, "The Doctrine of Calvin as Transmitted in the South African Context by Among Others the *Oude Schrijvers*," in *Calvinus Reformator: His contribution to Theology, Church and Society* (Potchefstroom: Potchefstroom University for Christian Higher Education, 1983), p. 260.

[11]*Christelijke Encyclopedie*, 2nd ed. (Kampen: Kok, 1959), 5:128.

[12]Martin H. Prozesky, "The Emergence of Dutch Pietism," *Journal of Ecclesiastical History* 28 (1977):33.

[13]For historical-theological connections between seventeenth-century English and Dutch Calvinism, see especially the writings of Keith Sprunger (*Dutch Puritanism: A History of English and Scottish Churches of the Netherlands in the Sixteenth and Seventeenth Centuries* [Leiden: Brill, 1982] and *The Learned Doctor William Ames: Dutch Backgrounds of English and American Puritanism* [Chicago: University of Illinois Press, 1972]). Cf. MacMillan, "The Connection between 17th Century British and Dutch Calvinism," in *Not by Might nor by Power*, 1988 Westminster Conference papers, pp. 22-31.

[14]"The Dutch Puritans," *Banner of Truth*, nos. 154-55 (July-August, 1976):3.

[15]"The Connection between 17th Century British and Dutch Calvinism," in *Not by Might nor by Power*, p. 24. Willem Jan op 't Hof also points out the influence of

Dutch refugee congregations in England, noting that "it can be justifiably concluded that it is chiefly the Dutch congregations in England which are in the background of the Puritanization of spiritual life in the Netherlands" (*Engelse piëtistische geschriften in het Nederlands, 1598-1622* [Rotterdam: Lindenberg, 1987], p. 639).

[16]"From 1598 to 1622 a total of 114 editions were issued of a total of 60 translations. These 60 translations concern works by . . . twenty-two English authors. . . . Two authors are numerically preeminent among them: Cowper (18 editions of 10 translations) and Perkins (71 editions of 29 translations). Indeed, Perkins alone eclipses all the others taken together. . . . Auction catalogues show that Udemans possessed 20 Puritan books in Latin and 57 in English. Similarly, Voetius possessed 30 works in Latin and 270 in English. . . . A rough estimate for the period from 1623-1699 gives 260 new translations, 580 editions and 100 new translators. Compared to the first quarter of a century of translational activity there is a considerable increase. . . . The flow of translations continued unabated during the whole of the seventeenth century, which is amazing. For what one would have expected was for translations, after a period of taking firm root and of blossoming in the absence of similar originally Dutch writings, to become decreasingly popular by the middle of the century when the Dutch Pietistic writings began to appear in large numbers" (ibid., pp. 636-37, 640, 645).

[17]Sprunger, *Dutch Puritanism*, p. 307.

[18]*Geschiedenis der Kerk* (Nijkerk: G. F. Callenbach, 1955), p. 228.

[19]Op 't Hof reaches the following conclusions: "First, the influence of Puritanism was largely embodied in writings, either in English or translated into Dutch. This is not to say that, secondly, the significance of personal contacts is to be underestimated. This applies both to Dutchmen in England and to Puritans in the Netherlands. Thirdly, the impact of Puritanism is nearly exclusively confined to exponents of the *Nadere Reformatie*. Fourthly, these men, Voetius and J. Koelman for instance, were no uncritical recipients of Puritan ideas. In the fifth place, in the course of the seventeenth century Puritan influence began to manifest itself in some new ways. In both Koelman and M. du Bois this is shown in the area of spiritual (auto)biography and in Koelman's case also in his resistance to fixed formularies. In the sixth place, most exponents of the *Nadere Reformatie* prove to have been substantially and in some cases even very decisively determined by the impact of Puritanism. In the seventh place, it was precisely the chief and the most influential exponents of the *Nadere Reformatie* who were most imbued with Puritanism. Finally, not only did Dutch devotional writers frankly confess their dependence on and orientation towards Puritans from England and Scotland, they also warmly recommended them and to the best of their ability promoted the reading of Puritan writings, which they also contributed significantly to by either undertaking translational activities themselves or stimulating others to do so. Having been nearly exclusively indebted to Puritanism for its rise and having been largely determined by it in its early period, the *Nadere Reformatie* during the whole of the seventeenth century remained exceedingly dependent on Puritanism. It is this dependence which explains why the large increase of *Nadere Reformatie* writings did not detract from the need of and the demand for Puritan works, either in English or translated into Dutch. The dependence was so great that the peak years of the *Nadere Reformatie*, 1650-1670, coincide with those of the Dutch translations of Puritan writings" (*Engelse piëtistische geschriften in het Nederlands, 1598-1622*, pp. 645-46; also, pp. 583-97, 627-35). Cf. Cornelis Graafland, "De Invloed van het Puritanisme op het Ontstaan van het Gereformeerd Piëtisme in Nederland," *Documentatieblad Nadere Reformatie* 7, 1 (1983):1-19. Graafland also details influences on

preaching, the art of meditation, casuistry, covenanting, the administration of the Lord's Supper, and eschatology.

[20]Ibid., pp. 2, 15-16.

[21]Gerstner, *Thousand Generation Covenant*, pp. 77-78.

[22]Beeke, *Assurance of Faith*, pp. 369-70.

[23]Pronk, *The Banner of Truth*, nos. 154-55 (July-August, 1976):6. Gerstner explains: "As orthodox Reformed in their doctrine as the English Puritans were, they were primarily pastors, not formal theologians. Thus one finds a remarkable scarcity of systematic theologies. Dutch Reformed thought while retaining a strong emphasis on the pulpit, produced a remarkable number of theological works, the majority addressed to the average person. Catechism preaching was perhaps part of the reason, but it seems they possessed a greater tendency towards system building. So the Continuing Reformation pastor strove for his parishioner's conversion, and at the same time to make him a dogmatician" (*Thousand Generation Covenant*, p. 78).

Sprunger notes that Ames found the Dutch somewhat too intellectual and not sufficiently practical, and therefore promoted Puritan piety "in an effort to make Dutchmen into Puritans" (*The Learned Doctor Ames: Dutch Backgrounds of English and American Puritanism*, p. 260). Cf. Hugo Visscher, *Guilielmus Amesius, Zijn Leven en Werken* (Haarlem: J. M. Stap, 1894).

[24]This term has been used more accurately to depict English-speaking Puritan churches in the Netherlands (cf. Douglas Campbell, *The Puritan in Holland, England, and America*, 4th ed., 2 vols. [New York: Harper and Brothers, 1892]; Sprunger, *Dutch Puritanism*; T. Brienen, *De prediking van de Nadere Reformatie* [Amsterdam: Ton Bolland, 1974]). Van der Linde prefers "English Puritanism in the Netherlands" to "Dutch Puritanism," since the English Puritans in the Netherlands confined themselves largely to their own circles (cf. "Jean Taffin: eerste pleiter voor 'Nadere Reformatie' in Nederland," *Theologia Reformata* 25 [1982]: 6ff.).

Moreover, the problem of using "English Puritanism" is compounded by the complexities of defining Puritanism itself (Beeke, *Assurance of Faith*, pp. 129-30n).

[25]*Thousand Generation Covenant*, p. 77.

[26]"The word 'Pietist' originally indicated 'an affected and indeed feigned kind of righteousnesss.' So K. D. Schmidt, *Grundriss der Kirchengeschichte*, 5th ed., Göttingen 1967, p. 416. M. Schmidt reports that the term became established after J. Feller, Professor of Poetry at Leipzig, used it with favourable connotations in two popular verses in 1689. See M. Schmidt, 'Pietismus' in *Die Religion in geschichte und Gegenwart*, 3rd ed., Tubingen 1961, v. col. 374" (Prozesky, "The Emergence of Dutch Pietism," *Journal of Ecclesiastical History* 28 [1977]:29-37).

[27]Stoeffler (*The Rise of Evangelical Pietism*, which attempts to define "Pietism" as embracing English Puritanism, the Dutch Second Reformation, and German Pietism, pp. 1-23) and James Tanis (*Dutch Calvinistic Pietism in the Middle Colonies: A Study in the Life and Theology of Theodorus Jacobus Frelinghuysen* [The Hague: Martinus Nijhoff, 1967] and "The Heidelberg Catechism in the Hands of the Calvinistic Pietists," *Reformed Review* 24 [1970-71]:154-61) follow German church historians in using the term, "Dutch Pietism," notably Heinrich Heppe (*Geschichte des Pietismus und der Mystik in der Reformierten Kirche, namentlich der Niederlande* [Leiden: Brill, 1879]) and Albrecht Ritschl (*Geschichte des Pietismus*, 3 vols. [Bonn: Marcus, 1880-86]).

For the influence of German Pietism on the Dutch Second Reformation, see Graafland, "De Gereformeerde Orthodoxie en het Piëtisme in Nederland," *Nederlands Theologisch Tijdschrift* 19 (1965):466-79; J. Steven O'Malley, *Pilgrimage of Faith: The*

Legacy of the Otterbeins (Metuchen, NJ: The Scarecrow Press, 1973); Stoeffler, *The Rise of Evangelical Pietism*. Cf. Martin H. Prozesky, "The Emergence of Dutch Pietism," *Journal of Ecclesiastical History* 28 (1977):28-37; Willem Balke, "Het Pietisme in Oost-friesland," *Theologia Reformata* 21 (1978):308-27.

[28]S. van der Linde, *Vromen en Verlichten: Twee eeuwen Protestantse Geloofsbeleving 1650-1850* (Utrecht: Aartsbisschoppelijk Museum Utrecht, 1974), p. 2; Gerstner, *Thousand Generation Covenant*, p. 76.

[29]Ibid., p. 76. According to Graafland, Dutch Second Reformation divines were united in emphasizing the importance of doctrine. Many of them (including even the Teellincks and the Brakels) viewed themselves as being free from "scholasticizing" in formulating doctrine, but nevertheless did frequently utilize scholastic terms and methodology, as is abundantly evident in this translation of *De Redelijke Godsdienst*. Flexibility and variety in terms of scholastic methodology were welcomed. Unlike German Pietists, none of the Second Reformation divines would subscribe to today's popular charges against Reformed scholasticism as being cold and irrelevant. Even Cocceius, known for his approach of biblical theology in a covenantal matrix, used a substantial amount of scholastic methodology. In fact, Gerstner subtitles the Voetian-Cocceian controversy, "The Battle of Two Scholastic Systems" (ibid, pp. 68-75). Richard Muller's conclusions relative to Reformed scholasticism (see Beeke, *Assurance of Faith*, p. 5n) hold true also for the Dutch Second Reformation divines.

Cf. Charles McCoy, "The Covenant Theology of Johannes Cocceius" (Ph. D. dissertation, Yale, 1957); H. B. Visser, *De Geschiedenis van den Sabbatstrijd onder de Gereformeerden in de Zeventiende Eeuw* (Utrecht: Kemink en Zoon, 1939); T. N. Hanekam, ed., *Ons Nederduitse Gereformeerde Kerk* (Kaapstad, 1952), p. 210; Prozesky, "The Emergence of Dutch Pietism," *Journal of Ecclesiastical History* 28 (1977):31ff.; H. Faulenbach, *Weg und Zeil; der Erkenntnis Christi. Eine Untersuchung zur Theologie des Johannes Cocceius* (Neukirchen: Neukirchener Verlag, 1973); Stoeffler, *The Rise of Evangelical Pietism*, pp. 113-15; C. Vogelaar, "The 'Unknown' Voetius Remembered," *The Banner of Truth* 55 (1989):182-83.

[30]"Deze termen suggereren een fundamentele eenheid, terwijl in werkelijkheid een zeer gedifferentieerde beweging voor ons staat met fundamentele verschillen in allerlei opzicht" (van der Linde, "Jean Taffin: eerste pleiter voor 'Nadere Reformatie' in Nederland," *Theologia Reformata* 25 [1982]:7; see also p. 28n). Cf. C. Vogelaar, "The Second or 'Further' Reformation," *The Banner of Truth* 52 (1986):40-41.

[31]W. van 't Spijker, "De Nadere Reformatie," in *De Nadere Reformatie: Beschrijving van haar voornaamste vertegenwoordigers*, pp. 6-16.

[32]"While they were not really state churches, they were folk churches. In such a church the tendency always exists to become so closely identified with the prevailing culture that its message becomes little more than a lifeless reiteration of prevailing values. This was overwhelmingly the case in the Reformed churches of the Netherlands...during the seventeenth century. Preaching was largely a matter of setting forth correct theological dogmas and generally accepted middle class virtues.... Any attempt to move in the direction of the spirituality and ethics of the New Testament was decried as 'precisianism' or worse" (Stoeffler, *The Rise of Evangelical Pietism*, pp. 115-16).

[33]*E Voto Dordraceno* (Amsterdam: Höveker & Wormser, 1905), 3:215.

[34]Jacobus Koelman, for example, "opposed governmental interference in church life on several fronts. He rejected the government's right to call ministers and to select elders and deacons. He fought against its low view of Christian living and its

lack of maintaining Christian discipline in conjunction with the administration of the sacraments. And he staunchly opposed the use of read forms and the observance of church feast days" (J. R. Beeke, "Jacobus Koelman," *The Banner of Truth* 55 [1989]:27).

[35]Genevan input came particularly through Jean Taffin, who studied under Calvin and Beza, and whose views are similar to those of the Teellincks, who were primarily influenced by English Puritanism. Balke feels that op 't Hof minimizes Taffin's influence in order to emphasize the role of the Teellincks in the Second Reformation (W. J. op 't Hof, *De Bibliografie van Eewout Teellinck* [Kampen: De Groot Goudriaan, 1988]; W. J. op 't Hof, C. A. de Niet, H. Uil, *Eewout Teellinck in handschriften* [Kampen: De Groot Goudriaan, 1989]). Cf. Stoeffler, *The Rise of Evangelical Pietism*, p. 116; van der Linde, "Jean Taffin: eerste pleiter voor 'Nadere Reformatie' in Nederland," *Theologia Reformata* 25 (1982):6-29.

[36]Graafland, "De invloed van het Puritanisme op het ontstaan van het Gereformeerd Pietisme in Nederland," *Documentatieblad Nadere Reformatie* 7 (1983):11-12; op 't Hof, *Engelse piëtistische geschriften in het Nederlands, 1598-1622*, pp. 599-600, 640.

[37]Stoeffler, *The Rise of Evangelical Pietism*, pp. 118ff. The *Devotio Moderna* was "a devotional movement of the fifteenth and sixteenth centuries chiefly associated with the Brethren of the Common Life; their founder, Gerard Groote; and their best-known writer, Thomas à Kempis" (P. H. Davids, "Devotio Moderna," in *Evangelical Dictionary of Theology*, ed. by Walter Elwell [Grand Rapids: Baker, 1984], p. 317). Cf. R. R. Post, *The Modern Devotion* (Leiden: E. J. Brill, 1968); T. P. van Zijl, *Gerard Groote, Ascetic and Reformer (1340-1384)* (Washington, D.C.: Catholic University of American Press, 1963); Albert Hyma, *The Brethren of the Common Life* (Grand Rapids: Eerdmans, 1950).

With regard to Anabaptism, op 't Hof concludes that the Second Reformation "was one of the answers to the Anabaptist reproach that Reformed doctrine did not lead to sanctity of life" (*Engelse piëtistische geschriften in het Nederlands, 1598-1622*, pp. 640-41; cf., pp. 606-607.).

[38]Dedication of his *Catechesatie over den Heidelbergschen Catechismus* (which underwent thirty printings in the seventeenth century!), cited in W. Verboom, *De Catechese van de Reformatie en de Nadere Reformatie* (Amsterdam: Buijten en Schipperheijn, 1986), p. 251.

[39]In the Second Reformation a desire for intimate Christian fellowship led to the development of "gatherings of the godly" in private homes to expound the Scriptures and to speak about spiritual truths in relation to the experimental leadings of God with His people. These became called *gezelschappen* (literally, "fellowships") in the Netherlands. "Fellowship," however, does not fully convey the Dutch meaning of *gezelschap*. Consequently, *gezelschap* is usually translated as "conventicle," the term ascribed to parallel meetings in Scotland. (In English Puritanism such meetings were known as *prophesyings* and in German Pietism as *collegiae pietatis*.)

Only in Scotland were conventicles more successful as a whole than in the Netherlands due largely to closer supervision by the presbytery on a long-term basis. In the Netherlands *gezelschappen* were also spiritually beneficial to many and were closely supervised for a time, but on occasion they turned into unsupervised, elitist groups which promoted critical assessment of sermons and highly introspective lifestyles (cf. van't Spijker, "De Nadere Reformatie," in *De Nadere Reformatie: Beschrijving van haar voornaamste vertegenwoordigers*, p. 14).

Stoeffler notes that conventicles were accepted by Second Reformation divines "as legitimate in many places. Voetius had recommended them and various ecclesiastical bodies among the Reformed churches had passed legislation to regulate them. They had started out as private meetings presided over by the pastor and held either on Sunday afternoon or on a weekday evening. The activities included singing, the reading of Scripture, discussion of a portion of Scripture, discussion of the sermon, and prayer. Gradually, however, they came close to being *ecclesiolae in ecclesia*, or small churches within the territorial church. While membership in the latter was based upon baptism and confirmation, conversion was considered the basic condition for acceptability within the *ecclesiolae*. Thus the conventicle in Pietistic practice developed into a closely knit religious fellowship" (*The Rise of Evangelical Pietism*, p. 160).

"The use of conventicles is instructive inasmuch as they were necessary adjuncts of the church where people could experience God in small group encounter. In these intimate fellowships discussion and other sharing was possible so that believers felt the presence of the Holy Spirit and were edified. Whereas the history of pietism has portrayed these 'holy clubs' as more bane than blessing, in the Netherlands, and also in the New World, they were often a creative instrument in the strengthening of personal relationships between God and his people and within the community as a whole. The 'communion of saints' is a necessity and, if the church in its ordinary ministry does not effect it, extraordinary measures must be taken. The use of conventicles was an extraordinary measure and one which proved its merit. When opened to all who desired to come, they became even more beneficial to the Christian community" (Osterhaven, "The Experiential Theology of Early Dutch Calvinism," *Reformed Review* 27 [1974]:189).

[40] *J. van Lodensteyn's Negen Predicatien*, ed. by Evarardus van der Hooght (Rotterdam: Gebr. Huge, n.d.), p. 197; cf. ibid., pp. 152ff.

[41] Pieter Proost, *Jodocus van Lodenstein* (Amsterdam: J. Brandt en Zoon, 1880), pp. 133-34.

[42] *Des Christens Eenige Troost in Leven en Sterven, of Verklaringe over den Heidelbergschen Catechismus in LII Predicatien; Benevens V Belydenis-Predicatien* (Middelburg: Ottho en Pieter van Thol, Den Haag, en A. L. en M. H. Callenfels, 1747), p. 336.

[43] For the ecclesiology of the Second Reformation, see S. van der Linde, *Opgang en voortgang der reformatie* (Amsterdam: Ton Bolland, 1976), pp. 189-200.

[44] "De Godservaring bij W. Teellinck, D. G. à Brakel en A. Comrie," *Theologia Reformata* 16 (1973):205.

[45] "Het Werk van de Heilige Geest in de Gemeente: Een appreciatie van de Nadere Reformatie," *Nederlands Theologisch Tijdschrift* 10 (1956):3.

[46] "De betekenis van de Nadere Reformatie voor Kerk en Theologie," *Kerk en Theologie* 5 (1954):216.

[47] Ibid., p. 218.

[48] *Het Gereformeerde Protestantisme* (Nijkerk: G. F. Callenbach, 1957), p. 9.

[49] Gerstner provides the following summary: "The movement viewed itself as a continuation of the first Reformation, indeed not as significant as the first one.... [Its] task was to apply these truths. Worship had to be purified so that only what was prescribed in God's word would stand. The State was constantly usurping the authority and even the material goods of the church. Above all the gospel must not be only intellectually understood, but people must be converted to saving faith through the preaching of the Word. They must also be instructed in the truths of God's Word and brought more and more closely in communion with him ethically and devotionally. One's time must be used for the glory of God. One's work must

be seen as a calling to glorify God and the Roman Catholic idea of 'time-killing' recreations had to be rejected. Thus this Continuing Reformation was seen as consistently applying the truths of the first" (*Thousand Generation Covenant*, pp. 75-76). Cf. J. R. Beeke, "'Nadere Reformatie,'" in *Making Confession and Then...?* by A. Hoogerland (Grand Rapids: Eerdmans, 1984), pp. 85-88.

[50]Cornelis Graafland, "Kernen en contouren van de Nadere Reformatie," in *De Nadere Reformatie: Beschrijving van haar voornaamste vertegenwoordigers*, al., pp. 351-52.

[51]*Geschichte des Pietismus und der Mystik in der Reformierten Kirche, namentlich der Niederlande*, p. 6.

[52]"The Doctrine of Calvin as Transmitted in the South African Context by Among Others the *Oude Schrijvers*," in *Calvinus Reformator: His contribution to Theology, Church and Society*, p. 260.

[53]*Herman Witsius: Bijdrage tot de Kennis der Gereformeerde Theologie* ('s-Gravenhage: Guido de Brès, 1953), p. 264; cf. pp. 220-25 for an exposition of this summary.

[54]"De Nadere Reformatie en haar culturele context," in *Met het woord in de Tijd*, ed. by L. Westland ('s-Gravenhage: Boekencentrum, 1985), pp. 117-38.

[55]*Die Nederduitse Gereformeerde Kerk, 1652-1824* (Pretoria: N. G. Kerkboekhandel, 1976), 1:83.

[56]"The Doctrine of Calvin as Transmitted in the South African Context by Among Others the *Oude Schrijvers*," in *Calvinus Reformator: His contribution to Theology, Church and Society*, p. 262. Hofmeyr's own pejorative assessment of the Second Reformation surfaces most strongly when he asserts that the writings of the "old writers" (*oude schrijvers*) reveal that "subjective experience is stressed... at the cost of objective truth and the truth of the Holy Spirit" (ibid., p. 263).

Derk Visser feels that most scholars of the Second Reformation give too much prominence to a small group of Reformed clergy and to the post-Dort decades: "For if the battle against the '-isms' of the 1600s [e.g., Remonstrantism, Cartesianism, Cocceianism, Labadism, JRB] was fought without the aid of the *Heidelberg Catechism* and Ursinus's *Exposition*, the *Heidelberg* had been the norm of correct doctrine before, though it continued to produce a large catechetical literature" (cf. the bibliography in Verboom, *De Catechese van de Reformatie en de Nadere Reformatie*, pp. 356-66).

[57]*Documentatieblad Nadere Reformatie* 7 (1983):109.

[58]Graafland, "Kernen en contouren van de Nadere Reformatie," in *De Nadere Reformatie: Beschrijving van haar voornaamste vertegenwoordigers*, p. 350.

[59]Balke is of the opinion that this spirit of religious-social activism only applies to the prologue of the Second Reformation. For the Second Reformation on mission work, see van der Linde, "De Nadere Reformatie en de zending," *Theologia Reformata* 10 (1967):5-16.

[60]The Labadists, followers of Jean de Labadie (1610-1674), promoted a Dutch separatistic sect in an attempt to establish "a congregation of the truly regenerate." Their decidedly separatist ecclesiology precipitated a deep crisis in the Dutch church. Cf. Heppe, *Geschichte des Pietismus und der Mystik in der Reformierten Kirche, namentlich der Niederlande*, pp. 240-374; Otto Ritschl, *Dogmengeschichte des Protestantismus* (Leipzig: Hinrichs, 1908), 1:194-268; Goeters, *Die Vorbereitung des Pietismus in der reformierten Kirche der Niederlande*, pp. 139-286; Stoeffler, *The Rise of Evangelical Pietism*, pp. 162-69; G. Frank, "Jean de Labadie, Labadists," in *The New Schaff-Herzog Encylopedia of Religious Knowledge* 6:390-91; C. Graafland, "De Nadere

Reformatie en het Labadisme," in *De Nadere Reformatie en het Gereformeerd Piëtisme*, pp. 275-346.

[61]Brakel issued strong warnings against separatistic pietists and their denigration of the church. The Second Reformation divines were church loyalists, not separatists, who sought to bring the apostate church back to God.

[62]Graafland, "Kernen en contouren van de Nadere Reformatie," p. 350. Cf. John Bolt, "The Imitation of Christ Theme in the Cultural-Ethical Ideal of Herman Bavinck" (Ph.D. dissertation, University of St. Michael's College, 1982), p. 55.

[63]Stoeffler, *The Rise of Evangelical Pietism*, p. 144.

[64]Graafland, "Kernen en contouren van de Nadere Reformatie," pp. 350-51.

[65]"De Godservaring bij W. Teellinck, D. G. à Brakel en A. Comrie," *Theologia Reformata* 16 (1973):198.

[66]Graafland, "Kernen en contouren van de Nadere Reformatie," pp. 354-65.

[67]The emphasis on personal experience frequently led to a decrease in communicant members, especially in the latter part of the Second Reformation. (Willem Balke, "Het Pietisme in Oostfriesland," *Theologia Reformata* 21 [1978]:324). Cf. Arie Blok, "The Heidelberg Catechism and the Dutch *Nadere Reformatie*," pp. 47ff.

[68]"Bernardus Smytegelt: Spiritual Advisor of God's Children," *The Banner of Truth* 53 (1987):210. Smytegelt lists 296 marks of the godly life in preaching 145 sermons on Matthew 12:20-21 (*Het Gekrookte Riet*, 2 vols. ['s-Gravenhage: Ottho en Pieter van Thol, 1744]).

[69]"Johannes Beukelman: A Clear Teacher of the Truth," *The Banner of Truth* 53 (1987):264-65.

[70]"The Experiential Theology of Early Dutch Calvinism," *Reformed Review* 27 (1974):180.

[71]Ibid., pp. 183-84.

[72]Stoeffler, *The Rise of Evangelical Pietism, p. 14.*

[73]Van der Linde, "De betekenis van de Nadere Reformatie voor Kerk en Theologie," in *Opgang en voortgang der reformatie*, p. 146.

[74]Graafland, "Van *syllogismus practicus* naar *syllogismus mysticus*," in *Wegen en Gestalten in het Gereformeerd Protestantisme*, pp. 105-122.

[75]"De Godservaring bij W. Teellinck, D. G. à Brakel en A. Comrie," *Theologia Reformata* 16 (1973):202-203. Cf. van der Linde, *Opgang en voortgang der reformatie*, p. 146.

[76]"Bronnen van de Nadere Reformatie," in *De Nadere Reformatie en het Gereformeerd Piëtisme*, p. 6.

[77]Ibid., p. 7. Ritschl's conventional caricature of pietism (that it represents an individualistic, ascetic, and anti-cultural Christianity) is not applicable to the Dutch Second Reformation — especially not to its earliest stage.

[78]Ibid., pp. 7-9.

[79]*The Work of the Holy Spirit*, pp. xii, 300.

[80]Cf. *Het Calvinisme* (Amsterdam: Höveker & Wormser); William Young, "Historic Calvinism and Neo-Calvinism," *Westminster Theological Journal* 36 (1973):48ff.

[81]Pronk, *The Banner of Truth*, nos. 154-55 (July-August 1976):7-10.

[82]*Dogmengeschichte des Protestantismus* 1:180.

[83]*Cultuurgeschiedenis van het Christendom* 3:337; cf. his *Prediking des Woords en bevinding* (Wageningen: H. Veenman & Zonen, 1950).

[84]"Het Zeeuwsche Mysticisme," *Gereformeerd Theologisch Tijdschrift* 17 (1916):141-62.

[85]"De Heilige Geest en het na-reformatorische subjectivisme," in *De Heilige Geest*, ed. by J. H. Bavinck, et al. (Kampen: Kok, 1949), pp. 228-63.

[86]*Het probleem der christelijke gemeenschap, Oorsprong en ontwikkeling der congregationalistisch geordende kerken in Massachusetts* (Amsterdam: Stichting Universitaire Uitgaven, 1951), p. 164.

[87]*De Prediking van de Nadere Reformatie* (Amsterdam: Ton Bolland, 1974). Brienen's study, which exaggerates the weaknesses of Second Reformation preaching, remains the most thorough on the subject. Brienen asserts that Second Reformation preaching no longer appeals to God's promises or takes His covenant seriously; rather, he claims that the stress is on the individual person by dividing and differentiating the listeners into various classifications. Though Calvin does not present the classification method of the Second Reformation divines, the reading of his sermons does not confirm Brienen's dichotomizing of Calvin and the "old writers."

[88]*Reformation, Orthodoxie und Rationalismus: Beiträge zur Förderung christlicher Theologie*, 2 vols. (Gütersloh: C. Bertelsmann, 1937-51).

[89]Vergunst, *Neem de wacht des Heeren waar* (Utrecht: Den Hertog, 1983), pp. 232-36.

[90]*Dutch Calvinistic Pietism in the Middle Colonies*, pp. 4ff.

[91]*Dr. Alexander Comrie, predikant van Woubrugge* (Utrecht: De Banier, 1964), pp. 185ff.

[92]*Thousand Generation Covenant*, pp. 68-79.

[93]"The Second Reformation is to be preferred above the Reformation in a variety of points" (*Engelse piëtistische geschriften in het Nederlands, 1598-1622*, stellingen no. 6).

[94]*The Rise of Evangelical Pietism*, pp. 178-79.

[95]Balke feels that the Second Reformation's theology was more irenic prior to the Synod of Dort (1618-1619), but that it became too rigid in "post-Dort" years. The Second Reformation depended too much on medieval philosophy and mysticism. This movement was in a different theological climate from Calvin, as can be evidenced by their promoting the syllogisms. Balke concludes: "Calvin would not permit himself to rigidly adhere to certain formulas, as is evident in his controversy with Caroli as well as in his contacts with Bullinger. His objective was to convey the message of Scripture as faithfully as possible. In doing so the *actus tradendi* is the *actus formulandi*. Time and again we must formulate anew and search to remain as close to the meaning of the Holy Scriptures as possible. Calvin did not want to be subordinate in any form or shape to any type of philosophy. Every attempt to find traces of Plato, Seneca, or Duns Scotus in his writings are to be rejected as incorrect interpretations. Calvin only desired to be a student of the Holy Scriptures" (personal correspondence; cf. "Calvin and the Theological Trends of His Time," in *Calvinus Reformator: His Contribution to Theology, Church and Society*, pp. 48-68; "Calvijn en Luther," in *Luther en het Gereformeerd Protestantisme* ['s-Gravenhage: Boekencentrum, 1983]).

[96]Cf. bibliography of Beeke, *Assurance of Faith*, for pertinent writings of each of these authors.

[97]Van der Linde, *Vromen en Verlichten* (Utrecht: Aartsbisschoppelijk Museum Utrecht, 1974), p. 2; cf. Graafland, "Het eigene van het Gereformeerd Pietisme in de 18e eeuw in onderscheid van de 17e eeuw," *Documentatieblad Nadere Reformatie* 11 (1987):37-53.

[98]"The Doctrine of Calvin as Transmitted in the South African Context by Among

Others the *Oude Schrijvers*," in *Calvinus Reformator: His contribution to Theology, Church and Society*, p. 260.

[99]Martin H. Prozesky, "The Emergence of Dutch Pietism," *Journal of Ecclesiastical History* 28 (1977):37.

[100]"The Experiential Theology of Early Dutch Calvinism," *Reformed Review* 27 (1974):182.

[101]"Licht- en schaduwzijden in de bevindelijkheid," in *Theologisch Werk* (Nijkerk: G. F. Callenbach, 1971), 3:43-60.

[102]Cf. Peter Lillback, "The Binding of God: Calvin's Role in the Development of Covenant Theology" (Ph. D. dissertation, Westminster Theological Seminary, 1985).

[103]Graafland, "Kernen en contouren van de Nadere Reformatie," in *De Nadere Reformatie: Beschrijving van haar voornaamste vertegenwoordigers*, pp. 352, 366.

[104]E.g., Theodorus G. à Brakel, Theodorus van der Groe, Adrianus Hasius, Abraham Hellenbroek, Nicolaas Holtius, David Knibbe, Johannes à Marck, Petrus van Mastricht, Gregorius Mees, Franciscus Ridderus, and Rippertus Sixtus.

[105]We trust that this English translation of Brakel's theological-devotional classic, *Redelijke Godsdienst*, which is representative of the Second Reformation as a whole, will open a major stream of the theological thought of this Dutch movement to English readers.

[106]*The Rise of Evangelical Pietism*, pp. 178-79.

[107]Hofmeyr, "The Doctrine of Calvin as Transmitted in the South African Context by Among Others the *Oude Schrijvers*," in *Calvinus Reformator: His contribution to Theology, Church and Society*, pp. 261-62; cf. Gerstner, *Thousand Generation Covenant*.

To the Congregation of God

Dearly Beloved Brothers and Sisters in Our Lord Jesus Christ,
Grace and Peace be Multiplied to You from God Our Father!

God wills that man be occupied. Prior to the fall He called him to an enjoyable task, and after the fall, to a difficult task. It is His will that everyone be faithful in the calling to which He has called him. Some callings are of a temporal nature, whereas others have a spiritual dimension. Even if a calling is of a temporal nature, this neither detracts from nor contributes to the spirituality of one's service of God in the discharge of this calling; rather, such spirituality is contingent upon the spiritual state of the individual as well as the manner in which he engages himself in his calling. A natural man deals even with spiritual matters in a natural manner which is not pleasing to God. The spiritual man, however, deals even with temporal matters in a spiritual fashion. He views his encounter with them as a dispensation of the Lord, embracing them as the will of God. He performs his temporal obligations in willing obedience as a service to his God, having God's glory as his objective.

Among all callings there is none so holy, excellent, necessary, and profitable as the office of shepherd and teacher in the church. Whomever God calls, qualifies, and renders faithful to be a minister of the New Testament is a marvel in this world. He is an instrument in the hand of God to save lost souls, to gather and edify God's church, thereby encouraging the church to promote God's glory upon earth.

An unqualified minister is the most despicable and harmful creature to be found in the world. He is a disgrace to the church, a stumbling block whereby many fall into eternal perdition, and the cause of the damnation of many souls. A faithful servant of Christ, on the contrary, is an ornament in the house of his God, a light upon a candlestick, a city upon a hill, a leader of the blind, a

terror to the ungodly, a joy to the godly, a comforter for the
sorrowful, a counselor for those who are perplexed, and a guide
for believers on the way to heaven. His life generally is of short
duration, during which his preaching reaches but a few and he
himself is consumed while illuminating others. The loss of a minister who is endowed with grace is inestimable.

God has wonderfully compensated for both the brevity of a
minister's life as well as the limited scope of his audience, by
having given man the wisdom to become acquainted with the art
of printing. It should be noted that this began during the time
when the church was about to depart from Babylon. This art was
brought to perfection precisely when the Reformation dawned at
the beginning of the sixteenth century. Now a single minister, even
centuries after his death, is capable of preaching to an entire
nation, yes, even to the entire world. With joyful readiness I seize
this opportunity to preach long after my death, according to the
measure of the gifts the Lord has bestowed upon me.

Prior to the invention of the art of printing, it was necessary to
dedicate one's work to an individual of distinction from whom the
various commissions would originate. This, however, is no longer
necessary. At times these were offensive in nature, and occasionally a work was too insignificant for consideration by the eminent
individuals to whom it was dedicated. In addition to this, such
dedications many times lent themselves to misinterpretation of the
author's intention. Therefore I have omitted this and rather address
myself to you, the Congregation of God, dedicating my work to you.

May this book particularly be of service to the congregation
which I am currently serving, the congregation which I previously
served, as well as the congregation which called me twice but was
not able to obtain me due to the condition of the congregation
which I was serving at that time. Receive it with much affection and
read it diligently and thoughtfully. Form small groups of acquaintances among yourselves for the purpose of reading a chapter or
portion each time, and may that which is read present subject
matter for edifying discussions.

I do not wish to comment upon the contents of this book as you
will be able to read it for yourself. You should know, however, that
whatever was useful from my previous works, such as *Halleluja*
[Hallelujah], *Scrupuleuze Communicant* [The Scrupulous Communi-
cant], and *Leer en Leiding der Labbadisten* [Doctrine and Government of the Labadists], has been included in this work, the
material rightfully belonging to me.

I will also rejoice if my work may be useful in giving direction to theological students, student preachers, and young ministers. May it enable them to comprehend the unique, distinct nature of divine truths so that they may safeguard and practice these truths in deed. May they present them to the congregation in such a manner that it results in the conversion and strengthening of souls and in the edification of the church of our Lord Jesus Christ.

May the almighty and good God, who repeatedly encouraged me when I had intentions of discontinuing this task and who is the Author of whatever good is to be found in this work, pour out His Holy Spirit upon all who will either read or hear this book read. May it be to the conversion of the unconverted, the instruction of the ignorant, the restoration of backsliders, the encouragement of the discouraged, as well as to the growth of faith, hope, and love in all who have become partakers of a measure of grace.

May the Lord preserve His church, causing it to increase in number and in godliness, and may He bless our nation for the sake of the church. May He live and walk in your midst, illuminate you with His light, supply you with manifold grace, and guide you by His counsel. And, upon having run your course, may He take you up into everlasting glory. I am, and remain your fellow brother and servant in Christ, to whom be praise, honor, and glory to all eternity.

Wilhelmus à Brakel
Rotterdam, February 2, 1700

Preface to the Third Edition

As was stated regarding the second edition, nothing was deleted, except that occasionally we have stated matters somewhat more concisely. Also, nothing was added which was worthy of mention, except here and there an explanation or a subject was treated somewhat more extensively. That edition became available on October 2, 1701.

This third edition has been enlarged considerably with the addition of the following material: 1) the life of faith relative to the promises; 2) a warning exhortation against Pietists, Quietists, and those who espouse similar errors which result in a religion which proceeds from nature being void of the Spirit, having, however, the appearance of spirituality; 3) an enlargement of the treatment of the Lord's Prayer, which is both expository and applicatory in nature.

If someone is displeased with the enlargement of the third edition, then let him transform his displeasure into generosity by giving his first or second edition to someone of humble means who could also be edified by it, and obtain a copy of the present edition for himself.

May the Lord also bless this edition. May it be useful in defending the truth and true godliness, both of which are under assault in these days. They are assaulted on the one side by people of a corrupt mind who propose reason to be the rule for doctrine and life; on the other side by people who, in striving for holiness and love, set aside the truth and stray towards a religion which proceeds from nature, revolving around the practice of virtue. The Lord shall preserve His church so that Satan and all his adherents shall not be able to prevail against her. As a servant in Christ to all of you, I remain

Wilhelmus à Brakel

THE CHRISTIAN'S
REASONABLE SERVICE

Theology:
The Doctrine of God

CHAPTER ONE

The Knowledge of God from Nature

The title of this book, *The Christian's Reasonable Service*, has been derived from Romans 12:1, "...which is your reasonable service." Religion[1] consists of four matters: 1) its foundation or basis, 2) its form or essence, 3) its regulative principle, and 4) its practical manifestation.

The Foundation of Religion

First, *the foundation* of religion is the character of God. The works of His omnipotence and benevolence are indeed reasons to stimulate man to serve God; however, they are not the basis for such service. This foundation is the very character of God. God possesses within Himself all glory and worthiness to be served, even if there were no creature. No creature could have its existence, except it be of Him and through Him. By its very existence the creature is obligated to God's majesty to exist for the purpose of serving God, having its origin in Him and existing by virtue of His influence. If this creature is rational, then God, because He is God, obligates him who has been placed directly under his Creator to honor and serve God and devote his entire existence to Him. The character of God eternally obligates the creature, and therefore also man, to this. "Who would not fear Thee, O King of nations? For to Thee doth it appertain" (Jer. 10:7); "Thou hast established the earth, and it abideth. They continue this day according to Thine ordinances: for all are Thy servants" (Psa. 119:90-91).

---

[1] à Brakel uses "religion" here since Romans 12:1 reads as follows in the Dutch Bible: ". . . welke is uw redelijke godsdienst," that is, ". . . which is your reasonable religion."

The Form or Essence of Religion

Secondly, *the form or essence* of religion consists of man's knowledge, recognition, and heart-felt endorsement of this binding obligation, which is to live unto God at all times and in all things with all that he is and is capable of performing. This is so because He is God and by virtue of His nature this is His worthy due. For this reason he willingly devotes and sacrifices himself unto God, surrendering himself to the service of God. He does so because He is his God, it is his obligation, and it constitutes his felicity. "O Lord, truly I am Thy servant; I am Thy servant" (Psa. 116:16); "One shall say, I am the LORD's; and another shall subscribe with his hand unto the LORD" (Isa. 44:5).

The Regulative Principle of Religion

Thirdly, essential to religion is the revelation of God's will as the regulative principle according to which man, as a servant, must engage himself. It has not been left to man to determine the manner in which he would serve God, for then he would stand above God. Anyone who engages himself in this way exalts himself above God and displeases the Lord in all his activity. "But in vain they do worship Me, teaching for doctrines the commandments of men" (Mat. 15:9).

Rather, the Lord Himself establishes for and reveals to man the regulative principle, indicating what He requires man to do and in which manner He wishes this to be accomplished. "Should not a people seek unto their God?...To the law and to the testimony: if they speak not according to this Word, it is because there is no light in them" (Isa. 8:19-20); "That ye may prove what is that good, and acceptable, and perfect, will of God" (Rom. 12:2).

The Practice of Religion

Fourthly, the essence of religion consists in an active agreement with, and execution of the will of God. All that God wills, the servant of God also wills, because the will of God is the object of his desire and delight. He rejoices that God desires something from him and that God reveals to him what He wishes to have done. This motivates him to perform it whole-heartedly as the Lord's will. "Doing the will of God from the heart" (Eph. 6:6).

As we consider the subject of religion, we shall not only discuss these four matters, but shall do so in the order which we have established. In the first place we must show that God is the foundation of religion, considering both His existence and the purpose for His existence. If man is to make God the foundation of his religion, recognizing his obligation towards Him, then he must know God. This makes it necessary first to demonstrate from which source the right knowledge of God must be derived.

God has decreed within Himself what He desires to reveal of Himself and the extent of this revelation of Himself. This knowledge of God is referred to as Θεολογία ἀρχέτυπα πρωτότυπα, *Theologia archetypa, protypa (Original and essential revelation)*. The knowledge in the rational creature which corresponds with this is referred to as Θεολογία ἔκτυπα, *Theologia ectypa (conferred revelation)*.

The manner by which this certain knowledge is instilled or granted to creatures varies according to the differences among rational creatures. The *angels* know God by an immediate beholding of the countenance of God. "Their angels do always behold the face of My Father which is in heaven" (Mat. 18:10). Such already is, and shall be, the knowledge of the elect in the state of glory. "For we walk by faith, not by sight" (2 Cor. 5:7); "For now we see through a glass darkly, but then face to face" (1 Cor. 13:12).

Christ according to His human nature knows God by virtue of His union with the Godhead as the Son of God, and thus in a more excellent way than can be comprehended by angels and men. "For in Him dwelleth all the fullness of the Godhead bodily" (Col. 2:9); "God giveth not the Spirit by measure unto Him" (John 3:34). *Man* upon earth knows God by revelation. "No man hath seen God at any time; the only begotten Son, which is in the bosom of the Father, He hath declared Him" (John 1:18). This revelation occurs either by means of nature in all men, or also by means of the Holy Scriptures, which the Lord grants only to some.

The Innate Knowledge of God

God has created within all men an innate knowledge that God is, that is, an acknowledgement that God exists.[2] This does not mean that man, in his existence, is immediately conscious of God; rather this consciousness comes gradually with an increase of age. Such knowledge is innate in man as reason is innate — which man also does not initially exercise. As time progresses, however, he begins to reason about matters which confront him. Both reality and mental exercises concerning the knowledge of God spontaneously proceed from his own nature, without external stimulation by means of instruction. This innate knowledge of God does not

---

[2] à Brakel here, as well as throughout the chapter, uses the word "Godserkennend-heid." In the Dutch text he admits that this word does not really exist in Dutch vocabulary, but has coined it for lack of a Dutch word to accurately describe this doctrinal concept.

necessarily manifest itself in action. Prior to birth children are not capable of engaging in the activity of hearing, seeing, speaking, and thinking; they can do neither good nor evil (Rom. 9:11). They cannot commit actual sins after the similitude of Adam's transgression (Rom. 5:14). Anyone who maintains the contrary does so without foundation. It is contrary to Scripture and experience.

Some, not being satisfied with ordinary expressions relative to the innate knowledge of God, wish to refer to it as a *mental image*. It is to be feared, however, that this notion is a cloak for strange sentiments. This would, for example, suggest that this uncreated mental image, as a mirror, would reveal to man all the perfections of God and His creatures, and that man passively, by mere observation or in response to this mental image, would be able to know all these perfections. What else does this suggest than that God is finite and the mental image within man infinite? Thus, the knowledge of God would not be obtained by man as created objects from God's revelations about Himself and His creatures, but from within ourselves, derived from this innate mental image. This is doing nothing else but attributing infallibility to every man. This would bring the infallibility of one person into direct conflict with the infallibility of the other by the opposing views they may have concerning this matter. From this it follows that all views concerning God are nothing but fantasies and waking dreams, which, to put it mildly, serve no other purpose than to generate confused and foolish ideas concerning this matter.

If, however, one understands this mental image to be nothing other than the innate ability to acknowledge God, that is, to perceive that God exists, is Creator and Ruler over all things, and is Lord over each person, such that each man is obligated to live according to His will and that whoever fails to do this must expect the just manifestation of His wrath notwithstanding that all this is impressed upon the conscience of every man — if such is the understanding, then this matter is viewed correctly. One should, however, avoid this terminology of "mental image"; it may, in addition to that mentioned, generate images of God within the mind similar to the external images Roman Catholicism creates, both of which are prohibited in the second commandment.

The inner perception of the form and image of all things is not innate in man. Unless there would be proof to the contrary, this must be emphatically denied. Man does not acquire knowledge about matters from within himself but rather from his own observation with his five senses. What image or perception do we have concerning the form of animals which live in other parts of the world, which we have never seen or heard mentioned? It is as if they neither exist nor ever existed. Does a child prior to birth or at the time of birth have a mental image of a lion, dog, or cat, as well as of their physical stature and nature? Of course not. To enable Adam to name the animals after their kind, the animals first had to be brought to Adam (Gen. 2:19). Man sees, hears, tastes, smells, and touches various objects from childhood on before he consciously takes notice of them. When he is accustomed to them, he will in time become knowledgeable concerning these things. The concept that he, without the conscious involvement of his five senses, acquires knowledge by means of innate imagery already being present prior to his birth, must be rejected as soon as it is formulated.

In similar fashion do we function within the realm of Christianity. From childhood on we observe the works of God in nature without reasoning about them or paying special attention to them. From childhood on we hear mention being made of God, which causes the innate knowledge of a god — or lest we be misunderstood, the acknowledgment of God — to be activated. It becomes reality and increases more and more, albeit unevenly, that is, in the one more than in the other. The idea that man, by observing the works of God, being instructed about God, or hearing about God, is able to develop this innate mental image of God, is irrational and entirely erroneous. Man, having been gifted with innate knowledge and created with the ability to reason as well as to acknowledge God, is capable of knowing God in due season. This is the very reason why God reveals Himself as is evident from Romans 1:19-20. That which may be known of God (which is not the full essence of God, nor that which God reveals and makes known to angels, the saints on earth, and the glorified saints in heaven, but that which the heathen are capable of knowing from nature by observing the works of God) is not evident to the heathen by way of innate, mental images, but by virtue of God's revelation to them. How? By means of mental images? No, but it is known to them from the works of God. "For the invisible things of Him from the creation of the world are clearly seen, being understood by the things that are made, even His eternal power and Godhead" (Rom. 1:20). Thus, in the absence of Holy Scripture, the heathen have had the knowledge of God, insomuch as they were able to obtain this from the light of nature. This consists of that which may be known of God in distinction to that which must be believed concerning God, according to the apostle's testimony in Romans 1:16-17.

That man possesses such innate knowledge of God is evident in the following passage, "For when the Gentiles, which have not the law, do by nature the things contained in the law, these, having not the law...shew the work of the law written in their hearts, their conscience also bearing witness, and their thoughts the mean while accusing or else excusing one another" (Rom. 2:14-15).

Here the apostle refers to people who do not possess the Holy Scriptures. He states that the law is written in their hearts and that they know by nature that they must live according to this law. Thus, they are a law unto themselves, their conscience the meanwhile accusing or excusing them in relation to whether or not they live according to the law written in their hearts. The knowledge of the Lawgiver is proportionate to the knowledge of the law. This knowledge obligates them to obedience, and teaches that the Lawgiver will justly reward the obedient and punish the disobedient. This Lawgiver, not being a man, is therefore acknowledged to be God.

Man's innate ability to reason enables him by way of research to become knowledgeable in various subjects as well as to increase in this acquired knowledge. Likewise the innate knowledge of God enables man, by observing the works of God in their created nobility, to increase in the knowledge of God and by means of the visible ascend to the invisible One. That which is visible could not possibly communicate to man that there is a God if prior to that he did not have an impression of God in his soul.

This internal knowledge of God can be increased by viewing the creatures and their experiences as being representative of the activities and government of God. This is therefore referred to as the external knowledge of God, it being derived from external matters (Rom. 1:19-20). Job testifies of this, "But ask now the beasts, and they shall teach thee; and the fowls of the air, and they shall tell thee: or speak to the earth, and it shall teach thee: and the fishes of the sea shall declare unto thee. Who knoweth not in all these that the hand of the LORD hath wrought this?" (Job 12:7-9). This is confirmed further in the following passages, "The heavens declare the glory of God; and the firmament sheweth His handiwork. Day unto day uttereth speech, and night unto night sheweth knowledge. There is no speech nor language, where their voice is not heard" (Psa. 19:1-3); "...who in times past suffered all nations to walk in their own ways. Nevertheless He left not Himself without witness, in that He did good, and gave us rain from heaven, and fruitful seasons, filling our hearts with food and gladness" (Acts 14:16-17). From all this it becomes evident that man by nature possesses both an external and internal knowledge of God.

The most brilliant philosophers have made much progress in

this knowledge as a result of the observation of creatures. One can increase in this knowledge in a threefold manner:

(1) by way of *negation*, barring from God all imperfection, frailty, finality and insignificance, all of which are to be found in the creature;

(2) by way of *excellence*, infinitely and perfectly ascribing to God all that can be observed as glorious, beautiful, and enjoyable in the creature, for the original cause will always excell that which is to be found in any created object;

(3) by way of *causality*, ascending from a simple matter to its cause, from thence proceeding to the higher cause, thus finally arriving at the ultimate cause which is God, and from thence descending by way of various causes to the lowest of all creatures.

Question: Is there such a knowledge of God in the natural man?

Answer: The Socinians deny all knowledge of God from nature and maintain that the knowledge of God has been passed on from generation to generation since the time of Noah or, by means of a special revelation of God, to certain individuals. Our response to this question, however, is positive.

First, it is evident from the texts previously referred to: Romans 2:14-15; Romans 1:19; Job 12:7-9; Psalm 19:1-3; Acts 14:16-17.

Secondly, it is evident from experience which teaches that there is not a nation under the sun which does not acknowledge a deity. The heathen themselves bear witness to this in their writings. Christians, who by virtue of maritime travel to Asia, Africa, and America have visited places where Christians have never been, have discovered that all nations, however savage they may have been, had an impression of a deity, albeit that some did not manifest any exercise of religion. Thus, the entire world exclaims: There is a God!

Thirdly, it is evident from man's inclination to honor something that is tangible. The religious worship of such things gives evidence that there is an external impression of the existence of a god. The lofty affections of men could not be persuaded to honor a piece of wood or stone, unless they would consider it as containing a deity or to be representative of the immediate presence of a deity who would be pleased by such service.

Fourthly, it is evident from the fact that one can teach a savage heathen, even if he is deaf and dumb, by means of signs and gestures to have respect for God and to animate his conscience concerning sin and virtue. This could certainly not occur if he did not have some initial internal knowledge concerning a deity.

Fifthly, if the knowledge of God in man were not innate and he lacked the ability by way of the visible to ascend to the invisible

God, then the heathen would be without sin. In the absence of a lawgiver there is also no law, and wherever there is no law there is no transgression; therefore, they could not be condemned. To hold to the latter is absurd, and thus it is certain that the heathen have knowledge of God.

Objection #1: All that comes naturally to man is to be found in all men at all times. The knowledge of God, however, is not to be found in all, since in some heathen it has been observed that not the least trace of religion was found. Such knowledge of God is not always present, for David states, "The fool hath said in his heart, There is no God" (Psa. 14:1). And Paul refers to ἄθεοι (*atheoi*) or atheists: "...without God in the world" (Eph. 2:12).

Answer: (1) It is *petitio principii*: this is precisely the point of contention. We maintain that the acknowledgement or impression of the existence of a god is at all times to be found in all, as we have proven in a five-fold manner. This is potentially true and also as far as man's rationality is concerned.

(2) Even if there might be people who do not give the least evidence of any religion, it does not necessarily follow that there is no impression concerning a deity concealed in their heart. Our discussion does not concern itself with the practice of religion, but with the propensity toward the acknowledgment of a deity.

(3) David speaks of fools, of ungodly persons given over to themselves who testify by their behavior that they neither honor, fear, nor serve a deity. By means of their wickedness they seek to erase the impression they have concerning God and rashly desire to silence their disturbed conscience. David, however, does not here address the innate knowledge of God.

(4) Paul calls such individuals *atheists* who neither have God as their reconciled God, Benefactor, or Salvation, nor as their Hope for eternal felicity. This text obviously does not relate to this matter.

Objection #2: There have always been atheists and those who utterly reject God. In our day atheism is clearly breaking forth in France, in England, and to some extent also in the Netherlands, primarily by means of various sects. There are even some who cleverly introduce atheism, secretly or openly, by way of their speech, writing, and lifestyle. Their objective is to distort Scripture by establishing reason as the expositor of Holy Writ, and in doing so remove its divine authority as well as its infallibility.

In order not to be despised, they use the word "God"; however, they do not understand this to refer to the Creator, Sustainer, and Governor of creation and all that is contained in Him who is eternally self-existent, independent, and Wisdom personified—

existing prior to the creation of creatures and the universe. They rather understand it to refer to the common nature of all things as if this were the origin and maintaining cause of all things, being governed in the same fashion as gears setting a clock in motion. Fortune and misfortune would then occur due to the motions of nature in specific objects, it being implied that one should be passive and quiet in response to these motions as they can neither be changed nor opposed.

Atheists acknowledge no law except the law of nature which they propose to be such as to endorse a pleasurable pursuit of their own lusts. They consider it sin when one does something contrary to his own interest and advantage; and they consider it a virtue if one engages himself in promoting the fulfillment of his lust. They consider salvation to consist merely in finding joy in eating, drinking, fornicating, boasting, indulging in pleasure, as well as yielding to one's lusts. Lying and deceit are considered honorable means to obtain such bliss, or to enable them to avoid whatever would disturb them in their bliss. They know of no punishment except when damage and shame are experienced, and no damnation except for a restless and melancholy frame of mind. Their motto is *Ede, bibe, lude, post mortem nulla voluptas!* that is, eat, drink, and play, for after death there is no pleasure. Irrespective of whether a man, horse, or any other creature dies, dead is dead. They ridicule the existence of a soul, angels, and devils and relegate them to the realm of fables. They are at peace with this conviction, having no acquaintance with a stirring and remorseful conscience. In this the wretched Jew, Baruch de Spinoza — born in December, 1633 and deceased in February, 1677 in The Hague — led the way. It is obvious that other atheists have borrowed sentiments from him.

It is thus evident that atheists do exist, and therefore there is no such thing as innate knowledge of a deity in the heart of man. If there were such innate knowledge, one would not be able to root it out as so many have done and currently are doing, or as many are attempting to learn how they may accomplish such a thing.

Answer: Such a conclusion is the consequence of establishing reason as the expositor of Holy Writ, as well as the arbiter in determining what to believe and what not to believe. How will those who hold to this principle be able to refute atheistical writings? The arrows fly back and they themselves will be wounded. These are the consequences of wresting and manipulating the Holy Scriptures, as well as the fruits of ridiculing the exercises of true godliness which are sneeringly referred to as lessons in morality. Those who do so are ignorant of the distinction between the virtues of the heathen, and those of Christians which proceed from faith in Christ, a knowledge of the truth, and are performed in love, godly fear, and obedience toward God. The acknowledging of the truth is after godliness (Titus 1:1). These are the fruits of dishonoring God and of denying the generation of the Son and the procession of the Holy Ghost. First they propose the existence of three collateral persons — that is, existing side by side — which is followed by the notion of three gods, and eventually this culminates in denying the existence of God. These fruits proceed from a distaste for the old paths which are unknown to them and from a hankering for the promotion of that which is new. Such are the fruits of doubting the existence of God.

The objection itself has no validity, for we do not deny that those persons who labor to erase the impression of God from their hearts will be given over by God to a reprobate mind (Rom. 1:28), and that He sends them a strong delusion (2 Th. 2:11) so that the knowledge of God is fully suppressed. Consequently, a person can become completely oblivious to the existence of God; however, from this it does not follow that God did not create this knowledge and consciousness within man. Is a person in a deep coma no longer a rational creature, even though reasoning itself is not evident? Is this person conscious of his ability to reason? When a person, due to a fall or a blow to the head, is deprived of his intellect, having neither knowledge, speech, nor his emotions — similar to a newborn child who shows signs of life in a limited sense — is he therefore without reason? Such is also the case with the ability to acknowledge the existence of a deity. In the absence of actually doing so, one cannot conclude that a person is without the propensity or the ability to do so.

Objection #3: Only by faith, and consequently not through nature, does one know that there is a God, which is evident from Hebrews 11:6, "He that cometh to God must believe that He is."

Answer: This issue of faith can be viewed in various ways. Nature teaches that God is who He is by virtue of the maintenance and government of all things; Scripture teaches that God is who He is in the face of Jesus Christ (2 Cor. 4:6). In Hebrews 11 the apostle refers to the latter, whereas in the previously quoted texts from Romans 1 and 2 he refers to the former. The recognition of the Godhead by faith does not exclude the knowledge of God from the realm of nature; rather, it includes and pre-supposes it.

Question: Relative to the natural knowledge of God the question must be posed: "Can man be saved by virtue of such knowledge?"

Answer: The Socinians answer this question in the affirmative.

The Arminians and some within Roman Catholicism also lean in this direction. We deny this emphatically, however, as is verified by the following:

First, all natural knowledge of God, whatever its measure may be, is cognizant of God's justice in punishing sin (Rom. 1:32), but is ignorant of the satisfaction of the justice of God and of the holiness with which one is able to stand in the just judgment of God. Without this satisfaction no one can be saved, as shall be shown comprehensively subsequent to this. Thus, for them God remains a God who will by no means clear the guilty, and who will recompense everyone according to his deeds.

Secondly, there is no salvation except in Christ and there is no other way unto salvation but by faith in Christ. "I am the way, the truth, and the life: no man cometh unto the Father, but by Me" (John 14:6); "Neither is there salvation in any other: for there is none other Name under heaven given among men, whereby we must be saved" (Acts 4:12); "But without faith it is impossible to please Him" (Heb. 11:6); "He that believeth not is condemned already, because he hath not believed in the Name of the only begotten Son of God" (John 3:36).

It is certain that the knowledge of Christ and faith in Christ are entirely absent in the natural knowledge of God. He is revealed only in the gospel, a revelation to which the heathen are not privy. "Even the mystery which hath been hid from ages and from generations" (Col. 1:26). Faith can only be exercised in response to the declaration of the gospel. "So then faith cometh by hearing, and hearing by the Word of God" (Rom. 10:17). It is therefore incontrovertible that the natural knowledge of God cannot bring about salvation for man.

Thirdly, the heathen, one as well as the other, even the wisest and most virtuous among them, are called:

(1) fools, "Professing themselves to be wise, they became fools" (Rom. 1:22);

(2) blind and dead, "Having the understanding darkened, being alienated from the life of God through the ignorance that is in them, because of the blindness of their heart" (Eph. 4:18);

(3) atheists, without promise or hope, "...strangers from the covenants of promise, having no hope, and Ἄθεοι ἐν τῷ κόσμῳ, *atheists*, without God in the world" (Eph. 2:12).

Their condition is denominated as, "and the times of this ignorance" (Acts 17:30).

Objection #1: "Because that which may be known of God is manifest in them...so that they are without excuse" (Rom. 1:19-20).

On this basis the following conclusion is made: Since the heathen by the light of nature already know what is to be known of God, and they, not walking according to this light, are without excuse, then in following this light, this knowledge should lead them to salvation.

Answer: (1) The apostle does not say that they knew all that is to be known of God, but merely that which is to be known from nature, which the apostle limits to "His eternal power and Godhead." It must be proved that such knowledge is sufficient unto salvation, for we deny it.

(2) That man is without excuse, because he is cognizant of God and his own duty, does not imply that he by the light of nature should be able to progress to such an extent that he should be without excuse, and therefore be able to come to salvation. It also does not imply that this light was fully sufficient, even if he had lived in accordance with it. The contrary must be inferred: the light of nature convicts man that God is just in condemning him, both because of the wickedness of his nature and because of his opposition to the light which is in him. Thus, this light has no other purpose than to convict him. Even if this light of nature were capable of excusing him in some measure, it should not be inferred that it would do so completely.

Objection #2: "...not knowing that the goodness of God leadeth thee to repentance" (Rom. 2:4); "That they should seek the Lord, if haply they might feel after Him, and find Him, though He be not far from every one of us" (Acts 17:27). These texts indicate that the knowledge of nature is adequate to bring about repentance, as well as to seek and find God. Salvation is promised upon repentance, and to find God is salvation itself. Thus, the knowledge of nature is sufficient unto salvation.

Answer: (1) In Romans 2:4 the apostle addresses those to whom he preached the gospel, Jews as well as Greeks, for he addresses them in the second person "thou," which he continues to do in the remainder of the chapter. This text is therefore not applicable to this situation.

(2) Contingent upon the extent of natural light, the natural knowledge of God also does indeed convict of sin, and shows the desirability and necessity of conversion from sin to virtue. Such a conversion, however, is not true conversion which results in a radical external and internal change in man — a transformation from death to spiritual life, without which no salvation is to be expected.

(3) In Acts 17:27, the idolatrous heathen were addressed who, in addition to their idols of wood and stone, had an altar with this inscription: "To the unknown God," whom they ignorantly served.

The apostle declared them to be ignorant and taught that the light of nature did not direct them to depart from God in favor of idols; rather, God had given them this light of nature for the express purpose of instructing them concerning their duty, which was to seek God "if haply they might feel after Him, and find Him." This communicates what man, having fallen away from God, must do, rather than what he is capable of doing, being guilty of having robbed himself of light and life. Man is obligated to seek God, if haply he might feel after and find Him; however, without the wondrous light which God grants to His children in the moment of regeneration, they shall never "feel after Him, and find Him" unto reconciliation and salvation, even though the light of nature may bring them to the realization that God truly exists and wishes to be served in spirit and in truth. This *feeling after and finding of God* to which the apostle refers, differs infinitely from that *feeling after and finding of God* by and in which salvation is experienced.

Objection #3: In Romans 2:14-15, the apostle states that the heathen by nature do things contained in the law, being a law unto themselves, but have the work of the law written in their hearts and their conscience excuses them. They in whom these things are found are doers of the law, and doers of the law shall be justified. Since these matters are to be discerned in the heathen who possess only the light of nature, they must be considered doers of the law, and therefore shall be justified. Thus, it must be inferred that the natural knowledge of God is sufficient to lead man to salvation.

Answer: To be a law unto one's self, to have the law written upon the heart, and to do the things which are contained in the law, is nothing more than to be cognizant of the relationship between man and God, as well as to be aware of the will of God. To be cognizant of this is to know that the law commands, forbids, promises, threatens, and convicts. The law, but also the light of nature does this even without having the written law, so that it does not imply the fulfilling of the law but shows what the law requires. Therefore if a person does not walk according to this light, it will then *accuse* him, and if he does so, it will *excuse* him, albeit not altogether as if he had fully kept the entire law at all times, thus being justified by God as Judge. The reference is to a specific deed, and only then in proportion to the measure of light received.

Objection #4: If the knowledge of nature in and of itself is not sufficient unto salvation, it is nevertheless salvific by virtue of its result. For example, if a man is faithful to the light of nature and lives accordingly, then God gives additional grace which is of such a nature that he can be saved according to this promise: "For whosoever hath, to him shall be given, and he shall have more abundance" (Mat. 13:12). This is further confirmed by examples such as Job, the centurion (Mat. 8:5, 10), and Cornelius (Acts 10).

Answer: (1) No one uses the natural knowledge of God rightly, for in reference to all who are in the state of nature it is written, "There is none righteous, no not one: there is none that understandeth, there is none that seeketh after God. They are all gone out of the way, they are together become unprofitable; there is none that doeth good, no, not one" (Rom. 3:10-12). All the virtues of the heathen lack the true essence of virtue. They do not proceed from faith, are not in true harmony with the law, and are not performed to the honor of God. Rather, they are so beset with sinful qualities and circumstances that these virtues are nothing but glaring sins.

(2) Even if a heathen were to live in full accordance with this natural light, there is not a single promise that God will therefore grant such a person saving grace. God is so free that He is debtor to no one, and His justice is so pure that no performance of a child of wrath — which necessarily misses the mark even if it were to conform with the light of nature — would move Him to draw such a person to Himself and to be gracious to him.

(3) Matthew 13:12 is not applicable here, as it does not refer to the gifts of nature, but to the gifts of grace which the Lord bestows upon His children in granting them grace to improve grace received, thus honoring them with additional grace. "In keeping of them there is great reward" (Psa. 19:11).

(4) The examples indicated are not applicable in this context since these individuals had the gospel and lived under its administration.

Even though the natural knowledge of God is not salvific, it nevertheless serves a purpose and is useful for the following reasons:

(1) It teaches that God exists; that He is an invisible, spiritual Being; is infinite; is the first cause of all things; in His Being is infinitely exalted above all that exists; and is holy, omnipotent, good, and just.

(2) It teaches that God is the cause of all things (also of him who meditates about God), and thus is sovereign Lord over all. It teaches that by His influence He upholds, governs, and directs all things according to His will, so that no one can stay His hand or say, "What doest Thou?"

(3) It teaches that every human being is obligated to Him with an irrevocable obligation to do His will as expressed in His law, which is revealed to him by virtue of the light of nature.

(4) By this man can view his sin and guilt against the background of God's justice.

(5) It also promotes the maintenance of human society.

(6) Man, by means of the revelation of Holy Writ, is a fit subject to be led in the way of true godliness by the Spirit of God.

The Origin of the Natural Knowledge of God and Morality

Question: Where do the natural knowledge of God and morality originate?

Answer: They do not originate from a new gift which God bestowed upon man after he lost the image of God. There is not a word in Scripture to suggest this. Reason neither teaches this, nor does necessity require it. It is also not a remnant of the image of God in its narrower sense, which consists of spiritual knowledge, righteousness, and holiness. It is a remnant, however, of the image of God in its wider sense, as far as this refers to the subject or essence of the image of God itself. In order to understand this correctly one must consider what the image of God actually is as well as what belongs to it. At the appropriate place these matters shall be discussed more extensively.

(1) Man was not first created *in puris naturalibus*, that is, he was not created as a purely natural and rational person, having no more than the five senses along with the instant ability to reason, the image of God being impressed upon him subsequent to his creation. It is my opinion that man would not have been truly man if the consciousness of God had not been present from the very outset. Rather, man was created in, and in possession of, the image of God. God, in creating man, created him in His image, generating this image in the very act of creating (Gen. 1:27). The existence of sensitivity as well as the capability for growth, both of which are inherent in the life of animals and vegetation, do not function as components united within a larger entity, but *virtualiter et efficaciter*, that is, by virtue of innate ability and propensity. The rational soul is also similarly capable of reasoning. Thus, in a similar manner the image of God contains within itself both the natural knowledge of God and morality. These are not individual entities; neither do they coexist as components of a larger entity, as if in Adam there were a distinction between a knowledge of God and morality which would be of a natural sort, and a spiritual knowledge of the same which would be the image of God. Adam possessed these by virtue of innate ability and propensity. The image of God permeated everything and energized all faculties and

motions of the soul; hence all that was within him and was performed by him was spiritual and holy in nature.

(2) Even though the image of God in Adam was indivisible, one can nevertheless distinguish three matters by way of intellectual deduction: 1) its basis or focal point, 2) its nature or essence, and 3) its consequence or purpose. The focal point of the image of God was the soul which is an invisible, immortal spirit, endowed with intellect, a will, and affections. The essence was spiritual knowledge, righteousness, and holiness. The consequence or purpose of the image of God was his glorious position and his exercise of dominion over the animal kingdom.

In reference to the focal point the following must be noted, which when properly understood will answer the initial question and eliminate much confusion concerning this matter. An artist cannot impress someone's image upon water or sand. To accomplish this he must have the appropriate base or medium. Similarly, the image of God could not have been impressed upon wood, stone, or an irrational creature. It required an intelligent, willing, rational soul, and a consciousness of God. The soul in Adam could not be separated from the image of God in its narrow sense, as the image of God permeated and energized the entire soul. We are merely making an intellectual deduction here. As a result of Adam's fall, the image of God in its narrow sense, consisting of spiritual knowledge, righteousness, and holiness, has been entirely removed from all the faculties and propensities of the soul. Nevertheless, Adam did not lose his human nature. He retained the soul in its essence and propensity, consisting of intelligence, will, disposition, reason, and consciousness of God. The consciousness of God is as natural to man as his ability to reason. This ability is at all times common to man, and to man only. One can therefore state this in reverse: every human being is conscious of a deity, and a being which is conscious of a deity is necessarily a human being. Yes, by virtue of his consciousness of God man distinguishes himself even further and more clearly from animals than by his ability to reason. In some animals one can discern a trace or semblance of the ability to reason, although such animals are not consciously aware of their activity. The impression of the existence of a deity is entirely absent and cannot be taught. Man's consciousness of God is innate, however. Even if someone no longer manifests any evidence of this, it does not require many hours, for example, to bring the most savage heathen to an acknowledgement of it, which proves that such is his natural propensity.

The consciousness of deity, viewed here as a propensity rather than the act itself, is not a remnant of the image of God in its narrower sense which consists of spiritual knowledge, righteousness, and holiness. To insist otherwise would create unsolvable difficulties. It is, however, possible to state that it is a remnant of the image of God in its wider sense, which includes the previously mentioned faculties of the soul, and those only. It therefore belongs to the essential nature of man, so that the natural consciousness of God, as well as the natural morality which proceeds from it, do not merely differ in degree from the essential elements of the image of God — that is, spiritual knowledge, righteousness, and holiness — but they differ in their very nature. This becomes evident from the following:

First, he who still possesses a remnant of the image of God [that is, in its narrow sense], or a measure thereof, is neither spiritually blind nor spiritually dead, for spiritual life consists in the possession of the image of God. A part is of the same nature as the whole; a drop is as truly water as is the entire ocean. Man however, possessing both the natural knowledge of God as well as morality, is entirely blind and dead. For verification of this blindness turn to Galatians 4:8, Ephesians 4:18, and 1 Corinthians 15:34. For verification of spiritual death turn to Ephesians 2:1-12. Consequently, there is neither a remnant nor a certain degree of the image of God in natural man. It is therefore evident that both natural knowledge and morality do not differ from the image of God in its narrow sense in degree, but in essence.

Secondly, if the natural knowledge of God were identical to the image of God in its narrow sense, and merely differed in degree, then man would be able to convert himself. A man in the state of nature is obviously capable, by virtue of his natural abilities, to progress very significantly in self-manufactured knowledge and virtue, thereby in some areas excelling the truly regenerate. Man, however, is not able to convert himself — a truth which we will consider more extensively at the appropriate place. Therefore, natural knowledge and morality are not synonymous with the image of God, merely differing in degree, but the image of God is of an entirely different nature.

Thirdly, in view of this we must consider that both knowledge and morality

(1) proceed from different causes, one being the original, creative power of God, and the other being the regenerating power of God;

(2) function through different means, one being nature, and the other being the gospel;

(3) have different objects, one being that which is known of God

by virtue of His revelation in the realm of nature, and the other being God's revelation of Himself in the face of Christ;

(4) have different results; the one renders man inexcusable, whereas the other results in salvation. Since there is a difference in all these aspects, there must also be a difference in essence rather than degree. If the restoration of the image of God does not consist in an increase of natural knowledge, but rather in a transformation resulting in knowledge and virtue, which are of an entirely different nature, then natural knowledge is not a remnant of the image of God in its narrow sense. This restoration does not consist in an increase of natural knowledge but in a transformation resulting in an entirely different sort of knowledge. Thus, natural knowledge is not a remnant of the image of God in its narrow sense, and differs with it not in degree, but in essence.

Even though these two are of a different nature, they are, however, not contradictory, just as one light does not clash with another type of light. His very nature makes man a qualified object to be the recipient of both spiritual and natural knowledge. Even though the natural propensity of man is confined to a limited realm of knowledge, and the spiritual is focused upon matters which are far loftier — they being viewed in another light and the subject under consideration being viewed with different eyes by the spiritual man who discerns other matters in it — it does not follow that natural and spiritual knowledge are therefore contradictory; instead, they complement each other.

Thus far we have demonstrated that all men have an impression of the existence of God. All that now remains is to answer the following concern.

Question: May one, in order to become more steadfast in his knowledge that God exists, temporarily set aside all the revelations concerning God in both nature and Scripture, and consider them to be non-existent? May one consider the inner conviction that God exists to be an advantage, thus enabling him to entertain the hypothesis that there is no God, so that by questioning everything and viewing the matter from all angles, he may with more steadfastness conclude that God exists? In sum, *may one doubt whether God exists?*

Answer: Since our intellect has been darkened, man is inclined to doubt whether a matter which presents itself is truly as it appears. This necessitates further research in order to be so conversant with the matter that all doubt is removed. Such, however, is not the case relative to the knowledge of the existence of God. This He has created in our nature and has further confirmed to every man by

Holy Writ, so that one is not permitted to doubt the existence of God, for the following reasons:

(1) It is a rejection of God willingly to maintain that God does not exist as well as willingly doubt His existence.

(2) It is tantamount to challenging God face to face and declaring Him a liar. He reveals both in nature and Scripture that He exists, and this revelation is so clear that man in his conscience from the very outset cannot keep himself deaf to the voice of God.

(3) The person who maintains this, being desirous to doubt, knows that he is lying. When he initially tries to doubt, it is impossible to do so.

(4) Willful doubt will never result in more steadfastness, as a corrupt intellect and an ungodly heart — being granted more room and strength to function — are capable of transforming a doubter into an atheist as far as such is possible. Thus he would rob himself of salvation. God, in response to all this, will at times execute this very judgment.

(5) The proper way, however, to increase in the knowledge of God is to believe that He is, and that He is a rewarder of them who diligently seek Him. To do what is right is to do what one knows to be right, for if any man will do God's will, he will know and confess that this doctrine is of God. The proper way is to seek the Lord, if haply one might seek after Him and find Him.

The knowledge of God in all men is so evident that even the most ungodly, as much as they may labor to do so, are entirely incapable of eradicating all knowledge and consciousness of God, even though they may temporarily succeed in rendering themselves insensitive to this consciousness, and thus become oblivious to the existence of God. May this be to the conviction of many so-called Christians who in addition to nature have the Word of God but reckon so little with God; yes, who in the consciousness of God and the practice of virtue do not proceed as far as many heathen do through the light of nature. How such heathen shall arise in judgment in the last day against such so-called Christians, approving of their damnation! How dreadful shall their judgment be, when God shall appear, "In flaming fire taking vengeance on them that know not God, and that obey not the gospel of our Lord Jesus Christ: who shall be punished with everlasting destruction from the presence of the Lord, and from the glory of His power" (2 Th. 1:8-9).

May everyone therefore strive earnestly to acquire the knowledge of God, without which there can neither be faith, love, religion, nor salvation. Do not be satisfied with only a natural knowledge which cannot lead you to a saving knowledge of God, but rather strive to behold God's glory in the face of Jesus Christ. Likewise, strive for the knowledge of the truth which is according to godliness.

From the foregoing, the godly may conclude that they are merely being tempted when they are troubled by atheistic thoughts. Their dismay concerning this is sufficient evidence that they know God and "believe that He is." Do not yield to such thoughts, but resist them. Even if for some time you cannot rid yourself of these temptations, still hold to your inner conviction. As troublesome as it may be to you now, it shall make you more steadfast later. Persevere in reading God's Word and join yourself to the godly in order to hear them speak about the delight they may have in God. Refrain from reading books authored by atheists or those who encourage atheism. Avoid interaction and disputation with confirmed atheists. Instead, turn to the Lord by continually engaging yourself in prayer; live in simplicity, knowing what the will of God is. In so doing you shall grow in the grace and in the knowledge of our Lord Jesus Christ (2 Pet. 3:18).

CHAPTER TWO

The Word of God

We have shown that the knowledge of God derived from nature is insufficient unto salvation. If man were ever to be brought to salvation, it was necessary for God to reveal a way whereby he could become a partaker of it. Although in retrospect we are able to deduce this truth, nature does not reveal it. It does disclose, however, that God is able to reveal something that is salvific in nature. This has encouraged some to claim to be the recipients of divine revelations and has caused people to believe such pretended revelations.

God, in His unfathomable goodness, being desirous to have a people of His own on earth whom He would lead unto salvation, has revealed to them a way of salvation, beginning with the first gospel declaration to Adam. The Seed of the woman would bruise the head of the serpent (Gen. 3:15). In addition to this, God repeatedly gave to His prophets more comprehensive and clearer revelations which they in turn proclaimed to the people who then believed these revelations unto salvation.

The Word of God Prior to Moses

Whether these revelations had been recorded prior to the time of Moses and had been forwarded to the church of that time in written form, we can neither affirm nor deny. Similarly, it is not known to us whether Moses, upon divine command and having been led by the Holy Spirit into all truth, had recorded those matters which transpired from the beginning of time to his time by means of holy and divinely inspired writings, or whether he received them himself by virtue of immediate revelation via the inerrant transmissions of men guided by the Holy Spirit. Since the fathers in the sacred lineage lived for the duration of several hundred years, such transmission could transpire more readily. Abraham, who faithfully made the way of salvation known to his seed, was able to learn third-handedly all that had transpired before him. Abraham was informed by Shem, with whom he lived contemporaneously, Shem from Methuselah, and Methuselah from Adam.

We know one thing with certainty: The church of that time was neither deprived of the Word of God nor of divine revelations. Moses conveys this to us in his first book, and the fact that the elect of that time were brought to salvation makes this a necessary prerequisite. The Word of God of that time is generally referred to as the *unwritten Word*, as it neither appears to have been recorded, nor to have been transmitted to us in written form. We are limited in our knowledge concerning this by what Moses conveys to us. Only Jude speaks of the prophecy of Enoch in verses 14-15, which is rendered credible by his account. To contrive the idea, however, that there is an unwritten Word in addition to the Holy Scriptures which would reveal things not recorded in the Bible — as Roman Catholicism does in order to make their traditions credible — would be an act which would invoke the curses pronounced upon those who would add something to the written Word.

The Names Assigned to God's Word

We generally denominate the written Word of God as *the Bible*, the word "Bible" itself being a Greek transliteration. In our language this word means "book," which corresponds with the fact that the Bible is the Book of all books. Such it is called in Isaiah 34:16, "Seek ye out of the Book of the LORD"; in Mark 12:26, "the book of Moses"; in Luke 4:17, "the book of the prophet Esaias"; in Acts 1:20, "the book of Psalms"; in Revelation 22:19, "the book of this prophecy"; in Psalm 40:7, "in the volume of the book," so called because at that time one did not make use of pages, but rather of a long strip of parchment which would be rolled up and tied together with a string.

The written Word is also called *the Holy Scriptures* in 2 Timothy 3:15-16. In Acts 8:32 it is referred to as *Scripture*. Since the art of printing had not yet been invented, everything had to be written by pen. Therefore, few possessed the entire Bible, the cost of a Bible at that time being thousands of dollars. Some only possessed a book of one of the prophets, one of the gospels, or one of the apostolic letters. In addition to this, many were not able to read. It was a wonderful mercy of God, upon which one cannot meditate without thanksgiving, that the art of printing was invented and put into practice a short time prior to the Reformation. As a result even a poor person can now own a Bible for a small price. Consequently, you will scarcely be able to find anyone of the Reformed faith who does not possess a Bible or at least a New Testament.

The Holy Scriptures are also denominated as *the Word of God.* In Romans 3:2 it is stated, "Unto them were committed the oracles of God."[1] God, in condescension to man, has revealed the way of truth in a manner consistent with humanity by speaking to holy men of God, who, moved by the Holy Ghost (2 Pet. 1:21), have spoken these things to the church, thus transmitting the words of God to her. "God, who at sundry times and in divers manners spake in time past unto the fathers by the prophets, hath in these last days spoken unto us by His Son" (Heb. 1:1-2).

The Necessity of the Written Word

After God enlarged the church to include Abraham and his seed, to which she was primarily limited until the time of Christ, it pleased Him to give to His church an immovable and everlasting rule for life and doctrine, by submitting His will in written form to her. This does not imply that such was necessary from God's perspective, as by His omnipotence He would have been able to reveal the way of salvation to His church without the written Word, and preserve the truth amongst her. From man's perspective, however, there was such a necessity, in order that the truth would be preserved so much better against the wickedness of man whose heart is inclined toward superstition and carnal religion, carrying within it the seed of numerous heresies. This was also necessary to protect the church against the wiles of the devil because his objective is always to use the smoke of heresy to tarnish the truth, knowing that without the knowledge of the truth there can be no true godliness. Finally, this was necessary so that the gospel might reach every individual member of the church more efficiently, be transmitted from father to children, and be distributed among the nations that much more rapidly. It was needful for Jude to write (Jude 3). The written Word is a light upon our path (Psa. 119:105). If they speak not according to the law and to the testimony, "it is because there is no light in them" (Isa. 8:20). Thus, the existence of the written Word is a necessity.

Roman Catholicism, in order to safeguard their traditions and superstitious legends more effectively, contradicts the necessity of Scripture, presenting the following arguments:

---

[1] The Dutch Statenbijbel reads: "Hun zijn de woorden Gods toebetrouwd," that is, "unto them were committed the words of God."

Objection #1: There have been particular churches which have existed without the written Word, such being the case when the apostles initially proclaimed the gospel among the heathen and established churches among them.

Answer: Such was the case only for a short period of time. Even if they were not in the immediate possession of the written Word, they had the word of the apostles who were infallibly moved by the Spirit of God. Nevertheless, in a general sense the church had God's Word in its possession, as one particular congregation would share it with another congregation (Col. 4:16). The Jews who were dispersed among the heathen had the written Word, and as you know, in many places they were generally the first to believe.

Objection #2: For the illiterate it is as if the written Word does not exist in written form.

Answer: They hear the Word read, as well as the quotation of Scripture passages by the minister, and thus their faith, and the faith of those who are able to read, is equally founded upon the written Word.

Objection #3: The Lord's people are taught by the Lord Himself and therefore are not in need of other instruction (cf. Isa. 54:13; Jer. 31:34, 1 John 2:27).

Answer: (1) It may similarly be argued that the church certainly has no need for her traditions and therefore they must necessarily be discarded.

(2) When God instructs His people by means of His Word, they are being instructed by Him.

(3) One does not exclude the other, as God grants His Holy Spirit by means of His Word (Acts 10:44).

The Bible is comprised of this written Word and consists of sixty-six books. Thirty-nine were written prior to the birth of Christ and are therefore referred to as the Old Testament (2 Cor. 3:14). It begins with the first book of Moses, generally referred to as *Genesis,* and concludes with *Malachi.* These books are divided in a variety of ways, such as "Moses and the Prophets" (Luke 24:27); and "Moses, the Prophets, and the Psalms" (Luke 24:44). Generally they are divided as follows:

(1) the books of the Law, that is, the five books of Moses;

(2) historical books, Joshua to Esther inclusive;

(3) poetical books from Job to the Song of Solomon;

(4) the prophets, consisting of the four major prophets from Isaiah to Daniel, and the twelve minor prophets from Hosea to Malachi.

The New Testament encompasses those Holy Scriptures which were written after the time of Christ, beginning with Matthew and concluding with the Revelation. These are divided as follows:

(1) the historical books, that is, the four gospels and the Acts of the Apostles;

(2) the doctrinal books from the Epistle to the Romans to the Epistle of Jude;

(3) a prophetical book, being the Revelation of John.

The Apocryphal, that is, the "hidden" books — being neither read in the churches nor recognized as divinely inspired — do not belong to the Bible. They are writings of human origin of which there are also so many today. They were composed prior to the time of Christ, neither by the hand of a prophet nor in the Hebrew tongue, but in the Greek language. They were neither given to the church, nor did the Jews to whom the oracles of God were entrusted (Rom. 3:2) accept them. They contain many errors and heretical statements contradicting the canonical books. For more comprehensive information you may refer to the excellent preface to the Apocryphal books by the Dutch translators of the *Statenbijbel*. It satisfactorily confounds Roman Catholicism which desired in later times to consider these books as canonical.

As the Holy Scriptures are the only rule for doctrine and life, the devil is intent upon overthrowing or obscuring this foundation to the utmost of his ability by means of instruments at his disposal. Therefore we shall engage ourselves to defend the Holy Scriptures, and for this purpose we shall consider, 1) their origin — both primary and secondary causes, 2) their contents, 3) their form, 4) their purpose, 5) the subjects to whom they are given, and 6) their profitableness. In considering each of these elements, we shall deal with matters of controversy which one can bring against them.

The Origin of the Holy Scriptures

With regard to the *origin* of the Holy Scriptures, we must consider the primary as well as the mediate causes. The primary, yes, the *only* essential cause is God. The evidence is as follows:

1) Throughout the entire Scriptures the following expressions are found: "God spake," "God said," "Thus saith the LORD," and similar words.

2) God Himself did not merely proclaim the law with a loud voice (Exo. 20), but also recorded it in two tables of stone (Exo. 34:28).

3) God expressly commanded the sacred writers to record His Word, "Write this for a memorial in a book" (Exo. 17:14); "Write thou these words" (Exo. 34:27); "What thou seest, write in a book, and send it unto the seven churches which are in Asia" (Rev. 1:11).

This is also expressed in several other texts, as Isaiah 30:8, Jeremiah 30:2, and Hebrews 2:2. Such is also the purpose of the preface to the various books containing the credentials of the writers, whether they be prophets, evangelists, or apostles.

4) The entire Scriptures bear testimony to this, "All Scripture is given by inspiration of God" (2 Tim. 3:16); "For the prophecy came not in old time by the will of man: but holy men of God spake as they were moved by the Holy Ghost" (2 Pet. 1:21); "The Spirit of the LORD spake by me, and His word was in my tongue" (2 Sam. 23:2).

This has been stated in rebuttal to Roman Catholicism, which denies that the Holy Scriptures were written upon divine command, but rather at this or that arbitrary occasion. The intent of such a notion is secretly to undermine the Scriptures and to give credence and respectability to Rome's traditions. They seek to prove this by maintaining that God would have caused an orderly book to be written, in which all creedal issues would have been recorded in an orderly fashion, the words and stipulations being such that no misunderstandings or heresies could issue forth from them.

Answer: (1) Who was the Lord's counselor? Who can say, "What doest Thou?" (Job 9:12); "For the wisdom of this world is foolishness with God" (1 Cor. 3:19). He makes foolish the wisdom of this world (1 Cor. 1:20); "Because the foolishness of God is wiser than men" (1 Cor. 1:25); "But the natural man receiveth not the things of the Spirit of God: for they are foolishness unto him" (1 Cor. 2:14).

Errors and heresies do not issue forth from the Holy Scriptures, but from the corrupt intellect of man. "For there must also be heresies among you, that they which are approved may be made manifest among you" (1 Cor. 11:19).

(2) We do not deny that some matters have been recorded at specified occasions; however, this does not eliminate the fact that God has inspired them and has caused them to be recorded.

The Inherent Divine Authority of the Holy Scriptures

Question: Are the Holy Scriptures truly the Word of God, having divine authority, both in regard to historical accounts where many words and deeds of the ungodly are related, and in regard to the rule for doctrine and life? It is necessary for man to be convinced of this and to esteem the Scriptures as the Word of God. Therefore, *how may man be assured that the Holy Scriptures are the Word of God?*

Answer: Roman Catholicism answers that we must believe it because the church says that it is so. We do affirm that the true church, which believes and declares that the Holy Scriptures are the Word of God, is a means whereby the Holy Spirit brings man to the Word, and thereby persuades man to believe it. The church is neither the foundation upon which rests the faith that Scripture is the Word of God nor whereby man is assured thereof. Rather, the Holy Scriptures, by virtue of the inwrought evidences of their divinity and the Holy Spirit speaking in that Word, are themselves the foundation and basis whereby we believe them to be divine. The authority of the Word is derived from the Word itself.

The church cannot be the foundation upon which one believes the Scriptures to be the Word of God.

First, the church derives all its authority from the Word. We cannot acknowledge a church to be the true church except by means of the Word of God — and only if it preaches the pure doctrine and has the credentials which Scripture expresses as belonging to the true church. "Built upon the foundation of the apostles and prophets" (Eph. 2:20); "If there come any unto you, and bring not this doctrine, receive him not into your house" (2 John 10); "...and avoid them" (Rom. 16:17).

If the Word of God is the only criterion by which we can determine a church to be the true church of God, then we must first acknowledge Scripture to be the Word of God before acknowledging the church to be the true church. Furthermore, we cannot receive the testimony of the church unless we acknowledge her to be the true church. Thus, we do not believe the Word to be the Word of God because the *church* affirms it, but on the contrary, we believe the church to be the true church because the *Word* validates her as such. A house rests upon its foundation, and not the foundation upon the house. A construction is subordinate to its cause rather than the cause being subordinate to what it has constructed.

Evasive Argument: The two can be interchangeable; Christ bore witness to John the Baptist, and John in return to Christ.

Answer: It is one thing to bear witness, but quite another to be the foundation of faith itself. Christ was Truth personified, and He testified with authority; John, however, was merely an instrument whereby the truth was disclosed, as every minister is today. God's servants are nevertheless not the foundation upon which the faith of the hearers is resting; that foundation is Jesus the Christ. Rather, with the Samaritans we must confess, "Now we believe, not because of thy saying: for we have heard *Him* ourselves, and know that this is indeed the Christ, the Saviour of the world" (John 4:42).

The basis for respecting someone's words is the person himself. The laws issued by the government derive their authority to demand compliance from the government itself. The laws do not receive this authority, however, from the person who publishes these laws either by reading or by displaying them. Thus, we acknowledge the Word to have divine authority solely because God is the One who speaks, "Hear, O heavens, and give ear, O earth: for the LORD hath spoken" (Isa. 1:2). The church merely functions as a herald.

If the Word derived its authority from the church, then we would have to hold the church in higher esteem than God Himself, for whoever gives credence and emphasis to someone's words is superior to the person who speaks them. God has no superior and therefore no one is in a position to give authority to His words. "I receive not testimony from man" (John 5:34), exclaimed the Lord Jesus. Even though John testified of Him, that is, declared that He was the Christ, it would nevertheless be contrary to the will of the Lord Jesus that someone would believe for that reason only. John's testimony was merely a means to an end. "But I have greater witness than that of John: for the works which the Father hath given Me to finish, the same works that I do, bear witness of Me, that the Father hath sent Me" (John 5:36).

Objection #1: "...which is the church of the living God, the pillar and ground of the truth" (1 Tim. 3:15). Whatever provides the truth with support and stability, provides it with the authority to be received as truth. Such is the relationship of the church to the truth.

Answer: I emphatically reject the conclusion of this proposition. The most eminent proponents of the church are called pillars, which is true in daily conversation as well as in Scripture. "James, Cephas, and John, who seemed to be pillars" (Gal. 2:9).

Nevertheless these men did not give to the church the authority to be recognized as the true church. Similarly, the church is the keeper, the defender, and the protector of the Word. If there were no church, the Word of God and the truth contained in it would almost entirely disappear from the world. The expression "a pillar and ground" has no reference to the giving of authority and credibility, but rather to preservation and protection. The oracles of God have been committed to the church (Rom. 3:2). Her calling is to preserve and defend them, as well as to publish them abroad. What credence does this give to the Word of God itself?

Objection #2: No one would know that the Bible is the Word of God if the church had not declared it to be so. God is not now declaring from heaven that the Bible is the Word of God; therefore there must of necessity be someone who declares such to be the case in order that the people can hear it.

Answer: (1) No one can know which law the government has issued forth, except for the announcement by a herald and yet he is not the person who gives these laws their authority. Such is also the case here.

(2) The argument that no one can know that the Bible is the Word of God except the church declares it to be so, does not hold. It occasionally occurs that someone born and raised far distant from other people, and being ignorant of the existence of a church, will accidentally find a Bible in his home. While reading it diligently, he finds delight in these matters and they are used as a means for his conversion. Consequently he acknowledges the Bible to be of God and he begins to love His Word. I have known such an individual, and what has happened to him can also happen to anyone else. Hundreds of people are ignorant concerning the church and thus have no regard for it. Yet they will acknowledge the Bible to be the Word of God and may even attempt to seek out the true church by means of the Word. Whether the church or some-one else gives us the Bible and declares it to be the Word of God is immaterial. In either case it can motivate a person to search, and while searching, he can discern evidences of divine authorship in it.

(3) The objector will claim the Roman Catholic Church to be the true church, thereby giving authority to the Word. We believe, however, that the Bible is the Word of God, but not because the Roman Catholic Church says it is, as we do not even recognize them to be the church of God. Thus, with how much more certainty — ten times more than they — can we declare that the Bible is the Word of God! And we are not basing this on the acknowledgement that the Roman Catholic Church is the true church. Scripture neither receives its divine authority from the pope, from papal assemblies, nor from the entire power structure of the Roman Catholic Church.

Objection #3: The church existed prior to the written Word and is better known than the Word; thus the church gives the Word divine authority.

Answer: The church is not older than the Word; the very opposite is true. The Word is the seed of the church. The first gospel message was issued forth prior to the existence of the church and was a means whereby the church came into existence. It is true that the church existed prior to the time that the Scriptures were fully contained in the Bible. Nevertheless, the church neither gave credence to the books of Moses nor to the Scriptures which followed. Today when someone is born under the ministry of the Word, Word and church are simultaneously present. Generally one acquires esteem for the Bible as the Word of God prior to comprehending what the church is and discerning what she has to say about the Word. From this it follows that the church does not have more recognition than the Word. The converse is true. Assuming that the church did precede the written Word and has more recognition, this fact would not give her the privilege above another to declare the Word to be divine.

Thus, the church does not give divine authority to the Word among men. We do not believe the Word to be divine because the church declares it to be so, but the Holy Scriptures themselves manifest their divinity to the attentive hearer or reader and this becomes clear from the following:

(1) The prefaces of the books of the Bible and apostolic letters, and such words as, "Thus saith the Lord," "The Lord speaks," "Hear the Word of the Lord," etc., touch the heart.

(2) Scripture manifests its divinity to man by its revelation of the lofty mysteries of God and divine matters, which nature does not reveal, no human could have conceived, and which, apart from the operation of the Holy Spirit, cannot be comprehended. The divinity of Scripture is also manifested in the holiness and purity of its injunctions as well as by the way in which man is commanded to conduct himself. Therefore, all other writings which are not derived from this Word are carnal, unrefined, vain, and foolish, whereas those writings which are derived from Scripture compare to Scripture as a painting resembles a living human being.

(3) The divinity of Scripture is further evident from the power it exerts upon the human heart, for wherever the gospel is preached, hearts are conquered and brought into subjection to Scripture. The more those who confess the truth of Scripture are suppressed and persecuted, the more the Word will exert its power.

(4) It is evident from the wondrous light with which the Word illuminates the soul, the internal and external change it engenders, and the manner in which it fills believers with sweet comfort and inexpressible joy. It enables them to endure all persecution in love and with joy as well as surrender themselves willingly to death.

(5) Finally, it is evident from the prophecies which, having declared thousands of years in advance what would subsequently occur, have been fulfilled in minute detail, thus validating these prophecies.

These and similar matters are rays of the divinity of the Word which illuminate and convince man of this divinity by its inherent light. However, the task of fully persuading someone, especially a person who uses his corrupt intellect to judge in this matter, is the work of God's Spirit who is the Spirit of faith (2 Cor. 4:13). He gives faith (1 Cor. 12:9), and bears witness that the Spirit speaking by means of the Word, is truth (1 John 5:6); "No man can say that Jesus is the Lord, but by the Holy Ghost" (1 Cor. 12:3).

The Mediate Causes Whereby God Has Provided
Man with His Word

Having considered the primary moving cause, we now will consider the *mediate causes* or the means the Lord has been pleased to use
in providing man with His Word. These were "holy men of God,
moved by the Holy Ghost" (2 Pet. 1:21). They received revelation,

(1) by means of immediate address, "With him will I speak
mouth to mouth, even apparently" (Num. 12:8);

(2) by means of a trance (Acts 10:10), and being "in the spirit"
(Rev. 1:10);

(3) by means of dreams in which God would speak (Mat. 1:20),
or in visions accompanied by verbal declarations (Gen. 18:13,17);

(4) by means of angels, be it during sleep, during a trance, or while
being awake (Gen. 18:2). In whatever manner the prophets received
their revelations, they, as well as the evangelists and the apostles,
wrote by the inspiration of the Holy Spirit who inspired them (2 Tim.
3:16), moved them (2 Pet. 1:21), and guided and directed them into
all truth (John 16:13), showing it unto them (verse 14).

These men, being guided by the Holy Spirit in regard to matters,
words, and style, wrote in the language in use by the church,
thereby enabling her to understand the Scriptures. The Scriptures
of the Old Testament were written in *Hebrew*, since at that time the
church existed within that nation. Only a few chapters have been
recorded in the *Aramaic* language which resembles Hebrew so
closely that whoever understands Hebrew will almost be able to
understand the Aramaic language fully. The Scriptures of the New
Testament were written in *Greek*, this language being most commonly in use among the Gentiles.

Both languages have remained so untainted in the Holy Scriptures that even though various manuscripts contain some writing
or printing errors, and heretics have sought to corrupt them in
various places, the Scriptures have nevertheless been fully preserved due to the faithful, providential care of the Lord, as well as
the meticulous attention given to the manuscripts by both the
Jewish and Christian churches.

Only the aforementioned languages are authentic, having the
inherent authority to be both credible and acceptable. It was in
these languages that it has pleased the Lord, by the inspiration
and direction of the Holy Spirit, to cause His Word to be
recorded. All translations into other languages must be verified
by means of the original text. Whatever is not in harmony with this
text must be rejected, as God did not cause His Word to be recorded

in the languages into which it is being translated, but only in Hebrew and Greek.

Roman Catholicism considers the common *Latin* translation to be authentic, albeit that some of the more educated among them, being conversant with Hebrew and Greek, are of a different opinion. Others among them would rather die in ignorance than come to the knowledge of the truth. Their efforts to whittle away the authenticity of the original texts are so fraught with ignorance that they are not deserving of a reply.

The Substance or Contents of the Word of God

The *substance* or *contents* of the Word is the covenant of grace, or to state it differently, it contains the perfect rule for faith and practice. This rule is comprehended in the Old and New Testaments. It is not true that part of this rule is to be found in each such that the Old Testament would not have been sufficient for the church of the Old Testament and that the New Testament would not have been sufficient unto salvation without the Old Testament, as if they of necessity belong together in the absolute sense of the word. This would suggest that if one book of Scripture were to be lost, part of this rule would be missing and therefore would not be perfect. One book or several together — for example, the books of Moses or the gospels — perfectly contain the complete rule for faith and practice. Someone being in possession only of these books would still be able to be saved, presuming he would understand them correctly. In giving us many Scriptures, however, authored by various prophets, evangelists, and apostles, all bearing witness to the same truth, the Lord is manifesting His wondrous goodness to us. One book will shed light upon one doctrine more comprehensively and more clearly, whereas another book will do so in reference to a different doctrine. Thus, all the books of both Old and New Testaments obligate us to believe and practice all that God commands, which implies that nothing may be believed or practiced which is external to the Scriptures. This confronts us with the following questions:

Question: Is the Word of God a complete and perfect rule for man in reference to faith and practice, thereby implying that nothing needs to be, or may be, added?

Answer: Roman Catholicism denies that the Word of God provides us with such a perfect rule, insisting that unwritten traditions must be accepted and believed with the same veneration and faith as the written Word of God. We, on the contrary, maintain that the written Word of God is a perfect and complete rule, thereby rejecting as human inventions all unwritten traditions which pertain to doctrine or practice. This is verified by, "The law of the LORD is perfect, converting the soul: the testimony of the LORD is sure, making wise the simple" (Psa. 19:7). David as prophet does not merely make mention of the perfection which is inherent in the minutest detail of the Word of God, but rather how this Word functions in reference to man: it can infuse man with wisdom unto salvation, which in turn results in his conversion. Thus, the Word contains all that is essential for doctrine and practice. If such were not the case, then it would neither be capable of converting a man nor providing him with suitable wisdom. The written Word has been given for the express purpose that we might procure life by it. "But these are written, that ye might believe that Jesus is the Christ, the Son of God; and that believing ye might have life through His Name" (John 20:31). Such an objective could not be attained if the written Word were neither sufficient nor a perfect rule for doctrine and life. Thus, it must be concluded that the Word is perfect.

The written Word is competent to teach the truth, to rebuke error, to correct evil, and to identify that which is good, so man may be made perfect, thoroughly furnished unto all good works. In one word, it is able to make man wise unto salvation. More one need not desire, for to have this is to have all. Indeed, the vitality and efficacy of Scripture is such that it is both perfect and sufficient. Observe this in 2 Timothy 3:15-17: "The Holy Scriptures... are able to make thee wise unto salvation. All scripture is given by inspiration of God, and is profitable for doctrine, for reproof, for correction, for instruction in righteousness: that the man of God may be perfect, thoroughly furnished unto all good works."

Evasive Argument #1: The word used is "profitable," not "sufficient." Ink is both profitable and necessary for writing, but not sufficient by itself.

Answer: It is written that the Word can make us wise unto salvation, and whatever is profitable unto salvation is of necessity also sufficient. In consequence of this there can be no additional requirements. The sun is profitable for illumination, which is equivalent to being sufficient, as no other light is either necessary or profitable when we are illuminated by the sun.

Evasive Argument #2: The apostle refers to the Old Testament. If the Old Testament were sufficient unto salvation, then the New Testament is not necessary. Since it is indispensable, however, then *profitable* here is almost identical to *advantageous* but it is not the equivalent of being *sufficient.*

Answer: (1) The Old Testament was sufficient prior to the coming of Christ who had been promised in the Old Testament. The New Testament does not propose a doctrine and practice which differs from that which is presented in the Old Testament, but rather confirms and augments that which was promised, and thus gives an exposition of its fulfillment. If the Old Testament were profitable to such a degree that it was sufficient for that time, then, due to their sufficiency, the combination of Old and New Testaments are all the more profitable.

(2) When Paul wrote these words to Timothy, several New Testament Scriptures were already available and therefore were included as well.

Addition to or Deletion from the Holy Scriptures Prohibited

It is forbidden to add to or delete from the written Word. All the curses recorded in this Word relative to such a practice confirm this. Thus the Word of God is a complete rule for doctrine and practice. This can be observed, as we read, "Ye shall not add unto the Word which I command you, neither shall ye diminish ought from it" (Deu. 4:2); "If any man shall add unto these things, God shall add unto him the plagues that are written in this Book: And if any man shall take away from the words of the book of this prophecy, God shall take away his part out of the book of life" (Rev. 22:18-19); "But though we, or an angel from heaven, preach any other gospel unto you than that which we have preached unto you, let him be accursed" (Gal. 1:8).

Evasive Argument #1: Moses makes reference to that which he spoke and not to that which he wrote. John only referred to his book, the Revelation, and not to the entire Bible.

Answer: That which Moses spoke, he, upon the Lord's command, also recorded as a faithful servant of God. In writing the book of the Revelation, John wrote the conclusion of the Word of God. John placed his prohibition at the very end of the Revelation as a seal upon the entire revealed and recorded will of God in His Word. The reason for this prohibition is identical for every book of Holy Writ, and thus for the entire Scripture, the reason being that God had inspired those writings and none other.

Evasive Argument #2: The prophets have added much to Moses, and the apostles have added to both.

Answer: This is not true in reference to the rule for doctrine and practice, but only as far as exposition, augmentation, and application are concerned, this being inspired and commanded of God. Paul declared all the counsel of God (Acts 20:27), and yet did not go beyond Moses and the prophets (Acts 26:22).

Evasive Argument #3: The texts refer to an addition or deletion which would contradict and corrupt that which has been recorded, but not to something which conforms to and complements the text.

Answer: Whatever one adds to a perfect work has a corrupting effect. The texts do not merely refer to all that is contradictory, but to all exceptions, as well as whatever is composed beyond the written text (Gal. 1:8).

All traditions which are extrabiblical are inventions and institutions of men. There are no traditions which have been handed down to us by Christ and the apostles. Never does Christ or an apostle direct us to unwritten traditions, but always to the Word (cf. Isa. 8:20, Luke 16:29, John 5:39, 2 Pet. 1:19-20). God condemns all institutions of men. "But in vain do they worship Me, teaching for doctrines the commandments of men" (Mat. 15:9). The institutions of Roman Catholicism are superstitious, erroneous, and contrary to God's written Word.

Objection #1: Many books of the Holy Scriptures have been lost, such as *The Book of the Wars of the Lord, The Book of the Just, The Book of the Chronicles of Israel, The Book of the Prophets Nathan and Gad, The Letter to the Laodiceans.* In addition, not all the words and deeds of Christ have been recorded. We may believe that the apostles also wrote additional letters which are not in our possession. Thus, we must conclude that the Bible is not complete.

Answer: (1) These books have never been regarded as a rule for doctrine and practice. Scripture mentions several other books which have been written by pagan authors (Acts 17:28; Titus 1:12).

(2) We believe that Christ has spoken and done many things. Furthermore, we believe that the apostles have written many letters to the congregations, also by inspiration of the Holy Spirit. Such particular congregations were obliged to receive these letters as being of divine origin. These were not in the possession of other congregations, however, and after the apostolic period were not preserved for the church of God. The Scriptures which we may now have are therefore not incomplete, but nevertheless are and remain a perfect rule for doctrine and practice. The entire gospel is contained in them, and apart from Scripture nothing else has ever been said or written about Christ and the apostles which has been recognized as a rule for doctrine and practice for the congregation. Indeed, even if we had fewer books in number, we would nevertheless be in possession of a perfect rule. It is the Lord's goodness, however, to give us the same gospel by the agency of

many persons, as well as by means of many amplifications, applications, and expositions — all being abundantly sufficient for us. A distinction needs to be made between the essence of a matter and the details of it.

Objection #2: "I have yet many things to say unto you, but ye cannot bear them now" (John 16:12). This indicates that many essential things have not been recorded. Thus, we must conclude that the Scriptures are not complete, and therefore need to be augmented by means of traditions.

Answer: After Christ's resurrection the apostles were stronger in faith and grace, and during the forty days of His presence among them He spoke about the things concerning the kingdom of God (Acts 1:3). Thus, Christ spoke to them about those things which they were previously not able to bear. They were moved by the Holy Spirit who guided them into all truth (John 16:13). This Spirit would teach them all things and bring to remembrance all things which the Lord Jesus had told them (John 14:26). Thus, tradition is eliminated and the Holy Scriptures are and remain perfect, the apostles having recorded "all that Jesus began both to do and to teach" (Acts 1:1), which encompasses all that is essential unto salvation.

Objection #3: "Hold the traditions which ye have been taught, whether by word, or our epistle" (2 Th. 2:15). Here the apostle expressly makes mention of traditions which were taught verbally, thus distinguishing them from traditions taught by letter. Consequently, there are traditions which have not been recorded, but which nevertheless must be adhered to.

Answer: The apostle did not only write but he also engaged in live preaching. The substance of his preaching, however, did not differ from the substance of his writing, and vice versa. It was in essence the same gospel. Therefore "by word or by letter" merely refers to different manners of presentation and not to matters which differ essentially. Therefore this does not lend support to the use of tradition.

Objection #4: The Jewish church also instituted various practices — passing them on to subsequent generations — which were not commanded, however, such as fasting in the fourth, fifth, seventh, and tenth month (Zec. 7:5 and 8:19); the days of Purim (Est. 9:21-26); and the feast of the dedication (John 10:22). In similar fashion the Reformed Church also has her traditions, which implies that also now we may and must uphold tradition.

Answer: The practice of fasting was commanded by God; the determination of necessity, time, and circumstances was left to the church (Joel 2). Special days of thanksgiving are also commanded, the occurrence and frequency of which are to be determined by the church. There is no basis in the Word, however, upon which the church may legislate the observation of such days for subsequent generations. Such practices should be denounced and the church should not observe them. This is true also for our so-called feast days which ought to be eliminated. Regarding feast days consult *Res Judicata* by D. Koelman, as well as his other scholarly and devotional writings. Other external religious ordinances and circumstances are principally commanded in the Word of God, the stipulations of which are left to each individual church, and consequently are alterable according to time and place. In doing so, however, all superstition must be avoided and such practices must not have an adverse effect upon doctrine and practice. Thus, the perfection of the rule of Scripture will not be violated, nor will the use of unwritten traditions be advocated.

The Old Testament: Binding for New Testament Christians

Question: Does the Old Testament continue to be a rule for doctrine and practice for Christians in the New Testament?

Answer: The Anabaptists reply negatively, whereas we reply in the affirmative. Our proof is as follows:

First, the Old and New Testaments contain the same doctrines and the same gospel; thus the Old and the New Testaments are one in essence, differing only in circumstances and the manner of administration. The church of the Old Testament anticipated the coming of Christ and therefore had a ministry of types and shadows. The New Testament church reflects upon Christ who has come and therefore has a ministry without shadows. The Old Testament is one in essence with the New Testament and therefore is as much a rule for us as is the New Testament. Subsequently we shall demonstrate more comprehensively that such is evident in both Testaments, which is the reason why the apostle, while preaching in the New Testament dispensation, said "none other things than those which the prophets and Moses did say should come" (Acts 26:22).

Secondly, there is but one church from the beginning of the world until the end of time. The books of the Old Testament were given to the church as her regulative principle, and such is therefore true for the New Testament church as well. Even the ceremonies, which were instituted to be practiced only for a period of time, are applicable to us in the New Testament — not to be practiced as such, but for the purpose of discerning in them the truth and wisdom of God, and also for the attainment of a better knowledge of Christ from the details of those ceremonies.

Thirdly, the church of the New Testament is built upon the foundation of the prophets as well as of the apostles. "Built upon the foundation of the apostles and prophets" (Eph. 2:20). Thus the writings of the prophets are as regulative for us as the writings of the apostles.

Evasive Argument: The word "prophets" should be interpreted as referring to the prophets of the New Testament, of whom we can read in 1 Corinthians 12:28, Ephesians 3:5, and Ephesians 4:11. This is indicated by the order in which they are mentioned, as the apostle first makes mention of the apostles and then of the prophets.

Answer: (1) The prophets of the New Testament, to whom reference is made in these texts, did not leave behind any writings. Consequently, the church cannot be built upon their writings.

(2) Whenever mention is made of prophets in the New Testament, the reference is generally to the prophets of the Old Testament (Luke 24:25, 27).

(3) The fact that the apostles are mentioned before the prophets lends no support to such a sentiment. The prophets are placed before the evangelists in Ephesians 4:11, and yet evangelists are superior to prophets in the New Testament.

Fourthly, Christ and the apostles substantiated their doctrine by means of the Old Testament. They direct us to the Scriptures of the Old Testament, demonstrating the profitability of the Old Testament for us who are in the New Testament dispensation. "Search the Scriptures; for...they are they which testify of Me" (John 5:39); "For whatsoever things were written aforetime [that is, the books of the Old Testament] were written for our learning" (Rom. 15:4); "They have Moses and the prophets; let them hear them" (Luke 16:29); "We have also a more sure word of prophecy; whereunto ye do well that ye take heed" (2 Pet. 1:19); "These were more noble than those in Thessalonica, in that they received the Word with all readiness of mind, and searched the Scriptures daily, whether those things were so" (Acts 17:11). All this demonstrates with exceptional clarity that the Scriptures of the Old Testament are as regulative for us as those of the New Testament.

Objection #1: "In that he saith, A new covenant, he hath made the first old. Now that which decayeth and waxeth old is ready to vanish away" (Heb. 8:13). Since it then already was waxing old and ready to vanish away, at the present time it has vanished long ago. Thus, we conclude that the Old Testament is no longer regulative for us.

Answer: In this text the apostle is not referring to the books of the Old Testament, for he commends them, declaring them to be profitable for instruction, reproof, etc., (Rom. 15:4, 2 Tim. 3:15-17).

Rather, his reference here is to the administration of the covenant which will be demonstrated in more detail later. Even though the ceremonies relating to the administration of the covenant have ceased, the books of the Old Testament do not therefore cease to be regulative.

Objection #2: "For all the prophets and the law prophesied unto John" (Mat. 11:13); therefore the prophecies of necessity ceased at the time when John appeared on the scene.

Answer: The prophets and the ceremonial laws proclaimed that Christ would come, whereas John proclaimed that Jesus had come. The fulfillment implies the cessation of the promise; as such these promises must no longer be understood to be prophetical in nature. Their prophecies continued to be valid in other respects, however. They prophesied concerning the suffering, death, resurrection, and ascension of Jesus, and of His return to judge the world. In this sense the prophecies could not cease with John, the reason being that they had not as yet been fulfilled. The Lord Jesus makes reference in this text to prophecies and their fulfillment, but not to the issue whether the prophetic Scriptures are regulative. The one terminated with the coming of Christ, and the other will always be valid.

Objection #3: "Christ is the end of the law" (Rom. 10:4). Therefore, the Old Testament ceased to function at the coming of Christ.

Answer: The apostle does not refer to the termination of its enduring validity, for Christ states, "Think not that I am come to destroy the law, or the prophets: I am not come to destroy, but to fulfil. For verily I say unto you, Till heaven and earth pass, one jot or one tittle shall in no wise pass from the law, till all be fulfilled" (Mat. 5:17-18). Rather, Paul refers to the objective in view, that is, that the function of the law is to lead to Christ, that through His fulfilling of the law by His life and passion one may become a partaker of justification.

The External and Internal Composition of the Holy Scriptures

The composition of the Holy Scriptures is both external and internal. To the *external* belong the orderliness, clarity, and suitability of the style of Scripture, most succinctly giving expression to each doctrine considered individually as well as conveying the internal harmony between the doctrines, and at the same time displaying the majesty of God by whose Spirit they have been recorded. A man of worldly wisdom seeks to use ornate vocabulary, but will rarely be able to adequately describe the wondrous fortitude, dignity, loftiness, and elegance of the style of Scripture. The language used in the most elegant speeches of orators is in comparison but the language of farmers and children. They are not learned enough, however, to perceive this.

The *internal* composition of Scripture relates to the orderly and precise meaning which corresponds with the thoughts and objectives of the Speaker, that is, God. The meaning of each word, affection, or argument is not two, three, or fourfold, but rather singular in nature. It is an accepted fact that the essential meaning of something can only be singular, as there is in essence only one truth. Thus, the Scriptures are clear and comprehensible, for the sincerity of the Speaker makes it a requisite that He express His meaning in a singular and simple fashion so that His hearer neither be confused nor misled by ambiguous words.

Such a meaning is referred to as the literal meaning which is expressed in either singular or compound form. The singular meaning of the sentence is expressed either precisely or metaphorically. The precise meaning of the sentence is expressed when one articulates his thoughts by using vocabulary which immediately expresses the substance of the matter at hand, such as, "God is just and man is sinful." The literal meaning is expressed metaphorically when one expresses himself with words from which the original and precise meaning is deduced, in order to express one's view that much more clearly, graciously, and forcefully. Such a manner of speech is frequently used which in the discipline of oratory is often illustrated by examples such as, "Herod is a fox," that is, he is cunning and crafty.

The compound meaning of the speaker is expressed when both type and antitype are placed side by side; the one part of the sentence contains the type and the other part the antitype. This is illustrated in the following text: "And as Moses lifted up the serpent in the wilderness, even so must the Son of man be lifted up" (John 3:14). Each element of the sentence when viewed individually has a well-defined meaning of its own; however, the true intent of the sentence is only expressed by joining both clauses together. The meaning of Scripture which the Holy Spirit wishes to convey is always singular in nature. One may and must rely upon this truth without any distrust. One and the same matter can be viewed from various perspectives, and therefore also be expressed in various forms. Every expression, however, fits precisely in the context in which it is found and in which it is to be comprehended. The views and expressions of Scripture are therefore internally related to each other. They fit together and are by no means different, much less contradictory in nature. Therefore, the Scriptures do not permit various interpretations of the same matter or text.

Scripture is not Subject to Various Interpretations

In order to facilitate the pope's placement upon the seat of judgment, Roman Catholicism maintains that one and the same text can have a fourfold meaning. First, there is the *literal* meaning which, incidentally, is the only meaning that we acknowledge. Secondly, there is the *allegorical* or figurative meaning, when matters of a temporal and physical nature symbolize those of a spiritual dimension, as in Galatians 4:24 where Hagar and Sarah are expressive of two covenants. Such is also the case when something from the realm of nature is used to instruct and motivate man to fulfil his obligation. This is illustrated in 1 Corinthians 9:9, where it is stated, "Doth God take care for oxen?" by which the congregation is exhorted to care for their ministers. Thirdly, there is an *analogical* or mystical meaning, such as when heaven is depicted by means of earthly objects. This is the case in Revelation 21:2 when "Jerusalem" refers to heaven. Fourthly, there is a *tropological* meaning which is established by an exchange of words, something which is resorted to when application is made to our daily walk or for the purpose of amending it.

If one were to maintain that in a particular text one meaning is evident, whereas in another text a different meaning must be advocated, we would readily submit to such a view. For then the literal intent of the Holy Spirit is taken into consideration, whether this is the case in a singular or a compound sense, primarily or metaphorically. However, the practice of assigning a fourfold meaning to every text, however, must be considered absurd. We can tolerate the occasional use of one text to make several applications, and we can cope with someone who acts foolishly in this regard and exceeds the limits of reason. To maintain, however, that in every text the Holy Spirit has four interpretations in view, is to make the Holy Scriptures ludicrous. Even though God is infinite and therefore capable of comprehending many matters of infinite dimension simultaneously, He nevertheless is not addressing Himself, but rather men who have but a puny and finite intellect. As He speaks, He is as desirous to be understood clearly as when man uses speech to express his thoughts to others. Man's ability to speak is not derived from the Bible; rather, the Bible is written in the language of man. It uses man's language in a more distinguishable, clear, and intelligible manner than the most brilliant lawyer is capable of, so that there is not the least reason for misunderstanding. Misunderstandings concerning Scripture are generated by the ignorance and obstinacy of man. Several questions need to be dealt with relative to this issue.

Question: Do the words in Holy Writ always convey every possible meaning which may be assigned to them?

Answer: Who could have ever imagined that anyone would arise who would answer this question in the affirmative? Yet today there are many individuals who believe this to be true. We emphatically answer in the negative for the following reasons:

First, this is evident from the four reasons which we stated in a previous paragraph, rejecting the concept that the Word has multiple meanings. Apply that principle to this situation.

Secondly, if this were true, then no certainties could be found in the entire Scriptures, and various opinions would simultaneously have to be accepted as truth. In such a situation a passage would have various meanings, one person accepting one and someone else another meaning, all being of equal value. We would then have to tolerate every opinion, since each person would be able to justify the meaning he selected for the words in question. It should be obvious to everyone that such is the logical consequence of this view. Whether there are some individuals who apply this concept in this fashion is known only to those who interact with them. Thus it would be possible to make the truth and the lie compatible.

Thirdly, the most denigrating and ludicrous expositions imaginable would have to be accepted as truth, as several persons have demonstrated with numerous texts in Scripture. Such expositions cannot be rejected by those who hold to this proposition, even if they themselves perceive that a given position is ludicrous. This notion is therefore a dreadful desecration of the Word and an affront to God. It would suggest that He would speak in an ambiguous manner or express many different and contradictory meanings in one and the same text.

Fourthly, we are not permitted to deal with human writings, such as wills, contracts, and financial receipts, in this manner. What a disgrace it would be to proceed in such a fashion! Much less may one deal in such a way with the Word of the living God, since He gives expression to every doctrine as well as His intent in a most fitting, orderly, clear, and forceful manner. Even if God were hypothetically (if I may speak of God in such a fashion) to express and aim at all that is true in one paragraph, He is nevertheless not addressing Himself, but men. Thus, He is speaking in a human fashion, in a way which men are best able to understand.

Evasive Argument: This principle applies only if the meaning of the text neither contradicts the rule of faith, nor is contrary to the Holy Spirit's sacred objectives, nor conflicts with the context.

Answer: (1) If we were to carry the true ramifications of this principle to their logical conclusion, it would constitute a *contradictio in adjecto*, for the latter assertion would refute the first. The implication would be that no word in all of Scripture could mean what it truly should, since the meaning would always be dependent upon the manner in which this principle is applied.

(2) This principle is flawed as has been demonstrated by several individuals in reference to various texts, since by the use of this rule the meanings of words can be arbitrarily established, and thus the biblical parameters of faith be redefined. Everything is acceptable, one exposition as well as another. According to this principle they can and must also maintain that the Holy Spirit has all these various meanings of the Word in view, thus enabling one to create a context as it pleases him. These stipulations are essential to discern the correct meaning of each text, and are potent medicine for those who maintain that every word does not mean what it potentially can mean. The meaning of a word can only be such as is congruent with the requirements of the specific circumstances in which it occurs.

Objection #1: Many texts will permit a two or threefold interpretation. One can find this to be true by consulting various scholarly expositors, and by what one hears from the pulpits. This is even true for those who object to this principle, suggesting that any given word can be understood to mean one thing as well as another. From this it is evident that even those who oppose this principle agree that words are subject to various interpretations.

Answer: When expositors in writing or speaking make mention of a variety of meanings associated with a word, they are not admitting thereby that this text, or the word within this text, has various meanings. They are merely admitting that because of their darkened understanding they are not able to interpret this text absolutely and do not dare to say with certainty which meaning the Holy Spirit has in view. If emphasis is under consideration, one should compare the translation with the original text.

Objection #2: This principle yields much light as one seeks to understand the Word of God; it enables one to perceive the full force and emphasis of the text.

Answer: (1) This principle will make it very difficult to understand the Word. Only if one were to dispense with his love for the truth, could such a principle enable one to understand the Word quickly. Anything will then be acceptable and one cannot err, as the words mean what is most conveniently suitable at the moment.

(2) God's Word always speaks with emphasis, and all words are used in full effect, so that the meaning of a word or sentence is never diluted. Those who wish to introduce heresy, or who desire to maintain the viability of their heresies, will use the full force and emphasis of a word, as if that were capable of altering the true meaning of a given text. Scholars are conversant with such trickery, and the simple must be on guard when they hear words used in such a fashion.

Additional objection: Everyone understands that words are sometimes taken in a narrower and a wider sense, thereby including a wide variety of meanings. Some words or sentences are viewed from such a broad perspective so as to include at once all the consequences which naturally flow out of them. From this it is evident that one can utilize words either with full force and emphasis or with less than full emphasis.

Answer: The issue at hand relates to the various meanings of words which have one meaning in one text and another in a different text. If a word has one meaning in one text, it does not necessarily follow that it has the same meaning in other texts. The meaning is determined by that particular text. Some words have reference to a special and unique doctrine, whereas some words are general or common, and in their meaning embrace everything which is comprehended in that general word. Sometimes this comprehensive meaning finds full expression and sometimes the meaning must be deduced from that which immediately follows. This process will yield the literal meaning of those words, and neither determines the magnitude of the force or the emphasis of them.

Question: Must all doctrines relative to faith and practice be established on the basis of words expressly recorded in Scripture, and are they to be disqualified as being according to truth if such is not the case? Can the meaning of a text be determined by applying the logical principle of necessary consequence?

Answer: Anabaptists, in order to deny infant baptism, hold to the first principle. We hold to the second with this understanding — that we do not accept what people deduce with their darkened and corrupt intellects, but that which is contained in the text and becomes evident by virtue of necessary consequence. This is verified as follows:

First, man is rational and his speech is rational. In all his interactions his verbal expression generally implies consequences. Since God speaks to man in a human fashion, His verbal expressions also imply consequences. Sometimes these consequences are verbalized, and at other times the matter is merely mentioned —

containing the consequence by implication. Among the innumerable consequences which are expressed consider this one: Christ, the Head of all believers, has risen from the dead. This proposition implies that all who are members of Christ must of necessity be spiritually alive. The latter is implied in the first and is consequently deduced from the first, "...that like as Christ was raised up from the dead by the glory of the Father, even so we also should walk in newness of life" (Rom. 6:4). Consider the following as an example of an implied consequence: "I am...the God of Abraham, the God of Isaac, and the God of Jacob" (Exo. 3:6). This implies

(1) that they who had been deceased long before the time of Moses are yet alive;

(2) that there shall be a resurrection from the dead. This is confirmed in Matthew 22:31-32: "But as touching the resurrection of the dead, have ye not read...I am the God of Abraham...God is not a God of the dead, but of the living."

Secondly, the purpose of Scripture is to be profitable for doctrine, reproof, correction, refutation of error, and for comfort (Rom. 15:4; 2 Tim. 3:16). No one can make application toward himself or someone else except by way of inference, which causes one to reason as follows: "Since God has expressed such and such in His Word, I must refrain from doing this, and I must do the other; I am in error as far as this opinion is concerned; in this area I ought not to consider myself defeated, but I ought to be encouraged." Since our names are not recorded in the Bible, how would anyone be able to use the Bible in a profitable manner except by way of application? All application, however, is made by way of inference.

Objection #1: If such were the case, then our faith would rest upon a fallible foundation, for in drawing conclusions one can be in error as human intellect often errs in the process. Whatever one claims to extract from a text by way of logical deduction may be refuted by another.

Answer: (1) It cannot be logically concluded that the potential for error will necessarily lead to error. Our eye can fail to perceive something correctly, even though such is generally not the case. That which one person cannot perceive clearly due to nearsightedness or failing vision, the other is able to perceive clearly.

(2) Our faith is not founded upon rational deduction extracted from a certain text, but upon the text itself. Our ability to reason is merely a means whereby one may perceive that a certain doctrine finds expression in the text. Such a conclusion cannot be drawn from the realm of nature, but only on the basis of revealed truth which is the foundation for faith. Our reasoning cannot deduce

anything from the text which was not already inherent in it, but can extract and unveil what is contained in the text already. Thus, faith is not founded upon reason but upon the Word of God.

Objection #2: "No prophecy of the Scripture is of any private interpretation" (2 Pet. 1:20). Thus, we must conclude that everything relative to faith must be based on actual words of Scripture itself, which makes private interpretation inappropriate.

Answer: Private interpretation is not the comprehension and knowledge of a given text acquired by reasoning. If such were the case then Scripture would not be profitable for doctrine, etc. (2 Tim. 3:16). Then the exhortations to search the Scriptures (John 5:39) and to compare spiritual things with spiritual (1 Cor. 2:13) would be without purpose, and one neither could nor should heed them. It is evident that everyone in particular should and must exercise discriminatory judgment in dealing with Scripture. Private judgment, however, consists of the fabrication of a person's own views — views which originate in his own intellect. It is the bringing of Scripture into subjection to such views and declaring as final authority on the matter, "I determine that such and such shall be the interpretation." Private interpretation is to assign a meaning to a text which is foreign to Scripture, is not extracted from Scripture, and is the product and conclusion of a person's own intellect.

Objection #3: "Beware lest any man spoil you through philosophy and vain deceit; lest any man should beguile you with enticing words" (Col. 2:8, 4). To engage in deductive reasoning is the practice of philosophy. We must refrain from making deductions which generate conclusions without substance.

Answer: The apostle warned against the abuse, not the lawful use of all things. Philosophy is the art of reasoning. It is innate in man to acquire knowledge about a certain issue by virtue of the process of reasoning, an ability which he utilizes in all his mental and verbal activities. The ability to reason improves by way of exercise. The desire to acquire wisdom by way of reasoning is denominated as philosophy, which in itself should not be labeled as vain deceit. Paul does not label philosophy as vain deceit but indicates that in their argumentation deceptive individuals can formulate that which has a semblance of being reasonable, which, however, very easily could beguile, deceive, and mislead the simple. One should be on guard for such people and their activity, and listen to Scripture rather than reason. All this, however, has nothing in common with the proper use of reason in attempting to understand Scripture — to use it as a means to extract what is concealed in every text, which is but drawing conclusions on the basis of the Word.

Objection #4: "Casting down imaginations, and every high thing that exalteth itself against the knowledge of God, and bringing into captivity every thought to the obedience of Christ" (2 Cor. 10:5). One must cast down imaginations and bring all thoughts into captivity. Thus, all conclusions drawn from the Word by way of thoughtful deliberation should be rejected.

Answer: (1) If man must cease to deliberate and think, he would have to dehumanize himself. He would even have to reject that which has been expressly recorded in Scripture, as he would not be able to do this without deliberation and thought processes.

(2) This text explains itself, for it speaks of imaginations and high things which exalt themselves against the knowledge of God. Such must obviously be cast down and be "brought into captivity." That is not true, however, concerning deliberations and thought processes by means of which one acquires knowledge about God and His Word, whereby one searches to discover what is contained in the Word and in every text — also what is discovered to the conscience by way of deduction.

The Perspicuity of the Holy Scriptures

Question: Are the Scriptures perspicuous?

Answer: Roman Catholicism maintains that the Scriptures are so obscure that they cannot be comprehended except by the use of unwritten tradition and authoritative declarations of the church; and that every text can only be understood in a manner which is congruent with the interpretation of the Roman Catholic Church, since she determines such and such to be the meaning of a given text.

We reply, (1) that some matters are beyond human comprehension, as for instance, the manner of God's existence, He being one in essence yet three Persons. This is also true for His eternity, His infinity — being without limitation, His unconditional goodness, the union of the two natures of Christ, and similar mysteries. These truths are presented to us and everyone can see with one glance that they are recorded in the Word. Since, however, these matters cannot be fully comprehended, they are believed.

(2) All men are not capable of understanding the Scriptures from a spiritual perspective, which nevertheless have been expressed clearly. Similarly, the sun cannot be seen by a blind person even though the sun is an illuminating body. One who is nearly blind sees only a glimmer of light and therefore is not able to distinguish things clearly. Even among those who are able to see there are degrees of clarity in the exercise of vision. This is not due to a flaw in the sun, but is to be attributed to man himself. Such is

also the case with spiritual light. A natural man is capable of discerning words in a natural way, as well as the meaning and much of the internal harmony of Scripture; however, he is not able to understand its spiritual dimension, for such is foolishness to him. He is as ignorant in this matter as a blind heathen. God favors some with general enlightenment whereby they are able to perceive the glory and preciousness of divine truths. Those who may be recipients of grace are favored by the Lord with enlightened eyes of understanding while reading or listening. Also here there is a difference in degree; there are children, young men, and adults. The least of them perceive the purpose of Christ and as they attentively read the Word, they comprehend all that is necessary for them unto salvation. They discern the truth contained in the Word; they know and believe it precisely because it is found in the Word. Others make more progress and discern more doctrinal truths, perceiving their interrelatedness. Still others receive even more light but yet remain pupils; their light is not comparable to the knowledge of the saints in heaven.

(3) One must recognize that many texts of Scripture, when considered individually, may be clearly understood in reference to godliness and salvation even though one may not be cognizant of their interrelatedness. Many texts no sooner become subject for consideration when more diligent study becomes necessary. The interrelatedness of many texts to other texts also cannot be immediately discerned — not because the text itself is neither clear, orderly, nor suitable, but due to the lack of light in the person studying.

(4) The knowledge of the Holy Scriptures is imperfect even in the most advanced, and in many is very limited. Such are in need of instruction, not due to any lack of clarity in the Word but in order that they might acquire the ability to see the light. Such instruction should not be given by conveying the judgment of the church, with the traditional arguments relative to the issue at hand, or by a resting in these, but it should occur when the issues are presented and explained in various ways so the recipient of this instruction may see for himself what Scripture has to say and thus come to an understanding of the issue itself.

Therefore we answer the question whether the Scripture is perspicuous enough to be understood in the affirmative. A regenerated person with the smallest measure of grace is able to understand that which is necessary unto salvation when he reads Scripture attentively. Not only is Scripture perspicuous as far as orderliness and manner of expression is concerned, but it is also intelligible for a converted person, the eyes of his understanding being enlightened (Eph. 1:18). This is evident from the following:

First, from express declarations by God Himself, "The commandment of the LORD is pure, enlightening the eyes" (Psa. 19:8); "Thy word is a lamp unto my feet, and a light unto my path" (Psa. 119:105); "A light that shineth in a dark place" (2 Pet. 1:19).

Secondly, God has given His Word to enlighten, govern, and comfort those who are His, as becomes evident from, "...enlightening the eyes" (Psa. 19:8); "...for our learning...comfort of the Scriptures" (Rom. 15:4); "And that from a child thou hast known the Holy Scriptures, which are able to make thee wise unto salvation...and is profitable for instruction" (2 Tim. 3:15-16); "Wherewithal shall a young man cleanse his way? by taking heed thereto according to Thy Word" (Psa. 119:9).

This objective of Scripture could not be achieved unless the perspicuity of the Scriptures is such that they can be understood.

Thirdly, a writer is flawed if he does not write in an intelligible manner. The more plain and clear his presentation of matters is, enabling the reader to discern the very marrow of the issue at hand, the more learned he is. One can then conclude that he thoroughly understands his subject matter and that the clearer he writes the better the result will be. God, however, is the Father of lights, an unapproachable Light, and He has given the Scriptures to make His mysteries known to man. It is therefore most certain that the Holy Scriptures incomparably surpass all other writings as far as clarity and perspicuity are concerned, and therefore are most supremely suitable for the instruction of mankind.

Fourthly, those who possess worldly wisdom, even though they are blind concerning the subject matter, shall be compelled to confess that many passages of the Holy Scriptures, as far as style and manner of presentation are concerned, can be comprehended by men of limited understanding without instruction. This enables such individuals to understand the matters themselves. This is true, for example, in statements such as, "There is one God, and one Mediator between God and men" (1 Tim. 2:5); "Christ died for our sins" (1 Cor. 15:3); "But now is Christ risen from the dead" (1 Cor. 15:20); "Blessed are all they that put their trust in Him" (Psa. 2:12); "He that believeth on the Son hath everlasting life" (John 3:36); "There shall be a resurrection of the dead" (Acts 24:15). Is there obscurity in expressions such as these? Since he does not have spiritual eyes, however, the natural man is not able to understand these matters in a spiritual fashion. Converted persons, on the contrary, have enlightened eyes of understanding (Eph. 1:18). They have received the anointing of the Holy Spirit who teaches them all things (1 John 2:27). They are taught of God (Isa. 54:13). For these reasons the Scriptures are clear and intelligible for them.

Objection #1: "In which are some things hard to be understood, which they that are unlearned and unstable wrest, as they do also the other Scriptures, unto their own destruction" (2 Pet. 3:16). Something which is of such a nature and has such consequences cannot be deemed clear, and is obscure to our understanding.

Answer: (1) The apostle was referring to some rather than all matters in Paul's letters — letters he had penned with divine wisdom.

(2) He was referring to matters and not to style and manner of presentation. These matters were lofty and deep mysteries, but were nevertheless presented in a most clear and exact manner.

(3) He was not speaking of men unlearned in the things of nature, but rather to unlearned and unstable men — men who are in the state of nature and are void of the Spirit — who are neither taught of God nor have spiritually enlightened eyes. He had unstable men in mind who do come to church and are somewhat acquainted with divine truths but who are without a spiritual foundation and are being tossed to and fro with every wind of doctrine. Such persons wrest not only the lofty doctrines expressed by Paul — which they cannot understand — but also wrest other Scriptures to their own destruction. "But these speak evil of those things which they know not: but what they know naturally, as brute beasts, in those things they corrupt themselves" (Jude 10).

Thus the text does not suggest that Scripture is obscure in the doctrines which must be known unto salvation; especially for those who are regenerated, which was the point of contention.

Objection #2: "And Philip ran thither to him, and heard him read the prophet Esaias, and said, Understandest thou what thou readest? And he said, How can I, except some man should guide me?" (Acts 8:30-31). Since Scripture cannot be understood without further instruction, it lacks the clarity necessary for it to be understood.

Answer: (1) Far be it from us to exclude the necessity of instruction. Those who are still unconverted are in need of instruction, as they are without knowledge concerning spiritual matters, however clearly they may be presented. Our reference here is not to what the Scriptures are for the unconverted. A blind person cannot read and therefore cannot become conversant with the contents of a book by means of reading. For everyone who has begun to receive spiritual eyesight and also for those who have made further progress — each one at his own level as no one comes to perfection in this life — instruction is a means whereby one may progressively advance. The necessity of instruction, however, does not imply obscurity in Scripture, but rather takes into account the loftiness of its doctrines and the incompetence of the person who is reading it.

(2) The purpose of instruction is not to make Scripture more clear but to make a person more capable of discerning the mysteries contained in Scripture.

Objection #3: "For now we see through a glass darkly" (1 Cor. 13:12).

Answer: This text does not refer to Holy Scripture, but to the believer, declaring that the knowledge he may possess in this world is but a glimmer compared to the knowledge which he shall have in heaven. This text therefore is not relevant to the issue at hand, namely, whether the godly can understand the Holy Scriptures to their comfort, direction, faith, and salvation, or whether the Scriptures are so obscure that the godly can barely understand anything.

Objection #4: The Word of God cannot be understood apart from the illumination of the Spirit of God. Thus we conclude that it is too obscure to be understood, as is evident in the following texts: "He opened to us the Scriptures" (Luke 24:32); "Open Thou mine eyes, that I may behold wondrous things out of Thy law" (Psa. 119:18).

Answer: (1) We readily admit that man needs to be enlightened by God's Spirit before he can understand Scripture in its spiritual sense. Apart from this illumination he cannot comprehend spiritual matters, as they are foolishness to him.

(2) The texts themselves indicate that the problem is not with the perspicuity of Scripture, but with man's intellect, which must be wrought upon by the Holy Spirit before he can understand the spiritual matters presented in Scripture.

The Pope Not the Infallible Judge of Scripture

Question: Is there a superior and infallible judge upon earth who can rule in disputes concerning the Holy Scriptures, to whom every one, upon God's command, should submit? And if there is such a judge, would this be the church, an ecclesiastical assembly, or the pope of Rome?

Answer: Roman Catholicism claims that God has appointed such a judge, this judge being the pope of Rome. Even if they occasionally make references to churches or ecclesiastical assemblies, they nevertheless surrender to the pope in the end. They have appointed him to be the head of the church and have elevated him above ecclesiastical assemblies, for the majority views him to be infallible when he makes a declaration from his papal chair.

We reply, (1) that many doctrinal heresies have originated from man's corrupt intellect, the one being of more and the other being of less significance. "For there must be also heresies among you, that they which are approved may be made manifest among you" (1 Cor. 11:19).

(2) Every individual church member, whether he be a government official or an ordinary citizen, as a member has the necessary discernment to understand Scripture.

(3) According to the rule of God's Word, the elders as representatives of the church and as servants of Christ, may render their judgment as office-bearers in an effort to settle disputes which concern external matters, and thus preserve peace and the unity of faith. According to Romans 16:17, they are also authorized to remove from the midst of the congregation those members who are unwilling to abdicate their heresies. It is not within the jurisdiction of the church, however, to judge concerning any member's conscience, neither can a person's faith be founded upon the judgment of the church. This is the jurisdiction of the Holy Spirit only. This Spirit speaks in and by means of the Word; and upon the Word alone may faith be founded.

(4) Thus, we deny that there is an infallible judge upon earth who rules in disputes and to whose judgment everyone must surrender. We deny even more emphatically that either the Roman Catholic Church, its ecclesiastical assembly, or the pope can be judge. We do so for the following reasons:

First, there is not one jot or tittle in the Bible which makes reference to such a prominent, superior, and infallible judge who is to judge in disputes and ascertain the meaning of the Holy Scriptures. Much less is there any reference that such authority is vested with assemblies of the Roman Catholic Church or with the pope. Let one proof text be produced! Paul in his letter to the Romans would certainly have made some mention of such a privilege — of such a weighty matter in which the very truth of Scripture is at stake. The apostle Peter also would have done or said something to indicate such a privilege and would have given some injunction that the pope of Rome should succeed him and have infallible authority to judge in disputes. He does not mention a word relative to this matter; in fact, Scripture tells us that Peter was rebuked by Paul (Gal. 2:11). At the first ecclesiastical assembly held in Jerusalem (Acts 15:13), Peter was not even the chairman, but the assembly acted according to the judgment of James. Thus, all the activity of the pope is nothing but a usurpation of authority. He presumptuously claims authority for himself which he has neither received nor can validate.

Secondly, the pope is not infallible in doctrine or in practice. Some have been exceptionally ungodly, having been fornicators, occultists, heretics, and atheists; this has been confirmed by papal chroniclers. How can such individuals function as infallible judges in disputes that relate to doctrinal issues? The secrets of the Lord are with those that fear Him (Psa. 25:14). Yes, also in our day the pope legislates in direct contradiction to Scripture. He forbids the use of foods which God has created and which are to be received with thanksgiving, and he also forbids marriage, both of which are contrary to 1 Tim. 4:3. He condones incestuous marriages which God has forbidden. He commands that a piece of bread be worshipped as God. He has instituted the religious worship of angels, deceased saints, and images — all of this being directly contrary to Scripture. Can such a man be an infallible judge? How abominable!

Thirdly, Roman Catholicism itself does not acknowledge the pope to be an infallible judge. To illustrate this we shall present a few small extracts from the *public proclamation made at the Court of Parliament, the great Chamber of Tournelle, gathered by papal edict on January 23, 1688, in France. This proclamation was printed in The Hague in the German language by Barend Beek.*

"We wish to make known in this commonwealth the new sentiments concerning the infallibility of the pope, which, in fact, is precipitated by his stubbornness. Who could have imagined that the pope, who is held before us as an example of holiness and virtue, would be so attached to his sentiments and so jealously guard the illusion of vain authority? The injunctions of the pope, as unjust as they were, only served the purpose of investigating their unjust claims. The pope jealously strives for the excelling of his papal office in ostentatious novelties. Furthermore, the addition of vain threatenings of excommunication to this edict has not succeeded in causing even the most fearful souls and those who have a most principled conscience to be the least frightened. The pope's use of spiritual weapons in an entirely secular matter is an intolerable abuse, thus causing such a scandalous novelty to have the illusion of righteousness. When Pope Gregory IV threatened French bishops with excommunication, they replied boldly that they would not be obedient to the will of the pope. Furthermore, if he would have come with the intention to excommunicate them, he in turn would have been exiled. 'Si excommunicaturus veniret, excommunicatus abiret.' Can anything more unreasonable and unjust be imagined — if not to say more abominable — than the issuance of this proclamation? Even the entire world is convinced that, rather than the zeal of God's house, envy and spite engendered the publication of this proclamation. In these circumstances there is nothing to fear from this clap of thunder from the Vatican. How expedient it would be if all the ecclesiastical matters in this commonwealth could be dealt with without one being under obligation to turn to Rome, and that the pope would be entirely subordinate to the ecclesiastical assemblies, who are authorized to correct him and modify his proclamations. Does such conduct emulate the care and meekness of the apostles in their governing of the church? What a strange matter it is that the pope, after having sat in the chair of St. Peter, has not ceased to negotiate with the disciples of Jansenius, whose doctrine was condemned by his predecessors. He has showered them with favors, has praised them, etc."

Such is the esteem Roman Catholics have for their pope. Far be it therefore from us to acknowledge him as infallible!

Fourthly, the objective is to have a tangible, infallible judge for the settlement of all disputes. This objective, however, is certainly not accomplished by the pope who elevates himself as an infallible judge. All Protestants refuse to acknowledge him as such. Whenever he pronounces his "anathema" upon them, they in turn pronounce it upon him. How can he, being one of the parties in the dispute, be the judge? And have the disputes between the squabbling factions of Dominicans and Jesuits, Jesuits and Jansenists, and Quietists and Operatists ever been settled? These sects are still alive and well within the pope's domain. From all this it becomes apparent that the pope is not, nor is he qualified to be, an infallible judge in disputes.

Fifthly, the Word of God teaches us that in reference to religion, doctrine, and practice one should not look to man, but only to the Word as the infallible rule, acknowledging it to function as judge in disputes and recognizing that Scripture is its own expositor. This logically follows since it is the Word of the only sovereign Judge of heaven and earth who is the most excellent Wisdom and lives to all eternity. No sovereign while still living on earth would tolerate his subjects to presume — whether subject to him in pretense or in truth — to be infallible interpreters of his commands, imposing their interpretations upon his subjects and requiring compliance with them. Much less shall the living God tolerate such presumption. He speaks with utmost clarity and does not refuse the illumination of His Holy Spirit to those who ask Him for it. He who refuses to be subject to God shall much less be subject to the declaration of a man who exalts himself against the Word of God, while he who wishes to subject himself to God only shall reject the heretical declarations of the pope with loathing.

Sixthly, it is God's will that everyone's doctrine and practice should be in accordance with His Word. This is evident from the following texts:

"To the law and to the testimony" (Isa. 8:20); "Search the Scriptures" (John 5:39); "Ye do err, not knowing the Scriptures"

(Mat. 22:29); "They have Moses and the prophets; let them hear them" (Luke 16:29). For this reason the Lord Jesus, although very God, confirmed His doctrine from the Scriptures, which may generally be observed in the gospels. Such was also the practice of the apostles as is evidenced by their sermons recorded in the Acts of the Apostles and by their letters. Indeed, Peter does not recommend himself as being infallible but recommends the word of prophecy in 2 Peter 1:19. Luke commended the Bereans who made the Word their standard of reference as they investigated whether the things spoken by Paul were truly so (Acts 17:11). Not one word in the Bible refers to an infallible earthly judge but Scripture itself is established as judge. To its declarations we are to give heed as being the oracles of God. Thus we conclude emphatically that neither the true church, much less the Roman Catholic Church, nor her ecclesiastical assemblies, nor the pope who is the focal point of her entire establishment, are to be the judge in disputes of doctrine or practice.

Seventhly, add to these reasons texts which emphatically establish the Word of God itself to be judge, "...the word that I have spoken, the same shall judge him in the last day" (John 12:48); "There is one that accuseth you, even Moses" (John 5:45); "All scripture...is profitable for doctrine, for reproof" (2 Tim. 3:16); "The Word of God...is a discerner of the thoughts and intents of the heart" (Heb. 4:12).

Thus the Word itself is arbiter in the disputes which arise concerning the Word of God, for it is the sovereign, living God who speaks in it, has spoken in it, and speaks by means of it until this very moment. Thus, the Word must be viewed as if God were continually narrating it to us with an audible voice from heaven.

Objection #1: Moses, the high priest, the prophets, and all the priests functioned as judges in doctrinal disputes in the Old Testament. Therefore the pope, cardinals, bishops, and ecclesiastical assemblies function similarly in the New Testament. "For the priest's lips should keep knowledge, and they should seek the law at his mouth: for he is the messenger of the LORD of hosts" (Mal. 2:7).

Answer: (1) Moses and the prophets received extraordinary revelations from God for the purpose of making these known and recording them. There was, however, no continuation of this practice in respect to common teachers, neither in the Old nor in the New Testament.

(2) None of them, much less the common teachers, had the authority to issue a superior judgment about that which had been recorded. They had ministerial and official discernment, however,

enabling them to apply the truth of the Word to individual persons and issues. In this discernment they were not infallible, as is also the case today.

Objection #2: There must of necessity be an earthly, infallible judge to arbitrate disputes, for otherwise the truth could not continue to exist in the church; neither could the church continue to exist according to the truth, and no disputes would ever be resolved.

Answer: (1) The truth will always remain in the Word, and the Word within the church.

(2) The church is preserved by means of the truth, just as the truth within the church is preserved by virtue of the ministerial discernment which the elders exercise on the basis of the Word of God. They are called to use the truth to combat heresies as well as deal with persons who are in error, instructing them thereby, and if they persist in their error, to exclude them from the fellowship of the church. In order to accomplish this there is no need for a superior and infallible judgment.

(3) There will never be an absence of disputes; neither will heresies disappear. They would not be eliminated even if there were an infallible judge upon earth. Such disputes continue to surface even in the papal domain, albeit the pope and the ecclesiastical assemblies are presumed to be infallible judges.

Objection #3: The Word is not capable of hearing the grievances of the opposing parties and therefore cannot function as arbiter in disputes. Consequently, there must of necessity be another judge.

Answer: Such can be true for human writings and of an individual who expresses himself inadequately, ambiguously, or obscurely. Such, however, is not true for the perfect law of the sovereign, omniscient, all wise and everlasting God who joins His Spirit to His Word, declaring all truths plainly, clearly, and accurately, and thereby rejecting all errors which present themselves in opposition to it. The Holy Spirit has foreseen whatever errors might arise. He who neither has eyes nor ears will be incapable of hearing the pronouncement of either a visible and audible judge, or of God in His Word. Even if the spirit of error concerns the spiritual realm, God nevertheless remains Judge, maintaining the truth by means of His Word and countering all error.

Objection #4: The dispute concerns the Word itself, referring to its meaning; therefore Scripture itself cannot make a pronouncement in this area but requires the services of an infallible judge.

Answer: If a dispute arises in reference to the laws of an earthly sovereign must there then be someone other than the sovereign who authoritatively declares what is the meaning of such a law?

May a subject do this or should this be the responsibility of the sovereign if he is still alive at that moment? Everyone can understand that this is the responsibility of none other than the sovereign alone. However, God lives, and He speaks clearly and perspicuously in His Word, doing so by means of various ways, methods, and texts, so that if a man is not able to understand the Word in one text, he may do so in another. For this purpose he must compare Scripture with Scripture which will lead him to the conclusion that God is the expositor of His own Word. Thus, Holy Scripture, or the Holy Spirit speaking by means of the Word, is the judge who renders a decision in the disputes which arise among men. To appoint another infallible judge is to elevate someone above God and His Word, which God will not tolerate.

Objection #5: One must hear the church, and whoever refuses to do so must be excommunicated (Mat. 18:17). Thus the church is capable of rendering infallible judgment in reference to disputes.

Answer: Such a conclusion does not necessarily follow from this. The elders[2] render a ministerial and applicatory judgment over particular circumstances, and only in harmony with the Word. In this context there is the obligation to hear them and whoever refuses to subject himself to the Word which the elders hold forth must be excommunicated.

The Function of Reason in the Exposition of Holy Writ

Question: Is not reason the expositor of Holy Writ?

Answer: The *Socinians*, and whoever concurs with them, maintain that the entire Word of God as well as every individual text must be examined in the light of reason, and that one should accept nothing as truth which is not congruent with reason. Whenever Scripture appears to contradict reason, then it must be understood as reason determines. In the event that Scripture does contradict reason, then, in opposition to Scripture, reason must be adhered to as an infallible principle.

We agree that intellect and reason are absolutely necessary to understand Scripture, and thereby to exercise faith. They are only the means, however, whereby we may know what God says in His Word, and this Word works faith and is the foundation of faith. Thus, intellect and reason may not be considered as a basis for, as a rule to go by, or as a touchstone, in determining whether that which God reveals in His Word is truth. We believe this solely

---

[2] à Brakel uses the word "opzieners" here. As used in 1 Timothy 3:1, this title relates to the office of elder — both teaching and ruling.

because God declares it to be so. Reason must surrender itself to the Word; the Word must never surrender itself to reason. Reason is to Scripture what Hagar was to Sarah; it is the servant and not the master. This is evident

First, from a consideration of the condition of man's intellect. It has not merely been affected by sin relative to natural matters — having a limited capability to perceive matters and much less to comprehend them — but particularly relative to spiritual matters, being completely blind in that respect. "Having the understanding darkened" (Eph. 4:18); "For ye were sometimes darkness" (Eph. 5:8); "But the natural man receiveth not the things of the Spirit of God: for they are foolishness unto him: neither can he know them, because they are spiritually discerned" (1 Cor. 2:14).

Such is the nature of man that Scripture cannot deal with such a conceited and clumsy creature any differently from the way the organ grinder treats his donkey. He slanders that of which he is ignorant and he corrupts himself with that which he has in common with the dumb animal (Jude 10). Who would venture to elevate man's darkened intellect to exercise judgment regarding the lofty mysteries which it has pleased the only wise God to reveal? Each source of light has a limited environment in which it shines. This is true for a candle, a torch, as well as for the sun. This also applies to man's ability to see. One with excellent vision can distinguish matters in the distance which a nearsighted person cannot distinguish at all. This is also the case with man's knowledge. Should someone with an undeveloped intellect judge concerning the mysteries and particulars of physics, metaphysics, geometry, and astronomy? Thus it is with man's intellect and reason. They have too many limitations, and therefore are not capable of penetrating the lofty mysteries of the divine Word. Consequently, they cannot sit in judgment over God's Word.

Secondly, the mysteries which have been revealed are far beyond the reach of our intellect; hence reasoning cannot even approach to within a thousand miles of their meaning. How then can it be the judge regarding them and be the bench mark by which these mysteries should be evaluated? "Canst thou by searching find out God? canst thou find out the Almighty unto perfection?" (Job 11:7); "Such knowledge is too wonderful for me; it is high, I cannot attain to it" (Psa. 139:6); "Lo, these are parts of His ways: but how little a portion is heard of Him? but the thunder of His power who can understand?" (Job 26:14). Whoever is to judge what the meaning of Scripture is, and determine what is to be accepted as truth and what should or should not be believed, must be able to understand all truth in absolute perfection. Man's intellect and his reason, however, are not capable of penetrating the lofty mysteries of God and thus are not qualified to render judgment in such matters. If we must reject all that our reason cannot comprehend, then we must reject the eternity of God and all His perfections such as His omnipresence, infinity, etc. We would also have to reject the Holy Trinity, so clearly revealed in God's Word, as well as the union of the two natures of Christ and the creation of the world itself. Reason cannot fathom how God created everything out of nothing; however, this is understood by faith. Indeed, would we not have to reject nearly everything?

Thirdly, that which can clearly be discerned and comprehended by way of reasoning for one person will appear to be contradictory to the reasoning of another, and a person will subsequently reject as false what he once considered to be true. Thus in many matters man cannot be certain. Whoever lies repeatedly no longer has any credibility. Our reason deceives us so frequently, however, that it cannot possibly function as either judge, bench mark, or expositor of Holy Writ.

Fourthly, faith and reason are totally different avenues by which one may determine the validity of something. If something is validated by reason, faith is necessarily excluded. If something is accepted as truth by faith, reason is necessarily excluded. Reason can only acknowledge that which has been stated by someone else, and then only if such a statement does not belong to the realm of the impossible. The truth of the matter, however, is validated by faith only. The divine mysteries of the Word of God must be accepted as certainty only by faith, by virtue of the fact that God has said it — He who is true and cannot lie (Acts 26:27; Heb. 11:1, 6; John 16:27). In this respect reason is useful only to determine whether a particular matter is to be found in the Word of God. If such has been determined, then there can be no suspicion or distrust as to whether it is true, for this would render God suspect — as if He were capable of lying. Faith accepts the infallibility of the issue at hand and if it is beyond reason's ability to determine the validity of a certain matter, this does not mean that this matter is contrary to reason. In such a case reason must be silent and admit that this matter is beyond its reach and that faith alone acknowledges it as truth.

Fifthly, God's Spirit reveals the mysteries of the Word to the heart, testifies that the Word is truth, and gives faith to embrace it. Thus reason is excluded from functioning as judge and arbiter in determining whether a matter revealed in Scripture should be believed or not. This is confirmed in the following passages: "Flesh and blood has not revealed it unto thee (that is, reason has not taught you this), but My Father which is in heaven" (Mat. 16:17); "Then opened He their understanding, that they might understand the Scriptures" (Luke 24:45); "For God, who commanded the light to shine out of darkness, hath shined in our hearts, to give the light of the knowledge of the glory of God in the face of Jesus Christ" (2 Cor. 4:6); "Open Thou mine eyes, that I may behold wondrous things out of Thy law" (Psa. 119:18); "And it is the Spirit that beareth witness, because the Spirit is truth" (1 John 5:6). Scripture testifies that reason must be brought into captivity (2 Cor. 10:5).

Sixthly, if reason were the judge over Scripture and were to determine which portion of the Word of God should or should not be believed,

(1) God would be subject to the judgment of man, thereby summoning God before man's judgment seat to give an account of what He has said;

(2) all religion would function in the realm of the natural rather than the spiritual and would be void of faith;

(3) the greatest philosophers and the most intelligent men would be the most enlightened divines, which is directly contrary to the word of Christ, "I thank Thee, O Father, Lord of heaven and earth, because Thou hast hid these things from the wise and prudent, and hast revealed them unto babes" (Mat. 11:25). Such absurdities necessarily follow from these propositions. They are as absurd as that which now follows.

Objection #1: Religion is a reasonable service according to Romans 12:1. Thus reason must judge in all matters of religion in order to determine how each text of Holy Writ is to be interpreted.

Answer: In the Old Testament dumb animals were sacrificed as types which, when considered apart from the antitype, could not be pleasing to God. However, God being a Spirit demands that He be served in spirit and in truth, with intellect as well as with reason. Here reason is a means in determining what God has revealed. Irrespective of whether the matter which God has revealed can be fully understood and comprehended or if it can be comprehended to such a degree as is necessary unto salvation, even though the matter itself transcends our comprehension — it is sufficient for man as far as believing is concerned. It may not be concluded, however, that reason is to function as judge over every doctrine and text. Reason is the servant and not the master.

Objection #2: Many doctrines can be deduced from the realm of nature, as the Lord Jesus generally taught in the parables. Hence, in matters of nature reason is the judge and therefore also the judge in reference to the doctrines contained in Scripture.

Answer: It is incorrect to state that any of the doctrines relative to faith can be deduced from nature. That which belongs to the realm of nature is used only to further explain the doctrines of faith and to impress them more deeply upon the heart. Furthermore, God has a most perfect knowledge of natural matters.

Objection #3: Many doctrines are not expressly defined in Scripture, but are formulated by way of logical deduction. Reason alone determines whether such deductions are correct or not. Thus, reason judges as to what one should or should not believe.

Answer: Those doctrines, which by way of sound argumentation may be deduced from a text, are contained in the text itself and one accepts them as true simply because God states them to be so. Consequently, the matter which may be deduced from this text is true, and therefore reason cannot be involved. Reason is the vehicle, however, by which one comes to the conclusion that a particular doctrine is contained in a given text, and by necessary consequence may be deduced from the text. Reason judges whether the proper conclusion has been made, but not whether the doctrine which has been deduced from the text is true.

Objection #4: Scripture defines certain doctrines which reason determines to be contrary to proper judgment, knowing that such cannot be the case. Thus, reason should judge what is congruent with or contrary to the truth, and consequently should determine what one ought to believe.

Answer: It is not true that Scripture proposes something which reason judges to be contrary to fact. Whatever God reveals in Scripture concerning the realm of nature is true and by virtue of His testimony is infallible.

Scripture does not Support the Erroneous Views of Men

Question: Does God's testimony in Holy Scripture concur with the erroneous opinions of men?

Answer: There are those who answer in the affirmative, but we emphatically deny this. It is πρῶτον ψεῦδος, that is, the original lie, to maintain that the earth revolves and the sun is stationary.

It should not be too surprising that heathen who are ignorant of God and His Word, or atheists who reject both, would speak in such a fashion. That those who know God and acknowledge the Holy Scriptures to be of divine origin speak in such a fashion, however, cannot but be heard with great consternation by anyone who loves God. Is not God the God of truth and therefore truthful? Is He a man that He should lie? Is not He the God who cannot lie, and shall a holy and truthful God lie? If God were to say something contrary to truth and against better knowledge, thereby verbally making Himself like unto men who are of erroneous judgment — would this not constitute lying and would He not, by speaking in like fashion, encourage men to adhere to their error? Is not the Holy Spirit the Spirit of truth and does not He lead into all truth? All Scripture is inspired by God. Holy men of God have spoken, being moved by the Holy Ghost. The Word of God is true and far be it from the Almighty that He should pervert judgment (Job 34:10, 12).

I ask you, "Where in the Holy Scriptures does God adjust His testimony to the erroneous opinion of men? Where can even the semblance of such a thing be found?"

Objection #1: The Holy Scriptures state in many places that the earth stands still, is stationary, and that the sun circles it, as it appears to be this way to men, and they have that erroneous notion. Nevertheless it is undoubtedly true that either the world circles a stationary sun or that the one as well as the other revolves and circles in an established circuit.

Answer: Who would concern themselves about the fact that philosophers and astronomers discuss this matter? To bring God's Word into this discussion, however, thereby generating the suspicion that God and His Word are guilty of erroneous statements, is something which cannot be tolerated. It is certain that God in His Word uses various and illustrious figures of speech. It is also true that God in His goodness condescends to the frail and limited comprehension of men, directing them by way of visible and natural things to the spiritual. To maintain, however, that God in His Word is guilty of untruth is a statement that can only be heard with great consternation. Would he who loves God not vehemently protest against such a statement?

The truth is that God states in many places in His Word states that the sun is in motion, her circuit resulting in both day and night, and that the world remains both motionless and stationary. Nowhere does God speak to the contrary, as we will demonstrate in chapter 8. Since God states it to be so, it is truth and we are to embrace it as truth. Is not God the Creator, maintainer, and governor of all things, who is much better acquainted with His own work than is man with his limited and darkened understanding? Should men not subject their judgment to the very sayings of God? Or should one attempt to bend and twist the clear declarations of God in such a way that they agree with our erroneous thinking? Whatever God declares, also concerning things in the realm of nature, is true. God says that the world is motionless and stationary, being circled by the sun, and thus it is a certain and incontrovertible truth.[3]

Objection #2: "And God made two great lights; the greater light to rule the day, and the lesser light to rule the night" (Gen. 1:16). Here sun and moon are denominated as two great lights, even though some stars are much larger than the sun or moon. Thus, God speaks in harmony with the erroneous opinion of men who judge sun and moon to be the greatest lights due to their external appearance.

Answer: (1) God does not make a comparison here, but merely refers to sun and moon as viewed individually, stating that the sun is a greater light than the moon. God does not call them the *greatest*, but *great* lights. Where is error or an erroneous statement to be found here?

(2) God does not make mention of celestial bodies, nor does He state that the sun and moon are larger in size as bodies than some stars, thus being the largest bodies. Note, however, that God makes reference to lights. Are not sun and moon greater lights, if not the greatest lights, even though the text does not state this? Which stars generate more light? There are none, are there? To speak of lights as bodies is to speak erroneously and to be guilty of error, and by virtue of this error to be guilty of the dreadful practice of attributing error to God Himself. If one engages in such activity, then which truth cannot be distorted?

Objection #3: "Sun, stand thou still upon Gibeon; and thou, moon, in the valley of Ajalon" (Josh. 10:12). The fact is that the sun was neither in Gibeon, nor the moon in the valley of Ajalon; rather, it merely appeared to be so. Thus, a statement is made which is congruent with erroneous opinion. This is also true for that which follows, that is, that the sun and moon stood still.

Answer: Were people at that time so naive to be of the opinion that the sun and moon were actually upon earth? Far be it from us to suggest such a thing! Therefore this is neither an example of an erroneous opinion nor of an erroneous statement. It merely indicates that to their perception the sun then appeared to be near Gibeon and the moon to be near Ajalon, and that they remained in those apparent locations. A miracle occurred here. This miracle did not occur in reference to the earth as if her circuit were interrupted, but it occurred in reference to the sun and the moon whose circuits were interrupted. All this clearly proves that sun

---

[3] It should be evident that this unequivocal conclusion of à Brakel must be viewed in its historical context.

and moon revolve around the earth.[4] There is neither the least indication of error, nor do we have a falsehood here.

Objection #4: "...about midnight the shipmen deemed that they drew near to some country" (Acts 27:27). [The Statenvertaling reads as follows: "...omtrent het midden des nachts vermoedden de scheepslieden, dat hun enig land naderde," that is, "...about midnight the shipmen deemed that *some country drew near to them.*"] This is an erroneous sentiment, for the country did not draw near to them; instead, the ship drew near to the country.

Answer: These men, had they been of the opinion that the ship was stationary and that the land drew near to them, would indeed have been ignorant mariners. They were, however, not that demented. This is but a common expression whereby it is indicated that the land is drawing near. Such an expression is still in daily use and is neither an erroneous sentiment nor a falsehood. It thus remains incontrovertible that God in His Word does not adjust His testimony to the erroneous sentiments of men.

Thus far we have discussed the origin, substance, and structure of the Holy Scriptures, upon which follows the fourth subject, namely, the purpose of Scripture. The purpose of Scripture is to provide man with a steadfast and unchangeable rule for doctrine and practice in order to lead him in the way of salvation. "But these are written, that ye might believe that Jesus is the Christ, the Son of God; and that believing ye might have life through His Name" (John 20:31); "For whatsoever things were written aforetime were written for our learning, that we through patience and comfort of the Scriptures might have hope" (Rom. 15:4); "Wherewithal shall a young man cleanse his way? by taking heed thereto according to Thy Word" (Psa. 119:9).

The highest and ultimate objective of all things, as well as of all that is recorded in the Word of God, is the glorification of God. Such is also true of the Word of God itself which contains the revelation of God's wondrous goodness, unsearchable wisdom, unchangeable truth, and omnipotent power. It particularly refers to the manner in which all these effect the conversion, the consolation, the joy, the wondrous light, and the salvation, of which the elect by means of this Word become partakers. "Praise ye the LORD:...(for) He sheweth His Word unto Jacob, His statutes and His judgments unto Israel" (Psa. 147:1, 19); "Seven times a day do I praise Thee because of Thy righteous judgments" (Psa. 119:164).

---

[4] See previous footnote.

The Holy Scriptures: To be Read by Every Member of the Church

The church is the recipient of the Word of God. "He hath not dealt so with any nation [as with Israel]: and as for His judgments, they have not known them" (Psa. 147:20); "Chiefly, because that unto them were committed the oracles of God" (Rom. 3:2); "...to whom pertaineth...the covenants, and the giving of the law" (Rom. 9:4); "...which is the church of the living God, the pillar and ground of the truth" (1 Tim. 3:15).

Question: May and must God's Word be read by everyone?

Answer: Since the Word of God has been given to the church and thus to every member of the church, it follows that it must also be read by everyone. Roman Catholicism expends much energy to make Scripture obscure and to remove it out of the hands of the people. Their errors become clearly evident in this practice because they seek to make the people entirely dependent upon the pope, his cardinals, ecclesiastical assemblies, bishops, and priests. In fact, the Council of Trent expressly forbade the reading of the Bible. We, on the contrary, consider this to be a dreadful act of ecclesiastical robbery, whereby the way to heaven is closed. We maintain therefore that every man, learned or unlearned, may and must read the Word of God. This becomes evident from the following:

First, since the reading of Scripture is nowhere forbidden, who would muster the courage to forbid this practice? The church has never forbidden this. This horrible edict finds its origin in the Council of Trent which was not an orthodox but an anti-Christian ecclesiastical assembly.

Secondly, from the time of Moses until Christ and from the time of Christ until this present day the Bible has always been read by every member of the church. Yes, some were so diligent in this practice that they were able to quote entire apostolic letters from memory.

Thirdly, God has expressly commanded the common man to read His Word. "And these words, which I command thee this day, shall be in thine heart: and thou shalt teach them diligently unto thy children, and shalt talk of them when thou sittest in thine house, and when thou walkest by the way, and when thou liest down, and when thou risest up. And thou shalt bind them for a sign upon thine hand, and they shall be as frontlets between thine eyes. And thou shalt write them upon the posts of thy house, and on thy gates" (Deu. 6:6-9). Observe to what extent they had to familiarize themselves with Scripture. "Search the Scriptures" (John 5:39); "Let the word of Christ dwell in you richly in all wisdom" (Col. 3:16); "I charge you by the Lord that this epistle be read unto all the holy brethren" (1 Th. 5:27); "We have also a more sure word of prophecy; whereunto ye do well that ye take heed" (2 Pet. 1:19). It is dreadful indeed to forbid what God has commanded!

Fourthly, those who read the Word are commended in Scripture, and a blessing is also pronounced upon them. "Blessed is the man...(whose) delight is in the law of the LORD; and in His law doth he meditate day and night" (Psa. 1:1-2); "These were more noble than those in Thessalonica, in that they received the word with all readiness of mind, and searched the Scriptures daily, whether those things were so" (Acts 17:11); "Blessed is he that readeth, and they that hear the words of this prophecy" (Rev. 1:3).

Fifthly, the nature and purpose of Scripture are such that it must be read by everyone.

(1) It is the testament or will of God; a will may and must be read by the heirs.

(2) It contains letters addressed to everyone in the church, this being evident at the beginning of every letter; a letter may and must be read by everyone to whom it is addressed.

(3) The Word is the sword with which every believer must defend himself against spiritual enemies (Eph. 6:17). Would one then rob the spiritual warrior of his weapons?

(4) It is the means unto conversion, the seed of regeneration (1 Pet. 1:23), as well as the source of spiritual illumination (Psa. 19:8), instruction, comfort, and the means unto spiritual growth (Rom. 15:4, 1 Pet. 2:2).

(5) It is written for the very purpose that everyone would read it. "Write the vision, and make it plain upon tables, that he may run that readeth it" (Hab. 2:2). From all this it has been incontrovertibly demonstrated that every individual may and must read the Word of God.

Objection #1: "Give not that which is holy unto the dogs, neither cast ye your pearls before swine" (Mat. 7:6). Thus it must be concluded that the Holy Word of God may not be given to everyone to read.

Answer: In this manner we might conclude that one ought not to preach to the unconverted. The reference here is not to the reading of Scripture, but rather to the instruction, exhortation, and reproof of those who become even more wicked in response to this, and might harm the one who is speaking. Such, however, is not applicable to believers and others who are desirous to hear the Word of God.

Objection #2: Many errors have been generated by common men who have read the Holy Scriptures. This has been to their own disadvantage as they wrest the Scriptures to their own destruction, as well as to the disadvantage of others who have been misled by these errors. Thus, it would be more beneficial to withhold the Holy Scriptures from them.

Answer: By means of the individual reading of Scripture, the errors of popery as well as other errors will be discovered and exposed. However, the reading of Scripture does not generate such errors. Errors are generally propagated by misguided scholars. Even though some abuse Scripture with their corrupt intellect, this does not negate the use of Scripture itself. Without the Word of God one will most certainly err.

Objection #3: If everyone is permitted to read the Word of God, preaching is unnecessary. Since preaching is a necessary practice, however, there is no need to read Scripture.

Answer: Reading and hearing function very well together (Rev. 1:3, Acts 17:11). Both preaching and reading instruct, motivate, lead to repentance, and comfort every believer; hence, reading and hearing have identical results. It is the same Word received in a twofold manner. Though there is a distinction between reading and hearing, they are not contradictory in nature.

Objection #4: We do not forbid the reading of Scripture categorically, as we give many permission to read it, that is, those whom we trust will not create problems by doing so.

Answer: This is directly contrary to the Council of Trent. This statement is made in an effort to avoid embarrassment for those who live among Protestants. Neither pope nor priest have the authority to withhold from anyone the privilege of reading the Bible. The privilege to read Scripture is a divine gift for which we owe gratitude neither to pope nor priest. To withhold Scripture from anyone is an act of ecclesiastical robbery as well as spiritual murder.

The Translation of the Scriptures into Other Languages

Since Scripture has been given to the congregation, to every individual member and must be read by everyone, and since the church of the New Testament is to be found throughout the world among various nations and languages (Rev. 5:9), it becomes a necessity to translate the Holy Scriptures into every language. This will enable everyone both to read and hear the Word of God in his own language, as was the case when the apostles spoke in tongues (Acts 2:8). For this purpose the Bible has already been translated into a large variety of languages. Three hundred years prior to the birth of Christ the Old Testament was translated from Hebrew into Greek by seventy-two men who were very conversant with both languages. This occurred under the direction and with the financial support of Ptolomeus Philadelphus, king of Egypt. During the apostolic era the Old Testament was translated into Aramaic, by Jonathan Onkelos, and other unknown translators; afterward it was also translated into the Syrian language. Later, a number of individuals translated the entire Bible into Latin which, next to Greek, was the most common language at that time. Among those Latin translations there is also one which is endorsed by the papacy as being valid. Subsequently, the Bible has been translated into almost as many languages as there are nations in which the church may be found. All translations, however, have not been derived from the original Hebrew and Greek languages in which holy men moved by the Holy Ghost have written. Such translations are derived from other Greek or Latin translations. They merely qualify as transcripts. Such is the case with various Dutch translations which are now referred to as the "old" translations.

In compliance, however, with the decision of the National Synod held in 1618 and 1619 in Dordrecht, a number of carefully selected scholars, being commissioned by the most honorable gentlemen of the General Assembly,[5] faithfully translated the entire Bible into Dutch from the original Hebrew and Greek texts. In order to do this as accurately as possible, additional scholars were commissioned to thoroughly inspect and verify the translation work of the initially selected scholars. Consequently, this translation greatly excels all other Dutch translations, including both the older and the newer.[6] It is such an accurate and careful rendering of the original text that scholars, friends, and even enemies are all astonished. Those who wish to quarrel about this only convey how inadequate their knowledge of the original languages is, for if a word could have been translated differently, the translators have made note of this in the margin. Thanks be unto the Lord for this unspeakable gift!

As accurate as a translation may be, it nevertheless is neither authentic nor infallible. The meaning of a given word can be inaccurate and therefore when there are differences of opinion, a careful comparison of each translation to the original text is a necessity. A faithful translation will convey all that is contained in the original text; however, since it is a different language, there will

---

[5] à Brakel refers to the Dutch legislature as "De Hoogmogende Heeren Staten-Generaal der Verenigde Nederlanden." Since these gentlemen of the "Staten-Generaal" (comparable to a western legislative assembly such as the U.S. Congress) commissioned the translation of the Bible into the Dutch language, this translation became known by its still current and venerated name, the "Statenvertaling" or the "Statenbijbel."

[6] We may voice similar conclusions regarding our King James Version in the English language.

also be distinct linguistic differences as far as vocabulary is concerned. The original texts are directly inspired by God and originate with God — both as to doctrinal content as well as the words. In translations, however, only the doctrinal content is divinely inspired, not the words. An unlearned person, being incapable of comparing translations with the original languages, can nevertheless be assured of the veracity of the doctrinal content of the translation if he may perceive the internal doctrinal cohesiveness and harmony of a translation. There is also the witness of the Holy Spirit who in speaking through this Word bears witness to the veracity of God's Word in its translated form. In addition to the approbation of both scholars and the godly, the veracity of the translation is also confirmed by the powerful effect the Word has upon one's own heart, as well as the hearts of others. Yes, even the enemies of true religion who are conversant with both languages must attest to the veracity of this translation, agreeing that it is both faithful and accurate. If anyone understands one or another word differently, he may be convinced by comparing it with the original language.

Concerning the Greek translation of the Old Testament by seventy-two translators (that is, the Septuagint [LXX]), as well as the common Latin translation called the Vulgate, the following needs to be asked: Are these translations as authoritative as the original texts? Do they have the same credibility, so that the choice of vocabulary must likewise be deemed infallible, as the recorded text of the prophets, gospel writers, and apostles who were inspired by the Holy Spirit?

Answer: Roman Catholicism maintains that such is the case; however, we deny this as will be evident from the following:

First, these two translations are no more the result of the infallible inspiration of the Holy Spirit than are all other translations. They are the result of the work of fallible people in spite of all their efforts not to fail in this task. Therefore, neither these nor any other translations may be placed on equal footing with the original text as far as esteem and infallibility are concerned.

Secondly, it is very evident to all scholars — even Roman Catholic scholars rendering their judgment in this matter — that considerable errors are to be found in both translations. It is evident that the Septuagint was misguided in several places, as the translators used a Hebrew Bible without vowel markings, which God, however, caused to be written with vowel markings. Think for instance of a letter written in which vowels are absent. One might be able to discern the main issues, but could also easily come to erroneous conclusions. It can readily be discerned that the common Latin translation of the Old Testament was from the Greek rather than the Hebrew. Both translations contain serious errors. Since this fact was acknowledged by papal scholars, the pope had ordered that the common Latin translation be somewhat corrected. This explains why many in Roman Catholicism do not recognize any translation as being authentic.

Objection #1: Christ and His apostles always made use of the Septuagint when quoting texts from the Old Testament. Thus, they acknowledged the validity of this translation, thereby rendering it authentic.

Answer: Christ and the apostles were concerned with the meaning of a text rather than the words themselves. They did not always make use of this translation, but frequently used the Hebrew text itself. They made use of the Greek translation since it was better known among the people, the Greek language being in more common use than the Hebrew language. Therefore, the fact that texts were quoted from the translation of the LXX does not prove that it was on equal footing with the original text.

Objection #2. Since both the Hebrew church as well as the Greek church had an authentic Bible in their respective language, the Latin church should also have an authentic Bible in her language.

Answer: This conclusion has a dual flaw. The Hebrew church possessed the Word as immediately inspired by God in reference to both doctrine and vocabulary. They did not have the Scriptures of the New Testament. The Greek church did not possess the Old Testament in its authentic language; they used a translation instead. They did possess the New Testament in its authentic form, however, since it also had been immediately inspired by God. The Latin church, on the contrary, was in possession of only a translation — not an original manuscript, such as both the Hebrew and Greek texts are. If this conclusion is correct, then each nationality, according to the same rule, ought to be in possession of an authentic translation.

Objection #3: Since both translations (LXX and the Vulgate) are the oldest translations and have been used over a long period of time, they should at least be viewed as authentic.

Answer: An error is not transformed into truth by virtue of the progression of time. As old as the Latin translation may be, there are many translations which are even older.

The Necessity of Scripture
Question: Is Scripture a necessity?

Answer: The last particular concerning the Word of God which must be considered is its *necessity* and *profitability*. The Word of God is necessary and profitable not only for beginners and little ones but also for the most advanced and spiritual believers here upon earth. It is a brook from which a lamb may drink and an ocean in which an elephant can drown. He who is of the opinion that he has advanced beyond Scripture is a fool. He gives evidence that he is ignorant of the spirituality of the Word as well as ignorant of himself. God by His omnipotence could have gathered and preserved His church and caused her to grow without the written Word. It is, however, according to the wisdom and goodness of God to care for His church in a most appropriate and steadfast manner, making His will known to her by means of a written document. In our day this is enhanced by the art of printing. Everyone can have God's Word in his home and thus be enabled daily to obtain guidance and nourishment from it. God has bound man to His Word to keep him from straying outside of its perimeter. Thus, the Word of God is necessary as well as profitable. This is evident from the following:

First, it is the only means instituted by God to faith and conversion. Without the Word none shall believe. "How then shall they call on Him in whom they have not believed? So then faith cometh by hearing, and hearing by the Word of God" (Rom. 10:14,17). Apart from the Word no one can be regenerated. "Of His own will begat He us with the Word of truth" (James 1:18); "Being born again, not of corruptible seed, but incorruptible, by the Word of God, which liveth and abideth for ever" (1 Pet. 1:23).

Secondly, the Word of God is the food which nurtures the spiritual life of the converted: "As newborn babes, desire the sincere milk of the Word, that ye may grow thereby" (1 Pet. 2:2). Since many persons use the Word so infrequently, they are in darkness, unsteady, tossed to and fro by all winds of doctrine, live in sorrow, suffer from weak faith, and experience the hiding of God's countenance.

Thirdly, the Word of God is the only rule whereby the condition of our hearts, thoughts, words, and deeds should be governed. "And as many as walk according to this rule" (Gal. 6:16); "To the law and to the testimony" (Isa. 8:20); "Then shall I not be ashamed, when I have respect unto all Thy commandments" (Psa. 119:6). If people neglect to retain the Word of God in mind and heart, they will begin to elevate their own intellect as their Bible, and thus will mislead themselves and be a cause for concern to others. Such neglect will result in a sinful life as well as much backsliding. Yes, many who do not establish the Word of God as their rule of life "will seek to enter in, and shall not be able" (Luke 13:24).

Fourthly, the Word of God provides a steadfast comfort. "That we through patience and comfort of the Scriptures might have hope" (Rom. 15:4); "Unless Thy law had been my delights; for they are the rejoicing of my heart" (Psa. 119:92, 111). This comfort which originates from the Word may come while reading or hearing it or during prayer and meditation. It may originate from a text of Scripture or when the soul, while engaged in sweet exercise, is directed to a text. Such comfort is generally of a much deeper and more fundamental nature, and more steadfast and durable than the comfort which the soul receives without any reflection upon the Word. One should refrain, however, from insisting upon the application of a specific text of Scripture at a specific moment of time, for such expectation will readily rob him of a sweet, spiritual frame. It is therefore desirable to read or hear the Bible read frequently so that one may have ready access to a supply of Scripture in time of need. Furthermore, while meditating, texts of Scripture may be impressed upon the heart to the comfort of the soul — yes, even during dreams. Such often occurs with passages which previously had not arrested one's attention, not even knowing where to find them in the Bible.

Fifthly, the Word is a special means for sanctification. "Sanctify them through Thy truth: Thy word is truth" (John 17:7). God's Word does not only work sanctification by means of continual exhortation by which the soul is inclined towards obedience by the very voice of God. It also works sanctification through a continual dialogue with God Himself while hearing, reading, and meditating upon His Word as the believer seeks to regulate his life by means of the Word. In addition to this the soul will be more exercised in faith and will become more established in the truth by virtue of its consistent use of God's Word. Faith then gives birth to love, and love in turn to sanctification. Yes, the soul is led further in this way into the mysteries of God's Word and perceives many matters which it previously was not able to discern. Every new acquaintance with spiritual mysteries, however, as well as each mystery itself, has a sanctifying influence. Those who are remiss in reading and lax in acquainting themselves with God's Word will be deprived to a considerable degree of these blessed fruits.

Sixthly, the Word of God is the spiritual sword which must be wielded at all times in our battle against the devil, heresies, and our flesh (Eph. 6:17); "For the Word of God is quick, and powerful, and sharper than any two-edged sword, piercing even to the dividing asunder of soul and spirit, and of the joints and marrow, and is a discerner of the thoughts and intents of the heart" (Heb. 4:12). Those who stand ready with this sword stand firm, provide themselves protection, and are victorious over their enemies.

Seventhly, to state matters comprehensively, the Word of God is the only means whereby we can be saved. "It is the power of God unto salvation" (Rom. 1:16); "The gospel of your salvation" (Eph. 1:13); "The engrafted Word, which is able to save your soul" (James 1:21). Therefore, whoever desires salvation will esteem and acknowledge the Word of God as necessary and profitable and will be desirous for this Word.

Our Obligations Toward the Holy Scriptures

Since we have shown the Word to have all these qualities, it obligates everyone to the following:

First, man must acknowledge, value, believe, and view the Word of God in this manner. Apart from this, the Word shall not be profitable. "The Word preached did not profit them, not being mixed with faith" (Heb. 4:2). At times our unbelieving heart, being incited by the devil, will cause us to doubt whether the Word of God is truly inspired by God. This at times can cause believers much grief and be very injurious to them. Even then they still perceive that the power of God's Word touches their heart, which no mere human manuscript can accomplish. And if human writings touch their heart, it is only insofar as it makes use of the Word and is taken from it. Even in this condition they readily perceive how the Word of God is a source of rest and comfort for the believer, how powerful a means it is unto the conversion of men, and that there is no purer, better, and more certain way unto salvation on earth. This ought to convince everyone to bring their thoughts into obedient captivity to the Word of God, nipping all wrong impulses in the bud, lest by permitting such thoughts to be multiplied the soul will become more distraught. This subject will be treated more comprehensively when considering the diseases of the soul in chapter ninety-three, "The Temptation whether God's Word is True."

Secondly, men ought to rejoice wholeheartedly in this most precious gift of God, embrace it with much love, and be joyful whenever they may either behold it or hold it in their very hands. Almost the entire world is deprived of the Word. Papacy deprives its people of it, burning the Bibles together with those who have read it. We, on the contrary, may have it in our possession and may hear and read it. How our hearts ought to rejoice over this fact! "I have rejoiced in the way of Thy testimonies, as much as in all riches. O how love I Thy law!" (Psa. 119:14, 97); "More to be desired are they than gold, yea, than much fine gold: sweeter also than honey and the honeycomb" (Psa. 19:10).

Thirdly, we should thank and magnify the Lord, who has given it for this. "At midnight I will rise to give thanks unto Thee because of Thy righteous judgments" (Psa. 119:62); "Praise the LORD, O Jerusalem; praise thy God, O Zion. He sheweth His word unto Jacob, His statutes and His judgments unto Israel" (Psa. 147:12, 19).

Fourthly, make use of the Word of God in prosperity, adversity, darkness, seasons of doubt, times of perplexity, and your entire walk. Nothing can befall you, nor is there any duty in which you must engage where the Word of God would not provide you with comfort, peace, counsel, and direction. "Thy testimonies also are my delight and my counselors; I have chosen the way of truth: Thy judgments have I laid before me; Thy word is a lamp unto my feet, and a light unto my path; Thy testimonies have I taken as an heritage for ever: for they are the rejoicing of my heart" (Psa. 119:24, 30, 105, 111).

Fifthly, purchase this inestimable jewel, and be diligent in giving it a place in your home. One of the current customs which I consider most desirable and praiseworthy is that of many prominent citizens having a large, beautiful Bible, together with a Psalm book, on display in every room. If only they would use them more frequently! One of the most appropriate acts of mercy is to provide the poor with Bibles, and to question them frequently whether they are also reading them daily. Those of limited means who do not wish to receive anything as a gift, must be diligent in saving all their pennies for the purpose of purchasing a Bible. Those who are not able to read must exert every effort to learn, with the objective to be able to read the Word of God. A home without a Bible is a ship without a rudder and a Christian without a Bible is a soldier without a weapon.

When the Reformation initially took hold in the Netherlands, it was customary for some prosperous citizens to visit the poor with a New Testament in their pocket for the purpose of reading a portion to them, as most people were not able to read. After this, they would give a charitable donation to them. Sea captains would do similarly upon returning home from a journey. In doing so they met the needs of those who either did not possess a Bible or who were not able to read. In this way there was mutual edification and it caused the Reformation to take hold. How profitable it would be if this practice would still be in vogue as many lack the qualifications to express themselves relative to Scripture!

Sixthly, read, search, and meditate upon the Word of God with all diligence and persistence. This should even be the practice of kings. "And it shall be with him, and he shall read therein all the days of his life" (Deu. 17:19). It is the duty of scholars as well. "Give attendance to reading" (1 Tim. 4:13). It is the privilege and obligation of the lowly and of every individual. "Search the Scriptures" (John 5:39); "Have ye not read?" (Mat. 12:3).

The eunuch read while riding in his chariot (Acts 8:28). The Bereans searched the Scriptures daily (Acts 17:11). How everyone ought to practice this in private, prior to going to work, both by himself alone, and with his family! At noon when one nourishes his body, he ought also to nourish his soul. In the evening after work, one must end the day by seeking some refreshment from the Word of God. In the meantime, while engaged in his occupation, by meditating upon what has been read, the soul will maintain communion with God. He will be enabled to understand the spiritual meaning as well as experience the power of God's Word. This will cause the soul to grow in grace, prevent vain thoughts from arising, control the tongue, suppress corruptions, and direct man to fear God.

Guidelines for the Profitable Reading of Scripture

For the reading of Scripture to be profitable, there must be preparation, practice, and reflection.

First, *the preparation for reading God's Word.* Each time when one engages himself to read:

(1) He must, with mental concentration, place himself in the presence of God. He must promote a reverent, spiritual frame, being conscious that the Lord shall speak to him. The consciousness of that reality should cause us to tremble with holy reverence. To promote such reverence, reflect upon Isaiah 1:2, "Hear, O heavens, and give ear, O earth: for the LORD hath spoken."

(2) He must lift up his heart to the Lord, beseeching Him who is the Author of this Word for His Spirit, that He may cause us to perceive the truth expressed in God's Word and apply it to the heart. Our prayer ought to be with Psalm 119:18, "Open Thou mine eyes, that I may behold wondrous things out of Thy law."

(3) He must also attentively incline the heart to obedience in order to exercise faith, be receptive to comfort, and comply with all that which the Lord shall proclaim, promise, and command, saying, "Speak, LORD; for Thy servant heareth" (1 Sam. 3:9).

Secondly, *the practice of reading God's Word.* As you read, it is essential to do so calmly and attentively rather than to do it hastily with the objective of bringing the exercise of this duty to a conclusion. If there is a lack of time, it is better to read less but to be attentive in doing so. One can read God's Word in a twofold manner, that is, either by personal study or by utilizing the research of others. This should be determined by both availability of time as well as ability.

In order to read God's Word in a studious and scrutinizing manner, one must observe the context preceding and following a given text and take notice of both the manner of speech and the objective of the text. The text must then be compared with other texts where the issue at hand is explained more comprehensively, and with texts which are similar in content. For this purpose it is advantageous to consult the excellent marginal notes,[7] which will shed much light upon the text. In following this procedure one will be able to search for and ascertain the literal meaning of the text. We should not merely cleave to the literal meaning, however, as so many literalists do. This is being merely satisfied with the rind of the fruit which provides neither strength nor food for the soul. One must penetrate to the kernel itself, seeking to perceive the internal essence of the matter. For this the natural man is blind, regardless of how learned, proficient in the Word of God, and able he may be to understand the context and convey the literal meaning of the text to others. A godly person, on the contrary, immediately begins to view the unique clarity, nature, and power of spiritual matters contained in the text and his perception increases the more he engages himself in observing and meditating upon these matters. Regardless of how often he may read the same words and chapters he will always perceive something of which he has not been aware before. The truth he finds in the Word is always new again and becomes increasingly sweeter. It is true that the process of ascertaining the literal meaning of the text is sometimes not accompanied with many spiritual exercises, but it qualifies a person to better understand the Holy Scriptures and afterward

---

[7] à Brakel here refers to the marginal notes or annotations of the Dutch "Statenbijbel," which is a compilation of notes by the translators. These notes are brief annotations which indicate various shades of meaning deduced from the original text. These notes are indicative of the honesty, sincerity, and integrity of these men as they endeavored to translate God's sacred Word with painstaking accuracy. They were translated into English by Theodore Haak and published in two volumes as The Dutch Annotations upon the whole Bible (London: Henry Hills, 1657), but have never been reprinted. Of English commentaries currently in print, the Dutch annotations would be most akin to Matthew Poole's Commentary on the Holy Bible, 3 volumes (London: Banner of Truth Trust, 1962).

to be wrought upon the more readily, and in a more thorough and powerful manner.

Four treacherous shoals must be avoided in this respect. Whoever runs aground on one of these will not be able to ascertain the correct meaning of the Word of God but will rather obscure the spirituality of the Word.

The first practice that needs to be avoided is *to assign every allowable meaning to a given word,* in consequence of which any meaning of the Word of God is acceptable as long as it does not violate the regulative principle of faith and the circumstances surrounding the text. Whoever adheres to such a practice makes a fool of himself and wrests the Scriptures. The meaning of Scripture is simple, clear, straightforward, and concise, expressing matters in a more organized manner than any man would ever be capable of doing. This obligates us to search out carefully what the specific intent and objective of the Spirit is in every text.

The second practice to avoid is that of *forcing everything into a framework of seven dispensations,* as the entire concept of seven dispensations is erroneous. It would be tolerable if this were limited to the Revelation of John; however, it would prevent one from ever ascertaining the correct meaning of the book of the Revelation. It is, unacceptable to search for seven dispensations throughout the entire Bible, subordinating every scriptural issue to a dispensation. That would take away the true meaning, spirituality, and power from the Word.

The third practice to avoid is to *relegate everything to the realm of prophecy,* relating everything to a special era in the New Testament dispensation and considering it as fulfilled or as yet to be fulfilled. This means that hardly anything remains which is of contemporary relevance. There are those who relate everything to the church and the antichrist. Even the parables of the Lord Jesus as recorded in the gospels are denominated as prophecies, and are considered to be references to the church and the antichrist. Whoever engages in such a practice wrests the Word of God, robbing it of its spirituality and power. It is true that all ceremonial procedures from Adam to Christ and all prophecies in the Old Testament are not explained in the New Testament. It is therefore an enjoyable and advantageous study to search out those things which are not explained in the New Testament, but nevertheless are certain and infallible. In doing so one will often discover singular declarations concerning the nature of the Lord Jesus and His execution of His mediatorial office, as well as prophecies which indeed have been fulfilled. In this way our faith is increased and is greatly strengthened. In the pursuit of this, wisdom and moderation should be exercised, however, while refraining from making radical statements by insisting on specific meanings. How often have others, and also we ourselves, been in error in the exposition of prophecy, discovering subsequently our adherence to an erroneous view! Godly humility is essential when engaging in such a study.

A fourth practice, insisting that no text in Scripture can be correctly understood unless viewed in its context, is also to be avoided. Apart from the fact that the context itself is usually obvious, it is generally easy to grasp even for an uneducated but godly reader — easier than some are ready to admit. Where the context is not so readily perceived — one interpreting the context differently from another — it is due to man's darkened understanding. A godly person, when reading Scripture in all simplicity and being capable of perceiving its spiritual dimension, will often be more capable of understanding the context than others, even though he frequently will not be able to prove his case as would a scholarly person who is in the state of nature. An awareness of the context is not always essential, however, to the correct understanding of a text or a passage. There are thousands of expressions in God's Word which, when heard or read individually, have a precise meaning, give full expression to their doctrinal content, and are sufficiently penetrating to stimulate faith, render comfort, and be exhortive in nature. This is illustrated in the following examples, "He that believeth on the Son hath everlasting life" (John 3:36); "Ask, and ye shall receive" (John 16:24); "Blessed are the poor in spirit...that mourn...the meek...who do hunger and thirst after righteousness," etc. (Mat. 5:3-12). Yes, many of the proverbs of Scripture are presented without an apparent context; whoever would search for a context in such a situation would be guilty of obscuring the matter. This much we state about ascertaining meaning in reading Scripture.

One can also read Scripture without engaging in studious research for the meaning of the text. This could be referred to as a practical reading of Scripture. Such is the case when, with a humble, hungry, and submissive spiritual frame, one places himself before the Lord while reading slowly and thoughtfully as if hearing the voice of God, and subjecting himself to the Holy Spirit to operate upon the heart as he reads. If he encounters something which is not immediately understood, he will put such a passage aside for the time being and continue his reading. Whenever there is a passage which has a special power upon the heart, such a person pauses in order that this Scripture might have its effect in the heart. Then he prays, gives thanks, rejoices, and is filled with amazement — all of which revive the soul and stimulate it to obedience. Upon concluding these exercises he will continue reading. After having read a chapter, he will meditate upon it, time permitting. When he encounters a remarkable text, he will mark or memorize it. In such a fashion both the learned and the unlearned should read the Word of God. In so doing, one will understand its spiritual meaning with increasing clarity and God's Word will increasingly become more precious to us. "If any man will do His will, he shall know of the doctrine, whether it be of God" (John 7:17); "If ye continue in My Word, then are ye My disciples indeed; and ye shall know the truth, and the truth shall make you free" (John 8:31-32).

The reflection upon reading Scripture consists in

(1) joyfully giving thanks that the Lord has permitted His Word to be recorded, that we may have it in our homes, that we can and were privileged to read it, and that it was applied to our heart;

(2) painstakingly striving to preserve this good spiritual frame which is obtained by reading God's Word;

(3) meditating while engaged in one's occupation upon that which one has read, repeatedly seeking to focus his thoughts upon it;

(4) sharing with others what was read, whenever possible, and discussing it;

(5) especially striving to comply with what was read by bringing it into practice.

If the Holy Scriptures were used in such a fashion, what wondrous progress we would make in both knowledge and godliness! Children would soon become young men, and young men would soon become men in Christ Jesus.

CHAPTER THREE

The Essence of God

We considered in the previous chapter the two principal sources from which the knowledge of God may be derived: nature and the Holy Scriptures. We will now proceed with a consideration of God Himself. This is a task which we must undertake with trembling, so that on the one side we may avoid entertaining unbecoming thoughts about God, and on the other side we may be properly exercised in response to appropriate considerations of God. May the Lord guide me as I write and may He reveal Himself to everyone who reads this chapter or hears it read. May this chapter also be to the establishment of professors of the truth and be a rebuttal against Socinians, Arminians,[1] and other proponents of error. Most importantly, may it guide us in the way of salvation.

As we consider the doctrine of God, we will discuss His Names, His divine essence, His attributes, and His divine Persons. Additionally, we will also consider the works of God: His intrinsic and extrinsic works as well as His works in the realm of nature and the realm of grace.

The Names of God

In order to speak about God to others, it is necessary to have a word to indicate of whom we are speaking — although it should be clear that such description is not needed to distinguish God from other gods as there is but one God. As it was sufficient for the first human to have but one name, "man," there being no other crea-

---

[1] The word "remonstranten" is here translated as "Arminians" since the latter word is used throughout the English-speaking world to refer to those who subscribe to the teachings of the father of the "remonstrance," Arminius.

ture like him, and as the Savior had no need of any other name but "Jesus," that is, Savior, there being but one such Savior, likewise God has no need for any other name but "God."

The Name JEHOVAH

Although a name cannot possibly express the infinite Being, it has pleased the Lord to give Himself a name by which He wishes to be called — a name which would indicate His essence, the manner of His existence, and the plurality of divine Persons. The name which is indicative of His essence is יהוה or *Jehovah*, it being abbreviated as יה or *Jah*. The name which is indicative of the trinity of Persons is אלהים or *Elohim*. Often there is a coalescence of these two words resulting in יהוה or *Jehovi*. The consonants of this word constitute the name *Jehovah*, whereas the vowel marks produce the name *Elohim*. Very frequently these two names are placed side by side in the following manner: *Jehovah Elohim*, to reveal that God is one in essence and three in His Persons.

The Jews do not pronounce the name *Jehovah*. This practice of not using the name Jehovah initially was perhaps an expression of reverence, but later became superstitious in nature. In its place they use the name אדני or *Adonai*, a name by which the Lord is frequently called in His Word. Its meaning is "Lord." When this word is used in reference to men, it is written with the letter *patach*, which is the short "a" vowel. When it is used in reference to the Lord, however, the letter *kametz* is used, which is the long "a" vowel. As a result all the vowels of the name *Jehovah* are present. To accomplish this the vowel "e" is changed into a *chatef-patach* which is the shortest "a" vowel, referred to as the guttural letter *aleph*. Our translators, to give expression to the name *Jehovah*, use the name LORD, which is similar to the Greek word κύριος *(kurios)*, the latter being a translation of *Adonai* rather than *Jehovah*. In Revelation 1:4 and 16:5 the apostle John translates the name *Jehovah* as follows: "Him which is, and which was, and which is to come." This one word has reference primarily to being or essence, while having the chronological connotation of past, present, and future. In this way this name refers to an eternal being, and therefore the translation of the name *Jehovah* in the French Bible is *l'Eternel*, that is, the Eternal One.

The name *Jehovah* is not to be found at all in the New Testament, which certainly would have been the case if it had been a prerequisite to preserve the name *Jehovah* in all languages. To maintain that this name cannot be pronounced in Greek confirms our view rather than renders it ineffective. Even though the transliteration of Hebrew words would conflict with the common elegance of the

Greek language, it is nevertheless not impossible. Since they can pronounce the names Jesus, Hosanna, Levi, Abraham, and Hallelujah, they are obviously capable of pronouncing the name *Jehovah*. I am not suggesting that the name *Jehovah* may not be used, but one may not make its use a prerequisite, as if its use were indicative of a higher level of spirituality and of superior wisdom. It is carnal to use this Name to draw attention to one's self, and thereby to display one's theological sentiments. *Jehovah* is not a common name, such as "angel" or "man" — names which can be assigned to many by virtue of being of equal status. On the contrary, it is a proper Name which uniquely belongs to God and thus to no one else, as is true of the name of every creature, each of which has his own name.

Question: Does Scripture ever assign the name *Jehovah* to a creature, or is this name uniquely God's own?

Answer: The Socinians, in order to avoid conceding that the Lord Jesus truly is God, maintain that others are also called by this name. We deny this, however; we maintain that this name uniquely belongs to God. Therefore no one but God alone may be called by this name. This becomes evident from the following:

First, it is evident when examining the composition of the word. Linguists maintain that this name has all the characteristics of a proper name. Therefore it never has anything in common with ordinary names. Since God is called by this name it is therefore of necessity the proper name of God.

Secondly, this name also cannot be applicable to anyone else but the LORD God, because it has reference to an eternal Being who is perpetually unchangeable and the origin of all beings.

Thirdly, the Lord appropriates this name as belonging exclusively to Him. "I am the LORD; that is My Name: and My glory will I not give to another" (Isa. 42:8); "The LORD is His name" (Exo. 15:3); "...and they shall say to me, What is His Name? what shall I say unto them? And God said unto Moses, I AM THAT I AM...I AM hath sent me unto you" (Exo. 3:13-14).

These words express the meaning of *Jehovah*, since *Jehovah* is a derivative of the verbal expression "I am." "But by My name JEHOVAH was I not known to them" (Exo. 6:3). This does not mean that the Lord was not known by the name *Jehovah* prior to this time, for even Eve already called Him by this name: "I have gotten a man from the LORD" (Gen. 4:1).

However, the Lord had not caused them to experience the meaning of this name — that He remains the same and is immutable regarding His promises. They would now observe this as He would lead them out of Egypt and bring them into Canaan.

Objection #1. Created angels are also called by this name. "And she called the name of the LORD that spake unto her, Thou God seest me" (Gen. 16:13). He who spoke to her was an angel, for he is previously referred to as such.

Answer: (1) It is credible that Hagar was cognizant of the fact that either a prophet or an angel had been sent to her by God, and thus considered these words as having been spoken by God Himself. For similar reasons the shepherds of Bethlehem also stated, "Let us now ...see this thing which is come to pass, which the Lord hath made known unto us" (Luke 2:15). Thus Hagar was not of the opinion that the angel's name was "Thou God seest me," but attributed it to the Lord who by means of this servant spoke to her.

(2) It was, however, undoubtedly the very Son of God who prior to His incarnation frequently appeared in human form and who, in reference to His mediatorial office, is called the "Angel of the Lord," the "Angel of the Lord's presence," and the "Angel of the covenant." He states in Genesis 16:10, "I will multiply thy seed exceedingly." This obviously cannot be accomplished by a created angel, but by God alone. Thus Hagar referred to *Jehovah* who spoke to her as "Thou God seest me," whether she perceived that this was *Jehovah* Himself or whether she identified Him as such by means of the messenger which spoke to her.

Objection #2. In Genesis 18 it is recorded that an angel came to Abraham, who nevertheless is referred to as *Jehovah* on several occasions.

Answer: It was the uncreated Angel, the Son of God Himself.

(1) He is expressly distinguished from the other two angels who are not called by the name *Jehovah*. This is true for Him alone.

(2) The Angel, being *Jehovah*, knew about Sarah's laughter in her tent (verse 13). He prophesied the birth of Isaac which from a natural perspective was impossible (verse 10). He knew that Abraham would command his children and his household to keep the way of the Lord (verse 19). All these incidents can be attributed only to God.

(3) Abraham acknowledged Him to be the Judge of all the earth (verse 25) while worshipping and supplicating before Him with utmost humility (verse 27).

Objection #3. Moses called the altar which he built, *Jehovah*. "And Moses built an altar, and called the name of it Jehovah-nissi" (Exo. 17:15).

Answer: Such an opinion is expressly contrary to the text. It is not stated that he called the altar *Jehovah*, for otherwise he would have terminated his statement at that point. Rather, he states, "Jehovah-nissi," that is, "Jehovah is my banner." As impossible as it is that he called the altar "banner," so impossible is it that he called it *Jehovah*. It was a verbal symbol which he appropriated to the altar — similar to the manner in which proverbs are placed over gateways and doors. By this he wished to indicate that the Lord, the God of the covenant, was their help, of which the altar, a type of the Lord Jesus, was tangible evidence.

Objection #4. The church is called by the name *Jehovah*. "…and the name of the city (that is, *Jerusalem*) from that day shall be" שמה יהוה or *Jehovah Shamma*, "The LORD is there" (Ezek. 48:35).

Answer: It is an expression which is used in reference to the church and in view of this it is stated concerning her, "The LORD is there." God dwells among her with His protection and blessing.

The Name ELOHIM

The name which refers to God's manner of existence or His divine personhood is אלהים or *Elohim*, which is equivalent to the Greek word Θεός *(Theos)*, and the English word *God*. It is rarely encountered in its singular form אלה or *Eloah*, and never in a dual sense. It is generally encountered in its plural form, that is, referring to two or more. This word is generally used in conjunction with a singular verb, as is true in Genesis 1:1, "In the beginning *Elohim* created," this being in reference to one God existing in three Persons (1 John. 5:7). A verb, an adjective, or a noun, however, are frequently placed in apposition to the word *Elohim* when used in its plural form, to which an *affixum pluralis numeri* is added. This becomes evident in the following passages: And *Elohim*, that is, God said נעשה *(Na'aseh)*: "Let us make man" (Gen. 1:26); When *Elohim* התעו *(hith'u)*, "caused me to wander" (Gen. 20:13); *Elohim* קדשים *(Kedoshim)*, "is an holy God" (Josh. 24:19); Remember now בוראיך *(Borecha)*, "thy Creator" (Eccl. 12:1); בעליך עשיך *(Bo'alaich 'osaich)*, "thy Maker is thine Husband" (Isa. 54:5); "I am *the LORD*" אלהיך *(Eloheka)*, "thy God" (Exo. 20:2).

Elohim is not a common name to which others have equal claim, but it is a proper name exclusively belonging to God. There is no one but the Lord who, as *Elohim*, exists in three Persons. In a metaphorical sense, however, it is also used in reference to others. Idols are called by the name *Elohim* due to the veneration and service which idol-worshippers afford them. Angels are called by this name since they reflect the glory and power of God. Governments are called by this name due to the territory allotted them over which they bear rule and whereby they reflect God's supreme majesty.

Many other names, descriptive and expressive of God's perfections, are attributed to Him in Scripture such as the Almighty, the Most High, the Holy One, etc.

The Essence of God

From the names of God we now proceed to the essence of God — His existence as God. But what shall I say concerning this? Jacob once asked the Lord His name, that is, to give expression to His essence, for in early history it was customary when assigning names to give expression to the essence of a matter. He received the following answer, however: "Wherefore is it that thou dost ask after My name?" (Gen. 32:29). God did not wish him to penetrate any further into the mysteries of God. In responding to Manoah the Lord said, "Why askest thou thus after My name, seeing it is secret?" (Judg. 13:18). In Isaiah 9:6 we read, "His name is Wonderful." You, who pretend to have some knowledge of God, tell me, "What is His name and what is His Son's name if thou canst tell?" (Prov. 30:4). All I can say is that the essence of God is His eternal self-existence. When Moses asked what he should tell the children of Israel if they asked him as to who had sent him, the Lord responded, אהיה אשר אהיה *(Ehjeh Asher Ehjeh)*: I AM THAT I AM. He added to this, "Thus shalt thou say unto the children of Israel, אהיה *(Ehjeh)*, I AM hath sent me to you" (Exo. 3:14). Job said concerning the Lord in chapter 12:16, "With Him is strength and wisdom"— חושיה *(Toeschia)* or essence. This is a derivative of ישה *(jashah)*, which in turn is derived from יש *(jeesch)*, and is expressive of steadfastness and continuity.

In the New Testament this is expressed by means of the words Θειότης *(theiotés)*, and Θεότης *(theotés)*, both of which are translated as "Godhead" in Romans 1:20 and Colossians 2:9. Additionally there are Φύσις *(phusis)*, which is translated as "nature" in Galatians 4:8, and μορΦὴ *(morphé)* which is translated as "form" in Philippians 2:6.

Whoever wishes to know more concerning God's essence should join me in worship as we close our eyes before this unapproachable light. It is in some measure revealed to the soul; however, we can only perceive the uttermost fringes of His Being by reflecting upon the divine attributes. At this point we will digress from the customary manner in which we treat our subject matter. We will not painstakingly deal with objections, lest we give someone the opportunity to entertain thoughts about God which are unbecoming, and thus imitate in this respect both the Socinian and heathen and their followers. We will nevertheless deal with and respond to objections in a very discreet manner by presenting the truth in an expository and affirmative manner.

The Attributes of God

Our gift of language belongs to the realm of the physical. Our words and expressions are derived from terrestrial objects. It is therefore a wondrous reality as well as a manifestation of divine goodness that man, in using sounds which are expressive of that which is tangible, is able to give an explanation about divine and spiritual matters by means of the vehicle of language. Our mind, being finite and having limited capacity, must function in the realm of concepts and ideas before comprehension can occur. It is the goodness of God that He adjusts Himself to our limited ability to comprehend. Since a harmonious concept of God — which would include all that could be said and thought about Him — is beyond our comprehension, it pleases God by means of various concepts and ideas to make Himself known to man. These concepts we describe and designate from a human perspective as God's essential attributes. This designation pertains to the various objects towards which God engages Himself and the deeds which He performs. We understand these attributes to be one from *God's* perspective, however, such that they can neither be divorced from the divine Being nor essentially and properly from each other as they exist in God, but are the simple, absolute Being of God Himself. We, however, relate these attributes as distinct entities by themselves. Justice and mercy are one in God, but we differentiate between them in reference to the objects towards which they are manifested, and the effects of these manifestations. Our God is inimitable and incomprehensible in His perfection, and consequently is simple and indivisible. In God there can be no differentiation between various matters, for whatever would be essentially distinct from God would render Him imperfect. Our limited comprehension must deal with each matter individually, however, and thus we assign distinct names to each attribute. Whatever we are capable of comprehending concerning God is according to truth and is consistent with His Being, but our finite understanding cannot penetrate its perfection and infinity.

The attributes or perfections of God are generally distinguished as being *communicable* and *incommunicable*. All God's attributes, being His simple, essential Being itself, are equally incommunicable as far as their nature is concerned. This distinction is merely made for the purpose of comparison. God has created man in His image and likeness and again renews fallen, but elect, sinners according to that image, making them anew partakers of the divine nature. This does not imply that such a sinner becomes divine and is a partaker of the very being and attributes of God. From a divine perspective God is incommunicable, and finite man from his perspective cannot comprehend God's Being, the Godhead being infinite, simple, and thus indivisible. Therefore, if man in some measure were a partaker of the divine Being itself or of one of the divine attributes, he would consequently be a partaker of the entire Godhead itself, and thus man would be God. However, when we speak of the image and likeness of God in man, we are merely referring to a reflection of some of God's attributes, which are infinite, indivisible, and incommunicable in God Himself. There is some measure of congruency between these attributes and the image of God in man; however, not as if there were full equality, but merely by way of faint similitude.

Nevertheless, some attributes are such that not even the faintest reflection of them can be observed in a reasonable creature. This being true, they are denominated incommunicable attributes. Some of the attributes of God of which there is a reflection and faint resemblance in man are therefore denominated *communicable attributes*. The *incommunicable attributes* include the following: perfection or all-sufficiency, eternity, infinity or omnipresence, simplicity, and immutability. The *communicable attributes* are those attributes which relate to intellect, will, and power. We shall discuss each of these individually in order to demonstrate what manner of God our God is, whom we serve.

The Perfection of God

The perfection of the creature consists in the possession of a measure of goodness which God has given and prescribed to all His creatures. All creatures, whatever the degree of their perfection may be, are dependent upon an external source for their being and well-being. God's perfection, however, excludes such a possibility, as He has no need of anything. No one can add to or subtract anything from His being, neither can anyone increase or decrease His felicity. His perfection consists in His self-sufficiency, His self-existence, and that He is the beginning — the first (Rev. 1:8). His all-sufficiency is within and for Himself, the שׁדַּי אֵל *(El Shaddai), the All-sufficient One* (Gen. 17:1). "Neither is worshipped with men's hands, as though He needed any thing" (Acts 17:25); "Is it any pleasure to the Almighty, that thou art righteous? or is it gain to Him, that thou makest thy ways perfect?" (Job 22:3). "My goodness extendeth not to Thee" (Psa. 16:2).

Thus there is no common ground between the perfection of God and of creatures — except in name. That which is in man is contrary to the perfection of God, however, and thus the perfection of God is an incommunicable attribute of God. The salvation of man consists in knowing, honoring, and serving God. Such is our God, who not only is all-sufficient in Himself but who with His all-sufficiency can fill and saturate the soul to such an overflowing measure that it has need of nothing else but to have God as its portion. The soul so favored is filled with such light, love, and happiness, that it desires nothing but this. "Whom have I in heaven but Thee? and there is none upon earth that I desire beside Thee" (Psa. 73:25).

The Eternity of God

We insignificant human beings are of yesterday, have a beginning, and exist within the context of time which progresses in a sequential fashion. We cannot even begin to comprehend eternity. By way of negation, we seek to comprehend eternity by comparing it with time, stating that it is without beginning, continuation, and end. If we go beyond this in seeking to comprehend the "how" and the "why," we shall spoil it for ourselves and be in darkness. If we wish to consider the eternity of God within the context of our conception of time, then we will dishonor God and entertain erroneous notions concerning Him. All that relates to and resembles time, and all that we denominate as eternal in a figurative sense, must be totally excluded from our concept of God. We call something eternal which,

(1) continues until it has fulfilled its purpose. In this context circumcision is referred to as an eternal covenant. "...and My covenant shall be in your flesh for an everlasting covenant" (Gen. 17:13). This means that it would last until the coming of the Lord Jesus who is the embodiment of all the ceremonies, in whom all shadows had their fulfillment and consequently no longer have a function. It can also be interpreted to mean that this covenant, being confirmed by circumcision, is an eternal covenant.

(2) The word eternity can also be expressive of the duration of a condition which is in force as long as man lives. "...he shall be thy servant for ever" (Deu. 15:17).

(3) The word eternity can also refer to something that has stability and endures. In this context hills are referred to as being eternal (Deu. 33:15; cf. Gen. 49:26).[2]

---

[2] In the KJV these eternal hills are called "lasting hills" or "everlasting hills," which implies eternalness.

(4) The word eternity is used in reference to that which will never end, such as felicity in the hereafter. "I give unto them eternal life" (John 10:28).

We use the word eternity in reference to all these things. There is, however, neither commonality nor resemblance with the absolute eternity of God. We cannot refer to it any differently than to define it as the existence of God which is without beginning, continuation, and ending, all of which are simultaneously true. This is expressed in the word יהוה (*Jehovah*), which defines a being for whom the past, present, and future are a simultaneous and concurrent reality — He is the One who is, who was, and who shall be. God's Being is eternity and eternity is God's Being. It is not fortuitous as time is in relation to the creature. There can be no chronology within the Being of God since His Being is simple and immutable. Such likewise cannot be true in reference to God's eternity; eternity is the very Being of God. The Holy Scriptures refer to God as the eternal God. "And Abraham . . . called there on the name of the LORD, the everlasting God" (Gen. 21:33); "The eternal God is thy refuge" (Deu. 33:27). It is stated concerning God that He is the beginning and the end (Rev. 1:8). Even though these are distinguished in God, they are a simultaneous reality. There is no intervening time nor anything that remotely resembles the progression of time. ". . . from everlasting to everlasting, Thou art God" (Psa. 90:2); "with whom is no variableness, neither shadow of turning" (James 1:17); "They shall perish . . . but Thou art the same" (Psa. 102:26-27); "For a thousand years in Thy sight are but as yesterday when it is past" (Psa. 90:4). Thus we conclude that God and time have nothing in common.

Even when years and days, or past and present time are attributed to God, and He is called the Ancient of Days and other similar expressions, such is merely done from man's viewpoint. The reason for this is that we, insignificant human beings incapable of thinking and speaking about eternity in a fitting manner, may by way of comparison — which in reality is a very unequal comparison — comprehend as much of eternity as is needful for us to know. Nevertheless, in doing so we must fully divorce God from the concept of time.

God unchangeably exists while time is in progression. God was yesterday, is today, and will be tomorrow. However, God does not measure time as the creature measures time, as He transcends time and is external to the concept of time. If He has wrought something in the past, will do it tomorrow, or is active at the present moment, this does not suggest that a change of time occurs in

God. Such an apparent change merely relates to the objects of His activity and the purposes which He has accomplished.

Therefore, do not elevate yourself beyond the reach of your comprehension, and do not limit God by your human conceptions. Acknowledge and believe God to be the One who dwells in incomprehensible eternity; lose yourself in this eternity; worship that which you cannot comprehend; and with Abraham call upon the name of the eternal God.

The Infinity and Omnipresence of God

A being, be it of a spiritual or a corporal nature, is considered finite if its existence has well-defined parameters. Such is true for the entire structure of heaven and earth as well as of every individual creature. The world is finite, and even though there is no other celestial body by which the parameters of the earth are defined, preventing it from expanding itself beyond its current limits, these parameters are nevertheless determined by its own mass. The earth's measurement from its center to its circumference is well-defined, and beyond this circumference is nothing but space which itself has its own parameters. God's Being, however, is inherently without any parameters, neither are any imposed upon Him externally and thus God in His Being is infinite in the absolute sense of the word.

Occasionally, when referring to something of which the limits are not known, we refer to infinity in a hypothetical sense, as when we speak of the total number of grains of sand, blades of grass, or stars. We also define as infinite that to which something can always be added, which for instance is true of a number. Regardless of how long one counts, the ultimate sum will either be even or uneven, a reality which changes as soon as one number is added — even if you were to count during your entire lifetime. When we define God to be infinite, however, we do so in the literal sense of the word, thereby conveying that His Being is truly without any parameters or limitations. His power is infinite, His knowledge is infinite, and His Being is infinite; and it is this latter truth which we are discussing here.

Eternity being an incomprehensible concept for us as creatures of time, as local and finite creatures we are equally incapable of understanding God's infinity. We relate to infinity by thinking of a vast expanse. God's infinity, however, excludes the concepts of quantity, dimension, and locality. In order to have any comprehension of the infinity of God's Being, we must, for instance, make a hypothetical comparison to a vast expanse while simultaneously denying such to be characteristic of God.

The infinity of God's Being is a logical consequence of,

(1) the perfection of God's Being. Whatever is limited and finite is imperfect, since expansion of parameters implies the approximation of a higher degree of perfection. Consequently, something without limits is better and excels in perfection that which has limits.

(2) It being evident that God is infinite in power — something which cannot be attributed to a finite being.

(3) God Himself bearing witness to this by His Spirit: "Great is the LORD, and greatly to be praised; and His greatness is unsearchable" (Psa. 145:3); "the heaven and heaven of heavens cannot contain Thee" (1 Ki. 8:27).

One of the friends of Job expressed himself concerning God's infinity, both as to His knowledge and His Being. "Canst thou by searching find out God? canst thou find out the Almighty unto perfection? It is as high as heaven; what canst thou do? deeper than hell; what canst thou know? The measure thereof is longer than the earth, and broader than the sea" (Job 11:7-9).

Infinity and omnipresence are identical in God. When we speak of His omnipresence, however, we are merely referring to the infinite God in regard to His presence at any given location. We are not defining His parameters as we would with corporal entities which have well-defined spacial limits. He is also not limited as other spiritual beings are who can be only at one place at one time. Rather, the reference is to the fact that with His Being He permeates everything, albeit not in a local, corporal, and dimensional sense.

God, by virtue of the hypostatic union in Christ, is in heaven with His glory, as well as in His church with His grace. He dwells in every believer with His life-giving Spirit, and is in hell with His just wrath. He is present everywhere in the created universe, not only by virtue of His power and knowledge — also in His Being, such not being partial or dimensional — but because His Being is infinite, simple, and indivisible. This is as incomprehensible for the creature as is God's eternity. We must therefore close the eyes of our understanding as to the manner of His existence and believe that God is such as He has revealed Himself in nature and in Scripture.

Nature itself instructs every man in this regard, and especially those who apply themselves with some diligence to become acquainted with God and religion. Such persons will become conscious of the omnipresence of God so that everyone simultaneously, regardless of what his location may be at any given time upon earth, not only will acknowledge God to be omnipotent and omniscient but also that He is near him in His essential presence. Even intelligent men in the secular realm have expressed themselves forcefully in reference to this reality.

God states very clearly in His Word, "The heaven is My throne, and the earth is My footstool" (Isa. 66:1). When such a statement is made in reference to a king, it is indicative of his immediate and corporal presence. Consequently, this is also true when God refers to Himself in such human terms in order that we might understand and acknowledge the presence of the very essence of God both in heaven and on earth. "Am I a God at hand, saith the LORD, and not a God afar off? ... Do not I fill heaven and earth?" (Jer. 23:23-24). "... though He be not far from every one of us: for in Him we live, and move, and have our being" (Acts 17:27-28). Add to these the texts which indicate that God not only fills heaven and earth, but infinitely transcends both (1 Ki. 8:27).

When it is stated that God is in heaven, this does not exclude His omnipresence upon earth. Nowhere can God either be confined or excluded. God manifests His glorious presence in a far more evident manner in heaven — it being His throne — than upon earth, which is His footstool. By using this manner of speech the lofty and exalted glory by which God transcends all creatures is made known to us. This is acknowledged by man when he prayerfully lifts his heart and eye upward, acknowledging thereby that God also is invisible and alien to all that is upon earth.

When it is stated that God was not present in the strong wind, the earthquake, and the fire, but rather in a still small voice (1 Ki. 19:11-12), the reference is not to His essential presence, but to the manner in which He addressed Elijah and revealed Himself to Him. When it is stated that God is not with someone or that He would not go up in the midst of Israel (Exo. 33:7), the reference is to the manifestation of His favor rather than to His essential presence. It is not unbecoming for God to be present in various vile and offensive places for His presence is not characterized by corporal involvement, but He is present as the energizing, preserving, and governing cause, just as He is in the ungodly and devils as an avenging Judge. The sun illuminates everything without being contaminated in the least. An object cannot contaminate a spirit, much less the infinite God. Whatever God deems suitable to be created and to be governed, He also deems suitable for His essential presence. God reveals Himself in the world by means of His works, not as a God who is afar off, but as a God who is invisibly present.

Believer, since the Lord is always present with you, compassing your pathway and your lying down, besetting you behind and before (Psa. 139:3-5), be careful to refrain yourself from doing anything that would be unbecoming of His presence. Set the Lord always before you. Acknowledge Him in all your ways. Fear Him.

Humble yourself before Him. Walk in all reverence and humility
before His countenance, for to sin in the presence of God greatly
aggravates the sin committed. The presence of people serves as a
restraint against the commission of many sins, and if the presence
of God does not accomplish the same, one reveals himself as having
more respect for people than for the majestic and holy God. What a
despising and provoking of God this is! Therefore, let your reverence for the presence of God prevent your sinning against Him
and let it motivate you to live a life pleasing to the Lord.

On the other side, believer, let the reality of God's presence be
your continual support and comfort in all the vicissitudes of life.
The Lord is at hand; He is a fiery wall roundabout you, and no one
will be able to touch you contrary to His will. If something befalls
you, seek refuge in Him and encourage yourself with His presence.
How this revived David's soul! "Yea, though I walk through the
valley of the shadow of death, I will fear no evil: for Thou art with
me" (Psa. 23:4). The Lord is pleased to comfort His children in this
manner. "When thou passest through the waters, I will be with
thee; and through the rivers, they shall not overflow thee; when
thou walkest through the fire, thou shalt not be burned, neither
shall the flame kindle upon thee" (Isa. 43:2).

The Simplicity of God

As we can neither comprehend the eternity of God because we are
creatures of time, nor the non-dimensional infinity and omnipresence of God because we are finite and local in nature, so we also,
being composite creatures, are not able to comprehend the simplicity
of God. Since we must recognize, however, that all composition
implies imperfection, dependency, and divisibility, we may not think
of God as being composite even in the remotest sense of the word.
Thus, we acknowledge God in every respect to be perfect and of
singular essence.

Philosophers recognize various types of composition, all of
which we deny to be applicable to God. Among these are:

First, *a logical composition*, (*ex genere et differentia*), that is, in reference to gender, nature, and distinction. For example, both man and
beast are animals as both have an animal nature in common and thus
belong to the animal kingdom.[3] In addition to their animal nature,

---

[3] The Dutch reads as follows: "De mens is een dier, en een beest is een dier; de
dierlijkheid is hun gemeen, beide behoren ze tot het geslacht der dieren." In
reading this statement one must bear its historical context in mind. Since evolutionary theory did not exist, no one would have suspected à Brakel of teaching
that man is an animal in an evolutionary sense.

however, there is also something by which they are distinguished from each other. Man possesses reason in addition to his animal nature, whereas a beast is without reason and intelligence. However, God has nothing in common with any creature, and by virtue of His Being, transcends all His creatures while remaining distinct from them. Whenever God is referred to as a Spirit, the word "spirit" does not imply that God and angels have a common nature of which both God and angels would be equal partakers. The resemblance is one of nomenclature only. God is called a Spirit in order that we would perceive Him as being invisible.

Secondly, *a physical or natural composition*, consisting of three elements: substance and form, a subject and its incidentals, and individual parts.

(1) *Substance and form.* Everything which has been created with a tangible form has, in addition to the matter of which it consists, something which identifies such a created object to be gold, a tree, an animal, or a human being. Far be it from us to entertain such notions about God who is without a body and infinitely removed from every possible notion of any physical characteristics, no matter how he is viewed by man. In order to distinguish Him as such, He is referred to as a Spirit. Such a composition as to substance and form simply does not exist relative to God.

(2) *A subject and its incidentals.* An angel, for example, has the nature of an angel, and in addition to this nature has a mind, intelligence, a will, holiness, and power. These qualities are not the angel himself, but they are complementary to his being. His being is the subject of these qualities, making him complete. Far be it from us to think of God in such a fashion. God is perfect in His Being and His perfection cannot be improved upon in any way. All that may be discerned in God is God Himself. His goodness, wisdom, and omnipotence is the good, only wise, and omnipotent God Himself.

(3) *Individual parts.* Parts by way of composition constitute a whole — such as is true for objects. Such is clearly not the case with God for God is a Spirit who has nothing in common with a body. If such were the case, there would be something less than perfection in God, as the composite whole would be more nearly perfect than each individual part.

Thirdly, *a metaphysical or supernatural composition.* Three aspects must be considered.

(1) *Ex essentia et existentia,* that is, there is an essential distinction between the essence and the actual existence of something. It is possible to comprehend the one without the other. It is possible to

describe a rose and to comprehend what it is, even during the winter when no roses are present. Thus, we distinguish between the essential nature of a rose and its actual existence. God's Being, however, is His actual existence, and His actual existence is His Being, a truth which is conveyed by His name *Jehovah*. One cannot be distinguished from the other and one cannot be comprehended without the other, for they are one.

(2) *Ex potentia et actu*, that is, there is a distinction between the potential and the actual deed. In discussing potential, we distinguish between active and passive potential. Active potential refers to the ability to accomplish something, even though one is not accomplishing it at the time. In the creature such potential is distinguished from the deed, and the excellence of a creature in action supersedes that of one who has the potential for such activity. Such, however, is not the case with God; in Him the potential for activity and the act itself are one. God is one singular, active force. Distinction and change in this realm can only be perceived in the creature which has been created, is maintained, and is governed. Such, however, is not true for God who is the Creator, Maintainer, and Governor. Latent potential — or to express it in more intelligble language — the possibility of existence, is to be found in creatures only, such being true in a threefold manner. In the first place it refers to something which as yet does not exist but which by virtue of the exertion of effort could be brought into existence. It also refers to something which already exists, but which by the exertion of effort can be changed. Thirdly, it refers to something that can be annihilated. It is obvious that all of this does not apply to God.

(3) *Ex essentia et subsistentia*, that is, there is a distinction between the nature or being and the existence or personhood. *Subsistentia* or the manner of existence is complementary to the existence of a being itself, by which it possesses something which makes it uniquely distinct from another being, having a unique existence of its own. Thus, we conclude the manner of existence to presuppose a being. *Suppositium*, or the existence itself, refers to that which can in nowise be communicated to someone else, nor can exist in someone else either in part or form. Something having such a distinct existence and being endowed with reason we refer to as a person. A person is an indivisible and independent entity endowed with a rational nature. A person is either a human being such as John, Peter, or Paul; or an angel such as Gabriel or Michael; or a divine Person, such as the Father, the Son, or the Holy Ghost.

In every created person there is a composition of essence, actual existence, and manner of existence. One is not the same as the other, but is distinguished from the other. Consider, for instance, the human nature of Christ, in which we can discern both essence and actual existence, but not a human personality. As such it has its existence within the Person of the Son of God, for otherwise Christ would consist of two persons: a human and divine person. He is, however, one divine Person. In God there is no composition of being and personhood, as every form of composition implies imperfection. Each divine Person is not to be distinguished from either the divine Being or from the other Persons as we would distinguish between various matters, nor as between a matter and the manner in which it functions, such being distinct from the matter itself. We insignificant human beings, however, try to comprehend this by relating to or defining a manner of existence. This does not indicate that there is composition in His Being, but merely enables us to distinguish between various matters related to God's Being. Whatever we cannot comprehend of it, we believe and worship, as it pleases God to reveal Himself in such a fashion. Believers, being illuminated by the Spirit of God, know as much concerning this attribute as is necessary to cause them to adore and glorify God, as well as to experience joy, confidence, and sanctification.

Scripture makes reference to this simplicity when referring to God in an abstract manner such as when it speaks of the Godhead, divinity, or when it refers to God as light, "God is light" (1 John 1:5); truth, "God of truth" (Deu. 32:4); and love, "God is love" (1 John 4:8). None of this can be stated concerning a creature.

When man is referred to as having his origin in God, belonging to God's generation, being God's son, or being a partaker of the divine nature, and when God is said to be the Father of spirits, this does not imply that man is of the same essence as God, as this would mean that God's Being is communicable. In such cases the reference is to creation and regeneration by which man receives some resemblance to some of the attributes of God. This creative act does not bring about a change in God but in the creature.

Similarly, the decrees, when viewed internally in God, are the decreeing God Himself. Also the relationship which God establishes relative to His creatures does not imply a change or composition within God, as this relationship is merely external and adds nothing to the essence of God's Being. Whenever human limbs, hands, eyes, and a mouth are attributed to God, such human terminology occurs in order that we insignificant human beings may comprehend the operations of God by comparing them to the manner in which we use those limbs, etc. Whenever anger, love, and similar passions are attributed to God, we must have the consequences and results in view such as occur when we have similar passions.

The Immutability of God

Mutability has reference either to a created entity, to incidents or circumstances, or to the will. Every creature in one way or another is subject to change and has within itself the potential for change or to be changed. The Lord our God, however, is absolutely, and in all respects, immutable in both His essence and His will. Yes, even the possibility of change is utterly foreign to God. This is evident from the following:

First, it is conveyed by the name of God, *Jehovah*, which means "eternal Being." By means of this name God shows Himself to be immutable. "...but by My name JEHOVAH was I not known to them" (Exo. 6:3), that is, I have made a promise to them concerning Canaan, which, however, I have not fulfilled in their time and have not shown to them in very deed that I am immutable, but I will now show to you that I am *Jehovah*, the immutable God, by fulfilling my promise to you, their seed.

Secondly, add to this these and similar texts. "Of old hast Thou laid the foundation of the earth: and the heavens are the work of Thy hands. They shall perish, but Thou shalt endure: yea, all of them shall wax old like a garment; as a vesture shalt Thou change them, and they shall be changed: but Thou art the same, and Thy years shall have no end" (Psa. 102:25-27); "For I am the LORD, I change not" (Mal. 3:6); "The Father of lights, with whom is no variableness, neither shadow of turning" (James 1:17); "God, willing more abundantly to shew unto the heirs of promise the immutability of His counsel, confirmed it by an oath" (Heb. 6:17); "And also the Strength of Israel will not lie nor repent: for He is not a man, that He should repent" (1 Sam. 15:29); "For the LORD of hosts hath purposed, and who shall disannul it? and His hand is stretched out, and who shall turn it back?" (Isa. 14:27).

Thirdly, the following reasons also make the immutability of God evident. All change occurs either because the principle of change is inherent in us, or because our nature is such that someone else is capable of bringing about a change in us.

God, however, is eternal, transcendent, and the original cause of all things. All change is either the result of a lack of wisdom, the perception of which necessitates a response to the error one has made in consequence of this; or it is precipitated by a lack of foreknowledge, by which one could not anticipate what would be encountered and thus is confronted with the unexpected. God, however, is supreme Wisdom Himself, the only wise God, who has foreknowledge concerning all things. "Known unto God are all His works from the beginning of the world" (Acts 15:18). He is cognizant of all that man will do or refrain from doing by the exercise of his free will, as man in all his motions is dependent upon God. He knows our thoughts from afar, our downsitting and uprising, as well as our speaking and silence. Change can also occur when we lack the ability to carry out our intent, being unable to overcome a given obstacle. God, however, is the Almighty, wonderful in counsel and excellent in working; consequently, not even the minutest change can take place with God.

Additionally, it should be considered that if God were to change, He would improve Himself or gain in wisdom. Neither possibility can be entertained concerning God as He always is and remains the infinitely perfect One.

It is according to God's will that certain things will change. This, however, does not bring about a change in His will. When repentance is attributed to God, this does not suggest a change in God Himself, but rather a change in activity (in comparison to a prior moment) towards the objects of that activity, this change being according to His immutable decree. Whenever God issues a promise or a threat which He does not carry out, this merely indicates that there was a contingency, either expressly stated or implied, which would determine whether or not the circumstances would take place. This fact was already known to God by virtue of His omniscience and His counsel. The fact that God is Creator, Maintainer, Governor, and Reconciler, and is a Father, does not indicate that any change occurs in God, but rather in the creatures. It conveys the relationship which God thereby establishes with His creatures. This relationship, however, does not suggest a change in the parties involved in this relationship.

Since God is immutable, how you should fear, unconverted sinner! For all the threatenings and judgments, both temporal and eternal, with which you have been threatened, will certainly and unavoidably come upon you if you do not repent.

Believers, be comforted by the immutability of the Lord, for all promises of which you are the heirs will most certainly be fulfilled. Not one of them will fall upon the earth nor be disannulled, even though the circumstances appear to be strange and so contrary to them and, in your opinion, the fulfillment of the promises is postponed so much longer than ought to be the case. God leads His children in these ways to cause them to trust in His Word alone. He makes the promise obscure and causes the opposite to transpire in order to demonstrate subsequently the immutability of His counsel that much more clearly. "...in those is continuance, and we shall be saved" (Isa. 64:5). This much for the incommunicable attributes.

The Communicable Attributes of God

The communicable attributes of God are not less infinite and are the simple[4] God Himself, as is also true for the incommunicable attributes. They are neither denominated "communicable attributes" because God communicates these attributes themselves nor because there is any equivalence between the Creator and the creature. Rather, He has communicated a slight resemblance of these attributes to His rational creatures. These communicable attributes can be organized under three headings: intellect or knowledge, will, and power.

The Knowledge of God

Though rational creatures possess a measure of knowledge, there is nevertheless an infinite difference between God's knowledge and the knowledge of His creatures, both in reference to the mode as well as to the objects of their knowledge.

First, let us consider *the mode of God's knowledge.* Man acquires knowledge by means of deliberation and rational deduction, deducing and drawing conclusions by viewing one fact in reference to another. The initial knowledge concerning an object is acquired by way of *species sensibiles,* that is, sensible observations, which are made regarding physical objects through the agency of the five senses, and by means of *species intelligibiles,* that is, intellectual observations which are made through the agency of one's intellect regarding matters about which man reasons. The knowledge of God, on the contrary, neither has its origin in the creature nor does it flow from the creature to God; rather it flows from God Himself to the creature. God does not become acquainted with things after the fact by virtue of their existence and function; rather, He knows matters in advance so that they will exist and function according to His decree. God does not decree His workmanship by considering cause and effect. He does not acquire His knowledge concerning His creature through the process of research and rational deduction; rather, He knows them since He

---

[4] The Dutch reads as follows: "de eenvoudige God zelf," and thus the reference here is to the incommunicable attribute of God's simplicity.

has decreed that they should exist and operate. His cognizance of everything is full and instantaneous in consequence of who He is. He views everything simultaneously, and each matter in particular; this pertains even to the minutest detail of its existence. Beyond this we cannot speculate about the mode of God's knowledge. We must confess, "Such knowledge is too wonderful for me" (Psa. 139:6).

Secondly, *The object of God's knowledge.* Also here there is an infinite difference between the knowledge of men and the knowledge of God. Man is knowledgeable about only a few things, and that which he knows is only known superficially, as he lacks the capacity to uncover the most profound and essential substance of a matter. "For we are but of yesterday, and know nothing" (Job 8:9); "Lo, these are parts of His ways: but how little a portion is heard of Him?" (Job 26:14).

(1) On the contrary, God knows Himself, and that perfectly. "...the things of God knoweth no man, but the Spirit of God" (1 Cor. 2:11).

(2) God is cognizant of His omnipotence, knowing that He can fully perform all that He would desire to do. All that he would desire to do can indeed come to pass and be accomplished by Him. This we would refer to as the possibility of all things. The Lord Jesus refers to this when He states, "I say unto you, that God is able of these stones to raise up children unto Abraham" (Mat. 3:9). This is generally referred to as *scientam simplicis intelligentiae*, that is, knowledge in its most simple or essential form.

(3) God is also cognizant of all things which currently exist or will exist — that is, prior to their existence. This is not merely true in a general sense, but it relates to each individual matter or action as if each were singular in its existence. This knowledge is generally referred to as *scientia visionis*, that is, visionary knowledge as it relates to the perception of things which shall be or currently exist.

God clearly testifies in His Word that He does not merely have a general knowledge concerning matters, but a specific knowledge of each individual matter. Such is not only confirmed by texts which refer to God's knowledge in a general sense, such as, "Known unto God are all His works from the beginning of the world" (Acts 15:18); "all things are naked and opened unto the eyes of Him with whom we have to do" (Heb. 4:13); "God...knoweth all things" (1 John 3:20) — also by texts which refer to God's knowledge concerning each matter individually, such as, "Neither is there any creature that is not manifest in His sight" (Heb. 4:13); "But the very hairs of your head are all numbered" (Mat. 10:30); "He telleth the number of the stars; He calleth them all by their names" (Psa. 147:4).

(1) The Lord observes and is cognizant of all things, both great

and small. He knows the heart of kings (Prov. 21:1) and takes notice of every sparrow (Mat. 10:29).

(2) He is cognizant of all good and evil things, "Thou hast set our iniquities before Thee, our secret sins in the light of Thy countenance" (Psa. 90:8).

(3) The Lord is cognizant of all secret things, "Thou, even thou only, knowest the hearts of all the children of men" (1 Ki. 8:39); "The LORD knoweth the thoughts of man" (Psa. 94:11); "for He knew what was in man" (John 2:25).

(4) The Lord has an infallible knowledge of all future things which will transpire due to the exercise of man's free will, and therefore knows all things which will occur relative to man. God knows everything, for all His works are known to Him from eternity and are naked and open before Him. This becomes evident from the following:

First, the word "all" comprehends everything. It includes all future events, including those which occur as a result of the exercise of man's free will. If God were not cognizant of such events, He would be ignorant concerning many things. The contrary is true, however, for He knows everything.

Secondly, what is more frequent in occurrence and more dependent upon the exercise of man's free will than his sitting down and rising up, as well as the function of thought and speech? The Lord knows all this from afar, however, even before one thinks or speaks. "...for I knew that thou wouldest deal very treacherously" (Isa. 48:8; see also Ps. 139:1-2); "Before I formed thee in the belly, I knew thee" (Jer. 1:5); "For I know the things that come into your mind, every one of them" (Ezek. 11:5).

Thirdly, this is true for all prophecies, even those which refer to such events which could only come about as a result of the exercise of man's free will. Examples of this are too numerous to mention here; the entire divine revelation exemplifies this. The Lord Jesus Himself says, "Now I tell you before it come, that, when it is come to pass, ye may believe that I am He" (John 13:19).

Fourthly, nothing exists or comes to pass apart from the operation of God. God sustains everything by His omnipotent and omnipresent power. Nothing can move without divine cooperation and thus everything transpires according to His decree, be it either by the Lord's initiation or permission, directing things in such a manner that they accomplish His purpose. Thus it becomes evident that the Lord has prior knowledge concerning all things. You will comprehend this with more clarity and be less confused if you keep in mind that God is omniscient and has decreed all that transpires. His knowledge is not derived from existing matters and secondary causes as is true for man. Keep in mind that from God's perspective, who is the first cause of all things, everything is an absolute certainty even though it appears to be uncertain when viewed from the perspective of secondary causes. From God's perspective there are no contingencies; such is only true from man's perspective. Thus, in defining the freedom of the will we must not think of it as functioning independently from God, on an equal plane with His will, or as a neutral entity; rather, this freedom is a function of necessity. Thus, the freedom of the will does not contradict the certain foreknowledge of God. Man, without coercion and by arbitrary choice, performs that which God has most certainly decreed, and of which He was cognizant that it would occur.

God speaks in the manner of men when it is recorded that He tries man in order to know what is in him, and also when He states, "... now I know that thou fearest God" (Gen. 22:12). He had knowledge of this already from eternity. He also speaks in the manner of men when it is recorded that He waits whether man will perform a particular duty. He does this in order to exhort and warn man that he must be aware that God takes notice of his actions; it is not that He does not know what will occur.

Jesuits, Arminians, and others who fanatically insist that man has a free will have concocted a *scientiam mediam*, that is, a mediate knowledge which would positionally be between the absolute, natural, and essential knowledge of God by which God is cognizant of the full potential of all things. His volitional, visionary knowledge would then be that knowledge whereby He has a particular and detailed knowledge of all things — having decreed them — as far as circumstances and occurence are concerned. Such a will, being in a mediate position relative to both [essential and visionary knowledge], would be a means whereby God knows one thing by means of the other, that is, that which takes place by means of causes and circumstances.

They define this mediate knowledge to be the knowledge of God whereby He is cognizant of future events which are not yet considered as certain, since no determination has yet been made by presupposing in what manner these events will be shaped by the exercise of man's free will. Let me illustrate by way of hypothesis. God, in envisioning that man would be created in perfection and would be confronted with a particular temptation of Satan, could foresee that man in the exercise of His free will would abuse His gifts. God further envisioned, after man had fallen, that the gospel would be proclaimed to him, urgently motivating him in various ways to believe it, this taking place at such a moment when man would be most pliable, attentive, and properly prepared. Thus, He would be enabled to foresee and know who would and who would not repent, believe, and persevere until the end of life. Such reasoning could also be applied to other situations in which angels or men would appear to exercise their free will in one way or another. The foolishness of such a hypothesis will be evident from the following:

First, if God had such a *mediate* knowledge, all knowledge of God relative to the actions of men would be fraught with uncertainty and mere assumptions. Even if every imaginable circumstance needed to induce man to a certain action would be brought into play, man, in their opinion, would still be free to do as he pleased. They reason that man would not be limited by a necessary cause, and thus it would be uncertain what he would do. Consequently, God's knowledge relative to such actions would be of a contingent nature. Far be it from us to entertain such a notion concerning an omniscient God!

Secondly, such mediate knowledge implies that God has no control over the voluntary actions of man. Such an assumption is an absurdity in reference to both the Creator and the creature. As far as the future is concerned, such voluntary actions would have no causal relationship to God at all, as there would neither be any decree concerning them, nor could they have been a contingent element of any decree. Then such actions would proceed entirely from man in the exercise of his free will. Indeed, in such instances God would be dependent upon the creature, unable to decree anything concerning man apart from the intervention of man's free will. Consequently, all decrees could only be executed upon the condition that it would please man to cooperate, he being lord over his free will and thus unable to be restricted by anyone but himself. Their view [the Jesuits and Arminians] implies that all that God has decreed is uncertain because man by the exercise of his free will is able to change it.

To be Lord over man's volitional action, it is not sufficient that God have control over the circumstances which can sway the activity of man's will, either causing or not causing certain things to take place, or to be in a given condition. These circumstances must not be contingent upon the exercise of man's free will for then it would be in man's power to dictate the circumstances either verbally or physically relative to other individuals. Apart from such a consideration, it must be recognized that such power and control would only involve the circumstances and situations which would induce man to exercise his free will but would not extend to the will itself. It would remain free and thus, independent from God, maintain control over itself rather than being subject to His control. Even if they allow that both the will and its freedom have their origin in God, they nevertheless maintain that man remains his own master relative to the exercise of his free will. Thus, he is not dependent upon God, nor can be controlled by Him. Such are the absurdities which follow from holding to a view that God has a mediate knowledge of things. Having concluded this, it must also be posited that consistent with this view such divine knowledge is merely related to circumstances which occur to man; this would then have an effect upon his will. This in turn would result in a given event, in response to which God would subsequently establish His decree. Such reasoning changes the very nature of both God and man as it consequently removes the creature from the realm of God's control. Since all of this is nonsensical, we conclude the existence of such mediate knowledge to be an absurdity.

Objection #1: In 1 Samuel 23:11-12 we read that the Lord, in response to David's question, replied that "He [Saul] will come down," and they [the men of Keilah] "will deliver thee up." This was not according to God's decree, although He was cognizant of it by means of His mediate intervention relative to the exercise of man's free will.

Answer: This was not a prediction concerning a future event, but rather a revelation about a current reality which from a human perspective could have resulted in an event which as yet had not occurred. Since God had not decreed this event, however, He consequently knew that it would not occur. David inquires about that which is hidden from him so that he may decide whether to stay or flee. God revealed to him that Saul would come down to Keilah and that the hearts of the men of Keilah were not inclined towards him; therefore, they would determine to deliver David to Saul when he would come down. Saul had already prepared himself accordingly and the hearts of the men of Keilah were already set against him. God revealed this to David, and upon viewing this from a human perspective, he could conclude that it was in his best interest to flee. Since God decreed the ultimate outcome of the event, He also decreed the means which would lead to this outcome. Thus, if one views this text relative to the outcome of events, it follows that God's knowledge concerning the ultimate outcome of events is a result of essential omniscience. It is the result of God's singular and comprehensive knowledge, whereby He is cognizant of every possibility, rather than an imaginary, mediate knowledge by which He would decree in response to the activity of man.

Objection #2: "...and if that had been too little, I would moreover have given unto thee such and such things" (2 Sam. 12:8); "Oh that My people had hearkened unto Me, and Israel had walked in My ways! I should soon have subdued their enemies" (Psa. 81:13-14). God had foreseen how David as well as Israel would conduct themselves, and thus concluded what would or would not occur to them even though He had not decreed it to be such. Consequently, there is such a thing as mediate knowledge.

Answer: It has pleased God to make conditional promises relative to the practice of godliness. He who lives godly will receive them and he who does not will not receive them. God makes the promise in order to incite man to action and man acquiesces and acknowledges it to be his duty. The obedience to such exhortations, however, is dependent upon the gift of divine grace which God either does or does not give according to His decree. David and Israel did not fulfil the necessary conditions, and thus the fulfillment of the promise was withheld from them. God had decreed that David would not receive beyond what had been given him and that He would not deliver Israel from its enemies. By virtue of this decree God knew that they would not receive blessings beyond those which were already theirs. This was according to His decree rather than in response to their behavior. God is cognizant of the result of all conditional promises by virtue of His decree, and not by virtue of man's exercise of his free will.

Objection #3: "And the man of God was wroth with him, and said, Thou shouldest have smitten five or six times; then hadst thou smitten Syria till thou hadst consumed it: whereas now thou shalt smite Syria but thrice" (2 Ki. 13:19). The frequency with which the Syrians would be smitten was dependent upon the frequency with which the earth was smitten. From the one event God concluded the other, which He evidently had not decreed.

Answer: Here is not even the slightest reference to mediate knowledge. What was the relationship between the smiting of the earth and the smiting of the Syrians? God had revealed to Elisha that Joash, the king of Israel, would defeat the Syrians just as often as he would smite the earth with arrows. He smote the earth three times in accordance with divine government, for God had decreed that Joash would defeat the Syrians three times. The prophet, being desirous of the total destruction of the Syrians who were the enemies of God's people, became angry that Joash had not smitten the earth five or six times. This does not suggest that the ultimate outcome was dependent upon the frequency with which the earth would be smitten. The prophet, not being cognizant of the counsel of God, merely had a general revelation that the Syrians would be defeated and that the frequency of these defeats would be revealed by the Lord by means of Joash's smiting of the earth. It was thus his wish that Joash would have smitten the earth more frequently so that the number of Syrian defeats would have exceeded three.

Objection #4: "...if the mighty works,...which were done in you, had been done in Tyre and Sidon, they would have repented long ago..." (Mat. 11:21).

Answer. The manner of speaking here is hyperbolic, which, rather than being conclusive, merely underscores something by way of overstatement, as is true in the following text, "I tell you that, if these should hold their peace, the stones would immediately cry out" (Luke 19:40). It is as if Christ said, "They [the inhabitants of Tyre and Sidon] are not as hardened as you are." This merely conveys that God in His omniscience acknowledged the possibility of their conversion.

Since God's omniscience extends to past, present, and future, and all things are naked and opened unto the eyes of Him with whom we have to do, how the ungodly ought to tremble! For,

(1) God perceives and knows your heart and its spiritual frame. He knows what is concealed in it as well as what can issue forth from it. He knows your thoughts, vain imaginations, and contemplation upon both habitual and spontaneous sins. He is cognizant of the motives of all your actions — whether it is your objective to end in yourself, to get your own way, or to harm your neighbor. He is aware of the hatred and contempt you foster for your neighbor, your wrathful emotions, as well as your envy regarding your neighbor's prosperity. In sum, God truly perceives all that transpires in your heart even though you may neither discern it nor be conscious of it.

(2) God is cognizant of your immoral inclinations, adulterous eyes, licentious words, secret promiscuity, fornication, immoral conduct, as well as all the persons with whom you have engaged in such activity.

(3) God is cognizant of your inequitable behavior, deceptive business practices, trickery whereby you seek to make the belongings of your neighbor your own, dishonest billing practices, idleness, as well as all your other acts of thievery.

(4) God is cognizant of your gossiping, slandering of your neighbor, defamation of his character, and the delight you have in hearing and speaking about these things.

(5) He is cognizant of your pride, ostentatious behavior, promenading in front of the mirror, and how self-satisfied you are.

(6) The Lord is cognizant of your dancing and revelling, your gambling and card-playing.

(7) He is cognizant of your hypocrisy within as well as outside of the realm of religion.

Be aware that,

(1) God records all the aforementioned much more accurately than if someone were to be continually in your presence recording with pen and ink all your thoughts, words, and deeds, along with the location, day, month, and hour when they occurred. As there is a book of remembrance before God's countenance on behalf of His elect (Mal. 3:16), there is likewise a book before the Lord's countenance in which the guilt of the ungodly is recorded. How conscious you ought to be of this!

(2) Be aware that the books will once be opened and you will be judged according to all that is recorded in them (Rev. 20:12). Be assured that the Lord will set all things in order before your eyes (Psa. 50:21).

(3) Consider it as an utmost certainty that God, the righteous Judge of heaven and earth who by no means will clear the guilty and whose judgment is according to truth, will punish you for all your sins (Psa. 7:12-13; 50:21). Not only will He pronounce the curse upon you with which He threatens transgressors of the law and say to you in the last day, "Depart from Me, ye cursed" (Mat. 25:41), but He will also assign you eternally to the lake of fire which burns with sulfur and brimstone if you do not make haste to repent. You are presently not concerned whether God sees you, as long as people do not see you, but how frightful it will be for you when the Lord Jesus shall appear as Judge and will summon you before His judgment seat, examining and reexamining you with His eyes which will be as flames of fire! How dreadful will that day be! "But who may abide the day of His coming? and who shall stand when He appeareth?" (Mal. 3:2); "For, behold, the day cometh, that shall burn as an oven; and all the proud, yea, and all that do wickedly, shall be stubble: and the day that cometh shall burn them up, saith the LORD of hosts, that it shall leave them neither root nor branch" (Mal. 4:1).

Therefore, repent before it is too late. May you presently fear the all-seeing eye of God, so that in that day you will not be terrified before His flaming eyes.

You, however, who take your refuge in the Lord Jesus, choose Him as your Surety, receive Him by faith, find all your hope and comfort in Him, and fear and serve the Lord — how the omniscience of God ought to be to your comfort! For,

(1) He is cognizant of your sincerity relative to Him and your desire to please Him. "For the eyes of the LORD run to and fro throughout the whole earth, to shew Himself strong in the behalf of them whose heart is perfect toward Him" (2 Chr. 16:9); "such as are upright in their way are His delight" (Prov. 11:20); "The LORD knoweth the days of the upright" (Psa. 37:18).

(2) The Lord knows of your religious exercises in secret, prayers, supplications, wrestlings of faith, sighs, weeping, cleaving to Him, reading, meditation, holy intentions, fear of God, and godly walk. He saw the eunuch reading (Acts 8:28-29), and Paul praying (Acts 9:11). "The eyes of the LORD are upon the righteous, and His ears are open unto their cry" (Psa. 34:15); "The LORD is nigh unto all them that call upon Him" (Psa. 145:18).

(3) The Lord knows of your secret strife; of your wrestling against unbelief; of your sorrow over your sins, lack of light, and being afar from God; and of all your spiritual anxieties. "Lord, all my desire is before Thee; and my groaning is not hid from Thee" (Psa. 38:9); "I dwell...with him also that is of a contrite and humble spirit, to revive the spirit of the humble, and to revive the heart of the contrite ones" (Isa. 57:15); "The LORD is nigh unto them that are of a broken heart; and saveth such as be of a contrite spirit" (Psa. 34:18).

(4) The Lord perceives your bodily needs, adversities, poverty, and tribulations. He saw the need of the widow of Zarephath, and provided for her (1 Ki. 17), as well as of another widow (2 Ki. 4). He saw Hagar in her misery (Gen. 16:13) and the tribulation of Israel in Egypt. "And the LORD said, I have surely seen the affliction of My people which are in Egypt, and have heard their cry by reason of their taskmasters; for I know their sorrows" (Exo. 3:7); "Thou tellest my wanderings: put Thou my tears into Thy bottle: are they not in Thy book?" (Psa. 56:8).

(5) The Lord is cognizant of your innocence when people with lies speak evil of you and slander you. May it be to your comfort that, "if our heart condemn us not, then have we confidence toward God" (1 John 3:21); "For our rejoicing is this, the testimony of our conscience" (2 Cor. 1:12). Oh, what strong consolation may believers derive from the omniscience of God, for He does not merely take note of their misery in an external sense, but He beholds them with compassion and is ready to help them in the time of His good pleasure!

If the Lord is omniscient and takes such careful notice of every matter and deed, then this ought to stir us up to engage ourselves as follows:

First, as Ezra, be ashamed, considering that the Lord has perceived all your sinful spiritual frames and has observed all your sinful deeds. "O my God, I am ashamed and blush to lift up my face to Thee" (Ezra 9:6). Be as the publican who stood afar off, smiting upon his breast, and "would not lift up so much as his eyes unto heaven" (Luke 18:13).

Secondly, beware of all arrogance and pride in your heart as you walk before God and man. Thus, seek to walk in all meekness and humility, for the Lord knows how despicable and abominable you are and how you have nothing of which you should be proud. "God resisteth the proud, and giveth grace to the humble" (1 Pet. 5:5).

Thirdly, commit all that you desire or fear into the hands of the Lord. "Thou hast seen it: for Thou beholdest mischief and spite, to requite it with Thy hand" (Psa. 10:14).

Fourthly, repeatedly confess your sins openly and conceal none of them as Adam did, for the Lord is nevertheless cognizant of them. "Thou hast set our iniquities before Thee, our secret sins in the light of Thy countenance" (Psa. 90:8).

Fifthly, fear the Lord and be disturbed when the least sin begins to make its presence felt, for the Lord sees you. How greatly it aggravates your sin if you have committed it in the presence of God! Who would dare to commit adultery in the presence of men? Should anyone then dare to sin before the very eyes of God? Such ought to be considered the height of wickedness. "And they were haughty, and committed abomination before Me: therefore I took them away as I saw good" (Ezek. 16:50); "For though thou wash thee with nitre, and take thee much soap, yet thine iniquity is marked before Me" (Jer. 2:22).

Sixthly, let the impression that God sees you continually accompany you in your walk, and by it be motivated to live in righteousness and humility before His countenance. Such is God's requirement. "... walk before Me, and be thou perfect" (Gen. 17:1); "In all thy ways acknowledge Him, and He shall direct thy paths" (Prov. 3:6); "I have set the LORD always before me" (Psa. 16:8).

The Will of God

The will of God also belongs to the communicable attributes of God. The ability to elect or reject, love or hate, and be pleased or displeased is referred to as the will. This being one of the special perfections to be found in man as a rational creature, it is therefore infinitely true for God. The will of God is the willing God

Himself. There is but one will of God; however, there is a distinction in the objects to which His will relates. Therefore in recognizing this distinction we differentiate between *the will of His decree* and *the will of His command.*

We understand *the will of His decree,* also referred to as *the will of His good pleasure* or *His secret will,* to be God's purpose and good pleasure which He will execute, either by Himself or by the agency of others. "He doeth according to His will in the army of heaven, and among the inhabitants of the earth" (Dan. 4:35); "Having predestinated us...according to the good pleasure of His will...who worketh all things after the counsel of His own will" (Eph. 1:5, 11); "Even so, Father: for so it seemed good in Thy sight" (Mat. 11:26). This good pleasure God executes irresistibly, and thus He always accomplishes His will. "...our God is in the heavens: He hath done whatsoever He hath pleased" (Psa. 115:3); "who hath resisted His will?" (Rom. 9:19). This refers to the ultimate outcome of all things which will be according to God's decree which He either has not revealed at all to man or which He reveals only after a period of time. This will can frequently be perceived only in retrospect, or in special situations by way of prophecy when specific elements of this will are revealed in His Word. Such is true for instance in reference to prophecies as well as the distinctive marks whereby one may conclude his salvation, being assured of this by the veracity of the promises.

The will of God's command is also referred to as His *preceptive will* or His *revealed will.*[5] This will has reference to the regulative principle of life as well as to the laws which God has made known and prescribed to man in order that his walk might be regulated accordingly. Inasmuch as God has decreed that it is His good pleasure to convey His will to man, this will could also be referred to as the will of His decree and good pleasure. As it is primarily descriptive of man's duty, however, it is associated with the will of God's command or His revealed will. Since God is holy, He has pleasure in, delights in, and approves of compliance with His precepts. He is displeased with and abhors deviation from His commandments. God commands obedience but also permits the violation of His commandments to demonstrate His justice in

---

[5] The Dutch reads as follows: "De gebiedende wil wordt ook genoemd de wil des bevels, des gebods." Since the words "bevel" and "gebod," as well as "gebiedende" of which "gebod" is a derivative, are all translated into English by the word "command," the entire phrase was translated by a single reference to the will of God's command.

punishment and His mercy in being gracious. It is God's will to give to His elect His Holy Spirit who removes their heart of stone and causes them to walk and behave according to the commandments of the Lord. Herein God always infallibly and irresistibly accomplishes His purpose. Man, on the contrary, does not always conduct himself in a manner pleasing to God. The duty imposed by God is frequently not observed by man. God's purpose and good pleasure, however, will prosper since He commands that which is pleasing to Him and also because the decree of His good pleasure is accomplished. Thus the secret and the revealed will of God function side by side. "The secret things belong unto the LORD our God: but those things which are revealed belong unto us and to our children for ever, that we may do all the words of this law" (Deu. 29:29). Paul also refers to the will of His command. "...doing the will of God from the heart" (Eph. 6:6); "...that ye may prove what is that good, and acceptable, and perfect, will of God" (Rom. 12:2). This is also stated in Ps. 143:10, where it reads, "Teach me to do Thy will."

In making a distinction in the will of God, we are not suggesting that God has two wills. In God the act of the will is singular. The difference rather relates to the objects towards whom His will is exercised. Much less do we suggest that God has two wills which are incompatible, as if God with His revealed will would desire something and His secret will would be opposed. When we consider the will of God as being either secret or revealed, this distinction pertains to decidedly different matters, some of which are revealed whereas others are not. The secret and revealed will of God neither relate to one and the same matter, nor should they be viewed from the same perspective. Let me illustrate. God commanded Abraham to sacrifice and kill His son Isaac; nevertheless, it was not God's will that Isaac would die. This became evident from the outcome. There is a distinction here between the command and the result. God's command was His revealed or preceptive will, which was the basis for Abraham's behavior. He had to do everything which would contribute to the death of his son, which he also did. The result — that the death of Isaac would not take place by Abraham's activity — was another matter and belonged to the secret will of God's decree which Abraham perceived afterward when the voice of God prevented him. There should therefore be no concern as to what will should govern our behavior, as the Lord's secret will is solely His domain and against it we cannot sin. God will accomplish His good pleasure. Nevertheless, it is expressed in God's revealed will that we are to exercise confidence and subjection towards His secret will. It is His revealed will, however, which must be regulative for our behavior and it is in regard to the latter that we are guilty of sin.

We can define the exercising of the will of God as being either a necessary consequence or as being volitional in nature. This necessity, however, does not imply compulsion, for God freely loves Himself, for "God is love" (1 John 4:8), and "the Father loveth the Son" (John 5:20). By virtue of His immutability God necessarily wills that all which He has decreed shall come to pass. "My counsel shall stand" (Isa. 46:10).

A volitional act is either an act of arbitrary determination or of one's own pleasure whereby one can opt for the one thing as well as its opposite, that is, to do or not do a certain thing. All that God wills He wills by virtue of His own pleasure, also that which He necessarily wills. In God there is a freedom to exercise His pleasure relative to many matters. He had the freedom of will either to create or not create, or to elect or not elect men. If God has decreed something, however, He wills it of necessity because He has decreed it. That which was a matter of sovereign prerogative before, God now wills of necessity, albeit voluntarily and as a matter of course.

The will of God issues forth from the very Being of God and is not caused by anything issuing forth from creatures. No creature can move God to will. All man's goodness cannot move God to will to do him good, for man's goodness rather has its origin in the will of God. If it is God's will to sanctify a person, he will become holy in consequence of this. God does not choose anyone unto salvation *because of* his good works, rather He chooses them *unto* good works.

Arminians and others who propose good works to be the moving cause of man's salvation, election, and reprobation, make the following distinctions relative to the will of God. They speak of an antecedent will and a will of consequence, of an efficacious and impotent will, and of an absolute and conditional will. To them the antecedent will is God's counsel concerning men whereby He, considering man as prior to and apart from his works, has chosen all men unto salvation. In God's will of consequence He takes man's works into consideration, thus choosing believers and those who persevere in good works unto salvation. The aforementioned parties perceive God's impotent will to be similar to His antecedent will. They understand this to relate to God's desire and inclination which neither find expression nor are executed, but are opposed by man and thus rendered impotent. They relate God's efficacious will to His consequent will, this efficacy issuing forth from his faith and good works whereby God is enabled to make him a partaker of salvation. God's absolute will, in their view, is not contingent upon any condition; instead, it considers man as prior to and apart from his works, which, however, is rendered impotent and futile by man. The conditional will of God relates to such blessings which He promises upon condition of faith and obedience, it being dependent upon the exercise of man's free will whether or not he meets these conditions, and thus whether or not he becomes a partaker of that which is promised.

For example, God decrees to save all men irrespective of their works; however, anticipating and presupposing their works, subsequently decrees not to save all men, but only those who believe. By virtue of His antecedent decree God willed to establish Saul in his kingdom; however, by virtue of His consequent decree He determined, in view of Saul's ungodly behavior, not to establish him but to reject him. God willed to save Judas if he believed; however, because of his unbelief He willed to damn him.

These distinctions are human inventions which are contrary to God's Word and replete with contradictions, as all this ascribes foolishness, impotence, and mutability to God. The suggestion that God truly, earnestly, and sincerely decrees to save all men, but subsequently changes His intent, is to maintain that this is the result of God not perceiving previously what He perceives subsequently. If prior cognizance would cause Him to change His decree, His decree could not have been true, earnest, and sincere. Or it suggests that His change of intent is due to His inability to execute His will either because man prevents Him from doing so, or because God's nature is mutable, thus causing Him to change His mind. Neither of the aforesaid can be true concerning God. He is the only wise God (1 Tim. 1:17) and the omnipotent One. "The LORD of hosts hath sworn, saying, Surely as I have thought, so shall it come to pass; and as I have purposed, so shall it stand. . . . For the LORD of hosts hath purposed, and who shall disannul it? and His hand is stretched out, and who shall turn it back?" (Isa. 14:24, 27). He is also the immutable One in whom there is no change nor shadow of turning (James 1:17). He says concerning Himself, "I am the LORD, I change not" (Mal. 3:6); "My counsel shall stand, and I will do all My pleasure" (Isa. 46:10). God is truth, and all that He wills He wills truly, earnestly, and sincerely. He is perfect. Far be it from the Lord to will something and yet be insincere; to will something and then to change it; to decree something and subsequently to be in error in this area, being neither desirous nor able to execute the said decree; and to be desirous while simultaneously not being desirous.

When the Lord states, "...for now would the LORD have established thy kingdom upon Israel for ever" (1 Sam. 13:13), He would have us understand that many of His promises are given conditionally. If a person does not meet these conditions which God certainly knows beforehand, God will consequently not grant that which He has promised. He also has prior knowledge when and to whom He will manifest His grace and enable to meet the conditions. Since Saul was disobedient towards God, it pleased God not to establish Saul in his kingdom. This was something the Lord would have done had he lived a godly life. Thus, there is no reference here to two wills in God, being an antecedent and a consequent will (for God had decreed to reject Saul and to establish David in his place), but rather to the will of God rejecting him due to his sin.

When the Lord Jesus says, "...how often would I have gathered thy children together...and ye would not!" (Mat. 23:37), it is neither suggested that there are two wills in God nor that He has an impotent will. Rather, Christ is here referring to His work which He executed according to His will, and to the opposition of the chief rulers of Jerusalem who were not desirous to enter in, and prevented the people from entering in as well.

When God is said to desire something which does not occur, such as when He states, "O that there were such a heart in them, that they would fear Me,...that it might be well with them, and with their children for ever!" (Deu. 5:29), or, "O that thou hadst hearkened to My commandments! then had thy peace been as a river" (Isa. 48:18), He is speaking in the manner of men. Strictly speaking, such can never be said concerning the omniscient, omnipotent, immutable, and most perfect God. Rather, it indicates God's displeasure toward sin and how He delights in holiness. It indicates that sin is the reason why those blessings are withheld from them — blessings which they, according to His promise, would have received as a reward upon godliness. The promises are made upon condition of obedience which is granted to the elect according to God's immutable purpose. When God says, "Have I any pleasure at all that the wicked should die? saith the Lord God: and not that He should return from His ways, and live?" (Ezek. 18:23), this does not suggest that God's will is impotent. Rather, it indicates that God has no pleasure in the destruction of men, inasmuch as they are His creatures. He has pleasure in the exercise of righteousness and godliness, and in blessing the godly.

Our Conduct and God's Will
Thus we have considered what the will of God is. Now we will

demonstrate how a person ought to behave himself relative to God's will as well as how he ought to make use of it. God's will is the foundation for quietness and peace within the heart in all circumstances. It is the foundation and substance of, and the most powerful motive for, a believer in the practice of true holiness. I am referring to a believer who receives Christ unto reconciliation and by grace commits Himself to the service of the Lord. An unconverted person neither loves the Lord nor delights in His will. Rather, he wishes to be independent and desires that God, and whatever else may be of use, might be subservient to the fulfilling of his own will. Believers, on the contrary, know God and delight in Him and therefore also love the will of God. Since they have but a small beginning of all this, however, they have need to be further instructed. Therefore in your meditations frequently pause to reflect upon, acknowledge, and delight in the will of God, extracting peace and godliness from it.

Let us first consider the will of God's decree. As God is sovereign Lord over all His creatures, His will is therefore also sovereign over all that happens to His creatures and extends to what they do and refrain from doing. Acknowledge then with your whole heart the supreme authority and absolute freedom of God's will. Approve of His will with delight and joy by saying: "Amen, yes Lord, Thy will is sovereign, being the primary, supreme, and only reason why everything must occur. It is Thy prerogative to deal with all Thy creatures, with all men, and with me and my household, according to Thy will. I rejoice in the fact that it is Thy prerogative to do with the army of heaven and among the inhabitants of the earth according to Thy will, and that there is no one who can stay Thy hand or say, 'What doest Thou?' It is Thy free will to make a vessel unto honor or unto dishonor from the same lump of humanity, and to show Thy wrath and power on the vessels of wrath fitted to destruction, as well as the riches of Thy glory on the vessels of mercy which afore have been prepared unto glory (Rom. 9:21-23). Thy will is sovereign to give kingdoms to whomsoever Thou wilt (Dan. 4:17), and to turn the hearts of kings whithersoever Thou wilt (Prov. 21:1). Thou art free and hast absolute power and jurisdiction, on the basis of Thy will, to exalt the one and abase the other, to fill one with joy by giving him the desire of his heart, while overwhelming others with various vicissitudes and sorrows and withholding the desire of their hearts from them. I rejoice in the fact that Thou art not accountable to anyone for the diversity of Thy actions. I rejoice in the fact that Thy will extends to other creatures, and even to me, and that therefore a creature, including myself in all that I encounter, may not end in anything else but Thy will only, finding delight in it. Should Thy will even be contrary to my natural desires, grant that in such circumstances I may persevere by focusing upon Thy will, recognizing it as Thine. May it be my confession, 'Not my, but Thy will be done;' I desire to subject myself, just as I am, to Thy hand, bowing under Thy sovereign will. May Thy will be fully accomplished in me, whether it be according to my wishes or not. In all the turmoil of the world, in stormy winds, in the destruction and sinking of ships, in floods of water upon earth, in the burning of cities, in regional upheavals due to earthquakes, in destructive warfare, in victories and defeats, in the oppression and persecution of Thy church, in the poverty and tribulations of Thy children — yes, in all of this I perceive the accomplishment of Thy will, and therefore I worship, bowing before Thee, and silently confessing, 'Amen, so be it, for this is the Lord's will.'

"With respect to the future, everything will also transpire according to Thy will. All the tumultuous activity of man, all their schemes and intents, will not transpire except it be according to Thy will, as Thou dost govern everything. This I acknowledge, this I desire, and in this I acquiesce. This I desire to do in reference to all things, particularly in reference to myself — not because I feel that Thy will can be opposed, neither because I believe that all occurs due to an unavoidable fate, nor because I believe all things must work for good both for the church as well as for myself, but rather because it is Thy sovereign will. This suffices for me and therefore my confession is, 'Amen, Thy will be fully done!' In regard to the future I shall be without concern; in prosperity and adversity I shall rejoice and be glad.

"If it pleases the Lord to avail Himself of means in the accomplishment of His will to enable me to discern His will that much more clearly in the final outcome, I shall evaluate and also use such means, since it is God's will that I use them, recognizing them to be merely means rather than the cause of things. I shall not depend upon them in such a way as if the final outcome were dependent upon them. Rather, I shall focus upon His will, and in retrospect, when the matter has come to a conclusion, and via the means which have served the accomplishment of Thy purpose, I shall ascend to Thy will by acknowledging that Thou hast accomplished the matter, and thus be satisfied.

"If it would please the Lord in His goodness to use me in the accomplishment of His good pleasure, then I offer myself willingly: 'Here am I; send me' (Isa. 6:8). Use me. For that purpose I am willing to sacrifice myself, my family, and all that belongs to me, as long as Thy will may be fully done by me and through me."

In addition to the acknowledgement of the sovereignty of God's will, the believer has the insight that all which God wishes to accomplish will be to the magnification of His power, justice, and goodness. It will be perceived by angels and men who will rejoice in the revelation of God's perfections and give Him honor and glory, saying, "Thou art worthy, O Lord, to receive glory and honor and power: for Thou hast created all things, and for Thy pleasure they are and were created" (Rev. 4:11). Such is the desire and delight of a believer which causes him to say all the more, "Thy will be done!"

Furthermore, the believer has the promise that all God intends to do and will do, however contradictory His ways may seem, will be for the best advantage of His church, of the elect, and of himself in particular. In spite of all that transpires he beholds the promise, believes it, embraces it, is satisfied with it, and entrusts its accomplishment to the goodness and wisdom of the Lord, saying, "Thy will be done!"

In reference to the will of God's command, the believer acknowledges that all that God wills pertaining to his walk proceeds from the sovereign will of God, a will which has the holiness of God as its foundation. For God cannot command something which would be contrary to His holy character, but rather He commands man in a manner consistent with His holiness. God did not create man in the image of His will, but in the image of His holy character, and has given unto man a law which is consistent with this holy character. As far as we are concerned, however, the law of God is the rule of holiness. We need not ascertain whether something is consistent with the holy character of God in order to establish a basis for obedience. Rather, we ought to ascertain what God has been pleased to command us, and thus we must "prove what is that good, and acceptable, and perfect, will of God" (Rom. 12:2). We are obligated to do everything according to the will of God. "Doing the will of God from the heart" (Eph. 6:6).

Having seen, upon considering His will, how His commandment is congruent with His holy character, this foundation for obedience also inherently obligates us towards God, in whose image we were created and are re-created, to follow Him and to manifest the presence of His image in us. Although our intellect is too limited to comprehend how every commandment is congruent with God's holy and righteous character as expressed in each commandment, the will of God is our regulative principle. If we are cognizant of this, we have a sufficient rule to live by. Even if the commandments of God did not issue forth from His holiness and justice, but merely from His majesty and sovereign prerogative to command — as was true for many special and ceremonial commands which proceeded only from the will and good pleasure of God — all creatures would still be obligated by the will of God. One need not search out whether all that God commands is just, for the will of God validates everything as just and good. God says, "I will," to which the believer responds, "Amen."

(1) Believers so love the will of God's command and consider it so sovereign that they esteem all His precepts to be right (Psa. 119:128). They join Paul in saying, "Wherefore the law is holy, and the commandment holy, and just, and good" (Rom. 7:12). The law of the Lord, being His will, is their joy, their delight, and the object of their love. "O how love I Thy law! it is my meditation all the day" (Psa. 119:97).

(2) A believer, loving that law, does not merely acquiesce in the will of God's command, but the soul offers himself to the Lord to do His will, willingly submitting himself to the Lord's will. God's will is his will and his will is swallowed up in God's will.

(3) The soul is ready and prepared to walk in the pathway of the Lord's commandments. He delights in the law of God according to the inner man, confessing with his whole heart, "I delight to do Thy will, O my God: yea, Thy law is within my heart" (Psa. 40:8).

(4) In his entire walk he focuses upon the will of God in order to regulate everything according to this will.

(5) The will of God is not merely a regulative principle. It is simultaneously an urgent motive, prompting the soul to be diligent, sincere, and persevering in doing God's pleasure.

(6) Even though there is great reward in the keeping of God's commandments and one may and must be quickened by it to a godly walk, the will of God is nevertheless the loftiest, most influential, and endearing object of affection. Blessed is he who relates to the will of God in such a manner, submitting himself to it in his walk both in prosperity and adversity.

Several attributes of God are considered in relationship to the will of God, such as holiness, goodness, grace, love, mercy, long-suffering, and justice.

The Holiness of God

Holiness is the pure essence of the character of God. Consequently, it relates to the brightness of all His perfections, for which reason He is called a "light, and in Him is no darkness at all" (1 John 1:5). The Lord continually reveals Himself as holy, in order that the heart of man may continually be filled with deep awe and reverence. "Who is like unto Thee, O LORD . . . glorious in holiness, fearful in praises?" (Exo. 15:11). "Let them praise Thy great and terrible Name; for it is holy. Exalt ye the LORD our God, and worship at His footstool; for He is holy. Exalt the LORD our God, and worship at His holy hill; for the LORD our God is holy" (Psa. 99:3, 5, 9); "Holy is His Name" (Luke 1:49).

The Lord is not merely called holy but is holiness itself. "Give thanks at the remembrance of His holiness" (Psa. 97:12); "Once have I sworn by my holiness" (Psa. 89:35); "Glory ye in His holy Name" (Psa. 105:3).

From the holy character of God proceeds the holiness of all His deeds. "He is the Rock, His work is perfect: for all His ways are judgment: a God of truth and without iniquity, just and right is He" (Deu. 32:4).

From His holy character proceeds His hatred and contempt for sin. "Thou art of purer eyes than to behold evil" (Hab. 1:13); "For Thou art not a God that hath pleasure in wickedness: Thou hatest all workers of iniquity" (Psa. 5:4-5).

From His holy character proceeds His delight in holiness. "For in these things I delight, saith the LORD" (Jer. 9:24); "But such as are upright in their way are His delight" (Prov. 11:20).

The Goodness of God

Goodness is the very opposite of harshness, cruelty, gruffness, severity, mercilessness — all of which are far removed from God. How unbecoming it is to have such thoughts about God! Such sinful emotions are found in man. The goodness of God, on the contrary, is the loveliness, benign character, sweetness, friendliness, kindness, and generosity of God. Goodness is the very essence of God's Being, even if there were no creature to whom this could be manifested. "The good LORD pardon every one" (2 Chr. 30:18); "Good and upright is the LORD: therefore will He teach sinners in the way" (Psa. 25:8); "There is none good but one, that is, God" (Mat. 19:17).

From this goodness issues forth lovingkindness and an inclination to bless His creatures. This is to the astonishment of all who take note of this, which explains why David exclaims twenty-six times in Ps. 136, "For His mercy[6] endureth for ever." In the following texts we read likewise. "Also unto Thee, O Lord, belongeth mercy" (Psa. 62:12); "All the paths of the LORD are

---

[6] The Statenvertaling uses "goedheid," which means "goodness."

mercy" (Psa. 25:10). From goodness and benevolence issues forth
the doing of that which is good. "Thou art good, and doest good"
(Psa. 119:68); "Rejoice the soul of Thy servant: and attend unto the
voice of my supplications. For Thou Lord, art good, and ready to
forgive; and plenteous in mercy unto all them that call upon Thee"
(Psa. 86:4, 6, 5).

This goodness is of a *general* nature in reference to all God's
creatures, since they are His creatures. "The LORD is good to all:
and His tender mercies are over all His works" (Psa. 145:9); "The
earth is full of the goodness of the LORD" (Psa. 33:5); "For He
maketh His sun to rise on the evil and on the good, and sendeth
rain on the just and on the unjust" (Mat. 5:45). The goodness
which is of a *special* or particular nature as it relates to God's
children is thus expressed: "Truly God is good to Israel, even to
such as are of a clean heart" (Psa. 73:1); "The LORD is good unto
them that wait for Him, to the soul that seeketh Him" (Lam. 3:25).

This goodness of God is the reason why a believer, even after
many backslidings, is motivated by renewal to return unto the
Lord. "The children of Israel shall return...and shall fear the LORD
and His goodness" (Hosea 3:5); "But I have trusted in Thy mercy"
(Psa. 13:5). This is why they call the Lord "the God of my mercy"
(Psa. 59:10, 17). In this goodness they rejoice and this goodness
they magnify. "I will sing of the mercies of the LORD for ever"
(Psa. 89:1); "Praise ye the LORD. O give thanks unto the LORD;
for He is good: for His mercy endureth for ever" (Psa. 106:1).

The Love of God

Love is an essential attribute of God by which the Lord delights
Himself in that which is good, it being well-pleasing to Him, and
uniting Himself to it consistent with the nature of the object of His
love. The love of God by definition is the loving God Himself, for
which reason John states that "God is love" (1 John 4:8). When we
view the love of God relative to its objects, however, several distinctions need to be made. We call this love *natural* when it refers to the
manner in which God delights in Himself as the supreme manifestation of goodness. "For the Father loveth the Son" (John 5:20). We
call this love *volitional* when it refers to the manner in which God
delights in His creatures. And thus this love is either the love of
benevolence or the love of His delight.

The love of His benevolence is either *general* as it relates to the
manner in which God delights in, desires to bless, maintains, and
governs all His creatures by virtue of the fact that they are His
creatures (Psa. 145:9), or it is *special*. This special love refers to

God's eternal designation of the elect to be the objects of His special love and benevolence. This finds expression in the following texts, "For God so loved the world, that He gave His only begotten Son, that whosoever believeth in Him should not perish, but have everlasting life" (John 3:16); "As Christ also loved the church, and gave Himself for it" (Eph. 5:25).

The love of God's delight has the elect as its object as they are viewed in Christ, being clothed with His satisfaction and holiness perfect and complete in Him (Col. 2:10); "According as he hath chosen us in Him ... according to the good pleasure of His will ... wherein He hath made us accepted in the Beloved" (Eph. 1:4-6). This also applies to the believer in his present state, having the principle of holiness within him. "For the Father Himself loveth you, because ye have loved Me, and have believed that I came out from God" (John 16:27).

This love of benevolence precedes all good works of man, whereas the love of God's delight concerns itself with men who presently either are partakers of or perform that which is good.

The Grace of God

Grace can be defined as being a perfection of God's character which has no relationship to an object — that is, who God was and would be even if there were no creature; namely, a compassionate God who would be capable of manifesting His benevolence to creatures apart from any merit. Grace can also be considered relative to creatures in the manifestation of undeserved benevolence. Concerning the grace of God we distinguish between *grace as a gracious gift*, or *grace as a gracious receipt*.

Gratia gratis dans (grace as a gracious gift) relates to God's perfection as being the fountain from which all His benefits issue forth. "For unto you it is given[7] in the behalf of Christ, not only to believe on Him, but also to suffer for His sake" (Phil. 1:29)! "There is a remnant according to the election of grace. And if by grace, then it is no more of works" (Rom. 11:5-6); "Being justified freely by His grace through the redemption that is in Christ Jesus" (Rom. 3:24).

Gratia gratis data (grace as a gracious receipt), relates to the received benefits themselves. This is true for common grace of which unconverted persons are the recipients to which Jude referred, "Ungodly men, turning the grace of our God into lasciviousness" (Jude 4). This is also true for saving grace which is frequently

---

[7] The Statenvertaling reads as follows, "U is uit genade gegeven," that is, for unto you it is graciously given.

referred to as the *gifts of grace* (cf. Rom. 5:15-16; 6:23; 11:29). The following texts speak of this: "Through the grace given unto me" (Rom. 12:3); "That ye might have a second benefit" (2 Cor. 1:15);[8] "For this is thankworthy, if a man for conscience toward God endure grief, suffering wrongfully" (1 Pet. 2:19).[9] Both perspectives of grace, that is, grace as a gracious gift and grace as a gracious receipt, are often conjoined in the Pauline benedictions. "Grace to you and peace from God our Father" (Rom. 1:7); "The grace of our Lord Jesus Christ be with you" (1 Cor. 16:23).

The Mercy of God

In man mercy is related to grief, sorrow, and pity. Such, however, is not the case with respect to God. Mercy, being the merciful God Himself, is an essential attribute whereby God is inclined to come to the aid of a creature in his misery. Even though a miserable one is the object of the manifestation of divine mercy, misery is nevertheless not the motivating cause of God's mercy, but it issues forth from the goodness of God, which in its manifestation towards a miserable one is denominated as mercy. When God revealed Himself to Moses, He called Himself merciful (Exo. 34:6). The Lord Jesus refers to this mercy as an example worthy of imitation. "Be ye therefore merciful, as your Father also is merciful" (Luke 6:36).

Divine mercy is either general or special in nature. The *general* manifestation of mercy extends to all the works of God, unconverted persons inclusive. "His tender mercies are over all His works" (Psa. 145:9). The Lord Jesus showed compassion towards all sorts of miserable persons (Mat. 14:14; Mark 6:34). The *special* manifestation of mercy extends to the elect who therefore are called *vessels of mercy* (Rom. 9:23). Since the manifestation of this mercy is purely volitional in nature — "I will have mercy on whom I will have mercy" (Rom. 9:15) — it is also inexpressibly great. This is not only because it extends from generation to generation (Luke 1:50), but also because of its intensity and magnitude. It therefore is emphatically referred to as great mercy: "According to His abundant mercy hath begotten us again unto a lively hope" (1 Pet. 1:3). It is further stated that God is rich in mercy, "But God, who is rich in mercy" (Eph. 2:4). God is spoken of as a God of multiple mercies. "The Father of mercies, and the God of all comfort" (2 Cor. 1:3). God's mercy is referred to as being tender. "Through the tender mercy

---

[8] The Statenvertaling reads as follows, "Opdat gij ene tweede genade zoudt hebben," that is, that ye might have a second grace.

[9] The Statenvertaling reads as follows: "Dat is genade . . . ," that is, for this is grace.

of our God; whereby the Dayspring from on high hath visited us"
(Luke 1:78).

The Long-suffering of God

This is an essential attribute of God whereby He refrains Himself from initially pouring out His full wrath upon the sinner, thus
postponing his punishment — meanwhile bestowing benefits upon
him. It is God's character to be long-suffering (Exo. 34:6). The Lord
is long-suffering towards sinners in a general sense. "Or despisest
thou the riches of His goodness and forbearance and longsuffering;
not knowing that the goodness of God leadeth thee to repentance?"
(Rom. 2:4). "What if God...endured with much long-suffering the
vessels of wrath fitted to destruction?" (Rom. 9:22).

God is long-suffering towards the elect prior to their conversion.
"The Lord...is long-suffering to us-ward, not willing that any should
perish, but that all should come to repentance" (2 Pet. 3:9); "To
declare His righteousness for the remission of sins that are past,
through the forbearance of God" (Rom. 3:25).

God is long-suffering towards His children, as considered in
their regenerate state, by not always chastising them for their sins
(it being understood that the elect are not punished in the definitive
sense of the word), but rather overlooking their failures and having
much patience with them. "I will spare them, as a man spareth his
own son that serveth him" (Mal. 3:17); "Like as a father pitieth his
children, so the LORD pitieth them that fear Him" (Psa. 103:13).

Such is the character of God, as we have extensively demonstrated to you. His character is holy, good, loving, gracious, merciful, and long-suffering.

You who are convinced of your miserable condition and are
desirous to be reconciled with God, be not discouraged from
coming to God. You need not be discouraged if your desire is to
approach unto Him in truth, with sincerity, and in the right way,
that is, only through Christ. Simply come: the Lord is not merciless, cruel, or pitiless. On the contrary, He is as He declares Himself
to be in His Name: "The LORD, the LORD God, merciful and
gracious, long-suffering, and abundant in goodness and truth"
(Exo. 34:6)! Just as the father of the prodigal son, the Lord runs to
meet all who turn to Him from afar. He calls you, manifests
Himself to you, and promises not to cast anyone out that comes to
Him. Do not let fear restrain you from doing so, but come boldly
to the Lord and His goodness.

And believers, how you do injustice towards the Lord when you
view Him as cruel, merciless, pitiless, and always angry, because He

neither immediately delivers you from your threatening and pressing circumstances, nor grants you your desires, nor answers your prayers. You dishonor God with such thoughts. You imagine things about God that are unbecoming of Him. Humble yourself for entertaining such sinful and God-dishonoring conceptions. Refrain yourself from and be fearful of such thoughts. How detrimental it is to you when you dwell upon such thoughts. It will prevent you from praying believingly. You will rob yourself of a quiet confidence in God, frustrate the expression of your love towards God, and bring upon yourself darkness, restlessness, the hiding of God's countenance, and a vulnerability towards sin.

Please conduct yourself no longer thus, but condition yourself to view God always in such a fashion as we have described Him to be on the basis of His Word. Acknowledge Him to be such and magnify Him in these perfections. If you have sinned or are in the way of affliction, believe firmly and seek to maintain a lively impression that God's character is truly of such a nature. Therefore frequently humble yourself before Him as a child and be at liberty to go to God believing Him to be such, not only as far as His character is concerned but also that He is such a God in regard to you. Rejoice in this and without fear commit both yourself and your case to Him. You will experience that it will be to your comfort and joy as well as promote intimate communion with Him, strengthen your faith, and result in progress in the way of sanctification. Then the holiness of God will not discourage you but generate a childlike reverence in you; and it will become your delight to be holy, since He is holy.

The Righteousness or Justice of God

The righteousness of God can be considered either in and of itself as referring to the justness, perfection, and holiness of the character of God; or in view of its manifestation toward the creature. As such the righteousness or justice of God consists in giving each his worthy due, either by punishment or reward.

Justice is executed either by way of mutual exchange or in a retributive fashion. Among men, the execution of *justice by way of mutual exchange* is practiced, as for instance when monetary remuneration is made according to an agreement. Such, however, is not true with regard to God, since none of our works, however perfect they may be, are by nature meritorious before God. Since none of our works are perfect, there can be no proportionate relationship between work and remuneration. God, always being independent, is not indebted to anyone. Man cannot take that which is his and bring it before God, for the good he performs originates in God. Since it is man's natural obligation to perform good works, he, having done so, can make no claims because of it. "So likewise ye, when ye shall have done all those things which are commanded you, say, We are unprofitable servants: we have done that which was our duty to do" (Luke 17:10).

Retributive justice must be ascribed to God, both in reference to reward as well as punishment. Whatever God does is just. "He is the Rock, His work is perfect: for all His ways are judgment: a God of truth and without iniquity, just and right is He" (Deu. 32:4). God is just when He acts according to either His promises or His threatenings. "That Thou mightest be justified when Thou speakest, and be clear when Thou judgest" (Psa. 51:4). God is just when He delivers and saves a person. "But now the righteousness of God without the law is manifested, being witnessed by the law and the prophets: even the righteousness of God which is by faith of Jesus Christ" (Rom. 3:21-22). God is just in damning sinners. "...the day of wrath and revelation of the righteous judgment of God; who will render to every man according to His deeds" (Rom. 2:5-6); "Righteous art Thou, O LORD, and upright are Thy judgments" (Psa. 119:137). The meting out of punishment is generally referred to as *the avenging justice of God*.

Question: In reference to the avenging justice of God, does God punish sin because it pleases Him, since He could refrain from doing so if He so desired, or is the punishment of sin a necessary consequence of the righteous character of God, so that He cannot but punish sin, that is, He cannot let sin remain unpunished?

Answer: The question is not whether God has the right and the authority to mete out punishment. Man is naturally cognizant of the fact that sin deserves punishment. The heathen know "that they which commit such things are worthy of death" (Rom. 1:32). Neither is it a question of whether God punishes sin by constraint or whether the avenging justice of God is so natural to Him that, just as fire always burns, there is an immediate response in meting out punishment upon the commission of each sin. God, doing everything independently, also does that which is natural to Him to the superlative degree. The freeness with which God exercises His will should not be construed to mean that it is a matter of indifference to Him whether or not He punishes sin. Rather, it should be viewed as a necessary consequence. Thus, God by virtue of His perfect, holy, and righteous character is inclined as the only wise God to punish sin at a time and in a manner suitable to Him. However, the question at hand is: "Is righteousness or punishment as an exercise of justice such that punishment cannot be avoided, and whether as God He cannot acquit without punishing sin, since such an act would be unjust and contrary to His holy and just character?" Our answer is "yes," which is confirmed by Scripture. "Shall not the Judge of all the earth do right?" (Gen. 18:25). God is a righteous Judge (Psa. 7:9); "Thou hatest all workers of iniquity. The LORD will abhor the bloody and deceitful man" (Psa. 5:5-6); "The LORD revengeth; the LORD revengeth, and is furious; the LORD will take vengeance on His adversaries, and He reserveth wrath for His enemies. The LORD is slow to anger, and great in power, and will not at all acquit the wicked" (Nahum 1:2-3). We will deal comprehensively with this subject in Chapter 17 which deals with the necessity of satisfaction.

Beware, oh sinner, whoever you are, for God is just! Do not imagine that you will be able to satisfy God by praying, "O God, be merciful to me a sinner," or by doing your utmost to refrain from evil and to practice virtue. To imagine such is to be on the broad way to eternal destruction, and causes millions, who live under the ministry of the gospel, to perish. If you could be delivered from this foolish imagination, there would still be hope for you. As long as you foster such an imagination, however, you are in a hopeless condition. Please consider that there can be no hope of grace and salvation without satisfaction of the justice of God, that is, by the enduring of punishment.

You have heard that God is gracious, which is true. You are guilty, however, of distorting the essential meaning of the grace of God by interpreting it to refer to remission of sin and absolution from punishment apart from satisfaction. Such, however, is not grace. There is no contradiction in God. The justice of God, which cannot be compromised to the least degree, of necessity demands the punishment of the sinner. God cannot deny Himself, and thus grace does not negate His justice. Grace is not incompatible with justice, but confirms it. This is the grace of God so highly exalted in His Word — that God, without finding anything in man, yes, contrary to his desert, gave His Son as a Surety. He transferred the sins of the elect from their account to His and by bearing the punishment justly due upon their sin, satisfied the justice of God on their behalf. This is grace, namely, that God offers Jesus as Surety in the gospel. It is grace when God grants faith to a sinner to receive Jesus and to entrust his soul to Jesus. It is grace when God converts a sinner, granting him spiritual life. It is grace when God permits a sinner to sensibly experience His favor. It is grace when God sanctifies a sinner, leading him in the way of holiness to salvation.

Please note how much the grace of God differs from your conception of grace. Put your erroneous conception aside and cease from trying to make all things well in the way of prayer and self-reformation. Perhaps you reply, "Then all my hope would be gone, and I would be given over to despair." My response is, "What can it profit you to flatter yourself a little with a false hope and thus perish forever? Instead, give up all hope and despair of yourself; believe and acknowledge the righteousness of God who cannot forgive sin apart from satisfaction and the bearing of punishment. Keep your sins and the justice of God clearly in view, as well as your inability to satisfy this justice. Freely fear and tremble, but do not remain in such a condition nor end in it. Allow the terror of the Lord to move you to faith. Seek salvation in a way whereby God's justice is satisfied. Therefore, flee to the Lord Jesus as Surety, receiving Him to your justification and sanctification. That is the only way by which you can be saved.

And believers, may you who know this way — the way by which you go to God — increasingly penetrate the truth of God's justice until you may perceive its purity, glory, and preciousness. Magnify God in His justice, and rejoice in the fact that God is just. Love His righteousness as you love His goodness and mercy, especially in that this righteousness has been satisfied on your behalf. Give thanks to God that the Lord leads you and all His elect along such a holy way unto salvation. Do not consider the justice of God to be against you, but as being for you — to give you salvation and justly punish your enemies.

The Power of God

In the foregoing we divided the communicable attributes of God into three main categories: intellect, will, and power. Having considered the first two, we shall now consider the attribute of power. The word *power* is ambiguous in our language, as it also refers to dominion, supremacy, and authority. Whenever it is attributed to God it refers to His omnipotence.

Power in its primary meaning is referred to in Greek as ἐξουσία *(exousia)*, and in Latin as *potestas*. Its meaning is to have a just claim upon someone, authority, and supreme jurisdiction. One can consider the power of God as an essential attribute, or use it in reference to the dispensation of grace. God is Lord and Master over all His creatures and has unrestricted, absolute power and jurisdiction over them. This necessarily follows from the fact that He is God and that the creature is dependent upon Him for existence and activity. In the exercise of this power He is not accountable to anyone; no one may demand a reason from Him by asking, "What doest Thou? Is this just?" We may often not be able to comprehend why God acts in a particular way; it should be sufficient for us that God is sovereign. This truth we are obligated to embrace. Consider the following texts: "Who will say unto Him, What doest Thou?" (Job 9:12). "For He giveth not account of any of His matters" (Job 33:13).

Nebuchadnezzar expresses this forcefully when he states, "He doeth according to His will in the army of heaven, and among the inhabitants of the earth: and none can stay His hand, or say unto Him, What doest Thou?" (Dan. 4:35). Also consider the following passages. "Is it not lawful for Me to do what I will with mine own?" (Mat. 20:15); "Nay but, O man, who art thou that repliest against God? Shall the thing formed say to him that formed it, Why hast thou made me thus? Hath not the potter power over the clay, of the same lump to make one vessel unto honour, and another unto dishonour?" (Rom. 9:20-21).

The Father has delegated His economical or executive power to the Mediator, Jesus Christ. Besides having given Him the church and all the elect in order to bring them unto salvation, He has also subjected all creatures unto Him so that He might use them to promote the salvation of the elect. This delegation of power, however, is not to the exclusion of the Father, so that the Father by virtue of this delegation would be deprived of power, for the Father executes all things by means of the Son. This power is referred to when it is stated, "All power is given unto Me in heaven and in earth" (Mat. 28:18).

The power of God in its second meaning, δύναμις *(dunamis)* in Greek, and *potentia* in Latin, refers to the power and strength of God whereby He is able to execute and accomplish everything which is in agreement with His character and His truth — also to create whatever is conceivable and to do whatever He wishes to do. From stones He is able to raise up children unto Abraham (Mat. 3:9), that is, to create human beings from a lump of clay as He did in the beginning, and make such human beings partakers of both the faith and life of Abraham. God could even create thousands of worlds. In a word, God's power is unlimited. One could imagine the creation of many things which would be contrary to the nature and truth of God. One could speculate about imaginary things which bear no resemblance to a creature. To relate this to the omnipotence of God and to ask whether God would be able to perform such things, is to entertain thoughts about God which are void of reverence and godly fear. Whatever is contradictory to the nature and truth of God, as well as contrary to the essential nature of a creature, is no reflection upon the power of God. Far be it from us to attribute this to the omnipotent and holy God. "Far be it from God, that He should do wickedness; and from the Almighty, that He should commit iniquity" (Job 34:10).

God can neither deny Himself (2 Tim. 2:13), nor can He lie or deceive (Titus 1:2). "It was impossible for God to lie" (Heb. 6:18). Even though God has eternally been capable of creating a world, it does not follow that the world could have existed eternally. "Yes" and "no" are at all times opposites and cannot be simultaneous realities. One and the same body, one and the same man, cannot be simultaneously present at many places which are far removed from each other. These and a thousandfold more things do not appertain to omnipotence. Nevertheless, we maintain that God by His omnipotence is able to accomplish whatever He will even beyond what He has willed, as well as whatever He would will. His arm is not shortened and therefore He is called the Almighty. "I am the Almighty God" (Gen. 17:1); "When the Almighty was yet with me" (Job 29:5); "...saith the Lord Almighty" (2 Cor. 6:18).

The Lord has no need of any objects, means, or anything which creatures require in order to function. "God...calleth those things which be not as though they were" (Rom. 4:17); "For He spake and it was done; He commanded, and it stood fast" (Psa. 33:9); "There is nothing too hard for Thee" (Jer. 32:17); "For with God nothing shall be impossible" (Luke 1:37). Whatever God wills, He shall accomplish irresistibly. "Our God is in the heavens: He hath done whatsoever He hath pleased" (Psa. 115:3); "His hand is stretched out, and who shall turn it back?" (Isa. 14:27).

Therefore, you who are ungodly should fear, for you have such an omnipotent God against you! You cannot prevail against Him. There is neither a hiding place or refuge, nor is there anyone who will be able to offer you protection against Him and deliver you out of His hand. "It is a fearful thing to fall into the hands of the living God" (Heb. 10:31). "Howl ye; for the day of the LORD is at hand; it shall come as a destruction from the Almighty" (Isa. 13:6).

And you, children of God, let the omnipotence of God encourage your hearts. If God is for you, who will be against you? Do you have any corporal needs and know not how to meet them? Even if there are no means available, God has the answer. He requires no means, and if the Lord desires to avail Himself of means, He will bring them about and make them available to you. Insignificant means are sufficient for Him for He is the Almighty One. He creates light out of darkness in order that the movement of His hand may be observed that much more clearly. In all your perplexities confess with Abraham, "The LORD shall provide." Does your soul stand in need of light, comfort, a change of heart, and strength against sin? Even if you see no solution, He is able to give you the desire of your heart with one word. Seek to maintain a lively perception of the omnipotence of God. This will strengthen you in all things, causing you to take refuge with Him and be free from concern, fear, and terror. "He that dwelleth in the secret place of the most High shall abide under the shadow of the Almighty" (Psa. 91:1).

The Duty of the Christian to Reflect upon the Attributes of God

Thus we have sought to present to you both the Being and the perfections of God. Such a God is our God. He is the object of our religion. Consequently, it is the duty of all who practice religion to reflect continually upon God as He is, to live in contemplation of Him, and to walk before His countenance, for it is this which the Lord requires from those that are His. "I am the Almighty God; walk before Me, and be thou perfect" (Gen. 17:1); "In all thy ways acknowledge Him, and He shall direct thy paths" (Prov. 3:6); "He hath shewed thee, O man, what is good; and what doth the LORD require of thee, but to do justly, and to love mercy, and to walk humbly with thy God?" (Mic. 6:8). "Acquaint now thyself with Him, and be at peace" (Job 22:21).

Such has been the continual practice of the saints who are held before us in Scripture as examples to be emulated. Consider for example Enoch, Noah, Moses, David, and Asaph. "And Enoch walked with God" (Gen. 5:24); "Noah walked with God" (Gen. 6:9); "For he (Moses) endured, as seeing Him who is invisible" (Heb. 11:27); "I (David) have set the LORD always before me" (Psa. 16:8); "When I awake I am still with Thee" (Psa. 139:18); "Nevertheless I am continually with Thee; but it is good for me to draw near to God" (Psa. 73:23, 28).

The most significant promise God makes to His people is when He promises that they will walk with Him, and He will walk with them. "They shall walk, O LORD, in the light of Thy countenance" (Psa. 89:15); "and We will come unto him, and make Our abode with him" (John 14:23); "I will dwell in them, and walk in them; and I will be their God, and they shall be My people" (2 Cor. 6:16).

This walking with God occurs,

(1) when the heart with holy determination separates and withdraws itself from all that is visible and tangible. "While we look not at the things which are seen" (2 Cor. 4:18); "Wherefore come out from among them, and be ye separate" (2 Cor. 6:17);

(2) in quietly turning toward God, while preparing oneself to be

illuminated by His wondrous light. "In the morning will I direct my prayer unto Thee, and will look up" (Psa. 5:3); "Truly my soul waiteth upon God" (Psa. 62:1);

(3) when we focus upon the attributes of God that we might gain an increasingly deeper understanding of them and perceive their influence in the heart. "Therefore I will look unto the LORD" (Mic. 7:7); "They looked unto Him, and were lightened" (Psa. 34:5). Moses endured as seeing Him who is invisible (Heb. 11:27);

(4) when we engage in all humility in intimate communion with God. One time this will consist in silently presenting ourselves before God, while at another time there will be a reverent bowing before Him in worship. Then there will be times of holy dialogue, prayer, humble submission, trusting, rejoicing and delighting in the Lord, as well as a willing surrender to the service of the Lord in order to live in a manner pleasing to Him. This is that sublime life; this is what constitutes a walking with God. It is the hidden way in which nothing but holiness and delight are experienced.

In order to motivate you to become enamored[10] with such a life, and to encourage you to stir yourself up to commence with such a walk and to persevere in it, you should be aware that walking with God engenders self-abasement and a spiritual frame which is pleasing to the Lord and desirable for yourself. It also engenders steadfast and abundant comfort, true joy and peace which pass all understanding, and genuine sanctification.

For when the soul is privileged to reflect upon God as his God in Jesus Christ, such a soul will be conscious of the *righteousness* of God. He will magnify and delight in this righteousness no less than in God's goodness and love. He will perceive in this attribute only light, purity, and extraordinary glory. Such a soul rejoices the more in this righteousness, since by virtue of the merits of Christ it is no longer against him unto destruction, but rather for his help and salvation, and to the damnation of the ungodly.

The soul beholding God's *goodness* and *all-sufficiency*, and tasting the power of these is so fully satisfied with this that all the goodness of the creature vanishes. It no longer has any appeal to him. He can do without it and confesses with Asaph, "Whom have I in heaven but Thee? and there is none upon earth that I desire beside Thee....but God is the strength of my heart, and my portion for ever" (Psa. 73:25-26).

The soul, irradiated by the *love* of God and ignited with reciprocal love, loses itself in this love and is silent in response to it. He

---

[10] à Brakel uses "verlieven," which most literally would be translated as "to fall in love."

stands in amazement of this love, and finds so much in it that all creature-love loses its appeal. He no longer perceives any desirability in the creature except where he perceives something of God in it. Therefore he no longer covets the love of others and is readily weaned from all that appears to be desirable upon earth.

Viewing the *holiness* of God, the soul, not able to endure its brilliant splendor, covers her countenance, exclaiming with the angels, "Holy, holy, holy is the Lord of hosts!" He thus becomes enamored with this holiness and desires to be holy as He is holy who has called him.

The soul perceives the *sovereignty* of the holy *will* of God, exalting, esteeming, and approving it as such. He rejoices in the full accomplishment of this will relative to all creatures as well as himself. He submits himself to this will which sweetens and makes all things well. He yields his own will to be swallowed up in the will of God. The Lord's will is his will both in what he endures and does, and he is thus ready to perform all that is according to God's will and is pleasing to Him.

Contemplating the *magnificence* and *glory* of God, the dignity and glory of all creatures vanish and are in comparison considered to be lowly, insignificant, and contemptible. He neither desires the splendor and glory of the world for himself, nor is he intimidated by the dignity of others who might cause him to act contrary to the will of His God. In that aspect he deems the dignified and honorable equal to the most insignificant and contemptible even though he will fully subject himself to all whom God has placed over him because God wills it. Rather, he bows in all humility before God the most High, rendering Him honor and glory. His heart and tongue are prepared and ready to speak of the honor and glory of His majesty.

Viewing the *omnipotence* of God in itself as well as in its manifestation in all creatures, the power of creatures which either is exercised for or against him vanishes. He will neither rely upon nor fear it, but dwelling in the secret place of the most High he abides under the shadow of the Almighty. In that shadow he rejoices over all his enemies, enjoys safety without fear, and is confident.

In contemplating the multifacetted and unsearchable *wisdom* of God as it is manifested in all His works both in the realm of nature and of grace, he loses his own wisdom, considering it to be but foolishness, as well as all esteem for the wisdom of friend and enemy. Such a soul is quiet and satisfied with the all-wise government of God, be it in relation to the whole world, the church, his country of residence, times of peace and war, or its effect upon him and his loved ones. He yields in everything to the wisdom of God who knows both time and manner, even though the soul has no prior realization or perception thereof.

The soul, viewing the infallible *truth* and *faithfulness* of God, refuses to rely upon human promises. They neither can cause him to rejoice nor can human threatenings terrify him, for he is aware of human mutability. However, He knows the Lord to be a God of truth who keepeth truth forever. He knows the promises and believes them, being so convinced of their certainty as if they were already fulfilled. He therefore rests in them and has a joyful hope in them.

Behold, is this not a joyful life — a heaven upon earth — to have such a God as your God who promotes both your welfare and your salvation? Can there be sorrow in such a soul? Does not He who has a God as the God of joy and gladness have every reason to experience immediate comfort? Does not such a walk with God cause the soul to manifest utmost meekness and humility, being cognizant of his own insignificance? This engenders in the soul a circumspect and un-wavering spiritual frame, a quiet and humble submission in all things, and a fearless valor and courage in the performance of his duties, even when the Lord calls to a duty which is extraordinary in nature. There is a delighting in that which he may have done for the Lord, submissively leaving the outcome to be determined by His government. Such a spiritual frame engenders genuine holi-ness. "But we all, with open face beholding as in a glass the glory of the Lord, are changed into the same image from glory to glory, even as by the Spirit of the Lord" (2 Cor. 3:18).

All virtue which does not issue forth from such a representation and contemplation of God in Christ is of little value for it lacks true essence. A view of God, as outlined above, elevates the soul above all creature activity and unites him with God and His will, which teaches him his duty as well as the manner in which he is to perform it. Such a view of God will bring forth the most effective and purest motives to stir up the soul. In this view of God the soul may find all sweetness and peace — indeed, it brings heaven in the soul and the soul in heaven. It prevents sinful lusts from issuing forth; and if they emerge, it enables the soul to subdue them. This is the fear of God, love to God, submission to God, and obedience to God, which causes the soul to radiate holiness as the counte-nance of Moses was radiant when for forty days he had commun-ion with God upon the mountain. "Blessed is the man whom Thou choosest, and causest to approach unto Thee, that He may dwell in Thy courts: we shall be satisfied with the goodness of Thy house, even of Thy holy temple" (Psa. 65:4). Oh, blessed eternity when we shall always be with the Lord, shall see Him face to face, and know Him as we are known! (1 Cor. 13:12).

Directions for Reflecting upon the Attributes of God

In order to be properly engaged in this contemplation of God, and thereby to increase in the knowledge and love of God, the following directions are to be observed.

First, maintain a lively impression that you are but an insignificant creature, and seek to persevere in such a spiritual frame. Realize that your soul's ability for comprehension is very limited and that a matter may readily exceed your understanding. Furthermore, our understanding having been darkened through sin, we are very unfit to comprehend anything about God who is an infinite Spirit. Can a small bottle contain an entire ocean? How then can a finite being comprehend an infinite Being? Can someone look directly into the sun without being blinded? How then will anyone view God who is an infinite light dwelling in the light unto which no man can approach (1 Tim. 6:16) and is clothed with the garment of light? Everyone therefore, when viewing himself from this perspective, must recognize himself to be but a great and foolish beast, not having a right human understanding because he has been so blinded by sin. Truly, to perceive that God is incomprehensible and to acquiesce in and lose one's self in this; to pause and reflect in holy amazement; to believe that the Lord infinitely transcends the capacity of our mind; to rejoice in the fact that God unveils to man that He exists and reveals something of Himself; and to be satisfied with that revelation — that constitutes knowledge of God and is the best frame to increase in this knowledge.

Secondly, be more passive in your contemplation of God and allow yourself to be more illuminated with divine light. Quietly follow that light with your thoughts and permit yourself to be influenced by it rather than wearying your soul with rational deductions, so the soul may move beyond the illumination granted at that moment. The reality and intensity of such mental activity will cause our thoughts to be more carnal than godly and will bring darkness upon the soul.

Thirdly, in doing so it is essential that the soul in all simplicity approves of God's revelation of Himself to her and refrains from hankering to comprehend this revelation. If one seeks to penetrate the manner of God's existence intellectually — that is, His eternity, infinity, omniscience, omnipotence, and internal motions — it will of necessity bring the soul in darkness and various temptations will emerge as a result, for the mind then contemplates things which are beyond its reach. Therefore, one should quickly resist any inclination to ponder about the "why" and the "how" of God's existence, nipping any temptations in the bud. Flee them by readily focusing upon your insignificance and darkness of understanding, and in all humility start again from the beginning.

Fourthly, in order for the soul to contemplate upon God in a manner which is becoming of Him, he must seek to be in a godly frame of mind and be emptied of sinful desires and world conformity, for "the secret of the LORD is with them that fear Him" (Psa. 25:14). "Blessed are the pure in heart: for they shall see God" (Mat. 5:8); "he that loveth me shall be loved of My Father, and I will... manifest Myself to Him. And we will come unto him, and make our abode with him" (John 14:21, 23).

Fifthly, in doing so historical faith must be very active. This means that as we come to the Word, we will read what God says about Himself, without contradiction accept it as the truth, and conclude and confess that God is such as He reveals Himself to be. Our thinking will remain within the context of God's Word without agonizingly seeking to move beyond the Word. We will then in all simplicity follow the Lord, until it pleases Him to lead us to a higher level of understanding.

Sixthly, it is essential that one considers God to be His God in Christ. The light of the knowledge of the glory of God is to be found in the face of Jesus Christ (2 Cor. 4:6). Outside of Christ God is a terror, and can only be viewed as a consuming fire. In Christ, however, one may have liberty; and God reveals Himself to such who approach unto Him in that way. Then one will be able to better endure the light of God's countenance, rejoice in it, and therein glorify God. One ought to be cautious, however, of becoming too free and irreverent when considering God as Father in Christ and in the contemplation upon His perfections which are unveiled by means of the covenant of grace. The proper frame for contemplation upon God is to be humble, reverent, and to tremble with awe before the majesty of the Lord.

CHAPTER FOUR

The Divine Persons

The Holy Trinity

Having considered the name, the essence, and the attributes of God, we will now turn to the mystery of all mysteries, the *Holy Trinity*. Throughout history all parties opposed to the truth have vehemently assaulted this article of faith. The ancient church has always confessed this article and defended it as a steadfast pillar of the truth against *Sabellians, Arians*, and *Valentians*. However much they may disagree with one another concerning other points of doctrine, they are united in their attack upon the Holy Trinity. Today we must defend this article against Socinians, Anabaptists, Socinian Arminians, and other proponents of error. Thanks be unto God who has always caused the church to be faithful to this truth. The church stands firm in this truth until this very day, and God will enable her to stand firm in it until the day of Christ, in spite of all who regret this.

Before we proceed with our consideration of this doctrine and before you meditate upon it, the following must be clearly perceived.

First, it must be understood that God is incomprehensible in His essence and existence. It should further be understood that we human beings, to whom God has been pleased to reveal Himself in a manner sufficient to lead us unto salvation, only know in part and are but able to grasp a fragment or the external fringes of the doctrine at hand. Believers must not, nor do they desire to, proceed with their minds beyond its defined limitations, that is, beyond that which the Lord has been pleased to shed light upon. Whatever cannot be fully understood and perceived, they believe.

They worship the Invisible One who dwells in the light which no man can approach unto.

Secondly, the entire written Word of God, having been given to man, uses human language and words which relate to tangible objects. Such is the wondrous wisdom, goodness, and omnipotence of God, that man by means of earthly expressions understands spiritual matters. Thus, that which is stated ἀνθρωποπαθῶς *(anthropopathós)*, that is, in a *human manner*, can be understood Θεοπρεπῶς *(theoprepós)*, that is, in its *divine* dimension. Such is the case with the language and vocabulary which are used to reveal the mystery of the Holy Trinity. Therefore one must be cautious not to cleave to the tangible matters from which the words have been derived, nor to bring divine matters down to the human level. Rather, we must ascend above tangible matters and expressions in order that, in a spiritual manner pleasing to God, we may understand what God states concerning Himself. May you thus maintain the spiritual frame which we have described in the previous chapter. Reread it attentively and apply it in this chapter.

Thirdly, it should be understood that the Holy Trinity cannot be known from nature, but has only been revealed in Scripture. Therefore one should refer only to Scripture and in all simplicity believe its testimony. One must not exalt his wisdom above that which has been written; he must set all human reasoning aside and avoid all imaginary comparisons to tangible objects. Such comparisons, rather than shedding light upon the issue, result in more obscurity and tend to divert from, rather than promote, a proper understanding of this mystery. May the Lord sanctify and guide me in writing, and you in reading or hearing.

The Singular Essence of God's Being

We maintain and state emphatically that there is but one, only God. "Hear, O Israel: the LORD our God is one LORD" (Deu. 6:4); "For though there be that are called gods...to us there is but one God" (1 Cor. 8:5-6); "But God is one" (Gal. 3:20); "For there is one God" (1 Tim. 2:5). There can of necessity only be one eternal, omnipotent, and all-sufficient Being. Even the most intelligent among the heathen have acknowledged this. The most barbaric heathen of our time, showing no external evidence of any religion, acknowledge but one God. The perception among the heathen that there are many gods seems to originate from the knowledge of the existence of angels, and perhaps also from an erroneous understanding concerning the Holy Trinity, and the plural name of God, *Elohim*.

Divine Personality Defined

This one and only God is Father, Son, and Holy Spirit. The divine Being has a threefold manner of existence, which expressed in intelligible language — lest heretics find here a pretext — is denominated in Scripture by the use of the word "person." In Hebrews 1:3 reference is made to "the express image of His person," or as it is stated in Greek, τῆς ὑποστάσεως αὐτοῦ *(Tés hypostaseós autou).* Since the word ὑπόστασις *(hypostasis)* refers to an intelligent, independent being, the reference is consequently to a person. We understand this to refer to a living, intelligent, incommunicable being who is fully independent, sharing no part with any other being. Such is true of angels and men who consequently are referred to as persons. By application of this concept the divine entities are called persons, so that, in perceiving the divine dimension of the anthropomorphism, we should be able to comprehend something about that which is incomprehensible. We can consider one of the divine Persons in an abstract sense, that is, outside of the context of the divine Being, as is expressed for instance in Hebrews 1:3, where it is stated that Christ is the express image of His Father's Person. We can also consider the Person in a concrete sense, that is, as viewed in union with the divine Being, such as is expressed in Philippians 2:6, where it is said "Who being in the form of God." According to His divine nature Christ is said to be ἐν μορφῇ Θεοῦ *(en morphé Theou),* in the form, that is, having the being and nature of God so that He is equal to God. As the form of a servant includes personhood, essential being, and characteristics, the Word of God similarly includes personhood, essential being, and attributes as constituting the form of God. The manner in which attributes are ascribed to God has been discussed in the previous chapter.

The Divine Essence Consists of Three Persons

This one divine Being subsists in three Persons, not collaterally or side-by-side, but rather the one Person exists by virtue of the other Person either by way of generation or procession. The fact that there are three Persons in the one divine Being is so clearly revealed in the Word of God that it cannot be contradicted. It is evident in both the Old and New Testaments.

First, it is revealed in the name אלהים *(Elohim).*

(1) *Elohim* is a plural form which does not refer to one or two persons, but always expresses a plurality which exceeds two. Since Scripture expressly refers to three, we ought to be convinced of its teaching that the one God subsists in three Persons. *Elohim* is

rarely used in the singular, never in a dual sense, but generally in the plural. Since we know that there is but one God, who in reference to His Being cannot be given a name with a plural dimension, the name *Elohim* clearly indicates that there is a trinity of Persons.

(2) It should additionally be noted that the plural form of *Elohim* is also used in conjunction with a plural *verbum* (verb), *adjectivum* (adjective), or *substantivum in appellatione* (pronoun), and that a plural number is always affixed to it (an *affixum pluralis numeri*). Such is true in the following texts. "And *Elohim* (God) said, נעשה *(Na'aseh)* let us make man" (Gen. 1:26); "When *Elohim* (God) התעו *(hith'u)*, caused me to wander" (Gen. 20:13). "*Elohim* קדשים *(Kedoshim)*, He is an holy God" (Josh. 24:19); "Remember בוראיך *(Boreecha)* Thy Creators" (Eccl. 12:1); "בעליך עשיך *(Ba'alaich 'osaich)*, Thy Makers are Thy husbands" (Isa. 54:5); "I am *Jehovah* אלהיך *(Eloheka)*, Thy God" (Exo. 20:2).[1]

It should be noted that the names *Jehovah* and *Elohim* often coalesce into the one name *Jehovah*, and that quite frequently these two names are used in conjunction with each other, indicating the unity of Being as well as the subsistence in three Persons. Whenever the plural name of God, *Elohim*, is used in a singular sense, the Persons are considered as one Being. Only once, in Psalm 45:7, is the name *Elohim* used in reference to a Person, when it is stated אלהים אלהיך *(Elohim Eloheka)*, that is, "Therefore God, Thy God, hath anointed Thee." This indicates περιεμχόρεσιν *(periemchoresin)*, that is, the internal coexistence, and that the divine Persons, are inseparable from the divine Being and from each other.

Secondly, the Trinity of Persons is also evident in texts,

(1) in which the Lord refers to Himself as being more than one or two. "Let us make man" (Gen. 1:26); "the man is become as one of us" (Gen. 3:22); "let us go down, and there confound their language" (Gen. 11:7). The reference here is not to angels, as they are not creators, nor has man having been made in the image of angels. Angels cannot be considered as being equal with God. The fact that the kings of the earth refer to themselves as "we" and "us" merely indicates their limitation, since they do not govern independently but in consultation with their senate and people *(senatus populusque)*. God, however, is sovereign, and thus has no need to express Himself in such a fashion. His use of the plural relative to Himself reveals the Trinity of Persons, for which reason He is referred to in the original Hebrew as *Creators* in Ecclesiastes 12:1.

---

[1] These quotations deviate somewhat from the KJV as à Brakel here gives a literal rendering of the original Hebrew.

(2) It is also evident in texts wherein the Lord speaks about Himself as if He were referring to another person. "Then the LORD rained upon Sodom and upon Gomorrah brimstone and fire from the LORD out of heaven" (Gen. 19:24). One of the three angels which spoke with Abraham was *Jehovah*, the Son of God. He who appeared on earth caused this rain to come down from the Lord in heaven. Both He who summoned this rain, as well as the One who caused it to rain, are referred to as *Jehovah*. As God is one in essence, the reference here cannot be to two different Beings, but rather to the Son and the Father, being the second and the first Persons of the Godhead. For it is the Father who works through the Son, and the Son works on behalf of His Father (John 5:19).

Thirdly, to further facilitate your inner conviction, consider with a believing heart those texts which expressly state that God is trinitarian, not in His essence but in Persons. In the blessing which the Lord enjoins to be pronounced upon His people the name *Jehovah* is repeated three times. "The LORD bless thee, and keep thee: the LORD make His face shine upon thee, and be gracious unto thee: the LORD lift up His countenance upon thee, and give thee peace" (Num. 6:24-26). In each repetition the name *Jehovah* is conjoined to an activity which in the administration of the covenant of grace is specifically ascribed to either the Father, the Son, or the Holy Ghost. Safekeeping is ascribed to the Father, the manifestation of grace to the Son, and the bestowal of peace to the Holy Spirit. The apostle Paul expressing this in his benediction mentions the three Persons in 2 Corinthians 13:14, clearly proving that the repetition of the name *Jehovah* must be viewed as being indicative of the three Persons. This threefold repetition is also found in Isaiah 6:3, where it is stated, "Holy, holy, holy, is the LORD." In the New Testament this text is used to refer to the Father, Son, and Holy Ghost (cf. John 12:41; Acts 28:25). Furthermore, consider the following texts: "The Spirit of the Lord GOD is upon Me" (Isa. 61:1); "I will mention the lovingkindnesses of the LORD...the angel of His presence (from Malachi 3:1 we know that this refers to the Son) saved them" (Isa. 63:7, 9); "But they rebelled, and vexed His Holy Spirit" (Isa. 63:10); "By the word of the LORD were the heavens made; and all the host of them by the breath of His mouth" (Psa. 33:6).

There is also clear evidence in the New Testament. "And, lo, the heavens were opened unto Him, and He saw the Spirit of God descending like a dove, and lighting upon Him: and lo a voice from heaven, saying, This is My beloved Son, in whom I am well pleased" (Mat. 3:16-17). "Baptizing them in the name of the Father, and of the Son, and of the Holy Ghost" (Mat. 28:19); "The grace of the Lord Jesus Christ, and the love of God, and the communion of the Holy Ghost, be with you all" (2 Cor. 13:14); "For there are three that bear record in heaven, the Father, the Word, and the Holy Ghost: and these three are one" (1 John 5:7).

We have thus observed that there are three Persons in the divine Being. This will become even more evident as we come to demonstrate that every Person is truly God, the Son being generated by the Father and the Holy Spirit proceeding from the Father and the Son. We shall first consider the divinity of the Son and His eternal and incomprehensible generation, and then the divinity of the Holy Spirit and His procession.

The Divinity of Each Person of the Trinity

That the Father is truly God is not disputed, which will become sufficiently evident as we progress. The indisputable proof that the Son as the second Person of the Trinity is also truly God, is to be found in His divine names, attributes, works, and the honor He receives.

First, let us consider His divine *Names*. He is called *Jehovah,* which is a name attributed to God alone, as has been previously demonstrated (cf. Jer. 23:6; Rom. 9:5; 1 John 5:20).

Secondly, let us consider His divine *attributes*. Whoever is eternal, omnipotent, and omniscient, is the only true God. All of these are attributed to the second Person, the Son (cf. Rev. 1:8; Mic. 5:2; Rev. 2:13).

Thirdly, let us consider His divine *works*. He who has created the world, maintains everything, and raises the dead, is truly God. All these works are attributed to the Son (cf. John 1:3; Col. 1:16-17; John 5:20-21).

Fourthly, let us consider His divine *honor*. He, who as the Father is to be honored, is to have baptism performed in His Name, is to be worshipped by men, and is to be believed in by them, is truly God. This honor is attributed to the Son (cf. John 5:23; Mat. 28:19; Phil. 2:10; Heb. 1:6; John 14:1). We shall deal with this comprehensively in chapter eighteen. That the Holy Spirit is truly God will be shown later.

These three Persons are neither different nor separate from the divine essence, nor from each other — so that the divine essence would be considered as one entity, a divine Person another; or that the Father would be one entity, the Son another, and the Holy Spirit yet another. This would constitute the existence of three or four gods. There is a distinction rather than an essential difference between the divine persons. Each Person is coequal and the divine

Being in the full sense of the word, existing in such a manner. Therefore whenever Scripture refers to the Persons of the Trinity it speaks of three, and whenever it refers to the divine essence existing in three Persons, it states that these three are one (1 John 5:7).

The Greek church used three words by which it gave expression to the unity and harmony between the three Persons. In our language we are not capable of being as precise in expressing this; however, we will attempt to approximate this as much as possible.

The first word is ὁμοουσία *(homoousia)* or *coessence,* which indicates that the three Persons have the same divine essence in common, one Person not being of a different essence from another Person, but one and the same. The Son is of the same divinity as the Father, and the Holy Spirit is of the same divinity as the Father and the Son. Of old, heretics have toyed with this word, and instead used the word ὁμοιουσία *(homoiousia)* or *co-similarity.* They maintained that the Son and the Holy Ghost are of an essence which resembles the Father's essence, which nevertheless is not the same essence. They suggested that there is but little difference between the two concepts as the two words differ only in one letter. We maintain, however, that the three Persons are of the same essence. "I and My Father are one" (John 10:30). The Son was ἐν μορΦῇ Θεοῦ *(en morphé Theou)*, that is, having the same form and nature as God (Phil. 2:6).

The second word is ἰσότης *(isotés)* or *coequality.* This expresses the fact that each Person is of the same divine essence in the full sense of the word. The divine essence is indivisible, that is, each Person possesses it in the full sense of the word — one Person not more than the other. The three Persons possess the divine essence equally; they are equal as far are possessing the complete, indivisible divine essence.

The third word is ἐμπεριχώρησις *(emperichórésis)*, or *coexistence.* Thereby is indicated that since God is a simple Being, there being neither diversity nor composition — that is, neither Essence and Person nor Person and Person constitute a composite entity — the three Persons, though distinguished from each other, are not different. They coexist as one God, in simplicity of Being. The Father exists in the Son, the Son exists in the Father, and the Holy Spirit exists in the Father and in the Son. "And the Word was with God, and the Word was God" (John 1:1); "He that hath seen Me hath seen the Father...the Father that dwelleth in Me...I am in the Father, and the Father in Me" (John 14:9-11).

Having established the equality of the Persons, we must nevertheless distinguish between the divine essence and the individual

Persons — lest we equate the divine essence with one of the Persons only, or view one Person as being another Person. The internal, natural distinction which exists within God, however, is incomprehensible. We only perceive the fringes of His Being — as much as it has pleased the Lord to reveal to us in His Word. That revelation is sufficient for us unto adoration, worship, sanctified use, and salvation. It is most certain that unconverted persons, as learned as they may be, know very little about this mystery. An uneducated but godly person, however, believes and perceives much more of this mystery — more than he can give verbal expression to — than an unconverted person or one who is opposed to the truth would be able to believe.

Thus we must distinguish here between the divine essence and divine Persons.

(1) There is one essence and three Persons.

(2) We must view the divine essence as being entirely nonrelational, [that is, not existing in an essential relationship with any other Being], whereas the divine Persons exist in an interpersonal relationship to each other and interact together.

(3) The same essence in its entirety is present in all three Persons; however, each Person has His own independent personality. As such we can say that the divine essence is communicable to the divine Persons in the manner just stated, whereas the personality of each divine Person is incommunicable. Thus, it is evident that we distinguish between the essence and the Persons, albeit not as if there were an actual and essential difference. Rather, we do so merely in reference to the manner of existence, which is a matter about which we can only stammer.

The distinction between the Persons can neither be defined as a single, intellectual concept, nor be made in reference to the works of God — as if God when He functions in one sense is called the Father; when He functions in a different sense is called the Son; and when He functions again in a different sense is called the Holy Spirit. This distinction also may not be perceived as if the three Persons function collaterally, that is, as if they function side by side without any interaction among each other, for then the Son could just as well be the Father, and the Father could just as well be the Holy Spirit. Their relationship and titles would then only have reference to the work of redemption. Rather, this distinction relates to the very nature of these Persons. It is God's eternal nature to exist as Father, Son, and Holy Ghost, the Father not being able to be the Son, and the Holy Spirit not being able to be the Father. Scripture makes a distinction:

(1) in personal properties, as being foundational to the interpersonal relationship, and which are the basis for our distinction;

(2) in names, which are Father, Son, and Holy Ghost;

(3) in order, as there is a first, second, and third Person;

(4) in manner of existence, as the Father is of Himself, the Son is of the Father, and the Holy Spirit is from the Father and the Son;

(5) in the manner of operation, as the Father works of Himself, the Son is engaged on behalf of His Father, and the Holy Spirit on behalf of both.

The personal properties of each Person are as follows: The Father generates; the Son is generated, and together with the Father sends forth the Holy Spirit; the Holy Spirit proceeds from the Father and the Son, whose manner of operation is described in Scripture as "breathing." Nowhere in the Bible are the three Persons ever referred to in a manner of absolute detachment from each other. The references are always relational in nature, indicated by the names which they have: Father, Son, and Holy Spirit. Even if in a given text reference is made to one, two, or three Persons, and even if the interpersonal relationship is not expressed therein — something which to our knowledge occurs only two or three times — then this relationship is expressed in other texts. Such is the case, for instance, when we compare Numbers 6:25-26 with 2 Corinthians 13:13, and Isaiah 6:3 with John 12:41 and Acts 28:25. To maintain that the three Names have no significance beyond the names themselves, or to maintain that these names merely refer to God's administration of the covenant of grace, is nothing less than a denial of the Holy Trinity. To maintain, however, that there are three entities which coexist simultaneously without the interpersonal relationship is to maintain that there are three Gods. It is thus necessary to examine the basis for this interpersonal relationship which is to be found in the eternal generation of the Son, as well as the procession of the Spirit.

The Eternal Generation of the Son as the Second Person of the Trinity

It is a personal property of the first Person of the Godhead to generate the second Person, and of the second Person to be generated in a manner fully congruent with God's perfect character. Scripture uses the word "begotten"[2] as it best expresses the manner of divine operation. This eternal and incomprehensible generation should not be compared to human generation, but human generation should be viewed as a reflection of divine

---

[2] The Statenbijbel uses the verb "genereren," which means "to generate."

generation. We must therefore remove any notion of human generation from our minds as we ascend to divine generation, and understand it to refer to such a generation of the second Person by the first Person, by virtue of which the first Person is Father and the second Person is Son. This is a truth which at all times has been acknowledged, believed, and defended by the church.

We shall demonstrate and confirm *this eternal generation* by presenting evidence in a twofold manner. The first proof will be derived from the terminology itself; the second, from the foundational concept that undergirds this terminology.

Proof #1: The only wise God, who in His Word reveals both Himself and the way of salvation with the clearest, most emphatic, and most suitable words, not only declares that He exists in a Trinity of Persons, but also calls the first Person Father, and the second Person Son "...in the name of the Father, and of the Son" (Mat. 28:19); "the Father loveth the Son" (John 5:20); "Grace be with you, mercy, and peace, from God the Father, and from the Lord Jesus Christ, the Son of the Father" (2 John 3).

"Father" and "Son" are words which by definition are related to each other. In hearing these words we comprehend the nature of this relationship, apart from which these words are devoid of meaning. In encountering the word "Father" we immediately think of a person who has begotten another person in his likeness, and the word "Son" immediately causes us to think of someone who has been begotten with the likeness and character of someone else. We can at once comprehend the relationship which exists between these two persons. God has particularly and actually revealed Himself as the object of our faith by means of the names Father and Son. Whereas these words immediately convey a specific relationship, being so understood by everyone, it is therefore a certainty that the Father has generated the Son and that the Son has been generated by the Father, in consequence of which there is this relationship between them. Angels, Adam, and believers are also called the sons of God, expressing at once their relationship to Him, having been begotten in the image of God — the first two by creation and the latter by regeneration. Christ's Sonship, however, is of a different nature and thus not comparable to this other sonship. In reference to this the apostle states, "For unto which of the angels said He at any time, Thou art My Son, this day have I begotten thee?" (Heb. 1:5). Christ is the Son by generation, who, transcending all creatures, is called κατ᾽ ἐξοχήν *(kat' exochén)*, the Son of God par excellence (Heb. 1:1, 8). He is furthermore called God's *own* Son which excludes the notion that His Sonship is merely figurative in nature. "He that spared not His own Son" (Rom. 8:32). "Own Son" is indicative of His Sonship by generation and thus of being equal with God, a truth which even the Jews understood. "But said also that God was His Father, making Himself equal with God" (John 5:18). More particularly, He is called the *only-begotten* Son. "The glory as of the only begotten of the Father" (John 1:14); "He gave His only begotten Son" (John 3:16). He is also called the *first-begotten* Son. "Who is the image of the invisible God, the firstborn of every creature" (Col. 1:15). To remove all objection, it is stated that He is the first-begotten Son who was born from eternity. "I was brought forth; when there were no fountains abounding with water" (Prov. 8:24). Thus, we conclude that He is the Son of the Father, His Sonship being infinitely different from angels and believers. He is the proper, only-begotten, first-begotten, and eternally begotten Son of God par excellence, who in His nature stands in a relationship to the Father by virtue of eternal generation. The second Person, however, is such that there is between the first and second Persons of the Godhead a relationship which has the eternal, incomprehensible generation of the Son as its basis.

Although this proof is fully convincing, Socinians and others, guided by corrupt intellects, attempt to conjure something whereby they may cast a shadow upon this truth. We shall seek to briefly expose their delusive tactics, defending the truth against all efforts to dilute it.

Evasive Argument #1: Relative to God, the words "Father" and "Son" are used figuratively. Consequently, one should neither focus on this figurative expression regarding God, nor conclude thereby the existence of a Trinity of Persons, existing in an interpersonal relationship to each other.

Answer: It is an untruth to suggest that these words "Father," "Son," etc., are used in a figurative sense in reference to God. These words are most emphatically used as properly referring to God Himself. In the most proper sense of the word the first Person is unequivocally the Father of the second Person, whereas the second Person most emphatically and in a most essential sense is the Son of the first Person. The eternal generation of the Son, being the basis for this relationship, is most emphatically and with utmost propriety consistent with the character of God. This expression, *generation,* is derived from human circumstances, as is done consistently in the entire Word of God, conveying spiritual matters by using vocabulary relating to aspects of human existence. This is done to facilitate the comprehension of insignificant human beings, knowing that whatever is stated from a human perspective must be understood from a divine perspective. No one would be so foolish to maintain that everything recorded in the Bible ought to be understood figuratively. God is said to have bodily parts such as eyes, ears, mouth, hands, etc., as well as to be subject to human emotions and engage in human activity. We know, however, that the mention of limbs and emotions are expressive of such attributes and activities in God as are manifested and performed by them. Who would maintain that these matters concerning God are only figurative? It is true with respect to God that they do not function in a human sense, even though these matters are expressed in a human manner. Nevertheless, they are most emphatically, and with utmost propriety, ascribed to God. Such is also the case here. "Father," "Son," and "generation" are words derived from human circumstances. These words, however, in a manner consistent with the incomprehensible character of God, express most emphatically and with utmost propriety both this relationship and their basis for it in God.

Evasive Argument #2: The second Person is called the Son by virtue of being coessential with the Father.

Answer: (1) This is stated nowhere in the Bible, and therefore we reject this as readily as it is stated.

(2) Even though a son may have the same nature as his father (for otherwise he would be no son), such similarity of natures is not the basis upon which someone is called a son, for then a father could be the son and the son could be the father. Then father and son would be brothers; people who are not even related to each other in the hundredth degree would be father and son, since they share the same human nature. This is convincing to all, and it is therefore evident that this argument has no plausibility. A father is someone who has begotten a person after his likeness; a son is someone who has been begotten after the likeness of his father — all of which is applicable to this mystery. Being of the same nature does not constitute a father-son relationship; rather this relationship is the result of generation and being generated.

Evasive Argument #3: The second Person is called the Son because He agreed to assume the human nature in the Counsel of Peace, and for the accomplishing of the work of redemption was manifested in the flesh as the visible image of the invisible God.

Answer: (1) By referring to a first and a second Person, one of necessity is referring to a relationship, and therefore cannot maintain the coexistence of three nonrelational entities. In seeking to establish a reason for calling the second Person "Son," and the first

Person "Father," we confess thereby that the words "Father" and "Son" are indicative of a relationship. Thus our proof derived from the relational terminology, "Father" and "Son," cannot be contradicted. We must admit that the three Persons of the Trinity exist relationally, that is, as Father, Son, and Holy Ghost. The only controversy remaining relates to the basis and reason for this relationship in consequence of which the first Person is called Father and the second Person Son. Scripture states that this is due to generation and birth. Not wishing to admit this, however, those advancing the argument relate this to the manifestation in the flesh, the assumption of the human nature — all of which is without foundation in the Word of God.

(2) Christ's manifestation in the flesh cannot be the basis for His Sonship, for His incarnation renders the second Person neither divine nor the only-begotten, proper, and first-begotten Son of God — He was already Son, the eternal Son of the eternal Father. He has been eternally begotten, thus prior to His manifestation in the flesh. Of necessity He had to be the Son of God; otherwise He could neither have assumed the human nature as the Son of God nor have manifested Himself in the flesh. "I was brought forth; when there were no fountains abounding" (Prov. 8:24). Since He was then already the begotten Son of God, His Sonship did not commence at the moment of His incarnation. Agur, the son of Jakeh, in amazement over the incomprehensibility of God's existence, asks among other things, "What is His Name, and what is His Son's Name, if thou canst tell?" (Prov. 30:4). Again, since He was already the Son of God at that time, He did not become the Son by His incarnation. "God sent forth His Son, made of a woman" (Gal. 4:4). Since the Son was sent to assume the human nature, He of necessity had to be the Son of God prior to being sent and thus not as a result of the assumption of the human nature. When it is said of Christ that "God was manifest in the flesh" (1 Tim. 3:16), this expresses beyond the shadow of a doubt that He was God prior to that moment and that He did not become God by virtue of this manifestation. Since it is also stated that the Son has been manifested in the flesh, and that the Son has been sent and was made of a woman, this undoubtedly expresses that He was the Son of God prior to His incarnation — not as a result of His incarnation.

(3) The Holy Spirit has also manifested Himself in the world when He descended as a dove (Mat. 3:16) at the baptism of Christ, when He was poured out in an extraordinary manner on the day of Pentecost, and later by way of His extraordinary gifts. Even now He manifests Himself daily in His gracious operations. No one will

maintain, however, that the Holy Spirit is the Son of God in consequence of this. Thus, Christ's manifestation in the world is not the basis for His Sonship. If one insists that the Holy Spirit was not incarnated, I reply that manifestation must be relinquished as a basis for Sonship. The remaining implication would be that one of the three Persons, it being a matter of indifference to them as to whether They would be Father, Son, or Holy Spirit, would have become the Son of God by virtue of His assumption of the human nature. Who would not detest such a conclusion? Does the human nature determine sonship? Or could we say that Christ's human nature is the image of the invisible God? Is not He the Son of God from eternity, being in the form of God? Is not He in His divine nature the express image of His Father's Person?

Additional Argument #1: To be born or to be revealed [or manifested] are equivalent in Scripture. Since someone becomes a son by birth, also being manifested renders someone to be a son. To be born and to be manifested are equivalent concepts, as may be seen in the following: "A brother is born for adversity" (Prov. 17:17); "Thou knowest not what a day may bring forth" (Prov. 27:1); "There thy mother brought thee forth: there she brought thee forth that bare thee" (Song of Sol. 8:5).

Answer: (1) "To be born" and "to be revealed" are not synonymous in meaning, so that they can be used interchangeably. One cannot state that whatever is manifested is born, nor can it be said that whatever is born is manifested, as this would have the most absurd consequences. If the same meaning is to be deduced from two words, then such words must be able to be used in the identical context, as well as interchangeably. Since this is not the case with these two words, the argument cannot support the proposed conclusion.

(2) If a word is used figuratively or comparatively in a given text, this does not mean that it should be understood figuratively in all other texts. In the subject under consideration, to be born is never viewed as being synonymous with manifestation, which consequently renders this argument futile.

(3) When manifestation is expressed by way of the verb "to be born," then the person who initiates this manifestation is never referred to as father, and that which is manifested is never referred to as son. Consequently this argument, by which one seeks to prove from the verb "to manifest" that Christ is called the Son in consequence of His manifestation, is not plausible. One should therefore not simply say that "to be born" is equivalent in meaning to "manifestation," for it must then be proven that someone is called a father due to initiating a manifestation, or that someone

is called a son due to having been made manifest. Only if that were possible, would one be able to maintain that Christ is the Son due to being manifested in the flesh.

(4) Let us consider Proverbs 17:17. Adversity is not the father of him who behaves himself as a brother, and a faithful friend is not the son of adversity, which would have to be true in order for this argument to have a semblance of validity. The meaning of the text is that a faithful friend loves not only in prosperity, but especially in adversity. While behaving himself as a friend in days of prosperity, he will behave himself as a brother in days of adversity. Let us next consider the meaning of Proverbs 27:1 which relates to the fact that one cannot know what one will encounter during a given day. That which one encounters is not a son of the day, and the day is not the father of that which one encounters. The word day relates to the time rather than the cause.

Finally, let us consider Song of Solomon 8:5. This text is not applicable, as the verb "to bear" means to bring forth rather than to reveal. The church as a mother, in conjunction with the ministers, labors painstakingly in order that Christ may be formed in the hearts of the people, this being achieved by the preaching of the gospel. This is the reason why the church bears the name of mother (Gal. 4:26). Faithful ministers are called the fathers of those who have been converted as a result of their ministry (1 Cor. 4:15). Believers are called the children of the church and of the ministers under whose ministry they were converted (cf. Zec. 9:9; Luke 13:34; Phile. 10). Since by virtue of spiritual nurture and birth the church is called a mother and believers are called children of the church, this text opposes those who have presented it. For it states "to bear" to be equivalent to generation and bringing forth, this being the basis for the relationship between a mother and her children, as well as between a father and his sons.

Additional Argument #2: The third Person in the Trinity does not owe His name to a personal procession from the Father and the Son, but due to His execution of the divine economy relative to the work of redemption, at which time He revealed and proved His divinity. Without assigning a name, the Holy Spirit, one would not be able to distinguish between first and second Person, as they are a Spirit and a Holy Spirit in reference to the divine Being (cf. John 4:24; Isa. 6:3, 8; John 12:39-41; Acts 28:25; Rom. 1:4; 1 Cor. 15:45; Heb. 9:14). However, if the third Person is called Holy Spirit only because He has revealed Himself as God in the ministry of grace, then the second Person is called the Son due to His manifestation in the flesh.

Answer: (1) We deny this conclusion, there being no logical connection. Truths are stated concerning each Person which cannot be said of the others. It can never be stated concerning the Father that He was born or that He was sent. Neither can it be said of the Holy Spirit that He was born or that He sent the Son.

(2) We also deny that either the first or second Person of the Trinity is the Holy Spirit. Nowhere, not even in the aforementioned texts is the Father or the Son called the Holy Spirit. It is true that God is a Spirit and that each of the Persons is holy, but the combination of "Holy" and "Spirit" is never used in reference to the other Persons.

(3) When God is called a Spirit and the third Person of the Trinity is called the Holy Spirit, then the word "Spirit" is not used in the same sense. The word "spirit" has numerous meanings. It is also used to refer to wind, the soul of man, and angels. When God is called a Spirit, it is to be understood negatively. It refers to such a Being who, in His simplicity, non-corporeality, and invisibility, is infinitely distinguished from all creatures. This cannot be expressed to us human beings any better than by means of the word "Spirit." The third Person of the Trinity is called the Holy Spirit, however, due to His manner of procession from the Father and from the Son, which cannot be expressed any better than by means of a word which is derived from "to breathe."[3] He is therefore called the Spirit of God, the Spirit of the Lord, and the breath of His mouth — and these have no reference to the work of redemption. This is confirmed in the following texts. "And the Spirit of God moved upon the face of the waters" (Gen. 1:2); "The Spirit of God hath made me, and the breath of the Almighty hath given me life" (Job 33:4); "By the word of the LORD were the heavens made; and all the host of them by the breath of His mouth" (Psa. 33:6). From these texts it is evident that the third Person is distinguished from the first and the second Person of the Trinity; that He is the Spirit; and that although the first and second Persons are holy, He is the Holy Spirit (cf. Mat. 28:19; 1 John 5:7). Whenever His activity manifests itself externally, He is operative in a manner congruent with His nature, which is by way of breathing (cf. John 3:8; John

---

[3] à Brakel here, as well as elsewhere in this chapter, uses the word "blazen" to convey the manner of the Spirit's operation, this being an obvious derivative from the vocabulary of the Dutch Bible. The literal translation of this word would be "to blow." However, since the KJV generally uses the verb "to breathe" in such passages (cf. John 20:22), and since the English word "Spirit" is derived from the Latin noun "spiritus," which means "breath," we have consistently translated "blazen" as "to breathe."

20:22). This breathing therefore relates to His manner of operation rather than His relationship to the Father and the Son, or the
basis for this relationship, which is His procession from both.

Evasive Argument #4: The words "Son" and "Word," as well as
"Son" and "King of Israel," are used interchangeably, and identify
one and the same. It is known that "Word" and "King of Israel"
have reference to the execution of His mediatorial office and not
to Christ's manner of existence. Consequently, the word "Son"
also has reference to His mediatorial office and not the manner of
His existence.

Answer: We deny emphatically that the words "Son" and "King
of Israel," as well as "Word" and "Son" are one and the same. Both
have reference to the same Person, but this does not mean that
they have the same meaning. Therefore, the one is not a necessary
consequence of the other. Many things are attributed to Christ, in
consequence of which He has numerous names, such as Wonderful, Counselor, the Mighty God, the Prince of Peace, the Everlasting Father, Immanuel, the Lord our Righteousness. Who would
maintain that all these names are synonymous in meaning because
they refer to the identical Person? Even though the title "King of
Israel" relates to His mediatorial office, it cannot be concluded
that the title "Son" also relates to this, much less that He is
denominated the Son by virtue of His mediatorial office. It is not
the Greek word ῥῆμα *(rhema)* which is used to denominate Christ
as the Word, but instead the word λόγος *(logos)*, the meaning of
which relates to reason, intellect, and wisdom. This is congruent
with the fact that Christ is the eternal and supreme manifestation
of Wisdom, who has eternally been begotten, whom the LORD has
possessed in the beginning of His way, before His works of old
(Prov. 8:22), etc. Even though Christ is called the Word relative to
the revelation of the gospel, it is neither the reason that He is the
Son nor why He is called the Son. Rather, it refers to His work as
the Son, consistent with His manner of existence.

Evasive Argument #5: The name "Son" encompasses the entire
Person of the Mediator as consisting of both the divine and human
natures. Since His mediatorial office is executed in reference to both
natures, His Sonship therefore does not relate to His divine nature
only. Also His title "the Son of Man" refers to the Person of the
Mediator in its entirety, and not to His human nature only. Thus, His
being called the Son is not due to His eternal generation. Rather, He
is the essential Son of God, the firstborn and the only-begotten Son
of God, the Branch, the Dayspring from on high, and the image of
the Invisible, by virtue of His wondrous incarnation, words, miracles,

ascension, as well as in reference to the outpouring of His Holy Spirit and His all-encompassing government.

Answer: (1) This is the old teaching of the Socinians, and it is peculiar that those who do not wish to be numbered with the Socinians must resort to Socinian proofs to prove their point. To such a degree one can be led astray by his prejudices. If you do not agree with the Socinians, why resort to argumentation which cannot but generate the suspicion that you are or ultimately must be in agreement with them?

(2) The Godhead is bound up in the entire Person. The human nature is neither the Person nor part of the Person of Christ, but has only been assumed by the Person of the Son of God. Already prior to the assumption of the human nature the second Person was the eternal Son of the eternal Father, as has previously been proven. Thus He is not the Son of God by virtue of His wondrous conception, etc. All of this proves that He was the Son of God, but it is neither the basis for, nor the reason why He is and is called the Son of God. This is expressed by the apostle, "And declared to be the Son of God with power, according to the Spirit of holiness, by the resurrection from the dead" (Rom. 1:4).

(3) Christ has two natures, the one being divine and the other human. The names, attributes, and manner of operation of both natures are attributed to the same Person, all of which are an essential dimension of His Personhood, some relating to His divine and some to His human nature. Thus, in Luke 1:32 Christ is called the Son of the Highest and the Son of David, the first referring to His divine and the second to His human nature. The eternal Son of the eternal Father has assumed the human nature. Since it was the Son of God who assumed the human nature, He consequently was already the Son of God prior to this event; He did not become the Son in consequence of His assumption of the human nature. It does not necessarily follow from the fact that He is the Son of man that He is therefore the Son of God. Neither is He not called the Son of man due to the fact that He is the Son of God. The use of these titles is not arbitrary. The Son of God and the Son of man are not one and the same, even though this is said of one and the same Person. As we have proven, He is the Son of God only in reference to His divine nature by virtue of His eternal generation, and He is the Son of man only by virtue of His human nature, having been born of the seed of the woman.

Evasive Argument #6: "This is my beloved Son, in whom I am well pleased" (Mat. 3:17), to which is added in Matthew 17:5, "Hear ye Him." Reference is made here to the entire Person of the Mediator, being God and man. In Him and in His sacrifice God the Father is well-pleased; He must be heard and obeyed as Prophet and King. It is when viewed from this perspective that He is called and is the Son of God.

Answer: We readily agree with all this, but it has no reference to the point of contention. The point of contention here is whether or not the second Person of the Godhead is called the Son of God because God delights in Him as God and man — as Mediator — is pleased with His sacrifice, and that we should obey Him as Prophet and King. This we deny. This text furnishes no proof whatsoever, nor does it advance a basis or reason why Christ is called the Son, but it merely indicates that the Father calls Him Son, because He was the eternal Son of the eternal Father by virtue of eternal generation. The statement, "Hear ye Him," does not suggest that Christ is therefore the Son of God. This is erroneous. In addition it should be noted that neither His human nature nor His office as Mediator is the basis for obedience to Him, but His Godhead only. His divine Sonship is a consequence of His Godhead, although He is united as such with the human nature.

Evasive Argument #7: The most significant reason why Scripture frequently ascribes the name Son of God to Christ is to teach us that "Jesus is the Christ, the Son of God; and that believing ye might have life through His Name" (John 20:31). To conclude that He has truly been generated because He so often is called the Son of God is a futile exercise.

Answer: How conclusive this text is! The objective of Scripture in calling Christ the Son of God is indeed to teach that Jesus is the Christ. If it were stated that Jesus is the Son of God due to His assumption of the human nature, this argument would be credible, but it merely states that Jesus is the Christ, the Son of God, whose Sonship is in consequence of His eternal generation rather than His incarnation, as has been proven. It is therefore not futile, but certain and irrefutable that the titles "Son," "Only-begotten Son," "Own Son," "First-begotten Son of God" lead us to conclude that He was not begotten in the corporal sense of the word, but in a unique manner, agreeable with the nature of God. He is the eternal Son of the eternal Father, which is the reason why Scripture so frequently calls Him the Son. Even if it occurred only once in the Bible, it would be sufficient for us to believe that Jesus is the Christ, the Son of God, and that believing we might have eternal life through His Name. The frequent repetition of this title should convince and unnerve those who contest this truth, and discourage them from doing so.

Proof #2: Thus far we have proven from the titles "Son," "My Son," "Own Son," "Begotten, Only-begotten, and First-begotten Son," that the second Person of the Trinity has eternally existed in a Father-Son relationship to the first Person and that He is the eternal Son of the eternal Father. We will now proceed with the second proof, which relates to the basis or reason for this relationship: how and why the second Person is the eternal Son, which according to Scripture is by virtue of eternal generation. We shall verify this from various passages of Holy Writ, examining them individually as well as effectively eliminating all arguments against it.

First, we shall consider Psalm 2:7, "Thou art My Son; this day have I begotten Thee." The first Person here addresses the second Person, calling Him His Son, which necessarily implies that the first Person is the Father of the second Person. The foundational phrase for maintaining that the first Person is the Father and the second Person the Son is expressed in these words, "This day have I begotten Thee." It must then be evident that the second Person is not called the Son simply because He is of the same essence, without any interpersonal relationship. We already have responded to this above in our rebuttal of *argument #2.* It is also equally and unquestionably certain from this that the second Person's being the Son and the first Person's being the Father are due to the second Person's assumption of the human nature, as the first Person did not generate the second Person in this. He was the second Person prior to His incarnation and thus the second Person was the Son from eternity. (This was dealt with above in our rebuttal to *argument #3*). In addition, Christ's human nature was created at the moment of His incarnation, which, however, is not true for His divine nature. The human nature would then be the Son of God rather than the divine nature; generation would not refer to the generation of a person according to the express image of His Father. It would refer to the generation or propagation of a nature which would infinitely differ from the nature of the Father. Such an argument is absurdity itself.

This text makes it exceptionally clear that these two propositions — the second Person is the Son because He is of the same essence as the first Person, or He is the Son due to His assumption of the human nature — cannot be harmonized as they are contradictory to each other. Two untruths cannot produce one truth. This text, in expressing itself concerning the first and second Person, states that there exists a relationship of Father and Son between them, of which generation is the foundational concept. This generation establishes the Father as the first Person and the

Son as the second Person, while it also establishes the second Person to be the Son and the first Person to be the Father.

Secondly, there is frequent reference to the words of Paul, "God was manifest in the flesh" (1 Tim. 3:16). From the argument of silence they wish to maintain that the reference is to the Son of God. They lack the courage to explain these words and apply them to the heart, the result of which would be most unclear. For the words, "God was manifest in the flesh," are not equivalent in meaning to *"Son of God."* Rather, it conveys that He who is God from eternity assumed the human nature in hypostatic union with His Person, without there being the least reference to the relationship between the Father and the Son, nor the basis for this relationship, which the text clearly states to be *generation.* Why is no use made of the words of Paul, "God sent forth His Son, made of a woman?" (Gal. 4:4). Here expression is given to this relationship and to the divine and human natures of Christ, as well as to His incarnation. They will have to acknowledge that this text moves beyond the point which they wish to discuss, as it indicates that Christ already was the Son prior to His being sent and before He was made of a woman, and that He did not become the Son as a result of His assumption of the human nature.

Thus the second Person is the Son in consequence of being generated by the first Person. Here we must ascend from the human to the divine. We must reflect upon it in a manner which is becoming of God, even though it is an incomprehensible mystery to us. We must believe that the first Person has brought forth the second Person in a manner which can best be described by the word "generation." Any thought of human generation must be far removed from our minds. A chronological distinction between first and last is nonexistent here; neither is there any transition from nonexistence to existence; nor is this relationship one of dependency. This relationship is eternal in nature, characterized by coequality of *being* as well as *essential existence,* for the existence of the Son of the Father is a constituent element of God's character, as it belongs to the perfection of both the divine Being and the divine Persons.

Evasive Argument: This generation mentioned in Psalm 2:7 should not be understood to be eternal in nature, but rather to refer to His incarnation. This generation was to occur at a specified time: "this day." These are words which never denote eternity.

Answer: (1) The incarnation is never denominated as generation, and generation cannot signify incarnation, for then the Fatherhood of the first Person would relate to the human nature of Christ, of which He would consequently be called the Father. Then the human nature would be the son of the first Person, and thus be the image of God, the express image of the Father's Person. Such a conclusion is absurd and should be rejected with utter contempt.

(2) The generation referred to here is from eternity whereby the first Person is the Father of the second, and the second the Son of the first. The second Person is the Son from eternity, having been brought forth before the creation of the world (Prov. 8:24), prior to which there was nothing but eternity. His "goings forth have been from of old, from everlasting" (Micah 5:2). If the second Person who is here denominated as Son is the Son from eternity, His generation is consequently also from eternity. Furthermore, since His generation is eternal, the words "this day" of necessity refer to eternity.

(3) It may be objected that this word never refers to eternity, to which I reply that generation never has reference to the assumption of the human nature, even though some would like to understand it in this fashion. Let it be shown that the words "this day" cannot have reference to eternity, just as I have shown that generation cannot refer to the assumption of the human nature. Allow the fact that on no other occasion the words "this day" were to denote eternity, yet if they denote eternity in this text, then it suffices for our argument. I admit that when the words "this day" are used in reference to people, they are used to describe a specified period of time. Man is a creature who functions within the parameters of time. However, when the words "this day" are used, relative to God (who is without chronological dimensions) — as is the case here, "This day have I begotten Thee" — then it must be interpreted in a manner congruent with the nature of God for whom everything is simultaneously in the present and for whom a thousand years are but as yesterday (Psa. 90:4). God continually exists in the present. This Son, having been generated eternally, is ordained and sent forth to be the King of Zion. To Him the heathen have been given as a heritage. This Son would rule the people of God and punish His enemies. This Son we must honor, fear, and kiss with humility and love. All of this has been entrusted to Him as a consequence of His Sonship. He did not become the Son because He had all the aforementioned entrusted to Him.

Secondly, we shall consider Proverbs 8:22-25, "The LORD possessed Me in the beginning of His way, before His works of old. I was set up from everlasting, from the beginning, or ever the earth was. When there were no depths, I was brought forth; when there were no fountains abounding with water. Before the mountains were settled, before the hills was I brought forth."

Since it is an incontrovertible fact that the title "LORD" refers to the first Person, and that the pronouns "I" and "My" refer to the second Person who is called Wisdom in this chapter, there is no need to prove this. The second Person states concerning the first Person that He possessed Him, and He [the second Person] states concerning Himself that He was set up and brought forth. It is therefore incontrovertible that there is an interpersonal relationship between them. The basis for this relationship, being brought forth, is essential to both the Father and the Son. "The LORD possessed Me;" "I was brought forth." The Hebrew word קָנָנִי *(kanani)*, does not refer to ordination here or elsewhere, but always refers to possession, ownership, attainment, purchase, or acquisition. Thus, from this the word "possess" is derived. The first Person is here said to possess the second Person, to be His Proprietor. This proprietorship was eternal: in the beginning of the way, before His works of old. The question is in what manner the first Person is the Proprietor of the second Person. The text itself answers the question by stating, "I was brought forth." This proprietorship was in consequence of being brought forth, for which reason the second Person is called God's own Son, the first-begotten Son, and the only-begotten Son, as the word קָנָה *(kana)* means a receiving "by birth." When Eve brought forth Cain, she declared, "I have gotten a man from the LORD" (Gen. 4:1). The first Person is Proprietor of the second Person in consequence of being brought forth. The second Person states, "I was brought forth," however, not in this time state, for the text states expressly, "before His works of old; when there were no depths." The latter is convincing and incontrovertible. One cannot claim that being brought forth is the equivalent of being manifested in the flesh, for His being brought forth was from eternity, whereas this manifestation in the flesh did not occur until approximately four thousand years after creation. Neither can it be asserted that to possess and to be brought forth signify being ordained. This is not the meaning of these words — neither as far as root meaning is concerned nor by way of usage. Furthermore, ordination does not imply ownership, but it presupposes ownership. In order to ordain someone, one must have legal authority over this person.

The second Person, being eternally possessed by the Father in consequence of being brought forth, is said to be "set up from everlasting"; that is, to be ordained in His mediatorial office in the Counsel of Peace, in which every Person consistent with His nature, manner of existence, and manner of operation is involved in the ordination of the Son and the work of redemption by Him.

Each Person neither exists in an interpersonal relationship nor receives the relational name of Father, Son, or Holy Spirit in consequence of their relation to the work of redemption. Rather, it is the interpersonal relationship in which these Persons exist with one another in the Godhead, the basis for this relationship being either generation or procession. Since this is the very character of God Himself, each Person has involvement in the work of redemption. The scriptural discussion of various subjects is often intertwined with references to the work of redemption. Therefore, it must be recognized that everything in a given chapter is not to be related to the work of redemption. Rather, if such matters are discussed outside of that context, they are also to be interpreted as being outside of that context. Such is also the case here. The focus of this discussion is the interpersonal relationship between the first and second Persons, generation being the basis for it. Furthermore, the Holy Spirit conveys how, on the basis of this relationship, these Persons of the Trinity interact with one another in this relationship and in the work of redemption. This interaction consists of the first Person — who possesses the second Person by bringing Him forth — setting up (cf. Prov. 8:23) the second Person; that is, ordaining Him to be Surety and Mediator.

Thirdly, we shall consider Micah 5:2: "Out of thee shall He come forth unto Me that is to be ruler in Israel; whose goings forth have been from of old, from everlasting." Matthew 2:6 establishes beyond doubt that the reference is here to the Lord Jesus. This text speaks of two different "goings or comings forth." The one would have its origin in Bethlehem by virtue of His birth from Mary according to His human nature, whereas the other would be "from of old, from everlasting," that is, according to His divine nature. Both are defined by the same word in Hebrew, יָצָא (yatsa'). This word means "to come forth by birth." "All the souls that came with Jacob into Egypt, which יֹצְאֵי (yots'é) came out of his loins" (Gen. 46:26; cf. Gen. 15:4; Gen. 17:6; Gen. 35:11, and numerous other texts). In a special sense this word is used in reference to the Messiah (cf. 2 Sam. 7:12; Isa. 11:1; and others). As the Messiah came forth according to His human nature in this time state by birth from Mary in Bethlehem, so was His going forth by birth from everlasting. This identical word occurring in the identical simile has the same meaning. There is, however, one exception. The eternal going forth is expressed in the plural, which according to Hebraic style conveys a going forth par excellence, superseding all other goings forth — as is true of the eternal, incomparable, and incomprehensible generation of the Son. In considering this text one cannot resort to *coexistence, incarnation,* or *ordination,* for the reference is to a going forth, a coming forth by birth, an eternal going forth, and an actual going forth. Thus the truth that the Son has eternally been generated by the Father remains incontrovertible.

Fourthly, we shall consider John 5:26, "For as the Father hath life in Himself; so hath He given to the Son to have life in Himself." Both the first and the second Person of the divine Being are spoken of here. The one is called the Father and the other the Son; and it is in this regard that a relationship exists between them. It is stated that the Father has life in Himself, life being His all-sufficient activity and His singular energizing power. This life the Father has in Himself, He being the Fountain of that life and thus having received it from no one. As He is self-existent, likewise does His life originate from Himself. He is the living God, as He is frequently denominated in Scripture. It is also written that the Son has life in Himself. This life is neither a similar life nor another life, but the same life, manifesting the same all-sufficient activity and the same singular, energizing power. As the Father has this life in Himself, the Son likewise has this life in Himself. Thus, the Father and Son are equal; identical life is in each of them and in this respect they are the same. The difference, however, consists in the manner in which they possess this life; the Father having life in Himself, has given to the Son likewise to have life in Himself. This He has done in a manner which is consistent with God's eternal nature, which excludes both the concepts of time and a transformation from nothing to something. From this it is evident that the Son's existence originates in the Father, this being the basis for both Fatherhood and Sonship.

Evasive Argument: As far as God is concerned, the reference to life here is not subjective in nature, but causal; that is, it refers to God as the origin of the spiritual life of the elect. The Lord can save whom He wills and He has also empowered the Son as Mediator, being God and man, to save and to impart spiritual life to whomever He wills. That it must thus be understood is evident from the circumstances of the text.

Answer: (1) It is first of all a certainty that the life which the Son has in Himself is not different from the life which the Father has in Himself. In this respect they are equal, being in possession of the same life which both have in themselves.

(2) It is a certain truth that the Son, being Mediator and having assumed the human nature, has life in Himself. We deny emphatically, however, that the Father has given Christ to have life in

Himself in consequence of either the mediatorship itself or the manner in which He executes this mediatorship.

(3) If the first and second Person of the Godhead are coexistent in their divinity, without being dependent upon each other, then we must conclude that the one Person has life in Himself as much as the other Person, and thus when the second Person assumed the human nature, He already possessed life in Himself. Consequently, as Mediator He could not have received life in Himself from someone else for He already possessed it. The second Person already had life in Himself and this qualified Him to be the Mediator. The Father in having life in Himself does not have this as Mediator, in order to communicate life to the elect in the way of suffering and death. This must therefore be true for the Son as well, as both have the same life and have it in themselves. Both the Father and the Son have life in an identical fashion and whatever is not true for the Father is also not true of the Son.

(4) In order to be the cause of life in someone else, a person must first possess this life subjectively in himself. The results [that is, the manifestation of life] identify the energizing cause. Since the Father as well as the Son is the Author of life, it logically follows that they have life in themselves, which is the thrust of Christ's argument in this chapter. Christ demonstrates that the Father has life in Himself by virtue of the fact that He gives corporal and spiritual life to others. Since Christ also imparts both corporal and spiritual life to others, He demonstrates thereby that He also has life in Himself. He adds to this that as God He has life within Himself by virtue of the Father giving it to Him. He adds to this that the Father — by virtue of the fact that the Son has life in Himself, thus qualifying Him to be Mediator — had sent Him to execute the office of Mediator, enabling the Father, Christ Himself, and the Holy Spirit to impart life to dead and death-worthy sinners.

Fifthly, we shall consider Hebrews 1:3: "Who being the brightness of His glory, and the express image of His person." It is the apostle's objective in this chapter to prove both the divinity of Christ and the fact that He is the Son of God in an incomprehensibly more glorious manner than the most glorious creatures, the angels. "Unto which of the angels said He at any time, Thou art my Son" (Heb. 1:5)? God did call them the sons of God, as He also did the regenerate. None of these were sons by generation, however; only Christ is Son by generation. "Thou art my Son, this day have I begotten Thee" (Heb. 1:5). This is also conveyed by these two expressions, "the brightness of His glory," and "the express image of His person." This can be said of none other than He who is the natural Son of God. It cannot refer to the human nature of Christ, for, as we have previously shown, this nature and the first Person of the Godhead have nothing in common. There are also those who do not wish to associate this sonship with His divine nature and consider Him to be a separate, self-existent, non-relational, and non-generated Person. Then it would follow that the second Person in union with the human nature could also not be the Son, for whatever is absent in each nature individually cannot be present by virtue of their union. From this it would have to be concluded that the second Person, in manifesting Himself in the flesh, would reveal Himself in this world as the brightness of His own glory and the express image of His own Person. The Son, however, is the manifestation of His Father's glory and Person, which consequently must be true relative to His divine nature.

The Son is here described as existing in a relationship with the Father, which first of all is expressed by the phrase, "the brightness of His Father's glory." Brightness is a reflection generated by light. The Father is a light which no man can approach unto, and thus the Son, as far as His Personhood is concerned, eternally proceeds from that light. The Council of Nicea, held in 325 A.D., has expressed it very well when it calls Him "Light of Light."

The text further refers to this interpersonal relationship as "the express image of His Father's Person." In Greek the word ὑπόστασις *(hypostasis)* is used, which literally refers to an independent entity, but when used to refer to an intelligent being, expresses personhood. Thus, it is not the divine essence which is under discussion here, but rather the first Person of the Godhead, as the Son is here said to be the express image of His Father's Person. Men generate sons after their image, and thus a son is the express image of his father. Fully removing the human element, it may therefore be stated that the second Person has been generated by the first Person. Both the relationship as well as the relational titles "Father" and "Son," have their origin in this generation, in consequence of which the Son is called the express image of His Father. To be the express image of the Father necessarily implies natural Sonship by way of eternal generation. It is for this reason that the Lord Jesus is called "the image of God" (2 Cor. 4:4), and "the image of the invisible God" (Col. 1:15).

Thus we have described this great mystery which God has revealed in His Word, a truth which always has been and will be known, acknowledged, believed, confessed, and staunchly defended by the church, in spite of all who regret to see this truth upheld.

The Holy Spirit as the Third Person of the Trinity

Thus far we have discussed the divinity and the interpersonal relationship of the Father and the Son. Now we shall proceed to consider the *third Person*, who in Scripture bears the title *Holy Spirit*. Of this Person we shall consider the following: 1) His Name; 2) His Personhood; 3) the veracity of His divinity and His divine Personhood; 4) the interpersonal relationship between His Person and the other divine Persons, as well as the basis for this relationship: the procession from the Father and the Son.

Scripture calls the third person *Holy Spirit* by means of the Hebrew word רוח *(ruach)*, and the Greek word πνεῦμα *(pneuma)*. This word is used in a variety of contexts, such as in reference to wind (John 3:8), angels (Heb. 1:14), the human soul (Eccl. 12:7), and the motions of the soul (Gal. 6:1). To give expression to the spiritual dimension of God's character there is no more suitable word for us than the word "Spirit." Sometimes this word is used in its essential sense, that is, in reference to the divine Being as it subsists in three Persons. "God is a Spirit" (John 4:24). Sometimes it is used in a personal sense, as in reference to the Son, "the last Adam was made a quickening Spirit" (1 Cor. 15:45), but most often the third Person is called by this name (cf. Mat. 28:19; 1 John 5:7). Occasionally the word "Spirit" refers to the operation of the Holy Spirit. "The Holy Ghost fell on all them which heard the Word... that on the Gentiles also was poured out the gift of the Holy Ghost" (Acts 10:44-45). When discussing the third Person of the divine Being, we do not merely refer to Him as "Spirit," but as *the Holy Spirit*, which is in accordance with Scripture.

The third Person is called the *Spirit,*

(1) because it is His personal property as the third Person to proceed from the Father and the Son, which cannot be expressed any more clearly than by the use of the word "Spirit" which means "to breathe." Therefore He is called "the breath of the Almighty" (Job 33:4), and "the breath of His mouth" (Psa. 33:6);

(2) due to His manner of operation which, as indicated above, is compared to breathing. When the apostles were filled with the Holy Spirit on the day of Pentecost, the entire house was filled with the sound "as of a rushing mighty wind" (Acts 2:2,4). When the Lord Jesus promised the Holy Spirit to His disciples, He breathed on them (John 20:22);

(3) in view of the consequences of His operation, which produce in His people a ready and diligent disposition towards the service of God. "Who maketh His angels spirits; His ministers a flaming

fire" (Psa. 104:4); "The wind bloweth where it listeth...so is every one that is born of the Spirit" (John 3:8).

He is called the *Holy Spirit*, not because He is holier than the Father and the Son — Isaiah uses the word "holy" three times in reference to the three Persons of the divine Being (Isa. 6:3) — but,

(1) due to His manner of operation by virtue of His procession from the Father and the Son, from which His name is derived. Therefore He is called the Spirit of both the Father and the Son. When considering the three Persons of the Godhead comparatively, then the first Person by virtue of His personal property, is called *Father;* the second Person, also due to His personal property, *Son;* and likewise the third Person, *Holy Spirit.* Since their manner of operation is a necessary consequence of their manner of existence, they are also referred to by these names in their execution of the work of redemption;

(2) due to the manner of His operation in the elect. "...being sanctified by the Holy Ghost" (Rom. 15:16); "...through sanctification of the Spirit" (2 Th. 2:13).

The Holy Spirit is not merely a good influence in man nor a gracious gift of God, but He is a *Person.* Properties and operations are attributed to the Holy Spirit which can only be attributed to a Person.

First, *intelligence* is attributed to Him. "For the Spirit searcheth all things, yea, the deep things of God. For what man knoweth the things of a man, save the spirit of man which is in Him? even so the things of God knoweth no man, but the Spirit of God" (1 Cor. 2:10-11). Here Scripture compares the spirit of man to the Spirit of God, knowledge being attributed to both. The one knows the things which are of man, whereas the other knows the things which are of God. Men who have become partakers of the Spirit of God are distinguished from the Spirit which is in them. "Searching what, or what manner of time the Spirit of Christ which was in them did signify," etc. (1 Pet. 1:11). 1 Corinthians 2:11 does not suggest that the spiritual man searches and knows the things of God, but rather the Spirit of God in contrast to the spirit of man.

Secondly, a *will* is attributed to Him. "But all these worketh that one and the selfsame Spirit, dividing to every man severally as He will" (1 Cor. 12:11). Apart from the fact that the Holy Spirit is distinguished from His gifts, He is said to be sovereign in the dispersion of these gifts. As such He is not accountable to anyone, but acts according to His sovereign good pleasure.

Thirdly, *works* are attributed to Him, such as the creation of the world (Psa. 33:6; Gen. 1:2), regeneration and the impartation of life (John 3:6; Gal. 5:25), and the commissioning of His servants

(Acts 13:2). When activities are attributed to particular persons, and these are acknowledged by all to be well-done, it is immediately evident that the reference is not to the cause of such activity, but rather to the means by which such a person works. When mention is made of the Holy Spirit's works, however, the primary reference is to Him as being the cause of this activity, who, while thus engaged, avails Himself of means.

Fourthly, He is said to appear by means of a visible sign, denoting both His presence and manner of operation, as at the baptism of Christ (Mat. 3:16) and on the day of Pentecost (Acts 2:1-4). A person's existence manifests itself by way of incidents; however, incidents do not manifest themselves as persons.

Fifthly, the Holy Spirit is expressly distinguished from His gifts, as being the cause of that which transpires. "Now there are diversities of gifts, but the same Spirit. For to one is given by the Spirit the word of wisdom," etc. (1 Cor. 12:4, 8). Even though the Spirit is referred to as the power of God in Luke 24:49, Acts 10:38, and Luke 1:35, it is nevertheless clearly indicated that He is a Person rather than the contrary. Christ is also called the power of God in 1 Corinthians 1:24. Whoever has power and exercises this power is of necessity a person. When it is said that the Father and the Son work through the Holy Spirit, it indicates that the said Person works through the Person which proceeds from Him.

Objection: The Holy Spirit is referred to as a gift.

Answer: This does not deny His Personhood, for Christ is also referred to as a gift (cf. Isaiah 9:6; John 3:16; John 4:10). Even when the Holy Spirit is referred to as a gift, He is described as a Person, the event being distinguished from the cause of the event. "Because the love of God is shed abroad in our hearts by the Holy Ghost which is given unto us" (Rom. 5:5).

The Divinity of the Holy Spirit

The Holy Spirit is not merely a Person, but He is a *divine* Person. He is the true, eternal God who has created the heavens and the earth. This becomes evident from the fact that divine names, attributes, works, and honor are attributed to Him.

First, we shall consider His *Names*. He who is called *Jehovah* is the true, eternal God, for no one else may bear this Name, nor is anyone else called by this Name (cf. chapter 3, page 85). In Isaiah 6:3, 9 the Holy Spirit is referred to as *Jehovah*. He who in verse 3 is called *Jehovah Sabaoth*, the LORD of Hosts, says in verse 9, "Go, and tell this people," etc. This *Jehovah* was the Holy Spirit according to the testimony of Paul. "Well spake the Holy Ghost by Esaias the prophet unto our fathers, saying, Go unto this people, and say," etc. (Acts 28:25-26). In Psalm 95:3-9, He who is referred to as "a great God," "a great King above all gods," who is JEHOVAH in whose hands are the deep places of the earth, who must be worshipped, before whom we must bow — of Him it is said, "To-day if ye will hear His voice," etc. (verses 7-8), "your fathers tempted Me, proved Me, and saw My work" (verse 9). This Person is the Holy Spirit, which is confirmed in the following passage, "But they rebelled, and vexed His Holy Spirit" (Isa. 63:10). This is also confirmed by the apostle, "Wherefore as the Holy Ghost saith, To day if ye will hear His voice" (Heb. 3:7).

Add to this, "...to lie to the Holy Ghost,...thou hast not lied unto men, but unto God" (Acts 5:3-4). To lie to the Holy Ghost is to lie to God. In order to remove all excuses, the Holy Spirit is called God in contrast to creatures or men. Ananias and Sapphira did not lie to men, nor to Peter and all those who were present — even though they were partakers of the gift of the Holy Spirit and were graced with special qualities — but they lied to God, thus tempting the Spirit of the Lord (verse 9). This truth is also confirmed in the following texts, "Know ye not that ye are the temple of God, and that the Spirit of God dwelleth in you?" (1 Cor. 3:16). "What? know ye not that your body is the temple of the Holy Ghost which is in you?" (1 Cor. 6:19). "Temple" and "God" are closely related to each other. A temple is designated for the service of God, and God dwelt in the temple in Jerusalem. Since God is the One who dwells in the temple and since the Holy Spirit dwells in us as in a temple, believers being temples of the Holy Ghost, it follows that the Holy Spirit is God (cf. Num. 6:24-26 as compared to 2 Cor. 13:14).

Secondly, we will consider His *attributes*. He who is eternal, omnipresent, omniscient, and omnipotent, is the true and eternal God. Such is true of the Holy Spirit.

(1) He is *eternal,* for He is the Creator of heaven and of earth, which we will prove shortly. The Creator is none other than the eternal God. Prior to creation there was only eternity in which God dwelt (Isa. 57:15). At the very outset of creation the Holy Spirit was already present, and moved upon the face of waters (Gen. 1:2).

(2) He is *omniscient.* "Whither shall I go from Thy Spirit? or whither shall I flee from Thy presence? If I ascend up into heaven, Thou art there: if I make my bed in hell, behold, thou art there" (Psa. 139:7-8). The psalmist confronts himself with the omnipresence of God, declaring that no one can hide himself from God as in His Being He is everywhere, whether it be in heaven, upon

earth, or in hell. Since, according to the psalmist, the Holy Spirit in His being is omnipresent, He of necessity is truly God.

(3) He is *omniscient.* "The Spirit searcheth all things, yea, the deep things of God" (1 Cor. 2:10). The Spirit Himself, in contrast with the spirit of man, searches and knows all things in an all-inclusive manner (1 Cor. 2:11), doing so in relation to the deep things of God — the most hidden things concerning God, His Being, His manner of existence, His perfections, and His secret counsel.

(4) He is *omnipotent.* He is the Spirit of might (Isa. 11:2), and the power of the highest (Luke 1:35). This omnipotence becomes evident in His works, which we shall presently demonstrate.

Thirdly, we shall consider His *works.* He who has created the world, regenerates the elect, imparts spiritual life, is the dispenser of all spiritual gifts, teaches the elect to pray and leads them, and raises the dead — He is the true and eternal God. Since the Holy Spirit does all this He is of necessity truly God.

(1) *He creates.* "The Spirit of God moved upon the face of the waters" (Gen. 1:2); "By His Spirit He hath garnished the heavens" (Job 26:13); "By the word of the LORD were the heavens made; and all the host of them by the breath of His mouth" (Psa. 33:6).

(2) *He regenerates and imparts life.* "Except a man be born of water and of the Spirit" (John 3:5); "The Spirit giveth life" (2 Cor. 3:6).

(3) *He dispenses spiritual gifts.* "But all these worketh that one and the selfsame Spirit" (1 Cor. 12:11).

(4) *He teaches how to pray.* "The Spirit of grace and of supplications" (Zec. 12:10); "The Spirit itself maketh intercession for us with groanings which cannot be uttered" (Rom. 8:26).

(5) *He leads believers to glory in the way of sanctification.* "For as many as are led by the Spirit of God, they are the sons of God" (Rom. 8:14).

(6) *He raises the dead.* "He that raised up Christ from the dead shall also quicken your mortal bodies by His Spirit that dwelleth in you" (Rom. 8:11).

Fourthly, we shall consider His *honor.* He is the true God, in whose name we must be baptized, from whom we must ask all things, and whom we must obey. Since we must be baptized in the name of the Holy Ghost, and must request all gifts from Him, the Holy Spirit must of necessity be truly God.

(1) The requirement of baptism in His name is expressed in Matthew 28:19, "...baptizing them in the name of the Father, and of the Son, and of the Holy Ghost." Baptism is a seal of the covenant of grace, the latter being established only between the true God and believers. In baptism we surrender ourselves to God

as the all-sufficient One who possesses all that is needful unto man's salvation; we surrender ourselves to the Most High in order to honor, fear, trust, and obey Him. In baptism we entrust our soul to God, desiring that He who is true to Himself would make us partakers of all the benefits of the covenant. In baptism we surrender ourselves to God, desiring to love and serve Him. Since all of this is comprehended in baptism, it necessarily follows that He in whose name we are baptized is truly God. This explains why the apostle so adamantly rejected the idea of anyone being baptized in his name (1 Cor. 1:14-15). Whereas the three Persons of the divine Being are actively engaged in the covenant — the Holy Spirit leading a believer to the Son, and by the Son to the Father, and the Father, through the Son and by the agency of the Holy Spirit works in believers — it therefore follows that these three Persons are expressly mentioned at baptism. In it the Holy Spirit receives the same honor as the Father and the Son, and thus He is the very same God, coequal with the Father and the Son.

(2) It is evident from 2 Corinthians 13:14 that we should petition the Holy Spirit for all gifts. "The grace of the Lord Jesus Christ, and the love of God, and the communion of the Holy Ghost, be with you all." Here the Holy Spirit is afforded the same honor as the Son and the Father, as the same act of worship is expressed in identical fashion to the three Persons of the Godhead. Consider also the worship expressed towards the Holy Spirit in the following passage: "Grace be unto you, and peace, from Him which is, and which was, and which is to come; and from the seven Spirits which are before His throne" (Rev. 1:4). Again the eternal God and the Holy Spirit are worshipped in identical fashion. If one wishes to view the latter part of this text as being explanatory of the first part — which frequently occurs — the text would read as follows: from Him which is, etc., which are the seven Spirits. This would then identify the Spirit as the One who applies all that is of Christ to believers. In this capacity the Holy Spirit would also be worshipped as the eternal God, for He is the selfsame eternal God. One should not understand the seven Spirits to be angels, as they ought not to be worshipped (Mat. 4:10), but rather the third Person of the divine Being who is referred to in this manner in view of His operation, imparting to the congregation numerous sufficient and perfect gifts.

(3) The obligation to serve and obey the Holy Spirit becomes evident from the fact that it is possible to sin against the Holy Ghost. We are exhorted not to grieve the Holy Spirit (Eph. 4:30). The ungodly Israelites rebelled and vexed the Holy Spirit, and thus

grieved Him (Isa. 63:10). Yes, the sin against the Holy Ghost — because He is the One who directly deals with and manifests Himself to the soul — is declared to be the greatest as well as an unforgivable sin (cf. Mat. 12:31-32; 1 John 5:16).

All these considerations, viewed individually as well as collectively, ought to convince the conscience that the Holy Spirit is truly God, being of the same essence as the Father and the Son.

The Procession of the Holy Spirit from the Father and the Son

Thus far we have proved that the Holy Spirit is a Person, and more particularly, that He is a divine Person, and of the same essence as the Father and the Son. We will now consider the interpersonal relationship which exists between the third Person and the other Persons of the Godhead. As the Son is a different Person from the Father, likewise the Spirit is a different Person from the Father and the Son.

(1) He is expressly called "another Comforter" (John 14:16).

(2) He is also described in such a way that He can be neither the Father nor the Son, but must necessarily be another (John 15:26). He who has been sent by the Father and by the Son, proceeds from the Father and testifies of the Son; He is another Person from the one who sends Him, from whom He proceeds and of whom He testifies.

(3) He is therefore referred to as a distinct Person in those texts in which mention is also made of the Father and the Son. (cf. Mat. 28:19; 2 Cor. 13:14; 1 John 5:7).

(4) It is also stated that the Holy Spirit works as well as the Father and the Son, and that in regard to both. "He will guide you into all truth: for He shall not speak of Himself; but whatsoever He shall hear, that shall He speak: and He will shew you things to come. He shall glorify Me: for he shall receive of Mine, and shall show it unto you" (John 16:13-14).

The Holy Spirit is not a coexistent Being, which implies that He exists simultaneously, is of the same essence, and is not in an interpersonal relationship with the Father. Rather, He is a divine Person, the nature of whose Personhood is to exist in an interpersonal relationship to the Father and the Son. The eternal *procession* from the Father and the Son is the basis for this relationship. The Son proceeds from the Father by way of eternal generation, and the Holy Spirit proceeds from the Father and the Son in a manner which can best be described by "to breathe."

(1) The word "Spirit" as it occurs in Hebrew and Greek conveys this idea.

(2) For this reason He is called the "breath of the Almighty" (Job 33:4), and "the breath of His mouth" (Psa. 33:6).

(3) This manner of operation is congruent with His manner of existence. The third Person works by way of breathing, and it is also the manner of His existence. "The wind bloweth where it listeth...so is every one that is born of the Spirit" (John 3:8). For this reason Jesus also availed Himself of such symbolism when He promised the Spirit to His disciples. "He breathed on them, and saith unto them, Receive ye the Holy Ghost" (John 20:22). In like manner also the apostles were filled with the Holy Spirit, an event which was accompanied with the sound of a rushing mighty wind (Acts 2:2).

The third Person proceeds from both the first and second Persons. This truth resulted in an intense and lengthy controversy between the Greek and Latin churches. The Greek church held the viewpoint that the Holy Spirit proceeds only from the Father. The Latin church opposed this position, defending the truth which had always been believed and confessed: the Holy Spirit's procession from the Father and the Son. In the Lord's goodness we may still believe and confess this truth which will always be believed and confessed by the church. Scripture confirms this.

First, it is confirmed by those texts in which the Holy Spirit is called the Spirit of the Son and the Spirit of Christ. "God hath sent forth the Spirit of His Son into your hearts" (Gal. 4:6); "Now if any man have not the Spirit of Christ, he is none of His" (Rom. 8:9); "Searching what, or what manner of time the Spirit of Christ which was in them did signify" (1 Pet. 1:11).

Secondly, it is confirmed by those texts in which the Son is said to send the Holy Spirit. "...I will send unto you from the Father" (John 15:26); "But if I depart, I will send Him unto you" (John 16:7). What is true for His manner of operation is also true for His manner of existence. The manner of His operation is a necessary consequence of His manner of existence.

Thirdly, it is confirmed in such texts in which it is stated that the Holy Spirit imparts to the elect that which He receives from the Son. "But whatsoever He shall hear, that shall He speak...He shall take of Mine, and shew it unto you" (John 16:13-15).

The operations of both the Father and the Son relative to the procession of the Holy Spirit should not be viewed as proceeding from two distinctly different origins, for it is one and the same operation and power. Both the Father and the Son ought rather to be viewed as the primary cause of all that transpires, rather than viewing the Son as a primary cause of lesser importance, implying that the Father would cause the Holy Spirit to proceed by means of the Son. If, however, we consider manner and order of both existence and operation, then the Holy Spirit proceeds from the Father and from the Son, as well as from the Father through the Son.

Objections to the Doctrine of the Trinity Refuted

From all the aforementioned it has been proven incontrovertibly to all who believe the Scriptures that the one divine Being subsists in three Persons, and also how they exist in an interpersonal relationship to each other.

All the objections which the corrupt intellect of man may present relative to this doctrine, such as is done by Socinians and all who sympathize with them, are merely the result of reasoning from a human and temporal perspective. Such reasoning cannot be associated with the eternal God and is thus easily refuted.

First, when God is said to be one in essence, and yet to subsist in three Persons, this is not a contradictory statement. Both elements of this statement are not equivalent in meaning, for God is one in essence subsisting in three Persons; not three in essence and not one Person.

Secondly, there are three Persons which are eternal, infinite, and omnipotent, and not three eternals, infinites, and omnipotents. Rather, there is but one eternal, infinite, and omnipotent Being.

Thirdly, when it is stated "...that they might know Thee the only true God" (John 17:3), this does not suggest that only the Father is truly God to the exclusion of the Son and the Holy Spirit, but rather that the Father is the only true God. The word "only" does not modify Father, but it modifies the word God. Both the Son and the Holy Spirit are the identical and only true God, a truth which has been proven above.

Fourthly, the words "generate" and "proceed" neither suggest superiority or inferiority nor the transformation from nothing to something, for all this is an eternal reality. It is consistent with God's eternal nature that the divine Being exists in Father, Son, and Holy Spirit. The Father generates, the Son is generated, and the Holy Spirit proceeds from both.

Fifthly, it does not suggest imperfection if that which is the unique property of one Person cannot be attributed to another Person. Rather, it is a perfection of each Person and of the Godhead to subsist in these Persons, each Person having its personal properties.

Sixthly, when Christ acknowledges His Father to be greater than He (John 14:28), the reference is not to His divinity, for as such He is equal to the Father (Phil. 2:6) and one with the Father

(1 John 5:7). This has reference to His office as Mediator, in respect to which the Father calls Him His Servant (Isa. 53:11).

Seventhly, when the Holy Spirit is said to be a gift, to be sent, to be poured out, and when believers are said to be baptized with the Holy Spirit, reference is being made to both His extraordinary and ordinary operations. The Son is also called a gift (cf. Isa. 9:5; John 3:16; John 4:10), and is also said to be sent (John 5:36). Furthermore, in the human realm men of equal status are commissioned or sent forth, which is true for instance when an official body delegates someone from its membership. Individual persons can also be viewed as gifts, as when a father gives his daughter to a man in marriage or when masters give their slaves to others.

Eighthly, when the Spirit is said to be not yet given (John 7:39), the reference is not to the Person of the Holy Spirit. He already existed as can be observed in the baptism of Christ (Mat. 3:16). This rather refers to the abundant gifts of the Spirit which believers would receive according to promise.

Ninthly, dependency is a reality among men, but not in God. The Son has life in Himself as the Father has life in Himself (John 5:26). The attribute of eternity excludes all possibility of dependency. In the execution of the covenant of grace each Person operates according to the manner of His existence. Thus, the Father's operation proceeds from Himself, the Son's from the Father, and the Holy Spirit's from the Father and the Son — all of which occur without dependency as this would suggest imperfection. This is the meaning of John 5:19 where it is stated that the Son can do nothing of Himself. Since as Son His existence originates in the Father and not in Himself, He cannot be operative as Father, but operates as the Son of the Father. Further, it is to be understood that as Mediator He receives everything from the Father and in that capacity does nothing by Himself.

If someone were to say, "This is far beyond me; I cannot comprehend it," I would respond that God is incomprehensible. There are things of much less importance which you cannot comprehend. What causes low and high tides? How does your soul affect your body? How are members of your body set in motion by the exercise of your will, etc.? Would you, insignificant "ant," comprehend the incomprehensible God? Believe what you cannot comprehend simply because God declares it to be so, and worship the incomprehensible. If you were a believer, you would already have more insight into these mysteries than you can presently imagine or would then be able to express.

The Profitableness of Reflecting upon the Mystery of the Trinity

Thus far we have expressed the truth concerning these great mysteries, namely, that the one divine Being subsists in three Persons, and that each Person is the eternal, true, and only God. We have also shown that these Persons are distinguished from each other,

(1) in their names: Father, Son, and Holy Spirit;

(2) in their personal properties: the Father as generating, the Son as being generated, and the Holy Spirit as proceeding from the Father and the Son;

(3) in their order of existence: the Father as the *first* Person exists of Himself, the Son as the *second* Person exists of the Father, and the Holy Spirit as the *third* Person exists of the Father and the Son;

(4) in their manner of operation: the Father operates from within Himself, the Son out of the Father, and the Holy Spirit out of the Father and the Son. All of this is with the understanding that all the works of God in their external manifestation are common to all three Persons. Beyond all this we did not wish to penetrate any further into this mystery.

We now wish to proceed to the practical application, which is both wonderful and profitable — yes, the entire spiritual life of a Christian consists in being exercised concerning this mystery, and is thus distinguished from the practice of civil virtue and natural religion. A godly person will never deny this mystery, even though all believers do not perceive this mystery with equal clarity. They may neither be equally capable of reflecting upon their knowledge concerning this doctrine nor be able to express in words what they understand about it. The believer believes it and is much more knowledgeable in this mystery than the most learned but unregenerate divine, although the latter may be able to express himself more eloquently about it. The believer in all his religious exercises operates from this principle. Guided by the Holy Spirit he goes to the Son, and through the Son to the Father. The oneness of the divine Being will thus shine round about him as he is exercised concerning the Trinity.

Even though Arminians make no effort to deny the Trinity, they nevertheless seek to curtail the significance of this doctrine by suggesting that it is not profitable for edification. The Word of God, however, bears witness to the contrary.

First, this becomes evident in texts which show that the knowledge and acknowledgement of God as being Triune in Persons is prerequisite unto salvation. "And this is life eternal, that they might know Thee (the Father, verse 1) the only true God, and Jesus Christ (the Son, verse 1), whom Thou hast sent" (John 17:3); "Ye believe in God, believe also in Me. He that hath seen Me hath seen the Father. Believest thou not that I am in the Father, and the Father in Me?" (John 14:1, 9-10). "Whosoever denieth the Son, the same hath not the Father" (1 John 2:23); "But these are written, that ye might believe that Jesus is the Christ, the Son of God; and that believing ye might have life through His Name" (John 20:31).

Secondly, this is also evident from our baptism which is performed in the name of the Father, and of the Son, and of the Holy Ghost (Mat. 28:19). To these three Persons we are surrendered in holy baptism, and in their name the covenant of grace is confirmed to us. Baptism obligates everyone to trust in their Names, to acknowledge them, to love and to serve them, and to allow ourselves to be governed, comforted, and wrought upon by the Father, the Son, and the Holy Spirit. Baptism also obligates us to worship these three Persons and to seek to be blessed by each of them. "The grace of the Lord Jesus Christ, and the love of God, and the communion of the Holy Ghost, be with you all" (2 Cor. 13:14).

Thirdly, the Father, the Son, and the Spirit reveal themselves, interact with, and exercise believers in an individual and distinct manner. "My Father will love him, and we will come unto him, and make our abode with him" (John 14:23). The Holy Spirit dwells in the godly as in a temple (1 Cor. 6:19). From all this it should be evident that God cannot be served except as being Triune in Persons, and that those who honor and serve Him as such are the truly godly in this life and will experience salvation hereafter. Thus, this truth is most profitable and essential.

As we seek to demonstrate how one may profit from this mystery, we shall follow the order of the divine Persons.

First, *God the Father* is viewed by believers as the origin of all things, and thus also of their salvation. They may perceive that He has chosen them from eternity to become the objects of His eternal love, to exalt them, and to make them partakers of an eternal and incomprehensible salvation; and that all is of Him, through Him, and unto Him. Secondly, they perceive how the Father has appointed His only-begotten and beloved Son to be Surety for the elect in order to make known to men and angels His perfect righteousness, incomprehensible mercy, wisdom, freeness in the dispensing of grace, and wondrous benevolence — the purpose of this revelation being to enhance their experience of salvation. Thirdly, they perceive that the Father in order to accomplish that purpose has created the world, and has decreed that man, due to his own fault, would fall into sin. By His providence He maintains and governs everything for the benefit and profit of His elect, whom He has appointed to be the inheritors or possessors of the entire world. Fourthly, they perceive that the Father, according to the Counsel of Peace, has sent His Son into the world to assume the human nature, to suffer and die as Surety, to place Him under the law in order to satisfy the Father's justice by His Son's perfect obedience, and thus deliver the elect from guilt and punishment, granting them a right unto eternal life. Fifthly, they perceive that the Father sends forth His Holy Spirit into the hearts of the elect to illuminate and regenerate them, to lead them to Christ, unite them to Christ by faith, and in the way of holiness lead them to glory. Sixthly, they perceive that the Father receives them as His children and heirs, and consequently loves and cares for them as His children.

Such reflection produces in the believer a childlike frame which causes the soul to sink away in humility. How the soul then rejoices and receives liberty to exclaim, "Abba, Father"! The soul will commit himself and his entire case into the hands of the Father, entrusting all to Him, living out of His hand, bringing all his needs to Him as his Father, making all his desires known to Him, being willing to obey his Father and to serve Him according to His will. We will deal with this more comprehensively in chapter 35, on "The Adoption of Children."

In considering *God the Son*, first, believers perceive Him to be the only qualified Surety to make the elect sons and daughters, and children of the Father, while in amazement they reflect upon the unsearchable wisdom of God in appointing such a qualified Person to be Surety. Secondly, they perceive the wondrous love of the Son towards man, who gave Himself in the eternal Counsel of Peace to be Surety in order to accomplish the great work of redemption. Thirdly, they perceive how He humbled Himself in the fullness of time, taking upon Himself the form of a servant and assuming their nature, not being ashamed to call them brethren, in order that they might enjoy communion and fellowship with Him. Fourthly, they perceive how He out of pure and voluntary love has taken their sins upon Himself, doing so as if He had personally committed them. They perceive how He Himself, with all willingness, bore the punishment which they deserved, thereby fully satisfying divine justice and reconciling them to God. Fifthly, they perceive that He has united them to Himself as members of a spiritual body, He being the Head and they the members, He being the Bridegroom and they His bride, so that in Him, the Son, they are sons and daughters. Sixthly, they perceive that He thus brings them to God, presenting them to the Father, saying, "Behold, I and the children whom the Lord hath given me." Here is the fountain of salvation and here all the perfections of God manifest themselves in an entirely different and more glorious manner than in the work of creation and providential maintenance. Believers, beholding the glory of the Lord as in a glass, will be changed accordingly, and thus, through the Son, may go to the Father. We shall subsequently deal with this in a more comprehensive manner.

God the Holy Spirit is for believers the One who, in a manifold and merciful manner, applies and makes them partakers of all that the Father has eternally decreed for their benefit, as well as all that which the Son has merited for them. We wish to deal with this somewhat more comprehensively, as there will be little opportunity to do so subsequent to this chapter.

The Father and the Son send forth the Holy Spirit into the hearts of believers, and the Holy Spirit dwells in them as in a temple. Prior to their regeneration the elect are by nature as all other men, "sensual, having not the Spirit" (Jude 19). As it is only the Spirit who makes alive, they are dead in sins and trespasses, living in total separation from God, having neither perception of their sinfulness and damnable state nor of salvation and spiritual life, and having no desire for these things. That which is of the earth is the focus of all their soul's activity and of all the members of their body. All their religious activity is of a mechanical nature, in order to quiet their conscience. They rest in what they have done, and hate all that which resembles light, spirituality, and true godliness — especially when their encounter with them is too close for comfort.

However, when the moment of God's good pleasure[4] arrives for the elect, God grants them the Holy Spirit, who illuminates and regenerates them and by faith makes them partakers of Christ and all His benefits. "And because ye are sons, God hath sent forth the Spirit of His Son into your hearts, crying, Abba, Father" (Gal. 4:6); "Ye have received the Spirit of adoption, whereby we cry, Abba, Father" (Rom. 8:15); "Now we have received the Spirit which is of God" (1 Cor. 2:12). At this point we must consider in what manner or in what regard believers receive the Holy Spirit.

Question: Do believers receive the gifts of the Spirit, or is the Person Himself communicated to them?

Answer: (1) The indwelling of the Holy Spirit in the believer is

---

[4] à Brakel frequently uses the expression, "Als der uitverkorenen tijd daar is." The literal translation of this phrase is, "When the time of the elect is there," which, however, is more commonly referred to as "the moment of God's good pleasure." To enhance clarity, we opted to use the latter expression.

not just a mere presence, such as is true for the omnipresence of His Godhead.

(2) Neither is it an external relationship, viewing them as children of God and the objects of His operation.

(3) Nor is it a communication of His gifts, such as faith, hope, and charity, etc.

(4) Rather, it is the Person Himself who is given to believers, dwelling in them in a manner which is incomprehensible and inexpressible to us. This presence infinitely exceeds the limits of their person, and yet is in an extraordinary manner within them.

First, this becomes evident in those texts where the Holy Spirit is expressly said not only to be given to them, but also to dwell in them. "And I will pray the Father, and He shall give you another Comforter, that He may abide with you for ever; even the Spirit of truth; whom the world cannot receive, because it seeth Him not, neither knoweth Him: but ye know Him; for He dwelleth with you, and shall be in you" (John 14:16-17); "...the Spirit of Christ which was in them..." (1 Pet. 1:11); "Know ye not...that the Spirit of God dwelleth in you?" (1 Cor. 3:16).

Evasive Argument: The gifts of the Holy Spirit are identified as being the Holy Spirit Himself (Acts 10:44-45).

Answer: (1) In those places where the Holy Spirit is mentioned, it is not always and everywhere to be understood as being the same as His gifts. Thus, this argument has no clout, for it must then be shown that in the aforementioned and similar texts the reference is to gifts and not to the Person Himself.

(2) A clear distinction is made between the Spirit Himself, who is given to God's children, and His gifts. These gifts neither teach, lead, comfort, bear witness, regenerate, nor work faith, but it is the Person, the Holy Spirit Himself who works and imparts these things to each person as is pleasing to Him.

(3) The gifts of the Spirit are also given to reprobates (Heb. 6:4). Nevertheless these gifts do not make the person a partaker of Christ, as does the indwelling of the Spirit. "If any man have not the Spirit of Christ, he is none of His" (Rom. 8:9). Thus, it is confirmed that the Person of the Holy Spirit Himself dwells in the believer in a manner which is inexpressible and yet consistent with God's Being.

Secondly, this indwelling is confirmed by such texts where believers are called the temples of the Holy Ghost. "Know ye not that ye are the temple of God, and that the Spirit of God dwelleth in you?" (1 Cor. 3:16). "What? know ye not that your body is the temple of the Holy Ghost which is in you, which ye have of God?"

(1 Cor. 6:19). God Himself, and not His gifts, dwelt in the temple at Jerusalem. "And I will dwell among the children of Israel" (Exo. 29:45); "In Salem also is His tabernacle, and His dwelling place in Zion" (Psa. 76:2); "Thou that dwellest between the cherubims" (Psa. 80:1). Since the Holy Spirit dwells in the believer as He formerly did in the temple, He Himself likewise, rather than His gifts only, personally dwells in the believer.

Thirdly, believers have an infinite desire which can only be satisfied with the Infinite One. The gifts of God are not infinite, and thus a believer cannot be satisfied with them. God Himself must be and is their portion, and they are united to God in Christ and are made perfect in one (John 17:23). Thus the believer does not merely have the gifts of the Spirit, but he has the Spirit Himself.

Objection #1. Since the Holy Spirit is infinite, He consequently cannot dwell in finite man.

Answer: The fact that God dwells in a place or a person does not imply that He is limited to that location, as if He could not simultaneously be elsewhere. We rather understand that He who is infinite and omnipresent truly resides within an individual — neither physically nor as is true for His omnipresence, but in an extraordinary manner. The second Person, the Son of God, is personally united to the human nature of Christ, and yet exists infinitely beyond the limitations of this nature. We do not advance the latter argument as if to suggest that the Holy Spirit is personally united with man in a manner identical to the union between the Godhead and the human nature of Christ. Far be it from us to entertain such thoughts. We rather advance it to render the objection to no avail, as God can be said to be present at a given location while yet not being confined within its limits, since He exists infinitely beyond these limitations. Therefore, the indwelling of the Holy Spirit indicates the incomprehensible and extraordinary manner of presence of the omnipresent Spirit.

Objection #2. As God is incommunicable and cannot communicate Himself to man, He rather communicates all His gifts. Therefore, when the Holy Spirit is said to dwell in someone, it must be understood to refer to the gifts of the Spirit.

Answer: We are not suggesting that the Holy Spirit communicates His Being and Person, as this would deify man and make him equal to God. With contempt we reject such an abominable thought. We are also not suggesting that the Holy Spirit essentially or personally is united to believers as the divine nature of Christ is united to His human nature, or as the soul of man is united to the body. Nor are we suggesting that the Holy Spirit is the actual cause of man's deeds, as if it were the Holy Spirit rather than man who believes, hopes, and prays. To hold to such an idea is foolishness. We do maintain, however, that the Holy Spirit is truly present in believers in an extraordinary manner of presence, which, though inexpressible and incomprehensible for us, is nevertheless personal and real. He dwells in them as He formerly dwelt in the temple, where He revealed His presence by His gracious operations. Angels upon assumption of a human body, or a pilot directing a ship, are present — not as *formoe informantes, sed assistentes,* that is, not in an animating fashion, but in such a manner which enables them to mobilize such bodies or the ship. Although the comparison is inadequate, the Holy Spirit dwells similarly in the believer and causes him to be active.

The Holy Spirit's Saving Operation Within the Believer

The Holy Spirit, having been given to the children of God, is not idle but works in them various spiritual gifts and graces. These are faith and regeneration, making believers partakers of Christ and all His benefits. He also teaches them how to pray, guides them, comforts them, seals them, and abides with them to all eternity.

First, the Holy Spirit works *faith* in them. "For by grace are ye saved through faith... it is the gift of God" (Eph. 2:8). Therefore the Holy Spirit is also called the Spirit of faith. "We having the same Spirit of faith" (2 Cor. 4:13); "To another faith by the same Spirit" (1 Cor. 12:9).

The Holy Spirit illuminates those whose understanding is darkened and who are alienated from the life of God through the ignorance that is in them, giving them enlightened eyes of understanding, whereby they begin to see their misery, the filthiness and sinfulness of their hearts, and the abominable emotions and thoughts which proceed from their heart. At once they perceive the abhorrent, hateful, and damnable nature of sin, which fills them with alarm and fear. This brings forth a desire in them to supplicate God for His grace. The Spirit, however, confronts them with the righteousness of God which will not permit the least sin to remain unpunished, but requires that it most certainly be punished with eternal damnation. This realization impedes those who seek for refuge with God, causing discouragement and despair. Having been brought to this place, the Holy Spirit reveals the necessity of a Surety if they would be saved — One who might pay for their sins, satisfy the justice of God, and merit for them the right to eternal life. He then immediately reveals that God Himself has found and sent forth such a Surety into the world, His only-begotten Son the Lord Jesus, revealing both the benefits of the covenant which are found in Him as well as their desirability. How this causes them lovingly to esteem this salvation and this Surety, being desirous to become a partaker of both! Along with this the Holy Spirit convinces them that salvation by this Surety is personally offered to them in the gospel, subsequent to which He generates in them a strong desire for this Surety. This causes Him to become the choice of their hearts, resulting in a yearning, longing, waiting, and praying for Him. While thus engaged, there is hope one moment, and then it again becomes dark and hopeless. Yet, they cannot but resume this sacred activity, and while struggling in this fashion they receive liberty to receive this offered Surety. With all their heart they acquiesce in the offer of this Surety; and without any reservation or delay, just as they are, they fully and irrevocably surrender themselves to Him to be justified, sanctified, and brought to salvation. Encouraged by the Word of God, they personally appropriate this Surety, rely upon His faithfulness and power, lean upon Him, and entrust themselves to Jesus — be it at one time with light and assurance, and then again with darkness and much strife. For since the day that they received Jesus, the activity of their soul continues to be focused on Him, making use of Him to obtain peace and holiness.

Secondly, the Holy Spirit is the Author of *regeneration.* Man by nature is spiritually dead and separated from God, being completely immersed in the things of the flesh. He is as full of sin as a dead body is full of worms. When the moment of good pleasure arrives for each of the elect, however, the Holy Spirit quickens and grants him spiritual life, this being the consequence of the soul's union with God in Christ. As a result of this, Christ is formed in them and the spiritual frame of their soul inclines towards Jesus. That which previously was so desirable to their eye has now become despicable. That in which they previously delighted now causes sorrow. Those activities they formerly sought out, they now flee. Their mind, will, and affections have been changed. They have become new creatures, and in consequence of this change wrought within the soul, thoughts concerning God and reflections upon heavenly things become prevalent. All this results in a different manner of speech, in godly conversation, in holiness of life, in having a delight in the godly, in dignified behavior, as well as in modest dress. In a word, this change can be compared to a dead person arising from the grave. In its initial manifestation, however, this new life has many imperfections. In its beginning it is feeble and grows slowly, which is also true for its external manifestation. It is all only in part, but nevertheless in truth. It is this life which the Holy Spirit works, "the Spirit giveth life" (2 Cor. 3:6); "and renewing of the Holy Ghost" (Titus 3:5); "Except a man be born of water and of the Spirit, he cannot enter into the kingdom of God" (John 3:5).

Even though the Holy Spirit could accomplish this without means, it pleases Him to use the Word as a means. Nevertheless He immediately (that is, without means) touches the soul in a manner not known to us, exerting a creative power similar as at the time of creation when He moved upon the face of the waters. The Hebrew uses the word מרחפת *(Merachepheth)*, which is indicative of motion that forms and brings forth. As I stated, the Spirit uses the Word in regeneration. "Of His own will begat He us with the Word of truth" (James 1:18); "Being born again, not of corruptible seed, but of incorruptible, by the Word of God, which liveth and abideth for ever" (1 Pet. 1:23).

Thirdly, the Holy Spirit makes believers partakers of *Christ and His benefits*. Prior to regeneration, they were not in possession of these benefits; although they were elected, salvation had been merited, and the ransom had been paid for them. When the Holy Spirit conquers them, however, He brings them to Christ, and gives them that faith whereby Christ dwells in their hearts (Eph. 3:17). Cleaving to Him, they become one spirit with Him (1 Cor. 6:17). They are united to Him as members are to a body, as a graft to the stem, and as a bride to her bridegroom, love being naturally inclined towards unity. This union results in the mutual use of possessive pronouns. "My Beloved is mine, and I am His" (Song of Sol. 2:16).

Union with Christ results in union with His benefits.

(1) The first benefit is His satisfaction resulting in reconciliation with God. "Who loved me, and gave Himself for me" (Gal. 2:20); "For if, when we were enemies, we were reconciled to God" (Rom. 5:10).

(2) A second benefit is His holiness. "That we might be made the righteousness of God in Him" (2 Cor. 5:21); "And ye are complete in Him" (Col. 2:10).

(3) A third benefit is His intercession. "We have an Advocate with the Father, Jesus Christ the righteous" (1 John 2:1).

(4) A fourth benefit is His glory. "Heirs of God, and joint-heirs with Christ; if so be that we suffer with Him, that we may be also glorified together" (Rom. 8:17).

(5) A fifth benefit is related to the covenant of grace and all that is promised in it, such as redemption and restoration. "How shall He not with Him also freely give us all things?" (Rom. 8:32).

Fourthly, the Holy Spirit teaches believers how to *pray;* therefore He is called the Spirit of prayer. "And I will pour upon [them]

...the Spirit of grace and of supplications" (Zec. 12:10); "But the Spirit itself maketh intercession for us with groanings which cannot be uttered" (Rom. 8:26). The Spirit shows them what they are lacking, and makes them sensibly conscious of it. He holds before them the desirability of that which is spiritual, causing them to esteem it highly. He prompts them to request these things from God by way of prayer, assuring them that God will hear them and grant them their desire according to His good pleasure. He produces in them a prayerful frame which manifests itself in a humble and believing frame of mind. He takes them by the hand and leads them to the throne of grace. He generates strong spiritual desires in them, putting the words in their mouth. If the matters for which they pray are too lofty, the desires too strong, or their heart so oppressed that they cannot speak one word, then the Spirit will help in their infirmities, causing them to utter their desires with groanings, which contain more than could be expressed with words, though they cannot be uttered.

Fifthly, the Holy Spirit *leads* believers. The way is narrow, and one step out of the way will cause the believer to stumble. It is a steep and ascending way which necessitates climbing. It is a slippery way, not in and of itself but to those that walk upon it, as their feet so easily slide from this pathway. It is a way in which they are encompassed by many enemies, refusing to let them advance; yet they proceed with much difficulty while continually doing battle. Furthermore, they are so often in the dark, hardly knowing the way. They are weak, ready to stumble, tired, and discouraged. They are so easily overcome by the enemy and know not how to persevere. The Holy Spirit, however, leads them along this way as one would lead a blind person. As one would lead an ignorant person along the way he must go, the Holy Spirit leads them in a way which they have not known (Isa. 42:16). He shows them this way, saying, "This is the way, walk ye in it" (Isa. 30:21). He inclines their will, making them willing to walk in this way. He encourages them, repeatedly stirring them up to walk in this way. Time and again He gives new strength. "He giveth power to the faint; and to them that have no might He increaseth strength" (Isa. 40:29). Thus, in His light they travel through darkness.

Sixthly, the Holy Spirit *comforts* them; He is called the Comforter (cf. John 14:16; John 15:26; John 16:7). The life of believers is one of many vicissitudes. At one time or another a troublesome darkness comes upon them, their corrupt flesh overwhelms them, Satan assaults with His fiery darts, or unbelief gains the upper hand. It can also be that God hides His countenance from them, while appearing to reject and to be angry with them. Moreover, one trial follows the other so that perseverance seems impossible. Then again they live in fear of death and the king of terror attacks them. In these and similar circumstances which potentially can overwhelm their souls, it pleases the Holy Spirit to sustain them with His comfort. He does so in a variety of ways.

(1) He shows them that the cross they must bear is so light that it is not worthy of being downcast over. This becomes especially evident when He focuses their attention upon the future glory which will be their portion. With this in view they are in agreement with Paul, "For I reckon that the sufferings of this present time are not worthy to be compared with the glory which shall be revealed in us" (Rom. 8:18).

(2) He shows them the brevity of cross-bearing, as being but for a moment. "For our light affliction, which is but for a moment" (2 Cor. 4:17). That which occurred yesterday is no more, and what will be tomorrow we do not know. We merely have the present which passes by as rapidly as the progression of time. What is our life when compared to eternity?

(3) He shows them the advantages concealed in their affliction. He shows them how it humbles them, makes them submissive, weans them from the world, teaches them to depend on God and to trust in Him, and how they increase in holiness according to the apostle's testimony, "For they [the fathers of our flesh, vs. 9] verily for a few days chastened us after their own pleasure; but He for our profit, that we might be partakers of His holiness...nevertheless afterward it yieldeth the peaceable fruit of righteousness unto them which are exercised thereby" (Heb. 12:10-11).

(4) He shows them that their way is God's way by which He leads all His children to heaven. He shows them that it is God's sovereign will, which He exercises with pure wisdom and goodness, to deal with them in such a fashion. Along with this He gives them love for the will of God so that they agree with His will, causing them to pray, "Nevertheless not as I will, but as Thou wilt....Thy will be done" (Mat. 26:39, 42).

(5) He assures them of the love and grace of God towards them and that they have found grace in His eyes. Such testimony is sufficient to cause them to consider their cross to be but insignificant. This is expressed by Paul: "And He said unto me, My grace is sufficient for thee: for My strength is made perfect in weakness. Most gladly therefore will I rather glory in my infirmities, that the power of Christ may rest upon me" (2 Cor. 12:9).

(6) He shows them that the ultimate outcome of their trial will

be consistent with what they have experienced so frequently already. He shows them that the rod of the wicked will not always rest upon the lot of the righteous (Psa. 125:3), and that their cross will neither be too heavy nor will they be required to bear it any longer than necessary. It will not overwhelm them, for He will be with them even when they must pass through water and fire. Then the rivers will neither overflow them nor the fire burn them. They will come forth as gold tried in the furnace and will thank the Lord that He has dealt with them thus, having afflicted them in faithfulness. Consider therefore this promise, "God is faithful, who will not suffer you to be tempted above that ye are able; but will with the temptation also make a way to escape, that ye may be able to bear it" (1 Cor. 10:13).

Upon having these matters presented to us, it makes a considerable difference whether we meditate upon them as such, or whether it pleases the Holy Spirit to reveal them to us with clarity, powerfully impressing them upon the heart. Only then will these truths become effectual, yielding comfort to the heart. Only then will the believer bear his cross joyfully.

Seventhly, the Holy Spirit *seals* believers.

(1) In the process of sealing a transmission of the image found on the seal occurs, which in this context is the image of God.

(2) As the image is imprinted in wax, so the image of God is imprinted upon the heart of man, who is re-created in this image.

(3) The transmission of this image occurs by the operation of the Spirit of God, who imprints the image of God upon man, causing Christ to be formed in them.

The process of sealing occurs for various reasons:

(1) A seal is applied to conceal something from the eyes of others. Letters are sealed for this purpose. In like manner a believer is sealed and thus hidden from the eyes of the world which cannot receive the Spirit of truth (John 14:17). "Therefore the world knoweth us not" (1 John 3:1).

(2) A seal is applied to preserve something in its inviolate form. Upon the occurrence of death crates and cupboards in a home are sealed for this purpose. Believers are in like manner "a garden enclosed...a spring shut up, a fountain sealed" (Song of Sol. 4:12).

(3) A seal is applied to identify the ownership of an object, thereby distinguishing it from other similar objects. Merchandise is sealed for this purpose. In this manner God also seals His children, thus acknowledging them to be His. "Nevertheless the foundation of God standeth sure, having this seal, The Lord knoweth them that are His" (2 Tim. 2:19). Others also recognize

them by virtue of this seal. "All that see them shall acknowledge them" (Isa. 61:9); "By this shall all men know that ye are My disciples" (John 13:35); "and they took knowledge of them, that they had been with Jesus" (Acts 4:13). By this seal believers also recognize themselves. "And hereby we do know that we know Him, if we keep His commandments" (1 John 2:3); "Examine yourselves, whether ye be in the faith; prove your own selves. Know ye not your own selves, how that Jesus Christ is in you?" (2 Cor. 13:5).

(4) A seal is applied for the purpose of confirmation. Business letters and contracts are sealed in this manner. In like manner the Holy Spirit seals believers, confirming to them the covenant of grace and assuring them that they are partakers of the same. "Who hath also sealed us, and given the earnest of the Spirit in our hearts" (2 Cor. 1:22).

This sealing, which confirms believers and assures them that they are partakers of the covenant of grace, occurs in various ways.

First, this occurs when the Spirit reveals to believers that He dwells in them as in a temple. The bride requested, "Set me as a seal upon Thine heart" (Song of Sol. 8:6); that is, let me thus be imprinted upon Thy heart, that Thou wouldest continually think upon me and that my appearance would continually be before Thy eyes. In like manner the Holy Spirit sets Himself as a seal upon the heart of believers, making them conscious of His presence and indwelling, whereby He assures them as clearly and powerfully that they are partakers of the covenant of grace as if they were sealed with a seal. "Hereby know we that we dwell in Him, and He in us, because He hath given us of His Spirit" (1 John 4:13). The Spirit Himself has been given them as a pledge that God will make them partakers of all promised benefits. They cannot be sealed and assured in a more excellent manner than this, for God Himself is their pledge, and as such is of infinitely more value than salvation itself. "In whom also after that ye believed, ye were sealed with that Holy Spirit of promise" (Eph. 1:13); "...the Holy Spirit of God, whereby ye are sealed unto the day of redemption" (Eph. 4:30).

Secondly, the Holy Spirit seals them by imprinting the image of God upon them, as well as by showing and revealing to them that the image of God is in them. He convinces them of the genuineness of their initial change, of their being ingrafted into Christ, of their faith whereby they truly received Christ and still do so daily both unto justification and sanctification. He convinces them of the genuineness of their insatiable desire to continually enjoy communion with God, of their spiritual life which, though feeble, is nevertheless genuine, and of their hatred for sin. He makes them aware how it wounds and grieves them when they perceive internal sin, imperfection in their performance of duty, as well as their failure to perform that which is good. He shows them that it is not only all their desire to be holy, but that their utmost effort is to do everything in faith, to be motivated by the love and fear of God, to live in childlike obedience, etc. The Spirit makes them conscious of all this, so that they perceive it in such a manner that they can neither deny it nor be deprived of its inherent comfort. "Now we have received, not the spirit of the world, but the Spirit which is of God; that we might know the things that are freely given to us of God" (1 Cor. 2:12).

Having on the one side revealed this to them, He leads them, in the consciousness of this received grace, not only to the Word of God but also to the promises which are made to such persons as they are. He sheds light upon such texts and causes them to acknowledge the infallible truth expressed in them. In this condition He ushers them into the presence of God and by virtue of two propositions — one being deduced from the grace they possess and the other from the Word of God — causes them to come to the conclusion that they are most certainly the children of God and thus will become partakers of eternal salvation. By way of such reasoning, the Holy Spirit not only labors to give clarity and assurance concerning both God's grace in them and the promises of Scripture for them, but also takes an active part in the formulation of this conclusion. By granting much light, He causes them to be steadfast and assured in this conclusion. By His sealing power He impresses this reality so deeply upon their heart that they believe it with such certainty as if they saw it with their eyes and touched it with their hands — yes, as if they were already in possession of salvation itself. "The Spirit itself beareth witness with our spirit, that we are the children of God" (Rom. 8:16).

Thirdly, the Holy Spirit also occasionally seals in an immediate manner by means of clear and powerful declarations within the heart, such as: "I have loved thee with an everlasting love; Thy sins are forgiven thee; Thou art an heir of eternal life," and similar passages. Such declarations occasionally occur by means of a Scripture passage which is powerfully applied. At other times this can occur without a specific text, bearing in mind that such a declaration will always be in agreement with Scripture, it being the touchstone for such a declaration. This immediate sealing does not only result in the confirmation of their spiritual state, but the Holy Spirit grants them the immediate enjoyment of the matter itself, which results in peaceful serenity, a pleasant and sweet frame of mind, and an exhilarating joy. This causes such a person to be saturated with love, be in a holy frame of mind, be lifted up in the ways of the Lord, be ready to heroically do battle with the enemy, and walk in the way of God's commandments. The bride refers to this as being kissed. "Let Him kiss me with the kisses of His mouth: for Thy love is better than wine" (Song of Sol. 1:2). She further testifies, "He brought me to the banqueting house, and His banner over me was love," etc. (Song of Sol. 2:4-6). Such was David's desire, "Say unto my soul, I am thy salvation" (Psa. 35:3). It is this blessing which Christ promises to believers. "I will love him, and will manifest Myself to Him. We will come unto him, and make our abode with him" (John 14:21, 23).

One should know, however, that, although all believers are sealed, this does not occur with equal clarity. Many are in the dark and remain there, as they cannot clearly perceive the indwelling of the Spirit nor the graces which are in them. They fear that they are neither partakers of the one nor of the other. They cannot formulate a conclusion from Scripture without many doubts, as they quietly fear self-deception. Many who are sealed do not experience being sealed by an immediate declaration to the soul. Moreover, many, who have enjoyed this immediate sealing in some measure, do not always live in this enjoyment. Those who with Paul have been drawn into the third heaven will also be buffeted by Satan. Those who with Peter walk upon the sea will subsequently sink due to unbelief. Those who have been enlightened will experience darkness, and those who have rejoiced will become sorrowful. Thus, those who previously had so much assurance, can again become subject to a doubtful frame and are kept from sinking away only by reflecting upon former days.

Fourthly, the Holy Spirit *abides with them to all eternity*. Even though the Holy Spirit often hides Himself and appears to suspend His operation so that with Job they must complain, "Behold, I go forward, but He is not there; and backward, but I cannot perceive Him: on the left hand, where He doth work, but I cannot behold Him: He hideth Himself on the right hand, that I cannot see Him" (Job 23:8-9), He nevertheless dwells in them and will abide with them. This is according to promise. "That He may abide with you for ever; even the Spirit of truth...for He dwelleth with you, and shall be in you" (John 14:16-17); "But the anointing which ye have received of Him abideth in you" (1 John 2:27). Since He is given to believers as a pledge, it is certain that He will abide as such until the promised benefits will be enjoyed in full perfection. "Ye were sealed with that Holy Spirit of promise, which is the earnest of our inheritance until the redemption of the purchased possession" (Eph. 1:13-14; cf. Eph. 4:30).

Being temples of the Holy Ghost, how holy ought the conduct of believers to be, in order that He might find delight in dwelling in them! How carefully one should seek to prevent the desecration of the temple of God, either by personally engaging in sin or by causing others to sin. "If any man defile the temple of God, him shall God destroy" (1 Cor. 3:17). How careful we should be not to grieve the Spirit by either blatantly sinning in spite of His warnings, by a careless walk, or by resisting the way in which He leads us. "Grieve not the Holy Spirit of God" (Eph. 4:30). Rather, acknowledge His indwelling, willingly yield to His operation, listen to His comforts, and willingly follow in the way of His leading, in order that He may delight Himself in you and may work in you with ever increasing efficacy.

Behold, must you not admit that faith in the Holy Trinity is profitable? Is it not the only foundation of a truly godly life and the fountain of all comfort? Therefore, consider God as being one in essence and existing in three Persons. Take notice of the operation of each Person in the administration of the covenant of grace, especially as it occurs within you. If you may entertain appropriate thoughts, make appropriate comments, and have appropriate exercises concerning each Person of the Trinity, you will experience considerable and consistent progress in godliness. There will be a wondrous illumination concerning the unity of the Godhead as you consider each individual Person, and of the Godhead in its Trinity as you contemplate its unity. If so much light, comfort, joy, and holiness may be derived from perceiving what is but an obscure glimmer of the Trinity, what will it be and how will the soul be affected when he may behold God's face in righteousness, and awake, satisfied with His likeness? (Psa. 17:15). Then they will walk by sight (2 Cor. 5:7), and they will see Him as He is (1 John 3:2). Therefore, "Blessed is that nation whose God is the LORD; and the people whom He hath chosen for His own inheritance" (Psa. 33:12).

CHAPTER FIVE

The Decrees of God: General Observations

Having considered the principal sources from which God may be known, and who and what He is in His Being, attributes, and the Persons of the Godhead, we proceed with a discussion of the extrinsic[1] works of God. These can be considered both as to their origin and manifestation. The extrinsic works of God originate in the decrees of God. This is true in a general sense, but also in a special sense, relating to man's eternal predestination, as well as the *Counsel of Peace* or the Covenant of Redemption, wherein the Son became Surety on behalf of His elect. The manifestation of the extrinsic works of God relates to nature — *creation* and *providence* — or grace, which is the execution of the great work of *redemption*.

We initially will consider *the decrees of God*, which is a doctrine from which a believing child of God may derive extraordinary comfort, delight, peace, and joy. God is all-sufficient in Himself, having had no need to create any of His creatures. The creature can neither add glory nor felicity to Him; however, it has pleased

---

[1]To clarify the meaning of extrinsic, we provide the chart found in *Reformed Dogmatics*, by Rev. G. H. Kersten, 1:106

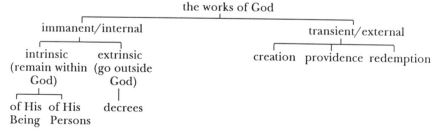

the Lord to create creatures in order to communicate His goodness to them and consequently render them happy. God in decreeing creation has eternally purposed and decreed within Himself where, when, how, and of what nature each creature should be, and what each should do and encounter. Whereas the doctrine itself can be deduced from the Word of God, the manner in which God decreed is hidden from us. In this respect we have hindsight rather than foresight. We discuss this doctrine in human terms, seeking to understand it in a manner consistent with God's Being.

Socinians and Arminians, considering the contingent nature of all that transpires, as well as the fact that man acts according to the free exercise of his will, are prepared to remove everything, particularly that which pertains to man, from under the domain of divine government, as they cannot comprehend how God could have decreed everything so precisely. They argue: "What happens to the concept of contingency and what remains of the freedom of man's will? How can prayer, exhortation, and diligence have any purpose, and how then can God be exempt from being the cause of sin and the damnation of man? If man cannot add anything to his salvation, he might as well cease all efforts and live in indifference." Consequently, they deny that God's decree extends to everything and that He has decreed specific events from eternity. We, however, being firmly grounded in the truth, maintain upon the basis of God's Word that there is such a decree of God, a truth which we confess and seek to use in a sanctified manner. In order to present this truth clearly to everyone, we shall consider the essential nature of God's decree and its particulars, confirm this from God's Word, respond to objections, and exhort one another to put this doctrine into practice.

We shall begin by considering the testimony of the Word of God. Scripture, in teaching that God has created, maintains, and governs all things according to a decree which He has decreed within Himself, uses a diversity of expressions to describe and represent this eternal decree.

(1) It uses the word *decree*. "I will declare the decree" (Psa. 2:7); "truly the Son of man goeth, as it was determined"[2] (Luke 22:22).

(2) It uses the verb *to appoint*. "For He performeth the thing that is appointed for me" (Job 23:14).

(3) It uses the phrase *determinate counsel and foreknowledge*. "Him, being delivered by the determinate counsel and foreknowledge of

---

[2] The Statenbijbel uses the word "besloten" which can also be translated as "decreed".

God" (Acts 2:23); "For to do whatsoever Thy hand and Thy counsel determined before to be done" (Acts 4:28).

(4) It uses the phrase *the counsel of His will and His pleasure.* "My counsel shall stand, and I will do all My pleasure" (Isa. 46:10); "who worketh all things after the counsel of His own will" (Eph. 1:11).

(5) It uses the word *purpose.* "Who are the called according to His purpose" (Rom. 8:28); "Having made known unto us the mystery of His will, according to His good pleasure which he hath purposed in Himself" (Eph. 1:9).

These texts do not merely provide us with the various designations for this decree, but convincingly and simultaneously confirm the truth of the doctrine that God has eternally made a decree, according to which proceeds all that transpires in this time state.

In human decision-making, people will view a matter from all angles, considering both pros and cons, in order to determine its feasibility. Often they cannot analyze the situation correctly, vacillate between two options, and ultimately must make a decision based on the facts as they appear to be at that moment and in similar situations. Far be it from us, however, to attribute such imperfections to the omniscient, only-wise, omnipotent, and immutable God; His ways are not as our ways. We cannot analyze in what manner the Lord decrees and establishes His counsel and purpose. We know, however, that He does so and that our human terminology gives expression to the unsearchable wisdom and immovability of God's purpose, as well as His comprehensive plan concerning all things as to the manner of their existence and the time of their occurrence.

The Decree of God Defined

We understand the decree of God to be *the eternal, volitional, all-wise, sovereign, and immutable purpose of God concerning all and every matter, comprehending both the time and the manner in which these matters will occur.*

Prior to the creation of the world there was only eternity, and thus matter, bodies, forms of life, and whatever else one may imagine, did not exist. God, who inhabited eternity, purposed to create a world, populate it with creatures, and maintain and govern them, thereby determining and stipulating the place, activity, and the course of events transpiring during the existence of each creature. This decree is the original cause whereby and according to which all things exist and occur in time, existing and occurring without deviation from this decree. Men first form a mental concept of that which they wish to make, adding and subtracting things which initially they have either partly or fully observed. Concerning God, however, there was no design external to Him imposed upon Him after which He would pattern that which He wished to create. All that He has created is an expression of His counsel. God's decree is the vehicle whereby He gives expression to His counsel; all that exists and transpires is the expression of that decree. The decree of God, being an intrinsic act of His will, is not incidental to God, but is the decreeing God Himself.

God's decree is from eternity. God does not decree things in response to issues which are already present; such is the manner of human decision-making. Rather, prior to the creation and existence of the world, He ordained all the events which He would bring into existence; that is, the time and place, means of execution, individual activities, and the individual circumstances from beginning to end for each. Scripture states emphatically, "Known unto God are all His works from the beginning of the world" (Acts 15:18). God, by virtue of His decree, has foreknowledge of all that will exist and occur in time, so that according to His will, by an act of His omnipotence, all matters are transferred from a state of potential existence to actual existence. It thus logically follows that God's eternal foreknowledge of all matters necessarily follows from the fact that He has eternally decreed them. "According as He hath chosen us in Him before the foundation of the world" (Eph. 1:4); "...to His own purpose and grace, which was given us in Christ Jesus before the world began" (2 Tim. 1:9). That which exists prior to time is necessarily exclusive of the concept of time. Prior to the existence of time there was only eternity. Should the thought occur concerning the moment when God made His decree prior to the existence of time, one is without knowing it already thinking within the parameters of time. Eternity necessarily excludes duration of time and chronology. Eternity is an incomprehensible concept for us as temporal creatures. Since God's decrees are existent prior to time, they are necessarily eternal. In the execution of things both duration of time and chronology are factors; however, also this chronology has been eternally decreed by God by a singular act of His will. In sequence and nature God Himself precedes His decree; however, in view of the eternal existence of this decree, such cannot be true in a chronological sense. Even among creatures the cause of an event does not always chronologically precede its effects.

In considering God's decree we must differentiate between viewing this decree relative to the decreeing God, it being a singular act of His will, or relative to the matters which have been decreed. In the latter there are as many dimensions to this decree as there are matters to which this decree relates.

The decree of God is in all aspects volitional and noncompulsory. It is also not motivated in the least degree by any internal or external necessary causes. It is purely an expression of His sovereign good pleasure. "Having made known unto us the mystery of His will, according to His good pleasure which He hath purposed in Himself" (Eph. 1:9), "after the counsel of His own will" (verse 11). Compulsion and volition are mutually exclusive, but necessity and volition can very well coexist. God's Being is of necessity volitional. The fact, however, that His will extends to matters which are extrinsic to His Being, that is, to create and govern them; to decree their manner of existence; to establish the course of events during their existence, that one will be rich and the other poor, that one will live in this locality and the other in that locality — all this is purely volitional. God could have decreed to create nothing; or if it were His will to create and govern, He could have created in a different fashion and have established a different course of events for His creatures. If a potter has power over clay to create a vessel purely by the free exercise of His will, if the head of a household has the prerogative to furnish his home as he pleases by placing one object here and another there, would then the sovereign Lord of all things not have the prerogative to deal with His clay and with His creatures according to His good pleasure? Would anyone be able to prevent Him, who is omnipotent, from doing so, thus having to adjust Himself to the whims of His creation? Would anyone be able to say, "Why hast Thou decreed it to be thus and not otherwise?" Would any creature be able to compel Him to establish a particular decree? This obviously cannot be so! His decree is the expression of His sovereign good pleasure, and it is for this reason that everything, transpiring as it does, is good because He wills it to be so. How blessed it is for the creature to acknowledge this, approve of it, and surrender His will to the will of God.

God has decreed everything with eternal, infinite, and unsearchable *wisdom*. When people construct something peculiar or extraordinary, we are amazed and exclaim, "How has man been able to conceive this?" Nevertheless, the idea is not truly original, having been derived from other principles which have been observed either in animals, inanimate objects, or in the work of other men. By way of subtraction or addition, or by a rearrangement of order, he has developed the concept for his creation. But "who hath directed the Spirit of the LORD, or being His counsellor hath

taught Him?" (Isa. 40:13). He, who is "the only wise God" (1 Tim.
1:17), whose "understanding is infinite" (Psa. 147:5), who in wisdom has made all things (Psa. 104:24), has also, before the existence of time, with wisdom ordained and decreed all things. "O the
depth of the riches both of the wisdom and knowledge of God!
how unsearchable are His judgments, and His ways past finding
out!" (Rom. 11:33).

The Characteristics of God's Decrees

The decrees of God are *independent, absolute, purely uncondi-*
tional, and not dependent upon secondary causes. Everything has
most certainly been decreed, will most certainly come to pass, and
will not have any other result or purpose than that which has been
decreed. God has indeed decreed that many things will come to
pass by virtue of secondary causes and means. These secondary
causes, however, are not conditional to the decree; as if God has
made a conditional decree which would change if these conditions
were not met; as if these conditions were subject to the control of
the creature or to chance. Rather, these secondary causes are
merely the means whereby the decree is executed. Both these
means as well as the ultimate outcome of the decree have been
most certainly decreed, even though there may be much uncertainty and contingency relative to these secondary causes. Such
contingency exists relative to the creature, but never with God.

Question: Did God decree many things conditionally, so that
their ultimate outcome depends on whether or not these conditions are fulfilled, the latter being dependent upon the manner in
which man exercises his power and free will?

Answer: Socinians, Arminians, and Jesuits answer in the affirmative, whereas we answer in the negative for the following reasons:

First, if God had made such a conditional decree, this would
have been either because He could not do otherwise as He could
be prevented from executing His decree or because He did not will
differently, leaving the fulfillment of the condition or the lack of it
in the hands of man. The first proposition cannot be true because
God is omnipotent, and He exercises this omnipotence in the
execution of His decree. "For the LORD of hosts hath purposed,
and who shall disannul it?" (Isa. 14:27).

The second is also impossible, because a creature is not able to
function independently from God; he cannot do anything apart
from His influence and government. "For it is God which worketh
in you both to will and to do of His good pleasure" (Phil. 2:13).

Evasive Argument: The nature of man is such that it is impossible for God to make a decree concerning those matters in which man exercises his free will. God has created the will of man in such a fashion that it cannot be compelled but always retains its freedom to will or not to will something. God could have decreed to save any individual unconditionally, regardless of how such a person would conduct himself. If God, however, elects a person who will believe and repent, then this choice must necessarily be conditional, being dependent on the exercise of man's free will as to whether or not he wishes to believe and repent.

Answer: (1) The freedom of the will does not consist of an arbitrary disposition in determining whether one will or will not do something; rather its function is a necessary consequence of one's judgment and inclination.

(2) Both a freedom of will which is arbitrary in nature and a freedom of will which is self-determining do not function independently from God. God causes man to will. He works in men to will and fashions the hearts of all men (Psa. 33:15). He turns the hearts even of kings as rivers of water whithersoever He will (Prov. 21:1). Is not He who has given man a will able once again to give him a good will if it so pleases Him?

(3) Faith and repentance are not conditions upon which the decree is made. Rather, God has decreed these means as well as the final outcome in order to accomplish His ultimate purpose. Thus, this argument neither applies nor renders the foregoing proof invalid.

(4) If the decree of God were contingent upon something which in turn was independent from Him, the Creator would be dependent upon the creature.

Secondly, God's decree was made purely according to His good pleasure, and therefore could not have been made contingent upon any conditions. "Even so, Father: for so it seemed good in Thy sight" (Mat. 11:26); "Having predestinated us unto the adoption of children by Jesus Christ to Himself, according to the good pleasure of His will" (Eph. 1:5). God accomplishes this good pleasure irresistibly. "My counsel shall stand, and I will do all My pleasure" (Isa. 46:10). In light of this, how can there be a condition upon which God's decree would be contingent? It would contradict the sovereignty, wisdom, and omnipotence of God.

Thirdly, all the decrees of God are immutable. "That the purpose of God according to election might stand" (Rom. 9:11); "For I am the LORD, I change not; therefore ye sons of Jacob are not consumed" (Mal. 3:6); "... the Father of lights, with whom is no variableness, neither shadow of turning. Of His own will begat He us ..." (James 1:17-18). That which is contingent upon a condition, however, not having been decreed, and which, as some parties insist, is contingent upon man's own control and the exercise of his free will, must of necessity be mutable. Consequently, the immutable decree of God cannot be contingent upon any condition. God does not change His decree in response to man's mutability, but all human changes occur in harmony with the immutable decree of God, who by means of human mutability immutably executes the comprehensive relationship which He has decreed between the means and the end, between sin and its punishment, and between godliness and the experience of salvation.

Objection #1: "But ye have set at nought all My counsel" (Prov. 1:25); "But the Pharisees and lawyers rejected the counsel of God against themselves" (Luke 7:30). From this it is evident that men can reject the counsel of God, rendering His decree impotent. Therefore, it must be concluded that God's decrees are of a contingent nature.

Answer: The word "counsel" as used in these texts does not refer to the decree of God, which at times is indeed referred to as "counsel," but refers to a directive accompanied either by promises or threats, which becomes evident from the texts themselves. In Proverbs 1:25 there is added, "and would none of my reproof." The counsel as expressed in verse 23 was to repent. It is presented with a reproof, "Turn you at my reproof," and with promises, "Behold, I will pour out My Spirit unto you." This exhortation they had not obeyed. The same is true for Luke 7:30. John the Baptist and the Lord Jesus had admonished the people of Israel to repent, for John preached the baptism of repentance, proclaiming that they should believe in Him who would come after him (Acts 19:4). They disobeyed this admonition, rejecting the counsel, the directive, this being evidenced by the additional clause "being not baptized of Him."

Objection #2: God's Word contains many conditional promises and threats. Since all promises and threats issue forth from one of God's decrees, there must of necessity be conditional decrees. Note these conditional aspects in the following texts, "If ye be willing and obedient, ye shall eat the good of the land: but if ye refuse and rebel, ye shall be devoured with the sword" (Isa. 1:19-20); "And it shall come to pass, if ye diligently hearken unto Me...then shall there enter into the gates of this city kings and princes...but if ye will not hearken unto Me...then will I kindle a fire in the gates thereof," etc. (Jer. 17:24-25, 27).

Answer: It is a well-known truth which we readily embrace, that God's Word contains many conditional promises and threatenings issuing forth from one of God's decrees. We deny, however, the deduction that God's decrees must then of necessity also be conditional. The one does not imply the other, for it only follows that God has decreed to make such conditional promises and threats. He has decreed the cohesive relationship between these matters to be such, that it will be well with the righteous and ill with the wicked. If someone improves, repents, and believes, it is the work of God. God converts (James 1:18), gives faith (Eph. 2:8), and works both to will and to do (Phil. 2:13). "Without Me ye can do nothing" (John 15:5). God's decree relative to all this is absolute and unconditional: to bring the elect to salvation in the way of repentance and faith, and to damn all others in consequence of their sins. The decree is absolute, but its execution is by means which have been decreed as certainly as the end itself.

Objection #3: God is said to change His decree if the condition is not fulfilled. Thus, the decree is conditional. This is to be seen in Scripture: "I said indeed that thy house, and the house of thy father, should walk before Me for ever: but now the LORD saith, Be it far from Me; for them that honour Me I will honour, and they that despise Me shall be lightly esteemed" (1 Sam. 2:30); "For now would the LORD have established thy kingdom upon Israel for ever. But now thy kingdom shall not continue" (1 Sam. 13:13-14).

Answer: In these texts there is no reference to the decree of God, but rather to the execution of the decree. God does not make a decree in this time state in response to the issues at hand, but His decree has been made from eternity (cf. Acts 15:18; Eph. 1:4). Thus, the execution of the decree is not contingent upon a condition which occurs in time. These texts merely demonstrate the relationship between sin and punishment, and between godliness and divine blessing. God uses these as a means to convince man of his duty, and of God's righteousness in punishing sin when man fails to perform his duty. He also uses such texts as means to lead the elect to godliness and thus to bestow the salvation which He had ordained. "I had said," that is, "I had promised you upon condition of obedience. You did not obey, however, and neither did I will to give you such an obedient heart. I was neither obligated to do so, nor did I decree to give you such a heart. Thus, the fulfillment of the promises will also not be yours."

God's decree is immutable. If God were to change His decree, it would either be because subsequent to the decree He perceived that it was not good, there being a better option, or because a circumstance presented itself preventing Him from executing His decree. Neither of these two possibilities can be true concerning God.

The first possibility cannot be true for He is the only wise God, and the second possibility cannot be true as He is the omnipotent One. Thus, it is certain that nothing can cause a change in God's decrees. Scripture confirms this in many places. "I am the LORD, I change not" (Mal. 3:6); "...with whom is no variableness" (James 1:17); "For the LORD of hosts hath purposed, and who shall disannul it?" (Isa. 14:27); "My counsel shall stand" (Isa. 46:10); "That the purpose of God according to election might stand" (Rom. 9:11); "Wherein God, willing more abundantly to shew unto the heirs of promise the immutability of His counsel" (Heb. 6:17).

Objection: God is said to repent, not to fulfill His promises and threatenings, presently to command something different than He did before, and to change His dealings.

Answer: Such statements are never made in reference to God's decrees. This manner of speech merely reveals the relationship between the matters and the condition, be it expressed or implied —all of which God has in each case most certainly decreed to propose or to command. Thus, He permits the ungodly in their wickedness to fail His requirements, in consequence of which they do not receive the promised blessing, but rather are partakers of the threatened punishment; whereas He causes the elect to fulfil the condition and thus obtain the decreed blessings.

Having considered the particulars of God's decree, we must now consider that which God decrees. His decree pertains to all matters in general and each individual matter in particular. No matter, no activity, meeting, no final results (whether they be great or small, good or evil) — be it that it all transpires in the common course of nature — are contingent upon secondary causes or happen accidentally. This is also applicable to the results of man exercising his free will, such as wars and their outcomes, marriages and all their related incidents, the times and places of our residence, our birthday and day of death — none of these matters are excluded. In a word, everything, every angel, every inanimate created object in heaven and upon earth, every man, every action, every result, and whatever may exist regardless of the name attributed to it — all function at a particular time and place according to a most certain and immovable decree. The one decree relates both to the intent and the execution of plans; the other relates to that which God permits and yet governs. This is taught throughout the entire Scriptures.

First, there are texts of an all-inclusive nature. "Known unto God are all His works from the beginning of the world" (Acts 15:18); "...Him who worketh all things after the counsel of His own will" (Eph. 1:11). The word "all" is all-inclusive, and there are no exceptions.

Secondly, there are texts which refer to specific matters, such as,

(1) the place and time of everyone's residence. "...and hath determined the times before appointed, and the bounds of their habitation" (Acts 17:26);

(2) all the events which occur in man's lifetime. "He performeth the thing that is appointed for me" (Job 23:14);

(3) the blessings which will be bestowed upon the elect. "Having predestinated us unto the adoption of children by Jesus Christ to Himself, according to the good pleasure of His will.... Having made known unto us the mystery of His will, according to His good pleasure which He hath purposed in Himself" (Eph. 1:5, 9);

(4) the election and reprobation of persons and nations. "That the purpose of God according to election might stand, not of works, but of Him that calleth; it was said unto her, The elder shall serve the younger. As it is written, Jacob have I loved, but Esau have I hated" (Rom. 9:11-13);

(5) that which is accomplished by the exercise of man's free will. This is evident from that which men did to Christ. "And truly the Son of man goeth, as it was determined: but woe unto that man by whom He is betrayed!" (Luke 22:22); "Him, being delivered by the determinate counsel and foreknowledge of God, ye have taken," etc. (Acts 2:23); "For of a truth against Thy holy Child Jesus, whom Thou hast anointed, both Herod, and Pontius Pilate, with the Gentiles, and the people of Israel, were gathered together, for to do whatsoever Thy hand and Thy counsel determined before to be done" (Acts 4:27-28);

(6) marriage. "Let the same be the woman whom the LORD hath appointed out for my master's son" (Gen. 24:44); "What therefore God hath joined together..." (Mat. 19:6).

Thirdly, the time, place, manner, and circumstances of the death of each man have been determined.

(1) This is expressly stated in Scripture. "Seeing his days are determined, the number of his months are with Thee, Thou hast appointed his bounds that he cannot pass" (Job 14:5). Job, referring to all men, speaks of a specified number of days and months which have been appointed, to which not one month or day will be added; that is, he will not live longer than this appointed time. David speaks likewise: "LORD, make me to know mine end, and the measure of my days, what it is; that I may know how frail I am. Behold, Thou hast made my days as an handbreadth" (Psa. 39:4-5). His reference here is not to the brevity of human life in general, but particularly that God has allotted him a measure of days, the duration of his life having its limits defined as it were by an handbreadth, so

that his life was but a very short, predetermined time. "...and hath determined the times before appointed" (Acts 17:26).

(2) As He determines the day of birth of every man, likewise God Himself takes man's life at His time. God has life and death in His hand, works everything according to His determinate counsel (Acts 2:23), and according to the counsel of His will (Eph. 1:11). Consequently, man's age has been determined. "My times are in Thy hand" (Psa. 31:15); "Thou turnest man to destruction" (Psa. 90:3); "He shall cut off the spirit of princes" (Psa. 76:12); "The Lord killeth, and maketh alive" (1 Sam. 2:6). Yes, even when someone dies due to an apparent accident, it is by divine government. If a man in passing is killed by an axe which has slipped from the helve (Deu. 19:5), God will have delivered that man into the hand of the hewer of wood (Exo. 21:13). God had determined Ahab's age, even though it appeared that the arrow of a marksman hit him accidentally (1 Ki. 22:28, 34). Did not God determine the age of the first world, and of the one hundred eighty-five thousand soldiers in Sennacharib's army?

Objection #1: The duration of life depends upon the good or evil behavior of man, according to which God either lengthens or shortens his life. Therefore the day of his death has not been precisely determined. "...that thy days may be long" (Exo. 20:12).

Answer: This lengthening of days is not related to the decree of God in which the terminus of each life has been determined. It rather expresses the relationship which God has established between godliness and blessing. Both have been decreed by God, the one as the end and the other as the means wrought in them by God Himself.

Objection #2: "Bloody and deceitful men shall not live out half their days" (Psa. 55:23). Thus, there is no established decree concerning the hour of man's death.

Answer: If this text refers to the decree of God, it obviously expresses that the precise duration of life has been determined, for if the half of such a life has been determined, the end has been determined with equal certainty. Then we would have to conclude that God had indeed determined the hour of each person's death, but that the person could yet resist and undo the determinate counsel of God. This is impossible, as we have shown. It is evident that this text does not refer to the decree of God, but rather to the natural resiliency of the body which potentially could enable man to live a much longer life. It could also refer to the possible notion of the ungodly that they will live a long life, but God — due to their ungodliness and according to His decree —joins the end and the means and thus removes them in the strength of their life. It is from this perspective that we must view Ecclesiastes 7:17, "Why shouldest thou die before thy time?"

Objection #3: "Behold, I will add unto thy days fifteen years" (Isa. 38:5). This proves that there is no established decree concerning the duration of man's life.

Answer: It is obviously stated here that the duration of Hezekiah's life is limited to an additional fifteen years. God had decreed that this illness would not be unto death, but that his death would occur fifteen years later, even though, if God had not miraculously healed him, according to his physical condition he should have died. He therefore received a message that he would die.

Objection #4: Man has his life in his own hand. He has the option to drown or hang himself, and thus, as some do, shorten the duration of his life.

Answer: If someone commits such an act, the time of his death was according to God's decree. The fact is that in judgment upon his sins he would be his own executioner and thus die an ungodly death. If it is not his time, however, such a person will neither commit this act, nor will he be desirous to do so, but rather make every effort to preserve his life. Someone may be able to shorten his life as far as the potential of his natural constitution is concerned, but not relative to God's decree.

Objection #5: If the hour of death has been determined for every person, from which follows that man will not die before his time, there is no need that one avail himself of the means. Then one does not need to eat, one can throw himself in water or fire, and in illness one need not avail himself of medicine, etc.

Answer: God, having decreed the end, has also decreed the means to that end, and thus will motivate man to use the means for both body and soul, and man will delight in them. One may not use the means, however, with the foolish objective to change the decree of God, but rather in subjection to God's counsel, since God has commanded us to use the means. "Except these abide in the ship, ye cannot be saved" (Acts 27:31); "I will yet for this be inquired of by the house of Israel, to do it for them" (Ezek. 36:37).

Objection #6: Since man is completely free to do or not to do a certain thing, the outcome of nearly every event depends upon the exercise of man's will. Since many things occur accidentally, the time and place of man's death could not have been decreed. To go a step further, therefore there cannot be such a decree of God pertaining to all things, for then everything would have to occur by unavoidable necessity.

Answer: (1) It is erroneous to maintain that the freedom of the will consists in doing or not doing something. Man's will does not function arbitrarily but of itself, so that man does everything with consent and inclination. God, who has created the will to function in this manner, inclines it, without compulsion and in harmony with its propensity, to function in accordance with His will.

(2) The outcome of events does not depend upon man, nor upon his activity, but upon God who grants the means, and according to these means brings to pass the outcome according to His good pleasure. He grants to one more strength, wisdom, and wealth than the other (Prov. 22:2), and provides one king with a larger army than the other. Even then, God often demonstrates that the final outcome does not depend on strength, wisdom, wealth, and number, but the ultimate outcome of events is from Him (cf. Prov. 21:31; Psa. 33:16).

(3) In respect to man and secondary causes, everything is contingent and accidental. Such however is not the case from God's perspective. He has most certainly decreed everything, and without impediment will execute His decree according to His good pleasure. This is even true for those events which appear to be most contingent in nature, such as an unexpected murder (Exo. 21:12-13), the casting of lots (Prov. 16:33), the falling of a sparrow from the rooftop, and the falling of a hair from our heads (Mat. 10:29-30).

(4) It is true that everything occurs by unavoidable necessity; however, it does not occur by compulsion. There is a threefold necessity. First, there is an internal necessity which proceeds from the very nature of a matter. Thus, fire burns of necessity, and that which is heavy necessarily falls downward. Secondly, there is a necessity which is the result of external compulsion, as for instance when a man compels a child, against his will, to go where he wishes him to go. Thirdly, there is a necessity stemming from dependence and the outcome of events. Every creature of necessity depends on God in all his activity, and the outcome of every event will necessarily be according to God's will. God, having most certainly decreed everything, executes everything irresistibly — not in an unnatural, compulsory manner, but in harmony with the nature of His creatures. Therefore, relative to God's decree everything happens of necessity, even though there is contingency relative to secondary causes.

Therefore refrain from the *Socinian, Anabaptist, Arminian, Jesuit,* and all who submit to natural reason, who are ignorant of God and His way, reject and contradict these truths, seek to dethrone God, and make man master of all. We cast down the imaginations and every high thing that exalts itself and bring every thought into captivity to the obedience of Christ (2 Cor. 10:5), and defend this doctrine which is so comforting and profitable for believers.

All believers, even though they believe these truths, do not have equal clarity concerning them but are often subject to temptation when they pray for a situation which they strongly desire. When things do not go well, when they experience adversity or are oppressed by various circumstances, they readily lose sight of the decree of God, being overcome by fear, and cannot submit themselves to God's decree with love and delight. They believe the Lord to be against them and to have decreed nothing in their favor. When they resort to prayer in these circumstances, they are sorely troubled by thoughts such as: "Of what use are my prayers, since I will neither receive what I request nor be delivered except it be decreed, and I fear that the decree is not in my favor." Such thoughts diminish their zeal. Prayer is impeded and becomes listless, clearly proving that we do not sufficiently love the decree of God, for we become more active to bring God's will in line with our desires, than our desires with God's will. We are more concerned to bring God's counsel in line with our will, than that our will be in line with His. This grieves believers and causes them to be much troubled within. They would gladly have faith in God's decree, delight in it, and believe that in all things it is for their good. They desire to use prayer and all available means to stimulate a holy desire to surrender to God's counsel, who by decreed means accomplishes the decreed end. They are much hindered, however, in this pursuit.

(1) Some are hindered by ignorance, having not been sufficiently instructed in these and other truths.

(2) Others are hindered by negligence, lacking the discipline to meditate upon this truth in order to become intimately acquainted with it.

(3) Some are hindered by strong and impure desires for earthly things.

(4) Others are hindered by failure to acquaint themselves with the Word of God whereby a text might readily be available when specific circumstances present themselves.

(5) Some are hindered by focusing too much on the circumstances, whether they are for or against them. All of this brings on darkness and yields opportunity for unbelief, thus allowing it to flourish.

Exhortation to Profit from this Doctrine

Do you desire to profit from this comforting doctrine?

First, seek to rid yourself of inordinate and close attachment to earthly things, and be diligent in renouncing your own will. The things of this earth are not your portion, and therefore cannot satisfy. Have you not often experienced that instead of resulting in more holiness, they rob you of your peace and spiritual liberty, hindering you from running your course with joy? Have you not often perceived in retrospect that it was God's wisdom and goodness that He did not give you the desire of your heart, and that at times you were uncomfortable when your desire was granted? Why then are you so set upon receiving your desire? Is it not much better to rest in God's decree?

Secondly, seek often to stimulate love for the sovereignty of God. Do you wish God to be your servant in order that you might receive your foolish desires? Or is it your joy that He is Lord, that He acts freely, and that as supreme Sovereign He rules everything according to His will, so that no one can stay His hand and say, "What doest Thou?" Would you wish God to be subject to you, and to do your bidding? Do you not rather desire that, without the least deviation, His will be accomplished, both in regard to all things and in regard to yourself, even if you would have to lose all that you possess? You would certainly approve of this if you would but quietly contemplate this.

Therefore, rejoice in His sovereignty and render Him honor and glory. You will then find sweet rest in His decree concerning the future, the present, and the past.

Thirdly, consider and believe unreservedly that all that God has decreed concerning His elect He has decreed to their benefit to such a degree that they could not have imagined or desired anything to be more profitable. Approve of this truth and apply it to your own situation. If you may believe yourself to be a partaker of Jesus Christ, God's decree will be precious to you. You will be able to find sweet rest in it, and you will be able to surrender everything into the Lord's hand with ease, saying, "He may accomplish in me whatever He has decreed concerning me, and it will be well."

Fourthly, you have no prior knowledge of what God has decreed concerning you in various specific circumstances. This much you know, however, that God works out His decree in the way of means, and has bound us to these means. Whoever refuses to use the means — which God will cause him to do if He has so decreed — has no right to complain, as he himself is to be blamed for it. "Ye have not, because ye ask not" (James 4:2). The promise is, "Ask, and it shall be given you" (Mat. 7:7); "Open thy mouth wide, and I will fill it" (Psa. 81:10). Keep yourself from using unlawful means, for then you are losing sight of God's decree, thus expecting it from the means. Use lawful means, and use them with the desire that God's counsel be accomplished rather than having the intent to change it. Let there then be no anxiety concerning the outcome of the matter, knowing that the outcome will be such as God in His counsel has decreed to be to your benefit. If this may be your practice, you will avoid or overcome many temptations, and preserve a quiet inner disposition.

By confirming and believing this truth while allowing yourself to grow accustomed to it through much meditation, you will be armed and strong in all circumstances of life; your desires will be holy, your concerns will be moderate, and you will use the means with more liberty, and yet carefully.

Should there be many evil circumstances, that you are threatened or oppressed with poverty, injury, disgrace, devastation by enemies, famine, pestilence, loss of property, loved ones, or life, the decree brings quietness since it is not inflicted by man, but is all according to God's eternal counsel, which you should neither desire to change, nor can be changed by anyone. Consider that His decree is for your good, even though you cannot perceive this beforehand. Then you will not fear, even if everything were to be turned upsidedown.

If you are currently desirous for something, meditation upon God's decree will not remove this desire, but will rather sanctify it, thus encouraging you to bring your desires before God more freely. Or it may cause you to bow before the Lord in holy submission, confessing, "Thy will be done!" without daring to insist strongly upon receiving your desire, but rather to have your desire swallowed up in God's will. It will soon become evident whether a person is entertaining any impure desires, which in such a frame will readily be extinguished. It will not only keep us from ever doing evil in order that good might come out of it, but rather it will motivate us to yield everything into the hands of the Lord, be satisfied with this, and thank the Lord in all things, confessing, "For of Him, and through Him, and to Him, are all things: to whom be glory for ever. Amen" (Rom. 11:36).

CHAPTER SIX

Eternal Predestination: Election and Reprobation

General Observations about Predestination

Having spoken of the decrees of God in general, we shall now proceed with a discussion of the specific decrees of God, speaking particularly of those relating to man's salvation and damnation. Due to repeated slander by individuals with evil motives, the word *predestination* gives some offense, triggers prejudice, and is repulsive to people who are both ignorant and filled with resentment against this doctrine. This has led some to be of the opinion that it is preferable not to speak of this mystery. Since Scripture, however, bears such abundant testimony to this doctrine; since it is a matter of supreme importance, yielding a proper understanding of the entire way of salvation; and since it is a fountain of comfort and genuine sanctification, nothing must be held back. The entire counsel of God must be declared. Everyone must strive to understand this doctrine well and apply it properly.

Scripture makes reference to election in a variety of ways.

(1) The Lord Jesus Christ is called *the Elect* (Isa. 42:1), "who verily was foreordained before the foundation of the world" (1 Pet. 1:20), to be the Surety and Savior of the elect.

(2) *The holy angels* have been elected to an eternal and permanent state of felicity. They are not chosen in Christ, and He is not considered to be their Mediator, as there was neither sin in them nor would there be. He is also not considered their Head to preserve and confirm them in their state, as Scripture makes no mention of this at all. The Lord Jesus has been given unto the

salvation of men and not angels. As God and man, however, Christ is exalted above the angels who worship Him, and whom He, as Lord, uses according to His will to the benefit of His elect. These holy angels have been chosen by God, which explains why they are called "elect" (1 Tim. 5:21), in distinction from other angels who have sinned, not having kept their first estate, and having left their own habitation, are therefore eternally damned (cf. 2 Pet. 2:4; Jude 6; Mat. 25:41).

(3) *Some people* are elected to a specific office, possibly in government, as Saul was chosen to be king. "See ye him whom the LORD hath chosen?" (1 Sam. 10:24). This was also true when he was rejected. "I have rejected him" (1 Sam. 16:1). Others are chosen to an ecclesiastical office, as Judas, who was also chosen to be an apostle. "Have I not chosen you twelve, and one of you is a devil?" (John 6:70).

(4) This manner of election is not under discussion here, but rather the election of some men *unto salvation*, in contrast to those who have been rejected by God.

Various words are used to give expression to the doctrine of election, such as.

(1) Προορισμός *(Proörismos)*, predestination, which in Latin is "predestinatio." It signifies a determination of a matter before it exists or transpires in order to bring it to a certain end. "For to do whatsoever Thy hand and Thy counsel, προώρισε *(proöórise)*, determined before (that is, predestined) to be done" (Acts 4:28). This is further confirmed in 1 Corinthians 2:7, "But we speak the wisdom of God in a mystery, even the hidden wisdom, which God ordained before the world unto our glory." It is this word which is used to refer to man's destiny relative to salvation, as well as the means whereby they obtain this salvation. "We...being predestinated...having predestinated us unto the adoption of children" (Eph. 1:11,5); "For whom He did foreknow, He also did predestinate to be conformed to the image of His Son.... Moreover whom He did predestinate, them He also called" (Rom. 8:29-30). This word not only relates to election, but also to reprobation, as confirmed in texts where the word is used in reference to Herod, Pilate, and Judas. "For to do whatsoever thy hand and thy counsel determined before to be done" (Acts 4:28). "And truly the Son of man goeth, as it was determined: but woe unto that man by whom He is betrayed" (Luke 22:22).

(2) Another word is Πρόγνωσις *(Prognosis)*, *fore-knowledge*. This word does not refer to a mere foreknowledge whereby God has prior knowledge of all things, including the end of men. "Known unto God are all His works from the beginning of the world" (Acts 15:18). It

rather refers to a foreknowledge characterized by love and delight. In this manner Christ is referred to as "the Elect of God," stating that He "was foreordained before the foundation of the world" (1 Pet. 1:20). In like manner "the LORD knoweth the way of the righteous" (Psa. 1:6), and "the Lord knoweth them that are His" (2 Tim. 2:19). Believers are therefore called "elect according to the foreknowledge of God the Father" (1 Pet. 1:2). It signifies election itself. "God hath not cast away His people which He foreknew" (Rom. 11:2); "For whom He did foreknow, He also did predestinate" (Rom. 8:29). This foreknowledge is contrasted with not being known, that is, being rejected. "I never knew you" (Mat. 7:23); "I know you not" (Mat. 25:12).

(3) Scripture also uses Πρόθεσις *(Prothesis)*, or *purpose*. This word does not refer to an impotent wish, but to a certain, immutable, unbreakable decree. It is used in reference to the election of the Lord Jesus as Surety. "Whom God hath sent forth to be a propitiation" (Rom. 3:25). It is also used relative to the elect, particularly in reference to both the means by which, and the end unto which they are made partakers of salvation. "...them who are the called according to His purpose" (Rom. 8:28); "...that the purpose of God according to election might stand" (Rom. 9:11); "...being predestinated according to the purpose of Him who worketh all things after the counsel of His own will" (Eph. 1:11).

(4) Then there is the word Ἐχλογή *(ekloge)*, that is, *election*. Even though it is used in reference to other matters, it also is frequently used to describe divine appointment unto salvation as well as the means whereby the elect become partakers of salvation. "The purpose of God according to election" (Rom. 9:11); "There is a remnant according to the election of grace" (Rom. 11:5); "Knowing, brethren beloved, your election of God" (1 Th. 1:4). In this respect believers are called the elect. "Few are chosen" (Mat. 22:14); "Who shall lay anything to the charge of God's elect?" (Rom. 8:33). They are even referred to as "the election" itself. "But the election hath obtained it" (Rom. 11:7). They whom God has chosen for a specific purpose He has also chosen in regard to the means, which is also referred to as "choosing." "Ye have not chosen Me, but I have chosen you, and ordained you, that ye should go and bring forth fruit. I have chosen you out of the world" (John 15:16, 19).

Predestination Defined

Having considered the word, we now proceed to consider the matter itself. We shall present it descriptively, and explain it point by point.

Predestination is an eternal, volitional, and immutable decree of God to create some men, concluding[1] them in the state of sin, and bringing them unto salvation through Christ, to the glory of His sovereign grace. He simultaneously decreed to create other men, also concluding them in the state of sin, to damn them for their own sin, to the praise of His justice.

Predestination is a divine decree. Whatever was stated in a general sense in the previous chapter concerning God's decrees must also be specifically applied to this decree: it is eternal, volitional, wise, and absolutely immutable.

This decree originates in God Himself. "Moreover whom He did predestinate" (Rom. 8:30); "Blessed be the God and Father of our Lord Jesus Christ....having predestinated us" (Eph. 1:3, 5). God is all-sufficient in and unto Himself; the creation of creatures was not a necessity with Him. It is solely due to His goodness that He wishes to make His creatures partakers of this goodness — indeed, that He has gifted both angels and men with intellect and volition, not merely to find sufficiency and delight within themselves, but to find their felicity in communion with God and in the reflection upon and acknowledging of God's perfections. Blessed is he whom God has chosen to be thus engaged!

The objective which God had in view with predestination is *the magnification of Himself in His grace, mercy, and justice.* This should not be understood to mean that anything can be added to the glory of God, but rather that angels and men, in perceiving and acknowledging this glory, would enjoy felicity. Even among men a wise individual does not proceed without a well-defined objective. A building contractor does not first gather bricks, wood, and various building materials without any intent and then subsequently decide what he will do with them. Rather, he first determines that he wishes to build a house, and in order to accomplish that objective he acquires the materials which serve his purpose. This leads us to affirm the following proposition: *The ultimate objective of a plan is conceived first and executed later.* This is much more true of the only wise God. Would God first have decreed to create men and to conclude them in sin without having any further purpose, only to decree subsequently what He would do with them? No, He first decreed the end: the magnification of His grace and justice. For this purpose God decreed the means to accomplish this objective: the creation of man and his conclusion in sin. This is clearly stated

---

[1] At the end of this chapter à Brakel refers to Romans 11:32 when using a similar expression. The Dutch phrase from this text "onder het ongeloof besluiten" is translated as "concluding in unbelief" in the KJV.

in Scripture. "What if God, willing to shew His wrath, and to make His power known, endured with much long-suffering the vessels of wrath fitted to destruction: and that He might make known the riches of His glory on the vessels of mercy, which He had afore prepared unto glory?" (Rom. 9:22-23). The apostle emphatically states God's objective: to manifest His wrath as well as the riches of His glory. He follows this up by stating which means He will use to accomplish this objective: the vessels of wrath fitted to destruction, and the vessels of mercy prepared unto glory.

Whatever God accomplishes in time has been decreed by Him from eternity. He selects some from the depraved mass of the human race to be the recipients of salvation, bringing them to Christ their Surety and saving them by Him. This presupposes that He decreed to do so from eternity. Yet, it is but a means to His objective, which is the magnification of His mercy and justice. It was for that purpose that God decreed the felicity of men; and for that purpose God decreed to create men, to conclude them in sin, and to deliver them through Christ. Therefore if we view predestination comprehensively — including both the end and the means whereby the end is accomplished — both sin and Christ are involved. Although we make a separate and sequential distinction between these various matters, we recognize that God has decreed everything with one singular, all-inclusive decreeing act. For the purpose of orderly presentation, however, we distinguish between the end and the means.

God has also decreed that He will be magnified in His justice. To accomplish that objective He decreed to create men, to permit them to sin volitionally, and to justly damn them for their sins. God did not create one human being to happiness and another to condemnation. Rather, He created the entire human race perfectly holy, and thus unto felicity — His objective in doing so. I repeat that we must here consider God's objective in creating man, for the felicity of man was the objective of the state of innocency. If man had remained in this state, it would have resulted in the felicity of all mankind. We should not confuse the objective of creation and the objective of the Creator. In creation it was not God's objective that all men would attain unto salvation; for as God's counsel will stand and His purpose will always be accomplished, all would then indeed attain unto salvation. God prevents no one from obtaining salvation, but man excludes himself since he sins willfully. The election of some unto salvation is not to the detriment of others. Reprobation is neither the cause that someone sins, nor why someone is damned, but the sinner himself and his sin are the cause. It is true that those who have not been elected will not be saved; it is equally true that none but sinners will be damned. It is also true that whoever repents, believes in Christ, and lives holily will not be damned but saved. Man is therefore to be blamed for not doing so. Likewise when God converts someone, brings him to Christ, and sanctifies him, it is to be attributed to His sovereign grace. It is thus evident that it is nothing but vicious slander to insist that the church teaches that one man is created unto felicity and the other unto damnation — and therefore someone who would be virtuous to the utmost degree would nevertheless be damned, whereas someone else who would engage in wickedness to the utmost degree would nevertheless be saved. Far be it from the Almighty to do unjustly! That He has determined to manifest His grace and justice to man proceeds purely from His goodness and holiness. It is a pure manifestation of holiness to deliver men through Christ and to lead them unto salvation in the way of holiness. It is also a pure manifestation of holiness to leave men who sin voluntarily in their sin, and to damn them for their sins. When a person becomes godly and a believer, this is not to be attributed to any efforts by man who, being evil, wishes only to do evil. It must rather be attributed to the work of God's grace which He only performs in the elect.

The Distinctive Characteristics of Predestination

(1) Predestination is *eternal*, that is, from before the foundation of the world. "...whom He did predestinate" (Rom. 8:30).

(2) Predestination is *volitional*. God was not moved by external or internal causes to predetermine man's destiny, but was solely moved by His good pleasure. "For so it seemed good in Thy sight" (Mat. 9:22). The fact that God has ordained to lead one individual unto salvation through Christ and to damn another individual for his sins is solely to be attributed to the free exercise of His sovereignty. "Hath not the potter power over the clay, of the same lump to make one vessel unto honor, and another unto dishonor?" (Rom. 9:21). This is infinitely more true of God.

(3) Predestination is an *act of wisdom* whereby God ordains suitable means to accomplish His end. "O the depth of the riches both of the wisdom and knowledge of God!" (Rom. 11:33). The apostle exclaims this concerning predestination, which he discussed in this chapter.

(4) Predestination is *independent, absolute,* and *unconditional.* God accomplishes His decree by the use of means, but the means are not the conditions. The decree is not contingent upon the means.

Thus, the means neither establish nor unsettle this decree. God Himself governs the means to accomplish His certain, immutable, and immovable purpose — a purpose which proceeds from within Himself according to His good pleasure. All means are subordinate to this good pleasure. "(For the children being not yet born, neither having done any good or evil, that the purpose of God according to election might stand, not of works, but of Him that calleth;) it was said unto her, The elder shall serve the younger. As it is written, Jacob have I loved, but Esau have I hated" (Rom. 9:11-13).

(5) Predestination is an *immutable decree*. Since God's purpose originates in eternity, it is not contingent upon the condition of goodness or evil within man, but proceeds solely from the good pleasure of God. It is thus impossible for this purpose to change. God Himself is immutable, wise, and omnipotent. Therefore Romans 8:30 states, "Moreover whom He did predestinate...them He also glorified" (cf. Rom. 9:21-23).

The Two Parts of Predestination: Election and Reprobation

Predestination consists of two parts: election and reprobation. This is evident from texts in which both are mentioned simultaneously. "...vessels of wrath fitted to destruction:...vessels of mercy, which He had afore prepared unto glory" (Rom. 9:22-23); "The election hath obtained it, and the rest were blinded" (Rom. 11:7); "For God hath not appointed us to wrath, but to obtain salvation by our Lord Jesus Christ" (1 Th. 5:9).

The Decree of Election

Various words are used to describe the decree of *election*, such as "purpose," "foreknowledge," and "predestination." "...them who are the called according to His purpose. For whom He did foreknow, He also did predestinate" (Rom. 8:28-29). It is also referred to as being ordained to eternal life: "And as many as were ordained to eternal life believed" (Acts 13:48); as being written in the book of life: "but rather rejoice, because your names are written in heaven" (Luke 10:20); as obtaining salvation (1 Th. 5:9), and by the word "chosen": "According as He hath chosen us in Him before the foundation of the world" (Eph. 1:4).

Election is the foreordination of God whereby He eternally, certainly, and immutably has decreed to lead some specific individuals, identified by name, unto eternal salvation, not because of foreseen faith or good works, but motivated purely by His singular and sovereign good pleasure, to the glory of His grace.

(1) Election is *a divine deed*. It has pleased the eternal God, who is all-sufficient in Himself, to communicate His goodness, having

chosen some men to be the recipients of that communication. "He hath chosen us" (Eph. 1:4); He hath appointed us "to obtain salvation" (1 Th. 5:9). It is for this reason that they are called "His own elect" (Luke 18:7). God must not be perceived here as Judge, judging the deeds of men to either justify or damn them in consequence of this, but He must here be considered as sovereign Lord, who deals with His creatures as it pleases Him, electing the one and rejecting the other.

(2) Election originates *in eternity*. In time, God sets some apart by His efficacious call, bringing them from a natural state into the state of grace. "I have chosen you, and ordained you, that ye should go and bring forth fruit" (John 15:16). This selective call, however, proceeds from God's eternal purpose (Rom. 8:28). Thus the decree of election was not made in time — in response to man's existence, faith, and godly life — but occurred before man performed any good deed (Rom. 9:11); that is, from eternity, before the foundation of the world. "According as He hath chosen us in Him before the foundation of the world, that we should be holy and without blame before Him in love" (Eph. 1:4); "According to the eternal purpose which He purposed in Christ Jesus our Lord" (Eph. 3:11); "...according to His own purpose and grace, which was given us in Christ Jesus before the world began" (2 Tim. 1:9).

(3) Election pertains to *specific individuals;* that is, God has made a distinction between men and men. "Many be called, but few chosen" (Mat. 20:16); "...but the election...and the rest..." (Rom. 11:7). The elect are specific individuals, identified by name, in contradistinction to other specific individuals. God neither chose individuals because of qualities or virtues nor because of faith or godliness, but His choice relates to specific identity only. "For whom He did foreknow, He also did predestinate" (Rom. 8:29); "The Lord knoweth them that are His" (2 Tim. 2:19); "...whose names are in the book of life" (Phil. 4:3).

(4) Election *did not occur by virtue of Christ's merits, foreseen faith, or anticipated good works.* These are fruits issuing forth from election. They are not the causes of election. They do not precede election but are a consequence of it. There is nothing which necessitates God to do anything. Nothing which would be in man, nor any future deeds, moved God to elect a person. The reason for election is nothing but the sovereign good pleasure of God. "...according to His good pleasure which He hath purposed in Himself.... having predestinated us unto the adoption of children by Christ Jesus to Himself, according to the good pleasure of His will" (Eph. 1:9, 5).

This alone is the fountain of election. In its execution, however, God uses means. God, having permitted the human race to become subject to sin and punishment, in time draws His elect out of this state and is gracious to them. Election is therefore called the election of grace. "Even so then at this present time also there is a remnant according to the election of grace. And if by grace, then it is no more of works" (Rom. 11:5-6).

Because God has elected some, He grants Christ to them in order to bring them to God and salvation in a manner consistent with His divine Being. "Thine they were, and Thou gavest them Me" (John 17:6). It is in this respect that election occurred in Christ. "According as He hath chosen us in Him.... Having predestinated us unto the adoption of children by Jesus Christ unto Himself... wherein He hath made us accepted in the Beloved" (Eph. 1:4-6).

This election is not a consequence of any foreseen faith or good works. These issue forth out of election, being the means to make the elect partakers of the salvation ordained for them. This is true for faith: "And as many as were ordained to eternal life believed" (Acts 13:48). Therefore faith is called the faith of the elect (Titus 1:1). Consider also what is stated concerning good works in Ephesians 1:5,4, "Having predestinated us [not because we were such and such or because God viewed us as such but] "...that we should be holy and without blame before Him in love." "For whom he did foreknow, He also did predestinate to be conformed to the image of His Son" (Rom. 8:29). These He called, justified, and glorified (Rom. 8:30).

(5) Election is *immutable*. Man will not change this decree, as this election was not made on the basis of conditions. God Himself works in His elect that which is pleasing to Him, thereby leading them unto salvation. God will not of Himself change this decree, since with the Lord there "is no variableness, neither shadow of turning" (James 1:17). The Lord's wisdom and omnipotence cause His counsel to stand. This is why Scripture speaks of the "immutability of His counsel" (Heb. 6:17); "That the purpose of God according to election might *stand*" (Rom. 9:11); "The foundation of God standeth sure" (2 Tim. 2:19); "Whom He did predestinate ...them He also glorified" (Rom. 8:30).

(6) *The purpose of election is the glorification of God.* This is not to *add* glory to Him, for He is perfect, but to reveal all His glorious perfections which manifest themselves in the work of redemption, to angels and men, in order that in reflecting upon them felicity may be experienced. Its purpose is, by glorifying and praising Him, to end with all things in Him in whom all things must end, and thus

to afford Him honor and glory. The purpose is "to be glorified in His saints, and to be admired in all them that believe" (2 Th. 1:10); it is to "the glory of His grace" (Eph. 1:6). In reference to this the apostle exclaims, "For of Him, and through Him, and to Him, are all things: to whom be glory for ever. Amen" (Rom. 11:36).

Reprobation Defined

The other element of predestination is *reprobation*, to which reference is made in a variety of ways, such as "to be cast away." "I have chosen thee, and not cast thee away" (Isa. 41:9); to be fitted to destruction (Rom. 9:22); to be appointed unto wrath (1 Th. 5:9); to be ordained unto condemnation (Jude 4); and not to be written in the book of life (Rev. 13:8). These texts prove at once that there is such a thing as reprobation.

We define reprobation to be the predestination of some specific individuals, identified by name, out of sovereign good pleasure to the manifestation of God's justice in them by punishing them for their sins.

(1) Just as we have shown and shall further prove that election pertains *to specific individuals*, so this is likewise applicable to reprobation. "...whose names were not written in the book of life" (Rev. 17:8). Christ said to specific individuals, "Ye are not of My sheep" (John 10:26). They are designated by the relative pronoun "who." "For there are certain men...*who* were before of old ordained to this condemnation" (Jude 4). This is the reason why some are specifically called by name, such as Esau (Rom. 9:13), Pharaoh (Rom. 9:17), and Judas Iscariot (Acts 1:25). The number of reprobates far exceeds the number of elect, who in contrast to them — even of those that are called — are referred to as "few" (Mat. 20:16).

(2) Reprobation proceeds solely from God's good pleasure. Although the ungodliness of the reprobates is the cause of their damnation, this nevertheless was not the reason why God, to the glory of His justice, was moved to decree their reprobation. It purely proceeds from the good pleasure of God who has the right and the power to do as He pleases with His own. Thus, no one is permitted to say, "Why hast Thou made me thus?" (Rom. 9:20). According to His good pleasure He conceals the way of salvation (Mat. 11:25-26); "He hath mercy on whom He will have mercy, and whom He will He hardeneth" (Rom. 9:18). His purpose stands firm. This is confirmed in Romans 9:11 where it is stated, "for the children being not yet born, neither having done good or evil." It is therefore according to God's sovereignty and good pleasure to manifest His justice towards some and His grace to others (Rom. 9:22-23). God shall maintain His holiness and justice. Believers

know that God is just and righteous in all His doings. Let him who wishes to strive with God concerning this do so.

(3) As the decree itself is a manifestation of the sovereignty of God, its purpose is the manifestation of God's justice which reveals itself in the execution of this decree. He who decrees the end simultaneously decrees the means unto this end. Sin is the only reason that God has decreed to damn specific individuals. God permits them by their own volition to turn from Him and to enslave themselves to sin. They, having sinned, become subject to the curse threatened upon sin. God, while delivering others from sin and its curse by means of the Surety Jesus Christ, bypasses them, and therefore they neither hear God nor believe in Him. "Ye therefore hear them not, because ye are not of God" (John 8:47); "But ye believe not, because ye are not of My sheep" (John 10:26). As a righteous Judge God punishes them due to their sin in "the day of wrath and revelation of the righteous judgment of God" (Rom. 2:5). Thus, God shows His wrath over "vessels of wrath fitted to destruction" (Rom. 9:22).

Up to this point we have explained this doctrine; however, this doctrine has many opponents, such as Roman Catholics (although not exclusively so), Arminians, Lutherans, and others.

Questions and Objections Answered

The *Arminians* appeared on the scene at the beginning of the seventeenth century. They were condemned by the national Synod — better referred to as the General Synod held in 1618 and 1619 in Dordrecht — and were subsequently expelled from the Reformed Church.[2] They, first of all, propose the existence of a universal, indefinite decree which relates to believers and their perseverance in good works, as well as the damnation of the ungodly. This is referred to as the will of divine precedence. Secondly, they propose that God, moved by universal philanthropy, ordained Jesus Christ to be a Savior of all men in general and each one specifically. They maintain that God has done so in consequence of the universal atonement of Christ as well as man's faith and perseverance in good works, both of which they consider to proceed from the exercise of man's free will which God anticipates by virtue of His mediate knowledge (see chapter 3) whereby He knows what everyone will or will not do. They maintain that this is the reason why God was moved to decree to save some, whereas due to foreseen

---

[2] Contrary to today, there was only one Reformed denomination in the Netherlands during à Brakel's time, which bore the name "The Reformed Church."

continuance in unbelief, ungodliness, and apostasy He was moved to damn others. They also propose that no person can be assured of his salvation because he knows not whether he will persevere or not, even though he is presently believing and godly.

Within *Roman Catholicism* there is no agreement concerning this doctrine, but rather vehement contention. Some are almost orthodox in this doctrine, whereas others agree with the Arminians. First the battle was waged between the Franciscans and Dominicans and afterwards between the Jesuits and Jansenists. Some hold to election by grace, whereas others promote election on the basis of works. Others hold to yet different opinions, the one maintaining that election unto grace is by grace only, but unto glory on the basis of works, whereas others insist that both are on the basis of works.

Lutherans do not strictly adhere to the sentiments of Luther who was pure in this doctrine in spite of his use of expressions which are a bit too crude. His followers, however — the one more than the other — deviate from his position. They propose the existence of two decrees. The first decree pertains to the election of Christ to be a universal Savior of the entire human race. They hold to an election of all men in order that all might be redeemed through Christ, may receive means which are sufficient unto salvation, be called to Christ, and be saved upon the conditions of faith and repentance. Thus, all could possibly be saved if they would but believe in Christ and repent; however, the majority of mankind would reject this offer and thus perish. In addition they propose a different decree of election: God from eternity and out of sovereign grace has chosen certain specific individuals unto salvation in Christ, He being the foundation of election, who as Surety would pay for them and merit salvation. Others wish to hold to a foreseen faith, be it as a moving cause or as a means similar to its function in justification. They furthermore propose that the elect upon birth are dead in sins and trespasses and thus are entirely impotent to repent and to believe in Christ. At God's time, however, in accordance with the decree of election, He converts them, grants them faith, and preserves them unto salvation. Thus, they maintain that the elect can completely apostatize after regeneration and again become dead in sins and trespasses. Nevertheless they cannot do so irrevocably, since God, according to His eternal and immutable decree, restores faith and regeneration prior to their death. Consequently, an elect person, having been regenerated, can be assured of his salvation.

Amyraut, and all who follow him, maintain to have found a middle position whereby the offense of the true doctrine can be removed. They hold to the existence of two decrees. One is a *universal* decree whereby God, being graciously disposed towards the entire human race, decreed to send Christ into the world so that He by virtue of His atonement would merit the forgiveness of sins and eternal salvation for all men — this being contingent upon faith in Him and their not neglecting this salvation. To some extent God would then will the salvation of all men and every man would be able to be saved if he would but exercise his will accordingly. To this they add a *special* decree whereby God out of sovereign grace has chosen certain specific individuals unto salvation. By virtue of this decree He will most certainly lead them to salvation, granting them (due to their natural inability) faith and repentance and preserving them in this state by His power. From all this a regenerate person may be assured of his salvation. As far as the first decree is concerned, Amyraldians are in agreement with Armininans and Lutherans, but are orthodox concerning the second decree. In the presentation of the sentiments of the various parties it becomes evident that there is not merely one point of contention, but that various points of contention are intermingled. We shall therefore consider and treat each point by itself.

Socinians maintain that there are two elections: one *universal*, eternal election of godly men, and one *particular* election which occurs in time.

Question #1: Has God from eternity purposed universally to have mercy upon the entire human race, having ordained Christ to be a Savior for each and every one, calling them all to Himself and blessed communion with Him?

Answer: The sentiments of the various parties and the manner in which they express themselves concerning this manner have been explained above. All agree, however, in this point that God has not ultimately intended and purposed to save all men, perceiving that then all men would most certainly become the recipients of salvation — a fact contradicted by reality.

We respond that God does not hate any creature other than because of sin, having a common affection for all His creatures as created beings, each after his kind. He maintains and governs them, in this way not leaving Himself without witness to sinners, doing good to them and filling their hearts with food and gladness (Acts 14:17). We also maintain that God is pleased with the conversion of men, their faith in Christ, their prayers, their alms, and their sanctification, as all of these are principal elements of the restoration of God's image in man. We deny, however, the existence of such universal grace or purpose to be gracious to all men, to give Christ to be a universal Savior for all men, and presenting Christ as such to all men.

First, we maintain that whatever God does in this time state, He has decreed from eternity. "...who worketh all things after the counsel of His own will" (Eph. 1:11). Thus, God, in this time state, is not gracious to all men. "He hath mercy on whom He will have mercy, and whom He will He hardeneth" (Rom. 9:18). God did not send Christ into the world to be the Savior of all, but only for His elect. Christ suffered as a Surety and High Priest, and the merits of Christ and their application are inseparable. The first is not broader in scope than the other, and Scripture ascribes the efficacy of Christ's death only to some. We will deal with this more comprehensively in chapter 22, "The Satisfaction of Christ." God does not offer Christ to all men, for he does not call all men. "He sheweth His word unto Jacob. He hath not dealt so with any nation: and as for His judgments, they have not known them" (Psa. 147:19-20). Christ confirms this in Matthew 11:25-26, "I thank Thee, O Father, Lord of heaven and earth, because Thou hast hid these things from the wise and prudent, and hast revealed them unto babes. Even so, Father: for so it seemed good in Thy sight." This reality is incontrovertibly confirmed by daily experience. We therefore conclude that in eternity God did not make a universal, gracious decree. He neither ordained Christ to be the Savior of all men, nor did He decree to offer Christ to all men.

Secondly, election and reprobation are the opposite of each other. Both relate to specific individuals. Both election and reprobation concern specific persons with specific names. All of this has previously been demonstrated. Thus, there is simply no room for a universal decree — to be gracious to all and to send Christ for all men. It cannot be maintained that this is a determination in a second or subsequent decree, and then suggest that this decree does not eliminate a prior decree which is universal in scope. Nowhere does Scripture speak of a first and a second decree, much less of a first decree which is nullified by a subsequent decree. God's decree is immutable. Since God in His eternal decree has appointed some unto wrath and destruction, it follows that there was no prior decree of God to be gracious to them.

Thirdly, the position that grace is universal in scope has several inherent absurdities, which in turn generate additional absurdities:

(1) To propose that there is a universal will to save all men implies that God wills contrary to His will. He who truly, sincerely, and fervently wishes to accomplish a task, will execute it if at all possible. God is able to actually save all men, but it is not according

to His will. This is confirmed by the outcome of events. If, however, it is God's desire to save all men, then He necessarily has willed to do so, which is also true for the reverse argument.

(2) This universal decree to save all men is either absolute or conditional. If it is absolute, God has failed in His purpose, for all men are not saved. If it is conditional, God will either execute this condition or merely demand that it be met. If God Himself were to execute this condition, all men would actually be saved. This is simply not true. If God does not wish to execute the condition, but merely demands that it be met, then He does not truly will the salvation of all men. God knows that it is completely impossible for sinful man to comply with this condition, since he is spiritually dead, blind, unwilling, and impotent. Then God would fervently and earnestly desire something which He simultaneously knows with certainty will never come to pass.

(3) If God were to universally will the salvation of all men, He would fail in His purpose and would be deprived from accomplishing His will, since He wills something which does not occur. He wills the salvation of all men; and nevertheless, they are not all saved.

It is quite different, however, when God commands something and declares that obedience to it would be pleasing to Him. There can obviously be no argument about the fact that men do not obey the will of God's command. It is again a different matter to decree something with a purpose, and it is this will of God's decree which is the point of contention here. It is the will of God's decree which is thwarted if that which He wills does not come to pass. If God had decreed the salvation of all men, He would be thwarted in His purpose, as He would not obtain that which He decreed according to His will and that which He wills according to His decree. Since all this is absurd, it is also absurd to maintain that within God there is a will to decree the universal salvation of all men.

The reasons advanced by those who hold to the view of universal grace are dealt with in our discussion concerning the satisfaction of Christ in chapter 22. Here we shall deal briefly with some of the reasons and demonstrate that they do not lend support to the idea of a decree of universal grace.

Objection #1: "As I live, saith the LORD God, I have no pleasure in the death of the wicked; but that the wicked turn from His way and live" (Ezek. 33:11).

Answer: The decree of God, which most certainly will be executed and whereby God always accomplishes His purpose, is not discussed in this text. It rather speaks of God's delight in the conversion of man whereby man is again restored in the image and likeness of God; also that God, by virtue of the fact that man is His creature, is displeased with both man's failure to repent as well as his damnation.

Objection #2: "For God so loved the world, that He gave His only begotten Son, that whosoever believeth..." (John 3:16); "...which I will give for the life of the world" (John 6:51); "God was in Christ, reconciling the world unto Himself, not imputing their trespasses unto them" (2 Cor. 5:19); "And He is the propitiation of our sins: and not for ours only, but also for the sins of the whole world" (1 John 2:2).

Answer: (1) These texts do not deal with the point of contention, which is the eternal decree of God, but rather with Christ's mission on behalf of man.

(2) The word "world" here refers to human beings, to the human race which is the object of God's love for men, the human race being the object of God's love and benevolence. This does not mean that God loves every individual human being in the world, that Christ imparts spiritual life to every man, and that sin is not imputed to everyone. All this is evident from the general language of the Bible. The first world perished in the flood (Luke 17:27); nevertheless, Noah and his family were preserved. The devil "deceiveth the whole world" (Rev. 12:9), "and the whole world lieth in wickedness" (1 John 5:19). Who would therefore conclude that there were no believers in the world and that there was not a single human being who was not deceived by the devil, nor lying in wickedness? Christ says, "I pray not for the world" (John 17:9), which does not imply that there is not a person on earth for whom Christ does pray. The word "world" cannot be understood as referring to each and every human being upon earth, but one should understand it to refer to those individuals which the text has in view. Sometimes the reference is to a multitude of people, "Behold, the world is gone after Him" (John 12:19), or to the ungodly in contradistinction to the elect (John 17:9). Sometimes it is used in regard to the elect in contrast with others. In 2 Corinthians 5:19, "world" is used to refer to those who are reconciled with God and to whom God does not impute their trespasses. This does not apply to the ungodly, but to the elect.

Objection #3: "For God hath concluded them all in unbelief, that He might have mercy upon all" (Rom. 11:32); "Therefore as by the offence of one judgment came upon all men to condemnation; even so by the righteousness of one the free gift came upon all men unto justification of life" (Rom. 5:18); "For as in Adam all die, even so in Christ shall all be made alive" (1 Cor. 15:22); "And that He died for all..." (2 Cor. 5:15); "Who will have all men to be saved....Who gave Himself a ransom for all..." (1 Tim. 2:4, 6); "...not willing that any should perish, but that all should come to repentance" (2 Pet. 3:9).

Answer: Our response to each of these texts can be found in chapter 22. The word "all" does not refer to all men who have existed, do exist, and will exist, but rather to all those who are under discussion in each individual text. Romans 5:18 speaks of all those who are in Christ, who will be the recipients of justification unto life. Romans 11:32 refers to the rejection and the restoration or repentance of the Jewish nation. 1 Corinthians 15:22 speaks of all who will be made alive in Christ. 2 Corinthians 5:15 makes mention of all believers who have died to sin and are partakers of spiritual life. In 1 Timothy 2:4-6, the reference is to all sorts of men, which is evident in verse 2 — all sorts of men rather than all men will come to the knowledge of the truth. Whatever God has decreed shall certainly come to pass and whatever does not occur is not according to the will of God's decree. Thus, all men are not saved, but only those in whose stead Christ has been given as a ransom. 2 Peter 3:9 refers to the elect who will come to repentance and who must first be gathered in before the world perishes. It also makes mention of the command and the declaration of the gospel which commands everyone who hears it to repent, speaking of both God's pleasure and displeasure relative to repentance or the lack of it.

Since we have demonstrated above that the proponents of universal grace make Christ the foundation and cause of election, it is necessary to answer the following question.

Question #2: Does the election of Christ precede in its order the election of men, so that God was moved by the merits of Christ to elect men, or does the election of men take precedence, and thus Christ was chosen to execute the election of men?

Answer: The proponents of a universal grace hold to the first position and we to the second position. Christ, as far as the decree of election is concerned, is the Executor of this election. He is the meriting but not the moving cause of the salvation to which the elect are ordained. We maintain this for the following reasons:

First, Christ has been chosen on behalf of the elect, to be their Mediator, Redeemer, and Savior. "Herein is love, not that we loved God, but that He loved us, and sent His Son to be the propitiation for our sins" (1 John 4:10); "For God so loved the world, that He gave His only begotten Son" (John 3:16). These texts state clearly that the gift of the Son proceeds and issues forth from the love of God towards the elect. It is a fact in the realm of nature that the cause precedes the effect, the end precedes the means whereby the end is attained, and the objective precedes any activity related to it. Thus, the love of God toward the elect as well as their election preceded the ordination of the Surety who is given to them (Isa. 9:5), is given them unto their redemption and salvation, and who was foreordained and manifested for them (1 Pet. 1:20). The Lord Jesus confirms this in John 17:6, where He states, "Thine they were, and Thou gavest them Me." They were therefore the property of the Father before they were given to the Son as Surety and Mediator, and thus their election precedes the election of the Surety who was chosen for the benefit of their salvation.

Secondly, election has no other cause than the good pleasure of God. "Having made known unto us the mystery of His will, according to His good pleasure which He hath purposed in Himself: that in the dispensation of the fulness of times He might gather together in one all things in Christ, both which are in heaven, and which are on earth; even in Him: in whom also we have obtained an inheritance, being predestinated according to the purpose of Him who worketh all things after the counsel of His own will" (Eph. 1:9-11). Election has precedence here, as the elect are said to be ordained according to the purpose of Him who works all things according to the counsel of His own will; that is, according to His good pleasure. There is here no other cause which would have moved God. To this is added the means whereby God would accomplish His purpose: "That in the dispensation of the fulness of times He might gather together in one all things in Christ." Thus, Christ is the ordained means whereby those who have been chosen according to God's sovereign good pleasure are made partakers of the salvation to which they have been ordained. He is therefore neither the moving cause nor the foundation of election. This is also confirmed by the following texts. "...it is your Father's good pleasure to give you the kingdom" (Luke 12:32); "Even so, Father: for so it seemed good in Thy sight" (Mat. 11:26); "...not of works, but of Him that calleth" (Rom. 9:11).

Objection #1: "According as He hath chosen us in Him" (Eph. 1:4); "...grace, which was given us in Christ Jesus before the world began" (2 Tim. 1:9).

Answer: (1) To be chosen in Christ is to be made partakers of all spiritual blessings in Christ (Eph. 1:3). The apostle clearly expresses this in 1 Thessalonians 5:9, where he states, "For God hath ...appointed us...to obtain salvation by our Lord Jesus Christ." Our appointment unto salvation is the issue at hand, and this appointment is executed by the agency of Christ. Thus "in Christ" does not mean "for Christ's sake," but rather *by means of* Christ. He has chosen us to be saved through Christ. Before anyone was in Christ, he already was the property of the Father. "Thine they were, and Thou gavest them Me" (John 17:6).

(2) Grace was given in Christ before the world began, although not in actuality, as the elect did not as yet exist. Rather, it was ordained that grace would be given them in time by Christ as the Executor of the plan of salvation. Thus, these texts do not afford the least proof that Christ is the moving cause and foundation of election.

Objection #2: "For whom He did foreknow, He also did predestinate to be conformed to the image of His Son, that He might be the firstborn among many brethren" (Rom. 8:29). The image to which there must be conformity precedes that which is conformed to this image. Thus, Christ was elected prior to men, and man is elected as He is viewed in Christ.

Answer: (1) The apostle states expressly that His foreknowledge of the elect has precedence. "For whom He did foreknow, He also did predestinate to be conformed to the image," etc.

(2) Conformity to the image of His Son occurs in this time state, and is not related to the decree but to the execution of this decree. The apostle states that God has ordained from eternity, and that those known from eternity would be conformed to the image of Christ in this time state. He does not say, however, that God, in electing, conformed His elect to the image of His Son. If there were such a text, their argument would have a semblance of validity, but this is not at all the case.

(3) Christ is said to be the firstborn among many brethren, but not the first elect. It is the latter that needed to be proven. The apostle here speaks of the beginning of the salvation of the elect, which is the Son of God, Jesus Christ, who is both the meriting cause of salvation as well as the example to which the elect are conformed in time, both in reference to His suffering and His life. In this respect He is the firstborn of all in the actual execution of God's decree, and in His excellence.

Question #3: Have some men been the specific object of God's choice; that is, has He chosen them by name?

Answer: The Arminians maintain that all men have been the object of God's choice, this choice being contingent upon faith, repentance, and perseverance, all of which in turn are contingent upon the exercise of man's free will. They insist that election is God's decree to save all who believe and are godly, and that reprobation is God's decree to damn all unbelievers and the ungodly, without specifying them by name. They furthermore maintain that God, by virtue of a mediate knowledge, knows who shall and who shall not be willing to believe. As a result of this knowledge God knows who will and who will not be saved.

We maintain, however, that God has chosen a predetermined number of specific individuals by name. He has furthermore decreed to send Christ to be a Mediator to lead them unto salvation. He decreed to call them irresistibly unto Christ, grant them faith and repentance, preserve them by His power, and thus in actuality save them. This is confirmed by the following proofs.

Proof #1: It is evident from the word Προοριζειν (*proörizein*), that is, to ordain beforehand, which is repeatedly used in reference to election (cf. Rom. 8:29-30; Eph. 1:5, 11). This word means "to ordain someone for a specific purpose." "For to do whatsoever Thy hand and Thy counsel determined before to be done" (Acts 4:28); "Him...by the determinate counsel and foreknowledge of God," etc. (Acts 2:23); "Again, He limiteth a certain day" (Heb. 4:7); He "hath determined...the bounds of their habitation" (Acts 17:26). Since God uses this word in reference to election, it therefore pertains to specifically identified individuals who are ordained unto salvation. The same is also expressed by the verb "to elect," which is the Greek word ἐκλογή *(ekloge).* He who takes the whole does not make a choice. To elect is to choose something from among many for oneself according to one's own pleasure. Since Scripture states that God from eternity has chosen certain men unto salvation, it does not imply that all men are ordained to this salvation, but rather that He has chosen specific individuals unto Himself.

Proof #2: It is evident from the fact that some names have been written in the book of life. The children of Israel had their genealogies from which they could prove their tribal origin. Likewise God is said to have such a book, which is called *the book of life* (Rev. 3:5). The names of the reprobate are not recorded in this book. "... whose names are not written in the book of life..." (Rev. 13:8). Rather, the names of those elected unto salvation are recorded in this book. "But rather rejoice, because your names are written in heaven" (Luke 10:20). In Revelation 21:27 it is stated that "they which are written in the Lamb's book of life" will enter the new Jerusalem. The Father has elected them, written them in His book, and has given them to the Son in order that He might redeem them. He in turn assumed responsibility for them, and has transferred their names into His book, which for this reason is called the "book of the Lamb." "...help those women which laboured with me in the gospel, with Clement also, and with other my fellow-labourers, whose names are in the book of life" (Phil. 4:3). It cannot be expressed any more clearly. There is here no mention of any virtue or condition. There is no general reference to evil and good, to believers or unbelievers, but the name of each individual is recorded in the book of life. Those whose names are recorded in this book are mentioned by name, as well as those whose names are not recorded. Thus, election relates to specific individuals.

Proof #3: This is also evident from the contrast between persons rather than virtues. "…many be called, but few chosen" (Mat. 20:16); "…the election hath obtained it, and the rest were blinded" (Rom. 11:7). It is nowhere recorded that God elects or rejects *virtues,* nor is it stated anywhere that God has elected or rejected individuals with a specific nature. Rather, the reference is always to specific persons. "Jacob have I loved, and Esau have I hated" (Rom. 9:13). Even though this may be applied to their descendants, as the descendants of the one were incorporated into the church and those of the other were rejected — even from the administration of the means of grace — the text nevertheless refers to individuals as far as eternal election and rejection is concerned. All of this is evident from the context of this text, for the apostle follows this proposition with a treatise concerning election and rejection. This is also confirmed by those texts which do not mention individuals by name, but which nevertheless use the pronouns "our," "those," and "these." "…as He hath chosen us…" (Eph. 1:4); "For whom He did foreknow, He also did predestinate …" (Rom. 8:29). These words do not refer to virtues, but rather to specific individuals. "The Lord knoweth them that are His" (2 Tim. 2:19).

Objection #1: If God had chosen specific individuals, their names would have to be recorded in the Bible, which contains the entire counsel of God (Acts 20:27).

Answer: The names of some are recorded as has been demonstrated. It is sufficient if their names have been recorded in the book of life. As far as the full counsel of God is concerned, Scripture reveals as much as we need to know to believe, to live holily, and to be comforted.

Objection #2: Since all the promises of God are conditional, then this is also true for election. God's manner of operation in this time state is consistent with His eternal decree, and if therefore election is conditional, it is neither absolute nor does it relate to specific individuals.

Answer: We reject this conclusion. There are conditional promises, but it does not necessarily follow that there is a conditional decree of election. The decree is one thing and the administration of the gospel another. It is true that whatever God accomplishes in time He has decreed from eternity. Since He makes conditional promises in time, He consequently decreed from eternity to make conditional promises. This is logical, but it does not follow that therefore election is also conditional.

Objection #3: If God has decreed such an election which is both absolute and specific, then He would not issue a conditional command to the elect relative to the acquisition of salvation, nor a threat of damnation upon disobedience to this command, which nevertheless does commonly occur in the Word of God.

Answer: This is not a logical argument. He who has most certainly decreed the end, has also decreed the means whereby He brings the elect to that end. This is the way which God holds before them: faith and repentance. He uses promises and threatenings, which are sanctified by His Spirit, to motivate them towards that end.

Objection #4: If there was such a thing as an election of specific individuals, the gospel could not be proclaimed to everyone unconditionally, nor could a reprobate be commanded to believe in Christ, with the promise of salvation annexed to it. It would be contradictory not to will someone's salvation and nevertheless to promise salvation to him if he believes in Christ. Consequently, God has not chosen specific individuals by name.

Answer: The fact that there is such a specific election has been proven beyond the shadow of a doubt. It is equally true that there is an unconditional offer of the gospel, to which the promise of salvation is annexed upon the conditions of faith and repentance. There is no contradiction here, for the one is absolute and the other conditional. The one is a decree, whereas the other is a command. There is a difference between the objective of the worker and the ultimate realization of his work. It is a manifestation of God's goodness to present the gospel to the unrepentant with a conditional promise, and it is man's duty to obey that gospel. Election does not prevent the unrepentant from obedience, but rather their own evil nature, and God is thus glorified when He damns them for their own disobedience.

Question #4: Did election proceed purely from the sovereign good pleasure of God, without any external influence, or was this decree made on the basis of foreseen faith and good works?

Answer: The latter is the view of many in *Roman Catholicism*, of *Arminians*, and of many *Lutherans*. We do maintain that faith and holiness constitute the way by which God accomplishes the decree of election. They are, however, in no way the moving cause nor the foundation of election which solely and purely proceeds from God's sovereign good pleasure.

First, this is evident from Scripture's express declaration that election has no other cause but God's good pleasure alone.

(1) "Who hath saved us, and called us with an holy calling, not according to our works, but according to His own purpose and grace, which was given us in Christ Jesus before the world began" (2 Tim. 1:9). The apostle speaks of persons (us), and not of virtues. He declares that God who saves them grants them eternal glory, and leads them there by means of the calling. He reveals the fountain from which the purpose and the means unto this purpose proceed. He affirms that this is not to be found in works but solely in the purpose and grace of God.

(2) "For the children being not yet born, neither having done any good or evil, that the purpose of God according to election might stand, not of works, but of him that calleth; it was said unto her....so then it is not of him that willeth, nor of him that runneth, but of God that showeth mercy" (Rom. 9:11-12, 16). The apostle here refers to two specific individuals, Jacob and Esau, and not to their descendants as if to imply that Jacob's descendants would constitute the church of God and Esau's descendants would be deprived of the means of grace. He speaks of these two, considering them not yet born, "neither having done any good or evil." It is the apostle's objective to exclude all consideration of works as the moving cause that one person is accepted and the other rejected. He wishes to confirm that God's purpose according to election is the only origin of election and rejection, and thus the decree is not based on works but originates in the God who calls. From God's dealings with these two men, the apostle draws the line to God's dealings with all other men. Thus the reason why someone is appointed for destruction is not to be found in man even though sin is the cause for damnation coming upon them. Likewise, the reason why anyone is prepared unto glory is neither to be found in man, but only in the good pleasure of the Lord (vss. 21, 22). The reason is not to be found in willing nor running, but in the mercy of God.

(3) "Fear not, little flock; for it is your Father's good pleasure to give you the kingdom" (Luke 12:32); "Even so, Father: for so it seemed good in Thy sight" (Mat. 11:26); "Having predestinated us ...according to the good pleasure of His will" (Eph. 1:5); "...there is a remnant according to the election of grace. And if by grace, then it is no more of works: otherwise grace is no more grace," etc. (Rom. 11:5-6). These texts expressly state God's good pleasure and

His sovereign grace to be the origin of election unto salvation, excluding all other things, particularly all works.

Faith, good works, and the perseverance in both of these do not originate in man himself, but in God. They proceed from eternal election. Consequently, election is not based on faith, good works, and perseverance. We will subsequently demonstrate in chapters 31 and 32 that these matters do not proceed from man himself. That election is not the result of faith, but faith the result of election, is evident from what follows.

First, "For whom He did foreknow, He also did predestinate to be conformed to the image of His Son, that He might be the firstborn among many brethren. Moreover whom He did predestinate, them He also called: and whom He called, them He also justified: and whom He justified, them He also glorified" (Rom. 8:29-30). Here the apostle posits election as being unto glory and grace, unto glory as the ultimate end, and unto the benefits as means whereby this ordained glory is obtained.

Evasive Argument: Paul makes mention of the cross and states that believers have been appointed to suffer as Christ has suffered in order that they may be conformed to the image of His Son. He further says that they are called to this and that patient cross-bearing has the approbation of God; in this way He brings them to glory in the sight of all men.

Answer: (1) It is obvious that the apostle is referring to individuals; that is, specific individuals, pointing them out as it were with his finger as he uses words such as, "this," "that," "those," "not such," and "such."

(2) Even though the apostle has previously made mention of suffering, his reference in these texts is not to suffering, but he establishes a firm foundation for comfort in suffering: their eternal election unto glory — the latter being attained by making them conformed to Christ, calling them, and justifying them.

(3) This conformity of believers does not consist in the cross itself, for the ungodly also encounter crosses, who nevertheless are not conformed to Christ. This conformity consists in holiness. "...we shall also bear the image of the heavenly" (1 Cor. 15:49); "My little children, of whom I travail in birth again until Christ be formed in you" (Gal. 4:19); "But we all...are changed unto the same image..." (2 Cor. 3:18).

(4) This calling is not a calling unto the cross, but unto faith, hope, and love, which occurs by means of the gospel and is to glory and virtue. "...Him that hath called us to glory and virtue" (2 Pet. 1:3); "But the God of all grace, who hath called us unto His eternal

glory" (1 Pet. 5:10). This calling proceeds from election, as the apostle confirms here. Those whom He has foreknown, He has predestinated, and those He has called. This is why those who are called are declared to be chosen and faithful: "And they that are with Him are called, and chosen, and faithful" (Rev. 17:14). In addition, the apostle speaks of such a calling which is inseparably linked to glory. The calling to bear the cross does not generally result in salvation, however, for God also brings crosses upon the ungodly. Many who are called externally, apostatize as a result of the cross (Mat. 13:21).

(5) The suggestion that justification would be God's approbation upon the suffering of believers does not contain a semblance of truth. To be justified means to be acquitted from sin and punishment for the sake of Christ's merits. "It is God that justifieth. Who is he that condemneth? It is Christ that died" (Rom. 8:33-34). Thus, justification is not God's public approbation upon the suffering and patience of believers.

(6) Likewise, glorification does not signify the granting of honor before men; rather, it refers to making one a partaker of eternal glory. Nowhere does glorification refer to the act whereby God exalts someone or gives him a position of honor among men. Furthermore, believers are not honored among men for their suffering; suffering causes them to be held in contempt and to be despised by the world. To be glorified is to be made a partaker of eternal glory. "... that we may also be glorified together" (Rom. 8:17). Peter refers to being glorified as receiving a crown of glory. "Ye shall receive a crown of glory that fadeth not away" (1 Pet. 5:4).

From all this it may be concluded that this argument is vain and invalid. Thus, this text confirms that conformity to Christ, calling, and justification proceed from eternal election, from which follows that God in His electing decree was not moved by faith and good works to elect one person rather than someone else.

Secondly, this is confirmed by texts specifically referring to faith, good works, and perseverance. These texts demonstrate that election is not *based* on these virtues, but that they are the *result* of election. In Acts 13:48 there is stated concerning *faith*. "And as many as were ordained to eternal life believed." Specific individuals are here said to believe, to which is added why they believed, whereas others did not. The origin of their believing was to be found in the fact that God had ordained them unto eternal life. Although it is not stated who ordained them, we nevertheless know that no one can ordain anyone unto eternal life but God alone. "God hath...appointed us...to obtain salvation" (1 Th. 5:9).

The objective was eternal life, to which some had been ordained. Although it is not stated here that they were *predestinated*, we nevertheless know that ordination to eternal life is from eternity (cf. Eph. 1:4; 2 Tim. 1:9; Eph. 3:11). They had been *ordained* to eternal life. This does not imply that they had a good, suitable inner disposition, for apart from the fact that this word is never descriptive of an internal spiritual frame — no man has such a suitable inner disposition to believe or to be worthy of eternal life as we will demonstrate at the appropriate time — it does mean "to ordain," "to determine," "to appoint," and "to be committed to something," which in 1 Corinthians 16:16 is expressed as "submitting one's self unto." Since God had ordained them unto eternal life, it necessarily follows that God granted them faith as the means to lead them to eternal life. When it is stated "as many as believed," it is neither suggested that the apostle knew the precise number, nor that there were no more elect in those localities to be converted later. It merely indicates that the word was fruitful and efficacious, causing many to believe, and that none but the elect did believe.

This is also confirmed in Titus 1:1, where the phrase occurs, "the faith of God's elect." This neither suggests that faith preceded election, nor was a moving cause for election, for then it would have been an election of faith. Since, however, it is referred to as the faith of the elect, it is evident that faith is subsequent to election and proceeds from it.

Thirdly, it is evident that *holiness proceeds from election.* "According as He hath chosen us in Him before the foundation of the world, that we should be holy and without blame before Him in love: having predestinated us unto the adoption of children" (Eph. 1:4-5). Although holiness is the objective for which God chooses someone, it is not therefore the moving cause why someone is chosen above someone else. That He has chosen us does not suggest that He has chosen us as believers, knowing by virtue of His mediate knowledge that we would believe, as a fruit of which we would exercise holiness. Then foreseen faith would be the moving cause of election, from which holiness would issue forth. The apostle rather speaks of those who now actually believe, and says of them that they were elected, since faith is given to someone because he is elect. This we have demonstrated and is also evident from verse 3, "...who hath blessed us with all spiritual blessings in heavenly places in Christ." All spiritual blessings proceed from election, which includes faith, it being a special blessing and gift of God. This is equally true of sanctification.

Fourthly, it is evident that *perseverance proceeds from election.*

"...that, if it were possible, they shall deceive the very elect" (Mat. 24:24). False prophets would have much power of deception and thus deceive many, but they would not be able to deceive any true believers, the reason being that they are elected. Such is also the case in Revelation 13:8 where it is stated, "And all that dwell upon the earth shall worship him (the beast), whose names are not written in the book of life." Why is it that others would not follow the beast? By comparison it is evident that it was because their names were written in the book of life, as is confirmed by the golden chain of salvation, out of which not one link can be removed. Those whom He has foreknown, predestinated, called, and justified, he has also glorified (Rom. 8:29-30). The apostle Peter extracts all blessing — also the perseverance of saints — from eternal election. In 1 Peter 1:2 he calls believers "elect," and in verse 5 he says about those elect that they "are kept by the power of God through faith unto salvation."

Objection #1: "For whom He did foreknow, He also did predestinate" (Rom. 8:29). Here it is expressly stated that foreknowledge precedes predestination. This means that God sees the faith, good works, and perseverance of believers prior to His election of them, and is thereby moved to elect them in deference to others.

Answer: Far be it from us to suggest that the apostle here states that God perceives the faith and good works of some in advance and therefore elects them. The apostle in using the relative pronoun "whom" speaks of persons and not of virtues. This foreknowledge is the eternal election unto salvation; it is a knowing of some to be His. "The Lord knoweth them that are His" (2 Tim. 2:19). It also relates to the election of Christ as Mediator, "...who verily was foreordained[3]..." (1 Pet. 1:20), as well as to the election of some individuals, "Elect according to the foreknowledge of God the Father" (1 Pet. 1:2). God did not randomly determine who would become godly and believing, but consciously chose specific individuals to be His own. The reason why the apostle here allows foreknowledge to precede predestination is due to the fact that he establishes foreknowledge to be the fountain of all things. From that point he proceeds to the means whereby God leads those who are foreknown to salvation. Those whom He has known to be His own, He has also predestinated to be conformed to the image of His Son, and those He has called, etc.

Objection #2: God has loved the elect from eternity, and there-

---

[3] The Statenbijbel reads, "Dewelke wel voorgekend is geweest," which literally translates as, "who verily was foreknown."

fore foresaw their faith, for "without faith it is impossible to please Him" (Heb. 11:6).

Answer: It is God's will that we love our enemies, that we bless those who curse us, and that we do well to those that hate us (Mat. 5:44). Nevertheless there is nothing desirable in these enemies which would move us to love them. God likewise loves His enemies and, motivated by love, gives them His Son (John 3:16). "But God commendeth His love toward us, in that, while we were yet sinners, Christ died for us" (Rom. 5:8). God's love has its origin in God Himself, and He chooses objects to whom He will manifest His love. The motivation for this love does not originate with man. "Herein is love, not that we loved God, but that He loved us, and sent His Son to be the propitiation for our sins. We love Him, because He first loved us" (1 John 4:10, 19). It is a known fact that one can exercise love in a twofold manner. One can love with the love of affection and benevolence, which can be exercised towards his enemy, or with a love of pleasure or delight.[4] God has eternally loved the elect with a love of benevolence, and in time with the love of His delight, finding delight in their holy deeds. From that perspective it is impossible to please God without faith. Thus, they whom it pleased God to elect from eternity, please God in time.

Objection #3: God has chosen the saints, the poor of this world, and those that are rich in faith. "As the elect of God, holy and beloved..." (Col. 3:12); "...because God hath from the beginning chosen you to salvation through sanctification of the Spirit and belief of the truth" (2 Th. 2:13); "Elect according to the foreknowledge of God the Father, through sanctification of the Spirit..." (1 Pet. 1:2); "Hath not God chosen the poor of this world rich in faith, and heirs of the kingdom?" (James 2:5).

Answer: In these texts sanctification and faith are not presented as the moving causes why God has chosen His elect, but rather as fruits of election and as evidences that the person who manifests these fruits has been chosen by God from eternity. Colossians 3:12 does not suggest that these matters coalesce within God's eternal purpose, much less that holiness precedes election as its cause. Rather, the apostle refers to the elect as they exist in time, already being partakers of sanctification. He advances election before time, sanctification in time, and the love of God towards them as reasons why they should be motivated to live worthy of these benefits. 2 Thessalonians 2:13 and 1 Peter 1:2 do not refer to

---

[4] à Brakel uses "welbehagelijkheid," which expresses love towards those with whom we are well-pleased.

holiness as either preceding election or as being its cause. It does not say, "God has chosen you in view of your sanctification," but rather that He has chosen them unto salvation and sanctification, this being the way in which they will be brought to salvation. In James 2:5 the apostle makes mention of the temporal condition of some believers as being the poor of the world. He admonishes not to despise them since God had also chosen them to be rich in faith and to be heirs of the kingdom.

As election occurred according to God's sovereign good pleasure, so likewise did reprobation occur for the same reason.

Question #5: Is the decree of eternal election mutable or immutable?

Answer: The *Arminians* are at a loss here, as they must yield to too many clear and irrefutable passages of Scripture in this regard. In an effort, however, to maintain mutableness — which they must do as they consider election to be contingent upon the exercise of man's mutable will — they have invented a distinction by proposing the existence of a *perfect* and an *imperfect* decree of election. They view the *imperfect* decree to be the will of God to save those who believe and are godly. All of this is contingent upon the exercise of man's free will which enables man either to believe or to apostatize from the faith. They consider the *perfect* decree of election to be the will of God to save specific individuals, since God has foreseen that they would believe and persevere in faith. The first decree is considered to be mutable and the second immutable — not due to election, but due to the sufficiency of man, which God most certainly and infallibly foresaw. We reject this distinction as being outside of and contrary to the Word of God, and contradictory to the doctrine itself. We therefore maintain that the decree of eternal election, by virtue of its nature, is immutable in the absolute sense of the word. In it God has most certainly decreed the end, as well as the means to that end, by which He irresistibly accomplishes one thing or another.

First, this is evident from all texts which testify of the immutability of all God's decrees, a truth which we have considered comprehensively in the previous chapter. "For I am the LORD, I change not" (Mal. 3:6); "...with whom is no variableness, neither shadow of turning" (James 1:17); "For the LORD of hosts hath purposed, and who shall disannul it?" (Isa. 14:27). "My counsel shall stand" (Isa. 46:10).

Add to this the texts referring to election. "...that the purpose of God according to election might stand..." (Rom. 9:11); "...God, willing more abundantly to shew unto the heirs of promise the immutability of His counsel..." (Heb. 6:17); "Nevertheless the foundation of God standeth sure, having this seal, The Lord knoweth them that are His" (2 Tim. 2:19). It cannot possibly be disputed that this last text refers to eternal election, for the apostle has just discussed the apostasy of Hymenaeus and Philetus. Following this he declares that although they had apostatized, those who are God's will not apostatize. This does not suggest that the foundation for perseverance is to be found in man, but rather that their being called and brought to faith rests upon a sure foundation — the sure foundation of God, which He Himself has laid. This foundation is His eternal counsel and the election of His own, whom He knows individually by name, upon whom is His eye from eternity (and also in time), and whom He keeps from apostasy by His power. Subsequent to this text the apostle gives us the reason for the apostasy of these two, so one will neither consider it to be strange nor be offended by it, as all sorts of people are to be found within the church — both good and evil — who afore are prepared unto glory or damnation. This compares to the situation in a large house in which various vessels of silver, wood, and stone are to be found, some to honor, and some to dishonor.

Therefore, everyone ought to be diligent in perseverance, adherence to the truth, and the practice of godliness, whereas those who are known by God most certainly must depart from iniquity. Whomever God chooses unto salvation, He also chooses unto holiness. The sanctification of the elect is the evidence that God has chosen them, for which reason they will remain with the truth and persevere in godliness. "For the gifts and calling of God are without repentance" (Rom. 11:29).

Secondly, Scripture binds election and salvation together with an unbreakable knot. Neither the immutable God, the evil one, the evil world, nor its powerful corruption will break this bond. Whomever God has chosen unto salvation will most certainly obtain it. Whomever God has foreknown, He has also predestinated, called, justified, and glorified (Rom. 8:29-30). The apostle speaks of glorification in the past tense, it being so certain as if it had already occurred. Consider also Romans 11:7, where it is stated, "The election has obtained it, and the rest were blinded." This eliminates any notion about virtue and the focus is upon God's work alone. The apostle states that from election issues forth that which is obtained, for God who does the one, also grants the other.

Thirdly, the perseverance of the saints as a consequence of God's immutable decree is confirmed by the Lord Jesus. "For there shall arise false Christs, and false prophets, and shall shew great signs and wonders; insomuch that, if it were possible, they shall deceive the very elect" (Mat. 24:24). It is therefore impossible that the elect will be deceived. The word "elect" refers to those whom God has eternally designated to be His, and set before Him as His property. The attack of the false prophets would also be focused on them, doing their utmost to deceive the elect also. They would not be successful, for it is impossible. The statement "if it were possible" does not mean, "if with much objection and great difficulty they would be able to do it," neither does it say, "if *they* [the false prophets] would possibly be able to," for the word "possible" does not refer to the false prophets and their work. Instead, it refers to the certainty of the spiritual state of the elect warranted by the decree of God. As the elect they could not be deceived, and therefore the labors of the false prophets would have no effect upon them.

Objection #1: Believers are continually exhorted to fear and diligence in order to make their calling and election sure. "Wherefore let him that thinketh he standeth take heed lest he fall" (1 Cor. 10:12). This refers to apostasy from God, as was the case with many of the Israelites. "Work out your own salvation with fear and trembling" (Phil. 2:12); "Let us therefore fear, lest, a promise being left us of entering into His rest, any of you should seem to come short of it" (Heb. 4:1); "Wherefore the rather, brethren, give diligence to make your calling and election sure" (2 Pet. 1:10); "Beware lest ye also, being led away with the error of the wicked, fall from your own stedfastness" (2 Pet. 3:17).

Answer: (1) These texts do not refer to a fear for damnation, but to a careful watch over our conduct.

(2) These exhortations are means to lead believers in the way of righteousness to the salvation to which they are ordained. Since election is unto glory and grace, it thus relates to the end as well as the means unto that end.

(3) Calling and election are made sure from our side; that is, we need to be assured that we are partakers of the heavenly calling, from which may be concluded that we are chosen by God. From God's perspective, however, election is not made sure by us, since it has been sure from eternity in God's immutable counsel.

Objection #2: Threatenings relative to damnation indicate that election is not immutable. "I tell you, Nay: but, except ye repent, ye shall all likewise perish" (Luke 13:3); "God shall take away his part out of the book of life, and out of the holy city" (Rev. 22:19).

Answer: (1) Threatenings, just as exhortations, are means to stir us up to abstain from sin and to practice godliness. Whoever does not repent will most certainly go lost, and therefore this threatening is applicable to all who are unconverted. If, however, a person is converted but is not assured thereof, then in his estimation this threat relates to his condition. If, however, a person is converted and is conscious of it, this should motivate him to make additional progress. If he becomes lax and his condition deteriorates, he needs to arouse himself for fear of chastisement in body and soul. All believers must carefully refrain from everything which brings the wrath of God upon the children of disobedience. They must give heed to all threatenings in such a manner that they flee from those sins to which the threatening pertains.

(2) To have one's part taken out of the book of life is synonymous with not being saved. Such a person is neither a partaker of life, nor does he belong to those whose names are written in the book of life. This does not imply, however, that they initially were partakers of salvation and had been recorded in the book of life, for then all men most certainly would be partakers of eternal life. Then even someone who, until that very moment, would have lived a very ungodly life from his youth, would have his name written in the book of life until he would mutilate the Word of God by eliminating some truths from its pages, and only then would be erased from the book of life. Not even those who object to the immutability of election would hold to such a view, from which they should be convinced that this text cannot be used to maintain the mutability of election.

Objection #3: Those whom God has given to Christ can nevertheless perish. Thus, the decree of election is not immutable. "Those that Thou gavest Me I have kept, and none of them is lost, but the son of perdition [Judas]" (John 17:12). Paul also testified that he was not sure of his spiritual state, as he could also be a castaway. "...when I have preached to others, I myself should be castaway" (1 Cor. 9:27).

Answer: (1) In John 17:12 there is no coalescence of Judas and the others who have been kept, they having been given to Christ by God. Instead there is a contrast. It is not stated that Judas had been given to Christ, but it is merely stated that even though Judas perished, others did not perish. Therefore the word "but" actually means "except," for the Greek phrase εἰ μη, *(ei mé)* is often translated with the word "except" (cf. Mat. 12:4; Gal. 1:7).

(2) Judas had never been given to Christ, for although he had been chosen to be an apostle, he was nevertheless a devil (John 6:70).

Refer also to our answers to the objections found in our discussion concerning "The Perseverance of the Saints" in chapter ninety-nine. The slanderous suggestion that one of the elect, living in the most ungodly manner, will nevertheless be saved, has been answered already.

Question #6: Can believers be assured of their election?

Answer: Those of *Roman Catholic* and *Arminian* persuasion, who propose a conditional election due to the mutability of man's free will, do not know whether they will persevere until the end, and consequently cannot be assured of their election. We do not maintain that all believers are in possession of assurance, neither do we maintain that assurance is always present in the same sensible degree, nor that a believer is assured during a season of spiritual desertion. Nevertheless, we do maintain that God has given marks of election in Scripture which are such, that a believer perceiving these in himself may conclude by the operation of the Holy Spirit that he is elect and may thus rejoice in the assurance of them. Therefore believers can be assured of their election and should strive to be assured thereof.

Election is also confirmed by its fruits, which are calling, faith, and sanctification. One can be assured that he is a partaker of these and may ascend higher, namely, that God has justified those whom He has called. And those whom He has called He has predestinated to be conformed to the image of His Son, and those He in turn has foreknown. That someone may be assured of his calling is confirmed in the following texts: "For ye see your calling, brethren" (1 Cor. 1:26); "Wherefore, holy brethren, partakers of the heavenly calling" (Heb. 3:1). One can also be assured of his faith. "I know whom I have believed" (2 Tim. 1:12). This is also confirmed by the purpose for which believers have received the Holy Ghost. "Now we have received, not the spirit of the world, but the Spirit which is of God; that we might know the things that are freely given to us of God" (1 Cor. 2:12). Furthermore, Scripture states expressly that believers are indeed assured. "The Spirit itself beareth witness with our spirit, that we are the children of God" (Rom. 8:16). We will treat the subject of assurance comprehensively in the chapter which deals with justification (chapter thirty-four).

Practical Applications of the Doctrine of Election

Aside from the fact that many are offended by these divine truths — the one rejects them, the other slanders them, and a third refuses to heed them — God's children are occasionally assaulted about whether or not they are of the elect. Some are overcome by a great fright due to an inner voice which says, "You are not called." Some gradually come into strife concerning this matter while thinking, "If I am not elected, I shall yet go lost, and I fear that in the end I shall find it to be true that I am not one of the elect." Sometimes the devil is the originator of this assault, who, without reason, suggests this and impresses upon them word for word, "You are not elected; God hates you; God has rejected you; you will not be saved; and all your prayer and activity are in vain. Therefore, simply give up." These suggestions torment and injure the soul, bringing it into a disconsolate condition. This causes the soul to be deprived of what he previously enjoyed: a lively faith, heartfelt prayer, a sweet resting and rejoicing in God, and a simple cleaving to and serving of Him. Sometimes these assaults proceed from man's own heart. In mentioning these assaults I am not referring to the struggles of him who as yet is not assured about his spiritual state, is greatly concerned, and is seeking a basis for assurance by which he would be able to ascend to the fountain of election itself. Rather, it is an assault which originates in our own evil and unbelieving heart. Due to a foolish inclination we then begin to gainsay, so that by way of gainsaying we would as it were compel God to assure us of our election. This in turn may generate fretting and resentful thoughts towards God. It is also possible that such disturbing suggestions can occur when the soul is in a better spiritual frame than the aforementioned. This occurs when the soul focuses upon the darkness within, unbelief, the power of inner corruption, and upon the fact that his prayers are not answered. Such a soul has been very desirous to be rightly and thoroughly assured of his state — and thus of his election — so that the issue is beyond question. In spite of having often prayed for this, however, he has never attained it. Initially this results in some passing thoughts whether or not one is one of the elect, or a reprobate. Subsequently, these thoughts become established thought patterns, and the reasons why one is not elected present themselves more clearly and more powerfully, thus increasingly disturbing the soul. At last such a soul draws the conclusion that he is not one of the elect. This results in a nearly complete neglect of the means, such as prayer, reading, and a laboring to receive Christ by faith. One can no longer engage himself in spiritual matters as previously, being continually confronted with, "You are not elected anyway; it is all for naught and in vain." From this arises despair, anxiety, the inclination to have hard thoughts about God, and whatever other inner turbulence there may be. What a sad condition this is!

What counsel is there for such? Who can better heal the wounds of the soul than the great Physician Himself? He does this in the way of means; therefore listen to my counsel, and allow me to quietly instruct you.

First, did these turbulent thoughts ever give you peace and quiet within? Are you now much better off than before? Have you increased in wisdom and understanding? Have you become holier? Has there been an increase in inner peace? If not, are you now filled with much more anxiety than before? Why then are you torturing yourself? Cast away all these suggestions. But you will reply, "I cannot rid myself of them, for they have a hold on me."

Do you not now perceive that you were initially too careless by entertaining these thoughts, and have too easily yielded to these assaults? It is therefore time to cease doing so and to do battle against all those reflections and thoughts about this matter. Allow other thoughts and activities to divert you from them in order that you may distance yourself from these assaults.

Secondly, consider what foolishness all this is, for you are mulling about matters which God has concealed within His own counsel and has not revealed to man. For even if you lacked the least evidence of your election, you still could not determine whether or not you are elected, as you have no reason to conclude that you will never be converted.

Objection: I feel within my heart that I am not one of the elect but rather a reprobate, and that therefore I shall never be converted.

Answer: This is an untruth and nothing but imagination. No man can know whether he is a reprobate because God has not revealed this in His Word. The Lord does not have such intimate communion with the ungodly that He would make this known to them in an extraordinary way.

Objection: Some have known this, such as Spira and others.

Answer: They had no knowledge of this but it was mere imagination. I am neither suggesting that their imaginations could not have been true, nor that they did not belong to the elect, all of which could be true. I am saying, however, that they neither knew this from Scripture nor from immediate revelations, but rather from their imagination. It has happened that some who with such certainty imagined themselves to belong to the reprobate, just as these others, were subsequently converted. Others who were already converted received much assurance concerning their election.

Objection: Those who have sinned against the Holy Ghost know that they are reprobates.

Answer: Those who have sinned against the Holy Ghost are indeed reprobates; however, such do not come to repentance after the commission of this sin, but persevere in their wickedness and without any sensitivity continue in their rage against God. Since therefore you neither know nor are able to ascertain this, and all this is but imaginary, why are you then so foolish to torment yourself with unfounded imaginations?

Objection: I know that I am unconverted, have once been enlightened, and that I have been hardened under the use of so many means. May I not conclude my reprobation out of all this?

Answer: Suppose that you are presently unconverted, have resisted previous enlightenment and conviction, and have hardened yourself against the Word of God; even then you may not conclude your reprobation, for you can still be converted. It is also possible that you are neither conscious of your own condition nor of the grace which the Lord has already granted you. It is one thing to be a recipient of the life of grace, but it is additional grace to be conscious of those things which God has granted us. No matter how you view your state, you cannot know whether or not you are a reprobate, and therefore ought to desist from this foolishness and reject it outright.

Thirdly, let the revealed will of God be your guide. In the gospel God offers His Son Jesus Christ, inviting all who are desirous to come to Him to do so. He promises that all who believe in the Son will have eternal life, while promising at the same time that none will be cast out who come to Him. God will never damn anyone but for his sins. God does not prevent anyone from repentance, believing in Christ, and salvation. God is not the cause of anyone's damnation. Man and his own free will are to be blamed for the fact that he lives an ungodly life, and it is therefore just when God punishes and damns him for his sins. Let the Word of God be your rule and cease from entertaining these haughty imaginations. Seek Christ, believe in Him, pray, do battle against sin, and believe, so that, by proceeding according to Scripture, you will be saved. This way is both a steadfast and safe way.

Objection: Faith and repentance are the work of God, which He grants only to His elect. If I am a reprobate, He will not bestow it unto me.

Answer: (1) It is likewise an established fact that you are to be blamed for your failure to believe and to repent. Therefore if you do not believe or repent, blame yourself rather than God, for He is under no obligation to grant these graces to anyone. Even if He grants them to some, He is therefore not obligated to do so to others.

(2) Even though God has not granted you these graces until this day, you nevertheless do not know if He will yet do so. Therefore, do not be fretful or resentful towards the Lord and His holy decree. Be humbled and start from the beginning, allowing yourself to be guided by Scripture. Thus, in dependence upon the blessing of the Lord you will prevail over these assaults while making more lively and steadfast progress in the way of salvation. We have dealt sufficiently with this matter, however.

Although one cannot be assured of his reprobation, we have already demonstrated that one can be assured of his election. It is thus the duty of every Christian to strive for assurance according to the exhortation of the apostle in 2 Peter 1:10, as this assurance is the fountain of much joy in God and results in much growth in sanctification. One does not obtain this assurance by ascending into heaven to examine the book of life for the purpose of ascertaining whether one's name is to be found in it (Rom. 10:6-7). Neither is this assurance obtained by imagining oneself to be one of the elect, so that by the duration of this imagination one could consistently maintain this assurance, being of the opinion that it is a sin to be doubtful about it even though one lacks the least foundation for this assurance. Rather, one obtains this assurance from the Word of God wherein is found a clear description of those who are of the elect. If these characteristics are discerned within, he may draw the conclusion that he is one of the elect.

The first characteristic is the *calling*. God calls internally and efficaciously only those whom He has chosen. This is a well-established truth. "Moreover whom He did predestinate, them He also called" (Rom. 8:30); "Yea, I have loved thee with an everlasting love: therefore with lovingkindness have I drawn thee" (Jer. 31:3). If, while bringing yourself into the omniscient presence of the Lord and examining yourself in truth, you may perceive that your mind has been illuminated to enable you to discern the spiritual dimension of the spiritual benefits of the covenant of grace; if you perceive within yourself a love and desire for spiritual frames within your soul such as the love and fear of God, willingness and obedience, spiritual liberty, and joy in the Lord; if you perceive within yourself a recurring stimulus, stirring you up to think upon God, to pray, to repent after backslidings, to walk in a way pleasing to God; and if you perceive that the nearness of the Lord is your life and His absence your grief — if all these things are to be found in you, then you may be assured of being called and drawn. Since all of this proceeds from election one may therefore conclude, "God has drawn me to Himself and His communion with a heavenly, internal, and efficacious calling, and thus I am also one of the elect." Blessed is he who deals truthfully with himself in this matter, neither denying what he has received nor glorying in things which he does not possess.

Secondly, the Word of God teaches that *faith* is a certain characteristic of election. "And as many as were ordained to eternal life believed" (Acts 13:48); "... the faith of God's elect ..." (Titus 1:1). If then you are assured that you find delight in God's counsel to reconcile sinners to Himself through the Surety, the Lord Jesus Christ; if, due to grief and sorrow over your sinful heart and deeds, fear for God's wrath, love for communion with God and a spiritual walk, and a sense of your own impotence to attain to these matters, you take refuge to this Surety who offers Himself; if you look to Him, long for Him, engage in transactions with Him, accept His offer, surrender yourself to Him, rest your salvation upon Him, and rely upon Him — be it one time with more, and then again with less intensity, with more clarity or more darkness, with more or less strife, continually or intermittently — if these things are to be found in you, then you are a partaker of true faith. If you may thus be assured of your faith, you may then consequently conclude your eternal election.

Thirdly, *sanctification* is also a sure characteristic of election. "According as He hath chosen us . . . that we should be holy and without blame before Him in love" (Eph. 1:4). If you then perceive within yourself a hatred, repulsion, and sorrow concerning both the secret sins of your heart, as well as your sinful deeds, and if you find an inner delight and love for a godly spiritual frame and the practice of all virtues in the fear, love, and obedience of God, as being His will; if you perceive within yourself the warfare between flesh and spirit so that sin does not have dominion over you, that is, that you are not governed by your evil will; if sin meets with internal resistance of your will, being restrained and often driven away by the fear of God; if you perceive within yourself the inclination to pray, wrestle for peace of conscience, and experience the nearness of the Lord; if, either privately or in the presence of men, you desire to let your heart, thoughts, words, and deeds be governed by the will of God; if, I say, these things be found in you, then you are a partaker of spiritual life and the principle of sanctification is in you. This is not the result of your natural disposition, but a gracious gift of God issuing forth from election. Thus, you may conclude your election from this spiritual condition.

Having made this conclusion, focus upon it and meditate upon the fact that this election is the primary fountain from which your life, godliness, and salvation issue forth. You would not presently exist, neither would you have been born into the world, had it not been for this decree. Since you do exist, however, must you not perceive how sinful and miserable you are in yourself? How great is God's goodness towards you that He, who passes by millions, condemning them for their sins, has eternally chosen you to be His child and the object of His incomprehensible grace and salvation! Why is the gospel proclaimed to *you*? Why are *you* called, drawn, and quickened? Why do *you* know Jesus and receive Him by faith? Wherefore may you have some delight in communion with God and are desirous to fear His Name? Does not all of this issue forth from this eternal counsel to save you? Lose yourself in holy amazement and confess with Hagar, "Have I also here looked after Him that seeth me?" (Gen. 16:13), and with the psalmist, "What is man, that Thou art mindful of Him?" (Psa. 8:4). And if there are any inner motions to rejoice, then rejoice in this that your name is written in the

Lamb's book of life. After having engaged yourself in such meditation for some time, proceed to consider each grace which you receive as issuing forth from this — yes, proceed to consider eternal salvation itself and link it to eternal election as Paul does in Romans 8:29-30. In doing so, consider the immutability of that decree and the certainty, steadfastness, and immutability of your spiritual state and salvation. Quietly rest therein and say with confidence, "Thou shalt guide me with Thy counsel, and afterward receive me to glory" (Psa. 73:24).

Here we may have the fountain of comfort in all the grievous trials and tribulations which the Lord causes us to encounter in this life. All of these occur according to "the determinate counsel and foreknowledge of God" (Acts 2:23). "For He performeth the thing that is appointed for me" (Job 23:14). All these trials and tribulations proceed from love and are for your good. "And we know that all things work together for good to them that love God, to them who are the called according to His purpose" (Rom. 8:28). He who has eternally loved you and has appointed you to be his child and heir to manifest all His goodness to you — would He allow anything harmful to come your way? Far be it from us to suggest such a thing. He chastises those whom He loves (Rev. 3:19). Bear therefore your cross joyfully and submissively, and be comforted by the prospect of a favorable end which as yet you cannot perceive.

Here is comfort against the sins which oppress a child of God and frequently rob him of all spiritual desire and liveliness. What wretched thoughts sin often produces within the elect. Notice, however, that He, who in sovereign goodness and love has chosen you without being moved to such a decree by your good works or faith; who never deviates in His goodness and love; who concluded you in sin that He might have mercy upon you (Rom. 11:33); and who most certainly glorifies those whom He has elected unto salvation, will therefore not reject you for your remaining sin over which you grieve. Therefore, stand firm in faith, do not succumb to the multitude of remaining enemies, but rather focus upon this eternal decree, the perfect atonement of the Lord Jesus Christ, and the covenant of grace. Rest in these, and although sin must continue to grieve you, do not let it cause you to be discouraged.

The assurance of one's election also affords much liberty and gives much support in prayer. One may approach unto God and say, "My Father! Hast Thou not known me by name and have I not found grace in Thine eyes? Hast Thou not eternally known me to be one of Thy own, chosen me to be Thy child and the object of Thy love, and wondrously to glorify me by Thy grace, mercy, and faithfulness, which manifests itself in the way in which Thou hast led me and wilt lead me? Therefore, oh Father, consider the trials and tribulations which I fear, the troubles which press me down, and my sinfulness which oppresses me. These matters I desire, these are the needs of my body, and these are my spiritual desires. May it therefore please Thee to look down upon Thy chosen one and upon the object of Thy favor. May it please Thee to hear me and to grant my desire." How this yields liberty, familiarity, faith that my prayer will be answered, and quiet submission!

The assurance of election is a significant means whereby sanctification is promoted. Although the natural man cannot comprehend this, is offended by this, and imagines that resting on such a foundation makes one careless, Scripture teaches the contrary: "Every man that hath this hope in him purifieth himself, even as He is pure" (1 John 3:3). This is the daily experience of the godly. The more they are assured of the love of God towards them, the more they are stirred up to love God in return. "We love Him, because He first loved us" (1 John 4:19). Since the believer knows that sanctification is not the cause of his election and salvation, but a fruit of election and a principal element of salvation, all his activity proceeds purely from love. While he thus loves God it ignites within him a desire to be conformed to His will and to be engaged in a manner pleasing to his Lord.

Finally, when the godly perceive that the beginning, middle, end, yes everything, proceeds only from God according to His eternal election — there being neither any contribution from him nor any reason within him — it will then stir up the soul to return everything to God and in all things to honor and glorify Him, most heartily thanking Him as the apostle did on behalf of others in this respect. "But we are bound to give thanks alway to God for you, brethren beloved of the Lord, because God hath from the beginning chosen you to salvation through sanctification of the Spirit and belief of the truth" (2 Th. 2:13). Here the attentive soul will perceive God's sovereignty, goodness, mercy, wisdom, power, and immutability. He will be deeply led into this in order to have an intimate view of these perfections in all their glory. Oh, how he will lose himself in this and sink away in sweet amazement, only to arise afterwards to worship, be at rest, and rejoice that God's glory so far exceeds his comprehension! This will cause him to exclaim, "For of Him, and through Him, and to Him, are all things: to whom be glory for ever. Amen" (Rom. 11:36).

CHAPTER SEVEN

The Covenant of Redemption
Between God the Father and God the Son
Concerning the Elect; or, the Counsel of Peace

Having considered the decrees of God in general, and the predestination of men in particular, we now proceed to the discussion of the covenant of redemption. The first Reformers and some subsequent writers have spoken with much reverence about this sacred mystery, some discussing it at great length. How I wish that such reverence would also currently prevail when either speaking of, or hearing this mystery discussed. Do not understand this to mean that this is a truth which only recently has become known, as some pretend who are ignorant of what has previously been written. Rather, it is a truth which of old has been known in the church. Everyone should strive to understand and use this truth correctly. We shall present the full ramifications of this covenant, also as it is presently administered by Christ. We shall consider,

(1) the parties in this covenant;

(2) the persons concerning whom, and for whose benefit this covenant has been made;

(3) the reality of this covenant transaction;

(4) the work of the one party, the Father, which we subdivide into the commands and conditions of this covenant, the promises related to the fulfillment of these conditions, and the confirmation of these promises by oath and sacraments;

(5) the work of the other party, the Lord Jesus Christ, which is subdivided into His acceptance of the conditions and the promises,

His fulfillment of the conditions, and His demand relative to these confirmed promises.

The Covenanting Parties of the Covenant of Redemption

First of all we shall consider the covenanting parties, who are God the Father and the Lord Jesus Christ. It will be easier to comprehend this matter if we primarily consider the execution of this covenant rather than the decree from which it proceeds. We maintain that the manner in which the Lord executes it in this time state is consistent with the manner in which He has eternally decreed it. We nevertheless treat this covenant as one of the intrinsic works of God, being repeatedly presented in such a manner throughout the Holy Scriptures. Concerning Christ it is stated that He "was foreordained before the foundation of the world" (1 Pet. 1:20). The elect are chosen in Him (Eph. 1:4), and grace has been given them "in Christ Jesus before the world began" (2 Tim. 1:9). Whatever Christ encountered in this world happened to Him according to the *eternal decree, foreknowledge, and determinate counsel of God* (cf. Psa. 2:7; Luke 22:22; Acts 2:23).

By virtue of this eternal covenant there has been an eternal relationship between the Son and His suretyship. This He demonstrated already in His government of the Old Testament church immediately after the fall, prior to His incarnation. This raises a question: Since the Father and the Son are one in essence and thus have one will and one objective, how can there possibly be a covenant transaction between the two, as such a transaction requires the mutual involvement of two wills? Are we then not separating the Persons of the Godhead too much? To this I reply that as far as Personhood is concerned the Father is not the Son and the Son is not the Father. From this consideration the one divine will can be viewed from a twofold perspective. It is the Father's will to redeem by the agency of the second Person as Surety, and it is the will of the Son to redeem by His own agency as Surety.

The persons on whose behalf and for whose benefit this covenant is made are those who have been elected in Christ. We have extensively discussed this matter in the previous chapter. Of the elect it is stated that they belong to the Father and have been given by Him to Christ. "Thine they were, and Thou gavest them Me." Therefore they are said to be written in the Lamb's book: "They which are written in the Lamb's book of life" (Rev. 21:27). The Lord, in a holy manner, would permit that they would sin by their own free will and thus would be concluded in sin, by virtue of which they are by nature children of wrath. In order that the infinite mercy and grace of God should be bestowed upon them in delivering from them this state and bringing them unto salvation, it was necessary that there be a Surety to satisfy God's justice. The Father thus gave the elect to His Son as Surety, and the Son accepted them, recorded their names in His book, became Surety for all of them — none excepted — and for them alone, and promised to accomplish His Father's good pleasure in bringing them to salvation.

The Existence of the Covenant of Redemption Scripturally Verified

That there was such a covenant made between Jehovah and the Lord Jesus concerning the elect can be verified as follows.

First, in Psalm 89:28, 34 it is recorded, "My mercy will I keep for Him for evermore, and My covenant shall stand fast with Him. My covenant will I not break." Proof that mention is made here of the covenant between God the Father and the Lord Jesus is clearly evident. It is a known fact that the Psalms contain many references to the Lord Jesus, and that David in many respects was a type of Him. Therefore, Christ is also referred to as *David* (Hosea 3:5). In this Psalm mention is made of David and of the Lord Jesus as He is typified by David. I have stated that it also refers to the Lord Jesus, for

(1) whatever is recorded up to verse 37 applies most eminently to the Lord Jesus. In other texts He is also identified as the Elect of God (Psa. 89:3; Isa. 42:1), the Holy One of God (vs. 19; Luke 1:35), One that is mighty (vs. 19; Psa. 45:3), the Anointed One who was anointed with oil (vs. 20; Psa. 45:8), the firstborn of God (vs. 27; Heb. 1:6), the King of kings (vs. 27; Rev. 19:16), One whose kingdom extends over the entire earth (vs. 25; Psa. 72:8), and One whose kingdom will endure as long as the sun and moon will be (vss. 36-37; Psa. 72:5).

(2) Everything in this psalm does not apply to David, such as being the firstborn Son of God (vs. 27), being the King of kings (vs. 27), and possessor of an eternal kingdom (vs. 36).

(3) The last part of the psalm, beginning with verse 38, presents us with a contrast between David's kingdom and that of the Messiah. This contrast points especially to the fact that the kingdom of the Messiah would extend over the entire earth and, as has been pointed out previously, would endure as long as the sun and the moon. The kingdom of David, on the contrary, would come to an end.

(4) That which is stated in 2 Samuel 7:12-16 and in verses 26-37 of this psalm refers to the identical matter, and therefore it is beyond doubt that it refers to the same history. The words of 2 Samuel 7 however, are expressly applied to Christ in the New Testament (cf. Acts 13:22;

Heb. 1:5), and it therefore follows that this is also true for vss. 26-37 of this psalm.

Taking all this into consideration, let us now reason as follows. The Psalms often refer to Christ, David frequently being a type of Christ in them. Everything eminently applies to Christ, but everything does not apply to David. A contrast is made between the kingdom of Christ (vs. 25-36), and the kingdom of David which, according to vs. 38, would be destroyed. It is thus very evident that mention is made here of the Messiah, Christ. He is here said to be in a covenant engagement with the Lord, and thus it is evident that there is a covenant between the Lord and Christ.

Secondly, this is also evident in Zechariah 6:12-13, "Thus speaketh the LORD of hosts, saying, Behold the man whose name is The BRANCH; and He shall grow up out of His place, and He shall build the temple of the LORD: Even He shall build the temple of the LORD; and He shall bear the glory, and shall sit and rule upon His throne; and He shall be a priest upon His throne: and the *counsel of peace* shall be between them both."

We cannot understand both to refer to Jews and Gentiles. They are indeed united in one church in the New Testament, but not the least mention is made here of them. Therefore this idea cannot suddenly be inserted here. The pronoun "them" indicates that mention is made of two who have previously been mentioned, who are none other than *Jehovah* and the *Branch*.

Neither can we understand both to refer to the two offices of the Lord Jesus, that is, His kingly and priestly offices. It is true that these offices were not to be united in one person. A king was neither permitted to be a priest, nor a priest to be a king. These tribes (Judah and Levi) and their respective offices had to remain distinct; however, in the Lord Jesus they coalesce in one person. It is equally true that these two offices coalesce in the execution of the mediatorial office, but one may therefore not conclude this text to refer to these two offices. This cannot be true, for,

(1) Christ is one Person, and there is mention of two.

(2) There is no reference here to two offices, but merely to "being a priest" and "ruling."

(3) Christ had three offices, which all function in unison for the building of the Lord's temple. Therefore, if the reference is meant to be to the offices, it should have stated "between these *three*."

(4) There can be no mutual consultation between offices, as this is the activity of persons. Such consultation occurred instead between individuals who held the three Old Testament offices; thus we should not understand the reference to be to the kingly and priestly offices.

"Them both," however, refers to *Jehovah* and the *Branch*, the latter being the Messiah. In one glance it can be discerned that the reference is to these two. "Thus, speaketh the LORD of hosts...the *BRANCH*...He shall build the temple of the LORD," which is the work of the Messiah. He who would build the Lord's temple, that is His congregation, would be endowed with the necessary qualifications: to rule and to be a priest. Therefore, rulership and priesthood are descriptive of the Branch who would accomplish this work, and thus it reinforces our contention. He, the Branch, would be engaged in the Lord's work to which He had been commissioned: the building of the Lord's temple. This required mutual understanding and consent as well as consultation, counsel, and wisdom. Thus the Father and the Son not only agreed to promote the *peace of the elect*, but they also agreed about the manner of execution, that is, it would be accomplished by the Prince of Peace, the Branch, who had the necessary qualifications for this task.

Thirdly, this is also confirmed in Luke 22:29, where it is stated, "And I appoint unto you a kingdom, as My Father hath appointed unto Me." It is not stated ὁρίζω *(horizo)*, nor διατάττω *(diatatto)*, but διατίθεμαι *(diatithemai)*. This word means as much as to promise something to someone by way of testament or covenant. From this word διαθήκη *(diatheke)* is derived, which means "testament" or "covenant." Thus, the verb "to appoint" includes the idea of covenant, and by virtue of this covenant He would receive the kingdom. This is expressly stated in Galatians 3:16-17, where it is recorded, "Now to Abraham and his seed were the promises made. He saith not, And to seeds, as of many; but as of one, And to thy seed, which is Christ. And this I say, that the *covenant*, that was confirmed before of God in Christ," etc. Thus, we have here the covenant, the promises, and the fact that these have been made to Christ, as well as the fact that this covenant has been confirmed in Christ. Therefore, there is a covenant between God and Christ.

Fourthly, this is also evident from words which implicitly refer to a covenant, such as "My God," and "My Servant." That was the promise of the covenant. "And (I) will be their God, and they shall be My people" (Jer. 31:33); "...My servants..." (Isa. 65:13-14). Members of the covenant, by virtue of that covenant, call God their God (Deu. 26:17-18). The Lord Jesus generally makes use of the same manner of speech: *My God, My Father.* "I ascend unto My Father, and your Father; and to My God, and your God" (John 20:17).

Fifthly, the existence of this covenant is also clearly evidenced by the fact that Christ is called "Surety" in both the Old and the New Testament. Only consider Hebrews 7:22, "By so much was Jesus made a Surety of a better testament." None can be a surety unless there is a contract and a covenant between the creditor and the surety of the debtor. The creditor must be satisfied with, and consent to the fact that such and such a person functions as surety. The surety in turn must obligate himself to the creditor to pay the debt. Since the Lord Jesus has become Surety by virtue of mutual consent and approval, there is a covenant between Jehovah and Christ.

Sixthly, it is also evident by virtue of the following conclusion. Whenever, on the one hand, there are requisite conditions and commands as well as promises and sacraments, and on the other hand, consent and acceptance of conditions and promises, satisfaction of conditions, and a demand for the promised benefits upon satisfaction of the conditions, then we have an incontrovertible reference to a covenant. All of this exists between God and the Lord Jesus Christ, and thus there is a covenant between both of them.

This we now wish to demonstrate, not only as proof for this doctrine, but also to describe the nature of this covenant. In doing so we shall first reveal the work of the one party, and subsequently of the other party.

Concerning the work of the Father we must consider separately: 1) the commands which function as the conditions of the covenant, 2) the promises of the covenant, and 3) the warranty of the covenant. The Father in electing the Lord Jesus to be Surety, Mediator, and Savior, presents Him to the elect and gives them to Him so that He may merit and accomplish salvation for them, as we have seen above. For this purpose He presented several conditions to Him and commanded Him to fulfill them. "...The Father which sent Me, He gave Me a commandment, what I should say, and what I should speak. And I know that His commandment is life everlasting" (John 12:49-50a); "This commandment have I received of My Father" (John 10:18). These commands, being the conditions, include among others the following:

First, that the Son would assume the nature of the sinner; however, without sin. "...A body hast Thou prepared Me" (Heb. 10:5).

Secondly, that He, as Immanuel (Θεάνθρωπος), God and man, having assumed the identical nature of elect sinners, would become their Substitute, remove their sins from them, and take their sins for His account as if he Himself had committed them. For this purpose He, being a divine Person and thus above the law, would place Himself under the law, which demanded punishment for the transgressors and perfect obedience to gain a right to eternal life. "God sent forth His Son, made of a woman, made under the law" (Gal. 4:4).

Thirdly, that on their behalf He would bear all the punishment which their sins had merited, and would suffer, die, and arise from the dead. "No man taketh it [life] from Me, but I lay it down of Myself. I have power to lay it down, and I have power to take it again. This commandment have I received of My Father" (John 10:18); "Him, being delivered by the determinate counsel and foreknowledge of God, ye have taken, and by wicked hands have crucified and slain" (Acts 2:23).

Fourthly, that on their behalf He would have to fulfil all righteousness in order to make them righteous. "...So by the obedience of one shall many be made righteous" (Rom. 5:19); "God was in Christ, reconciling the world unto Himself.... He hath made Him to be sin for us, who knew no sin; that we might be made the righteousness of God in Him" (2 Cor. 5:19, 21).

Fifthly, that He would make the elect partakers of this merited salvation, by declaring the gospel to them, regenerating them, granting them faith, preserving them, resurrecting them from the dead, and ushering them into heaven. Thus the execution of this great work would rest upon His shoulders. "And this is the Father's will which hath sent Me, that of all which He hath given Me I should lose nothing, but should raise it up again at the last day" (John 6:39). This then is a general presentation of some of the conditions of this covenant.

To these conditions the Father added glorious promises, both in reference to the Surety as well as in reference to the elect.

First, the Father promised that God's good pleasure would prosper through Him. "When Thou shalt make His soul an offering for sin, He shall see His seed, He shall prolong His days, and the pleasure of the LORD shall prosper in His hand" (Isa. 53:10).

Secondly, the Father promised that He would be King over all the elect, not merely from among the Jews, but also from among the Gentiles. "Yet have I set My King upon My holy hill of Zion. Ask of Me, and I shall give Thee the heathen for Thine inheritance, and the uttermost parts of the earth for Thy possession" (Psa. 2:6, 8); "He shall have dominion also from sea to sea, and from the river unto the ends of the earth.... All nations shall serve Him" (Psa. 72:8, 11).

Thirdly, the Father promised that He would have power over all creatures in order to govern them to the benefit of His elect. "All power is given unto Me in heaven and in earth" (Mat. 28:18); "For He hath put all things under His feet" (1 Cor. 15:27).

Fourthly, the Father promised that He would be glorified in an exceedingly magnificent and wondrous manner which would be observed and acknowledged by the creatures. "...When He had by Himself purged our sins, sat down on the right hand of the Majesty on high" (Heb. 1:3); "...I also overcame, and am set down with My Father in His throne" (Rev. 3:21).

Fifthly, the Father promised that He would be the Judge of heaven and of earth. "And hath given Him authority to execute judgment also, because He is the Son of man" (John 5:27); "Because He hath appointed a day, in the which He will judge the world in righteousness by that man whom He hath ordained" (Acts 17:31).

Sixthly, relative to the elect, the Father promised to Him that the elect would receive all the benefits of the covenant of grace through Him: forgiveness of sin, reconciliation, adoption unto children, peace, sanctification, and eternal glory. "...It is your Father's good pleasure to give you the kingdom" (Luke 12:32); "He that spared not His own Son, but delivered Him up for us all, how shall He not with Him also freely give us all things?" (Rom. 8:32).

God confirmed all these promises to the Son by means of both sacraments and extraordinary declarations.

(1) He confirmed this to Him by oath. "The LORD hath sworn, and will not repent, Thou art a Priest for ever after the order of Melchizedek" (Psa. 110:4); "Once have I sworn by My holiness that I will not lie unto David [Christ]" (Psa. 89:35).

(2) He sealed this to Him by means of the Old and New Testament sacraments which we will discuss shortly.

(3) God assured Him of this by means of extraordinary and immediate revelations and declarations. "This is My beloved Son, in whom I am well pleased" (Mat. 3:17). This declaration is repeated in Matthew 17:5. God was not only pleased with His Person, but also with His qualifications as Surety and Mediator, and in His work of redemption.

This then is the work of the one party, the Father. We shall now consider the work of the other party, the Lord Jesus Christ, which consists in 1) His acceptance of both the conditions and the promises, 2) His fulfillment of these conditions, and 3) His demand that the promises be fulfilled on the basis of these conditions being fulfilled.

First, the Lord Jesus Christ, who is very God and a holy man, in hearing these conditions according to His human nature, neither would nor could but accept these conditions due to His perfect holiness and love for God. With full joy He wholeheartedly accepted them, as it is stated in Psalm 40:6-8, "Burnt offering and sin offering hast Thou not required. Then said I, Lo, I come: in the volume of the book it is written of Me, I delight to do Thy will,[1] O

---

[1] The Statenbijbel reads as follows, "Ik heb lust, o mijn God! om Uw welbehagen te doen," which translates as, "I delight to do Thy good pleasure, O my God."

My God: yea, Thy law is within My heart." The apostle also quotes this text in Hebrews 10:5-7, and extends its application more fully to Christ.

Secondly, He also accepted the promises. This acceptance is confirmed by the fact that the Father strengthened Him in the execution of the covenant by means of its promises, oaths, and seals. "He is near that justifieth Me; who will contend with Me?" (Isa. 50:8). In like manner He is said to be justified in the Spirit (1 Tim. 3:16). In what manner is Christ justified? The Father reaffirmed and assured Him of the fact that His suffering and death was a perfect ransom for all the sins of the elect, that the Father was perfectly satisfied with the execution of His suretyship, and that He merited a complete salvation for all the elect. Therefore, He who manifested Himself in the likeness of sinful flesh during His sojourn upon earth (Rom. 8:3), and who had all the sins of His elect imputed to His account, will "appear the second time without sin unto salvation" (Heb. 9:28). It is also evident that Christ strengthened Himself with these promises, for in His suffering He anticipated the glory which was promised to Him. "...who for the joy that was set before Him endured the cross" (Heb. 12:2).

Question: In what manner did the Lord Jesus use the sacraments? We have a dilemma here, for the sacraments were instituted for believers in order to seal to them that they are partakers of the benefits of the covenant on the basis of His suffering and death, whereas Christ was perfect and knew of no weakness of faith.

Answer: It is a certainty that He partook of the sacraments such as circumcision, the passover, and also holy baptism; this is not as evident regarding the Lord's Supper. To solve this dilemma the following must be considered.

(1) Both the sinless as well as sinners may make use of the sacraments. Prior to the fall the Tree of Life was a sacrament for Adam. This is true, considering that a sacrament, a) repeatedly and vividly brings to mind the promised matter; b) repeatedly reconfirms the certainty of the promises; c) provides a sweet foretaste of the matter signified; and d) rekindles and quickens the approbation of the conditions of the covenant as well as the person's pledge to fulfil these conditions. All of these are applicable to a sinless person. Since Adam could use the sacrament in this fashion, the Lord Jesus was able to use them likewise.

(2) The sacraments, being the seals of the covenant, sealed to Christ all the promises of the covenant of redemption. For believers, the sacraments seal the covenant of grace in Christ, but for Christ they sealed the covenant of redemption, assuring Him that

He, on the basis of His perfect obedience and satisfaction, would merit all the promised benefits for Himself and His children. It was thus sealed unto Christ that His sacrifice was pleasing, His satisfaction was efficacious to remove the sins of the elect which He had taken upon Himself, and His perfect righteousness was efficacious to acquire the right to eternal life for them.

Thirdly, as the Lord Jesus had promised to fulfil all that the Lord demanded of Him, He therefore came and perfectly accomplished this in very deed. "Who, being in the form of God, thought it not robbery to be equal with God: but made Himself of no reputation, and took upon Him the form of a servant, and was made in the likeness of men: and being found in fashion as a man, He humbled Himself, and became obedient unto death, even the death of the cross" (Phil. 2:6-8). Therefore He said, "I have glorified Thee on the earth: I have finished the work which Thou gavest Me to do" (John 17:4), and "It is finished" (John 19:30).

Fourthly, upon fulfillment of the condition, the Lord Jesus demanded the fulfillment of the promises both for Himself and for the elect. He does so first of all for Himself. "I have glorified Thee on the earth: and now, O Father, glorify Thou Me with Thine own self with the glory which I had with Thee before the world was" (John 17:4-5). He also does so on behalf of the elect. "Father, I will that they also, whom Thou hast given Me, be with Me where I am; that they may behold My glory, which Thou hast given Me" (John 17:24).

Question: Did Christ merit something on His own behalf, since He did and suffered everything on behalf of the elect?

Answer: These matters are not contradictory, as one thing can be pursued with various objectives. In suffering on behalf of the elect and in fulfilling all righteousness for them the Lord Jesus manifested such a perfect obedience and love toward God and the elect, that He, according to the covenant of redemption, has merited the promised benefits for Himself as Mediator.

First, when considering a covenant which contains conditional promises, the party which fulfills the conditions merits the matter which has been promised. Here there is also a covenant with conditional promises. Since the Lord Jesus has fulfilled the condition, He has consequently also merited the fulfillment of all the promises which have been made to Him as well as the elect.

Secondly, Christ anticipated the payment of His wages. "...surely My judgment is with the LORD, and My work with My God" (Isa. 49:4).

There is a gracious reward which is not according to merit, and there is a just reward which is according to merit and on the basis of accomplishment. In reference to Christ we have here a contract which justly requires the payment of wages upon the accomplishment of a task. In view of this, Christ has merited a reward for Himself.

Thirdly, the Lord Jesus had His glory in view as a prize which was set before Him. "...Who for the joy that was set before Him endured the cross, despising the shame" (Heb. 12:2). We thus observe that joy was set before Him upon the condition of submitting to the cross. That joy He had in view and therefore He endured the cross, thereby meriting that joy for Himself.

Fourthly, this is also confirmed by all those texts in which His work is stated to be the cause of His exaltation. Christ humbled Himself, and *therefore* God exalted Him. "He shall see the travail of His soul. *Therefore* will I divide Him a portion with the great,... *because* He hath poured out His soul unto death" (Isa. 53:11-12); "Thou lovest righteousness, and hatest wickedness: *therefore* God, thy God, hath anointed Thee with the oil of gladness above Thy fellows" (Psa. 45:7); "And being found in fashion as a man, He humbled Himself, and became obedient unto death, even the death of the cross. *Wherefore* God also hath highly exalted Him" (Phil. 2:8-9). The use of such language is so common, and so clearly presupposes merit, that the mere observation of these texts confirms that Christ did not only obtain glory in consequence of what had previously transpired, but He also merited the same.

Practical Observations Concerning the Covenant of Redemption

We have thus seen that relative to the eternal salvation of the elect there is a covenant of redemption between the Father and the Lord Jesus. We have considered the specific conditions and promises which it contains, how willingly the Lord Jesus has accepted them, and how perfectly He has finished everything. One should not be of the opinion that all this is mere intellectual speculation, and that, having perceived all this, one can let the matter rest, for it is the foundation for all sure comfort, joy, holy amazement, and the magnification of God. Therefore we must strive to understand this doctrine well, and to make use of it continually. For your guidance, consider the following matters.

First, the salvation of the elect is unmoveably sure. They are therefore in an unchangeable state — indeed, as confirmed in this as the elect angels. For both parties, God the Lord and Christ, are fully and mutually satisfied concerning the salvation of the elect and the way in which they will become partakers of it, the conditions for this having been fulfilled by the Surety. They need not keep themselves, but according to this decree they are in Christ's keeping and thus they are kept by a sure, almighty, and faithful hand. Therefore, "Who shall separate us from the love of Christ?" (Rom. 8:35). Who shall disannul the covenant which has been established between them both? "O death, where is thy sting? O grave, where is thy victory?" (1 Cor. 15:55).

Secondly, the elect neither need to accomplish nor merit salvation, nor add anything to the acquisition thereof, for by this covenant all the weighty conditions were laid upon Christ. He would bear the punishment; He would fulfil the law on their behalf; He would keep them; and He would lead them to salvation. He would perform all that pertained to the covenant, and has also accomplished it. On the other hand, all the merits of Christ extend to God's children, and all graces are theirs: the adoption unto children, justification, sanctification, perseverance, and glorification. All these, at the appropriate time, manner, and measure, are administered to them in accordance with the contents of this covenant. Therefore, in recognition of this, how they ought to cry out, "Not unto us, O LORD, not unto us, but unto Thy Name give glory, for Thy mercy, and for Thy truth's sake" (Psa. 115:1)!

Thirdly, the covenant of grace and our covenant transaction with God in Christ has its origin and basis in this covenant of redemption between God and Christ. From this covenant issue forth the beginning, continuance, and end of man's salvation. Before anyone existed, and before the gospel was proclaimed to them, it had already been decreed and established in this covenant when each of the elect would be born; when and by what means they would be brought into the covenant, the measure of grace, comfort, and holiness; and the quantity and nature of the tribulations and crosses they would have to endure in this life. All this has been determined and all the aforementioned matters issue forth from this covenant. Therefore the elect on the one hand need but be still and to let the Lord work. They need but to open their mouths to receive, for whatever is comprehended in the articles of this covenant will most certainly be given to them. On the other hand, they must focus upon this covenant, be active in entering into the covenant of grace, and living therein, they must make it the foundation of their life. This will motivate the godly to proceed with understanding and steadfastness, neither resting in the steadfastness of their faith or godliness nor, as one so often is inclined to do, being tossed to and fro when both appear to diminish. In consequence of this, they will acknowledge that the manifestation of every grace and influence of the Holy Spirit proceeds from this covenant. They will be enabled to exclaim feelingly, joyously, and lovingly, "For of Him, and through Him, and to Him, are all things: to whom be glory for ever. Amen" (Rom. 11:36).

Fourthly, this covenant reveals a love which is unparalleled, exceeding all comprehension. How blessed and what a wonder it is to have been considered and known in this covenant, to have been given by the Father to the Son, by the Son to have been written in His book, and to have been the object of the eternal, mutual delight of the Father and the Son to save you! The parties of this covenant were not moved to include any of the elect on the basis of foreseen faith or good works. They were not moved by necessity or compulsion, but by eternal love and volition. "Yea, I have loved thee with an everlasting love" (Jer. 31:3). Love moved the Father and love moved the Lord Jesus. It is a covenant of love between those whose love proceeds from within themselves, without there being any loveableness in the object of this love. Oh, how blessed is he who is incorporated in this covenant and, being enveloped and irradiated by this eternal love, is stirred up to love in return, exclaiming, "We love Him, because He first loved us" (1 John 4:19).

Fifthly, by virtue of this covenant the Lord Jesus is the Executor of the salvation of the elect. The Father has given them into His hand and entrusts them to Him. The Son in love has accepted them and has committed Himself not to lose one of them, but to raise them up again at the last day (John 6:39). The Lord Jesus is omnipotent, faithful, loving, immutable, and possesses everything which is necessary for their salvation. How safely one may therefore surrender everything to Him, and rest therein, confessing, "The LORD is my shepherd; I shall not want" (Psa. 23:1); "The LORD will perfect that which concerneth me" (Psa. 138:8); "Thou shalt guide me with Thy counsel, and afterward receive me to glory" (Psa. 73:24); "Blessed are all they that put their trust in Him" (Psa. 2:12)!

CHAPTER EIGHT

The Creation of the World

Having considered the intrinsic works of God, we proceed to consider His extrinsic works — in the realm of nature and in the realm of grace. His works in nature are *creation* as well as His *providence* in regard to His creation. We shall first discuss creation.

Creation Defined

The verb "to create" has various meanings.

(1) It can refer to God's common government of things. "I form the light, and create darkness: I make peace, and create evil" (Isa. 45:7).

(2) It can refer to extraordinary acts of God. "For the LORD hath created a new thing in the earth, A woman shall compass a man" (Jer. 31:22).

(3) It can refer to regeneration and renewal of heart in conversion. "Create in me a clean heart, O God" (Psa. 51:10).

(4) Generally we understand the verb "to create" to refer to the generation of matters, either out of nothing as was the case on the first day, or out of formless matter created on the first day, the latter being the method by which God created on the five succeeding days.

In travelling reversely through time, one will ultimately arrive at the beginning, beyond which one cannot proceed. Beyond this there is nothing but God only who inhabits eternity. No temporal human being can comprehend this eternity, and those who seek to view it as a very long time, view it erroneously. The eternal God, being desirous to reveal Himself and to communicate His goodness, has according to His eternal purpose and by His wisdom and omnipotence, created the universe and all things belonging to it. Thus, whatever exists has a beginning, prior to which nothing existed except God Himself. There was no infinite light. Neither were there elements, formless mass of matter, matter in motion, nor anything else which one could possibly name or conceive. "In the beginning God created the heaven and the earth" (Gen. 1:1). "In the beginning" does not refer to the moment before anything existed, but it refers to the first moment of time which coincided with the appearance of the very first element of creation. This is confirmed in Psalm 90:2: "Before the mountains were brought forth, or ever Thou hadst formed the earth and the world." Prior to the existence of the world, there was a "before," not in reality, but only when viewed from the perspective of the beginning of creation. In this "before" the world did not exist, but this "before" was eternity itself. "...even from everlasting to everlasting Thou art God." The world which did not exist was brought forth. That which has been brought forth, however, of necessity has no prior existence, but rather a beginning. This is confirmed by the use of the word "before" in other texts. "...before the foundation of the world..." (Eph. 1:4); "...before the world began" (2 Tim. 1:9). Both texts imply that there is a beginning of time and a beginning of the world. Consequently, the world has not existed eternally.

As the world *did* not exist eternally, neither *could* it have existed eternally. God was indeed eternally capable to create, however that which is created cannot be without beginning, and thus cannot be eternal. This is true for the following reasons:

First, it could then not have been stated that the world was created, for to create is to bring forth matter which had no prior existence. Since in this formation there is a transition from nothing to something, there is of necessity a beginning.

Secondly, there is progression of time during the existence of a created entity. Progression of time logically implies, however, that there be an initial moment, and therefore the existence of a created entity must of necessity have a beginning.

Thirdly, if the world would have eternally existed, then it either must eternally have been self-existent, or it must exist by virtue of God's eternity. If it existed by virtue of its own eternity, then of necessity there would be two collateral eternal entities, and God would neither be the only eternal One nor the original cause of everything. Scripture, however, consistently attributes these to God as being unique to Him alone. If the world would have eternally existed by virtue of God's eternity, then it would be God Himself, and thus also be omnipotent, omniscient, simple in essence, immutable, etc., for in every perfection of God all other perfections are comprehended. Within God these perfections cannot actually be distinguished, but they are all one and the same. It thus follows that the world could not have existed eternally.

In calculating retroactively from our time, the beginning can be dated approximately 5750 years ago. I say "approximately," for this date cannot be determined exactly, since this chronological calculation is not based on the course of the stars, but must be solely deduced from the genealogies of the patriarchs which are recorded in Holy Scripture, all of which only record the years, without reference to months and days. It is therefore uncertain during what season of the year the world was created. The suggestions that it occurred 1) either when the sun was at its zenith or lowest point, 2) at the point when during fall or spring both day and night are of equal length, or 3) during a different season of the year, are entirely speculative. Most often it is suggested to have been at the time of the spring equinox. Those who claim that it occurred at the time of the fall equinox seem to have the better arguments. I personally do not know which view is correct.

The world did not come into existence of itself for nothing can bring forth itself. Instead, the world has been created by God who is the Creator of all things. "...The Creator of the ends of the earth ..." (Isa. 40:28); "For in six days the LORD made heaven and earth" (Exo. 20:11); "My help cometh from the LORD, which made heaven and earth" (Psa. 121:2); "In the beginning אלהים *(Elohim)* (the triune God) created" (Gen. 1:1).

Creation, the Work of a Triune God

Since God is one in essence, and the three Persons are the one God, their will and power are one and the same. *All God's extrinsic works are common to the three Persons*, being the work of a triune God. Nevertheless, each of these extrinsic works is attributed to individual Persons according to the relationship which each Person has to the particular work. Consequently, creation is attributed to the Father, redemption to the Son, and sanctification to the Holy Spirit. In doing so, however, the other Persons are not excluded but expressly included in the same work, so that any extrinsic work attributed to one of the Persons, is also attributed to the other Persons. Thus, creation is attributed not only to the Father, but also to the Son and to the Holy Spirit.

The Son has created the world. "All things were made by Him (that is, the Word, the Son of God); and without Him was not anything made that was made" (John 1:3); "For by Him were all things created" (Col. 1:16). In doing so He did not *assist*, nor did it occur through Him as a *means*, but He is the *moving cause* Himself, for the word "by" refers to the original cause. "...Through Him...are all things" (Rom. 11:36). "God is faithful, by whom ye were called" (1 Cor. 1:9).

Creation is also attributed to the Holy Spirit. "And the Spirit of God, מרחפת (Merachepheth) moved (in a forming, creating, and generating manner) upon the face of the waters" (Gen. 1:2); "By the word of the LORD were the heavens made; and all the host of them by the breath of His mouth" (Psa. 33:6).

Since creation is the work of the Holy Trinity, it is stated in Genesis 1:26, "Let US (נעשה Na'aseh, plural) make man." "Remember thy בוראיך (Boreëcha), Creators" (Eccl. 12:1); "בעליך עשיך (Bo'alaich 'osaich), thy Makers is thine Husbands" (Isa. 54:5).[1]

Creation, the Proper Work of God

Creation is the proper work of God; He and He alone has created. The angels are not "co-creators," nor can this creative power be communicated to anyone. Some wish to make such a proposition to protect their view concerning transubstantiation. Others do so to deny the Holy Trinity. However, this neither is nor can be true.

First, Scripture states expressly that creation is exclusively the proper work of God alone. "I am the LORD that maketh all things; that stretcheth forth the heavens alone; that spreadeth abroad the earth by Myself" (Isa. 44:24); "I have made the earth, and created man upon it: I, even My hands, have stretched out the heavens" (Isa. 45:12).

Secondly, God distinguishes Himself from everything else by a power which, as it is in Him, is both inherent and incommunicable. "The gods that have not made the heavens and the earth, even they shall perish.... But the LORD is the true God, He is the living God, and an everlasting King.... He hath made the earth by His power, He hath established the world by His wisdom, and hath stretched out the heavens by His discretion" (Jer. 10:11, 10, 12); "For all the gods of the nations are idols: but the LORD made the heavens" (Psa. 96:5).

Thirdly, creating is the manifestation of infinite power. "For the invisible things of Him from the creation of the world are clearly seen, being understood by the things that are made, even His eternal power and Godhead" (Rom. 1:20). This infinite power is the infinite God Himself. If God were capable of communicating this infinite and eternal power, then God could cause other eternal

---

[1] It should be understood here that à Brakel wishes to give expression to the plurality of these words in the original Hebrew.

gods to exist, which is absurdity itself. On the other hand, the creature is finite and therefore cannot comprehend nor perceive the infinite. It is true that the work of creation relates to finite creatures, but the power of creation is and remains infinite.

Fourthly, in order to make a certain thing, a creature must work with something which already exists, and in addition that substance must be suitable to be used for given purposes. A painter, for example, cannot paint a picture on water. To create, however, is to bring forth something out of absolutely nothing — from something that in an absolute sense has not been formed, to something that has form. It is therefore impossible that the power of creation could be communicated to a creature.

When men are said to have performed miracles which necessitated the exercise of infinite power, then they themselves did not do it. They did not possess such infinite, inherent power, but were merely the moral causes of such power. Being inwardly convinced of God's will and being moved by God to declare His will, they thus stated, "Arise," "Receive thy sight," or "Walk." Upon such declarations God performed a miracle by His power. Peter confirms this when he states, "Why look ye so earnestly on us, as though by our own power...we had made this man to walk?" (Acts 3:12). The performance of miracles is the proper work of God alone. "Thou art the God that doest wonders" (Psa. 77:14); "Blessed be the LORD God, the God of Israel, who only doeth wondrous things" (Psa. 72:18). Thus it is evident that this creative power cannot be communicated to anyone, and therefore only God is the Creator.

As infeasible as it is for this creative power to be communicated to anyone, so infeasible it is that any instruments were used during creation. What would be the purpose of an instrument, when God, by the use of one word, brings forth something out of nothing? In the transition from nothing to something neither matter nor time play a role. The use of an instrument, however, necessitates the presence of both.

Objection: The angels were "co-creators." "Let us make man" (Gen. 1:26). God could not have addressed Himself, and thus He addressed the angels.

Answer: This text proves the Trinity of Persons. Man was not created in the image of angels.

God did not create the world from an infinite air mass, neither from indivisible elements, from an eternally formless mass of matter, nor from anything else, whatever name one would wish to attribute to it. This is a pagan fabrication derived from the fundamental principle: *only nothing can come out of nothing.* This is true in reference to the finite creature and natural forces, but not as far as the infinite and omnipotent God is concerned. He has brought forth everything out of nothing. The determining factor here is this "nothing," and not the matter from which things were formed.

The apostle demonstrates this in Hebrews 11:3, where he states, "Through faith we understand that the worlds were framed by the Word of God, so that things which are seen were not made of things which do appear." Natural reason teaches that by virtue of causal relationships one ultimately must come to God as the original cause of all things. Natural reason, however, cannot understand the "how"; that is, how something can come into existence out of nothing, how God with one word and with one single command has caused everything to come into existence. All this we accept by faith. By faith we also accept the order described by Moses, in which all things were brought forth. The pagan physician *Galenus*, upon reading the first chapter of Genesis, stated, "Moses says much, but proves little." By faith we understand and maintain with utmost certainty that τα βλεπόμενα *(ta blepomena)*, were made μὴ ἐχ φαινομένων *(mee ek phainomenon)*, that is seeing that which does not appear, the latter being a Greek manner of speech. It is as if it were stated, "τά ὄντα ἐξ οὐχ ὄντων, *(ta onta eks ouk onton),*" that is, being out of what is not, which is equivalent to "out of nothing." This manner of expression is found in Matthew 9:33: "It was never so seen in Israel," which does not imply that anything of this nature had existed before, but rather that something of this nature had never existed before. Our intellect can readily understand that something can be created from something, but faith is required to conclude that things which exist have been brought forth out of nothing by God "who...calleth those things which be not as though they were" (Rom. 4:17); "For He spake, and it was done; He commanded, and it stood fast" (Psa. 33:9).

(1) If anything existed prior to creation, then of necessity it either had to be created, or it was not created. If created, it necessarily was created out of nothing, and if not created, it was necessarily eternal and independent and thus was itself God. Then God would have created the world out of something which was external to His own existence and until this day the matter of the universe would be unrelated to God's Being. Added to that which we have already stated, this is the absurdity of absurdities.

(2) Scripture states clearly, "Thou hast created all things" (Rev. 4:11). This statement is all-inclusive.

The creation of the world came to pass

(1) by the exercise of *omnipotent power*, merely by a singular

verbal command of God's omnipotent will, all of which occurred without the least exertion. "Let there be light," etc. "Hast thou not known? hast thou not heard, that the everlasting God, the LORD, the Creator of the ends of the earth, fainteth not, neither is weary?" (Isa. 40:28).

(2) by virtue of His absolute sovereignty. God was able to create the world, and He could have also refrained from doing so. He could have created prior to 5750 years ago, at a later date, or also could have created several worlds. He only made this one world, however, brought forth at the precise moment according to His volitional decree.

(3) as a result of His infinite wisdom. This wisdom can neither be searched out anywhere in the entire universe, nor by examining the orderliness, motion, and interrelatedness of secondary causes; nor can it be traced even in a simple flower — although all of these reveal a glimmer of it. Here one must end with the exclamation, "In wisdom hast Thou made them all" (Psa. 104:24). This wisdom is wonderfully manifested in the orderly fashion in which everything that has been created continues from the beginning.

The Orderly Progression of God's Creative Activity

Immediately upon creating the formless mass of matter, God in one moment could have created everything in the perfect state which existed on the seventh day. It has pleased Him, however, to create sequentially within the time frame of six days, thereby providing man with an example to labor six days and to rest on the seventh day. This reason is stated in Exodus 20:11: "For in six days the LORD made heaven and earth...and rested the seventh day: wherefore the LORD blessed the sabbath day, and hallowed it."

It is, however, not recorded whether God devoted an entire day to each task, or whether the accomplishment of each day was created in one moment. God could indeed have commanded it into existence in one moment, and in one moment have created everything out of nothing. Due to one thing being created out of the other, however, that which was created needed time to set itself in motion. Air, as it issued forth from the shapeless mass of matter — which was but small in comparison to the globe in its final form — needed time to expand from the very center of this mass to form the immeasurable firmament. Time was needed for the division of the waters which were under the firmament and the waters which were above the firmament. Time was needed for trees to spring forth from the earth and to come to full height, etc. The quantity of time required each day for all this cannot be determined, however. It appears probable to me that an entire day was used for the accomplishment of each daily objective in order to give the angels reason each day to shout for joy (cf. Job 38:7) in response to their observation of the wisdom and power of God in the creation of things. It is also probable — in order for the six day duration of creation to be an example to man to perform his labors in six days, and because God observed and approved His work at the end of each day and is said to only have rested upon the seventh day.

Since the Lord has described creation for us in such a detailed fashion, it is therefore our duty to attentively observe all this. To facilitate this, we shall make the following general remarks.

First, it should be noted that the first verse of Scripture, "In the beginning God created the heaven and the earth" is not a superscription, nor is it a summary statement relative to creation, but it represents a stage of creation. By "heaven" we understand the third heaven, and by "earth" we understand the globe and the visible universe.

Secondly, on the first day God created out of absolutely nothing, and on the other days God formed everything from this formless, inert mass of matter.

Thirdly, God was initially — that is on the first four days — occupied with the creation of lifeless objects: on the last two days He created living creatures.

Fourthly, in the creation of lifeless objects God began with that which is most sophisticated: light, from which He proceeded to air, from air to water, and from water to the earth, which is the least sophisticated structure. In creating living creatures, however, God began with the lowest degree of complexity, the irrational animals, and ended with His most magnificent creature, man.

Fifthly, on each day of creation the following is to be observed: (1) There is a command: Let there be...; (2) there is a chronological equation: And it was there; (3) there is an approbation: "It was good"; (4) there is a definition of purpose, and (5) there is a blessing.

Sixthly, three matters must be considered in the creation of each thing: (1) Its generation, whereby it came into existence; (2) its formation, identifying it as a specific creation; and (3) its adornment, making it both beautiful and pleasant.

Seventhly, in considering the entire work of creation, it should be noted that it was God's objective to create man and to exalt man in a most extraordinary manner. For this purpose He prepared such a large and spacious edifice, arranged everything in an orderly fashion, and adorned it in every possible manner. Having prepared everything, God then created man, placing him in dominion over the works of His hands.

In proceeding to the creative work of each day, we discern that God created three things on the first day: the third heaven, the shapeless mass of matter, and light.

God created *the third heaven* upon the first day. "In the beginning God created the heaven." This refers neither to the atmosphere nor the firmament, which were created subsequently, but to this heaven which is also called *the heaven of heavens* (1 Ki. 8:27), *the third heaven* (2 Cor. 12:2), *Paradise* (by comparison) (Luke 23:43), *the Father's house* (John 14:2), and *on high* (Heb. 1:3). Concerning this place I dare not say much, as nothing has been written about it (I am referring to its locality and not to the benefits and felicity to be enjoyed there). We do know, however, that the third heaven was created. "For we know that...we have a building of God, an house not made with hands, eternal in the heavens" (2 Cor. 5:1); "For he looked for a city which hath foundations, whose Builder and Maker is God" (Heb. 11:10). In Matthew 25:34 it is stated, "Inherit the kingdom prepared for you from the foundation of the world," which confirms that this third heaven was created at the beginning of the six-day creation. Aside from knowing that it was created, it can be deduced from Revelation 21 that this heaven is exceedingly glorious, not merely due to the heavenly blessings with which the souls of men will be saturated as they enjoy perfect communion with God, but also in respect to the place itself. Man in his glorified state will retain his body, and whatever is most delightful for the body will therefore be found in this place, which is God's artifice (Heb. 11:10). We are therefore of the opinion that this third heaven, compared to the earth and to the earthly Paradise, will be superior in a manner exceeding our imagination. The particulars of this place, however, have been concealed from us.

The second activity of the first day was the creation of the *formless mass of matter*. We refer to this as "formless" in view of the formation which followed. This first mass was "תהו ובהו *(thohu wavohu)*, without form and void" (Gen. 1:2). Everything was brought forth from this original matter — not due to divinely induced activity whereby everything formed itself or had the potential for formation — and has thus been created from this mass by the omnipotent power of God, for it is expressly stated, "The Spirit of God מרחפת *(Merachepheth)*, moved (in a creative manner) upon the face of the waters"; that is, upon this mass of matter which was fully enveloped by water. The pagans refer to this mass of matter as "chaos," that is, the conglomerate mass of matter containing the original elements of all things.

The third activity of the first day was the creation of *light*. This light was not an effect without a cause; such would be contrary to the nature of an effect. It was also not an illuminating cloud, for clouds had not as yet been created. Its existence was also not exterior to this mass of matter, for exterior to this matter there was no space. Rather it was something which at its most extreme edge revolved around this mass of matter during a twenty-four hour period thus creating day and night. It is easier to describe what light is in its manifestation than to define its internal form and essence. Paul states, "For whatsoever doth make manifest is light" (Eph. 5:13).

On the *second day* God created two matters. First, He created the *firmament*. This mass of matter was neither suited to be a dwelling place for man nor did it manifest as yet the extraordinary wisdom of God. Consequently, God created additional space, bringing forth an air mass from this matter, limiting it by means of an immeasurable circumference, outside of which neither space nor anything else existed. Thus, the boundary of this air mass was not defined by something exterior, but its boundary was defined by the air-mass itself. From the very center of this mass of matter to its utmost extremity there was a remoteness established by God Himself, beyond which there was and is no space. This firmament is subdivided into two heavens, as the paradise of God is the third heaven. The first heaven extends from the earth to a specified point in the atmosphere which is unknown to us. The second heaven extends far beyond the point where the first heaven terminates, which is the space in which sun, moon, and stars have their place; this is referred to as the firmament. We will leave speculation about any further divisions of the firmament to astronomers.

The second activity of the second day was the *division of the waters* which are above and under the firmament. One should not imagine that there are waters beyond the stars and beyond the extreme circumference of the firmament, for beyond this extreme circumference there is no space, it being the ultimate boundary. It is probable that the farther air is removed from center, the thinner it is. The waters above the firmament, however, are the clouds, some of which float higher than others. They have, as far as altitude is concerned, a boundary beyond which they cannot move. This text (Gen. 1:7) uses the word מעל (*Mé'al*), "above," that is, in the higher regions of the firmament לרקיע (*Lerakia'*), and thus neither beyond nor in the lower regions of the starry heavens, but at the highest boundary of the first heaven. Since Moses refers only to two levels of water, dividing them in lower and upper waters, it negates the suggestion that there would be waters above the stars, as Moses would then have spoken of three levels of water: an upper, middle, and lower level.

On the *third day* God accomplished two things. First, *He separated the lower waters of the earth*. At various places He made cavities in which the flowing waters would collect so that dry land would appear everywhere and would be a suitable dwelling place for man and beast. This gathering together of the waters the Lord called *seas*, for which He established definite boundaries. Even if these waters rise higher than the shores which enclose them, they would nevertheless not move beyond these shores by virtue of the order which has been established. These waters, together with the earth, constitute a globe.

As the second activity of the third day, God *adorned the dry land with trees and every imaginable type of vegetation*, greatly beautifying the face of the earth with their delightful colors and scents. This was true in a far more glorious manner than presently is the case upon an earth which the Lord has cursed. Every plant had its elegance — even thistles, thorns, and poisonous herbs, which prior to the curse were not that abundant, but by virtue of the curse were multiplied to the disadvantage of man and beast.

On the *fourth day* God made *sun, moon, and stars*. Sun and moon are called the two *great lights*. It does not say the two greatest bodies, but they are referred to as lights. We will let astronomers argue about whether they are the largest bodies. The Bible calls them great lights, and it should be incontrovertible to all men that such is the case.

The idea that these lights and the stars, or the sun alone, would be stationary, and that the earth would revolve is a fabrication of men whose heads are spinning too much. We believe the Holy Scriptures, and by that faith we understand "that the worlds were framed by the Word of God" (Heb. 11:3). Scripture states that the earth is stationary. "Who laid the foundations of the earth, that it should not be removed for ever" (Psa. 104:5). Scripture states that the sun has a circuit. "Which (the sun) is as a bridegroom coming out of his chamber, and rejoiceth as a strong man to run a race. His going forth is from the end of the heaven, and his circuit unto the ends of it" (Psa. 19:5-6). When the sun stands still, it is due to a miracle. "And the sun stood still, and the moon stayed" (Josh. 10:13).[2]

---

[2] See footnote 6 in chapter two.

These lights have a threefold purpose: 1) to divide the day from the night, 2) for signs, for seasons, for days, and for years, and 3) by their influence to make the earth fertile. "I will hear the heavens, and they shall hear the earth" (Hosea 2:21b).

God does reveal extraordinary signs in the heavens to warn and to startle (Mat. 24:29-30), or for the purpose of instruction (Mat. 2:2). In observing the light of the stars and the moon one can even discern whether the air is stable or unstable, from which one can conclude whether good or unsettled weather is imminent (Luke 12:54-55).

By them to predict future events, however, which will transpire by the exercise of man's free will, as well as the outcome of wars, the death of this or that individual, prosperity or adversity, etc., is

(1) a vain practice which is refuted by reality. If someone accidentally makes a correct guess, this is not due to the stars, but mere guesswork or the secret influence of Satan by which he seeks to confirm people in their superstition and thus draw them away from God;

(2) also contrary to the express command of God. "Thus saith the LORD, Learn not the way of the heathen, and be not dismayed at the signs of heaven; for the heathen are dismayed at them" (Jer. 10:2).

Question: How could God have created the two great lights on the fourth day since He created light on the first day?

Answer: The light which God created on the first day, He, on the fourth day, caused to be transmitted by the sun — similar to the manner in which one places a candle inside a lantern. And since the sun illuminates the moon, it communicates that light to the earth by way of reflection.

On the *fifth day* God began the creation of living animals: the fishes and the birds. The fish were brought forth from the water, and the birds perhaps partly from the water (Gen. 1:20) and partly from the earth (Gen. 2:19). The amphibians, which live both on land and in the water, apparently were brought forth out of both.

On the *sixth day* God created four-footed animals with all their peculiar natures and shapes, as well as insects, be it with or without feet. We also believe that all vermin, which in the opinion of many exists as a result of decay or came into existence due to heavenly influences, was created on this day.

God gifted the animals of the earth with five senses, and thus also with feeling. Even though they cannot respond intelligently to these feelings (as is true for men), they nevertheless feel in their own way. Who would deny that a dog sees, smells, hears, tastes, walks, and conveys a friendly or angry disposition, albeit not in a human manner? This is also true for feeling, which manifests itself as clearly as the other senses. Scripture also confirms this in many texts (cf. Job 39:6-7; Psalm 104:11).

Finally, God created the most glorious of all creatures upon earth — *man*. Of this we will speak separately in a subsequent chapter.

After having completed everything in six days, the Lord added the seventh day, conveying to us His activity upon this day, namely, that He rested "from all His work which He had made" (Gen. 2:2). The perfection of His work was such that nothing was lacking, neither was there any necessity for Him to add anything to it. He rested, and thus no longer created any new creatures. He was not weary, for "the Creator of the ends of the earth, fainteth not, neither is weary" (Isa. 40:28). Humanly expressed, however, He examined all that He had made, and delighted Himself in His work. "For in six days the LORD made heaven and earth, and on the seventh day He rested, and was refreshed" (Exo. 31:17b).

The Lord has thus united the first seven days into one unit, thereby holding His work before man as an example to be followed, while simultaneously commanding man, by virtue of His example, to work six days and to rest on the seventh day.

The number *seven* throughout the word of God is generally referring to this seven, which is expressive of the perfection of a matter. By taking note of this, light will be shed upon those texts in which the number seven occurs and it will prevent one from drawing erroneous conclusions in seeking to distill other mysteries from this number.

Whatever we have stated concerning creation was neither done merely to enhance your knowledge concerning these things nor to satisfy your curiosity. Rather we did so to direct you by way of the visible to the Invisible One, that you might observe and acknowledge the Lord's greatness, power, glory, and goodness. "Whoso is wise, and will observe these things, even they shall understand the lovingkindness of the LORD" (Psa. 107:43). How clearly creation reveals the perfections of God! The heathen discern them, putting many Christians to shame. How they ought to be convicted that they have never been exercised with this, never having beheld the Creator in His creatures!

Exhortation to Meditate Upon the Wonder of God's Creative Work

Come, behold this magnificent edifice and Him who has made all this. Behold His majesty and supremacy and consider especially that you are His creature. He therefore has absolute power over you and you are thus obligated, because of what you are, to devote yourself to your Creator. How dreadful, unnatural, and unspeakably horrible it is that you, who are so needy and dependent upon your Maker, dare to sin against such a God! How appalling it is that you dare to despise and reject Him, neither desire communion with Him nor fear Him and His wrath. Added to this is your abuse of His creatures, the use of which you have forfeited through sin. How suitable this consideration therefore is to perceive the magnitude of sin, to abhor oneself, and to sink away in shame, fear, and trembling.

The contemplation of God as Creator first of all makes it very evident that all your security, freedom, rest, peace, and happiness consist in the goodness and love of your Maker towards you. While you remain the object of His wrath, all His creatures will be opposed to you, and every one as it were waits for permission to destroy you. Whatever you touch will resist you with displeasure. It does not want to be touched by you, but rather wishes to be used against you. Nothing will give you peace as long as your Maker is displeased with you, and therefore the fear of Cain ought to be upon you. When, however, your Maker is again reconciled with you in Christ, your Father now being pleased with you, you are then free indeed, for everything will be at peace with you. "For thou shalt be in league with the stones of the field: and the beasts of the field shall be at peace with thee" (Job 5:23). Strive therefore with all your heart to be thus reconciled by receiving this precious Savior Jesus Christ. "Therefore being justified by faith, we have peace with God through our Lord Jesus Christ" (Rom. 5:1).

Secondly, I wish to address you, children of God — both the strong and the weak, and you in whom there is but a small beginning of true spiritual life. What a steadfast foundation for comfort and confidence in the Lord you may have, both in prosperity and adversity, in abundance and in poverty, in times of peace and persecution, and in the present time as well as in the future! "For Thy Maker is thine husband" (Isa. 54:5); "The earth is the LORD's, and the fulness thereof" (Psa. 24:1). Since the Lord, your Father, is Creator and Proprietor of the entire world and all that it contains — which willingly avails itself for His service — how can you lack anything? How can the creature harm you? "If God be for us, who can be against us?" (Rom. 8:31). "When He giveth quietness, who then can make trouble?" (Job 34:29). Therefore distill your own comfort from this and reason as follows: The Lord has known me and accepted me to be His child. This I know by the Holy Spirit who has been given to me, and has wrought light and life in my soul, however small it may be. The Lord is the Creator of heaven and of earth; everything belongs to Him and is at His disposal. Thus, I shall not lack anything and all will therefore be well, for on the one hand the Lord loves me and on the other hand He desires and is able to help me. He has promised and declared, "I will never leave thee, nor forsake thee" (Heb. 13:5). Therefore, acquiesce in this, and if things do not proceed according to your wishes, then look unto your Maker and submit yourself to His holy will. Approach Him as His creature, as His child; pray, wait upon Him, lean upon Him, and always let the Lord, who has made heaven and earth, be your reliance.

Thirdly, children of God, therefore as God's creatures make use of everything, for the world is yours both in respect to property and usage (1 Cor. 3:22). All of this, however, is only so because you are the property of Christ, and God ultimately remains the Proprietor of everything. Refrain from cruel behavior towards the creature and from its unnecessary and deliberate destruction, because it is the Lord's property. Refrain from abusing the creature through revelling, drunkenness, and ostentatious and adulterous behavior, for it is God's property. Rather, use it freely for necessary purposes, as well as for honest enjoyment by seeing, hearing, tasting, smelling, touching and adorning it. Realize that three words are written upon each creature by which you are continually reminded: *Accipe, Redde, Fuge*, that is, *take, return, and avoid*. Take and receive whatever God gives you, return it with thanksgiving to Him from whom it originated, and avoid misuses and sinful abuse.

Fourthly, accustom yourself to behold creation in such a fashion that you may behold God in it. May you thus be stirred up to praise Him, to glorify Him with your heart, mouth, and deeds for His magnificence, power, wisdom, and goodness, exclaiming, "O LORD, how manifold are Thy works! in wisdom hast Thou made them all: the earth is full of Thy riches" (Psa. 104:24). As you consider these perfections of God as manifested in creation, seek to cultivate a reverent, spiritual frame, and to bow yourself with reverence before Him. "O come, let us worship and bow down: let us kneel before the LORD our Maker" (Psa. 95:6). This is the work of angels. "Where wast thou when I laid the foundations of the earth? When the morning stars sang together, and all the sons of God shouted for joy?" (Job 38:4a, 7). The man after God's heart found his delight in this and he praised God as he beheld His creation. "O LORD our Lord, how excellent is Thy Name in all the earth! who hast set Thy glory above the heavens. When I consider Thy heavens, the work of Thy fingers, the moon and the stars, which Thou hast ordained; what is man, that Thou art mindful of him? and the son of man, that Thou visitest him? Thou madest him to have dominion over the works of Thy hands" (Psa. 8:1, 3, 4, 6); "The heavens declare the glory of God; and the firmament showeth His handywork. Day unto day uttereth speech, and night unto night sheweth knowledge" (Psa. 19:1-2).

Fifthly, although the Lord reveals Himself in a much more special and glorious manner in the work of redemption than in His works of creation and providence, heaven and earth have not been created in vain. They do not exist merely to be at man's disposal for the duration of his existence, but they exist for the glory of their Creator.

(1) An unregenerate man views heaven and earth, and God's government of them, in a natural way. His focus remains upon the creation and he rarely ascends to the Creator. If he does so, it is with a carnal heart and eye, perceiving little of God in it. And whatever he does perceive of God in it, he does not glorify God in response to it.

(2) The person, however, whose eyes of his understanding have been enlightened, who now knows, loves, and esteems God to be His God, now beholds everything — every creature and every motion — as so many books and mouths to declare the glory of his God and Father. And since his focus is not on creation itself, it does not concern him so much if the natural is inferior to the work of grace in the realm of the spiritual. His concern is how God, by means of creation, reveals Himself to the soul.

[1] Did not heaven and earth and God's government serve as a mirror to Adam after He was created, and prior to the fall, having as yet no knowledge of redemption? Did it not enable him to behold the glory of His Creator and to glorify Him in response to this?

[2] The heathen who are scattered throughout the entire earth, and have no knowledge of the Holy Scriptures, nevertheless behold God in the works of nature. "For the invisible things of Him from the creation of the world are clearly seen, being understood by the things that are made, even His eternal power and Godhead" (Rom. 1:20).

[3] God often directs His church to behold His works of creation and providence for the purpose of knowing Him. "Fear ye not Me? saith the LORD: will ye not tremble at my presence, which have placed the sand for the bound of the sea? Neither say they in their heart, let us now fear the LORD our God, that giveth rain, both the former and the latter, in his season: He reserveth unto us the appointed weeks of the harvest" (Jer. 5:22a, 24); "I have made the earth, and created man upon it: I, even my hands, have stretched out the heavens, and all their host have I commanded" (Isa. 45:12).

[4] Holy men of God have often focused upon the works of

nature and magnified God in them. "And blessed be Thy glorious Name, which is exalted above all blessing and praise. Thou, even Thou, art LORD alone; Thou hast made heaven, the heaven of heavens, with all their host, the earth, and all things that are therein ... Thou preservest them all" (Neh. 9:5-6). David does likewise in Psalm 104. He begins as follows, "Bless the LORD," upon which he demonstrates how the glory of the Lord reveals itself in the maintenance and government of both His inanimate and animate creation. He ends in like manner: "Bless thou the LORD, O my soul. Praise ye the LORD." The prophet made this reflection a foundation for the confidence of the church by saying, "Our help is in the name of the LORD, who made heaven and earth" (Psa. 124:8).

Therefore, you who love to magnify God, seek to observe God freely in His creation and wondrous government of heaven and earth. Do not easily let opportunity pass by, as if such a practice were childlike and less spiritual, and as if nothing worthwhile could be observed in this. The latter is the practice of many people who in doing so, follow the example of the irrational animals of the earth. Instead, may you take intelligent notice with a spiritual eye, and thus either from the observance of creation ascend unto God — thereby stirring up your soul to a lively frame to glorify God — or from living spiritually near to God, descend from the Creator to the creature and observe them. You will discover more in such reflection than a man could possibly express. If, however, it pleases the Lord not to stir up your soul by His Holy Spirit, the entire edifice of creation, His government inclusive, will be a closed book to you, which under such circumstances will likewise be true for the Holy Scriptures. If God's Spirit leads you into it, however, you will perceive God in an incomprehensibly glorious manner.

If, with an attentive soul, it is your desire — the soul now seeking to accustom itself to continually have God in view and to glorify Him — to observe all God's works, then do the following:

First, in a godly frame of mind go outdoors and lift up your eyes on high to observe the immeasurable dimensions of the universe (as far as man is concerned) as well as its enormous space, and consider yourself as a grain of sand surrounded by all this.

Secondly, observe heaven's beautiful countenance. How delightful are the distant heavenly blue, the fluffy clouds, the elegant moon, the innumerable multitude of glittering stars, the comprehensive view of the countenance of heaven; the quiet evening, the pensive night, the lovely sunrise; the sitting or walking under the canopy of a lush forest, the sweet rustling of the wind in the trees, the dimension of immensity presented by rows of lofty trees; and

the immensity of a plain when viewed either from a lonely eleva-
tion or from a distant point! Here one observes green meadows
filled with cattle, and there cultivated fields with either lovely,
multi-colored, and aromatic growth, or delicious fruits; while yonder are mountains interspersed with valleys. Then again one walks
along the seashore, and yonder one sits down by a quietly babbling
brook, everywhere hearing the joyful sound produced by the
voices of birds of various plumage. If a soul is to some degree
spiritual, will he not be drawn towards his Creator and Father, and
will it not stir up a variety of emotions within? Will he not observe
more than he can possibly express, and will not such exhilarating
excursions both during the morning and the evening cause him to
return home joyfully with a heart filled with praise?

Thirdly, observe the infinite diversity of colors, smells, tastes,
voices, and shapes of birds, fishes, animals, insects, leaves, and
grasses in the field. Seek to find two that are fully identical!

Fourthly, observe the infinite chain of secondary causes, and
how one thing serves and assists the other; how heaven and earth
interact, as is stated in Hosea 2:21-22, "I will hear the heavens, and
they shall hear the earth; and the earth shall hear the corn, and the
wine, and the oil; and they shall hear Jezreel." When you sit down
at your table to eat, has not the entire edifice of heaven and earth
been in motion to set this table before you? What an innumerable
multitude of people have served you in this, who have labored to
provide you with a table, a table cover, knives, dishes, spoons,
glasses, bread, meat, fruits, wine, and beer? Through how many
hands did all these things pass before coming to your table? But
who sets all of this in motion and who caused them to serve you in
the sweat of their brow? Behold, oh, behold the good hand of your
Father! It is He who gave life to the bird, the animal, or the fish. It
is He who gave them food with the intent to raise them for your
benefit, and who directed men to catch them, to deliver them to
your home, and to prepare them for you. It is He who causes a
little tree to be planted on your behalf, and prevents all His
creatures from picking that apple, cluster of grapes, etc., rather
directing them to leave it until, being ripe, it be delivered to your
home, even if it were thousands of miles from your residence. Is
all of this not suitable to prompt you to observe the hand and glory
of God in a variety of ways? Does this not draw the soul which loves
God towards Him?

Fifthly, observe the mountain peaks, the crowns of the trees, the
church steeples, and blades of grass, and consider in which direction they point. Do they not point upward? Does all this not teach

you not to focus on creation itself, but rather, to turn away from it to know the Lord God, love Him, delight yourself in Him, and give Him honor and glory?

No education is required to discern what one may observe in, and learn from, creation. The Holy Spirit, having given God's child a sanctified soul, reveals with great clarity many glorious attributes of God, revealing them in a clearer and different manner than the brightest physicist would be capable of doing. Yes, a godly farmer can observe a thousandfold more than a secularly trained astronomer, herbalist, or biologist.

Sixthly, we hereby conclude that *God is,* all of which is manifested in a clear, incontrovertible, and immanent manner. This concept of God's existence transcends our ability for verbal expression. It declares and reveals to us "His eternal power and Godhead" (Rom. 1:20). The fact that He created everything with one word, and by the influence of His power energizes in its existence and activity every one of the innumerable multitude of His creatures, is a reality too wonderful for our comprehension. In this we may observe the unsearchable wisdom, the infinite power, and the wondrous goodness of God, a view which will cause us to lose ourselves in amazement.

These and other attributes of God are observed by a godly person with an attentive disposition, doing so not simply by way of reasonable deduction or by mere observation. It is not so that he simply concludes God to be such and such and nevertheless remains in darkness. Rather, the Lord reveals Himself to the soul by way of His creation and the manner in which it functions, doing so as clearly as light manifests itself to the bodily eye. The fact that we neither observe all this nor lift up our hearts to the Lord with wonder, delight, and joy, or, when reasoning deductively, do not discern the glory of the Lord in all this and thus do not glorify Him in this, is but a sign of our lack of spirituality. It is a natural rather than spiritual reaction to imagine that we cannot observe God's creation from a spiritual perspective. Perhaps this is due to the fact that one ends in creation itself, drawing but obscure conclusions from such observations, and having no experience in observing the glory of God either inductively or deductively[3] with a heart which has been spiritually illuminated.

Seventhly, when a person who loves God ascends from creation to God Himself, he will observe far more of the glory of God than

---

[3] The Dutch reads as follows: ". . . of van onderen op, of van boven neder."

the creature itself can externally convey to him. He loses sight of the creature and ends in the Creator, acknowledging that His glory far exceeds the narrow confines of the creature. "But will God indeed dwell on the earth? behold, the heaven and heaven of heavens cannot contain Thee" (1 Ki. 8:27). Should he attempt to express the honor and glory of His majesty, then all mental capacity is too limited and all words are inadequate, causing him to exclaim, "His greatness is unsearchable" (Psa. 145:3). He concludes that if God has created this lowly earth, the firmament, and the entire universe in such a glorious fashion and to His honor, His glory must be much more manifest in the third heaven, in that city whose Builder and Maker He is. There glory is to be observed in all its dimensions. It is there that the Lord Jesus was received in glory and is seated at the right hand of the Majesty in the heavens. There the angels are the most excellent creatures, excelling in glory. There the bodies of the godly will be conformed to the glorified body of Christ, be fully manifested in glory, and receive the crown of glory which will not fade away. The glory of God illuminates the New Jerusalem in its entirety — a glory which is so great that Paul, having been lifted up into the third heaven, only shares with us that He heard unspeakable words, which are not lawful for a man to utter; that is, which cannot possibly be expressed. Thus, a person viewing this by faith, in believing meditation can join himself to this glorified multitude in heaven, with them prostrate himself before the Lord, take his crown and cast it down before Him, and join in exclaiming, "Hallelujah to Him who sits upon the throne, to whom be honor and glory!" Even then one could say that all of this is as nothing compared to the infinite glory which God has within Himself. And thus we must end in amazement and exclaim, "Thou, who hast set Thy majesty above the heavens, Thy glory is infinite! Therefore, to Thee be glory and majesty, dominion and power, both now and for ever! Amen."

CHAPTER NINE

Angels and Devils

Since angels and men have the highest measure of perfection among all creatures, we shall consider them separately. First, we shall consider the angels.

The Name "Angel" Defined

The name *Angel* (Hebrew: מלאך *Maleach)* is used for a variety of persons in the Word of God.

(1) The Lord Jesus Christ is called the *Angel,* of whom it is stated, "My Name (Jehovah) is in Him" (Exo. 23:21), that He is "the Angel of His presence" (Isa. 63:9), and "the messenger of the covenant" (Mal. 3:1).

(2) Ministers are called angels. "...for he is the messenger (angel)[1] of the LORD of hosts" (Mal. 2:7).

(3) Messengers are referred to as angels (Job 1:14).

(4) Incorporal personal entities are referred to as "angels." "And David lifted up his eyes, and saw the angel of the LORD stand between the earth and the heaven, having a drawn sword in his hand stretched out over Jerusalem" (1 Chr. 21:16).

In Greek Ἄγγελος *(Angelos)* is used two or three times to denote a messenger; otherwise it is always in reference to incorporal personal entities which are denominated as "angels." This name is not in any way related to their mission. It is a name which belongs as uniquely to these creatures as the name "man" belongs to the human race. Thus, this name does not refer to an office, but signifies spiritual, personal entities in contrast to human beings.

---

[1] In both Malachi 3:1 and Malachi 2:7 the Statenvertaling uses the word 'engel', which is translated as 'messenger' in the KJV.

"For we are made a spectacle unto the world, and to angels, and to men" (1 Cor. 4:9); "Though I speak with the tongues of men and of angels..." (1 Cor. 13:1). Men are compared to angels, Ἰσάγγελοι *(Isangeloi)*. "But they which shall be accounted worthy to obtain that world, and the resurrection from the dead, neither marry... for they are equal unto the angels" (Luke 20:35-36; cf. Mat. 22:30). These incorporal personal entities are also called *spirits*, which in Hebrew is רוּחַ *(ruach)*, and in Greek πνεῦμα *(pneuma)*. This word is also used in a variety of ways.

(1) It refers to God (John 4:24);

(2) to the third Person in the divine essence (Psa. 33:6; 1 John 5:7);

(3) to the soul of man (Psa. 77:3, Acts 7:59);

(4) to the wind (Psa. 1:4; John 3:8);

(5) however, most frequently it refers to angels, that is, incorporal personal entities. "A spirit passed before my face" (Job 4:15); "Are they not all ministering spirits?" (Heb. 1:14). "And the evil spirit answered..." (Acts 19:15).

Both this name and the name "angel" are proper to their being, and are not assigned to them on the basis of comparison with other creatures. God who gave everything a name according to His will has given these specific names to these personal entities, and those names are synonymous with these personal entities. The use of these names is as common as our use of money; it is not necessary to anxiously and cunningly search for hidden meanings. We know what the word "angel" or "spirit" means, and what we understand by it.

Anyone who believes Scripture and does not impudently reject human histories and witness accounts, needs no proof for the existence of angels. If anyone wishes to join the Sadducees, however, in stating "that there is no resurrection, neither angel, nor spirit" (Acts 23:8), let him not object to being numbered among them.

The angels were created, for whatever exists is either Creator or creature. Since they are not the Creator, they are creatures and have been created. Paul confirms this when he states, "For by Him were all things created, that are in heaven, and that are in earth, visible and invisible, whether they be thrones, or dominions, or principalities, or powers: all things were created by Him, and for Him" (Col. 1:16). Although it cannot be stated with certainty on which day of creation they were created, we do know that they were not created prior to "the beginning." Prior to the beginning there was nothing but God Himself who inhabiteth eternity, whereas all creatures have a chronological existence, making them increasingly distant from the initial moment of their existence. It is equally true that they were not created after the initial six days, since God perfectly completed everything within this time frame. It is most probable that as the heavenly host (Luke 2:13) they were created on the first day with the third heaven, for when the Lord in subsequent days brought forth everything from that shapeless mass of matter, they were already present. "Where wast thou when I laid the foundations of the earth?... When the morning stars sang together, and all the sons of God shouted for joy?" (Job 38:4, 7).

In the beginning God created but one person, from whom He created a second, and out of these two the innumerable multitude of human beings has been brought forth. However, He created the entire, unfathomably large multitude of angels in one moment. There is "an innumerable company of angels" (Heb. 12:22); "The chariots of God are twenty thousand, even thousands of angels" (Psa. 68:17); "Thousand thousands ministered unto Him, and ten thousand times ten thousand stood before Him" (Dan. 7:10).

The Existence of Angels Defined

An angel is an incorporal, personal being which God has created and gifted with an extraordinary intellect, will, and power.

An angel is a personal being based on the following evidence. Everyone will admit that whatever possesses intellect, a will, and power, and engages in intelligent and energetic activity, is a personal being. All this is true for angels — which we will subsequently support with abundant evidence — and they are therefore personal beings. As their form and manner of existence are unknown to us, however, their internal essence is likewise unknown to us. But we do know that their attributes, such as intellect, will, power, goodness, and wisdom are to be differentiated from their essential being, for "simplicity" is one of the incommunicable attributes of God. Beyond this we cannot delve into the essential nature of their being, since it has not been revealed to us. As it is beyond the reach of our intellect, we do not wish to deal with matters which have been hidden from us, but must wisely be moderate so that our own thinking and that of others may not be tainted.

Angels are *incorporal* personal beings; that is, beings which exist without a body. It is their very nature to be spirits, and thus there is no essential union with a body. A body is *trinam dimensionem*; that is, three-dimensional, having length, breadth, and height. We emphatically deny this to be true for angels, even if one were to think of a body of the minutest dimensions. There is not the least relationship between angels and that which is corporal. "...a spirit hath not flesh and bones..." (Luke 24:39). They have been created by God to exist independently, without being united to a body.

As is true of the angels, the soul of man is also incorporal, that is, a spirit. The concept of three-dimensionality is also entirely absent here, for the soul can exist without a body, as is true after man's death. This does not mean that the soul is then an angel, but as there are various bodily forms, the soul is likewise a different kind of spirit. It has spirituality and incorporeality in common with the angels, albeit in a lower degree, as the essential difference between the two is hidden from us. We also are not fully cognizant of the form of existence of our souls. We do know this, however, that they are not angels, nor are they ever referred to as angels. Rather, they are expressly distinguished from angels. "But ye are come unto...an innumerable company of angels...and to the spirits of just men made perfect" (Heb. 12:22-23).

Although there is no essential union between angels and bodies, they do appear in bodily form. They did not appear as apparitions or shadows during their frequent appearances, but the bodies in which they walked, sat, spoke, ate, wrestled, or touched other bodies, were true bodies. The saints to whom they appeared were not mentally impaired, did not sleep (although they did appear to them corporally in dreams or during a state of mental ecstasy), but were awake, spoke, moved, and interacted with them as if they were human beings. However, I neither know the origin of the bodies which they temporarily possessed, nor do I wish to make a guess. Although the bodies by which they interacted with men were true bodies, the angels were not essentially united to those bodies as the soul is united to the body. They set those bodies in motion, not *formaliter,* that is, in essence, but *efficienter;* that is, as operative agents of those motions, such as when a man moves the gears in his watch. This occurred for the purpose of enabling the angels to meet with man in a manner consistent with his own form of existence, and thus to interact with man in a manner familiar to him.

Although the angels are incorporal — and thus not surrounded by the atmosphere, etc., as is true for human bodies — they nevertheless, in a manner consistent with their nature, exist in one locality, although we as corporal beings cannot comprehend how. We nevertheless know that they exist *elsewhere,* for that which exists nowhere does not exist, and whatever exists everywhere and without dimensions is God. If they are in one locality, they are not simultaneously elsewhere. Whenever our bodies change locality, our souls likewise change locality. Whenever a godly person dies, his soul does not remain upon earth, but has its residence in the third heaven. Whenever an ungodly person dies, his soul goes to hell and does not remain upon earth. Thus a spirit changes locality and the angels do likewise. When the angel was stationed at the east of Paradise, he was at that location and not in heaven (Gen. 3:24). When the angel of the Lord spoke to Zachariah while standing at the right side of the altar (Luke 1:11), he was not in Nazareth. When the angel Gabriel was sent to Nazareth and visited Mary (Luke 1:26, 28), he was not in Jerusalem. When the angels of God ascend and descend (John 1:51), they are changing location. Thus, they are always in a specific locality and move from place to place.

It is even more absurd to think that a spirit is wherever he thinks himself to be. This presupposes of course that he is in a specified locality at that moment. The devil would still be in heaven, since he can think of having been there. Then man would be without a soul whenever he is mentally present in another place. Then the soul of a deceased person would still be within his body upon earth, since he could still think of being there. Whenever the soul of man removes itself mentally to other places it does not go there in actuality, but man brings such distant places and matters into his imagination; thus the soul reflects upon that which is manifest in the imagination. Similarly, an angel also thinks about matters which are remote, doing so in a manner consistent with his nature, but which is concealed from us as we do not know his form of existence.

Angels are *intelligent* creatures in a manner far exceeding the intelligence of man. This is why the wise woman of Tekoa said to David, "My lord is wise, according to the wisdom of an angel of God" (2 Sam. 14:20). Their knowledge is either natural or acquired.

By virtue of their nature, the angels from the initial moment of their existence have always beheld the countenance of the Father (Mat. 18:10). They do, however, acquire knowledge concerning matters of which they had no prior knowledge, either by *revelation* or by *experience*. The Lord Jesus revealed the mystery of "things which must shortly come to pass" to an angel, sending him to reveal this to John (Rev. 1:1). By constant exhortation, the church makes known to principalities and powers in heavenly places the manifold wisdom of God (Eph. 3:10).

Their knowledge is finite and therefore they do not know all things, as many things are hidden from them.

(1) They are not naturally capable of themselves to perceive future events which will transpire by the exercise of man's free will or which will result because of secondary causes. This attribute properly belongs to God alone. "Shew the things that are to come hereafter, that we may know that ye are gods" (Isa. 41:23); "But of

that day and that hour knoweth no man, no, not the angels which are in heaven" (Mark 13:32).

(2) They have no knowledge of the heart, free will, and thoughts of men by way of an extrinsic act of the intellect. Such knowledge is in the first place attributable to God alone. "For Thou only knowest the hearts of the children of men" (2 Chr. 6:30); "The heart is deceitful above all things, and desperately wicked: who can know it? I the LORD search the heart, I try the reins" (Jer. 17:9-10a). Such knowledge is never attributed to an angel. Secondly, the reasonable will is subject to God alone and is immediately dependent upon Him. He only is capable of influencing the will. "The king's heart is in the hand of the LORD, as the rivers of water: He turneth it withersoever He will" (Prov. 21:1); "He fashioneth their hearts alike" (Psa. 33:15).

If angels are cognizant of the will and opinion of men, this is neither due to immediate nor prior knowledge. Rather, they perceive this in retrospect, observing all the circumstances and manifestations of man's movements and thus they conclude the probability of man's thoughts and will. However, the probability of being in error concerning these matters always remains. One must always distinguish here between the will and the manifestation of the will. The angels are conscious of the latter from which they conclude the former.

Nevertheless, God does reveal to both good and evil angels some of the things which will come to pass — either to the benefit of the godly or as a trial and punishment upon the ungodly. The angels utilize these revelations for the purpose of comfort and exhortation. The devils, however, use them to deceive, to cause men to acknowledge that they are capable of predicting future events, and to induce men to believe them.

Our little children often ask when they begin to reason, "Why is this?" and "How does this work?" In regard to these matters they ask, "Does an angel have eyes?" Answer: No. "How is he then able to see? How is he able to read the Bible and thus know what it contains as well as what transpires in the world? Does he have ears?" Answer: No. "How then is he capable of hearing what we say? Does he have hands and feet?" Answer: No. "How then is he capable of moving from one place to another? How is he capable of doing anything?" We respond that all this is known to us from God's Word. Since, however, we are ignorant of the manner of their existence, we are also ignorant of the "how" of their existence. Being unable to understand the "how" of a matter does not mean that we must deny the matter itself. All we can say is that they do not see, hear, and function as man does, but rather in a manner which is consistent with their nature.

The angels are in possession of superior and extraordinary power, enabling them to execute great matters which far exceed the ability of men. "Whereas angels, which are greater in power and might..." (2 Pet. 2:11). It is stated that they "excel in strength" (Psa. 103:20); they are called "His mighty angels" (2 Th. 1:7); they are referred to as "the heavenly host" (Luke 2:13), and as "horses and chariots of fire" (2 Ki. 6:17). All this is evident from the acts which they perform, as recorded in God's Word.

The Interaction of Angels and Physical Entities

Question: Is it possible, and has it truly occurred that an angel has interacted with a physical entity since they are neither compatible nor have anything in common?

Answer: By positing that there is no compatibility between the two, one thereby presupposes that there are angels as well as men.

First, if this were an impossibility, the impossibility exists either in relation to God, to the physical entity, or to the angel. The impossibility is not with God for He is omnipotent and can empower a creature to a degree that is pleasing to Him. This also is not true relative to the physical entity which can be set in motion, nor is it true relative to an angel, as both God's Word and experience confirm this to be so. No one is able to state in what manner this interaction occurs, however, unless he were to have a perfect and thorough knowledge of the nature as well as the manner of an angel's existence — which man does not have. Poor, insignificant man! How can men who hardly understand how one physical entity interacts with another even entertain the notion to argue about the power of angels? I said "hardly," for there be many things of which they have no knowledge at all; they are not able to tell us how sun, moon, and stars influence whatever transpires upon earth, nor the cause of low and high tides, and many other such phenomena. Explain that first to us and then you may explain to us how our soul is united with and influences the body, as well as proceed to state what is either possible or impossible relative to angels. Or else, believe the Word of God, as well as experience, which is the teacher of fools.

Secondly, it is certain that God — who is a Spirit and is distinctly different from physical entities to a far greater degree than is true for angels — interacts with physical entities. Therefore the fact that an angel is a spirit does not prevent him from interacting with a physical entity. If you reason that God is omnipotent whereas an angel is not, and thus disallow the aforementioned conclusion, I respond that this is true as far as omnipotence is concerned. The congruency between God and angels consists, however, in the fact that both have nothing in common and are incompatible with physical entities. From this we draw the incontrovertible conclusion that this incompatibility and incongruency does not prevent a spirit from interacting with a physical entity. The entire foundation of this logical construction collapses, and thus all reasons for denial are nullified.

Thirdly, our soul is a spirit, and as such is as distinct from the body as an angel is from a physical entity. Our soul interacts with the body, however, and thus an angel is capable of the same. Upon the suggestion that a soul is united to its own body and therefore interacts with its own body — and by the agency of this body with other physical entities — I respond that the fact whether the spirit does or does not belong to a physical entity is not the issue here. The soul is a spirit and as spirit it immediately interacts with the body. You can suggest as many indirect contacts between body and soul as you wish, but one must ultimately arrive at the point of immediate contact in their union. Thus, we conclude that a spirit interacts with a physical entity. Once more, is God not able to give a body to an angel, temporarily assigning him a body? Would this angel be able to interact with his own body as the soul interacts with its body and, by virtue of its body, with other physical entities? As this is true for the soul, it is obviously true for angels as well. Having eliminated every reason for the objection, it is certain that an angel can interact with a physical entity.

Fourthly, the interaction between angels and physical entities is so clearly and abundantly attested to by Scripture that it merely suffices to read about this. From a large number of Scripture references let me select the following example. "Then the angel of the LORD went forth, and smote in the camp of the Assyrians a hundred and fourscore and five thousand" (Isa. 37:36). An angel performed this task; no other creature was capable of performing a task of this magnitude. People, and that in respect to their bodies, were the object of his activity; they were killed by the angel. This certainly is an example of interaction with physical entities. "My God hath sent His angel, and hath shut the lions' mouths" (Dan. 6:22). Did not an angel of the Lord announce the birth of Christ to the shepherds with heavenly clarity using the language of men (Luke 2:13)? The act of speaking sets air particles in motion, and thus the angel, as well as the multitude of the heavenly hosts which joined him, interacted with physical entities. It was an angel who spoke with the Lord Jesus Christ in Gethsemane (Luke 22:43).

Angels appeared to the guards and the women at the resurrection of Christ (Mat. 28:2-5). "And, behold, the angel of the Lord came upon him, and a light shined in the prison: and he smote Peter on the side, and raised him up, saying…" (Acts 12:7). Is it possible to express the interaction between a spirit and a physical entity any more clearly? Also in verse 23, "And immediately the angel of the Lord smote him [Herod]." From all these examples it is undeniable that angels interact with physical entities.

Objection #1: The angels were not involved, but were merely bystanders to enhance the luster of God's work.

Answer: Is there a single text where this is stated? Allow for the enhancement of glory that they would manifest themselves to men in human form; they nevertheless, in this manifestation, were interacting with physical entities. In addition to this it is expressly stated, however, that angels performed all these things. Who dares to contradict what God affirms?

Objection #2: One could ask in what manner angels interact with physical entities. Is it merely by means of their will, or are the exercise of power and exertion of influence also factors?

Answer: (1) The will is the initiating principle for the activity of a rational creature. To bring anything to pass by the mere exercise of the will, however, is an act of God rather than of the creature. God says, "I will: be thou clean" (Luke 5:13); "God…calleth those things which be not as though they were" (Rom. 4:17); "For He spake, and it was done; He commanded, and it stood fast" (Psa. 33:9).

(2) It is nowhere stated in the entire Bible that angels have executed tasks merely by the exercise of their will. Who therefore dares to state such a thing, and what is the basis for such a statement?

(3) God's Word states that they excel in strength, have power, killed, smote Peter's side, closed the mouths of lions, spoke, and did everything in a manner as one would describe the activity of men. This proves that in addition to the exercise of their will there also was the exercise of power.

(4) If one wishes to maintain that angels are merely active in exercising their will, such a statement would imply the negation of the fact that angels truly interact with physical entities. By such reasoning one would not be able to rebut those who deny this very interaction itself, thereby confirming the very thing he wished to negate. Since they truly and actually interact with physical entities, however, they are thus not merely exercising their will, but the exercise of power and exertion of influence are added to this. Yet as far as the manner of operation is concerned, we readily remain silent. It should be observed that all this haggling and manipula-

tion is expressive of a subtle inclination to completely deny the existence of any spirit.

As angels interact with physical entities, they likewise interact with each other, as 1) there is among them no incompatibility of natures, 2) Scripture states it to be so, "And one cried unto another . . ." (Isa. 6:3), and 3) if such were not the case, they would each exist in solitude and would be less perfect than man. It is also to their well-being to see and hear each other and to speak to and interact with each other.

These then are general observations concerning both good and evil angels.

Concerning the Good Angels

In the beginning all angels were created in a holy state; however, a large portion of them have apostatized so that presently both holy angels and devils exist.

The good angels are also referred to as *elect* (1 Tim. 5:21), proving that there is an election of angels as well as of men. They are generally referred to as *holy angels* (Mat. 25:31; Jude 14), *angels of the Lord*, or also, without the use of an adjective, *angels*. They are also called *ministering spirits, cherubims, appearances* (due to their visible appearances to men), and *seraphims* (aflame) because of their zeal and readiness. In reference to their service they are called *holy watchers, sons of God, morning stars, heavenly hosts, thrones, principalities, powers, and rulers*. In one text they are called *Elohim* (Psa. 8:5), which the apostle, in view of their radiation of divine power, translates as *angels* in Hebrews 2:7.

The third heaven is the residence of the angels. ". . . in heaven their angels do always behold the face of My Father which is in heaven" (Mat. 18:10); ". . . but are as the angels of God in heaven" (Mat. 22:30). Therefore they are called the *angels of heaven* (Mat. 24:36). It is from heaven that they are sent forth to perform those things which they are commanded to do. "For the angel of the Lord descended from heaven, and came . . ." (Mat. 28:2); "And there appeared an angel unto Him from heaven. . ." (Luke 22:43).

There is a very orderly relationship between the angels. Since God is a God of order, there can be no disorderliness in the holy environment of heaven. The manner of this order and the nature of the hierarchy are not known to us. We only know that there are thrones, principalities, powers, and rulers. The orders or ranks suggested by some are a pure fabrication.

Generally, their task is to execute God's commands. "Bless the LORD, ye His angels . . . that do His commandments, hearkening unto the voice of His Word" (Psa. 103:20). God specifically sends them forth to serve the elect (Heb. 1:14). They preserve them, "for He shall give His angels charge over thee, to keep thee in all thy ways. They shall bear thee up in their hands, lest thou dash thy foot against a stone" (Psa. 91:11-12). They warn them against danger (Mat. 2:13); they rebuke them for committed sins (Rev. 22:9); they exhort them (Rev. 19:10); they give them direction as to what their course of action must be (Acts 10:5); they reveal future events to them (Dan. 8:16); they carry their souls to heaven after death (Luke 16:22), and they will be used to gather them prior to the final judgment (Mat. 24:31). God uses them for these and many other special tasks to the benefit of the elect, and uses them on the other hand to punish the ungodly. An angel slew 185,000 men in one night (Isa. 37:36), and an angel smote Herod the King and he died (Acts 12:23).

Someone may ask whether every country, every city, every home, and every person has its special guardian angel. Our response is that nothing of the sort is to be found in God's Word, and therefore our wisdom must not go beyond the boundaries of what is written. Scripture does state that an angel is present with a godly person (Acts 12:7). Sometimes more angels are present with a godly person (2 Kings 6:17), and sometimes one angel is present with several godly persons (Dan. 3:25).

Practical Exhortations Concerning the Doctrine of Angels

If the angels interact with man in such a fashion, the godly must believe and acknowledge this and behave themselves accordingly for the activity of angels has not been recorded without purpose.

First, one should carefully avoid attributing anything to them which is not revealed in God's Word and which we are forbidden to attribute to them. They must neither be acknowledged as intercessors nor must we desire that they intercede for us, as such activity is not according to God's Word. We must neither serve nor worship them for the following reasons:

(1) It is idolatry to serve anything which by its very nature is not God (Gal. 4:8). One may serve and worship only God. "Thou shalt worship the Lord thy God, and Him only shalt thou serve" (Mat. 4:10).

(2) It is expressly forbidden. "Let no man beguile you of your reward in a voluntary humility and worshipping of angels" (Col. 2:18).

(3) It is sharply condemned. "See thou do it not...worship God" (Rev. 19:10).

Secondly, one should observe and acknowledge this, and by way of frequent meditation seek to increase both observation of and faith in the fact that it pleases God to accomplish so many great things by their agency. We must stand amazed at the interrelationship of secondary causes and God's government of them in relation to the influences of sun, moon, and stars upon earthly things, as well as in relation to the interaction between terrestrial objects. While observing the wisdom and goodness of God in all these things, we must also be amazed about God's use of the angels. Although we do not know everything, we can deduce many other things from that which has been recorded. We would know even more if we would more frequently contemplate upon it. This would render us more fit to acknowledge and praise God joyfully concerning His wisdom and goodness in His use of the angels.

Thirdly, one must refrain from and be fearful of offending, despising, and grieving the godly, for they have such holy guardians who are displeased with such behavior — standing ready to punish their offenders, as has been demonstrated in the past (cf. Isa. 37:36; Acts 12:23). It is for this reason that the Lord Jesus states in Matthew 18:10, "Take heed that ye despise not one of these little ones; for I say unto you, that in heaven their angels do always behold the face of My Father which is in heaven."

Fourthly, how safe God's children are! It is true that only God by His power and supervision protects and preserves His people. Thus, one may neither trust in nor rely upon a creature. Nevertheless, God uses means in this preservation, as He provides nourishment for the maintenance of life and armed forces for the protection of cities and countries. God therefore is to be acknowledged in the provision of means. And we ought to stand amazed and rejoice in the manner whereby He directs the holy angels, in that He uses such glorious creatures to preserve such minuscule and insignificant human beings. Since God has commissioned them to guard, protect, and keep the godly, one ought to be quiet and without fear, even when all things appear to be against us. "For they that be with us are more than they that be with them" (2 Ki. 6:16).

Fifthly, in view of their presence we, even when not being observed by man, ought to conduct ourselves holily and without blame. Although God's omnipresence and omniscience alone ought to sufficiently restrain us, God nevertheless uses the presence of men, due to our respect for them, as a means to keep us from many sins and to stir us up to the practice of virtue. Thus, it also behooves us to be holy and without blame in our behavior in view of the presence of angels, considering them to be fellow servants and our "company" (Heb. 12:22). We shall thus cause them to rejoice, and by virtue of their communication of this there will be joy in heaven (Luke 15:7, 10). Consequently, the apostle exhorts that "for this cause ought the woman to have power (a covering) on her head because of the angels" (1 Cor. 11:10).

Concerning the Devils

God created all angels in a state of holiness; however, a large multitude apostatized. "For if God spared not the angels that sinned..." (2 Pet. 2:4); "And the angels which kept not their first estate, but left their own habitation..." (Jude 6). They are referred to as *angels* (sometimes without the use of any adjectives) by virtue of their nature — a nature which they have corrupted through sin, but have nevertheless not lost. "For I am persuaded, that neither death, nor life, nor angels...shall be able to separate us from the love of God" (Rom. 8:38-39). Sometimes the term is modified by a reference to the sin which they have sinned; that is, as those "which kept not their first estate," or by a reference to their leader, βεελζεβούλ *(Beelzebul)*, "the prince of the devils" (Mat. 12:24), "the angel of the bottomless pit" (Rev. 9:11). They are consequently called the angels of the devil (Mat. 25:41), the angels of the dragon (Rev. 12:7), and the messengers of Satan (2 Cor. 12:7).

In view of their nature they are also referred to as *spirits*. "They brought unto Him many that were possessed with devils: and He cast out the spirits with His word" (Mat. 8:16). Due to their abhorrent nature they are called "unclean spirits" (Mark 3:11). "And in the synagogue there was a man, which had a spirit of an unclean devil" (Luke 4:33). Due to their internal activity in men they are called "dumb and deaf spirits" (Mark 9:25), "spirits of infirmity" (Luke 13:11), that is a spirit which makes one dumb, deaf, and ill. They are also referred to as practitioners of "spiritual wickedness" (Eph. 6:12).

In Hebrew the devil is called שטן, and in Greek, Σατᾶν, Σατανᾶς *(Satan)*, that is, *one who opposes, resists, and contradicts*, since he is in opposition to God, Christ, believers, and all that is good. "...There was given to me...the messenger of Satan..." (2 Cor. 12:7); "And the great dragon was cast out, that old serpent, called the Devil, and Satan" (Rev. 12:9). For this reason he is called ᾿Αντίδικος *Antidikos*, or "adversary" (1 Pet. 5:8).

In Greek he is called Δαίμων, Δαιμόνιον *(Daimon, Daimonion)* (demon). These words are derived from δαίω *(daio)*, to know, since he leaves no stone unturned in his quest to know where and in what manner he can perform the ultimate in evil. He is also cognizant of many matters which are hidden from man, which he by divine permission at times reveals, and sometimes guesses on the basis of probability. He is subtle in all his evil practices. "That ye may be able to stand against the wiles of the devil" (Eph. 6:11); "...as the serpent beguiled Eve through his subtilty..." (2 Cor. 11:3).

He is also called Διάβολος *(Diabolos)*, or *Devil*, which is derived from διαβάλλειν *(diaballein)*, to slander. The devil is a slanderer, for he slanders God by casting fiery darts in the heart of the believer, and he slanders believers in the presence of God (Job 1:9, 11). "Although thou movest Me against him..." (Job 2:3). For this reason he is called Κατηγορος *(Kategoros)*, *(*accuser) (Rev. 12:10).

The idea that the words *Satan, devil, unclean spirits, angels that sinned* should be translated with words such as *sin, sickness, evil moods, fantasy, imagination, and evil men*, is ludicrous. Such an obvious absurdity is contradicted by the Bible, by all Hebrew, Greek, and Latin writers, as well as writers in other languages. Whenever these words occur we know that they do not refer to these abstract ideas, but rather to evil, spiritual, and personal entities. They are mentioned in contradistinction to such things. "And to have power to heal sicknesses, and to cast out devils" (Mark 3:15). Knowledge, the knowledge of Christ, and the ability to reason and to speak, are all attributed to the devils. This will be abundantly evident as we proceed, all of which cannot be attributed to other abstract things. The exception occurs when the Lord Jesus once called Peter Satan, an adversary (Mat. 16:23), because he withstood him and thereby engaged in the work of Satan. Judas, the traitor, was called a *diabolus* or a devil (John 6:70) since the devil would enter into him and he thus would be a tool of the devil.

To pagans and Christians and to both the godly and the ungodly it is very evident that devils do exist. Scripture makes mention of it so frequently and clearly that no one can doubt this truth unless one wishes to stubbornly contradict the common view of men as well as God's Word. Such a person would not deserve to be answered with one word, nor to be engaged in a discussion.

Devils do exist, and their number is very large. Scripture frequently speaks of devils, occasionally using the adjective "many" (Mark 1:34), and "seven" (Mark 16:9), as well as referring to the presence of a legion of devils in one person (Mark 5:9, 15). Whenever the reference to the devil is singular, this occurs either because there was only one devil present; because the reference was to his identity, as one would say, "man lives by food and drink"; or because the reference is to the chief of devils.

Whatever has been stated generally concerning the angels also applies to the devils, who are angels. This means that they are personal entities, endowed with intellect and power, and interact with physical and human beings. The fact that they are personal entities is confirmed by all those texts which state that they speak, know Jesus, tempt, tear people, cast them about, kill swine, etc. It is confirmed in Mark 1:34, among other texts, that they possess intellect, "And (He) suffered not the devils to speak, because they knew Him." This is also shown in the following texts, "And the evil spirit answered and said, Jesus I know, and Paul I know; but who are ye?" (Acts 19:15). "But I fear, lest by any means, as the serpent beguiled Eve through subtilty..." (2 Cor. 11:3).

The fact that devils interact with physical and human beings is confirmed first of all from all those texts which we have previously used to prove that such is true for angels, (the devils being angels), as well as from many other texts of which we merely mention the following, "Now the serpent...said unto the woman" (Gen. 3:1), and, "The serpent beguiled me" (Gen. 3:13). The one being engaged in this activity is here referred to as a serpent. It is common knowledge that the creeping animal which bears the name "serpent" neither possesses intellect nor the ability to speak, so that it was not the animal which spoke, but it was merely a means used by another. It is also certain that Eve in her holy state was neither subject to illness, melancholy, vain imaginations, nor to any other sinful condition, nor was this an imagination, such as in a waking dream. It was a true historical event. It was also not possible for Eve, due to her holy state, to entertain evil thoughts concerning God in her imagination, to do battle against them, and ultimately to be conquered by them. Who then did speak to Eve? The text states that it was the serpent whose head would be bruised by the seed of the woman; that is, it is the one who would be conquered by the Lord Jesus Christ — the devil. "That through death He (Christ) might destroy him that had the power of death, that is, the devil" (Heb. 2:14). It was therefore the devil who spoke to Eve and tempted her, and it is he who presently lives and engages in battle against the congregation of God. "But I fear, lest by any means, as the serpent beguiled Eve through his subtilty, so your minds should be corrupted..." (2 Cor. 11:3). The Lord Jesus clearly states that it was the devil. "He (the devil) was a murderer from the beginning, and abode not in the truth..." (John 8:44). Thus, the devils at one time abode in the truth, sinned, did not keep their first estate, and are murderers of men. He is called "that old serpent,...the devil, and Satan" (Rev. 12:9). It is therefore undeniable that the devil knew Eve, spoke with her, and thus is capable of interacting with a human being.

Secondly, such interaction is confirmed in the following passages, "And the LORD said unto Satan, Behold, all that he hath is in thy power...so Satan went forth from the presence of the LORD" (Job 1:12); "And, behold, there came a great wind from the wilderness, and smote the four corners of the house, and it fell upon the young men, and they are dead" (Job 1:19); "So went Satan forth from the presence of the LORD, and smote Job with sore boils from the sole of his foot unto his crown" (Job 2:7). Here the active agent was neither an illness, an evil temper, a sin, nor a man, but Satan. It was Satan, the devil (he is one and the same), who caused the wind to arise from the desert, by which he smote the house and killed Job's children. It was also he who smote Job with sore boils. It is thus confirmed that Satan interacts with human beings as well as with physical entities.

Thirdly, add to this what is stated in Matthew 4:1-11, "Then was Jesus led up of the Spirit into the wilderness to be tempted of the devil," etc. All this activity, such as reasoning, tempting, resisting, the showing of the glory of kingdoms, was not mere imagination, but truly historical. The agent of this activity was not an evil temper, sin, nor a man. Aside from the fact that all of the aforesaid neither are nor ever are called the devil, they obviously do not fit this context. The Lord Jesus was holy and therefore could neither tempt Himself nor imagine all these things in such a fashion that He would thus reason with His own imagination in order to prevail against that temptation. God also was not the author of that temptation, since He does not tempt man (James 1:13). The text, however, states expressly that it was the devil, or Satan. The devil, although he is a spirit, interacts with human and physical beings.

Fourthly, add to this all the histories — recorded in the gospels — of those possessed with devils. Those spirits are generally referred to as "devil," "spirit," "evil spirit," but never as "sickness," "sin," "madness," "imagination," or "temper." They are said to know Jesus, which was true for almost none but the disciples of Christ only, and their knowledge was but a glimmer. These devils were fearful of being tormented before their time, they prayed for permission to enter the swine — which they did after permission was granted — and killed them. They tore the bodies of those who were possessed, casting them about, all of which are known truths. The casting out of devils were miracles whereby Christ confirmed and manifested His mediatorial office. Paul was buffeted by a messenger of Satan (2 Cor. 12:7). Even though Satan has neither fists nor a body, he can make use of a body by divine permission. From all this it has been clearly proven that devils do exist, are present upon earth, and interact with human and physical beings.

Fifthly, the devils are still continually engaged against man, particularly the godly. This is evident from the exhortations to manfully resist the devils. "Put on the whole armour of God, that ye may be able to stand against the wiles of the devil" (Eph. 6:11); "Be sober, be vigilant; because your adversary the devil, as a roaring lion, walketh about, seeking whom he may devour" (1 Pet. 5:8).

The methods of Satan's assaults are manifold. They can, however, be reduced to three main headings.

(1) Sometimes his activity is focused upon man's five senses. He does so either by impeding their function while simultaneously stimulating the imagination — whereby a person is of the opinion to have truly seen those things — or his presence is audibly or visibly perceived due to a physical appearance.

(2) Sometimes he only stimulates the imagination, be it when man is either awake or is dreaming — during daylight or darkness.

(3) Sometimes he operates by speaking directly to the soul, which is all the more evident when he presents nonphysical matters and arguments to the soul.

The Practice of Fortunetelling and Witchcraft

Thus, we have observed that devils do exist, are operative in this world, and interact with human beings. When devils practice their evil by the agency of men who surrender themselves to the devil for this purpose or otherwise willingly allow themselves to be His tools, we refer to this as fortunetelling or witchcraft.

Fortunetelling is that practice whereby man, assisted by the devil, unveils current matters which are hidden from man but known to the devil, or foretells future matters which the devil can either deduce from the course of nature — concerning which he makes a guess — or which may have been made known to him by God.

Witchcraft is that practice whereby man through the agency of the devil performs strange things which are beyond the capacity of human ability. Such is the case when he causes deceased persons to appear, tormenting men in their bodies. Many texts in Holy Writ confirm that he is capable of such activity, and engages in this. "And the soul that turneth after such as have familiar spirits, and after wizards, to go a-whoring after them..." (Lev. 20:6); "A man also or a woman that hath a familiar spirit, or that is a wizard, shall surely be put to death" (Lev. 20:27); "Now the magicians of Egypt, they also did in like manner with their enchantments" (Exo. 7:11); "Thou shalt not suffer a witch to live" (Exo. 22:18). The witch of Endor caused the form of Samuel to appear and predicted Saul's death (1 Sam. 28:9-19). Likewise we read of Simon the sorcerer (Acts 8:9), and of Elymas the sorcerer (Acts 13:6-8). We do not wish to concern ourselves with the manner in which the devil accomplishes this, nor how men accomplish these evil deeds by the devil's agency. We know from God's Word that there are witches who have performed strange things, and it is sufficiently confirmed by experience, which is the teacher of fools. This suffices us, although we must admit that very many of such accounts belong entirely to the realm of fables and fabrications.

Exhortations Relative to the Doctrine of Devils

It is not sufficient merely to have knowledge of these things, but we have dealt comprehensively with all these matters for the express purpose that it might be to our benefit. The devil is a prince of darkness and generally wishes to remain unknown and concealed as this enables him to engage effectively in his evil designs. Those who assist him in concealing himself do him a considerable service. Therefore there is profit in this doctrine for unconverted and converted alike, as both are the objects of his activity.

First of all I wish to address myself to the unconverted, stating that as long as you remain unconverted, you are subject to the power of the devil, having the devil as your father. "Ye are of your father the devil, and the lusts of your father ye will do" (John 8:44). The devil is lord and master over you and he is at work in you. "The spirit that now worketh in the children of disobedience" (Eph. 2:2). You are his captive and in bondage to him. "And that they may recover themselves out of the snare of the devil, who are taken captive by him at his will" (2 Tim. 2:26). He frequently moves you to commit acts, the commission of which you would have never deemed possible. He thus moved Judas to betray the Lord Jesus and afterward to hang himself. The devil often keeps you out of church, especially when he knows that the sermon to be preached could be a choice means to your conversion. During the sermon he seeks to detract you by infusing other thoughts, holding such matters before you which he knows you delight in, thereby facilitating your meditation upon them. If you hear something that makes an impression upon you, he seeks in every possible way to rob you of this impression (Mat. 13:19). The devil prevents you from comprehending the power of the gospel. "But if our gospel be hid, it is hid to them that are lost: in whom the god of this world hath blinded the minds of them which believe not, lest the light of the glorious gospel of Christ, who is the image of God, should shine unto them" (2 Cor. 4:3-4). Do not think that this renders you innocent, for you yourself are also blind and of an evil disposition, willingly rejecting the gospel. The devil, however, often creates the occasion for this, stimulates you, and you then obey him.

Carefully meditate upon all this and apply it to yourself. Consider that you are a slave of the devil, that he is your lord and master, that he controls you, engages you to be active in his cause, and will soon drag you as his prey to hell to be eternally tormented there. What a dreadful condition to be subject to such an abominable tyrant — the archenemy of God, Christ, and also yourself — who in bitter hatred murders your soul and eternally separates you from God and His blessed Christ! Therefore have mercy upon your own soul, wake up, hate the devil and his work, flee from him, bid his kingdom farewell, and surrender yourself to the sweet, easy, and lovely government of the Lord Jesus Christ — a government which will culminate in eternal salvation. Oh, that you would hear me! May the Lord save you.

In accordance with God's declaration, "And I will put enmity between thee and the woman, and between thy seed and her seed" (Gen. 3:15), there is a special hatred between the devil and believers, the members of the Lord Jesus Christ. The hatred from the side of the devil is as bitter and evil as possible. It is only a lack of power which hinders him from executing his evil intent, as God continually prevents him from executing his premeditated intentions. How I wish that I could be instrumental in causing the hatred of believers towards the devil to be more lively and intense, that they may be more careful against being beguiled by his subtle temptations or cooperating with him in other ways! That all of this would motivate believers with bitter hatred for, and antipathy against, the wicked enemy of our Lord Jesus, to be courageous and to do battle against his assaults. "Whom (the devil, vs. 8) resist steadfast in the faith" (1 Pet. 5:9).

Anthropology:
The Doctrine of Man

CHAPTER TEN

Concerning Man, Particularly the Soul

Having discussed the most eminent creatures of heaven, the angels, we will now proceed to consider the most eminent creature upon earth, *man*. In the original language, the Hebrew tongue, man is called אדם (*Adam*), which is derived from a word which means "to be red," man being of a reddish color when he is healthy and most elegant in appearance. "They were more ruddy in body than rubies" (Lam. 4:7). The word אדמה (*Adamah*, red earth) is derived from this. In Greek man is called ἄνθρωπος (*Anthropos*, of an erect posture). After the fall man is also called אנוש (*Enos*, wretched one).

After the Lord had created everything and had adorned the world in a most elegant manner, He said, "Let us make man" (Gen. 1:26). Such a statement not being made at the creation of other things, we can deduce that the glory of man excels that of all other creatures. God did not address Himself to angels for they cannot be considered as being of equal stature with God. They were not "cocreators," as the act of creation is unique to God only; man was also not created in the image of angels. This statement, made in the manner of men, is expressive of the deliberations of a triune God concerning the creation of something significant. Thus, upon the sixth day God created the final creature, man. He gave him no other name but "man," as there was but one such creature which in and of itself was sufficiently distinct from all other creatures. God created all angels simultaneously; there is no procreation among them. He created but one man, however, and has filled the earth with men by way of procreation. "And did not He make one? Yet had he the residue of the Spirit. And wherefore one? That He might seek a godly seed" (Mal. 2:15).

Man consists of two essential elements, *body and soul.* God formed the body out of the *earth.* "And the LORD God formed man of the dust of the ground" (Gen. 2:7). It has not been recorded whether man was created in or outside of Paradise, and thus we cannot state anything concerning this. This, however, is recorded, "And the LORD God took the man, and put him into the garden of Eden to dress it and to keep it" (Gen. 2:15). When someone is appointed to a specific task in a specific location, it is not implied that he previously was external to this locality. It does say, "Therefore the LORD God sent him forth from the Garden of Eden, to till the ground from whence he was taken" (Gen. 3:23). The earth within and outside of Paradise, however, is one and the same. His task was, with sorrow and in the sweat of his face to cultivate the earth from which he was formed and which now had been cursed by God, in order to support his life from it.

After Adam had been created, had been prohibited from eating from the tree of the knowledge of good and of evil, and God brought all the animals and fowl to him to be named, Adam observed that they all came in pairs. Adam perceived that he was alone and without a helpmeet. "And the LORD God caused a deep sleep to fall upon Adam, and he slept: and He took one of his ribs, and closed up the flesh instead thereof; and the rib, which the LORD God had taken from man, made He a woman, and brought her unto the man. And Adam said, This is now bone of my bones, and flesh of my flesh: she shall be called Woman, because she was taken out of Man" (Gen. 2:21-23). Adam was thoroughly acquainted with the nature of the animals and thus gave every animal a name consistent with its nature. How Adam knew that Eve had been taken from his rib — whether he inferred this from Eve's nature, or whether he became aware of having one less rib than before, or whether God made this known to him — is unknown. Thus, the first marriage became a reality. This was not a type of the spiritual marriage between Christ and His congregation, for Adam neither possessed nor knew Christ, nor was an example available to him. The apostle Paul, however, refers to the first marriage for application purposes and in order to explain spiritual marriage (Eph. 5:29).

Together with Adam, the woman was created on the sixth day, for concerning man's creation on the sixth day it is stated, "Male and female created He them" (Gen. 1:27). "And on the seventh day God ended His work which He had made; and He rested on the seventh day from all His work which He had made" (Gen. 2:2). Subsequent to this day God did not create any new creatures. The narration that follows the seventh day is only a clearer description of what God had created previously; this was but touched upon with a few words.

The Body of Man

God constructed the *body of man* both wondrously and in an artful manner with an elaborate system of bones, arteries, nerve cells, and various other parts, all of which proportionally and efficiently contribute to whatever is required for the well-being and functioning of the entire body. He then covered it with a smooth skin, so that the external appearance greatly exceeds all other physical creatures in elegance. Thus, man can justly be referred to as a small world. The Lord has equipped man with *five senses*: vision, hearing, smell, taste, and touch. By means of these senses all that pertains to the body is communicated to the soul's intelligence, enabling the soul to exert external influence on matters related to the body, thus becoming cognizant of these things. Some matters can only be perceived with one of the senses, some by several, and some by all five. If one of the five senses does not function well internally, or if the intermediate space or distance is not proportionate, one could easily judge a matter incorrectly if he were not to research the matter more thoroughly. A square tower when viewed at a distance appears to be round, as our vision is not capable of distinguishing distant features. A straight stick of which the end is in the water appears to be crooked or broken. The color white appears to be yellow or greenish when light shines through colored glass; however, after carefully investigating everything, a correct understanding is attainable. When by means of the proper functioning of various senses, and being within reasonable proximity to the object, there is unanimous agreement among all, a definite conclusion can be drawn. Thus, from the experiential use of our senses we know that two times two equals four; one object is straight and the other crooked; one long and the other short; one hard and the other soft; one white and the other black; one heavy and the other light; and one hot and the other cold. On this basis men have been able to deduce several principles and fundamental rules, the contradiction of which would be ludicrous. So much about the body.

The Soul of Man

The other constituent element of man is the *soul,* also referred to as his *spirit.* In Hebrew it is called נפש (*Nephesh*), and in Greek πνεῦμα (*Pneuma*).

Both words are derivatives of "to breathe," either because it was created by a symbolic act of breathing, is the cause of nasal breathing, or due to its invisibility and mobility.

The soul is a spiritual, incorporeal, invisible, intangible, and immortal personal entity adorned with intellect and will. In union with the body it constitutes a human being and by virtue of its inherent propensity is inclined to be and remain united with the body.

The soul is a *personal entity*. This is evident, first because it possesses both intellect and will, by which it actively loves, hates, rejoices, and mourns. "My soul is exceeding sorrowful" (Mat. 26:38); "My soul doth magnify the Lord, and my spirit hath rejoiced in God my Saviour" (Luke 1:46-47). Secondly, since the soul is separated from the body, it continues both in its essence and existence, and will either rejoice in heaven or be grieved in hell.

It is therefore a self-contradicting heresy to maintain that the soul is a thought, thus denying the existence of the soul.

(1) If the soul is a thought, thinking being an activity, there must necessarily be a personal entity from which this thought proceeds. If it be maintained that the soul is an essential and independent thought, we have a contradiction, as much as if we were to call that which is black white. An activity and a personal entity are *toto genere*, that is, too distinctly different from each other, for whatever is an activity is not a personal entity, nor is the contrary true.

(2) Since man repeatedly thinks of new things and generates new thoughts, he would then repeatedly have a new soul, which is absurdity itself.

(3) This is also not consistent with the Word of God which never refers to the soul as a thought.

It is also incorrect to state that the soul is a rational essence.

(1) Reasoning is not the essence of the soul, for an activity cannot be the essence of a personal entity, since the former is a consequence of the latter.

(2) The soul is not always engaged in thinking, as is the case during a coma or when it first unites itself to the body prior to the birth of man. What would the unborn fetus be thinking about? And if it were capable of thinking, man would commit actual sin prior to his birth, whereas Paul states, "For the children being not yet born, neither having done any good or evil..." (Rom. 9:11). Instead, the soul is a personal entity which is capable and inclined to think.

Each human being has but *one soul*. There are three types of souls. There is *anima vegetativa*, which we wish to refer to as the *soul of growth*, whereby trees and herbs are said to exist. There is *anima sensitiva*, or the *soul of sensitivity*, whereby animals exist and are sensitive to their environment. This, according to Scripture, is to be found in the blood of animals. "For the life of the flesh is in the blood" (Lev. 17:11); "For the blood is the life" (Deu. 12:23). There is *anima rationalis*, or the *rational soul*, which we have just described and referred to as *rational* since by its agency man reasons and makes decisions. Man grows, moves consciously from one locality to another, and reasons — not by virtue of a different soul for each activity, but due to the singular activity of the reasonable soul within man. Thus, man has neither three, nor two, but one soul. This is first of all confirmed by the Word of God which, in giving a detailed description of the constituent elements of man, states nowhere that man has two or three souls. This concept must therefore be rejected.

Secondly, Scripture makes mention of only one human soul, such reference always being in the singular as is also true of the body. "...And man became a living soul" (Gen. 2:7); "Or what shall a man give in exchange for his soul?" (Mat. 16:26); "...which is able to destroy both soul and body in hell" (Mat. 10:28); "...glorify God in your body, and in your spirit..." (1 Cor. 6:20). Man is only alive when the soul resides within the body. "Trouble not yourselves; for his life is in him" (Acts 20:10).[1] When the soul is absent from the body, man is dead. "For as the body without the spirit is dead..." (James 2:26).

Thirdly, every animal exists independently by virtue of his soul and is thus an independent being. If man were also to have a sensitive soul apart from a rational soul, either the sensitive or the rational soul would constitute the personal entity, or, man would consist of two or three personal entities. The sensitive soul is not the constituent element of man's personhood, for man would then be animal-like. These two souls do not constitute a human being, for then man would not be one but two persons. Since man is but one person, he consequently has but one soul.

Fourthly, if man were to possess two or three souls, this would likewise be true for Christ, "wherefore in all things it behoved Him to be made like unto His brethren" (Heb. 2:17). Christ would thus not only have assumed the human nature, but also the nature of trees and animals, which is most absurd. While dead, Christ in His divine nature would then have been separated from the nature He assumed, while maintaining the singularity of His personhood, since these two souls are fully annihilated in death.

Fifthly, if man had two or three souls, there would be no

---

[1] The Statenvertaling reads, "... want zijne ziel is in hem," that is, "... for his soul is in him."

resurrection of this body from the dead, for the two souls are fully annihilated in death. Whatever has been fully annihilated cannot be restored *eodem numero*, that is, in its original form. Thus, in addition to the rational soul, a new soul would have to be created, which would then be glorified or damned without prior existence or commission of a deed.

Sixthly, if man were in possession of an animalistic soul, man would be able to live without a rational soul. This is contrary to the Bible which, as we have just demonstrated, teaches that man is dead when the rational soul is absent. If man were able to live in such a condition, one would not know if children possess a rational soul or whether they would subsequently receive one. On what basis would one then be able to baptize them? One would not know whether man, giving evidence of being alive, possesses a rational soul at that time, and thus be a rational creature. The soul could be absent and away from home on a journey to the East Indies, for according to the sentiment of some, the soul is present wherever it thinks itself to be. Behold, this error is replete with absurdities and essentially is a denial of the existence of the soul.

God created this singular soul of man out of nothing and in the process of procreation, each time anew, creates a soul within the body. The fact that God brought forth the soul of Adam out of nothing rather than from some dust is confirmed in Genesis 2:7. When God formed the body of man from the dust of the earth, it was lifeless. God, however, "breathed into his nostrils the breath of life; and man became a living soul." This breathing into the nostrils does not indicate that the creation of the soul occurred externally to the body and subsequently was brought into the body, but rather conveys both the manner and the symbolism of its creation. Likewise, we read in John 20:22, "And when He had said this, he breathed on them, and saith unto them, Receive ye the Holy Ghost." It expresses the wind-like mobility of the soul, its invisibility, its spirituality, as well as the energy of the soul which enables man to breathe through his nostrils. "The Spirit of God hath made me, and the breath of the Almighty hath given me life" (Job 33:4). Thus, the soul of the first man was created in his body out of nothing.

Question: How are the souls of men brought forth? Does this occur by seminal procreation or by transmission and ignition as one candle transmits light to another candle? Or does God create the soul whenever man by procreation comes into existence?

Answer: First, the soul is a spiritual entity, and thus is not physical in any sense. Therefore the soul cannot be brought forth by means of corporal and seminal procreation, for that which is causal cannot bring forth something which is *toto genere*, that is, of a nobler generation than the cause itself. If one maintains that the soul does not proceed from the body, but from the soul, I would ask, "Is it from the soul of the father, the mother, or from both?" It neither proceeds from both, for there is no mixture of souls, nor does it proceed from one of the two, for then the question remains, "Does it proceed from the father or the mother?" This question one will not be able to answer. In what manner would it be transmitted from the soul of the parents? If the personal soul of one of the parents would be transmitted in its entirety, the parent would be without a soul. If the transmission were partial, the soul would be divisible, and having parts it would not be a spirit but a body. If one maintains that the soul is brought forth *causaliter*, that is, as the effecting cause, by the souls of the parents, the question must be asked, "Out of what?" It is neither produced seminally nor by the complete or partial transmission of the soul. It would then of necessity be brought forth out of nothing, which is not possible for that is a creative act which is the proper work of God alone. The comparison of a burning candle igniting another candle and thus transmitting its flame is not applicable here, as fire is material in nature. Thus, one candle transmits its flame to the other by way of molecular transmission, since it finds matter to feed upon.

Secondly, Scripture states clearly that God creates a new soul each time within the fruit of the womb. "Then shall the dust return to the earth as it was: and the spirit shall return unto God who gave it" (Eccl. 12:7). Thus, we have two matters under consideration, the body and the soul, and the destiny of both — the one to the earth and the other to God. This agrees with their origin — from the earth and from God. As the body originates from the earth, the soul has its origin in God. "The burden of the Word of the LORD for Israel, saith the LORD, which stretcheth forth the heavens, and layeth the foundations of the earth, and formeth the spirit of man within him" (Zec. 12:1). As God brought forth heaven and earth by His omnipotence and without any secondary cause, He has also formed the soul within the inner recesses of man, that is without intervention of secondary causes in this formative act. Consider also Hebrews 12:9 where God is called the "Father of spirits," in contrast to "fathers of our flesh" (cf. Isa. 63:16; 1 Pet. 4:19).

Thirdly, the soul, subsequent to the death of man, exists independently, and is therefore also independent from the body at the very beginning. The soul is immortal and cannot be killed. "And fear not them which kill the body, but are not able to kill the soul" (Mat. 10:28). If the soul had its origin in man, it could be killed by man as is true for the body, for the effecting cause can destroy its creation, but man is not able to destroy the soul and thus he is not the effecting cause of the soul.

Objection #1: If only the body of man would be generated and not the soul, man would not bring forth another man, since man consists of body and soul.

Answer: This generation does not consist in bringing forth either matter or form. Neither matter nor body are brought forth since man does not create that which previously had been created by God, nor is the form or soul brought forth as has been demonstrated in the first proof. Rather, this generation is an act of those who generate, and through this act substance and form are brought together; in this way the entire composition is brought forth. Thus, the generation of man is the result of human activity which results in the union of soul and body, and the fruit of the womb thus receives and is brought forth with its inherent nature, its humanity. Consequently, a man brings forth a man, although he brings forth neither the substance of the body nor the soul. Observe this for instance in the birth of the Lord Jesus, the God-man, who was born out of Mary.

Objection #2: "All the souls that came with Jacob into Egypt, which came out of his loins..." (Gen. 46:26). Here it is stated expressly that the souls of Jacob's descendants had their origin in him.

Answer: It is a common, metaphorical manner of speech, in Scripture as well as in daily conversation, to refer to persons as "souls." The entire matter is named after one of its constituent parts. One also says, "so many heads," thereby referring to so many people. These persons came forth out of Jacob by generation. The union of their soul and body and their existence issued forth from him, be it immediately as with his own sons, or mediately as with his grandchildren.

Objection # 3. God fully completed the work of creation in the first six days (Gen. 2:2). Consequently, God does not create the soul on a daily basis.

Answer: During the first six days God created every species, subsequent to which He no longer creates new species. Rather, He maintains His creation either by special continuation, as with the angels, or by continuing the species, as He does with the human race which maintains its stability by generation. Thus, God daily creates the souls of men which are *individua,* that is, unique personal entities within the same human species.

Man's Intellect

This unique spiritual entity, having been created by God out of nothing, is gifted with *intellect*. This *intellect* consists of *comprehension, judgment,* and *conscience* or *joint knowledge*.

The very essence of *comprehension* is perception of a matter without giving verbal expression to it. It relates to that which can be deduced with one's intellect and thus could be considered as only intellectual. Man, however, when actually understanding a matter, verbalizes it even though he is not conscious of how his intellect judges and responds to it.

Comprehension is like a mirror which reflects matters under consideration. A mirror does not reflect anything unless something is placed before it. Even if something is placed before it, it will not reflect anything in complete darkness; something will only be faintly visible if there is but a small light source, or if the mirror is covered with condensation. This will prevent one from determining whether something is crooked, upside down, or of a different shape or color. All of this depends on the condition of the glass or the manner in which it was ground. This is likewise the case with the intellect of corrupt man. Many matters which it should comprehend, it does not comprehend at all. Others are but faintly and confusedly observed, so that the intellect cannot perceive what is at hand. Many matters are perceived erroneously as to form and appearance.

It is obviously erroneous to state that *the intellect of man, being in the state of sin, cannot err*. This is directly contrary to Scripture, where we read expressly that man is *blind* (Rev. 3:17), "having the understanding darkened" (Eph. 4:18), and that spiritual matters are hid from the wise and the prudent (Mat. 11:25). It also states that one can have a zeal, "but not according to knowledge" (Rom. 10:2), that "the natural man receiveth not the things of the Spirit of God: for they are foolishness unto him" (1 Cor. 2:14), and that there are "men of corrupt minds" (1 Tim. 6:5).

This proves that *the ability to comprehend clearly and discerningly cannot be regulative as far as the truth is concerned*. The ability to comprehend clearly and in a discerning manner, that is, to have appropriate and fitting thoughts agreeable to the matter at hand, is certainly a reality. Simply because one is able to understand clearly and discerningly, however, does not mean that what is comprehended is truth, even though the truth is inherent in the subject under consideration. Often we cannot know whether the matter has been comprehended clearly and discerningly, since we have frequently been deceived when we were of the opinion to have comprehended clearly and discerningly. Since our darkened understanding can imagine a small glimmer of light to be as the noonday sun, a person who makes the ability to comprehend clearly and discerningly regulative for truth must remain a *doubter* all his life. He will not acknowledge the phenomena of the tides, the existence of the soul, and many other matters, as he is not able to understand them. Yes, if one wishes to judge the matters revealed in God's Word on the basis of one's ability to comprehend clearly and discerningly and to accept only as truth that which can be comprehended, such a person must be called an atheist. His darkened intellect will never acknowledge the perfection of God, the Holy Trinity, God's influence in the preservation and governing of all things, the hypostatic union of the two natures of Christ, the Holy Spirit's operation in regeneration, nor many other matters. If we have knowledge of what God has revealed in His Word, however, then we must believe it to be true and act accordingly. It must be an infallible truth, for else all faith and religion is rendered ineffectual (cf. chapter 2).

Judgment is also a constituent element of the intellect whereby one evaluates a matter to be either true or false, good or evil. This *judgment* is either a *cognitive judgment* whereby in a general sense one acknowledges a matter to be such and such without any further response — the matter not being pertinent to us; or it is a *judgment of relevancy* which does not merely indicate what is true or false, and what is good or evil, but rather what currently must or must not be our course of action under the circumstances, supplementing this with motives to persuade and stimulate the will.

To make judgment a constituent element of the will is contrary to the concept of judgment itself.

(1) Let me express myself in harmony with those who hold to such an opinion. If the ability to comprehend clearly and discerningly is regulative for the establishment of truth, and if such comprehension is a constituent element of the intellect, then judgment is most certainly also a constituent element of the intellect. For the ability to comprehend clearly and discerningly gives some indication of the matter — whether it is true or false, good or evil. Without this comprehension there cannot be a clear and discerning understanding concerning a matter, nor can it be regulative for the truth. To state a matter to be such and such, however, is to make a judgment concerning this matter. Thus, judgment is a constituent element of the intellect.

(2) Judgment very frequently opposes the will by conveying to the conscience, "This is sin; God sees it; God shall punish it," and thus causes the will to be restless and anxious. Man frequently wishes that such an impression were not so lively; however, in spite

of all opposition, judgment frequently continues to make its presence felt, and thus is not a constituent element of the will.

(3) Scripture also establishes judgment as a constituent element of the intellect. "I speak as to wise men; judge ye what I say" (1 Cor. 10:15).

(4) If judgment were a constituent element of the will, man would then determine a sin not to be sin. This would be to the liking of the sinner, and his deeds would then be harmonious with his judgment since it would coincide with his will. It is true that a man will not render judgment in a matter unless he wishes to do so. This does not imply, however, that judgment itself is a constituent element of the will. Man similarly does not engage his intellect unless he is desirous to understand. One would thus, by the same token, be able to say that the intellect is a constituent element of the will. The latter is absurd, however, and therefore also the former.

Man's Conscience

The *conscience* is also a constituent element of the intellect, for the term itself implies this, knowledge being a constituent element of the intellect. "Conscience" translated into the Dutch language (mede-wetenschap) means "knowledge of concurrence." *The conscience is man's judgment concerning himself and his deeds, to the extent he is subject to God's judgment.* The conscience consists in three elements: *knowledge, witness, and acknowledgement.*

First, there is *knowledge* of the will of God, commanding or forbidding every man with promises and threats. This is not only true in a general but also in a specific sense, and not only in reference to a given matter, but also relative to the circumstances of here and now. Thus, the conscience prescribes what must either be refrained from or be done. The more clearly and powerfully it does this, the better the conscience functions.

Secondly, there is the element of *witness.* After man's obligation is held before him, it determines whether or not he has acted according to light and knowledge. The more painstakingly the conscience takes note of man's deeds and his conformity to the commandment held before him, the more it keeps a precise record thereof, and the more clearly and powerfully it witnesses to man, the better it performs its duty.

Thirdly, there follows an *acknowledgement* that the righteous God is also cognizant of this and will reward or judge him accordingly. The more clearly the conscience acknowledges the knowledge of God and is sensitive to it, and the more it either reassures itself concerning this or is powerfully affected as a result, the more faithfully the conscience performs its task. These three activities the apostle places side by side. "...the Gentiles, which have not the law...are a law unto themselves: which shew the work of the law written in their hearts" (Rom. 2:14-15). The first activity is expressed by the fact that they have *knowledge* of God's will and law. The second activity — the *witness* to their conformity or lack of conformity to the law — is described by the apostle when he states, "their conscience also bearing witness." This is followed by the third activity: the *acknowledgement* that God is cognizant thereof and shall either reward or punish, "...their thoughts the mean while accusing or else excusing one another" (Rom. 2:15). These activities of the conscience can also be observed in the following texts. "My conscience also bearing me witness in the Holy Ghost" (Rom. 9:1); "For oftentimes also thine own heart knoweth that thou thyself likewise hast cursed others" (Eccl. 7:22); "For if our heart condemn us...if our heart condemn us not..." (1 John 3:20-21).

The conscience is either *good or evil*. It is good when it performs its duty well.

(1) This is true when it clearly and immediately reveals and represents the will of God, obligating and stirring us up to do the will of God. "Let every man be fully persuaded in his own mind" (Rom. 14:5).

(2) It is true when it carefully keeps record of our deeds, and clearly and powerfully convicts us in reference to these deeds.

(3) This is also true when it either troubles or reassures us. Both of these aspects are exemplified in the following texts. "And it came to pass afterward, that David's heart smote him, because he had cut off Saul's skirt" (1 Sam. 24:5); "For our rejoicing is this, the testimony of our conscience" (2 Cor. 1:12). Someone is said to have an evil conscience whenever the commission of abominable deeds fills one with anxiety, fear, and remorse. This is not to say that the conscience is evil, as it is performing its duty well, but it is called evil because it convicts of evil deeds. If the conscience does not perform these three tasks well, it is evil in and of itself, being remiss in its duty either in all three or in one or two of these activities.

Question: Can the conscience be in error?

Answer: We must presuppose the following:

(1) In this discussion we do not consider man in his perfect state before the fall, but in his imperfect state after the fall.

(2) Our discussion neither relates to adherence to nor to any reflection upon such knowledge whereby one is cognizant of his objective and activity, and is thus conscious of these deeds.

(3) Neither are we discussing here whether or not man responds to the witness of his conscience.

(4) Nor do we maintain that the second and third acts of the conscience are the first to err.

We do maintain, however, that the conscience in its first act — which relates to man's knowledge of the law and will of God — is capable of error. It is capable of presenting something as the will of God which is not the will of God — yes, is even forbidden. This is the first error and when it prevails, it is followed by the second act of conscience, that is, its witnessing act. The error is not precipitated by the conscience bearing witness or man responding to this witness. The error is rather in having witnessed that man has done well, whereas in reality he has done evil, even though according to his knowledge he has done well. Someone can bear false witness before the court without speaking contrary to his conviction by testifying that a certain person has committed a given deed, being in error as far as that person is concerned. The person he mentions is not guilty, but rather someone else. He expresses his opinion, his conscience testifying that his witness is correct, and thus it is satisfied. He is mistaken, however, and his witness is erroneous even though his conscience bears him witness that in this erroneous matter he has been both correct and good. Thus his conscience is in error, acquitting him even though he should have been condemned. The conscience can similarly bear witness that a person has acted correctly in various matters when in reality he has sinned most grievously. When the conscience errs in its first act as to its knowledge of the will of God, it must err in the other two acts as well.

God's Word also confirms irrefutably that the conscience can err, as is confirmed in the following and many other passages. "Howbeit there is not in every man that knowledge: for some with conscience of the idol unto this hour eat it as a thing offered unto an idol; and their conscience being weak is defiled. For if any man see thee which hast knowledge sit at meat in the idol's temple, shall not the conscience of him which is weak be emboldened to eat those things which are offered to idols?" (1 Cor. 8:7, 10). Here the apostle does not speak of an opinion, nor of a lust, but of the conscience, making reference to it several times. He states that the conscience is in error, for he calls it a "conscience of the idol." This leads one to believe that an idol is important and needs to be honored. Is this not a very serious error? The conscience can be "emboldened" in its error in order to persevere in the sin of idolatry with all the more freedom. Add to this that which is stated in John 16:2: "Whosoever killeth you will think that he doeth God service," and in Acts 26:9, "I verily thought with myself, that I ought to do many things contrary to the name of Jesus of Naz-areth." The word "conscience" is not mentioned here, but the reference is to the activity of the conscience. Whenever a matter is described, the name need not be mentioned. It was a serious and heinous sin to murder the godly and to be in battle against Jesus. This sin did not proceed from an evil principle, but from error; that is, from an erroneous understanding of God's will. This erroneous understanding motivated them to be faithful to this perceived illumination, and thus to perform the task before them. Having finished this task, their conscience bore witness that they had acted correctly, giving them peace and delight in this work. In reality, however, they had engaged in an abominable evil, and the conscience should have convicted them that they had done evil; it should have brought forth contrition and terror within them. We can thus observe that the conscience can err. Someone may object by stating that it is more correct to maintain that one errs in his views. My response is that an erroneous view is equivalent to an erroneous intellect and judgment whereby a certain course of action is suggested to be the will of God, which, however, is not the will of God. When acting accordingly, it then satisfies man that he has acted correctly. All of this is identical to the conscience being in error. One should therefore hold to common language usage, for strange expressions generally conceal strange sentiments. If there is essential agreement in this matter, all of this would at best be a matter of semantics.

The Will of Man

The soul of man is also gifted with a *will, which is a faculty by which we can either love or hate*. This faculty is called a blind faculty. This does not imply that man ignorantly loves or hates, but rather that it is the intellect, not the will, which judges in a given matter. It is the intellect which presents a matter to the will as being either desirable or contemptible, prescribing the course of action to be taken under the current circumstances. The will embraces this practical judgment blindly and acts accordingly. If one judges erroneously, the will functions erroneously as well. At times the intellect suggests something to the will which is enjoyable and advantageous but not according to truth. The will then embraces it as such, even though it is contrary to God's law.

The will is free and cannot be compelled. This freedom is not *arbitrary* in nature; that is, one cannot simultaneously will or not will to do something. The holy angels are free in the exercise of their will, and yet they cannot but do the will of God. Rather, this freedom is one of *necessary consequence* whereby one is motivated and inclined to either embrace or reject something. Even the will of a child cannot be compelled to function in a certain manner. As long as a child does not want to go to school, he will not go there, no matter what one may try. Although he may not go when considering his situation independently, circumstances, promises, or threats can, however, bring about a change of will, thus causing the child to go because he is now willing.

The Immortality of the Soul

The soul of man is *immortal*. God could have annihilated it if He had so desired. He has, however, established an eternal ordinance that He shall not do so. The soul can neither be destroyed by any creature nor can it self-destruct by virtue of some internal principle, for the soul is a spirit and thus of eternal existence. There is an indelible impression in man that such is the case. God Himself in His Word expressly and irrefutably states this to be so in regard to the souls of both the godly and the ungodly. This is confirmed in a general sense in the following passages: "Then shall the dust return to the earth as it was: and the spirit shall return unto God who gave it" (Eccl. 12:7); "And fear not them which kill the body, but are not able to kill the soul" (Mat. 10:28); "I am the God of Abraham, and the God of Isaac, and the God of Jacob. God is not the God of the dead, but of the living" (Mat. 22:32); "And I give unto them eternal life" (John 10:28); "...having a desire to depart, and to be with Christ..." (Phil. 1:23); "...the souls of them that were slain...cried with a loud voice..." (Rev. 6:9-10). Such is also stated concerning the souls of the ungodly. "And these shall go away into everlasting punishment" (Mat. 25:46); "By which also He went and preached unto the spirits in prison" (1 Pet. 3:19); "And in hell he lift up his eyes, being in torments" (Luke 16:23). We thus conclude that the soul is immortal.

The Intimate Union Between Body and Soul

God neither creates the soul outside the body nor does He first cause it to exist independently. As the soul is created within the body, it is united to the body with an incomprehensible but essential union so that together they form a *suppositium,* that is, a person or a human being. They are not united in their manner of existence, as angels were temporarily united to bodies. Be careful not to deem the soul to be an angel when considering it independently, for such is not the case. Be careful not to view this union as a matter of indifference, it being immaterial whether or not it is united with the body, or as if it would be better or preferable if it existed independently. Also be careful not to view the union between soul and body as a marriage. All such propositions contain within them dangerous consequences and errors. Be careful not to view the body as an instrument or tool of the soul, for one essential element cannot be the instrument of the other. This union is much more intimate than can be comprehended. Together soul and body constitute a human being. It is natural to the soul to be united with the body, and contrary to her nature to be separated from the body through death. It does exist and experience joy or sorrow; however, it is not in a *complete, fulfilled condition*. In separation from the body, the soul is referred to as an *incomplete* personal entity. This does not imply that there is imperfection in the soul itself, but rather that it is a constituent element of the whole man. Neither does it cease to have the nature of a constituent element, and thus it continues to be inclined to be united with its body.

The soul being so intimately united with the body, is and remains in the body as long as man lives. *It is not where it imagines itself to be*. This is proved by the following:

First, the body, at that moment and thus most of the time, would then be without the soul, and consequently would be dead. Both nature and Scripture teach that man dies when the soul departs, as we have proven before.

Secondly, experience teaches that when the soul is elsewhere mentally, the body is moved and affected by whatever occurs there, or by whatever the soul imagines to see and hear there. This results in change of blood pressure, heart palpitations, tears, laughter, etc. If the soul at that time were to be hundreds of miles away from the body, why would there be such emotions? Can the soul operate *in distantia,* that is, from a distance? It is thus certain that the soul is not in the place where it imagines itself to be.

Thirdly, if someone wishes to maintain that the soul is there where it thinks itself to be, such a person would refute himself by his displeasure which he would manifest if one were to state that he was without a soul. Distant places and matters are represented by the imagination, and the soul thus thinks upon such matters.

I cannot state where the soul resides in the body. I do not know whether it encompasses the body in its entirety, or whether in its entirety it encompasses every part, or whether it resides in the heart, the brains, or in the pineal gland. As the union of soul and body is a mystery, so likewise is its location in the body. By limiting the soul to a specific location in the body, one must be careful neither to undo the intimate union between soul and body, nor should one, in an attempt to define it more expressly, be misled by not limiting the soul to a locality at all.

The Image of God

Man, consisting of a body prepared in such a skillful and elegant fashion, as well as with such a noble soul, was created in a state of perfection. All that God created was good. The goodness of every creature consisted in the measure of perfection required to function as such a creature. The goodness of man consists in the *image of God.* This term is sometimes used in reference to the Son, the second Person of the divine essence, who is "the brightness of His [the Father's] glory, and the express image of His Person" (Heb. 1:3); as well as "the image of the invisible God" (Col. 1:15).

In this case, however, we use this term in reference to the perfection of man, which consists in a faint resemblance to the communicable attributes of God. We use the word "resemblance," for God's attributes themselves cannot be communicated or transferred. Only their resemblance can be communicated. Scripture speaks of this when it states, "So God created man in His own image, in the image of God created He him" (Gen. 1:27). In vs. 26 the word "likeness" is added. "Let us make man in our image, after our likeness." These two words are synonymous and express as much as an image of great resemblance. The image of God does not consist in the perfection of the body, for God is a Spirit. It does not primarily consist in the exercise of dominion which was bestowed as a consequence of this image, but rather it exists in the soul.

In order to have a correct understanding of the image of God, three matters need to be considered separately: the basis for, the form, and the consequences of this image. The *basis,* or that which is prerequisite, is the spirituality and rationality of the soul. The *form* relates to the quality of its inherent powers. The *consequence* is the exercise of dominion. Let me illustrate. If a painter wishes to make a good picture, he must first have a proper and well-prepared canvas. He cannot paint a picture in water, in air, or in dry sand. He either needs a piece of wood, canvas, or some other solid material, which in turn must have been properly prepared. Having all these, he then must have a suitable model for that which he wishes to express.

The basis — or canvas — for this image is the spirituality, rationality, and immortality of the essence of man's soul, and more particularly the faculties of the soul such as intellect, will, and affections. The soul had to be of such a nature in order for the image of God to be impressed upon it. This does not constitute the form of the image of God, however, for man possessed these before as well as after the fall. Even the devils possess these at the present time. When God forbids man to murder, man having been created in God's image (Gen. 9:6), this refers to both what he did possess as well as the background which he still possesses, upon which the image of God at one time was impressed. God did not wish this background to be destroyed. The spirituality and the faculties of the soul belong to the image of God as a background belongs to a painting. The latter can still exist and remain, even though the image upon it has been so erased that any resemblance of the same can no longer be detected; nevertheless it can still be seen that something had been impressed upon it.

The essential *form*, the true essence of the image of God, consists in knowledge, righteousness, and holiness, they being the qualities that regulate the faculties of the soul: intellect, will, and affections.

(1) The intellect was pure and transparent, immediately beholding God in His essence and manner of existence in the Holy Trinity. This immediate beholding of God constitutes the felicity of angels and men. "As for me, I will behold Thy face in righteousness: I shall be satisfied, when I awake, with Thy likeness" (Psa. 17:15); "For now we see through a glass, darkly; but then face to face" (1 Cor. 13:12); "for we shall see Him as He is" (1 John 3:2). Although Adam's vision was not of the same degree as that vision glorified saints will enjoy in heaven — this having been held before and promised to him upon obedience — his knowledge of God was nevertheless perfect and sufficient to enable him to rejoice in God, greatly excelling that which we are currently able to imagine. Adam's possession of such illumination is evident from the fact that he was created after the image of God which consists in knowledge. "And have put on the new man, which is renewed in knowledge after the image of Him that created him" (Col. 3:10).

(2) Additionally, the will was holy and righteous, being satisfied and delighted with God. It was joyful and fervent in love, having no desires outside of God. It readily, joyfully, and perfectly performed the will of God, doing all things in purity, luster, and glory, both in an external and internal sense. This was the image of the holy God, as it is stated, "And that ye put on the new man, which after God is created in righteousness and true holiness" (Eph. 4:24).

(3) The affections were fully regulated, never preceding the exercise of the intellect and the will, but being an orderly consequence thereof. All desires were Godward, in order to continually enjoy Him, and toward the performance of His will.

(4) His memory was excellent and active. As he took note of

everything, he likewise remembered everything; and in reflecting thereupon by comparing the past with the present he could observe God's wisdom, goodness, and power, and magnify Him in response to this.

(5) All members of his body were instruments of righteousness by which this holiness could be manifested and translated into action. In one word, all that was to be found in Adam and which proceeded from him, was pure light, holiness, righteousness, and orderliness.

The *consequence* of the image of God is the exercise of *dominion* over the entire earth. "Let us make man in our image, after our likeness: and let him have dominion over the fish of the sea," etc. (Gen. 1:26). Man having been created in God's image, God said to man, "Have dominion" (Gen. 1:28). Adam exercised this dominion by giving a name to every animal (Gen. 2:20). God is awe-inspiring to all His creatures, and whatever conveys a ray of His divinity is awe-inspiring as well, which is evident when a holy angel appears to men. God vested Adam with the power to exercise dominion, while endowing the animal kingdom with the inclination to be in subjection. By virtue of sin man lost this authority. Nevertheless, God said to Noah, "And the fear of you and the dread of you shall be upon every beast of the earth,…into your hand are they delivered" (Gen. 9:2). David praised the Lord in reference to this. "Thou madest him to have dominion over the works of Thy hands; Thou hast put all things under his feet" (Psa. 8:6). The unconverted exercise dominion over some animals, and do so by force. God's children, however, have again received a right to all things, although the use of a part of this authority is not permitted them as yet.

Man possessed the image of God from the first moment of his existence and was not initially created *in puris naturalibus*, that is, *in a purely natural state* — without knowledge, righteousness, and holiness — having only body and soul (that is, intellect, will, inclinations, and memory), and lacking either good or evil in them.

(1) Scripture nowhere states this, and therefore this concept is to be rejected.

(2) Man was created after God's image. A painter who intends to paint the likeness of a man does not first create something void of any resemblance and then add form and resemblance subsequently. Rather, he seeks to express the image of this man in every stroke of the brush. God created man in like manner, creating him after His image, to which he gave expression in the act of creating.

(3) This is also confirmed by the fact that the creation of man was very good (Gen. 1:31). "Lo, this only have I found, that God

hath made man upright" (Eccl. 7:29). Without this image man would not have been good and upright, for he would have lacked the essence of his perfection and would not have been much better than a beast. Indeed, the absence of the image of God would have been tantamount to sin.

(4) Man was created to magnify God both as He is in Himself and in His works. He could not have attained to this purpose without that image, that is, without knowledge, righteousness, and holiness.

(5) What man attains in recreation, Adam must have been, and has been. Since man is recreated after God's image, Adam was therefore created in like fashion.

Although man was created with and in this image, it was not bestowed upon him above and beyond his nature — as if this would prevent disharmony from arising between the superior and inferior faculties of the soul such as intellect, will, and affections; or (so absurd is the argument) as if this would prevent the marriage between soul and body from not becoming a contentious marriage. It was, however, a natural element of man's nature. It did not belong to the essence of the soul, and was not one of the constituent elements of man, nor an essential property. Thus, when man lost the image of God, he did not lose his nature. As health naturally emanates from the well-being of soul and body, likewise the image of God was natural to man and belonged to his well-being. This is consequently referred to as original righteousness and is evident from the following:

(1) In the state of perfection, if Adam had affections which were contradictory to his intellect, he would not have been perfect, but would have been naturally opposed to the tenth commandment which forbids dissatisfaction and covetousness.

(2) From his very beginning man was very good and possessed the image of God. His original righteousness was thus one of his natural components.

(3) Conformity to the law of nature is not supernatural to man, but natural (Rom. 2:14-15). This is much more true of the perfect conformity to the law which was impressed upon the first man.

(4) Had man not sinned, whatever would have been transmitted by procreation, would have been natural to him. Since his original righteousness would have, however, been transmitted to his descendants, it was thus natural to him.

(5) Man, being deprived of the image of God, is now naturally depraved. "...and were by nature the children of wrath" (Eph. 2:3). Thus, this propensity emanating from original righteousness was natural to man in his perfect state.

Man's Residency in Paradise

Man, having been created in so holy and glorious a state, was placed in *Paradise* which was his residence. The word "paradise" does not occur in the Old Testament, with the exception of the Song of Solomon 4:12 [Dutch *Statenbijbel*]. It is generally referred to as *Eden,* which is a derivative of "delightful." This garden was created by God on the fourth day and was the most delightful area of the delightful earth. Its apparent location is inferred by men to have been east of the Mediterranean Sea. Its actual location and size are uncertain, however. I believe that it has been so totally destroyed, either by the flood or other means, that it is no longer recognizable, even if one were to be standing on the location itself. It was so fully enclosed and impenetrable that no man or beast was able to go in or out, except by a way upon which an angel had been placed to bar entrance for fallen man (Gen. 3:24). The delightful nature of this garden was such that the third heaven is called paradise by comparison (cf. Luke 23:43; 2 Cor. 12:4; Rev. 2:7).

In the midst of this Garden of Eden was the *tree of life,* which we do not consider to have belonged to a certain species, but was a tree singular in nature. "And out of the ground made the LORD God to grow every tree...the tree of life also in the midst of the garden" (Gen. 2:9). Thus, this tree was not to be found at other locations.

This tree did not typify the second Person of the Godhead, that is, the Son, for the following reasons:

(1) There is no evidence substantiating this anywhere.

(2) It is not congruent with the Godhead to be typified by a physical image, and then especially by a tree. God has forbidden to make any physical likeness of Himself, and has not done so Himself.

(3) It would not have been advantageous to man in his perfect state, since he knew God rightly.

(4) The Lord Jesus Christ, the Mediator of the covenant of grace, is called the tree of life (Rev. 2:7; 22:2). He is not called thus because He was typified by this tree, for Adam in the state of perfection neither had need of a Mediator nor had it been revealed to him that a Mediator would come. Although he was capable of believing everything which God would present to him as an object to be believed in, he nevertheless did not believe in Christ, who had not been revealed to him. If the tree had been a type of Christ, Adam, being in the covenant of grace, would have been permitted to eat from this tree, which, on the contrary, he was forbidden to do. Christ, however, is called the tree of life by way of application and by way of comparison due to the efficacy of his mediatorial office, by virtue of which He is the life of His

people and grants them eternal life. The tree of life was a type and *sacrament* of this for Adam.

This tree did not have inherent power to preserve man so that he would not die, for:

(1) Immortality did not originate from this tree.

(2) There is not a single word to substantiate this in Scripture.

(3) How would all the descendants of Adam — if he had remained in the state of perfection and if they would have populated the entire earth — have survived without this tree, there only being one located within Paradise? Would they then have died?

(4) All other trees had been given to him for food, and his body was created in such a perfect condition that it was not subject to any sicknesses and therefore had no need of medication. Thus, the tree was merely a sacrament of eternal life.

In Paradise there was also the *tree of the knowledge of good and evil,* which man was not permitted to touch nor to eat from. "But of the tree of the knowledge of good and evil, thou shalt not eat of it" (Gen. 2:17; cf. Gen. 3:3). As there was only one tree of life, so there was also but one tree of the knowledge of good and evil. It is not stated that this refers to the type of tree, but rather to the number. It is simply referred to as "the tree." The reason for this name can be deduced from the name itself.

(1) It was a probationary tree whereby God wished to try man whether he would persevere in doing good or whether he would fall into evil, as is found in 2 Chronicles 32:31, "... God left him, to try him, that He might know all that was in his heart."

(2) Man, in eating from this tree, would know how good he had it and in what a sinful and sad condition he had brought himself.

The Lord placed Adam and Eve in this garden *to dress it and keep it* (Gen. 2:15) so that the animals would not intrude and trample and feed upon the beautiful plants, elegant flowers, and aromatic herbs. He would also dress the garden by pruning the trees in order to make them fruitful, sow seed here, and plant something there. All these activities would neither be burdensome and tiresome, nor would he perform them in the sweat of his face, but would engage therein with pleasure and delight, for a perfect man was neither permitted nor desirous to be physically idle. The *Sabbath* was the exception, for then he was required to rest and refrain from labor according to the example which his Maker had given him and had commanded him to emulate.

Thus Adam had all things in perfection and to the delight of body and soul. If he had perfectly persevered during his probationary period, he would, without seeing any death whatsoever, have been translated into the third heaven, into eternal glory. We have already confirmed the immortality of the soul in this chapter. Although the body had been constructed from material elements, its condition was such that it was capable of being in essential union with the immortal soul, and capable of existing without ever being subject to sickness or death.

Had he not sinned, man would not have died, but would rather have ascended into heaven with body and soul.

First, this is evident from the promise of eternal felicity, the fulfillment of which was contingent upon rendered obedience. This subject we will discuss subsequent to this chapter. Man, however, upon having been obedient, would never have died, but according to God's truth would have lived eternally.

Secondly, this is evident from God's threatenings, "For in the day that thou eatest thereof thou shalt surely die" (Gen. 2:17). If man would have died regardless of what occurred, the threatening would not have been a threat. Since death was threatened upon the commission of sin, death entered for no other reason than sin, which is confirmed in Genesis 3:17-19. "Wherefore, as by one man sin entered into the world, and death by sin" (Rom. 5:12); "The wages of sin is death" (Rom. 6:23); "...and sin when it is finished, bringeth forth death" (James 1:15).

Man: Created to Enjoy Felicity Eternally

God thus created Adam — and in him human nature in all its dimensions, as well as all men as created in him — in such a glorious and immortal manner. He skillfully prepared his body for him and promised him eternal life. Where are they now who slander Reformed doctrine by stating that we maintain God to have created one man unto the enjoyment of felicity and another unto damnation? We insist that God created all men in Adam for the enjoyment of felicity, and that man himself is to be blamed for his damnation.

Here is reason to glorify and praise God for creating man with such excellent capabilities in body and soul. For He established man in a state of such holiness and glory, to the honor of His Maker, for the purpose of exalting and praising Him for all His works, as well as for the creation of man and the manner in which God endowed him with faculties. Here we perceive the abominable nature of sin, whereas man, being endowed with such excellent faculties and being united to His Creator with so many bonds of love, has departed from Him, and despised and rejected Him. He did so in order that the Creator would not be master over him, but that he might be his own lord and live according to his own will.

Here is reason to approve of the justice of God if He requites the sinner according to his ways and condemns him. Here the incomprehensible goodness and wisdom of God shines forth in that He reconciles such evil human beings — although not all of them — with Himself again through the Mediator Jesus Christ. He caused this Mediator to come forth from Adam as holy, having the same nature which had sinned, to bear the punishment of the sin of man's own nature and thus to fulfil all righteousness. Such human beings He again adopts as His children and takes to Himself in eternal bliss. To Him be given eternal praise and honor for this. Amen.

CHAPTER ELEVEN

The Providence of God

The Providence of God Defined

Having considered the creation of all things in general and the creation of angels and men in particular, we will now proceed to consider the *providence of God* concerning all His creatures. We understand this to be neither the singular foreknowledge of God nor the immutable decree of God concerning all that would transpire (see chapter 5), but rather the execution of that decree; that is, the immediate provision for, and dispensation of all things. This is to be observed in Genesis 22:8, "God will provide Himself a lamb for a burnt offering." Providence is also referred to as *ordinance* (Psa. 119:91), *God's way* (Psa. 77:13), *God's hand* (Acts 4:28), *God's upholding* (Heb. 1:3), *God's working* (Eph. 1:11), *God's government* (Psa. 93:1), and *God's care* (1 Pet. 5:7).

The Heidelberg Catechism clearly and devoutly describes providence as follows:

> The almighty and everywhere present power of God; whereby, as it were by His hand, He upholds and governs heaven, earth, and all creatures; so that herbs and grass, rain and drought, fruitful and barren years, meat and drink, health and sickness, riches and poverty, yea, and all things come, not by chance, but by His fatherly hand; that we may be patient in adversity; thankful in prosperity; and that in all things, which may hereafter befall us, we place our firm trust in our faithful God and Father, that nothing shall separate us from His love; since all creatures are so in His hand, that without His will they cannot so much as move.

Providence is a *divine power*. This is not merely due to providence being executed by the omnipotent One, but particularly in reference to the extrinsic execution of this power towards His creatures. It is therefore stated with emphasis, "And Jesus, immediately knowing in Himself that virtue had gone out of Him…" (Mark 5:30).

Providence is an *omnipotent power*. When perceiving the magnitude of the work of creation; the innumerable number of creatures; the unfathomable diversity of their natures and appearance; the existence and continuation of each created object according to its own essential nature; the movement of animate, rational, and inanimate creatures; the precise order of all things both as to movement and the manner in which one object initiates the motion and progression of another object — one must lose himself in amazement regarding the infinite power and wisdom of God by which all things are maintained and governed. By this power God irresistibly executes whatsoever He wills, and no one can prevent Him from doing so. "For the LORD of hosts hath purposed, and who shall disannul it? and His hand is stretched out, and who shall turn it back?" (Isa. 14:27); "My counsel shall stand, and I will do all My pleasure" (Isa. 46:10).

Providence is an *omnipresent power of God*. This is not merely true in reference to the omnipresent Being of God, but particularly in reference to His energizing power in all His creatures. This power of God does not merely manifest itself generally in all things. Neither does it merely affect the initial secondary causes, which in turn further initiate motion and activity in all other secondary causes. This power of God penetrates the existence of every creature, and thus, in an immediate sense and via all secondary causes, affects the ultimate outcome of all things. The power of God is therefore in all things and manifests itself in all that exists and moves. If we had clear perception, we would observe this power in everything.

That the providence of God pertains to everything is so clearly revealed in nature and in Scripture that whoever denies the providence of God is no better than an atheist, or at best, must be considered as blind as a mole.

First, consider the testimony of nature as expressed by Job. "But ask now the beasts, and they shall teach thee; and the fowls of the air, and they shall tell thee: or speak to the earth, and it shall teach thee: and the fishes of the sea shall declare unto thee. Who knoweth not in all these that the hand of the LORD hath wrought this?" (Job 12:7-9).

(1) Reflect upon whatever you encounter, viewing it from every perspective until you observe the omnipotent and omnipresent power of God in it. Every object testifies that its being and existence do not originate within itself; rather, it has been created by

God and is therefore neither capable of existing by itself nor of generating itself, as the same power is needful for both. If it were independent from God, it would not be subject to Him, but would exist and function on the same level as God.

(2) Observe the orderly arrangement of the universe, and how everything has its purpose and functions accordingly. Observe how one thing does not interfere with another, but cooperates with the function of the other. Consider the absence of confusion among creatures of various sorts and mobility. Notice how inanimate objects maintain their motion in such a precise and orderly fashion without either understanding this or its purpose. How precisely do sun, moon, and stars know their courses and the time to rise and to set. How precise is the time schedule of low and high tides. The birds know when to arrive and when to depart; every flower knows when it must sprout; every species remains consistent both in its being and in its manner of procreation, so that from the creation of the world until now not one is missing. "Lift up your eyes on high, and behold who hath created these things, that bringeth out their host by number: He calleth them all by names by the greatness of His might, for that He is strong in power; not one faileth" (Isa. 40:26).

(3) Consider the rise and fall of kingdoms, the outcome of wars, and unexpected occurrences which can have significant consequences. Consider also the prophecies and the manner in which they are fulfilled, the extraordinary plagues which come upon those who are particularly ungodly, the unexpected deliverances of the godly, the answers upon their prayers, and all the wondrous ways in which various matters come to pass in nature and in grace. Whoever will not observe God's hand in all these things must be entirely blind.

(4) Add to this the common sentiment and the acknowledgment of all men in whose heart, due to the innate knowledge of God, there is an impression of this. Even though by observation one person may acknowledge this more than another, and some labor to become atheists by attempting to deny everything, this awareness nevertheless remains in their heart and cannot be entirely erased.

We desire that whoever is as void of understanding as the animals of the field and cannot observe God's providence in all this, may come to his senses as Nebuchadnezzar did, and confess with him, "And all the inhabitants of the earth are reputed as nothing: and He doeth according to His will in the army of heaven, and among the inhabitants of the earth: and none can stay His hand, or say unto Him, What doest Thou?" (Dan. 4:35).

(5) Yes, whoever acknowledges the existence of God must also acknowledge His providence, for the one confirms the other.

Secondly, as the providence of God is evident from nature, so it is abundantly expressed in Holy Writ. No person who considers the Bible to be the Word of God has ever dared to deny this doctrine. Some, however, twist and distort the Scriptures to such an extent that they, while adhering to the same expressions, seek to divorce the matter itself from its content. As we proceed, this will be confirmed by many texts, of which we here only mention Ephesians 1:11, where it is stated, "...who worketh all things after the counsel of His own will."

Only one who is void of understanding would dare to suggest that his own government of the world would be more wise and better than is presently the case. He would not allow it to rain upon the sea, since there is sufficient water there. He would not tolerate the existence of so many mountains, rock formations, and barren territories. He would do well to those that are good, and bring evil upon the wicked. Poor man! With *Icarus* and *Phaeton* he would immediately plunge from his lofty position and turn everything up-side-down. God does nothing in vain; unsearchable wisdom may be discerned in every work of God, and every one of them has a wonderful and useful purpose. The angels observe this and magnify God for it. Those with an enlightened understanding observe all this perceptively, believe everything at once, and search it out afterwards. Everything is beyond the reach of a fool. "For the ways of the LORD are right, and the just shall walk in them: but the transgressors shall fall therein" (Hosea 14:9). Observe what sin causes in the world, and this will confirm it for you.

The acts of God's providence can be arranged under three headings: *preservation, cooperation, and government.*

The First Act of God's Providence: Preservation

Preservation is *defined as the immediate, energizing power of God whereby all creatures in general and every creature in particular is preserved in its being and existence.* God does not merely preserve living creatures by providing them with their prescribed food and drink. He also energizes them immediately by bestowing upon each creature the energy needed to preserve its existence, apart from which food would serve no purpose. "For in Him we live, and move, and have our being" (Acts 17:28); "And by Him all things consist" (Col. 1:17); "...upholding all things by the word of His power" (Heb. 1:3).

If this preserving and immediate influence were to be withheld for but one moment, the creature would at once be reduced to nothing, as no creature can of and by himself exist independently from God. This is implied in the word "creature." "That He would let loose His hand, and cut me off" (Job 6:9); "Thou hidest Thy face, they are troubled: Thou takest away their breath, they die, and return to their dust" (Psa. 104:29).

God has created some creatures in such a fashion that apart from this energizing and preserving power they need no other means to maintain their existence. Others He has created such that they are in need of a variety of other terrestrial means. Between these means there is a relationship of secondary causes which exceeds our comprehension. The lesser of these secondary causes is frequently the means which the superior of these secondary causes utilizes. They in turn are causal in relation to the secondary causes which are inferior to them. "I will hear the heavens, and they shall hear the earth; and the earth shall hear the corn...and they shall hear Jezreel" (Hosea 2:21-22).

God has ordained that living creatures be preserved by food and drink, and He himself provides this for them. "O LORD, Thou preservest man and beast" (Psa. 36:6); "He giveth to the beast his food, and to the young ravens which cry" (Psa. 147:9). God does not need to avail Himself of means, neither can the means preserve the creature without His preserving influence. However, God uses the means to manifest His wisdom, power, and goodness, so that rational creatures would the better discern His hand, rejoice in this, and magnify God because of it.

God ordinarily uses the means, but occasionally He acts in an extraordinary manner to demonstrate His majesty and sovereignty:

(1) At times He preserves by means which otherwise are insufficient. In this manner God preserved Elijah, the widow, and her son for a long time by means of a small measure of flour and oil (1 Ki. 17:10ff.) In like manner the Lord Jesus fed five thousand people with five loaves and two fishes (John 6:9-10).

(2) God preserved some for a period of time without food and drink — for example, Moses, Elijah, and Christ, each for a period of forty days (Exo. 34:28; 1 Ki. 19:8; Mat. 4:2).

(3) God has preserved some by holding natural powers in abeyance. God preserved the three young men in the fiery furnace in this fashion (Dan. 3:17). He delivered Israel out of Egypt by causing the water of the sea to stand as walls on both sides until Israel had proceeded through on dry land (Exo. 14:22); this also occurred at the Jordan (Josh. 3:16). The Lord caused the sun to stand still (Josh. 10:13) and to move backwards by ten degrees (2 Ki. 20:11).

The Second Act of God's Providence: Cooperation

The second act of providence is *Cooperation, (concursus)*, that is, *the concurrence of the power of God with the motions of His creatures.* All creatures have received an independent and unique existence from God so as to move in a manner unique to themselves. They set themselves in motion, as man for instance walks, speaks, and works — all of which he does of himself. Since every creature exists, however, by the energizing and preserving power of God, and would not be able to exist without this, each creature's activity comes about by the influence of God's cooperative power, without which it would not be able to move. As is its manner of existence, so likewise is its manner of motion; both existence and motion are dependent upon God.

(1) The cooperation of God must not be understood to mean the energizing power of God which preserves the existence and faculties of all creatures but then ceases to function, leaving further activity and government to the creature. We rather understand it to be a *preserving, initiating, and persevering power* within the moving creature that influences its motion.

(2) Neither do we understand this cooperative power to be a general, discriminating, or proportionate influence which does not determine the creature's activity, so that time, location, and manner of activity are determined by the creature, and thus would have its effect whenever it would please him. This would then be similar to the sun which has a general influence upon earthly matters, such as the growth of plants, the procreation of beasts and men, a rotting cadaver, and a sweet smelling flower. In this case the object and the effects are different, but the energizing influence is always the same. One should not be of the opinion that He who is supreme in sovereignty and wisdom cooperates with various creatures in such a general and detached manner — not regulating the creature, but being regulated by the creature, thus giving the Creator the opportunity to cooperate according to the good pleasure of the creature. In this fashion we use the sun, wind, water, and fire according to our pleasure. God, however, energizes by a wise, sovereign, and special cooperative act, in which His activity precedes the activity of every creature, thus determining the time, location, and manner of activity, while preserving the creature in his motions until the act has been performed.

(3) Neither do we understand cooperation to be a suggestive influence which is either positive or negative in nature, nor an operation whereby opportunities and objects are made available. It rather refers to a physical (if we may use this word in this

context), natural, immediate, and powerful influence which causes the creature to move voluntarily.

(4) This cooperation is also not mediate in the sense in which a craftsman uses his tools, and as the moon by means of reflected light from the sun affects earthly objects and illuminates the earth. This cooperation is immediate; God energizes mobile creatures by His own power and by virtue of His own Being. This is not merely true for the initial secondary cause which directly proceeds from Him, leaving it to itself to set everything else in motion, but with identical power He is involved in all secondary causes. Thus He is immediately involved with all consequences of the initial secondary cause, although creatures in respect to each other must be viewed as means in the hand of God.

(5) One should also not understand this cooperation to be such as if God were collaterally involved in the activity of the creature, as is true when two horses draw a wagon. This would mean that the creature by virtue of a God-given innate ability would then function independently rather than that God would energize the creature in order for it to be in motion. This would additionally mean that God would merely join Himself to the activity of the moving creature, executing this task jointly, each by exercising power independently. God's initiative precedes the motion of the creature, however, stipulating the creature to a specific object, place, and time. Having initiated and determined the creature's motion in this manner, God then proceeds to further involve Himself in the creature and its motion, thus accomplishing what He has purposed.

We therefore understand the cooperation of God not merely to refer to His omnipotent and omnipresent power whereby He preserves the existence and faculties of all creatures but also to be a special, *physical*, natural, immediate, and tangible operation by which He precedes the creature in every motion, directing this motion and preserving the created object while in motion. Thus He permeates all secondary causes and their motions to their conclusive effect.

Socinians, Roman Catholics, and *Arminians* deny this, and therefore we must give further explanation. This truth is confirmed by both Scripture and nature.

It is first of all evident throughout the entire Bible. Consider for instance Acts 17:28, where a clear distinction is made between the *being* and the *motion* of the creature. It is confirmed that the creature both moves in God and has its being in God. To move in God is being active due to the influence of divine power. This is also exemplified in the following passages. "Thou hast covered me in my mother's womb. I will praise Thee; for I am fearfully and wonderfully made" (Psa. 139:13-14); "Hast Thou not poured me out as milk, and curdled me like cheese? Thou hast clothed me with skin and flesh, and hast fenced me with bones and sinews" (Job 10:10-11); "The king's heart is in the hand of the LORD, as the rivers of water: He turneth it whithersoever He will" (Prov. 21:1). Water follows its own course, but God directs it whithersoever He wills. Although the heart of the king may be highly exalted above his subjects, it nevertheless does not function independently from God. The king may have as many plans as he wishes, but the Lord nevertheless inclines him towards His will and causes him to act accordingly. Add to this Isaiah 10:15, where it is stated, "Shall the ax boast itself against him that heweth therewith? or shall the saw magnify itself against him that shaketh it? as if the rod should shake itself against them that lift it up?" The prophet says that as an axe, saw, and rod cannot set themselves in motion, but must be set in motion by someone else, so it is likewise for every creature and man. God sets them in motion in harmony with their nature by means of His cooperative influence. The Lord causes "His sun to rise" (Mat. 5:45). The Lord caused "the stars in their courses" to fight against Sisera (Judg. 5:20). David acknowledged, "For Thou hast girded me with strength unto the battle: Thou hast subdued under me those that rose up against me" (Psa. 18:39). "For it is God which worketh in you both to will and to do of His good pleasure" (Phil. 2:13).

Secondly, this is also evident from reason and nature itself.

(1) It is an irrefutable principle that the *manner of operation proceeds from the manner of existence*. Since each creature is dependent upon God in its existence, it is likewise dependent in its motions.

(2) Either man is entirely independent from God — which is most absurd to maintain, as it would be contradictory to be a creature and yet be independent of the Creator — or if man is dependent, then he is also dependent in all his motions. For otherwise he would be independent in this area, and if he were able to be independent in one area, he would also be able to be independent in other areas, and consequently in every area; this is contrary to the nature of a creature.

(3) If God did not energize the motions of every creature, it would not be necessary to pray, "Create in me a clean heart" (Psa. 51:12); "Thy Spirit is good; lead me into the land of uprightness" (Psa. 143:10); "Keep the door of my lips" (Psa. 141:3). There would be no need to pray for victory in war or for any other matter. Since, however, we are commanded to pray, it is evident that God ener-

gizes by His cooperative power. Then (if God did not energize the motions of every creature) there would also be no need to thank God upon receipt of a blessing for body or soul; for if God had not done it, one would not be permitted to give thanks to Him, but would rather have to express his thanksgiving either to himself or to another creature who had bestowed the blessing.

(4) Then God would not be Lord, but rather a servant of the creature — similar to the sun which man uses as and when he pleases. God would then have to be readily available with His general influence when the creature specified it, the creature determining in which manner His influence was to be used. Then one would not be able to say, "I shall do this, the Lord willing," but rather, "The Lord will have to exercise His influence according to my will." Then it would not be as God wills, but as man wills, contrary to James 4:15.

God is not the Author of Sin

The thought might occur as to whether the consequence of such cooperation would not be that *there is but one cause of all motions and activities*. Then God would be the only active agent and man and all creatures would be entirely passive, being set in motion as the strings of a musical instrument which are entirely passive and whose motion is caused solely by the player.

My response to this is: "Not in the least!" For even though creatures function as means in relation to each other, God using them in the execution of His work and purpose, they are nevertheless the primary cause of their motions and activities. This is not true in respect to God as if they were independent from Him, but in respect to other subordinate causes as well as the results of their activities. There is no inconsistency in the fact that two causes of a different order have the same result, especially since the result is one and the same, proceeding from both sources in a different manner.

The designation of God as the sole cause of all motions, deeds, and activities, and the proposition that man is therefore passive and inactive is the result of blindness and ignorance concerning God's power and wisdom. It is an error which is refuted by both Scripture and nature.

First, since God has imposed a law upon man to which promises as well as threatenings are appended, man is therefore not passive, but is himself the moving cause of his deeds. God can neither impose a law upon Himself, make promises to Himself, nor threaten Himself. Since the law with its promises and threatenings has been given to man for the purpose of regulating his conduct, man must therefore be active himself and thus receive either what has been promised or threatened.

Secondly, if man were merely passive in all his motions, he could not be subject to punishment, for punishment is the execution of justice in response to transgression of the law. If man had not committed anything but was merely a passive object of God's activity, he would not have committed any evil, and thus, on the basis of justice, could not have been punished and condemned.

Thirdly, if man were merely passive and God was the only active agent in his motions and deeds, all motions and deeds, both natural as well as sinful (far be it from God, that He should do wickedness) would have been committed by God and would have to be attributed to Him. Then God rather than man would be walking, speaking, writing, or reading. Man would neither pray nor believe, but God would be praying to Himself, and believing in Himself through Jesus Christ. Man would not be guilty of making idols; man would not use God's Name in vain; man would not break the Sabbath; man would not be disobedient to his parents; man would not be guilty of hatred, wrath, and anger towards his neighbor, etc. Man would not be a hater of God, since he would be but passive and thus inactive. All of this would have to attributed to God which would be the ultimate act of blasphemy.

Fourthly, Scripture states plainly that man walks, sees, hears, speaks, believes, and prays. It also states that man sins, and is thus righteously subject to punishment. It is unnecessary to quote all the texts which mention this. Paul states, "For we are labourers together with God" (1 Cor. 3:9). This is also confirmed when he states, "Work out your own salvation with fear and trembling. For it is God which worketh in you both to will and to do of His good pleasure" (Phil. 2:12-13). God is the efficient cause of this activity, but man is the subjective cause of that same work, *producing these activities from within himself.* These activities must therefore be attributed to man according to the following principle: *The name is attributed to the formal cause.* In Philippians 2:12-13 man is exhorted to be active towards his salvation, being convinced and stirred up concerning his duty. He is simultaneously instructed, however, concerning his sinfulness and spiritual impotence, so that he would entertain no notion concerning the goodness of his will, nor be encouraged to be active towards this in his own strength. On the other hand he ought not to be discouraged when he perceives his weakness, but should rather be encouraged by the fact that God helps him by being the initiator of his action, working powerfully in him to take hold of this power and be engaged by virtue of this power.

Objection #1: Does not such cooperation make God a cause of sin?

Answer: By no means! One needs to make a distinction between the activity itself, such as understanding, willing, seeing, hearing, speaking, working, and the context in which this activity must occur: the law of God. The activity itself is natural and as such neither good nor evil; however when viewed within the context of the law, according to which it ought to be judged as far as subject, time, and manner are concerned, this activity becomes either good or evil. When discussing God's cooperation we understand this to refer to the natural dimensions of this activity or motion itself. This is neither true, however, in reference to the misuse of this activity, to the lack of conformity to the law, nor to the evil in this activity. One person can be the cause of activity in another person, but not of the evil which accompanies it. The government causes the executioner to scourge the thief, but is not the cause of the cruel manner in which he may do so. A player causes the strings to bring forth sound, but not the dissonance; this proceeds from the string. A rider may drive his horse and thus cause progress. He is not the cause of its limp, however; this is due to a flaw in the horse. Such is the case here. The activity itself proceeds from God, but man spoils it due to his inner corruption. Consequently, it is not God but man who is the cause of sin.

Objection #2: Does this initiating and definitive cooperation of God not eliminate the freedom of man's will?

Answer: By no means! The freedom of the will is not one of *neutrality;* that is, of indifference whether or not to do something, but of *necessary consequence,* coming forth from one's own choice, pleasure, or inclination to do or not do something. God's cooperation enables man to be active in harmony with his nature, that is, by the free exercise of his will. There is thus harmony between God's cooperation and the will of man. God activates the will and man then exercises his will.

The Third Act of God's Providence: Government

The third element of the providence of God is *Government, whereby God governs all things in general and each thing in particular for purposes predetermined by Him.* God's Word teaches throughout that God governs and directs all things. "The LORD reigneth" (Psa. 93:1); "...Him who worketh all things after the counsel of His own will" (Eph. 1:11); "I am the LORD that maketh all things" (Isa. 44:24). We can organize all these things under four particular headings: the independent entities, the greatness or insignificance, the goodness or evil, and the outcome of all matters.

The first heading is concerned with independent entities which are either animate or inanimate. The animate entities are either rational or irrational. The *rational* entities are angels and men. God governs the angels for they are "sent forth to minister" (Heb. 1:14). God governs the entire conversation of man. "The preparations of the heart in man, and the answer of the tongue, is from the LORD. A man's heart deviseth his way: but the LORD directeth his steps" (Prov. 16:1, 9). *Irrational* creatures either live sensibly or merely have a vegetative existence. The Lord governs all that which is sensibly alive, such as the birds. "Behold the fowls of the air ...your heavenly Father feedeth them" (Mat. 6:26). The Lord governs the animals. "...the LORD sent lions among them..." (2 Ki. 17:25). The Lord calls the locust, the cankerworm, the caterpillar, and the palmerworm, "My great army which I sent among you" (Joel 2:25). He governs the fish of the sea. "Cast the net on the right side of the ship, and ye shall find" (John 21:6). The Lord also governs all vegetation such as plants, trees, and herbs. "He causeth the grass to grow for the cattle, and herb for the service of man" (Psa. 104:14). The Lord governs all inanimate creation, such as sun, moon, stars, rain, hail, snow, thunder, lightning, wind, the mountains and all their natural resources, and the sea and rivers (cf. Psa. 148; Psa. 29:3; Jer. 10:13).

The second heading concerns the magnitude or insignificance of matters. Large objects are as incapable of governing themselves as are the small objects, and therefore are in need of divine government. Small objects, to the very least of them, are governed by God in all circumstances, occurrences, and motions. It is to the glory of God that He who has created all things — even the very smallest objects — and causes them to exist by His influence, also governs them. This is true for the buttons on our clothing, the shoes on our feet, and the hairs on our heads. "But the very hairs of your head are all numbered" (Mat. 10:30); "Neither were their coats changed, nor the smell of fire had passed on them" (Dan. 3:27); "Your clothes are not waxen old upon you, and thy shoe is not waxen old upon thy foot" (Deu. 29:5).

The third heading concerns the goodness or evil of a matter. Whatever is good in nature or in grace is of the Lord. "Every good and every perfect gift is from above, and cometh down from the Father of lights" (James 1:17). The evil is either the evil of punishment or of sin. *The evil of punishment* proceeds from God. God sends and governs the evil of punishment either as a righteous Judge or as a loving Father. "Out of the mouth of the Most High proceedeth not evil and good?" (Lam. 3:38); "Shall there be evil in a city, and the

LORD hath not done it?" (Amos 3:6). *The evil of sin* does not proceed from God, for He is holy (Isa. 6:3) and light (1 John 1:5). "He is the Rock, His work is perfect: for all His ways are judgment: a God of truth and without iniquity, just and right is He" (Deu. 32:4); "Far be it from God, that He should do wickedness; and from the Almighty, that He should commit iniquity" (Job 34:10); "...there is no unrighteousness in Him" (Psa. 92:15). Since God prohibited evil and will punish it, He is therefore not the cause of sin. This we wholeheartedly proclaim and declare before the entire world. It is therefore slanderous to maintain that the Reformed Church teaches that God is a cause of sin.

God's Government and Sin

Nevertheless God's government also encompasses sin, for otherwise the entire human race, being sinful in its deeds, would be removed from God's government. God's government regarding sin cannot be denied by someone who believes God's Word, from which we will prove this with utmost clarity.

For a correct understanding of God's government relative to sin we must take notice of three matters which pertain to every sin: the natural activity, the deviation in this activity, and God's government in bringing this activity to a good end.

(1) The natural activity, considered in and of itself, proceeds from God. This has been demonstrated in discussing the second act of providence, cooperation.

(2) We shall soon demonstrate that God governs sin to a good end.

(3) The deviation, the abuse of the energizing power of God, the corruption of this power, and the irregularity of the activity as far as manner and objective are concerned — whether such activity is internal or external — do not proceed from God, but from man himself. Man is nevertheless not independent in the act of sin for he corrupts the energy upon which he depends for his activity. God's government concerning sin relates 1) to its commencement, 2) to its progression, and 3) to its ultimate outcome.

First, God initially permits the occurrence of sin. "So I gave them up unto their own hearts lust: and they walked in their own counsels" (Psa. 81:12); "Who in times past suffered all nations to walk in their own ways" (Acts 14:16). God permits sin, but not in such a manner as if the sinner were discharged from the demands of the law, for then God would approve of sin and would not be able to punish sinners. He permits it in such a fashion, however, that He does not prevent the sinner from sinning. He is, nevertheless, capable of preventing sin, and at times also does. "For I also withheld thee from sinning against Me; therefore suffered I thee not to touch her" (Gen. 20:6).

This is not a matter of indifferent observation, whereby the sinner is merely allowed to go his own way. *It is rather an active permission,* not relative to sin as proper object itself, but relative to the circumstances. This does not merely consist in God refusing to coerce the free will of the sinner by forcing him to renounce his will. (Even when God prevents the sinner and does not permit him to sin — as we just observed with Abimelech — He nevertheless does not eliminate the freedom of his will.) Rather, God influences man in a manner agreeable with his nature so that he arbitrarily acts or does not act. This active permission consists of the following acts:

(1) Man's activity as far as his faculties and activity are concerned originates with God who restricts and sustains him with His powerful influence, enabling him to exist and move so that he works and is active.

(2) God permits situations to occur, of which man would make correct use if he were still perfect. He is still under obligation to utilize such situations correctly. Due to his corruption, however, he abuses them. David's lust was kindled when he observed Bathsheba (2 Sam. 11:2); Ahab's wrath was kindled in response to the words of the prophet Elijah (1 Ki. 21:20). Lusts are even kindled by the law itself. "But sin, taking occasion by the commandment, wrought in me all manner of concupiscence" (Rom. 7:8).

(3) In withholding from man the ability to withstand sin, God righteously and sovereignly refuses to impart new grace to man when he has the opportunity and is inclined to sin. He wills to leave him in his evil frame, rendering him capable and inclined to commit all manner of sins. "There shall ye serve other gods day and night; where I will not shew you favour" (Jer. 16:13).

(4) As a righteous judgment upon past sins, God does withdraw His restraining power which is normally exercised towards the sinner, leaving him to himself. "Howbeit in the business of the ambassadors of the princes of Babylon ... God left him, to try him" (2 Chr. 32:31).

(5) As a righteous judgment, God gives the sinner over to his own lusts and thus punishes sin with sin. "And even as they did not like to retain God in their knowledge, God gave them over to a reprobate mind, to do those things which are not convenient" (Rom. 1:28); "... because they received not the love of the truth, that they might be saved. And for this cause God shall send them a strong delusion, that they should believe a lie" (2 Th. 2:10-11);

"Let him alone, and let him curse; for the LORD hath bidden him" (2 Sam. 16:11).

(6) God gives the devil free play to focus all his efforts upon man, whom he drives from one sin to another, taking advantage of man's lusts which have been aroused. "But the Spirit of the LORD departed from Saul, and an evil spirit from the LORD troubled him" (1 Sam. 16:14); "Thou [lying spirit] shalt persuade him, and prevail also: go forth, and do so" (1 Ki. 22:22).

(7) God hardens the heart, causing it to be as stone, thereby permitting the sinner to persevere in sin without being sensible of it. God Himself uses such expressions, saying that He does this. "And I will harden Pharaoh's heart.... And He hardened Pharaoh's heart" (Exo. 7:3, 13). This act of hardening is not an infusion of some evil or sinful frame, but a holy and secret operation whereby common but abused gifts are withdrawn in an extraordinary manner. The Lord then fully withdraws Himself so that there is neither impression nor feeling concerning God or the conscience. God leaves the sinner over to his own raging lusts and allows the devils to have free play so that the sinner in this state cannot do anything else but sin and is hardened as a result of continual sinning. Therefore that which is attributed to God is also attributed to Pharaoh. "But when Pharaoh saw that there was respite, he hardened his heart" (Exo. 8:15). Such is God's government relative to sin at the outset of its commission.

Secondly, God's government also extends to the progression of sin. God determines the measure, time, and limitations; that is, thus far and no further, to such an extent and no more, and for such a duration and no longer. This we observe with Laban. "It is in the power of my hand to do you hurt: but the God of your father spake unto me yesternight, saying, Take thou heed that thou speak not to Jacob either good or bad" (Gen. 31:29). Esau was determined to kill Jacob, but must kiss him instead (Gen. 33:4). Baalam desired to curse in order to earn the wages of unrighteousness, but each time he was compelled to bless (Num. 24). The devil desired to eliminate Job, but each time the Lord determined his deliverance. "...only upon himself put not forth thine hand" (Job 1:12); "...but save his life" (Job 2:6).

Thirdly, God's government also extends to *the ultimate outcome of sin*. He governs sin either to declare His righteousness, to show forth His grace, longsuffering, and mercy, or to benefit His children, keeping them humble and making them careful. "But as for you, ye thought evil against me; but God meant it unto good, to bring to pass, as it is this day, to save much people alive" (Gen. 50:20); "O

Assyrian, the rod of Mine anger, and the staff in their hand is Mine indignation. I will send him against an hypocritical nation . . . and to take the prey. Howbeit he meaneth not so . . . but it is in his heart to destroy and cut off nations not a few. I will punish the fruit of the stout heart of the king of Assyria, and the glory of his high looks" (Isa. 10:5-7, 12). "Howbeit for this cause I obtained mercy, that in me first Jesus Christ might show forth all longsuffering, for a pattern to them which should hereafter believe on Him to life everlasting" (1 Tim. 1:16).

Such results do not naturally issue forth from sin; neither does God first determine to extract good results from sin after it has been committed. Having decreed to glorify Himself in such a fashion and to bestow certain benefits upon His children, God rather uses the wickedness of man in a sanctified manner to accomplish the outcome. As the sun is not defiled by the rotting of a stinking cadaver, God likewise, while men and devils commit sin, remains holy and operates in a holy manner relative to the commencement, progression, and ultimate outcome of sin. God uses sinners as if they were executioners, lions, and bears, in order to execute His judgments by means of their fury, and thus with a crooked stick He strikes with straight strokes.

The fourth heading concerning the providence of God relates to the *outcome of all matters*. These results are either necessary consequences or are contingent in nature. Therefore these also include whatever occurs as a result of such matters as the free exercise of man's will, the outcome of wars, marriage, and the day of one's death.

First, some results are certain and a matter of course, being determined by the law and order of nature. Such is true for the circuits (trajectories) of sun and moon, for eclipses, for the occurrence of low and high tides, and for the fact that fire ascends and that whatever is heavy descends. All these are governed by God. This is confirmed in the following texts. "He appointed the moon for seasons: the sun knoweth his going down. Thou makest darkness, and it is night" (Psalms 104:19-20); "They continue this day according to Thine ordinances: for all are Thy servants" (Psalms 119:91).

God can, however, intervene in this established plan and cause progression contrary to the course of nature. Upon the prayer of Joshua the Lord caused the sun and moon to stand still (Josh. 10:13) and He caused the sun to return ten degrees upon Hezekiah's request (2 Ki. 20:11). The Lord caused iron to float (2 Ki. 6:6), and the three young men to be unharmed in the fiery oven (Dan. 3:25). The prophecies also have a certain and determined fulfillment which

God is not willing nor are His creatures able to change. "But how then shall the Scriptures be fulfilled, that thus it must be?" (Mat. 26:54).

Secondly, the results of some matters are *contingent.* This is not true in reference to God, for not the least thing happens by chance. His counsel shall stand and He will do all His pleasure. They are contingent, however, both relative to secondary causes (relative to which they could have turned out differently) and relative to the connection between causes and their effects, for which the results were neither planned, regulated, nor expected. God, however, governs all these contingent results according to His counsel and will, executing them with certainty and without any impediment. This is exemplified by unexpected manslaughter in which God caused this blow to come upon the slain person (cf. Deu. 19:5; Exo. 21:13). Is there anything more unpredictable than the casting of the lot? God's government nevertheless extends to this, and He causes the result to be according to His will. "The lot is cast into the lap; but the whole disposing thereof is of the LORD" (Prov. 16:33). This is evident in the lot which fell upon Jonah (Jonah 1:7) and upon Jonathan (1 Sam. 14:42). What is more unpredictable in nature than the falling of a sparrow from the roof or a hair from the head? God's government, however, also extends to these. "One of them shall not fall on the ground without your Father. But the very hairs of your head are all numbered" (Mat. 10:29-30).

Thirdly, God also governs all actions which occur as a result of *the free exercise of the will of man.* God does not remove the freedom of the will, nor does he coerce man to act contrary to his will. Rather, He inclines and governs this will, be it by internal inclination or by external circumstances and events, so that man accomplishes those matters decreed by God by virtue of his own arbitrary determination and inclination. This is confirmed in the following texts. "He fashioneth their hearts alike" (Psa. 33:15); "...the answer of the tongue, is from the LORD...the LORD directeth his steps" (Prov. 16:1, 9); He turneth it (the king's heart) whithersoever He will" (Prov. 21:1); "...God which worketh...to will..." (Phil. 2:13).

Fourthly, God governs the *outcome of wars*, sending one nation to punish the other or to be a punishment to each other. He does not always give the victory to the nation which is strongest numerically, most clever, and most courageous, but to whomsoever He will. "How should one chase a thousand, and two put ten thousand to flight?" (Deu. 32:30a); "It is nothing with Thee to help, whether with many, or with them that have no power" (2 Chr. 14:11); "There is no king saved by the multitude of an host: a mighty man is not delivered by much strength. An horse is a vain thing for safety" (Psa. 33:16-17); "The horse is prepared against the day of battle: but safety is of the LORD" (Prov. 21:31). All texts in which God is said either to sell or give one nation into the hand of another nation, or to deliver a nation, serve to illustrate this (cf. Judg. 3:8; 6:1).

Fifthly, God's government also extends to *marriage,* directing a partner to every man. Some He joins together in judgment as punishment upon their sins, some for the purpose of chastening, and some for the mutual comfort of soul and body. How unsearchable are all those peculiar ways and unusual events relative to marriages! God, however, governs them all according to His determinate purpose, and as long as the world remains there will be some marriages in which such providences will be evident. "LORD...send me good speed this day...let the same be she that Thou hast appointed for Thy servant Isaac" (Gen. 24:12-14); "...a prudent wife is from the LORD" (Prov. 19:14); "What therefore God hath joined together..." (Mat. 19:6).

Sixthly, God determines every person's age. No one will die any earlier nor live any longer than God has decreed. He will die at such a location and in such a manner as God has determined. Until that moment God will provide food and shelter, preserving his body. But then all the doctors in the world will not be able to prolong His life by one hour. "...and hath determined the times before appointed, and the bounds of their habitation" (Acts 17:26); "Seeing his days are determined, the number of his months are with Thee, Thou hast appointed his bounds that he cannot pass" (Job 14:5); "Behold, Thou hast made my days as an handbreadth" (Psa. 39:5). (Cf. chapter 5.)

God's Providence and the Use of Means

We have thus observed that everything, without exception, is governed according to God's decree. God generally executes all these things by way of means, however, having bound man to them. Whenever the means are properly used, God generally blesses His own ordinances. An ungodly farmer who properly prepares his land generally has a fruitful harvest, and a godly farmer who has been lax in his preparation will have to witness the harvest with empty hands. When a godly person does his best, however, God surely blesses the most insignificant means. A person tempts God when he does not wish to use the means and nevertheless desires to see results.

This doctrine of the providence of God is of great benefit to those who make proper use of it. A blind, natural, and unconverted person can neither extract any benefit from this doctrine nor obtain comfort from it. He cannot do so even though he observes and believes in the providence of God and desires to strengthen himself by means of it when an extraordinary trial comes his way. His patience is a coerced patience, as he is not able to do otherwise. He resigns himself to a *fatum Stoicum*, that is, stoical fate, saying: "Circumstances had to be this way and nothing can change them." When he cannot do as he pleases, he tries to make the best of it. How will an unconverted man comfort himself with the providence of God, since God is against him? Whatever befalls him serves to his perdition if he is not converted. Therefore it is a terror unto him.

However, all the benefits which may be derived from this doctrine are for the children of God. The clearer they may know themselves to belong to God, the more benefit they may extract from the providence of God. Come therefore, all you who mourn greatly, inwardly, and continually over sin; who continually flee to the Lord Jesus to be justified by His blood; who yearn for communion with God; whose desire it is to love, fear, and obey the Lord, even though this is often accompanied with much darkness and sin. Come, I say, sit beside me for a moment, listen, and let my words enter into your ears and hearts.

Practical Exhortations Concerning the Doctrine of Providence

Accustom yourself by frequent meditations, attentive observation, and diligent exercises to believingly observe God's hand in all things. As you would observe the rays of the sun entering a room through a window, observe His preservation, cooperation, and government, concerning both creatures and their activity. Accustom yourself continually to discern God's active hand when you observe the sunrise in the morning and the shining moon and stars at night in their respective circuits; as you observe everything sprouting forth from the earth; when you take note of what occurs in the earth; and when you observe both victory and defeat in time of war, as also the extraordinary events and turn of events in time of peace. Do likewise regarding your own life, whether you are healthy or ill, whether you continually encounter tribulation, one cross following another; whether you experience deliverance and prosperity; whether a person looks at you either in a friendly or sullen manner, speaks either gruffly to you or helps and comforts you; or whether someone turns his back to you, seeks to trap you, opposes you, speaks well or evil of you. All these things, from the least to the greatest, are under God's control. It is not enough merely to state this and believe it to be true, for this will have but little effect upon you.

I beseech you, however, to endeavor by constant activity and by continually focusing vividly upon and viewing it to familiarize yourself with this truth. May you thus continually perceive God's hand working in and by secondary causes in such a manner as if these causes did not exist, but as if God worked these things immediately. Endeavor by thus being continually exercised to acquire a habitual frame of mind which will make it clear and easy for you to see God at work. Believe me, this requires more effort to learn than you may think. Our atheistic and worldly hearts continually detract us from such observations and acknowledgement, and this will bring on a darkness which will hamper us. Therefore, apply yourself in this matter, praying for much light to enable you to be attentive and to be continually engaged in such observations. You will experience that your soul will derive great benefit in every way. Beware, however, of too much effort spent in searching out the manner in which God preserves, cooperates, and governs, for this would have a detrimental effect upon you, it being an unsearchable mystery. Rather, believe and observe this doctrine each time with new attentiveness. Speak about it and communicate this to others, and you will perceive that your journey through this world will be attended with more comfort and holiness.

Secondly, do not merely focus on the acts of providence, but accustom yourself to perceive therein God's majesty, power, wisdom, righteousness, and goodness. Acknowledge these attributes with astonishment and joy. All creatures are His; all activity proceeds from Him; and He governs everything in heaven and on earth. This is true regardless of how large the universe may be, how many creatures (great or small) it may contain, and how diverse all activity may be. May this acknowledgement engender a humble fear and reverence in you. Is not He, and He alone, the Lord? Are not all things in His hand to use them either for or against you? Are not all creatures His servants who look unto the hand of their Master? Stand therefore in awe of Him and bow before Him in godly fear while exclaiming, "The Lord is God," and "the Lord reigns." God demands this. "Fear ye not Me? saith the LORD: will ye not tremble at My presence, which have placed the sand for the bound of the sea by a perpetual decree, that it cannot pass it: and though the waves thereof toss themselves, yet can they not prevail; though they roar, yet can they not pass over it?" (Jer. 5:22). Oh, how sweet it is in contemplation of the fact that God is the moving cause of all things to bow before Him and to worship Him!

Thirdly, no longer depend upon secondary causes; no longer rely upon your belongings, strength, wisdom, and ability; no longer concern yourself with friend or foe; do not depend upon naval forces, fortifications, and soldiers; do not look so much to this or that individual or to the means, as if your only expectation were to be from them. If God so pleases, He will overturn[1] all your dependencies and expectation from the means. He will turn everything upside down; what you thought to be your deliverance will prove to be your ruination, and what appeared to be your ruination will be your deliverance. Since creatures cannot but move otherwise than through His energizing power, what can they give to you or take from you? Why then do you look to them, since everyone of them bears this testimony, "It is not to be found with me"? Moreover, to depend upon the help of creatures is to be guilty of idolatry and departure from the Lord. "Cursed be the man that trusteth in man, and maketh flesh his arm, and whose heart departeth from the LORD. Blessed is the man that trusteth in the LORD, and whose hope the LORD is" (Jer. 17:5, 7). Oh, learn this great lesson! Let those who do not know God look to the creature and to the means and depend upon them. You, however, must expect everything from the Lord, carefully using the means as means and looking beyond all creatures to God Himself. This will engender both steadfastness and strength within your heart. "They that trust in the LORD shall be as mount Zion, which cannot be removed, but abideth for ever" (Psa. 125:1).

Fourthly, be not fearful of creatures, as they cannot initiate their own motion. It is God alone who governs and controls them. If you have an encounter with them, God who controls them has sent them. They cannot do anything but execute God's will. God obstructs them in their activity and causes them to depart again. Who would fear a sword, stick, or stone when it is lying upon the ground and does not move since it is not in anyone's hand? If it is God's will, anyone desirous to curse you will bless you; if they desire to slander you, they will praise you; and if they desire to kill you, they will kiss you. "If God be for us, who can be against us?" (Rom. 8:31). And since He is for you, children of God, why do you fear? For all your enemies it is true that it is but as if a terrifying mask conceals the countenance of a friend. "When He giveth quietness, who then

---

[1] The Dutch reads: "...zoo blaast Hij in al uw afhangen..."; literally, "He thus blows in all your dependency."

can make trouble?" (Job 34:29). Therefore, "Fear not them which kill the body" (Mat. 10:28). How quiet a soul may be which, while conscious of his enemies, "dwelleth in the secret place of the most High" and abides under the shadow of the Almighty (Psa. 91:1)!

Fifthly, do not be angry and vengeful towards those who have harmed you, for it is according to the Lord's command (2 Sam. 16:11). "Who is he that saith, and it cometh to pass, when the Lord commandeth it not?" (Lam. 3:37). It is true that they have done so with evil intention, but the Lord uses their evil deeds as a rod to chastise you (Isa. 10). We must not act as a dog which bites the stone that has been cast at him, but must look higher to the hand of Him who uses our enemies against us and refrain from murmuring against the Lord. To be vengeful or angry against the means used is to be opposed to the One who used them. Therefore never focus upon the evil-doing of man alone, as if he functioned independently, but rather "hear ye the rod, and who hath appointed it" (Micah 6:9), and turn to Him who chastises you (Isa. 9:12).

Sixthly, possess your souls in patience. This is so needful, for evil things do not come upon you by chance even if they are caused by people. Yes, even if your own foolishness and sin are the cause, it is nevertheless of the Lord who hath decreed this concerning you, who controls it, and who executes it. Therefore with quiet submission say, "For He performeth the thing that is appointed for me" (Job 23:14).

(1) Is He not the absolutely sovereign Lord? Do you begrudge Him this? Do you not rejoice that He is so? Would you not defend Him if anyone were to challenge His absolute right to govern? Would you desire that the link of His providence would break for your sake, desiring that His will not govern you, but that your will would govern Him? If so, how do you dare to resist Him? Be quiet therefore, and let His will — simply because it is His will — be fully accomplished towards you.

(2) Is He not your Father? Has He not loved you with an everlasting love? Behold, in love He caused this evil to come upon you. "As many as I love, I rebuke and chasten" (Rev. 3:19). He has compassion upon you, is merciful towards you, is with you in your affliction, knows your distress, sees your tears, and hears your cries. He will deliver you at His time and in His manner.

(3) The result will be to the further glorification of His power, faithfulness, and goodness. This will cause you to be that much more humble and holy. The more abundant the tribulation will have been, the more abundant the comforts will be.

Therefore, deny yourself and take up your cross, and follow

Jesus (Mat. 16:24). Do not be fretful and "despise not the chastening of the LORD; neither be weary of His correction" (Prov. 3:11). "Rest in the LORD, and wait patiently for Him" (Psa. 37:7). Say with David, "I was dumb, I opened not my mouth; because Thou didst it" (Psa. 39:9). Surrender yourself as clay in the hands of your Maker, and let Him mold you as it pleases Him. He shall guide thee with His counsel, and afterward receive thee to glory (Psa. 73:24). Is all not well then, regardless of whether He has led you in a way of sorrow or joy? To be blessed is to be blessed indeed.[2]

Seventhly, the proper use of God's providence will render you an exceptional measure of gratitude and will teach you to end in the Lord as the only Giver of all the good which you may receive for soul and body. It will cause you to observe God's goodness, faithfulness, and benevolence. This will cause you to rejoice, to praise and magnify God, to speak to others about His attributes, and to place yourself with a willing heart in God's service. He it is who, out of pure love bestowed His goodness upon you. At times He has done so in a most remarkable way and a marvelous manner. Since it came from God, we must also end in Him. "For of Him, and through Him, and to Him, are all things: to whom be glory for ever" (Rom. 11:36). "In every thing give thanks" (1 Th. 5:18). Continually follow David's example and say, "Bless the LORD, O my soul, and forget not all his benefits" (Psa. 103:2). Oh, how sweet it is when contemplating upon former affliction, helplessness, and our unworthiness to receive anything, to then perceive that the Lord Himself thinks upon us and delivers us! What desire this engenders to magnify the Lord in it and to rejoice in Him!

Eighthly, such proper use of providence yields to the soul a proper perspective and a quiet confidence in God concerning the future. The passionate lusts of the flesh are held in check, and the cross will not be feared. One will cease with the intense, immoderate, and sinful use of the means and surrender the matter in the Lord's hands. One will then be satisfied with the manner in which He performs it, knowing that it will be well. "Commit thy way unto the LORD; trust also in Him; and He shall bring it to pass" (Psa. 37:5); "Casting all your care upon Him; for He careth for you" (1 Pet. 5:7); "The LORD will perfect that which concerneth me" (Psa. 138:8). Behold, such benefits may be derived from the providence of God. Therefore, "Whoso is wise, and will observe these things, even they

---

[2] The Dutch reads, "Zalig is zalig." The profound dimensions of this statement are simply not translatable. à Brakel implicates that eternal felicity is the ultimate outcome of all God's ways with His children, regardless of what these ways may be.

shall understand the lovingkindness of the LORD" (Psa. 107:43);
"Who is wise, and he shall understand these things? prudent, and
he shall know them? for the ways of the LORD are right, and the
just shall walk in them" (Hosea 14:9).

CHAPTER TWELVE

The Covenant of Works

In the eighth chapter we have depicted Adam in his eminent, holy, and glorious nature. We shall now speak of him as being in covenant with God — the covenant of works. Acquaintance with this covenant is of the greatest importance, for whoever errs here or denies the existence of the covenant of works, will not understand the covenant of grace, and will readily err concerning the mediatorship of the Lord Jesus. Such a person will very readily deny that Christ by His active obedience has merited a right to eternal life for the elect. This is to be observed with several parties who, because they err concerning the covenant of grace, also deny the covenant of works. Conversely, whoever denies the covenant of works, must rightly be suspected to be in error concerning the covenant of grace as well.

The Covenant of Works Defined and its Existence Verified

The covenant of works was an agreement between God and the human race as represented in Adam, in which God promised eternal salvation upon condition of obedience, and threatened eternal death upon disobedience. Adam accepted both this promise and this condition.

Question: Was such a covenant between God and the human race represented in Adam?

Answer: Our answer is an unequivocal "Yes!" In order to consider a matter in an orderly fashion, it is necessary first to determine whether the matter exists and then to consider its nature. In this situation, however, we need first to consider the nature of this covenant, since the truth of the existence of such a covenant must primarily be proven from its nature. In that way we must seek to arrive at a conclusion.

Proof #1: If God gave Adam a law which is identical in content to the ten commandments; promised him eternal life (the same which Christ merited for the elect in the covenant of grace); appointed the tree of the knowledge of good and evil for him as a means whereby he would be tested and the tree of life to be a sacrament of life to him; and Adam, having accepted both the promise and the condition, thus bound himself to God — then a covenant of works between God and Adam existed. Since all of this is true, it thus follows that such a covenant existed.

We shall first consider the one party and His engagement, and subsequently the other party and his engagement. The one party is God who, in this covenant, manifests Himself as follows:

(1) as being *the foremost, eternal, supreme, and sovereign Lord,* who has power over His creatures to prescribe, command, and promise as He pleases. He is the "one Lawgiver" (James 4:12).

(2) as being *holy* and *righteous,* not being able to be pleased with anything other than holiness in His rational creatures, and cannot allow unholiness to remain unpunished.

(3) as being *infinitely good,* having a desire to communicate His goodness to man. His participation in the covenant consists of the issuance of a law, the promise of felicity and the threat of damnation, and the appointment of a sacramental tree and a probationary tree.

The Covenant of Works and the Law of God

The first matter to be proved is *that God gave a law to Adam,* this being such a law which in content is identical to the ten commandments. *The law is given of God to be a regulative principle for man as far as his inner man and actions are concerned. It declares what is good and evil, and by virtue of its divine authority obligates man to obedience.*

Man's rational intellect, be it ever so perfect and capable of a proper perception of the requirements of the law, is not a rule for good and evil. A matter is neither good nor evil merely because a proper perception determines it to be so. A proper perception does not obligate man to obedience; it is merely a means to know and acknowledge both the law and one's obligation. The divine law and its divine authority are the rule for good and evil, and obligate to obedience.

As I previously remarked, God gave a law to man. It is only His prerogative to do so.

Question: Are the laws which God issues the expression of His nature or of His free will?

Answer: They proceed from His will in harmony with His nature. They do not arbitrarily proceed from the will of God, as if God were able to command that which is contrary to Himself: to hate God and our neighbor; or that wrath, envy, hatred, vengefulness, and other sins would be holy in nature — God being able to promise eternal felicity upon the commission of sin. All of this would be contradictory to God's nature and thus also to His will. It would also be contradictory for Him to let a rational creature exist without a law.

That God gave Adam a law is confirmed as follows:

First, "...these (the heathen), having not the law, are a law unto themselves: which shew the work of the law written in their hearts" (Rom. 2:14-15). If men even after the fall have a law written in their hearts and are thus a law unto themselves, be it imperfectly and in obscurity, much more so would Adam in the state of rectitude have had a law. The reason for this conclusion is that the law of nature proceeds from the knowledge of God. Since Adam, after the fall, had a far superior and clearer knowledge of God than the heathen, he therefore also possessed the law in a far superior way. Knowledge of the law and conformity to it is a perfection of man's nature. He, who after the fall has the most knowledge of and is most conformable to the law, is superior to others. Since Adam was perfect, he consequently was superior in knowledge of and conformity to the law, and thus a law was given to him.

Secondly, "For what the law could not do, in that it was weak through the flesh, God sending His own Son in the likeness of sinful flesh, and for sin, condemned sin in the flesh: that the righteousness of the law might be fulfilled in us, who walk not after the flesh, but after the Spirit" (Rom. 8:3-4). The apostle concludes that there is a law which pertains to all men, this law having the inherent potential to justify a man which it finds to be perfect. He declares, however, that the law is weak, and that it is impossible for the law to justify, the reason being that through the flesh, that is, through sin, it has become weak. Wherever there is transgression of the law, it cannot acquit from transgression, for the law is truth. If the law has become weak, it implies that at one time it was strong. This however was never the case subsequent to the fall, and therefore was true prior to the fall, when sin was absent.

Thirdly, the nature of God as well as the nature of Adam requires that Adam have a law. By virtue of His nature God is the foremost and supreme Lord who is worthy to be honored and served. As soon as a creature appears upon the scene, He stands above that creature and the creature is subordinate to Him. This is also true for man as a rational creature, not merely because He has created man or has entered into a covenant with him or even because man has sinned, but more particularly due to God's nature, since He is *Jehovah*. Adam, being a creature, was of necessity dependent upon His Maker in all things, for otherwise he would be God himself. One cannot view the nature of the creature as being anything but dependent.

If Adam is dependent upon God, this is not only true for his being, but also for his motions. This is not merely true in relation to the motions he has in common with the animals, but also relative to his rationality enabling him to function intelligently. If God by virtue of His nature is supreme and independent, worthy to be honored, served, and feared ("Who would not fear thee, O King of nations? for to Thee doth it appertain") (Jer. 10:7), and since man is dependent in his nature, activities, and intellect, then man in his perfection had a rule by which his nature and activities had to be regulated, that is, a law. This law was embedded in Adam's nature so that he did not have to search for it as one who was ignorant of his obligations, or be concerned that being weak he would be led astray by his lusts to do otherwise. Knowledge of and conformity to the law were embedded in his nature.

Objection #1. "The law is not made for a righteous man, but for the lawless and disobedient" (1 Tim. 1:9).

Answer: The law can be viewed as a desirable, obligatory rule, or as a tool of coercion to generate fear and terror in view of punishment. The righteous view the law as a desirable, obligatory rule, and acknowledge with joy that they are subject to it. They are free from terrifying coercion, for, "...perfect love casteth out fear" (1 John 4:18). The unrighteous, however, are subject to the terrifying coercion of the law, which demands punishment upon their deeds. *Oderunt peccare boni virtutis amore; oderunt peccare mali formidine poenoe*; that is, *the good, out of love to virtue, desire not to sin, but the evil refrain from sin out of fear for punishment.*

Objection #2. Adam had a perfect love for God and thus there could not have been a law since he did everything spontaneously, voluntarily, and naturally.

Answer: (1) The law is love (Mat. 22:37-39). If Adam had perfect love, he necessarily had the perfect law.

(2) The law is liberty. "...the perfect law of liberty..." (James 1:25). Being in a state of holy liberty, Adam was thus subject to the law of liberty.

(3) There is no contradiction between doing something naturally and doing it in harmony with a law. The heathen also by nature do those things contained in the law.

(4) Is not the violation of love a sin and unrighteousness? Therefore, the law is intrinsic in perfect love.

(5) In the state of perfect love, Adam was threatened with death; whenever there is a threat upon transgression, there is a law. It thus follows that Adam had a law.

The question now presents itself, *What law did Adam have?* My response is that Adam, except for the prohibition pertaining to the tree of the knowledge of good and evil, had, as far as content is concerned, the *Law of the Ten Commandments.*

First, Adam doubtlessly had the most perfect law. The most perfect law is the law of love, however, and that is the law of the ten commandments (cf. Mat. 22:37-39). Adam therefore was in possession of the law of the ten commandments.

Secondly, all agree that the law which is embedded in the nature of the heathen and is a remnant of that law which Adam had embedded in his nature, is identical to the law of the ten commandments. Thus, Adam's law is the law of the ten commandments.

Thirdly, this is confirmed in Romans 8:3, which has already been quoted. Paul speaks there of a law, referring to it as "the law" without any further description. Without a doubt "the law" is the law of the ten commandments. This law Adam possessed in full strength, which after the fall had become weak, as has been demonstrated. Adam was thus in possession of the law of the ten commandments.

Fourthly, there is but one holiness, for holiness is the image of God, which is singular in nature. The law is thus also singular in nature, for man's perfect conformity to the law of the ten commandments is holiness. Therefore, as far as content was concerned, Adam in his perfection had the ten commandments as his law.

In addition to the law of nature God gave Adam a command which in His sovereignty He could or could not have given: the command *not to eat of the tree of the knowledge of good and evil,* the name of which we have referred to previously. This may readily suggest the question, *Why did God give this commandment to Adam?* Had God not given this commandment to him, he would not have sinned. My response is:

(1) That it does not necessarily follow that he then would not have sinned. Adam was holy, but mutable, and thus he could also have sinned in a different situation.

(2) God does not always give an account of His deeds. If anyone wishes to meditate somewhat upon this commandment, it will become evident that much is comprehended in this commandment. It declared that God alone was the Lord and thus entitled to command Adam as He pleased, and that Adam was thus required to obey blindly without asking why.

(3) In it was also comprehended that man should desire nothing else but the will of God, and that everything should be defined as desirable or undesirable in relationship to God only.

(4) This commandment comprehends man's felicity consisting in the enjoyment of God Himself — an enjoyment not to be found in anything outside of Him. Therefore, Adam had no need of what would seem to be most desirable, but could do without it.

(5) It also implies that man was to be satisfied with the present degree of perfection which God was pleased to confer at that moment. The question, *Why did God give such a commandment?* cannot be answered by man other than by saying, "It was God's sovereign good pleasure." We have thus observed that Adam had a law.

The Covenant of Works and the Promise of Eternal Life

The second matter which must be proven is that *Adam had the promise of eternal felicity.*

First, this is confirmed by contemporary heathen. As God has impressed upon the human heart that He exists, as well as the manner in which He wishes man to conduct himself, it has likewise been impressed upon the heathen that there is a reward for them that are good and punishment for those that commit evil. The diaries of seafaring men confirm this. When they came into heathen territory where Christians had never been, such heathen, by gesturing either upward or downward with their hands, would indicate that those who are good would go to heaven and those who are evil to hell. Paul testified that the conscience of the heathen either accuses or excuses them (Rom. 2:15). If the heathen have knowledge of the fact that reward and punishment are related to their behavior as measured by the law impressed upon their hearts, how much more is this true for Adam who had a perfect knowledge of the law and the promises of reward.

Secondly, in the foregoing we have shown that the law given to Adam was the law of the ten commandments. The law of the ten commandments has the promise of eternal life appended to it, as can be observed in Matthew 19. A young man asked, "What good thing shall I do, that I may have eternal life?" Christ answered, "If thou wilt enter into life, keep the commandments" (Mat. 19:16-17). This is also confirmed in the following texts: "Ye shall therefore keep My statutes, and My judgments: which if a man do, he shall live in them" (Lev. 18:5); "The commandment, which was ordained to life" (Rom. 7:10); ". . . and in keeping of them there is great reward" (Psa. 19:11). Thus Adam had the promise of eternal life.

Thirdly, this is confirmed by the fact that Christ has merited eternal life for the elect by subjecting Himself to the law, satisfying it by bearing the punishment of the law and by perfect holiness in both nature and conduct. This is evident in Romans 8:4, where the apostle declared that by virtue of Christ's satisfaction "...the righteousness of the law might be fulfilled in us (the elect)." This is also stated in Galatians 4:4-5: "God sent forth his Son, made of a woman, made under the law, to redeem them that were under the law, that we might receive the adoption of sons." Notice that here reference is made to a law — the same law Adam had. To this law the Lord Jesus subjected Himself, *and in doing so* He merited redemption and adoption of sons for the elect. "And if children, then heirs; heirs of God, and joint-heirs with Christ...that we may be also glorified together" (Rom. 8:17). Thus, eternal glory necessarily follows upon obedience to the law. Consequently, Adam, having the same law, had the promise of eternal felicity.

Fourthly, the same life which is granted upon the receiving of Christ by faith is promised upon perfect obedience to the law. Since eternal life is granted to the elect upon faith in Christ, this is likewise true for perfect obedience to the law. The apostle confirms that the same promise applies to both matters. "For Moses describeth the righteousness which is of the law, that the man which doeth those things shall live by them. But the righteousness which is of faith speaketh on this wise, That if thou shalt confess with thy mouth the Lord Jesus, and shalt believe in thine heart... thou shalt be saved" (Rom. 10:5-6, 9). "...The just shall live by faith. And the law is not of faith: but, The man that doeth them shall live in them" (Gal. 3:11-12). Here is one and the same promise: *life,* eternal life. This is stated in Matthew 19:16-17 as explained above. Concerning faith it is stated in John 3:36, "He that believeth on the Son hath everlasting life." The apostle demonstrates that there are two ways by which this goal can be reached, one being the law, and the other faith. From this follows that Adam, having the law, had the promise of eternal life, which now is obtained by faith.

Fifthly, this is confirmed by the threat. "In the day that thou eatest thereof thou shalt surely die" (Gen. 2:17). Death is threatened here without any limitation. Someone who insists that here death is limited to temporal death must prove that this is necessarily so. He will never succeed in doing so, as no trace of such evidence is to be found. Moreover, it is common knowledge that

(1) death refers to eternal damnation as well as to temporal death. "To the one we are the savour of death unto death" (2 Cor. 2:16); "There is a sin unto death" (1 John 5:16); "On such the second death hath no power" (Rev. 20:6);

(2) the death threatened was a punishment upon sin. The punishment upon sin is not only temporal, however, but also eternal death, which is placed in contradistinction to eternal life. "The wages of sin is death; but the gift of God is eternal life through Jesus Christ our Lord" (Rom. 6:23); "These shall go away into everlasting punishment: but the righteous into life eternal" (Mat. 25:46);

(3) the apostle states expressly that by eating from the forbidden tree condemnation has come upon all men: "The judgment was by one to condemnation...by the offence of one judgment came upon all men to condemnation" (Rom. 5:16, 18). No one can deny that this offense was the eating from the forbidden tree. Upon this eating, however, condemnation would follow, and thus condemnation was threatened by the word "death." Let us reverse this argument. If upon transgression Adam was threatened with eternal condemnation, then, by applying the rule of opposites, eternal life was promised upon obedience. This threat of death contained in it the promise of life if he did not sin. This reason is all the more credible, for who is able and would dare to think that a good God would threaten eternal punishment upon disobedience and not at the same time promise eternal felicity upon obedience? Who would dare to think that His judgments are incomprehensibly greater than His goodness?

The Covenant of Works and the Tree of Life

Sixthly, this is also confirmed by the *tree of life*. Here two trees are contrasted with each other. Since the one symbolizes eternal death, why would the other one not symbolize eternal life? The name also indicates this, for it is expressly called the tree of *life*. What else can be deduced from this than that it was a sacrament, that is, a sign and seal of life? There is not the least indication that the meaning here is limited to corporal life, and thus we may not do so either. Moreover, if Adam lost corporal life, he at once also lost the spiritual life which he possessed. Therefore, by the word life we must understand both the corporal and spiritual life which he then possessed, as well as eternal felicity which generally is comprehended in the word "life," even though the word "eternal" is not added to it. "If thou wilt enter into life..." (Mat. 19:17); "Narrow is the way, which leadeth unto life" (Mat. 7:14). This is stated in many other texts as well. For this reason, after Adam had lost this life, the Lord no longer wanted him to be a partaker of this seal of eternal life. By means of an angel the Lord expelled him from Paradise, "...lest he put forth his hand, and take also of the tree of life, and eat, and live for ever" (Gen. 3:22).

When he had sinned by eating from the one tree, which he had no right to do, God was not willing that he should also eat from the other tree. Would he have lived eternally if he nevertheless would have been able to gain access to this tree and have eaten from it? Most certainly not, for there was no inherent power in this tree to restore the spiritual life and communion with God which had been lost. Adam certainly knew this. What could corporal life have benefited him without spiritual life? Neither was there any inherent power in the tree to nullify and rescind God's threat, "Thou shalt surely die." Even if he were able to preserve his corporal life, Adam knew very well that he would not be able to do so. Why then did God say, ". . . and live forever"? My response is that this is a rebuking and reprimanding manner of speech, as is evident in that same verse, "Behold, the man is become as one of us" (Gen. 3:22). It is as if God said, "Behold the man, who thought that by eating of the forbidden tree he could become as one of us. Behold, how he now resembles us!" God said as it were, "How he has been deceived in his objective, for instead of becoming like one of us, he has become unlike us." This is also the manner of speech in the phrase, "and live forever," meaning, "for he would again be deceived in his objective and opinion, if he were to think that by eating of this tree he would live forever." "And live forever" therefore refers to that which he would imagine, as if after having sinned this tree would continue to be a sacrament of life. God did not want him to abuse the sacrament since he had forfeited the matter itself, that is, eternal life. It was the Lord's will that he would now turn away from the broken covenant of works, and, being lost in himself, would put all his hope in the seed of the woman, which was promised to him immediately after the fall.

Adam's Acceptance of the Conditions and Promises of the Covenant of Works

We have thus observed the activity of the one party: God giving the law to Adam, which in content was identical to the ten commandments, promising him that same eternal felicity which Christ has merited for the elect and grants unto them upon faith. We have observed that God gave the tree of the knowledge of good and evil as a sign of a probationary nature, and the tree of life as a sign of a sealing nature. Thus all the required conditions have been shown as far as the one side of the covenant is concerned. We must now in addition bring into view the other party and his engagement, this being a prerequisite for a covenant transaction.

The other party is the human race in Adam who was adorned

with the image of God, consisting of a flawless knowledge of God, righteousness, and holiness. He therefore certainly knew both condition and promise, and was capable of fulfilling the condition. Since nothing is written concerning this, the question is, *"Did he acquiesce in this covenant?"* My response is that even though it is not expressly stated in Scripture, it can nevertheless be clearly deduced from it.

It is evident that Adam accepted the condition and the promise. First of all, it occurs in Scripture that the promise of the covenant is mentioned relative to one of the parties, even though the reference is to the entire covenant. For Genesis 3:15 states, "It (the Seed of the woman, Christ) shall bruise thy (the serpent's) head." It is certainly known that the covenant of grace was established here, and yet there is not one word mentioning Adam and Eve's acceptance of this covenant. Since all the conditions of a covenant are mentioned as far as the one party is concerned, this necessarily implies the acquiescence of the other party.

Secondly, Adam was perfect and therefore, since God could rightfully command, and Adam, due to his perfect obedience could not refuse, he could not do otherwise than accept this condition and promise. Could a rational creature, having a perfect knowledge of communion with God in a lesser degree, be anything but in love with and desirous for a higher degree of this most blessed communion? He could not do any differently — unless he were dehumanized through loss of intellect and love for his own well-being. Therefore, when such matters were promised to him, he could not but delight in, desire, and embrace them with all his heart — matters which, as we have just observed, were indeed promised to him. This is likewise true for the condition, for this was not only the way leading to felicity, but was his present felicity itself. This consisted in a perfect love for a most amiable God and subjection to a sovereign Lord who was worthy of obedience. This Adam possessed and this was his love, joy, and delight. Since he could not but accept the promise for the reason just mentioned, he also could not but accept the condition, since the promise and the condition did not differ in essence but merely in degree.

Thirdly, this is also evident from the conduct of all men. Human nature teaches us to speak as follows: "I approve of the law as holy, just, and good. I approve of it; I conclude that I am obligated toward it, and acquiesce in this obligation, and deem this to be my duty. I willingly obligate myself to it, embracing the promise that upon obedience I shall receive heaven. Thus in seeing that natural man after the fall as yet acquiesces in both the promise and the condition, therefore much more could man in his perfection not do otherwise than accept both condition and promise.

Fourthly, the fact that Adam and Eve accepted the promise and condition is also evident in their refraining from and refusal to eat from the forbidden tree, the Lord having forbidden them to do so. When there is obedience in response to a prohibition and a refusal to transgress, there is an acceptance of promise and condition. Such is the case here, as is evident from the history in Genesis 3. Consequently Adam and Eve accepted the condition and promise, and it therefore follows that there was a genuine covenant between God and man.

We may thus draw the conclusion which we have sought for and found. Whenever there is a law as a condition, promises related to the fulfillment of that condition, signs of a probationary as well as a sealing nature, namely, the acceptance of both condition and promise, there is then a covenant. All of this is true here, and thus there was a covenant between God and Adam. We make no mention here of Paradise nor the Sabbath, since we do not acknowledge either of these, nor the tree of the knowledge of good and evil, to be sacraments.

Additional Proof to Verify the Validity of the Covenant of Works

Proof #2: Having established the former, the following proof is that much more clear. We base our proof on Hosea 6:7, "But they like men[1] have transgressed the covenant: there have they dealt treacherously against me." Here mention is made of a covenant — a covenant with Adam — and the breaking of a covenant. Two difficulties must be removed here: whether the word "Adam" ought to be translated as "man" here, the reference not being to Adam but rather to other men, and whether the word ברית (*Berith*) should not be translated as "law"; so that there is no reference to a covenant here at all.

My response to the first difficulty is as follows: Since the word "Adam" can be and frequently is translated as "man," it does not therefore follow that it must be translated in such a manner here. Whoever insists on this must prove it, and this he will not be able to do. We maintain that in this text the word "Adam" is the proper name of the first man. Our reasons for this are as follows:

---

[1] The Statenvertaling reads as follows, "Zij hebben het verbond overtreden, als Adam," that is, "They have transgressed the covenant as Adam." The argumentation which follows focuses on the fact that in à Brakel's opinion the English translation "as men" is incorrect, and should have been translated as "as Adam."

(1) If one were to translate it with the word "man," it would take away the emphasis of this text, for the words "as Adam" are added here to maximize rather than minimize the crime. What force of emphasis, yes, what purpose would there be to state that they had broken the covenant like other men who also are but members of the covenant. In order for them to transgress a covenant, they of necessity must be in the covenant; that is, they would have to transgress the covenant as they or their fellow members of the covenant did. This certainly makes no sense, and therefore Adam here refers to the first man.

(2) Frequently in the first book of Moses, and in Deuteronomy 32:8 and 1 Chronicles 1:1, the Holy Scriptures use the word "Adam" as the proper name of the first man, and we find this coalescence especially in Job 31:33. "If I covered my transgressions כאדם (ke Adam) as Adam..." This is an express reference to Adam's covering up his crime, and since the reference is to the first man, the proper name Adam must be used here. Since the reference in Hosea 6:7 is to a sin which Adam had committed, that is, a sin of a similar nature, why then not translate כאדם (ke Adam) as "Adam"?

(3) The original text also does not present any reason to prevent us from using the proper name. No ה (emphaticum, a symbol for emphasis) may be placed next to a proper name. If, however, this word means "man" it is frequently accompanied by an ה. An ה is not used here, which would be most appropriate if the reference were to other men, whereas the word "Adam" is used with great emphasis here.

(4) The matter in question is true in regard to Adam. He was involved in a covenant as we have observed above. He has broken the covenant, and therefore we must maintain that the reference is to Adam as long as necessity does not compel us to conclude otherwise.

(5) It fits the context very well. It is God's intent to demonstrate the magnitude of the sin of Judah and Ephraim by identifying the origin as well as the example for this sin. This sin was not only evil in and of itself, but it also had an evil origin, which made it all the more evil. This also amplified David's sin, as is recorded in Psalm 51. This breach of covenant was a sin proceeding from the original covenant breach in Adam, and therefore all the more abominable. Having been abundantly blessed both corporeally and spiritually, Adam lightly, recklessly, and faithlessly broke the covenant. They, whom God had blessed so abundantly in body but also in soul by granting His Word and all the means of grace, followed in the similitude of Adam's transgression by treacherously breaking God's covenant. Thus, the words "as Adam" cause us to focus upon the

first covenant breach of Adam, which is referred to here in order to amplify the sin of Judah and Ephraim.

The second argument, namely, that ברית (*Berith*) can be translated as "law" is also invalid, for we cannot logically conclude the actual meaning of a word from a possible meaning. Apart from this, however, I deny that the word *Berith* means "law." Until this moment I have not encountered any example of this, although I do admit that it is called a covenant, viewing the law as a rule of the covenant. To my knowledge, however, this word never means "law." This therefore confirms that the reference here is to covenant — a covenant which has been transgressed as Adam transgressed the covenant. Hence there was a covenant between God and Adam.

Exhortation to Reflect upon the Covenant of Works

Meditate frequently upon this covenant, in order that you may perceive to what a blessed state God had appointed the human race — and thus also you as far as your original state was concerned. How perfect, fitting, and even desirable are its conditions! How glorious are the promises, and how glorious it is to be in covenant with the all-glorious and infinitely good God! The dimensions of this are infinite. Then proceed to the breach of the covenant and the needless, reckless, and wanton nature of the same. What an abominable deed it was! From this perspective proceed to the righteousness of God and let the punishment and rejection of such covenant breakers meet with your approval. When considering the glory of this covenant, seek to amplify your actual and original sins. This beautiful covenant has now been broken, and an unconverted person who as yet has not been translated into the covenant of grace is still in the actual covenant of works. Therefore, as often as he sins, he breaks the covenant by renewal, remains subject to its curse, and increases it time and again. Therefore look away from the covenant of works. It has been broken and salvation is no longer obtainable by it. This exhortation is necessary since even God's children are often inclined to dwell upon their works, and accordingly, are either encouraged or discouraged. The unconverted are always desirous to perform something, being of the opinion that all can be made well with prayer and reformation; however, in this way they shall be deceived. Let the covenant of grace be precious to you. Turn to the Mediator of this better covenant. Enter into this covenant, give heed to it, and consider the first man to be dead.

CHAPTER THIRTEEN

The Breach of the Covenant of Works

The fact that Adam sinned and thus broke the covenant of works needs no other proof than the sinful condition of all men as well as the Scriptures, which bear witness to this fact everywhere.

The Time of Adam's Fall

However, the question arises, *when did Adam fall?* Man, having been created so magnificently, and being in such a blessed covenant with His God, in all probability did not remain long in this holy and blessed state. The duration of this state is not recorded and is thus unknown. That he did not fall immediately on the day of his creation is evident for the following reasons:

First, the seventh day is added to the sixth in the same manner as the previous days are joined together. There is no mention of any interval, or of the fall of either devils or man. The imposed chapter divisions have no bearing on this matter at all, for the chapter divisions did not originate with the holy writers themselves, but were established by others as a memory aid and for instructional purposes.

Secondly, the fall is recorded as having occurred after the seventh day. The first seven days and what occurred on those days, are described in chronological order in Genesis 1 and 2, whereas the fall is recorded subsequent to this in Genesis 3.

Thirdly, upon conclusion of the sixth day, everything was still very good. "And God saw every thing that He had made, and, behold, it was very good. And the evening and the morning were the sixth day" (Gen. 1:31).

Fourthly, when God saw man's sinfulness, "it repented the LORD that He had made man on the earth, and it grieved Him at

His heart" (Gen. 6:6). However, on the seventh day the Lord rested; that is, He ceased creating new creatures. He observed all His work with delight, rejoicing in His own works, and humanly speaking, was refreshed by this. "For in six days the LORD made heaven and earth, and on the seventh day He rested, and was refreshed" (Exo. 31:17). This proves that man neither fell prior to nor upon the seventh day.

Fifthly, it is also not conceivable that man, who had just opened his eyes upon this world, would immediately have fallen, and thus not have had time to delight himself in God, rejoice in his holy and glorious state, and magnify God concerning all this. He then would neither have had time to be experientially acquainted with his blessed state, nor have been able to reflect upon it after the fall. From this it may be deduced that God allotted him some time to experience that which is good, and that man did not fall until after the seventh day. It is unknown, however, after how many days, weeks, or months it did occur.

Satan's Role in the Fall

After a large number of angels had sinned and become devils, the devil conspired to cause Adam and Eve to fall in order to prevent them from glorifying God, whom he hated with a dreadful hatred as He had rejected the devils and eternally excluded them from grace.

The devil first attacked Eve when she was alone, probably standing near the tree of the knowledge of good and evil. There he deceived her, and she, having been deceived although not yet conscious of it, also deceived her husband Adam. He was not deceived due to love for his wife, but rather due to her deception, and only then the eyes of both of them were opened (Gen. 3:7). The devil was thus the suggestive cause of the fall, and for this reason is called "a murderer from the beginning" and "a liar" (John 8:44).

For this purpose the devil used a serpent, judging it to be a suitable instrument for him. He spoke to Eve through the serpent. He was neither invisible when he spoke, nor did he simulate a speaking voice. He did not communicate personally with the soul of Eve, but spoke through the serpent, of which he had taken possession. One should neither view this matter as being a metaphor, nor as a parable or an illusion. Neither did the devil appear as an apparition in the similitude of a serpent, but this is genuine history — an event which has truly occurred. Both the devil and the serpent were actively involved in this matter. It was a serpent in the true sense of the word, that is, a genuine animal. This is evident:

(1) From the history itself. "Now the serpent was more subtil than any beast of the field... And he said unto the woman..." (Gen. 3:1);

(2) Also from verse 14 where the following is stated concerning the serpent, "Because thou hast done this, thou art cursed above all cattle." It cannot be contradicted that the serpent was an irrational creature, and thus incapable of making intelligible and intelligent speech. It is therefore certain that a rational creature spoke through the serpent, and that this intelligent creature was evil and sinful. Hence it could not have been anyone else but the devil, who for this reason is frequently called "serpent," "dragon," or "that old serpent" in Scripture. "...the dragon, that old serpent, which is the devil, and Satan" (Rev. 20:2). It was he who deceived Eve: "...as the serpent beguiled Eve through his subtilty" (2 Cor. 11:3). It is his head which was bruised by Christ, "that through death He might destroy him that had the power of death, that is, the devil" (Heb. 2:14).

Since Moses is very brief in recounting the events of the first world, the method of deceit is not recorded. Therefore all conjecture in this case is but idle speculation, such as whether the devil spoke only once or on several occasions with Eve; whether he dealt with Eve in an entirely different manner; whether he came as a messenger of God, declaring that the time of probation had been concluded, and therefore they were now permitted to eat; whether he came as friend and teacher to counsel and convey to her what benefit could be derived from eating from this tree; or whether he came as an enemy of God, wishing to deprive her of that which would make her happy and equal to Him. These are all conjectures. It is also possible that he produced other pretexts or deceptive rationale. I would rather be silent about these and similar matters than to mislead you with what only appears to be rational. Whatever the wisest and greatest teacher has not been pleased to reveal to us, we should not be desirous to know. This is a safe practice by which one will avoid many temptations.

I am convinced that Eve knew very well that animals, also the serpent, have neither a rational intellect nor are capable of speech. Though she was ignorant of the fall of the angels, she could have deduced that this occurrence was of an extraordinary nature. I am also convinced that Eve was permitted to desire a higher level of knowledge and communion with God, this having been promised to her in the covenant of works. She was also permitted to aspire after increased knowledge concerning the realm of nature, which she could gain in the way of experience, just as the manifold wisdom of God might be known to the angels by the church (Eph. 3:10).

I am also convinced that she did not ignorantly eat from this tree, but knew very well that she was neither permitted to eat from it nor touch it. Being desirous to increase in understanding, Eve was seduced to eat from this tree. She was not coerced but did so of her own free will. Eve was not immediately conscious of this deceit, but became aware of this only after she had deceived Adam. Furthermore, Adam was neither the first to be deceived nor was he deceived by the serpent, but as the apostle states in 1 Timothy 2:14, by a deceived Eve — and thus subsequent to her. I am convinced that had Adam remained standing, Eve would have borne the punishment alone. Since Adam also sinned, however, the entire human nature, the entire human race, became guilty, as Paul said, "Wherefore, as by one man sin entered into the world..." (Rom. 5:12). He does not merely refer to Eve's sin, but to the sin of the entire human race, which is fully and entirely comprehended in Adam and Eve who were one by virtue of their marriage. Rather, he specifically refers to the sin of Adam who was the first man, the first and only source, both of Eve and the entire human race.

The eating from this tree was not a minor sin, even though the eating of the fruit itself was a small matter. Rather, it was a dreadful crime in which the breaking of the entire law was comprehended. It was a breach of love, obedience, and the covenant, resulting in the perdition of himself and all his descendants. This sin is aggravated by the fact that,

(1) it was committed against God Himself whom they knew in His majesty and His glory, and who in His manifold goodness had united them to Himself;

(2) it was committed by a holy person who had the necessary ability to refrain from doing so, and to resist all temptation;

(3) to refrain from eating from this one tree was but an insignificant and easy requirement, since they had everything in abundance in this beautiful garden;

(4) the felicity or condemnation of himself and his descendants hinged upon it. Therefore, in Romans 5 this eating is correctly denominated, "sin" (vs. 12), "transgression" (vs. 14), "offence" (vs. 15), and "disobedience" (vs. 19).

Unbelief Identified as Man's Initial Sin

When we consider this sin and its commission comprehensively, it is evidently a fusion of all sins. This is not merely so because whoever transgresses in one commandment is guilty of all — every sin being an act of apostasy towards the lawgiver and a transgression of the law — but also because many specific sins are combined in this sin. If someone were to ask, *"Which was the first sin?"*, I respond that a particular sin may not have been first chronologically, but first in order of importance. Also, before the external deed manifested itself, a fusion of various sins had already occurred. Thus the initial sin is neither to be found in the external act, in the emotions, affections, and inclinations, nor in the will. In a perfect nature will and emotions are subject to the intellect, as they do not precede the intellect in their function but are a consequence of the same.

The *initial sin* must be sought in the intellect, which by deceptive reasoning was prompted to conclude that they would not die and that there was an inherent power in that tree to make them wise, a wisdom which they were permitted to desire without being guilty of sin. This tree bore the name of *knowledge,* which was desirable to them. It also bore the name *good and evil,* even though it was hidden from them as to what was comprehended in the word *evil.* The serpent makes use of this name as if great matters were concealed in these words. As the intellect focused on both the desirability of becoming wise, as well as the tree by which either as a means or as a cause this wisdom could be transmitted to them, the intense and lively awareness of the prohibition not to eat and the threat of death tended to diminish. The faculty of judgment, suggesting that it would be desirable to eat from this tree, aroused the inclination to acquire wisdom in this manner. Added to this was the fact that "...the woman saw that the tree was good for food, and that it was pleasant to the eyes" (Gen. 3:6).

The deception of the intellect was not in consequence of the nature of the tree and its fruit, but due to the words of the serpent and the words of the woman to Adam. Thus, the issue at hand — namely, *not to die, but to gain in wisdom by eating of this tree* — was confirmed by faith, this being the act whereby one holds the words of someone else for truth. Therefore the first sin was *faith in the serpent,* believing that they would not die but instead gain wisdom. This act implied a disbelieving of God who had threatened death upon eating from this tree. Thus Eve by virtue of unbelief became disobedient, reached out, and ate. In doing so she believed the serpent and was thus *deceived* and beguiled, this sin being denominated as such in 1 Timothy 2:14 and 2 Corinthians 11:3. In like manner she beguiled Adam. Therefore, the first sin was not pride, that is, to be equal with God, also not rebellion, disobedience, or an unwarranted appetite, but unbelief.

Adam's Fall not due to Imperfection in His Nature

Question: How was it possible that a perfect person, who was entirely free from the principle of sin, could fall into sin?

Answer: Tell me first of all how it was possible that the angels, who had a higher degree of perfection, could have sinned? If you respond by saying that you know they have sinned, but not how they sinned, you have already answered your own question concerning Adam. The fact that Adam sinned is a certainty. That he was free from the least innate inclination towards sin is also certain, for 1) if that were not true, God would be designated as the author of sin; 2) such an innate inclination towards sin is inconsistent with being created perfectly and in the image of God; and 3) such an inclination is contrary to the tenth commandment.

Secondly, God created man as a rational creature, gifting him with intellect and a free will, thus enabling him to govern his actions and refrain from yielding to external temptations and guile. Instead, man permitted himself to be deceived in the manner stated earlier. Since we are now subject to it, let us be more concerned how we may be delivered from sin rather than how we became involved in it.

The fact that God from eternity foreknew the fall, decreeing that He would permit it to occur, is not only confirmed by the doctrines of His omniscience and decrees (chapter 5), but also by the fact that God from eternity has ordained a Redeemer for man, to deliver him from sin: the Lord Jesus Christ whom Peter calls the Lamb, "who verily was foreordained before the foundation of the world" (1 Pet. 1:20).

Question: Did Adam in sinning act independently from God, and did the fall therefore occur apart from the providence of God?

Answer: My answer is an emphatic "No." We have dealt comprehensively with this matter in chapter 11. There we have shown that no creature can be independent from God, neither in its existence nor in its actions. We also confirmed that the cooperation of God controls man and activates him relative to each specific deed, while supporting and sustaining him in this. Thus God, as far as natural motion is concerned, energizes man's intellect, will, and activities in a manner agreeable with his human nature, causing him to act by his free will. This will, though sustained, controlled, and governed by virtue of God's cooperation, is itself the initiator and cause of his deeds. In sinning, man abuses all this, by not engaging himself in conformity to the law appointed him. Such was the case with Adam. God had given him sufficient strength to resist all temptation, but God did not prevent him from sinning. He could have done the latter, but was not obligated to do so. God did not withdraw this given strength from Adam, but permitted man to be active in the exercise of his free will. Consequently the blame is man's and not God's. He who wishes to penetrate this matter with his puny, darkened understanding, summoning God before the bar of his intellect and judgment, to declare Him guilty and man innocent (which in all probability such a person would desire to do), attributing to man an innate inclination towards sin, or declaring him independent from God — such a person shall be rewarded for such audacity with great darkness and will fall victim to foolish and sinful notions about God. Therefore, I wish to advise you to acquiesce in what we have stated and to consider that the Lord's thoughts and ways are not as ours. God's ways are holy whether we understand them or not.

The Covenant of Works and its Obligations After the Fall

By sinning, man has broken that glorious covenant and has forfeited the promise. It is therefore now impossible for the law to justify him and to grant him the right to, and possession of, eternal life, "in that it was weak through the flesh…" (Rom. 8:3).

Nevertheless this covenant remains in full force, obligating the entire human race (that is, all who have not been translated into the covenant of grace) to obedience and subjecting men to punishment, since the fulfillment of the promise continues to be contingent upon obedience. "This do, and thou shalt live." Although man cannot obtain the promise since he does not fulfil the condition, the promise nevertheless remains part and parcel of this covenant.

First, this is evident by the fact that God by His very character obligates man to obedience, also that the creature is naturally obligated to obey, even if there were no covenant. God, however, created man in the covenant relationship, having embedded the knowledge and approbation of this covenant in his nature so that from the very first moment of his existence he never was outside of this covenant. Therefore the human nature remains under the original obligation towards this covenant.

Secondly, also among men, covenants remain in force even after the first transgression. A succession of kings and authorities will not merely recall the initial transgression of a covenant by others, but will also bring out how frequently the existing covenant has been transgressed. A woman, having committed adultery, remains in covenant with her husband and is not released from it. As often as she involves herself with someone else after the first commission of sin, so often she commits adultery and each time again breaks the covenant. This clearly proves that transgression of a covenant does not release the transgressor from the covenant relationship.

Thus also the covenant of works remained in force after the transgression.

Thirdly, it is naturally understood by all men, and Scripture teaches likewise, that the law, the promise, the threatenings, and the acceptance of the covenant remain in force; therefore the covenant of works also remains in force. Every man knows that there is a God and is conscious of the law written in his heart. He judges this law to be good and concurs with his obligation to be obedient to it. He acknowledges that he shall be rewarded if he obeys and be punished if he disobeys, which is confirmed in Romans 2:14-15 and 1:32. Since such a conditional law is in force, a covenant also is and remains in force. The sinner therefore continues to be obligated to this covenant, since he is a debtor to the entire law (Gal. 5:3). "The law hath dominion over a man as long as he liveth" (Rom. 7:1). Therefore, as often as he transgresses the law, so often he transgresses the covenant.

However, when God permits man to exit this covenant of works and enter into the covenant of grace, he is no longer under obligation to that covenant. "For ye are not under the law, but under grace" (Rom. 6:14). "For if the (first) husband be dead, she is loosed from the law of her husband" (Rom. 7:2). To the believer the law is no longer a condition of the covenant of works, but a most desirable rule of life. Thus, when he sins, he no longer breaks the covenant of works, as he is no longer obligated toward it. Rather, he sins against this most desirable rule of life which has been given to him in the covenant of grace. Such sin is not committed by the new man within, but by the flesh which remains in him. And although these sins themselves are worthy of punishment, believers shall not be subjected to punishment since the Surety has taken their sins upon Himself and has fully paid their debt.

One might think that since at the very first sin the promises were cancelled and the punishment was meted out, the covenant of works can therefore no longer be in force. Our reply is as follows:

(1) Both promises and threatenings are inherent in the covenant, and it continues to retain them. Therefore, the covenant remains in force, since in reality the promises and the threatenings already constituted the covenant.

(2) Neither the promises nor the threatenings, considered independently, constitute the essential nature of the covenant, but rather the interdependent relationship of the covenant. And since this remains in force, the covenant remains in force.

(3) There are also degrees as far as reward and punishment are

concerned. This already having been conceded, the covenant can remain in force.

(4) Man continues to be under obligation to delight himself in God, to believe in Him, to view Him as his highest good, and to seek Him in the way of obedience. No one wishing to be called a Christian would dare to deny this. Therefore, the covenant which obligates man to all this also remains in force.

The Misery of Man due to his Breach of Covenant

Numerous sinful and painful miseries have resulted from Adam and Eve's breaking of this covenant.

First, man was immediately deprived of the image of God, the reformation of which begins in regeneration (Col. 3:10; Eph. 4:24). These texts confirm that this image was lost, which immediately manifested itself by the consciousness of shame.

Secondly, there was consciousness of *shame*. Due to the shame of their bodily nakedness, they did not dare to come nakedly into the presence of God (Gen. 3:7, 10). They were also ashamed of themselves and in each others presence. This is not indicative of impure lusts in these married persons, but their consciences made them aware that their members were too shameful to be seen. They therefore attempted to conceal them, finding no better and more appropriate means than the leaves of fig trees. These leaves probably were not as small as here and in Spain, but lengthwise reached from a man's chin to his knees. Similar size leaves still grow today in Ceylon. These they attached to each other as best as they could, and girded themselves with them.

Thirdly, added to this was a *terrified conscience*. The Lord revealed Himself in the cool[1] of the day which arose at sunrise to moderate the heat — which especially occurs in many countries where it is hot. It is possible that at that time the Lord normally revealed Himself to Adam in a special manner, something with which he already was experientially acquainted. It is also possible that something extraordinary occurred, whereby Adam became aware of the Lord's arrival. At any rate, Adam and Eve were now conscious of having committed sin; hence they also feared the punishment of sin. The presence of God, which previously rendered them such joy, now caused them to fear, so that they fled, hiding themselves among the nearest trees (Gen. 3:8).

Fourthly, Adam manifested a *sinful self-love* by seeking to excuse himself, as well as his lovelessness by accusing his wife, Eve (Gen.

---

[1] In Dutch: "de wind des daags," that is, the breeze of the day.

3:12). Job spoke of this. "If I covered my transgressions as Adam, by hiding mine iniquity in my bosom" (Job 31:33). Eve also excused herself by stating that she had merely been deceived, blaming the serpent.

Fifthly, this was followed by 1) the sentencing of the serpent, which had been misused. "Thou art cursed above all cattle," etc. (Gen. 3:14), and 2) the sentencing of Satan who was the cause of the temptation: the seed of the woman "shall bruise thy head" (Gen. 3:15). This was accomplished by Christ (Heb. 2:14).

Sixthly, after the Lord had announced the covenant of grace to Adam and Eve by testifying of the seed of the woman (rather than of the man) — which is Christ, who would come to "destroy the works of the devil" (1 John 3:8), who is "the fruit of (Mary's) womb" (Luke 1:42) and who was "…made of a woman" (Gal. 4:4) — it was the Lord's will that man would always remain conscious of sin. Thus He announced to him the chastisement of miseries which would remain upon him and which for the unconverted would be punishment resulting in death.

(1) The special plagues with which particularly the female sex would be afflicted are: "I will greatly multiply thy sorrow and thy conception; in sorrow thou shalt bring forth children; and thy desire shall be to thy husband, and he shall rule over thee" (Gen. 3:16).

(2) The special punishments which God imposed upon the male sex are as follows: "Cursed is the ground for thy sake; in sorrow shalt thou eat of it all the days of thy life. Thorns also and thistles shall it bring forth to thee; and thou shalt eat the herb of the field; in the sweat of thy face shalt thou eat bread" (Gen. 3:17-19).

(3) The common punishment to which both the man and the woman would be subject was death. "For dust thou art, and unto dust shalt thou return" (Gen. 3:19).

One might think: Not one word is mentioned here of eternal damnation; it appears that this was neither threatened nor merited. I reply: first, in the above we have shown that eternal damnation was threatened upon sin. We will subsequently show how it has been merited by all sins, and that upon death it shall be the portion of the unconverted. Secondly, the reason eternal damnation is not mentioned here is because the covenant of grace by virtue of the seed of the woman, which is Christ, was announced to Adam and Eve (vs. 15) prior to the announcements of the sorrows to which they would be subject (vss. 16-19). Adam and Eve therefore had already been delivered from condemnation, and the sorrows imposed upon them were as chastisements.

Objection: There is no proof that Adam and Eve were saved by

Christ. The very opposite appears to be true in Hebrews 11:4, where Abel is presented as the first believer, as well as in Matthew 23:35 where he is presented as the first righteous man.

Answer: First, Abel is indeed mentioned in these texts, but not as the first righteous man, neither as the first believer. Thus, Adam is no more excluded there than when Abraham is called the father of the faithful — as if that were to exclude all believers before him. Secondly, in these texts Abel is placed in contrast to the ungodly, since there is reference to the superiority of his sacrifice over Cain's and he was the first martyr. Thirdly, that Adam believed in the promised seed is proven

(1) by virtue of the established covenant which could not exist without there being a partaker of this covenant. If Adam had not been a partaker of this covenant, it would have been without a partaker until Abel and Seth, who was born 130 years after Adam's creation. When God established a covenant with Abraham, he was himself included. Would God establish the covenant of grace, referring to the seed of the woman which would bruise the head of the serpent, and not include Adam and Eve in this covenant? Would this covenant then not be efficacious for so many years in the absence of partakers of this covenant? Would God have made announcement to Adam and Eve concerning the covenant of grace, and then have excluded them from it?

(2) It is evident from the enmity between man and the serpent, for wherever there is enmity with the devil there is peace with God.

(3) Eve immediately focused upon the promise after she bore Cain, saying, "I have gotten a man from the LORD" (Gen. 4:1).

(4) Add to this the godly upbringing and faithful instruction of Adam's children, which was the means whereby Abel received faith.

The Covenant of Works and the Covenant of Grace

Having established the covenant of grace with Adam and Eve, and having imposed upon them as chastisements the various trials and tribulations of this life as well as temporal death, the Lord clothed them with better garments than those made of fig leaves, namely, coats of skins. Prior to the fall Adam killed no animals. Not meat, but herb-bearing seed and the fruit of a tree yielding seed was given to him for meat. I cannot tell you where these skins came from. We do not read that they came from sacrificed animals, and it is of no profit to know this. It was God who made coats of skins for them, clothing them in order to cover and warm them. In doing so, however, He sharply rebuked them concerning the breach of the covenant of works and their objective in transgressing it, by saying, "Behold, the man is become as one of us, to know good and evil" (Gen. 3:22).

Whereas the covenant of works had been broken and rendered impotent so that felicity was no longer to be obtained by it, and the covenant of grace had replaced this covenant for believers, God did not want Adam to yearn for the covenant of works or its sacrament, the tree of life, as this covenant was no longer efficacious. Rather, the Lord wanted them to turn from this covenant, putting all their hope and seeking all their comfort in the promised seed of the woman. "Therefore the LORD God sent him forth from the garden of Eden, to till the ground from whence he was taken. So He drove out the man; and He placed at the east of the Garden of Eden Cherubims, and a flaming sword which turned every way, to keep the way of the tree of life...lest he put forth his hand, and take also of the tree of life, and eat, and live for ever" (Gen. 3:23-24, 22).

We have already shown that there was no efficacy in the tree of life to preserve life eternally. It no longer served a function as a sacrament of the covenant of works since the promise no longer could be obtained by way of this broken covenant. Why then was the way to the tree of life barred so that Adam would not approach it to eat of it? It is possible that the devil had given Eve a wrong impression concerning this tree of life, or that afterwards the devil might convince man that if he were to eat of the tree of life, he would not die — doing all of this to draw man away from the covenant of grace and to direct him by renewal to the covenant of works as the way in which felicity was to be sought. It is also possible that Adam himself would have such inclinations by having a wrong objective and impression in view. From this God wished to keep him and therefore not only forbade him to eat of this tree, but also prevented him from coming to this tree.

Thus the covenant of works has been broken and it would be to the advantage of God's children to look away from this covenant. How much yearning there still is for the covenant of works! This becomes evident both in the manifestation of unbelief when falling into sin — as if sin would nullify all the promises and as if one must find something within himself before coming to Christ — and by secretly resting in our own works, being more encouraged when things go reasonably well. Therefore one must make Christ in the covenant of grace the foundation for all rest and comfort and seek holiness from Him as a principal element of salvation.

CHAPTER FOURTEEN

Original and Actual Sin

Sin Defined

Having broken the covenant, Adam did not only become sinful himself, but also all his descendants with him. We understand the word "sin" here to refer neither to the *punishment of sin* nor to the *sacrifice for sin* (even though these are occasionally denominated as sin), but to that which both in essence and in deed is *contrary to God's good pleasure*. Scripture refers to this as: *revolt, iniquity, wickedness, disobedience, unrighteousness, transgression, treachery, rebellion, etc.* Each particular sin has its own particular name.

Sin is not something that has essence and exists independently. Whatever has essence has been created by God and as such is good. Furthermore, the essence of man's personhood was not changed due to sin. Sin, however, has polluted and corrupted the essential, moral character of the faculties of the soul.

The essential nature of sin also does not consist of the *voluntary and immediate acquiescence of the will*, as if sin were absent as long as there is no immediate acquiescence of the will — an idea which has been construed to deny original sin:

(1) Lot was guilty of incest, and Paul blasphemed Christ and persecuted the congregations. They, however, did so without their wills acquiescing in the commission of incest and blasphemy, since they did it ignorantly.

(2) The sin of covetousness (Rom. 7:7), prohibited in the tenth commandment, is already present in the soul prior to the will's acquiescence.

(3) In fact, all sins which are committed ignorantly (which are many) are committed without the will's acquiescence, for the will

in the act of acquiescence responds to the application of man's judgment. In tracing back this voluntary acquiescence to its origin, however, we conclude that man's nature and will are not opposed to sin, but rather are favorably disposed towards it. This is already true from the very first moment of man's existence, as yet having neither acquaintance with sin nor any real inclinations towards the same. The essence of sin also does not consist in *guilt*, that is, to be worthy of punishment, for guilt is a consequence of sin and as such can be removed, while sin remains. This occurs by virtue of the atonement of Christ for the sins of believers.

Sin also does not merely consist of *actions*, but is also inclusive of the propensity toward sin and a deviant disposition; that is, not having the faculties which ought to be present but instead having a disposition which ought not to be there.

The essence of sin consists in Ανομία (*anomia*) — *lawlessness, unruliness, and unrighteousness*, "... sin is the transgression of the law" (1 John 3:4). In relation to this a distinction must be made between man's sinful nature and his sinful acts relative to the law. In this respect a distinction is made between *inherited* and *actual sin. Inherited sin* is that sin which, by way of inheritance, has been transmitted from Adam to his descendants, having come forth from him by natural generation. Christ is the exception here, who came forth from Adam, but not in the way of natural generation. Inherited sin is also referred to as *original sin*, having its origin in Adam; it is in man from the moment of conception and origin. The other type of sin is called *actual* sin, since it is committed either in thoughts, words, or deeds.

Original Sin

Original sin consists of imputed guilt and inherent pollution. We do not understand *imputed guilt* to mean that man, due to his inherited corruption, must be viewed as being in the same condition as Adam; that is, as if he in actuality had committed the same deed which Adam had committed. This would not be the imputation of someone else's crime, but rather of one's own. This would be nothing more than a comparison between specific sins of specific people, and a comparison between sins as far as guilt and punishment are concerned. Then our sinfulness could just as well be measured against the sins of others, instead of against Adam's sin. Rather, by imputed guilt we understand the imputation of the original breach of the covenant itself, as was committed by Adam. By denying or distorting this truth the foundation is laid also to deny the pollution of sin as inherited from Adam, and thus of all original sin. This in turn leads to the denial of the imputation of the righteousness of Christ.

Imputation occurs because of a *personal crime*, whereby he who personally commits a sin by virtue of the deed righteously makes himself worthy of punishment commensurate therewith; or, this imputation occurs because of the crime of another person with whom one exists in a relationship, and thus by virtue of this relationship participates in the same sin. The sin of someone with whom we have no relationship whatsoever can also not righteously be imputed.

The relationship with someone else can exist in three different aspects.

(1) There can be a *natural* relationship, such as between a father and his children.

(2) There can be a *civil* relationship, such as between a government and its subjects.

(3) There can be a *voluntary* relationship, such as is established by a contract or mutual agreement between a creditor, debtor, and guarantor.

The latter relationship is not applicable here. The second relationship, that is, the civil relationship, when viewed per definition, is also not applicable here. It is true that Adam, by divine ordinance, without any necessity that descendants designate him as such, was the head of the human race. However, to say that Adam in sinning brought eternal condemnation upon his descendants solely on the basis of being head of the human race, places us before a dilemma, since Adam, also after the fall, remained the head of the human race. Consequently, in addition to the first covenant breach, all sins which Adam committed after the fall should then for the same reason also be imputed to his descendants. The apostle denies this when he speaks of *one* offense in Romans 5:18.

This leaves us with only the first type of relationship, that is, the natural relationship. This relationship, when considered in and of itself, is also not applicable to this situation. It is true that all men have come forth from Adam, who as it were was the trunk from which the human race has proceeded. With Adam, all are partakers of the same nature. To maintain, however, that Adam's sin is imputed to us solely because we are partakers of Adam's nature presents us with the same difficulty. Since Adam is the father of all men both prior to and after the fall, and all are therefore partakers of the same nature, then by the same argument all Adam's sins which he has committed after the fall would have an equal effect upon man as the original breach of covenant. This would be contrary to Romans 5:18. Then why wouldn't all the sins of our ancestors subsequent to Adam be imputed to us, since we were also in their loins, they also being our ancestors as well as Adam? Here it holds true, however, that "the son shall not bear the iniquity of the father" (Ezek. 18:20).

The Imputation of Adam's Sin due to Our Covenant Relationship to Him

The relationship with Adam consists in this, that the human nature of the human race, at that moment solely existing in Adam, was created as being in *the covenant of works*. Adam did not enter into the covenant of works subsequent to his creation, but was created in this covenant, being in this covenant from the very first moment of his existence. At the very moment that he formulated his first thought, he was conscious of God and the covenant, and could not but approve of this covenant. Therefore, the human nature in its totality, as well as the entire human race in Adam, were created in that covenant. For this reason all men are still born within this covenant of works discussed above. Upon Adam's breach of covenant, the human nature in its totality, that is the entire human race, broke the covenant. It is therefore righteous that this nature of the human race is rendered guilty, and that every human being, every person, by virtue of having this same nature, has the covenant breach imputed to him, and is deemed worthy of condemnation. From this it is clear that only Adam's breach of covenant and not his subsequent sins are imputed to his descendants. This is not merely because they are partakers of the same nature but because they were created in the covenant of works in Adam and have broken it in him.

Question: Is Adam's deed, that is, the original breach of covenant, imputed to the entire human race, and thus to every human being which has naturally proceeded from him, so that they are considered guilty of the covenant breach?

Socinians and Anabaptists deny this. They maintain that Adam's sin only affected him and not his descendants. *Arminians* also lean in that direction. We maintain, however, that this is certainly and irrefutably true.

The righteous imputation of the covenant breach to all men is evident from the following:

First, it is confirmed in Romans 5:12, 15-18, a passage containing several proofs.

Proof #1: "Wherefore, as by one man sin entered into the world, and death by sin; and so death passed upon all men, for that all have sinned" (Rom. 5:12).

(1) We do not read that all men are *sinful*, but that all men *have sinned*. The reference is not to *propensity*, but to the commission of an act. This text therefore can not be applicable to the corruption of the human nature, nor that man by means of his corruption would be subjected to the same punishment. Since the reference here is to a *deed*, that which follows also refers to this one *deed* (or *offense*).

(2) It is clearly stated here that sin is the cause of death, also of corporal death, and it is therefore not true that death is the result of man's sinful nature, even if no sinful act had been committed (cf. chapter 10).

(3) It is thus evident that little children prior to birth also must be guilty of sin, for they die. According to verse 14 they are not guilty of actual sin. They are therefore guilty of a sin which has been imputed to them, and no other sin is imputed to them than Adam's covenant breach.

(4) All men have sinned "in him," ἐφ' ᾧ (*eph hoi*). These little words can have numerous meanings, depending upon the manner in which they are used. In a context such as this, they mean "in him." Consider the following examples: ἐπ' αὐτοῖς (*ep autois*) — "and *in them* is fulfilled the prophecy of Esaias" (Mat. 13:14); ἐφ' ᾧ (*eph hoi*) —"the bed wherein the sick of the palsy lay" (Mark 2:4); ἐπὶ τῷ ὀνόματι (*epi toi onomati*) —"in the name of Jesus Christ" (Acts 2:38); ἐπὶ βρώμασι (*epi bromasi*) —"in meats and drinks" (Heb. 9:10); ἐπὶ νεκροῖς (*epi nekrois*) — "For a testament is of force after[1] men are dead" (Heb. 9:17). Such is also the case here, that is, men having sinned *in him*. All men were comprehended in Adam in the covenant, and therefore when he sinned, all men sinned in him in consequence of being in him.

Some might ask why these words ἐφ' ᾧ (*eph hoi*) could not be translated as "therefore," or as "because," since they are translated as such in other texts.

My reply is: The reference is here to the antecedent noun "man," which is a *masculine* word. The relative pronoun ᾧ (*hoi*), refers to this, and therefore it may not be used in the *neuter* (such as "that," "because," "therefore"), but rather in the *masculine* gender, in *him*, that is, *in a man* (a human being). It is also evident that these words, "for that all have sinned," are part of Paul's argument, namely, that by virtue of Adam's sin, death has come upon all men.

---

[1] The Statenvertaling translates this as "in de dooden," i.e., "in dead men".

It cannot be Paul's argument here that death, due to Adam's sin, has come upon all men because all men have personally sinned. This would merely prove that every man must die because he has sinned, which is not the argument of the apostle. Rather, the apostle argues that all men die by virtue of Adam's sin. If men die due to Adam's sin, however, there must be participation in Adam's sin as well as in his punishment. The apostle establishes the fact that all men are partakers of Adam's sin by these words, "for that all have sinned." The apostle first of all asserts participation in Adam's punishment, and then gives the reason for this: participation in his sin. All men die in Adam, and therefore all have sinned in him. Since no one has personally committed Adam's sin, however, there is therefore an imputation of Adam's sin by virtue of being comprehended in the covenant in him.

Proof #2: The imputation of Adam's covenant breach is also confirmed: "For if through the offence of one many be dead" (Rom. 5:15); "For the judgment was by one to condemnation" (Rom. 5:16); "For if by one man's offence death reigned by one" (Rom. 5:17); "Therefore as by the offence of one judgment came upon all men to condemnation" (Rom. 5:18). It is clear that the reference is here to one single sin, and thus to a deed rather than a propensity, and that sin was committed by only one man. By that *one* sin committed by *one* man, that is, Adam, judgment to condemnation has come upon all men. Since these are the very words of the text, this point needs no further proof.

In what manner does all this transpire?

(1) Not by imitation, for no one witnessed Adam's sin, for according to Romans 5:14 small children, who are also "men," had not sinned after the similitude of Adam. Imitation does not render anyone guilty of the sin of the person he is imitating. He is guilty of his own personal sin, which he commits by way of imitation.

(2) "Judgment to condemnation" is also not the result of *natural corruption*, which we receive from Adam for the same reason. This corruption does not render one guilty of the commission of Adam's sin, from which this corruption arises. Rather, one incurs guilt by virtue of personal corruption.

(3) "Judgment to condemnation" is also not due to the actual and personal activity in conspiracy with Adam. We did not then exist as yet and it would also not have been the *one* offense of *one*, but the offenses of many.

(4) Judgment to condemnation upon all men is rather due to the *one* offense of the *one* Adam by way of *imputation*, since they were created in the covenant in Adam.

Proof #3: It is clear beyond all controversy that in this chapter the apostle continually contrasts Adam to Christ. Adam is the cause of judgment to condemnation for all who are in him. Christ is the cause of redemption and salvation for all who are in Him. Since justification through Christ occurs by imputation (which we will prove at the appropriate moment), therefore, by virtue of the contrast, judgment to condemnation comes upon all men by imputation of Adam's breach of covenant.

Secondly, the imputation of guilt is also confirmed by 1 Corinthians 15:22, where we read, "For as in Adam all die..." It is not merely stated here that all men die. We also do not read that they die in their fathers or grandfathers, but only that all die *in Adam*. To die "in someone" means to be a partaker of the judgment resulting in the death and condemnation of this individual. If all men die, all have also sinned, "For the wages of sin is death" (Rom. 6:23). Furthermore, if all men die in Adam, they have also all sinned in him. Since they are punished, they must necessarily have sinned. If all men are justly subject to the threatened punishment — that is, "For in the day that thou eatest thereof thou shalt surely die" — they are also truly guilty of the same sin upon which the punishment was threatened. Since it is evident that all men are subject to the threatened punishment and not only die, but are also all subject to all the miseries due to the breach of covenant as enumerated in Genesis 3, all men are guilty of that sin. It is true that no one, neither by imitation, nor due to having inherited his corruption, has committed this sin personally along with Adam. In this manner no one can be said to sin or to die in someone. It thus remains certain that since all men die in Adam, they have sinned in him by way of imputation.

Thirdly, if all men were not guilty of Adam's breach of covenant, sin thus not being righteously imputed to them, each man would necessarily enter this world as perfectly as Adam did, that is, adorned with the image of God. Such would have to be the case since God creates the soul immediately, and in creating an innocent rational creature, does so in harmony with His holy nature. What relationship would then exist between Adam and subsequent human beings, since every one would be on his own? All men would then have a perfect existence as Adam had, and thus every man would be able to remain in this state of perfection. What reason would there be that many could not continue in this state of perfection? How can it be explained that all men, without exception, are in the same sinful state? Their corruption could not be derived from Adam if they had not sinned in him, for how else could they derive their corruption from him? It does not emanate from the body, for when viewed strictly in a physical sense, it is not subject to sin; otherwise the Lord Jesus could not have been formed in a holy fashion from the seed of the woman. This corruption also does not proceed from the soul, for the soul is created by God, and if there were no guilt, men would enter this world in a holy state, adorned with the image of God. Where then, I ask, does sin originate? Since man, however, is corrupt in his very nature and enters this world in a sinful condition, it is certain that he is guilty of the covenant breach in Adam.

Fourthly, add to this that the sins of the fathers' nearest of kin would be visited upon the children, and they would be punished for their fathers' sins. "For I the LORD thy God am a jealous God, visiting the iniquity of the fathers upon the children unto the third and fourth generation of them that hate Me" (Exo. 20:5); "That upon you may come all the righteous blood shed upon the earth, from the blood of righteous Abel unto the blood of Zacharias son of Barachias, whom ye slew between the temple and the altar" (Mat. 23:35). This is also confirmed by the examples of Achan (Josh. 7:24-25); Jereboam (1 Ki. 14:9-10); Ahab (1 Ki. 21:21); and Mannaseh (2 Ki. 24:3). This is also confirmed by a proof to the contrary when *Levi,* who was still in the loins of his father Abraham, paid tithes. It is true that the children themselves were sinful, and thus worthy of all manner of punishments. It is recorded here, however, that they were punished with temporal punishments for the sins of their forefathers. This is much more true then for all men, who, being in the loins of Adam, were comprehended in the covenant of works in him.

Objection #1: It is contrary to God's will that earthly judges should punish the son for the crime of the father. God even declares that He Himself does not do so. "The fathers shall not be put to death for the children, neither shall the children be put to death for the fathers: every man shall be put to death for his own sin" (Deu. 24:16); "The soul that sinneth, it shall die. The son shall not bear the iniquity of the father, neither shall the father bear the iniquity of the son" (Ezek. 18:20). Thus, the sin of Adam cannot be imputed to his descendants.

Answer: Deuteronomy 24:16 is a law which God has given to man. From this we may not draw a conclusion as far as divine justice is concerned. The text refers to violations of the law and not to a breach of covenant. The one is not a necessary consequence of the other. The text refers to the sins of specific individuals. Adam, however, was the head of the covenant which was established in him with the entire human race. This sin was the sin of the entire human race, for outside of Adam and Eve there were no other human beings. The entire human race was comprehended in Adam, and thus that same human race bears the punishment of their own sin.

Ezekiel 18:20 also speaks of specific sins of specific people, and is therefore not applicable to Adam and his descendants who are in covenant relationship with him. The text refers to adult children who do not follow the footsteps of their parents. God convinced them that they themselves were committing these sins, and thus would be punished for their own sins with the same manner of punishment. It is incontrovertible that God punishes children for the sins of their parents, as is to be observed in the flood, in the destruction of Sodom and Gomorrah, and in the children of Eli. God very expressly states the following about Himself: "...visiting the iniquity of the fathers upon the children unto the third and fourth generation" (Exo. 20:5).

Having considered original sin as far as the imputation of guilt is concerned, we will now proceed to consider the inherited corruption.

The Corruption of Sin as it Relates to the Absence of God's Image.

Inherited corruption consists in the absence of the image of God and in a propensity towards sin.

Let us first of all consider the *absence of the image of God*. Man is without the image of God, *not merely by way of denial*, nor due to a lack of original righteousness, but due to being *deprived of* something which presupposes the prior possession of a propensity to the contrary. All men, having sinned in Adam, are robbed of the image of God, so that every man is born void of spiritual light, love, truth, life, and holiness.

All glory and holiness are absent in man. "For all have sinned, and come short of the glory of God" (Rom. 3:23); "For I know that in me (that is, in my flesh,) dwelleth no good thing" (Rom. 7:18); "...dead in trespasses and sins" (Eph. 2:1); "Having the understanding darkened, being alienated from the life of God" (Eph. 4:18).

Secondly, this is confirmed by the fact that the image of God is restored in regeneration. Whatever is restored was once lost, and whatever is given was not previously in possession. "And have put on the new man, which is renewed in knowledge after the image of Him that created him" (Col. 3:10); "And be renewed in the spirit of your mind; and that ye put on the new man, which after God is created in righteousness and true holiness" (Eph. 4:23-24).

This inherited corruption also consists in a *propensity towards sin.*

Original sin does not only consist in the absence of original righteousness, but *also in the possession of a propensity to the contrary*. As an illness does not merely consist of the absence of health and good circulation of blood, but also in having an indisposition of character and mobility, such is also the case in the realm of the spiritual.

In view of this, original sin is called *the old man* (Rom. 6:6), *flesh* (John 3:6), *sin* (Rom. 7:11), *the law of sin* (Rom. 7:23), *covetousness* (Rom. 7:7), *lust* (Gal. 5:17), *uncleanness* (Col. 3:5), *filthiness* (James 1:21), and *filthiness of the flesh and spirit* (2 Cor. 7:1).

This original sin, found in all men who have proceeded naturally from Adam, is present from the moment of their conception. There are no exceptions — not even Mary. Even though God's children are born again, they are not regenerated to perfection in this life, but much corruption still remains within them.

Question: Do all men, by virtue of Adam's fall, have a propensity towards sin and a corrupt nature from the moment of their conception and birth, entering this world in a sinful condition?

Answer: Socinians and Anabaptists deny this entirely. Even if they are convinced by corruption manifesting itself in small children before they can learn by imitation of an evil example, they resolve this by saying that something is evidently present, but refuse to acknowledge this "something" to be sin. *Arminians* minimize original sin and lean towards *denial*. We, however, wholeheartedly answer this question in the affirmative.

That all men from the moment of their conception are in a state of degeneracy and corruption is evident:

First, from clear passages of Scripture which express this truth in a variety of ways.

(1) "Behold, I was shapen in iniquity, and in sin did my mother conceive me" (Psa. 51:5). There is no evidence that David here referred to the sin of his mother. This is equally clear in both the original text and in our translation. David was referring to himself: "I was." He humbled himself before God about the commission of his sin. However, in order to view the nature and magnitude of this sin and be humbled even more by it, he focused on the origin of this deed, confessing that his sin was not an incidental act, but that it proceeded from the wicked condition of his heart. He confessed to having this wicked condition already from the first moment of his conception, and thus was naturally inclined towards this sin. He acknowledged that from this evil condition nothing but pollution could come forth, and he was thus abominable in nature and in deeds. He was a man as all other men, and all other men are as he. Together they have the same origin, and therefore are in the

same sinful condition. Each person must therefore say the same about himself.

(2) Add to this such texts in which it is demonstrated that it is impossible to enter this world in any other condition but a sinful one. "Who can bring a clean thing out of an unclean? not one" (Job 14:4); "That which is born of the flesh is flesh" (John 3:6). Adam was sinful, and therefore could not do otherwise than bring forth a son in his own likeness rather than in the likeness of God (Gen. 5:3). All men are sinful, and no cause is capable of generating something which is superior to itself. Consequently, a sinner will bring forth a sinner: "neither can a corrupt tree bring forth good fruit" (Mat. 7:18).

(3) This is also confirmed by those texts which declare that man from his earliest childhood is nothing but evil in thoughts and deeds. "Every imagination of the thoughts of his heart was only evil continually" (Gen. 6:5); "For the imagination of man's heart is evil from his youth" (Gen. 8:21). Such evil thoughts are very clear evidence that the fountain is corrupt (James 3:11).

(4) This is also confirmed by the apostle: "and were by nature the children of wrath, even as others" (Eph. 2:3). There we see that all men are children of wrath, being so by nature. They are therefore not children of wrath only due to their sinful deeds, but are already the objects of wrath prior to that. Man's nature, as soon as it comes into existence, is the object of and the reason for divine wrath. Since they have this nature, they are children of wrath. However, no one is an object of God's wrath but by virtue of sin. Man is therefore by nature sinful, guilty in Adam, and has in himself a propensity towards evil.

Secondly, experience teaches that man by nature is corrupt. One can detect crossness and anger in children when they cannot have their way even prior to the use of their intellect. They also manifest vindictiveness before they can understand language, and before they can be taught even what it is. Children are pleased when others are scolded or receive corporal punishment — yes, they will even show delight by laughter. When it is admitted — since this cannot be denied — that something like this does exist, I respond that this is sin (Rom. 7:7-8). They are rational creatures and are subject to a law, and this law forbids wrath and vindictiveness. Moreover, if a child were to be educated without seeing any evil example, yes even if such were done by a holy person in a desert, this child would spontaneously commit every kind of sin, as experience will verify.

Thirdly, it is a known fact that children die even prior to their birth. However, death is a judgment upon sin, as is confirmed in Romans 5:12 and has been demonstrated above. It is therefore a certainty that they are sinful.

Fourthly, it is also confirmed by the fact that children are in need of Christ, for without Christ there is no salvation. All who are in need of a Redeemer are of necessity sinful, and this is therefore also true for children. Circumcision was a clear proof of this, for this sealed the putting off of the body of sin (Col. 2:11). This is also confirmed by the necessity of the new birth, for if all were well at the first birth, there would be no need for a second birth. This second birth, however, is a necessity if one is to be saved (John 3:5).

Objection #1: All sin must necessarily be committed consciously and with the acquiescence of man's free will. Original sin is not committed consciously and with the acquiescence of the will. It can therefore not be considered a sin.

Answer: It is not true that all sin is committed consciously and with the acquiescence of the will. Not only is this idea extra-biblical but it is also contrary to Scripture. It is one thing to do something against one's will and another to sin without the conscious acquiescence of the will; and indeed, the first sin was committed with the full acquiescence of the human nature.

Objection #2: It is written in 1 Corinthians 7:14, "Else were your children unclean; but now are they holy." Children are therefore without original sin.

Answer: This text expressly declares all children to be unclean, and thus as having original sin. It also states, however, that children of members of the covenant are holy. This holiness is not the holiness of God's image, but consists in being separated from other children, and in being incorporated in the church and the covenant of grace, so that they must be viewed as true members of the covenant until the contrary manifests itself.[2] In Ezekiel 16:21 they are called, "My children."

Objection #3: Children are harmless and cannot discern between their right and left hand (Jonah 4:11). They are innocent (Psa. 106:38), and have done neither good nor evil (Rom. 9:11). The man who was born blind, was blind neither because of his sins nor the sins of his parents (John 9:3).

Answer: These texts refer to sinful deeds and not to the sinful nature which already begins to manifest itself from the very outset. Neither the man born blind nor his parents were without sin, nor

---

[2] To understand this statement correctly it is advisable to read à Brakel's treatment of infant baptism in chapter 39.

were they perfectly holy. It was not the Lord Jesus' intent to infer this, but He wished to state that they were neither greater sinners than others, nor that it was for that reason he was born blind.

The Transmission of Original Sin from Adam to His Descendants

We have thus considered original sin relative to its imputed guilt as well as its inherited corruption. This surfaces the following question: *How is original sin transmitted from Adam to his descendants?* The manner in which guilt is imputed we have already demonstrated earlier so that the only question remaining is to show how man's natural corruption is inherited. One could be of the opinion that this cannot occur via the body, since it is not the actual object of sin. It also cannot occur via the soul, which, having been created by God, is good. It can also not occur via both body and soul, and thus not by generation. Since the soul is not generated, and since whatever is not true for either part can also not be true for the whole, it could not have come forth in this manner. My answer is: First, why do we need to know how sin is transmitted, since Scripture and experience confirm so clearly that such is the case? A fool can ask more questions than many wise men are able to answer. Tell me then how the body is formed with all its component parts; how the soul is united with the body; how by generating sound with the tongue one can cause someone else to understand abstract concepts; and how high and low tides return at a set time? You will reply that you do not know this, and that you cannot comprehend the "why" and "how." Who would be so foolish to deny something which he can visibly confirm, simply because he cannot understand it? Such is also the case with original sin.

Secondly, it is certain that God neither is nor can be the author of sin. It is also certain that souls are not reproduced, but are created by God.

Thirdly, the obscurity of this matter is often the result of separating generation of soul and body too much, as if God created a soul apart from the body, causing it to exist externally to the body for some time, and then uniting it with the body subsequent to this. God, by virtue of His *cooperative providence*, being the energizing cause of man's generation, forms the soul in union with the body so that it does not exist for one moment apart from the body. From the very first moment of the soul's existence, a man exists — a man who is guilty of the covenant breach in Adam. From this it is clear how the imputation of guilt is transmitted to descendants.

Fourthly, the soul, being formed during the generative process in union with the body, has the essence of a soul and thus is very good and without sin. However, the soul, coming into existence in union with the body and from that first moment forming a human being, is not more noble than the souls of the generating parents and thus is without the image of God. God was not obligated to restore this image to the soul after man had cast it away. It is therefore written in Genesis 5:3, "And Adam...begat a son in his own likeness, after his image," and thus not after the image of God.

Fifthly, man now being guilty of the covenant breach, not having the image of God according to his soul, and the body (which influences the soul and is united to the same) by generation having an evil state of mind, is in a state of separation from God. As such, man is subject to inner emptiness, and being dissatisfied with himself, is unfulfilled, miserable, craves for something, is restless, and lacks purpose in his activities. He is desirous, but not after God, for he has separated himself from Him; his desires are without restriction, focusing on whatever may appear to be desirable. Such a condition cannot but spawn a variety of lusts as man grows and develops. These lusts in turn spawn self-love, sorrow, wrath, hatred, and envy, which focus on a variety of wrong objects without restraints. Thus one human being generates another human being of like passions, and one sinner another sinner; in like manner the sin of Adam is transmitted to his descendants.

Actual Sin

Original sin produces all kinds of *actual sins*. This is confirmed in James 1:14-15, where we read, "But every man is tempted, when he is drawn away of his own lust, and enticed. Then when lust hath conceived, it bringeth forth sin." Since lust draws away, entices, and brings forth sin, it is sin itself. That which is not sin cannot generate sin. The apostle also expressly denominates covetousness as sin (Rom. 7:7). When covetousness is said to bring forth sin, this refers to actual sins.

Actual sin is unrighteousness or a deviation from God's law by an internal or external act of omission or commission. Relative to this sin a variety of distinctions are made.

First, there are sins against the *first table of the law*, requiring love towards God, and against the *second table of the law*, requiring love towards our neighbor.

Secondly, there are sins of *omission and commission*. A sin of *omission* is committed whenever one does not perform that which is commanded. Although many neither give heed to this nor are disturbed hereby, it is a great sin, for it proceeds from unwillingness and lovelessness in relation to the will of God. The apostle denominates both omission and commission as sin. "Therefore to him that knoweth to do good, and doeth it not, to him it is sin" (James 4:17). It is noteworthy that only sins of omission are recorded as causes for damnation in Matthew 25:42-43. A sin of *commission* is committed when one does that which is forbidden, or whenever one performs that which is good in and of itself in an evil manner or with an ulterior motive. "He that committeth sin is of the devil" (1 John 3:8).

Thirdly, there are sins which are committed:

(1) in *thoughts,* which are not concealed from the all-seeing eye of God, and are hated by Him: "An heart that deviseth wicked imaginations" (Prov. 6:18);

(2) in *words,* "But I say unto you, that every idle word that men shall speak, they shall give account thereof in the day of judgment" (Mat. 12:36);

(3) in *deeds,* "Depart from Me, ye that work iniquity" (Mat. 7:23);

(4) in *gestures* made with eyes, face, hands and feet, "A naughty person, a wicked man...winketh with his eyes, he speaketh with his feet, he teacheth with his fingers" (Prov. 6:12-13).

Sins committed in thoughts are the most numerous; however, those committed in deed excel in magnitude, since they occur in conjunction with the thoughts, doubling the magnitude of the sin. They are committed with more premeditation and are injurious to others.

Fourthly, there are sins which are committed presumptuously, and those which are committed *ignorantly.* "And that servant, which knew his lord's will...shall be beaten with many stripes; but he that knew not...shall be beaten with few stripes (Luke 12:47-48). In a certain respect all sins can be said to be committed in ignorance, since no one — unless he is a devil — commits sin with the perception of it being sin, but does so under a pretense of necessity, honesty, advantage, and delight. By ignorance we understand here that darkness in and carelessness of the sinner by which no attention is paid to whether his actions are sinful or not — that inattentiveness which fails to reckon with God and gives no heed to his actions. This is the reason that there is neither acknowledgement nor remorse concerning the committed sin. However, ignorance does not provide one with an excuse. He should have had knowledge concerning the matter, and in many instances he could have been knowledgeable about a particular sin, but with ignorant passion, yielded to his lust. "Who can understand his errors? cleanse thou me from secret faults" (Psa. 19:12); "For had they known it, they would not have crucified the Lord of glory" (1 Cor. 2:8). "...because

I did it ignorantly in unbelief" (1 Tim. 1:13) — otherwise it would have been the sin against the Holy Ghost. Such is true for all heresies.

There are degrees of wickedness relative to sins which are committed consciously, this being contingent upon the measure by which the light of either nature or Scripture illuminates the sinner. The most grievous of sins is committed when God immediately reveals His presence and omniscience, thereby discouraging and warning the sinner who is inclined to sin, and when, in spite of this, he proceeds with the commission of this sin.

Fifthly, there are *secret* sins which one commits either alone or in the presence of a few. There are other sins which are committed *publicly,* that is, in the presence of many. "For thou didst it secretly: but I will do this thing before all Israel, and before the sun" (2 Sam. 12:12).

Sin's Dominion over the Ungodly

Sixthly, there are *sins which have dominion over a man*, and *sins which are committed due to weakness*. Only the unconverted are under the dominion of sin.

Sin, first of all, has dominion whenever there is no union with Christ by faith. When one is *without Christ*, he is without God (Eph. 2:12), *dead in trespasses and sins* (vs. 1).

Secondly, sin has dominion when there is not that internal resistance of the heart towards sin resulting from union with God in Christ — and thus not proceeding from true faith, love, fear, and obedience; and thus in turn not from the Spirit. "If ye through the Spirit do mortify the deeds of the body" (Rom. 8:13). Natural man can be controlled and be resistant towards the commission of a specific sin as the result of the illumination of the conscience, and also due to a love for natural virtue. This virtue is truly desirable to someone who sees but a glimmer of it, although he neither perceives the spiritual dimension nor the required spiritual parameters. This love for natural virtue may also be due to fear of punishment, fear for shame and disgrace, or upbringing and habit. All of this can result in a virtuous life in the natural sense of the word. Those who know of no other virtue but this, consider it to be godliness. Hence proceeds the illusion that one is capable of converting himself. However, a heartfelt resistance towards sin, proceeding from the mentioned union and advancement in this area, which would restrain them from the commission of sin, is not to be found in them. They are then not motivated to be virtuous, and therefore all is of no value, and they are thus under the dominion of sin.

Thirdly, sin has dominion when the heart fully and willingly acquiesces to a life without God and Christ, being ignorant thereof and not desirous for nor seeking this union. It is satisfied without this union, and thus is united to the world and sin. All life outside of God and Christ, which from a natural perspective may appear to be as civil and religious as one could imagine, is purely sin. From such a frame proceeds lust, love, desire, and sinful meditation — the measure thereof being dependent upon one's state of mind, inclination, habit, and opportunity. "For they that are after the flesh do mind the things of the flesh" (Rom. 8:5); "If any man love the world, the love of the Father is not in him" (1 John 2:15).

Fourthly, sin has dominion when there is an outpouring of sinful lusts, a succession of sinful deeds, and a complete and voluntary yielding to one's lusts as far as possible, and when one is not hindered even by the natural motives mentioned above. Peter refers to this as "the same excess of riot" (1 Pet. 4:4). Consider also the following texts: "Who being past feeling have given themselves over unto lasciviousness, to work all uncleanness with greediness" (Eph. 4:19); "Woe unto them that draw iniquity with cords of vanity, and sin as it were with a cart rope" (Isa. 5:18); "And they... sold themselves to do evil" (2 Ki. 17:17). This is referred to as being "servants of sin," and to yield "your members servants to uncleanness" (Rom. 6:20, 19).

Fifthly, sin has dominion when there is immediate inner resistance towards those who are genuinely godly, who give evidence that they neither belong to this world nor are under the dominion of sin, but who are united with God in Christ and walk in the light. Natural men do find delight in natural virtue, this being consistent with their own nature. Even if one corpse appears to be more attractive than the other, death remains death. When, however, the regenerate not only lead a virtuous life, but in their speech reveal their light — it being the basis for and the essential nature of their virtue, as well as their excellency above others — then the heart is at once repulsed by this and there will be hatred towards this first and foremost by temporal believers, and in those who lead a civil life. Scripture states this plainly, "For every one that doeth evil hateth the light, neither cometh to the light, lest his deeds should be reproved" (John 3:20); "If ye were of the world, the world would love his own: but because ye are not of the world, but I have chosen you out of the world, therefore the world hateth you" (John 15:19). This hatred and heartfelt opposition is clear evidence of the dominion of sin, for it uncovers a contradiction as that which exists between light and darkness, and between life and death. By way of the five matters we have presented, the unconverted can examine themselves and be convicted of their unconverted state. They may also serve to the discovery of the converted in order that sin may not have dominion over them.

Sin Has no Dominion over the Godly

The converted detect much of the old Adam within themselves. They observe how they frequently fall — indeed, even continue in sin, being captured and captivated by sin. By this their faith easily falters, fearing that sin still has dominion over them. In order that they may know that sin has no dominion over them, but that it merely battles them as an enemy, we will further demonstrate when sin does not have dominion.

(1) Sin has no dominion when there is a union with Christ by faith, be it that this union manifests itself more clearly, strongly, and sensibly; or that it primarily manifests itself in activity to be reconciled with God in Christ consisting in desires, prayers, embracing, believing reception, and wrestlings, so that the soul cannot be at peace apart from the sensible enjoyment of this reconciliation and union, even if it cannot attain to the sensible assurance of this union. Since truth, love, and spiritual exercise manifest themselves, however, the essence of this union exists. Christ is the life of the soul (Col. 3:4). Being thus united to life itself, death has no dominion, but rather life, as feeble as it may be.

(2) Sin has no dominion when this union results in lively, spiritual exercises. All exercises which do not proceed from this union are deemed of no value by a converted person. All his efforts are focused on living by virtue of this union, be it in the enjoyment of this union, or in seeking after and focusing upon this union. Such a person desires to do everything out of God, through God, for God, before God, and unto God. They are only refreshed when all their deeds "are wrought in God" (John 3:21). This union cannot be passive, for faith "worketh by love" (Gal. 5:6), purifies the heart (Acts 15:9), "overcometh the world" (1 John 5:4), resists the devil (1 Pet. 5:9), and is fruitful unto good works (James 2:17). The issue here is not the measure of faith, but its genuineness.

(3) Sin has no dominion when this union brings forth internal opposition and hatred towards all that is sin (by virtue of its very nature) whether it be great or small. This attitude does not only pertain to that which is external, but especially concerns itself with what they perceive in their own heart. As a result of this they abhor themselves more than anyone else. "For that which I do I allow not.... If then I do that which I would not...it is no more I that do it, but sin that

dwelleth in me" (Rom. 7:15-17); "I hate vain thoughts...I hate every false way" (Psa. 119:113, 128). This will bring forth sorrow and humiliation concerning the inner condition of the heart, the sins of omission, and sinful deeds. The soul is immediately wounded and experiences sorrow. This is an evidence of the presence of a living principle which is diametrically opposed to sin.

(4) Sin has no dominion when, due to said union, internal resistance and hatred towards sin translates into actual opposition and strife against sin. Time and again there is a new resolve to do battle against sin; there is prayer for strength, and, desiring to be strengthened, there is a receiving of Jesus by faith unto sanctification. The godly fear that sin may take them by surprise and thus they seek to be watchful. They seek to avoid opportunity to sin, resisting it when it does occur. At times there is victory and at other times they will be overcome by one particular sin. "For the flesh lusteth against the Spirit, and the Spirit against the flesh: and these are contrary the one to the other: so that ye cannot do the things that ye would" (Gal. 5:17). It cannot therefore be denied that where there is a battle against sin, sin has no dominion.

(5) Sin has no dominion when this union results in a delight, a love for, and a desire to do whatever pleases the Lord. This opposition towards sin is all-inclusive, no sin being excluded. Similarly, the acquiescence with the will of God is also all-inclusive. "For I delight in the law of God after the inward man" (Rom. 7:22); "O how love I Thy law!" (Psa. 119:97). Yes, not only is there a love for and acquiescence with the will of God, but also a love for all those whom one deems to be loved of God and who love God. They are repulsed by and displeased with those that belong to the world, since at heart they are separated from the world. "In whose eyes a vile person is contemned; but he honoureth them that fear the LORD" (Psa. 15:4); "We know that we have passed from death unto life, because we love the brethren" (1 John 3:14).

Consider all these evidences together and compare them with those which are evidences of the dominion of sin. If someone comes to the conclusion that the evidences of being under the dominion of sin are not present, but perceives those evidences to the contrary, be it not in the measure which he would desire, he can be assured that sin has no dominion over him. Such a person should rejoice and not permit his faith to falter due to the power of internal corruption which still remains. Rather, he will persevere in that inner life — however feeble it may be — with sincerity and cheerfulness in order that he might increase in sanctification.

The Unpardonable Sin: The Sin Against the Holy Ghost

There are *pardonable* and *unpardonable* sins. Some sins are called *pardonable*, but not because their nature is such that they neither merit punishment nor can be forgiven without complete satisfaction. Such a sin does not exist, however seemingly insignificant it may be. Even though sins differ in degree and merit punishment commensurate with this degree, the least sin is worthy of eternal damnation. "For the wages of sin is death" (Rom. 6:23); "For whosoever shall keep the whole law, and yet offend in one point, he is guilty of all" (James 2:10); "Cursed is every one that continueth not in all things which are written in the book of the law to do them" (Gal. 3:10). They are called "pardonable" simply because they are forgiven to all who believe and repent.

Unpardonable are all the sins of those who have lived in sin and die in it. For them there is no ransom, and thus eternally no forgiveness. Such sins are unpardonable in view of the ultimate outcome.

In addition to these sins, however, there is one unpardonable sin, called the sin against the Holy Ghost (Mat. 12:31).

The sin against the Holy Ghost is spoken of in Matthew 12:31, where we read, "The blasphemy against the Holy Ghost shall not be forgiven unto men." "But he that shall blaspheme against the Holy Ghost hath never forgiveness, but is in danger of eternal damnation: because they said, He hath an unclean spirit" (Mark 3:29-30); "There is a sin unto death: I do not say that he (someone other than the person who has committed it) shall pray for it" (1 John 5:16). Thus a godly person, in praying for others, ought not to pray for a sin unto death, (that is, if he knows that someone has committed such a sin). This can be none other than the sin against the Holy Ghost, even though it is not identified as such in the last text. The sin against the Holy Ghost is not so much against the Spirit's Person, but against His operation; that is, His illuminating, sanctifying, and comforting work in God's children, as well as His mighty operation in the occurrence of miracles, by which true doctrine and personal convictions are confirmed.

This sin does not consist in lack of repentance, as every sinner who dies in sin did not repent of even one sin. It also cannot be said that there should be no prayer for such a sinner, since there is no prior knowledge whether such a common sinner shall repent or not. From 1 John 5:16 it is evident that this sin was not only committed during the time of Christ, but also afterwards. This sin consists in a complete rejection of confessed truth and in hatred and opposition towards the truth and godliness, all proceeding purely from bitter enmity.

A truly converted person can never commit this sin, since he is kept by the power of God unto salvation (1 Pet. 1:5), and it is impossible for the elect to be deceived (Mat. 24:24), the foundation of God being sure (2 Tim. 2:19).

It is also not a sin commonly committed by the unconverted, but is of an extraordinary nature and thus infrequently committed. We nevertheless believe that some take a step or two in the direction of that sin, even if not perceived by others. It is believed to be most frequently committed where the power of the Holy Ghost in the conversion of sinners manifests itself the most. In order to understand the very nature of this sin, take notice of the following propositions.

First, there is clear knowledge and conviction in such a sinner that what he opposes was of God and was the truth. I do not dare to maintain that for the commission of such a sin there needs to be a clear and powerful conviction of the heart concerning all points of true religion. Neither do we maintain that such a sinner is a professor of this truth and a member of the church. I do maintain that at least there must be a knowledge and conviction of the heart that the doctrine and life, as well as the religion of those with whom he has fellowship, is according to truth and godliness, and thus from God. As far as we know, the Pharisees and scribes who committed this sin never were disciples of Christ. They also did not know that Christ was truly the Messiah (1 Cor. 2:8). It is also not certain whether they had a proper knowledge of the divine persons. The Holy Spirit, however, had convinced them that Christ's doctrine, life, and miracles were from God and performed by God. Christ was acknowledged to be "a prophet mighty in deed and word before God and all the people" (Luke 24:19). Pilate himself "knew that the chief priests had delivered Him for envy" (Mark 15:10).

Secondly, such a sinner becomes filled with wrath and hatred against those in whom God's Spirit works mightily by granting them illumination, joy, holiness, zeal, and much opening in speaking, etc. This wrath and hatred can express itself against the congregation of Christ in general, a specific congregation, a specific company of godly persons, or a specific person, be it a minister or a member. This opposition is neither related to temporal matters nor to a general or specific difference of opinion, but is in response to the truth and to that life and activity which this sinner knows to be from God and to occur by His agency. This was evidently the case in the entire behavior of the Jews towards Christ recorded throughout the gospels (cf. Mat. 12; John 8). This enmity also manifested itself towards Stephen. "When they heard these things, they were cut to the heart, and they gnashed on him with their teeth" (Acts 7:54).

Thirdly, in such a sinner there is an evil opposition towards and a desire for the persecution of those in whom the Holy Spirit is so mightily at work. If this person previously functioned within the community of the church or within a specific fellowship of godly people, he will depart from them, not being able to endure them any longer. He wickedly opposes them, and persecutes them as much as possible because of the truth, godliness, and activity manifesting themselves there. This he accomplishes by slander, defamation, offending, contradiction, and by calling the work of the Holy Spirit in them the devil's work, the work of the flesh, hypocrisy, pride, etc. If he is in a position of authority, he will oppose them, try to root out the work of God, rob them of their good name, their possessions, and even life itself. All of this can be observed in the Pharisees and scribes as they continually slandered and tempted the Lord Jesus, and sought to kill Him — in which they finally succeeded. To this the apostle refers when he writes, "For if we sin wilfully after that we have received the knowledge of the truth, there remaineth no more sacrifice for sins, but a certain fearful looking for of judgment and fiery indignation, which shall devour the adversaries. He that despised Moses' law died without mercy under two or three witnesses: of how much sorer punishment, suppose ye, shall he be thought worthy, who hath trodden under foot the Son of God, and hath counted the blood of the covenant, wherewith he was sanctified, an unholy thing, and hath done despite unto the Spirit of grace?" (Heb. 10:26-29).

Fourthly, this is followed by an irreversible absence of remorse and a refusal to repent. I have stated that this is a consequence of this sin, for it does not belong to the nature of this sin. They do not come to themselves, for God gives them over to themselves and to their evil inclinations. Their anger propels them as a turbulent sea, and as chaff driven by wind, and they proceed in the manifestation of their hatred as long as they live or have the opportunity. Even if they settle down to some extent (which will cause them to perceive their sin), this is immediately accompanied by a feeling of despair. They perceive that heaven is closed for them and that Christ is not for them. For this reason there is no sorrow, no seeking, and no prayer. Instead, they feel the pangs of hell, and the terror of God consumes them. They either end their lives as *Judas* did, or they die, as *Julian,* with curses upon their lips.

Fifthly, added to this is the fact that this sin is unpardonable. This is neither due to the sin viewed in itself, nor because the mercy of God or the merits of Christ are insufficient, but solely because God wills not to forgive this sin. "The blasphemy against the Holy Ghost shall not be forgiven" (Mat. 12:31); "But he that shall blaspheme against the Holy Ghost hath never forgiveness" (Mark 3:29).

One may wonder: how is it possible that someone can fall into such a sin — that man can behave himself thus in response to revealed truth, godliness, and the operation of God's Spirit?

I answer: It is indeed true that no one either will challenge the truth as truth, or commit sin as sin, for then he would have to be the devil in the flesh. However, it can be that a graceless person, who is nevertheless illuminated by and convinced of the truth as the result of the operation of the Holy Spirit, may join himself to the godly, giving the impression of being one of them. However, when he perceives that his deception is evident and that he, contrary to his will and to his grief, is not accepted when he perceives that, due to the light by which he becomes acquainted with himself, he is not honored and esteemed as others or above others, but that his influence is curtailed, so that others are esteemed and loved above him; when others reckon him to be ignorant of spiritual mysteries, to yet be unconverted, and to be in a state of misery as a hypocritical, temporal believer and an imposter; when he is continually rebuked and is of the opinion that everything which is spoken applies to himself, or that people, whenever he speaks or acts, despise him in a nasty and provocative manner, ridiculing and continually correcting him — then, I say, his wicked heart will stir itself in anger and envy, will be stimulated, will begin to manifest itself, and he will engage in active opposition. Such a person will first take issue against persons as having been wronged by them, after which he will take issue with these persons for the matter at hand and the power of the Holy Spirit which manifests itself in them. From this proceeds the avoidance of God's people and of the truth of God he confessed and it is followed by slander, defamation, opposition, and persecution — due to the light, truth, godliness, and activity of the godly. Thus the first cause of this sin is generally self-love, and a desire to be honored and esteemed. If the latter is not attained, and such a person instead is discovered, rebuked, and rejected, his wickedness gradually increases until he commits the sin described above.

People may think that since all the unconverted hate the light of truth and oppose it, that therefore the sin against the Holy Ghost is something different from what we have explained.

My answer is:

(1) The seed of all sin, and thus also of the sin against the Holy Ghost, is to be found in all men by nature. If circumstances were favorable and if the restraining power of God were not to prevent it, this sin would be committed by all. The sin against the Holy Ghost is therefore a sin which in principle is rooted in the nature of man.

(2) All men do not come to the acknowledgement of the truth and of godliness, neither do they become acquainted with the powerful operation of God's Spirit, nor come to the conviction that this is of God.

(3) This hatred and the inclination to oppose all these do not burst forth in every person, but is controlled, either due to absence of opportunity, to other natural convictions, or to the restraining power of God.

(4) The sin against the Holy Ghost is not common hatred and opposition, but an extraordinary explosion of hatred and wickedness, accompanied by slander and persecution.

Instruction for Those Who Fear They Have
Sinned Against the Holy Ghost.

From that which has been said, the misunderstanding of some concerning this sin becomes evident. Being ignorant of the nature of this sin, and perceiving within themselves that they frequently sin against better knowledge and a speaking conscience, they imagine that they have committed the sin against the Holy Ghost. Therefore they do not dare to pray for forgiveness, their reason being that prayer for such a sin is not permitted, and that this sin is unpardonable. All this greatly terrifies them, causing much anxiety. Such persons need to be instructed on the basis of what has been stated.

(1) The sin against the Holy Ghost is not directed to the sinner himself as being the object, but it focuses upon others who manifest truth, godliness, and the powerful operation of God's Spirit, all of which humbles the godly, but grieves such a sinner.

(2) The injunction forbidding prayer for such persons does not pertain to oneself, but to others. Yes, even he who commits this sin remains under obligation to pray and to repent, but is not willing to do so.

(3) This sin is accompanied by a great explosion of hatred and anger towards others due to the light emanating from them, as well as by persecution of them through slander and oppression.

(4) There is neither sorrow over this sin, nor a seeking of forgiveness and repentance. Therefore those who are concerned

can perceive from this how mistaken they are, and that they have thus not committed this sin. They are merely being deceived by their darkened heart, even though their concern proceeds from a tender disposition. Moreover, the devil joins in to cast such souls to and fro and if possible to bring them to despair.

How each person ought to take warning in view of all this — that when meeting with opportunities which could give rise to this sin, he ought not to give free reign to his heart. One must refrain from impetuously assaulting someone who has spirit and life, or appears to have, but whose behavior may perhaps be unbecoming, lest by way of gradual progression one would come to the commission of this sin. Under such circumstances a person should always remind himself of the dreadful judgment upon those who commit this sin.

In view of this, how careful everyone ought to be of dealing imprudently by neither continually rebuking a person who opposes him, nor by despising and provoking him. One should also not attempt to passionately and forcefully bring such a person to repentance, whether this be one's spouse, children, parents, relatives, or others with whom one has a familiar relationship, lest they be afforded an opportunity to commit this sin.

The application concerning the doctrine of sin in general, which ought to humble all men, will follow in the next chapter.

CHAPTER FIFTEEN

Man's Free Will or Impotency and the Punishment Due Upon Sin

Free Will Defined

Having considered original and actual sin, we must also consider man's total inability to lift himself out of this sinful state and to restore himself in a state of holiness. This subject is generally considered under the heading "free will."

In Greek *Free Will* is referred to as αὐτεξουσία (*autexousia*). This word is not to be found in Scripture, but was introduced into the church by Platonic philosophers who had been converted to Christianity. In its essential meaning it means as much as *self-determination, self-worthiness*, or *to be one's own master*. As such it can only be properly used in reference to God. However, in some respects it may be used in reference to man as well. In Latin the words *liberum arbitrium* are used, which translates as *free judgment* or *free will*.

God has gifted the soul of man with intellect and a will. The intellect consists of comprehension, judgment, and conscience. The faculty of judgment makes either a general determination about the validity of a matter and what sort of a thing it is, or it applies itself to the will of man suggesting and determining what is or is not to be done, or what is to be loved or to be hated. The will of man consists of the ability to either love or hate something. A comprehensive treatment of these matters is to be found in chapter 10, where the nature of the soul, the intellect, and the will are discussed.

The Freedom of the Will: Not Neutrality but One of Necessary Consequence

In our discussion of *free will* it should be noted first of all that man's free will is not independent from God. Man is totally dependent upon God in regard 1) to his being, 2) to his activity, 3) to God's prerogative to obligate him to His will and laws (so that His commands must be loved and what He has forbidden is to be hated), and 4) to the foreknowledge and decree of God, for He infallibly knows and has decreed that every matter and deed will have a certain outcome and none other. This foreknowledge cannot be thwarted; and this decree cannot be changed. These matters have been discussed comprehensively in chapters three, five, and eleven.

Secondly, the will does not function independently from the judgment faculty of the intellect. The will cannot possibly function apart from the intellect, neither can it do otherwise than follow the dictates of the intellect, for man is a rational being and therefore functions rationally. Otherwise the will would be able to reject that which is good as well as that which is perceived as being good, and find delight in sin as sin — all of which is irrational.

Thirdly, the will of man is not free from human peculiarities, for man functions according to his nature. A man who is perfectly holy in his nature will be a servant of righteousness, and the will shall respond likewise (Rom. 6:18). However, if man is nothing but sin in all his characteristics, he is a servant of sin (John 8:34). The will responds and functions in harmony with man's sinful nature. To a holy nature belongs a holy will, and to a sinful nature a sinful will.

Even though the will is necessarily dependent upon the matters mentioned, this *necessity* does not eliminate the freedom of the will, nor is this necessity compulsory in nature, since the will responds spontaneously.

(1) The will is free from external compulsion. All the people on earth cannot force someone's will or cause him to do something which he is not willing to do. In order to cause someone to do another's will, however, the matter must be presented in such a manner that the person voluntarily chooses and wills, and thus functions according to his own will.

(2) The will of man is also free from natural instinct, by which animals, without being conscious of it, are motivated to function according to their purpose, for the will responds to the intellect and functions rationally.

Having considered in which respects the will of man is either free or not free, the question now presents itself: *Wherein does the freedom of the will actually consist? Does it consist in neutrality so that it makes no difference whether or not we do something, or whether we do a certain thing or act to the contrary? Or is this freedom one of "necessary consequence," man doing what he does by virtue of personal choice, personal desire, and thus spontaneously?*

Roman Catholics and *Arminians* respond by saying that this freedom consists in being neutral as far as either doing or not doing something, or doing a certain thing or acting to the contrary. Our response is that the will of man when considered in its essential nature, not being subject to any conditions, is neutral and unrestricted as far as doing a certain thing or the contrary thereof. It remains in this neutral position until the faculty judgment determines what ought or what ought not to be done. Once such a determination has been made by judgmental application, the will can no longer remain neutral, can no longer but will to do this, and cannot refrain from willing to do the one thing rather than the contrary. Thus, the freedom of the will does not consist in neutrality; that is, the ability to will or not to will, or to will either one thing or the contrary, even if all requirements and restrictions were in place. Rather, the freedom of the will is one of necessary consequence.

This is first of all evident from the nature of God, the angels, the glorified in Christ, and also the devils. God cannot but be holy, righteous, and true. His will cannot but desire this and cannot act to the contrary. However, is not God's will free to the superlative degree? The holy angels and glorified saints cannot will to either do good or evil. They can only will to be good and to do good. Is not their will entirely free? The Lord Jesus Christ could not will to be either obedient or disobedient to His Father. He could not do anything but be willing to obey His Father. Was not His will absolutely free? It is impossible for devils to will that which is good. They cannot but will to do that which is evil. In all these things there is an absolute freedom of will, but there is no neutrality as far as being willing or not willing to do something, or to will a certain thing or just its opposite. Thus, the freedom of the will does not consist in neutrality, but is one of necessary consequence.

Secondly, even though one can speculate about the will in its abstract nature, the will at no time functions outside the parameters of God's providence, the faculty of judgment, and natural inclinations. Therefore, even when all requirements for its functioning are present, the will cannot arbitrarily function or not function, or do a certain thing or the contrary. Rather, it voluntarily embraces that to which it is limited by God and the faculty of judgment, and thus it does not remain neutral.

Thirdly, it is entirely absurd to define the freedom of the will as consisting in neutrality. If this were so, man could desire his damnation and to be eternally miserable, never to partake of supreme felicity; or he could choose the opposite: to acquire this felicity, the will being neutral towards both options. It would then be in vain to pray for conversion, for then even by divine operation the will could not be nudged from its neutral position, and man would always be able to will that he remain unconverted. Then God would have no power over the human will, but the will would remain independent, having as much control over itself as God does. This of course is absurdity itself.

Since the freedom of the will does not consist in neutrality, it is therefore clear that the freedom of the will is one of necessary consequence. This is not an irrational instinct as in animals, but by one's own intelligent choice, willing, desiring, and embracing that which one by way of the faculty of judgment perceives as necessary or desirous at this particular place and time.

Man's Free Will After the Fall

Now the question is: Is man such a slave to sin that he wills nothing else, and cannot will, but to live in sin? Our reference here is to the will and not to desire. Also, can man both will to convert himself and to keep the law by powerfully and actively engaging his will? Or is man's will after the fall still neutral as far as repenting or not repenting, doing good or doing evil? In short, did sinful man retain sufficient natural ability to enable him to truly repent?

Roman Catholicism and Arminians answer affirmatively; we respond negatively. In order to understand this clearly, we must distinguish between various kinds of goodness and various states of man. There are four types of activity which can be considered good.

(1) There is natural goodness: eating, drinking, walking, standing, speaking, sleeping, etc.

(2) There is civil goodness: being courteous, friendly, helpful, sincere, and upright in daily conversation.

(3) There is external religious goodness: hearing and reading God's Word, offering of a mentally formulated prayer, the giving of alms, etc.

(4) There is spiritual goodness proceeding from internal union with God in Christ, and thus from the principle of spiritual life. This consists in faith, love, godly fear, obedience towards God as Father, complete submission to and acquiescence with God's will, and the performance of this will. The question does not relate to the first three kinds of goodness, but to the latter.

There is also a fourfold distinction in regard to man's state. There is 1) the state of *perfection* prior to the fall, 2) the *unregenerate* state after the fall, 3) the *regenerate* state, and 4) the state of *glory*. The question neither pertains to the first nor the last two states, but only to the second one. The question therefore is: *Is an unconverted person able to convert himself, regenerate himself, truly believe in Christ, and live a truly holy and spiritual life?* We emphatically deny this. This is evident first of all from man's evil condition prior to conversion, being blind, ignorant, evil, and unwilling. He is hostile, unable, unwilling to subject himself to the law of God, and spiritually dead. "Because the carnal mind is enmity against God: for it is not subject to the law of God, neither indeed can be" (Rom. 8:7; cf. chapter 30).

Sin and Punishment

Conversion is a work of God, consisting in creating, regenerating, drawing, the removal of the stony heart and the giving of a heart of flesh, etc. (cf. chapter 30).

Having considered man's misery relative to his first fall, original sin, actual sin, and his spiritual impotency, we will also consider his misery in respect to deserved punishment.

Punishment presupposes the existence of a rational creature which is subject to a law. Thus, the evil which comes upon animals in reality is not a punishment inflicted upon them, but either is executed in regard to man as proprietor of the animal, to prevent them from being able to harm man, or due to the curse resulting from the first sin, God thereby revealing His just wrath against the sin of mankind. For this reason the pushing ox had to be killed, Achan's cattle were killed along with him, and all the animals died in the flood.

All punishment proceeds from God. God does not punish a holy creature — He punished Christ only because He as Surety had taken sin upon Himself — but punishes the sinner as a righteous Judge. "For the wrath of God is revealed from heaven against all ungodliness and unrighteousness of men" (Rom. 1:18); "...against the day of wrath and revelation of the righteous judgment of God; who will render to every man according to his deeds" (Rom. 2:5-6). To that end God uses all such creatures as pleases Him, such as the sun, moon, and stars (Judg. 5:20), rain and wind (Psa. 148:8), angels (Acts 12:23), devils (Job 1-2), man (Isa. 10:24), and insects (Joel 1:4; 2:25).

Sin is the cause of and reason for this punishment. "For the wages of sin is death" (Rom. 6:23); "Thine own wickedness shall correct thee, and thy backslidings shall reprove thee" (Jer. 2:19). Yes, every sin merits eternal condemnation. "For whosoever shall keep the whole law, and yet offend in one point, he is guilty of all" (James 2:10). Every sin is a complete rejection of the eternal God, and by its very nature causes the sinner to remain in an eternally sinful condition. This is the reason for the righteous threatening found in Galatians 3:10, "Cursed is every one that continueth not in all things which are written in the book of the law to do them."

We can make a twofold distinction relative to punishment: temporal and eternal.

Temporal punishments are either corporal or spiritual in nature. There are many *corporal* punishments, such as bodily want, sickness, discomfort, pestilence, war, times of scarcity, and death. For the godly these are fatherly chastisements which proceed from love and are inflicted for their welfare. For the ungodly they are judgments which proceed from the avenging justice and wrath of God. "I will reprove thee, and set them in order before thine eyes" (Psa. 50:21).

Spiritual judgments include:

(1) The withdrawal of abused spiritual illumination. "... their foolish heart was darkened" (Rom. 1:21); "Because they received not the love of the truth, that they might be saved. And for this cause God shall send them strong delusion, that they should believe a lie" (2 Th. 2:10-11).

(2) The giving over of man to himself, whereby he falls from one sin into the next. "But my people would not hearken to my voice; and Israel would none of me. So I gave them up unto their own hearts' lust: and they walked in their own counsels" (Psa. 81:11-12); "Wherefore God also gave them up to uncleanness through the lusts of their own hearts" (Rom. 1:24).

(3) The hardening of the heart. "And I will harden Pharaoh's heart ...and Pharaoh's heart was hardened" (Exo. 7:3, 22). From these texts it is evident that God in His holiness punishes sin with sin.

Eternal punishment is referred to as death (Rom. 6:23), the second death (Rev. 20:6), the damnation of hell (Mat. 23:33), hell fire (Mat. 5:22), and everlasting fire (Mat. 25:41). It is also expressed by way of the place where this punishment will be endured, such as, the place of torment (Luke 16:28), the deep (Luke 8:31), and the lake of fire burning with sulfur and brimstone (Rev. 19:20). This place is generally referred to as "hell." In Greek two words are used, one of which is ᾅδης (*hades*), which is also used by pagans to refer to hell. The other word is γέεννα (*gehenna*), which is used in Scripture only. This word is derived from "the valley of the children of Hinnom," which was an accursed place where the Israelites burned their children in the fire in honor of the idol Moloch, and which Josiah transformed into a valley of horror by causing all manner of abomination to be brought there, so that, due to this horrendous sin, this valley would be abhorred (2 Ki. 23:10). (In Hebrew hell is called שׁאול [*sheol*], which is a pit.)

The place where eternal punishment will be endured is not fictitious, merely existing in man's imagination. It is a place which truly exists at this very moment and does not still need to be created. The devils are exiled to this place, even though they will be released prior to the final judgment (2 Pet. 2:4). The Sodomites suffer the vengeance of eternal fire (Jude 1:7). The souls of the ungodly upon departing from the body at the moment of death are always sent to this place (Luke 16:23).

The Punishment of the Ungodly Does not Consist in Annihilation

This raises the following question: Does eternal punishment consist in the annihilation of soul and body? Will the essence of both soul and body of the ungodly continue to exist and be in inexpressible pain to all eternity?

Socinius held to the first view, whereas we hold to the latter.

This is first of all confirmed by the resurrection of the ungodly. "There shall be a resurrection of the dead, both of the just and unjust" (Acts 24:15). All men upon the face of the earth will be divided into two categories, there being no third category. The unjust will be resurrected as well as the just. They will together appear before the Judge of all the earth, being resurrected for that purpose. "...and they that have done evil, unto the resurrection of damnation" (John 5:29). *The Father has vested Christ with the authority to execute judgment.* Since Christ will judge all men, it must be that all men will be present, and since most have already died, it follows that they must be resurrected. The Lord Jesus testifies of this in John 5:28, "For the hour is coming, in the which all that are in the graves," etc. This is true for all who have died, in whatever manner it might be, even if they have returned to dust and their dust has mingled with the earth. In vs. 29 He identifies both the person and his destination. No mention is made here of a spiritual resurrection, as there is in vss. 24-25. Rather, mention is made of those who have no part in the spiritual resurrection. All men are not regenerated, and those who are resurrected spiritually cannot be resurrected unto damnation, as is stated for those who have done evil. Thus it remains certain that mention is made here of a corporal resurrection and also of the resurrection of those who have done evil. Since the ungodly will be resurrected and also appear in the judgment, they were not annihilated in death. This is true of the souls of Cain and Judas who went to their own place. Likewise all the souls of the ungodly still exist in their essence, and are in prison with the spirits of the ungodly of the first world (1 Pet.

3:19). Neither have they been annihilated subsequent to their entering this prison.

Secondly, the soul of man is immortal in nature. Man cannot kill it, and God will not kill it. "And fear not them which kill the body, but are not able to kill the soul: but rather fear Him which is able to destroy both soul and body in hell" (Mat. 10:28). When the soul is joined together with the body, or contrasted with it, this indicates nothing else than the one essential element of man. (The nature of the soul was discussed in chapter 10.) This essential element of man cannot be killed by men. All human violence is directed towards the body, and the ultimate possibility is the killing of the body. If the soul were to be annihilated at death, man would be able to kill the soul as well as the body. Since man is not capable of doing this, however, it remains clear and certain that the soul continues to exist after the body dies. This is the force of Christ's argument: one need not fear man, but must fear God, who is able to destroy both body and soul in hell. The verb ἀποκτεῖναι (apokteinai), that is, to *kill* (which refers to a human act) is not used here, but rather ἀπολέσαι (apolesai), that is, to *destroy* in hell. The body will be resurrected and united to the soul, upon which the ungodly with body and soul will be cast into hell to be tormented there, this being an everlasting destruction (2 Th. 1:9). At first glance the meaning of Matthew 10:28 appears to be this: God ought to be feared more than man, since man can harm the body but not the soul. God, however, can punish both body and soul eternally in hell, the place of the damned. Thus the soul is not annihilated at death, but the ungodly will be tormented eternally.

Thirdly, Matthew 26:24 also confirms that the ungodly will not be annihilated, but will be in eternal misery. We read there: "It had been good for that man if he had not been born." Nowhere do we read about Judas' misery in this life, for in the end he even received money which could have fully rewarded him. He could have enjoyed the favor of the enemies, and his death was sudden and accompanied with little pain. If this were to have annihilated him, why would it have been better if he had never been born? Rather, these words clearly indicate that his miseries after death would be dreadful and unbearable. Thus the ungodly continue to exist after death in torment.

Fourthly, this is also confirmed by all the texts which state expressly that the ungodly will eternally endure pain. "Depart from me, ye cursed, into everlasting fire, prepared for the devil and his angels," ". . .and these shall go away into everlasting punishment: but the righteous into life eternal" (Mat. 25:41, 46). Fire in Scripture does not always refer to physical fire, but to pain of the severest sort. The devils are subject to this, upon whom physical fire has no effect. They themselves understand it to be so. "Art thou come hither to torment us before the time?" (Mat. 8:29). The Lord Jesus Himself explains it as such. That which He calls "fire" in vs. 41, He refers to as "punishment" in vs. 46. This fire, this punishment, is referred to as being eternal. The word "eternal" occasionally refers to a very long period of time, but it generally refers to infinity. Even if one were to use the first meaning, it still would be evident that the ungodly are not annihilated — neither in death nor in the judgment. The reference here is to infinity, as is indicated by way of contrast. *Eternal life* unquestionably refers to an endless state of felicity, and it is contrasted with another state, namely, of punishment. Therefore the Sodomites are said to suffer "the vengeance of eternal fire" (Jude 7). Sodom was completely destroyed by fire; her inhabitants, however (the name of the city refers to its inhabitants who were guilty of fornication), will eternally suffer punishment.

Add to this Mark 9:43-44, where we read, "...go into hell, into the fire that never shall be quenched: where their worm dieth not." It is obvious that this does not refer to what man encounters in this life, but to what he will experience after his death in hell, in the place where the rich man was after his death (Luke 16). Hell, the place of the damned, is referred to as *fire* due to the severity of the pain. It is said to be *unquenchable* since it will endlessly endure. Without end it will torment the ungodly who will also endure forever. The worm of the ungodly, that is, their conscience, will *never die*. If the conscience of the ungodly endures forever, this is necessarily true also for the ungodly themselves. Therefore, the word "unquenchable" neither means "until it has accomplished its task" nor "as long as there is something on which to gnaw," that is, during this life. Rather, it is written that this will not occur here, but in hell, that is, after this life. Christ contrasts pain caused during this life by the cutting off of hands and feet, with eternal pain, exhorting to endure the first in order to be delivered from the latter. No one enters hell in this life, but only after death.

Fifthly, if eternal punishment were to consist of annihilation, the animals would also be enduring eternal punishment and it would be correct to join with the Epicurians in saying, "Let us eat and drink; for to morrow we die," which is contrary to 1 Corinthians 15:32. Then the following would not be a true statement: "Seeing it is a righteous thing with God to recompense tribulation to them that trouble you" (2 Th. 1:6), since this does not always occur in this life.

It thus remains absolutely certain that eternal punishment does not consist in the annihilation of soul and body, but that both will endure while experiencing eternal torment.

The Infinite Duration of God's Judgment upon Sin

Objection #1: God's mercy cannot permit His creatures to be tormented eternally. Such punishment would not be commensurate with sin, and thus even God's justice could not demand eternal punishment.

Answer: Such thoughts are the result of ignorance concerning God's character and the nature of sin, as well as from an attitude of disrespect and unbelief concerning God's Word. Since God's Word states it to be so, who are you to argue against it? God's avenging justice is natural to His character, so that He, as we have demonstrated in chapter three, cannot but punish sin. Sin is inherently infinite due to being committed against an infinite God. It is a total rejection of God and a radical act of divorcement from Him. The sinner will eternally continue in a sinful state, and therefore God's wrath will also justly continue to rest upon him. There is no contradiction between God's mercy and His justice, for both have different objects. The sinner, due to his sin, is the object of God's justice; believers, for whom Christ has satisfied divine justice, are the objects of God's mercy.

Eternal punishment consists in *deprivation* and *sensibility*. The damned will have an eternal and essential existence; however, they will eternally *miss* all that which constitutes felicity, such as all light, communion with God and Christ, peace, rest, joy, love, and holiness. Yes, they will one day be deprived of all good things which God in His longsuffering permitted them to enjoy in this life. Then the damned, who will continue to exist as rational creatures, will no longer be insensitive to the fact that they are without God — as is currently the case because they now divert themselves with the enjoyment of temporal things. Since, however, they will then be deprived of all things and be unable to find satisfaction within themselves, they will be in a most horrible and grievous condition. Since there will neither be any expectation of fulfillment of their needs nor of refreshment throughout eternity, they will be filled with unrest and anger towards God who will deprive them of all things, as well as despair, since this will endure forever without the least expectation of relief. Even if hell were to consist only of deprivation, it would already be unbearable. We cannot comprehend this now, since here we are never without some measure of relief. Paul spoke of this state when he wrote: "Who shall be punished with everlasting destruction from the presence of the Lord, and from the glory of His power" (2 Th. 1:9).

Eternal punishment also consists in sensibility, which we have already demonstrated extensively above. However, the nature and dreadfulness of that which will be experienced is incomprehensible. Paul expressed it as follows, "Indignation and wrath, tribulation and anguish..." (Rom. 2:8-9). Daniel refers to it as "shame and everlasting contempt" (Dan. 12:2). It is generally referred to as "fire," "pain," "weeping and gnashing of teeth." God, in the totality of His Being, will be against them, and they will forever be filled with the wrath of God. We will demonstrate shortly how unbearable this will be. What an utter despair this will generate, since there will be no relief and no expectation that this will be diminished in the least unto all eternity! Along with this the body will endure pain of the severest degree, the nature of which, however, is not known to us.

To the question, "Will there be fire in hell?", we answer affirmatively, for Scripture states it to be so. The manner in which it will be present is not known to us, however, neither do we gain anything by knowing it. Happy is he who will not have to experience it. The location of hell I do not wish to investigate.

To the question, "Will one person endure more pain than another?" we also answer affirmatively, for Scripture clearly states this to be so. Even though it is common to all that there will eternally be neither annihilation, refreshment, nor deliverance, hell will be more unbearable for the one than for the other, all of this being commensurate with the degree in which they have sinned. "But I say unto you, It shall be more tolerable for Tyre and Sidon at the day of judgment, than for you" (Mat. 11:22); "Therefore ye shall receive the greater damnation" (Mat. 23:14). In Luke 12:47 and 48 few or many stripes are mentioned in relation to the degree of sin.

Our Misery: A Reflection upon our Sinfulness

Thus we have demonstrated to you the misery of man from various perspectives. We have done so in reference to the fall of Adam, original sin, actual sin, man's impotency, and punishment upon sin. Do not rest in a mere external knowledge of all this, but make practical use of it, applying it all to yourself, and view yourself as such. Be it known to you, and impress it upon your heart, that you are the most miserable creature upon the face of the earth. If you could but perceive a glimmer of your misery, your hair would stand up straight from terror, your eyes would never fail to weep, and you would continually gnash your teeth and wring your hands. Therefore listen attentively to me as I address you. May the Lord cause you to see and feel all this, for you are miserable in many respects.

First, you are miserable *in respect to your sinfulness*. Go to Paradise and behold how ingeniously and gloriously you were created in Adam, enjoying sweet communion between God and your very own nature. Behold how willfully you have fallen away from God and have joined ranks with the devil. Having thus sinned, you have forfeited the glory of God. The image of God in which you were created in Adam has departed from you. Neither life, truth, love, holiness, nor glory are to be found in you. Instead, the appearance of a wretched black devil is within you. Your soul is in an evil, devilish condition, and is blind and unable to receive the things of the Spirit of God. It is alienated from the life of God through ignorance, dead in sin, capable of devising and committing all manner of evil, having no other desire but for that which God hates, and having no contempt for anything but that which God delights in. Your soul wallows in filth, stench, abomination, and in that which is despicable and intolerable.

Your soul is a pool teeming with all manner of hateful, envious, wrathful, evil, impure, unrighteous, deceitful, and proud thoughts — thoughts by which you forget, depart from, and despise God, all of which are abominable in nature.

Your throat is an open sepulcher; with your tongue you use deceit. The poison of asps is under your lips, and your mouth is full of cursing and bitterness. Your eyes, ears, hands, feet, and all the members of your body are instruments of unrighteousness; you are a servant of sin in the fullest sense of the word. You are of your father the devil, a prisoner of Satan, and the property of the devil. You are thus separated from God, desiring also to remain separated from Him, finding delight in your evil frame and deeds. In one word, inwardly and outwardly you are in a state of direct opposition and enmity towards the high, holy, and glorious God.

What aggravates the abominable nature of your existence, however, is that there is not one honest person to be found in your generation, but rather you belong to a generation which is despicable, hateful, evil, and impure. There is not one single individual in your entire genealogy — even if you trace back your genealogy for five thousand years, and thus to Adam — who by nature is not a liar, a murderer, a thief, a fornicator, and a horrendous monstrosity at heart. You are an unclean thing out of an unclean (Job 14:4), of the earth earthy (1 Cor. 15:47), by nature a child of wrath

(Eph. 2:3), evil from your youth (Gen. 8:21). Give careful attention to these and similar passages of Scripture, and come into the presence of God. Hear these words as coming from the mouth of the Lord, hearing Him declaring you to be such a person. Impress this upon your heart, and be convinced beyond any doubt that this is descriptive of you, since He declares you to be such.

It is necessary that the view of your sinfulness exceeds that view which is the result of a mere believing in the Word of God. In order to be truly humbled and to be a suitable recipient of grace in Christ, there must be a sensible perception of this. For this purpose it is essential that you do not merely examine yourself in the mirror of the law of nature, measuring your deeds by that which nature teaches to be good or evil, but that you seek to acquire a thorough knowledge of your virtues and vices in light of the law of *the ten commandments*. For this purpose you should carefully read Lord's Days 34 through 44 of the Heidelberg Catechism. Do not merely seek to acquire an extensive knowledge of the subject matter itself — that is, do not merely seek to discern what are good or evil thoughts, words, and deeds — but also consider their very nature as commandments, and consider that every deed must proceed:

(1) from a consciousness of being reconciled and united to God, so that one does not serve Him as a strange God and provoked Judge, but rather as an appeased Father;

(2) from a conscious submission of one's self as creature to Him who only is Lord, who by virtue of His and our natures obligates us to be subject to Him in all things;

(3) from joyful willingness and obedience;

(4) from pure love;

(5) from a view and consciousness of His supremacy and majesty, and thus in the fear of His Name;

(6) from a joyful embracing of His will, solely because it is His will, so that our will is also swallowed up in His will;

(7) from an intense yearning that He alone be glorified, and that He alone is worthy of all honor and service, this being our sole objective;

(8) from an earnest zeal and devotion, until each deed be accomplished in all its particulars.

In one word, all things must be performed as proceeding from God, in dependence upon Him, and as before His countenance; and all must end in Him. With this in mind one will not be satisfied with the mere performance of one good deed, but will perceive how dreadfully one has fallen short — even in his best deeds, and thus how dreadful every sin is.

Be frequently engaged in this fashion, and examine your entire conversation both as to its internal and external dimensions. During the entire day give heed to your thoughts, words, and deeds, and sit down every evening to review the history of your behavior on that particular day. Proceed from hour to hour, from place to place, from one person to the next person with whom you have been in contact, from incident to incident as it occurred, and then consider your behavior in all these circumstances in view of each commandment. Identify the corruption of your nature as the fountain of all these things, and consider all that would have proceeded from this fountain if opportunity and inclination had given occasion for this. Add to this the aforementioned qualifications which are required for every action, in order that you may become acquainted with yourself. However, even that will not engender a truly perplexed, sensitive, and contrite frame, unless the Lord were to give you a view of His majesty, holiness, righteousness, and truth. He must cause you to see that sin is an act of denial, rejection, and contempt towards God, while simultaneously giving you an impression of the dreadfulness of its punishment. Only then will sin truly become a reality, and the sinner be perplexed. Only then will he need help and be driven to the Mediator, Christ. Behold, thus you are a horrendous and abominable monstrosity smothered in your sins.

Our Misery: A Reflection Upon the Punishment to Which We Are Subject

Secondly, you are miserable in view of *being deserving of punishment*. Proceed further to the consideration of the temporal and eternal punishments which are the consequences of sin. Contemplation upon the state in which you have come due to sin ought to make you shudder and tremble, considering that therefore you are not worthy to walk upon the face of the earth. It is a wonder that the earth still bears you and does not open its mouth to devour you alive. It is a wonder that fire does not come down from heaven to consume you with Sodom and Gomorrah and that the devil is not permitted to tear you to pieces and to drag your soul to hell. You are not worthy of inhaling air through your nostrils, of seeing the sun, and of having the canopy of heaven stretched out over you. You are not worthy of having a piece of bread to put in your mouth, nor a thread to cover your skin.

Lift up your eyes and think for a moment about God, the

majestic, holy, and glorious God who is a terror to the sinner. Consider what David said regarding Him: "For Thou art not a God that hath pleasure in wickedness: neither shall evil dwell with Thee. The foolish shall not stand in Thy sight: Thou hatest all workers of iniquity. Thou shalt destroy them that speak leasing: the LORD will abhor the bloody and deceitful man" (Psa. 5:4-6). Paul spoke likewise: "But unto them that...do not obey the truth...indignation and wrath, tribulation and anguish [shall come][1] upon every soul of man that doeth evil" (Rom. 2:8-9). Hear the thundering declaration in Galatians 3:10, "Cursed is every one that continueth not in all things which are written...to do them." Consider also 2 Thessalonians 1:8, "In flaming fire taking vengeance on them that know not God, and that obey not the gospel of our Lord Jesus Christ." Oh my unconverted fellowman who does not wish to be drawn and wooed by the goodness of God, may God once cause you to perceive what His wrath is, to which you are subject, in order that you may be saved with fear!

Let me present this in more detail to you, hoping that in some measure it may move you.

(1) Take note of God's own expressions in this regard. "Thou, even Thou, art to be feared: and who may stand in Thy sight when once Thou art angry?" (Psa. 76:7); "Who knoweth the power of Thine anger? even according to Thy fear, so is Thy wrath" (Psa. 90:11); "It is a fearful thing to fall into the hands of the living God" (Heb. 10:31).

(2) Consider the anxiety of the saints when God hides His countenance from them and when He causes but a glimpse of His anger to be seen by them. David feared this and therefore prayed, "O LORD, rebuke me not in Thine anger, neither chasten me in Thy hot displeasure" (Psa. 6:1). Jeremiah could endure anything, but he feared the wrath of God, for he said, "Be not a terror unto me" (Jer. 17:17). How Job complained of this! "For the arrows of the Almighty are within me, the poison whereof drinketh up my spirit: the terrors of God do set themselves in array against me" (Job 6:4). Heman expressed his anxiety as follows, "Thy fierce wrath goeth over me; Thy terrors have cut me off" (Psa. 88:16).

(3) Observe and consider how the Lord Jesus, the Surety of the elect, became a curse, and how He endured all misery and anxiety. Consider how He was assaulted by the devil, was rejected, despised, and mocked of men, was condemned and put to death on

---

[1] The words inside the brackets are printed in italics in the Statenvertaling. Since they clarify the meaning of the quote they have been included.

the cross. Consider how the wrath of God pressed Him down and caused Him to be sorrowful unto death. He was engaged in a fierce battle, and was sorrowful and very heavy. He sweat an abundance of blood which fell in drops from His face to the earth; He crawled as a worm upon the earth. He prayed and mourned, "My God, my God, why hast Thou forsaken Me?" Such was the heaviness of His task in atoning for the sins of His elect.

(4) If this does not move you, proceed to observe the dreadful pit of damnation, and listen to the gnashing of teeth, the weeping, the frightful shriek, "Woe, woe, woe," the terror, and the violent raging of the conscience of the damned in the eternal fire. Consider that to all eternity they will never enjoy one beam of light, nor one quiet moment, but will eternally be overcome with inexpressible despair knowing they will never be delivered as well as be subject to an inexpressible perception of the wrath of God.

In all quietness you ought to meditate upon the state of damnation. First of all, what will it be to have a soul and body which cannot find fulfillment within itself and thus cannot be satisfied unless this fulfillment comes from elsewhere, which, however, will be lacking to all eternity. There will not be the least refreshment, neither will there be food, drink, light, sleep, nor companionship by which one could find some delight in conversation. On the contrary, there will be an infinite separation from God, angels, the godly, joy, and glory. At the present time one may be able to forget his unhappiness and sorrow by a variety of means and thus feel no sorrow concerning that of which he is deprived. Then, however, it will be unbearable when these various means are removed. What dreadful despair will this yield for the unfulfilled and sorrowing soul!

Secondly, consider how the soul, against its will, will continually be compelled to think upon all the benefits which it had received of God in this life as far as the body is concerned. He will also be compelled to think upon the means of grace received, and the sermons and ministers by which he was admonished and rebuked, exhorting him to repent, and indeed, constraining him to do so. The soul will think upon all divine conviction within the conscience, as well as the deliberate rejection, despising, opposition towards, and contradiction of all the means of grace, as well as towards those who with words and deeds convicted them.

Thirdly, consider how dreadful it will be when all committed abominations will continually come to mind, and when these, one by one, will be vividly recalled together with all the abominable circumstances attending each of them.

Fourthly, consider what it will be when the ungodly will blame

God for not having converted them as others, and for not having ushered them into heaven as others, but instead depriving them eternally of all grace. Consider what it will be when, in their wickedness, they will lash out at God with every imaginable blasphemy.

Fifthly, consider how dreadful and terrifying it will be when the eternal wrath of God will continually overwhelm the soul, causing it unbearable pain, and all the perfections of God will simultaneously manifest themselves against the soul. How dreadful and terrifying this will be! What eternal despair this will engender!

Behold, you who hear or read this, you have deserved all this. Perhaps many of you, due to your failure to repent and the hardness of your hearts, will experience this and have your portion in this lake which burns with sulfur and brimstone. Perhaps this will be your portion within a few days. Be alarmed, tremble, and repent, in order that you may escape the manifestation of this wrath.

Perhaps all of this may not even affect you. This one or that one may perhaps think that he is too strong mentally to be seriously disturbed by all these things. Perhaps such a person can rationally respond to all this and quiet his conscience. I assure you, however, that when God causes one's heart to tremble, he most certainly will become aware that a terrified conscience alone will cause him unbearable distress. Even a rustling leaf will cause him to tremble. Oh that you would quietly and intelligently consider and believe these things, applying all this to yourself if you are still unconverted — in order that your heart might be appalled by all this, as to whether it would please the Lord to grant you conversion!

Perhaps someone else, in response to the presentation of these matters, may think, "Since God is gracious and merciful, I hope for better things. I hope that He will keep me from hell." My response to this is that, first of all, mercy must have an object which is pitifully miserable. You, however, are hatefully miserable, and there is nothing in you which would move God to be merciful. You are Lo-ruhamah: no more to have mercy (Hosea 1:6), hateful (Titus 3:3), "the generation of His wrath" (Jer. 7:29), to be loathed and not to be pitied by anyone (Ezek. 16:5), an abhorrence (Psa. 5:6), and a generation of vipers (Mat. 3:7). Who would have compassion upon an injured toad or snake? Man either continues to kill them or at least gets rid of them. In like fashion you are hateful and abominable, and therefore you are not to comfort yourself with the mercy of God. God is just and cannot allow any sin to go unpunished. God's grace does not consist in permitting any sin to go unpunished. Grace is God's ordination and sending forth of a Surety whom He has punished in the stead of His elect. It is grace that He, by means of the gospel, causes this Surety to be proclaimed and offered. It is grace that He bestows the gift of faith on someone, enabling him to receive this Surety. It is grace when He converts someone and sanctifies him. It is grace when He, by virtue of the merits of this Surety, leads someone to eternal felicity in the way of sanctification. Therefore you who are not upon this way have no reason to comfort yourself with grace, for that is deceiving yourself to your eternal damnation. In addition to your hatefulness, God can also not tolerate you because you neither cease from sinning, nor from provoking, reviling, and despising Him continually. Furthermore, you also exalt yourself above God. By all this you demonstrate that you ignore God's threatenings, and rather continue boldly in sin. It is as if you are saying, "God may do whatever He wishes, but I don't care. I will live as I please, and I will refrain from or do whatever I wish." In addition to this you show that you desire to be honored, feared, loved, obeyed and served by men — desiring that with all these deeds they would end in you. Do not you thus establish yourself as a god? Therefore, abominable and intolerable creature, do not imagine that your misery will move God to be merciful.

Secondly, God's justice will not permit sin to go unpunished. God's majesty, which you have trampled under foot, His holiness, and His truth demand satisfaction by the bearing of punishment. Therefore the sinner can neither hope for grace, nor for mercy — and he will certainly find himself deceived in his hope — unless he has an interest in the Surety Jesus Christ. Therefore, oh man, be alarmed about your condition and be convicted of your abominable and damnable nature, for to be sensible of this is the initial manifestation of grace.

Our Misery: A Reflection upon our Impotency

Thirdly, you are miserable in view of *your impotency*. Your condition is that you are abominable, condemnable, and forsaken of God and all creatures. Come then, be a hero and save yourself if you can. This is, however, absolutely impossible, for your salvation requires the perfect satisfaction of God's justice by the bearing of all temporal and eternal punishments, and a perfect holiness. This the justice of God requires, for God can only justify a just man and can by no means clear the guilty. He cannot grant the right to eternal life to a man unless the conditions of the covenant, upon which eternal felicity was promised, have been fulfilled. And now, oh miserable one, what will you do? What can you give as a ransom for your soul? You cannot bring that which is eternal to a conclusion, neither by suffering punishment can you make full satisfaction and be acquitted as one who has satisfied the requirements of justice. You are not able to deliver yourself from the pollution of your sinful state and adorn yourself with internal and external holiness which is both perfect and pure. Thus you cannot present yourself before God as pleasing in His sight, saying with boldness, "Here I am; enter into judgment with me and judge me according to Thy justice." If only you may perceive this to some degree (I do not even mention the things which precede this), you must be convinced of your impotency and cry out, "Oh, wretch that I am! I cannot help myself, and I sink away in my misery. Where must I go? Woe unto me!"

Now consider all this together, and take some time to meditate on how completely abominable, condemnable, and hopeless your situation is. If you are unconverted, it may be a means to stir you up to seek and to ask, "Is there yet help? Is there no hope? Is there yet a way whereby I may be saved?" If you are then directed to Jesus Christ as the way, He will become precious, and you will earnestly seek to become a partaker of Him by faith. If you are converted, the contemplation upon the state of sin, no matter what it may have been for you prior to your conversion, will make and keep you humble; it will teach you to esteem Christ highly and to make use of Him continually. It will motivate you to glorify God, this being an expression of gratitude for sending His Son to deliver poor sinners through Him and to lead them to eternal felicity.

CHAPTER SIXTEEN

The Covenant of Grace

In previous chapters we have depicted man in his holy nature, and as being in relationship with God in a glorious covenant of works. Subsequently, we have depicted man in his misery, being subject to sin and its punishment as a result of breaking the covenant of works. We will now consider man as being subject to grace, and therefore we will first discuss the *covenant of grace*.

The Word "Covenant" in Old and New Testaments

The Hebrew word for "covenant" is ברית (*berith*). It is more consistent with the nature of that language to view this word not as a derivative of ברא (*bara*), that is, to *create*, but rather of ברה (*barah*), that is, to *elect*, for in a covenant there also is a selection of persons and conditions. It was customary to dedicate and confirm such a covenant with various ceremonies, to which also belonged the slaughter of animals. These animals would be hewn in half, and the pieces would be placed opposite each other. The covenanting parties would then walk between the pieces, thereby testifying, "Thus must I be hewn in pieces if I break this covenant." This is to be observed in Genesis 15:9-10 and also Jeremiah 34:18, 20 where we read, "And I will give the men that have transgressed My covenant...which they had made before Me, when they cut the calf in twain, and passed between the parts thereof." This is why the act of covenanting in Hebrew is called כרת ברית (*karat berith*) (cf. Psa. 50:5), and in Latin *percutere foedus*, that is, *to cut a covenant*. It was also customary to eat a meal in conjunction with the act of covenanting (cf. Gen. 31:44-46). For this purpose salt was used, which is pure and stable and keeps food from spoiling. This may possibly be the reason why a sure and desirable covenant is called *a covenant of salt* in 2 Chronicles 13:5.

The Greek refer to a covenant as διαθήκη (*diatheke*). The Septuagint uses that word to translate בְּרִית (*berith*). In the New Testament it is either translated as *covenant* or as *testament*. There is no basis for — and it is contrary to the Greek writers, the Septuagint, and several texts in the New Testament — insisting that διαθήκη (*diatheke*) is not to be translated as covenant, but solely as testament. In a subtle manner this undermines the covenant transaction with God and the exercise of faith.

The difference, among others, between a testament and a covenant is that in the making of a testament there is no permission needed from the heir, whereas mutual acquiescence of both parties is a necessary prerequisite to a covenant. διαθήκη (*diatheke*) is most certainly very suitable to describe the covenant of grace, for it is a covenant which has the element of a testament in it, and it is a testament which has something of a covenant in it. *It is a covenantal testament, and a testamental covenant.*

In our language "covenant" is derived from the verb "to bind,"[1] whereby things which previously were not connected, are joined together and united. In a covenant, parties which previously were not one but existed separately, are bound together and thus united.

The word "covenant" has many connotations in God's Word, due to the nature of the agreement or covenant:

(1) It can refer to *an immutable promise.* "And I, behold, I establish My covenant with you, and with your seed after you; and with every living creature that is with you, of the fowl, of the cattle, and of every beast of the earth with you; from all that go out of the ark, to every beast of the earth" (Gen. 9:9-10). No mention is made of any acquiescence by the animals, but it is nevertheless stated that the covenant was made with them. This is nothing less than a promise, at least as far as one of the parties is concerned, promises being a constituent element of a covenant;

(2) It can refer to *a sure and unbreakable ordinance.* "Thus saith the LORD; if ye can break My covenant of the day, and My covenant of the night, and that there should not be day and night in their season..." (Jer. 33:20).

(3) Peace is a result of a covenant, and therefore, by way of comparison, "covenant" is used to designate peace. "For thou shalt

---

[1] In Dutch the connection between the noun and the verb is more obvious: "Verbond in onze taal komt af van binden." This agrees with the English definition of covenant: "a formal, solemn, and binding agreement."

be in league with the stones of the field: and the beasts of the field shall be at peace with thee" (Job 5:23).

(4) He who partakes of a covenant must take great care not to conduct himself contrary to the covenant. Therefore the act of careful observation is referred to as a covenant. "I made a covenant with mine eyes" (Job 31:1).

(5) A covenant includes laws which are conditional requirements, and therefore *a command* is called a covenant. "And He declared unto you His covenant, which He commanded you to perform, even ten commandments" (Deu. 4:13). Actually, these ten words did not constitute the covenant, for the covenant already had been established earlier. However, they were laws to which members of the covenant were obliged to adhere.

(6) *The administration of the covenant* is occasionally also referred to as the covenant. "This is My covenant.... Every man child among you shall be circumcised" (Gen. 17:10). Thus, the new administration of this singular covenant, which already was established with Adam and Eve immediately after the fall, bears the name "covenant." "I will make a new covenant with the house of Israel, and with the house of Judah" (Jer. 31:31). These are all the figurative meanings of "covenant."

The Covenant of Grace Defined

In its literal sense a covenant consists in *a mutual, binding obligation between two or more individuals, who, contingent upon certain conditions, promise certain things to each other.* Between God and man there is therefore such a covenant of grace in the true sense of the word. *This covenant is a holy, magnificent, well-ordered, and eternal agreement or treaty between the all-sufficient, good, omnipotent, righteous, faithful, true, and immutable God on the one side, and on the other side with the elect, who by nature are sinful, condemnable, impotent, abominable, hateful, and intolerable. In this covenant God promises deliverance from all evil and the bestowal of full salvation by grace through the Mediator Jesus Christ. Man, fully delighting himself in these promises, with all his heart acquiesces in and accepts the way revealed in the Word of God, whereby these promised benefits are to be obtained. In doing so, the sinner, by way of the covenant, surrenders himself to God, which God, for the assurance of covenant partakers, seals by means of the sacraments, all this to the magnification of His free and unfathomable grace.*

It will be necessary and profitable for us to analyze these matters a bit more carefully.

In order for someone to have dealings with God by way of a covenant, and to extract the proper advantage from this established covenant, this person must be clearly convinced in his heart that God establishes a covenant with man; invites man to enter into a covenant with Him; and that man is permitted to have, can have, and indeed does have covenant dealings with God.

In order to convince your soul of this, pay careful attention to all those texts in Holy Writ where reference is made to a covenant, establishment of a covenant, and entering into a covenant. It is true that these covenant transactions are comprehended in the acts of believing, receiving Christ, and surrendering to Him. The upright who in this manner have dealings with God through Christ, are thus partakers of that covenant and its benefits. Therefore the delineation of the covenant transactions should not hinder and grieve them if they perceive that they have not conducted themselves as being conscious of all this, and thus not in an entirely proper manner. Such covenant transactions with God yield more clarity, steadfastness, comfort, and consistent growth. We wish therefore to exhort everyone to proceed to transact with God in the consciousness of entering into a covenant with God, since the Holy Scriptures so clearly and frequently make mention of this.

Scriptural Evidence for the Existence of the Covenant of Grace

Genesis 15 describes, along with various noteworthy circumstances, the covenant transaction between God and Abraham. In it God, accommodating Himself to the manner of men, commanded Abraham to slaughter animals, cut them in half, and place the pieces opposite each other. Abraham was obedient, acquiesced, and prepared everything. God then allowed a smoking furnace and a burning lamp to proceed between these pieces, and thus established a covenant with Abraham. "And I will establish My covenant between Me and thee and thy seed after thee in their generations for an everlasting covenant, to be a God unto thee, and to thy seed after thee" (Gen. 17:7); "...I will make a new covenant with the house of Israel...this shall be the covenant...I will put My law in their inward parts...and will be their God, and they shall be My people" (Jer. 31:31, 33); "And they shall be my people, and I will be their God: And I will give them one heart, and one way, that they may fear Me for ever, for the good of them, and of their children after them. And I will make an everlasting covenant with them" (Jer. 32:38-40).

The New Testament also makes frequent mention of this covenant. Among others, this is confirmed in the following texts: "To perform the mercy promised to our fathers, and to remember His holy covenant" (Luke 1:72); "...being aliens from the covenants of promise..." (Eph. 2:12); "By so much was Jesus made a Surety of a better testament" (Heb. 7:22); "the Mediator of a better covenant" (Heb. 8:6).

Consider also those texts which speak of men entering into that covenant. "Yield yourselves unto the LORD" (2 Chr. 30:8); "And they entered into a covenant to seek the LORD God of their fathers with all their heart and with all their soul" (2 Chr. 15:12); "and I will bring you into the bond of the covenant" (Ezek. 20:37); "And because of all this we make a sure covenant" (Neh. 9:38). This is also the meaning of Isaiah 44:5: "One shall say, I am the Lord's...and another shall subscribe with his hand unto the LORD."

All these texts clearly confirm that there is a covenant transaction between God and believers, and that it is initiated from God's side by way of proffer and promise, and from the side of man by acceptance and surrender.

The teaching and practice of the church, not only prior to the Antichrist but also immediately subsequent to the Reformation, has always been consistent with the manner in which this covenant transaction is presented to us in Holy Writ. The Reformers have presented and inculcated this doctrine verbally as well as in writing. It is presented in the forms for Holy Baptism, the Lord's Supper, and marriage. A number of ministers who served subsequent to the writing of these forms have extensively and forcefully written on the subject. Therefore this is not a truth — as some suggest it is — which was defined clearly only a few years ago. Those individuals did this to be honored for it and were perhaps ignorant both of the matter itself and of former authors.

The Parties in the Covenant of Grace: God and Man

In order to gain a clearer understanding about the essence of the covenant, and to lose oneself in astonishment concerning this matter, it is needful to attentively consider the *parties* which come together and are joined in this covenant. Never have such opposite parties been appeased, and never have such unequal parties been united. The parties are God, the Creator of all things and a holy Lord, and an abominable sinner.

Let us now consider each of these parties in particular, in order that this doctrine may be acknowledged to be all the more glorious and be admired for its all-surpassing excellency, so that everyone may be allured to enter into this covenant. May it serve to excite those who have entered into it to the joy and glory of God.

The one party and covenant initiator is *the Lord God* who in this covenant must be viewed as *the all-sufficient One*. God is all-sufficient in Himself, and does not need the worship of man's hands. Man's goodness does not extend to Him. He does not profit from the fact that someone enters into this covenant and lives righteously; such profit is limited to partakers of the covenant. As He is all-sufficient in Himself, He is also שדי (*shaddai*), that is, *all-sufficient* for each and every partaker of the covenant, to fill them to overflowing with so much light, love, peace, joy, and felicity, that they do not and cannot desire anything but God alone. Yes, they experience that they can only perceive a small drop of that all-sufficiency. When a soul experiences but the least of all this, it will say, "Whom have I in heaven but Thee? and there is none upon earth that I desire beside Thee" (Psa. 73:25); "But it is good for me to draw near to God" (Psa. 73:28); "In Thy presence is fullness of joy" (Psa. 16:11); "I shall be satisfied . . . with Thy likeness" (Psa. 17:15); "They shall be abundantly satisfied with the fatness of Thy house" (Psa. 36:8). This all-sufficient God establishes a covenant with the man who lacks everything. Oh, how happy is he who may be in covenant with this God! Who would, and who can refuse to enter into a covenant with such an all-sufficient God? Who would not be motivated to do this at once?

In addition to this, God is revealed to us as a *good* God. God is truly good. "The LORD is good" (Nahum 1:7); "The LORD, the LORD God, merciful and gracious, longsuffering, and abundant in goodness and truth" (Exo. 34:6); "Thou art good, and doest good;" (Psa. 119:68); "O give thanks unto the LORD; for He is good: for His mercy endureth for ever" (Psa. 136:1). This is the very nature of God, and from this goodness issues forth the good which He does, manifested particularly in this covenant of grace. "Through the tender mercy of our God; whereby the dayspring from on high hath visited us" (Luke 1:78); "But after that the kindness and love of God our Saviour toward man appeared . . . He saved us" (Titus 3:4-5).

It cannot but grieve those who love God that there are many who always appear to entertain false notions concerning Him, considering this good God as being harsh, merciless, compassionless, unyielding, and as having no concern for the little and timid ones in grace. This view is rooted in their heart, and confirmed by their deeds. With such a heart they engage in prayer and have little or no hope of being heard. This is the condition of their heart for an entire day after they have sinned, as if grace were no longer available. Thus they dishonor God, and bring misery upon themselves. Let those who depart from God, who have no desire for Him nor seek Him, tremble before Him as an avenging God. You, however, whose heart goes out after Him and His grace, view Him as a good God. For it is in this manner that He reveals Himself in nature, in Scripture, and to other believers — and He has frequently manifested Himself in this manner also to you. "The LORD is good unto them that wait for Him, to the soul that seeketh Him" (Lam. 3:25). Therefore, whoever you are, come, fearing "...the LORD and His goodness" (Hosea 3:5). With such a good God man has dealings when entering into the covenant. Who then would not be desirous and have freedom to enter into a covenant with the Lord?

In this covenant God is also revealed to us as an *omnipotent* God, who not only is desirous to communicate His all-sufficiency and goodness, but is also able to do so. When the Lord made a covenant with Abraham, He prefaced this by saying, "I am the Almighty God" (Gen. 17:1). Mary sang, "For He that is mighty hath done to me great things" (Luke 1:49). The Lord says, "I am...the Almighty" (Rev. 1:8). He "is able to do exceeding abundantly above all that we ask or think" (Eph. 3:20). Whoever therefore is in covenant with such a God, how secure he is! How quietly he may rest in Him and with what assurance he may anticipate the fulfillment of His promises!

In establishing this covenant God also reveals Himself as the *faithful one*, who will neither forsake those who are in covenant with Him, nor allow them to be wanting in anything. He is the faithful Creator (1 Pet. 4:19), "which keepeth truth for ever" (Psa. 146:6). "Great is Thy faithfulness" (Lam. 3:23); "He will not suffer thy foot to be moved: He that keepeth thee will not slumber. The LORD shall preserve thee from all evil: He shall preserve thy soul" (Psa. 121:3, 7). Behold, whatever this faithful God does is characterized by faithfulness. Indeed, when He afflicts, He does so in faithfulness (cf. Psa. 119:75). "If we believe not, yet he abideth faithful" (2 Tim. 2:13). I will not "suffer My faithfulness to fail. My covenant will I not break, nor alter the thing that is gone out of My lips" (Psa. 89:33-34). Believe this and entertain no suspicion. Rest in this all you who have entered into this covenant, for your God is a faithful God. He will perfect all things concerning you.

God is also *truthful* and *immutable*. He is *Jehovah*, the I AM THAT I AM (Exo. 3:14). "For I am the LORD, I change not; therefore ye sons of Jacob are not consumed" (Mal. 3:6). "...also the strength of Israel will not lie nor repent" (1 Sam. 15:29); "...the gifts and calling of God are without repentance" (Rom. 11:29). Therefore, a partaker of this covenant may expect these benefits as certainly as if he possessed them already, and without anxiety ought to rejoice in them as Abraham did. "He staggered not at the promise of God

434   The Christian's Reasonable Service

through unbelief; but was strong in faith, giving glory to God; and being fully persuaded that, what He had promised, He was able also to perform" (Rom. 4:20-21).

In this covenant, God is also revealed as *holy* and *righteous*, for He "...will by no means clear the guilty" (Exo. 34:7). When Joshua caused the people to enter into a covenant with God, he said, "Ye cannot serve the LORD: for He is an holy God" (Josh. 24:19). Someone may think, "This discourages me, for who would dare to enter into covenant with such a holy and righteous God?" You should know, however, that this ought to attract you, since this righteousness has been satisfied by the Surety. God's righteousness now favors those who are in covenant with Him, and the covenant therefore remains unmovable. "He is faithful and just to forgive us our sins, and to cleanse us from all unrighteousness" (1 John 1:9).

Meditate to some length upon these aforementioned attributes of God, and consider God to be such until your soul is truly convinced that God in truth proves Himself as such in the establishment of this covenant. May you thus enter into this covenant with freedom, and having entered, rest with much assurance in this God. Thus this God is one of the parties in the covenant.

The other party is man, as miserable, sinful, condemnable, and impotent as we have previously depicted him to be. Compare, however, these two parties with each other. Is it possible to believe that between two parties who are so unequal there could ever be such a covenant, unless God Himself had revealed this to be so? Is the fact that such a covenant has come into existence between them not reason for astonishment and joy? Let angels, heaven, earth, and man be astonished that the majestic, holy, and glorious God enters into covenant with such abominable, evil, and unprofitable creatures, establishing such an intimate covenant of friendship with them, and leading them in this divine way to eternal felicity.

The Conditions or Promises of the Covenant of Grace

In order that we might attain to a clearer knowledge of this glorious covenant, it is needful that we examine the *conditions* or the *promises* of this covenant.[2] We shall first of all consider the benefits and promises which are offered and presented from God's side, and then which conditions are to be fulfilled from man's side.

---

[2] For a proper understanding of à Brakel's terminology here, i.e., his repeated use of the phrase "conditions (requirements) of the covenant," it is most helpful to refer to Abraham Hellenbroek's booklet for catechetical instruction. In chapter six, Hellenbroek asks, "What does God require in this covenant?" He replies, "That which God requires in it, is also a promise of the covenant, namely, faith in Jesus Christ."

Whoever you may be, take careful note of the articles of this covenant, whether it might arouse in you desire, astonishment, and joy. Is not this covenant God's covenant? That alone is sufficient reason to study it. Furthermore, the promised benefits are so numerous and great, that they transcend all comprehension. There is infinite bliss in each benefit. We shall only briefly describe the main benefits, reducing them to fourteen articles. The first seven represent the miseries from which the Lord promises to deliver those who are in this covenant. The second group of seven deals with the benefits which God promises to bestow. May God grant us to consider these promised benefits of the covenant with a wise and believing heart, rather than hearing or reading about them in a mere casual manner. May we contemplate so long upon them until we can say "Amen" upon them and they would be most precious to us! Take heed therefore, as these are the conditions of this covenant.

To all who desire to enter into this covenant with Him, God promises deliverance from the following seven evils:

God first of all offers as a condition of the covenant *deliverance from all sins*. "But this shall be the covenant that I will make with the house of Israel, saith the Lord...and I will remember their sin no more" (Jer. 31:33-34).

God promises to forgive sin in such a manner:

(1) He does not retain one single sin, but forgives them all; that is, the little, great, public, secret, and brazen sins, as well as those sins which are frequently repeated — due either to weakness or enticement — those which continually cleave to us, and also the sinfulness of our nature. He makes no exception. "And I will cleanse them from all their iniquity, whereby they have sinned against Me; and I will pardon all their iniquities" (Jer. 33:8).

(2) God promises that this forgiveness shall be of eternal duration, and that He will never recall these sins again. "I will remember their sin no more" (Jer. 31:34); "I...will not remember thy sins" (Isa. 43:25); "I have blotted out, as a thick cloud, thy transgressions, and, as a cloud, thy sins" (Isa. 44:22).

(3) God promises to forgive sin in such a manner that He will no longer view the sinner as a sinner, but as if he had never transgressed against Him — as if he had fully atoned for all his sins and fulfilled all righteousness. "Ye are complete in Him" (Col. 2:10); "...that we might be made the righteousness of God..." (2 Cor. 5:21).

(4) God promises to forgive sin in such a manner that from henceforth He will behold their sins with pity — as a father does when his weak child falls. Blessed is he whose sins are forgiven.

Secondly, God promises deliverance from His wrath. Due to sin every man is subject to wrath. "...and were by nature the children of wrath" (Eph. 2:3). This wrath is unbearable, for "...who may stand in Thy sight when once Thou art angry?" (Psa. 76:7). From this wrath all partakers of the covenant are fully delivered. "...which delivered us from the wrath to come" (1 Th. 1:10).

Thirdly, God promises deliverance from the curse which is upon every man. "Cursed be he that confirmeth not all the words of this law" (Deu. 27:26). God fully removes this curse. "Christ hath redeemed us from the curse of the law, being made a curse for us" (Gal. 3:13).

Fourthly, God promises deliverance from all corporal trials and from death; that is, to the extent that these would harm the partakers of the covenant and not be to their benefit. "I will redeem them from death" (Hosea 13:14).

Fifthly, God promises deliverance from the power of the devil. Every man by nature is a captive in the snare of the devil at his will (2 Tim. 2:26). God delivers His own out of this snare by virtue of this covenant. "To open their eyes, and to turn them from darkness to light, and from the power of Satan unto God" (Acts 26:18).

Sixthly, God promises deliverance from the dominion of sin. "For sin shall not have dominion over you: for ye are not under the law, but under grace" (Rom. 6:14).

Seventhly, God promises deliverance from eternal condemnation. "There is therefore now no condemnation to them which are in Christ Jesus" (Rom. 8:1).

What do you think of these conditions — you who have ever felt what sin, wrath, curse, death, the power of the devil, the dominion of sin, and condemnation are? Are not these matters precious, and are not these conditions worthy of acceptation? Is it actually possible to reject them?

However, the Lord was not satisfied merely to deliver those who are in covenant with Him from all these evils. He proposes other conditions in which He promises all blessings which can be subservient to the felicity of the partakers of the covenant.

First, God offers Himself to be the God of a poor, contrite sinner. "I will establish My covenant...to be a God unto thee" (Gen. 17:7); "But this shall be the covenant...I will be their God, and they shall be My people" (Jer. 31:33).

This is the sum and substance of all true felicity. No one knows what this is, however, except those who enjoy it. This felicity does not consist in receiving a benefit from God, but in having God Himself as one's portion. "The portion of Jacob is not like them: for He is the former of all things" (Jer. 10:16). This was the joy of the church. "The LORD is my portion, saith my soul; therefore will I hope in Him" (Lam. 3:24). Herein Asaph found rest and encouraged himself in all tribulations. "Whom have I in heaven but Thee? and there is none upon earth that I desire beside Thee. My flesh and my heart faileth: but God is the strength of my heart, and my portion for ever" (Psa. 73:25-26).

Who can give expression to the magnitude of this felicity? It consists in being overshadowed with God's gracious *presence;* to be surrounded with His supporting and preserving *omnipotence;* to rest in His unfailing *faithfulness;* to rejoice in God's eternal *fullness, majesty,* and *glory:* to be enlightened by His *light, goodness,* and *love;* to be satisfied with His *all-sufficiency;* to lose oneself in His *infinity* and *incomprehensibility;* to *bow* before Him with delight and love; to be *subject* to Him; and to *worship* Him. This felicity consists in rendering Him *honor* and *glory* with heart, tongue, and deeds — being conscious of His perfections and because He is so worthy of this. It consists in *fearing* Him, in serving Him, and a complete and full acquiescence in His will because He is God. This felicity is such that I can neither comprehend it, nor can you define it. Rather, we must lose ourselves in its infinity, exclaiming, "Hallelujah!", "Blessed is the nation whose God is the LORD" (Psa. 33:12)!

This is all-inclusive in and of itself. Nevertheless it has pleased the Lord to convey this and other special blessings as conditions and promises of the covenant. These conditions we will now consider in order that we may gain a better understanding and be more exercised concerning them.

Secondly, God promises to give *His Spirit* to those who are in covenant with Him. "I will pour My spirit upon thy seed" (Isa. 44:3); "And I will put My Spirit within you" (Ezek. 36:27); "And it shall come to pass afterward, that I will pour out My Spirit upon all flesh" (Joel 2:28); "And because ye are sons, God hath sent forth the Spirit of His Son into your hearts" (Gal. 4:6).

Thirdly, God offers His *friendship,* which is as intimate as between a *father* and his *children.* By virtue of this covenant Abraham was called "the friend of God" (James 2:23). Christ says of His disciples, "Ye are My friends" (John 15:14). "Behold, thou art fair, My love"[3] (Song of Sol. 4:1). The church in return calls Jesus *Friend* (Song of Sol. 5:16). Yes, God desires to be a Father to them, and they shall be His children. "And will be a Father unto you, and ye shall be My

---

[3] The Statenvertaling reads, "Ziet, gij zijt schoon, mijne vriendin," that is, "Thou art fair my friend."

sons and daughters" (2 Cor. 6:18). What a privilege, and how wondrous and sweet it is to be able to exclaim, *"Abba, Father!"*

Fourthly, God offers *peace.* "Great shall be the peace of thy children" (Isa. 54:13). This peace is with God, with angels, and with one's conscience. The person is in such a frame as if all of creation were at peace with him. The sweetness of this frame is such that it cannot be expressed, as it passes all understanding (Phil. 4:7). It is a foretaste of heaven, for the kingdom of heaven is peace (Rom. 14:17).

Fifthly, God offers *sanctification,* including all its elements, such as:

(1) illumination — "And all thy children shall be taught of the LORD" (Isa. 54:13); "But this shall be the covenant...they shall all know Me" (Jer. 31:33-34);

(2) life — "My covenant was with him of life" (Mal. 2:5);

(3) truth — "I will direct their work in truth, and I will make an everlasting covenant with them" (Isa. 61:8);

(4) freedom — "...where the Spirit of the Lord is, there is liberty" (2 Cor. 3:17);

(5) willingness — "Thy people shall be willing in the day of Thy power, in the beauties of holiness" (Psa. 110:3);

(6) joining everything together — godliness, faith, hope, love, godly fear, obedience, humility, meekness, wisdom, etc. "But this shall be the covenant that I will make...I will put My law in their inward parts, and write it in their hearts" (Jer. 31:33); "A new heart also will I give you, and cause you to walk in My statutes, and ye shall keep My judgments, and do them" (Ezek. 36:26-27). All that the godly so deeply long for — and the absence of which they mourn so deeply — is promised here.

Sixthly, God Himself guarantees that He shall *preserve* those who are in covenant with Him in the state of grace and friendship, so that neither they themselves nor any creature shall be able to rob them of it. The certainty of the state of partakers of the covenant is not dependent upon them, for they would fall from such certainty one hundred times a day. The Lord Himself promises that He will never forsake or reject them. "And I will make an everlasting covenant with them, that I will not turn away from them, to do them good; but I will put My fear in their hearts, that they shall not depart from Me" (Jer. 32:40). How sure and steadfast is the state of that person who may be in covenant with God! Such a person can confidently say, "Who shall separate us from the love of Christ?" (Rom. 8:35).

Seventhly, as a condition of this covenant God offers eternal *felicity.*

"And I appoint (by way of covenant or testament) unto you a kingdom, as My Father hath appointed unto Me" (Luke 22:29);

"And I give unto them eternal life" (John 10:28); "Come, ye blessed of My Father, inherit the kingdom prepared for you from the foundation of the world" (Mat. 25:34).

We have thus presented to you the articles of the covenant. Consider these fourteen articles together, and determine now whether there is one article which does not suit you, and which you would wish to be deleted. Consider whether there isn't something you would wish in addition to this. In doing so, you will discover that the perfection and glory of this covenant excels anything that all men together would have devised or dared to request. Is it not sufficient to be delivered from all the evil to which we are subject, and instead eternally to enjoy complete felicity? Does it not sufficiently motivate you to acquiesce fully in a resolution to enter into this covenant with God? What do you think — is he not robbed of all his senses who refuses to enter into such a covenant, a covenant with God Himself, and upon such conditions? Otherwise God would require something from man which is unreasonable.

The Unconditional Nature of the Covenant of Grace

Let us now consider which conditions God places upon man anew. I am not referring to conditions which man presents, for man is neither interested in a covenant nor inclined to enter into covenant with God. He therefore neither proposes such a covenant nor makes any request or promise for the purpose of moving God to enter into covenant with him. But God wondrously makes the initial proposal, and promises benefits in order to motivate and allure man to enter into covenant with Him.

The question is: What are the conditions which God requires from man, and which He also promises to fulfil?

I answer: God places no conditions upon man at all, nor does man promise anything as a condition upon which he would enter this covenant. Your heart needs to be instructed concerning this matter so that you might have more freedom to enter into this covenant, and with fewer doubts be more steadfast in this covenant. I therefore repeat that from man's side no conditions whatsoever are imposed upon him by God — conditions which man promises to fulfil.

This is first of all confirmed by several specific texts. "He that hath no money; come ye, buy, and eat; yea, come, buy wine and milk without money and without price" (Isa. 55:1); "I will give unto him that is athirst of the fountain of the water of life freely" (Rev. 21:6); "And whosoever will, let him take the water of life freely" (Rev. 22:17). It cannot be stated any more clearly than this.

Secondly, what would a poor son of man be able to contribute or promise? He has nothing and can do nothing. Even if he promised something, it would prove to be a falsehood. Whatever he would promise, he would have to be able to deliver, for he cannot promise concerning that which belongs to another. Man, however, possesses nothing, and God cannot be satisfied with a deceitful promise. God knows man, and He knows well that he can do nothing and will do nothing by his own initiative. God desires truth within.

Thirdly, this covenant is entirely of grace, excluding the covenant of works in its entirety. Consequently, all conditions to be met from the side of man are absolutely excluded. "And if by grace, then is it no more of works: otherwise grace is no more grace" (Rom. 11:6).

Fourthly, if any condition were imposed upon man, and were to be promised by him, the covenant of grace would be breakable and mutable; for whoever does not fulfil the condition breaks the covenant established on the basis of this condition. If man were to promise something, he would not keep his promise and would thus break this covenant and would never become a partaker of salvation by virtue of this covenant. Then the saints would be able to fall away, which is contrary to the Bible.

Fifthly, if man were able to do something and make promises accordingly, what would it be? Would it be conversion, love, holiness, obedience? Aside from the fact that man cannot do so, these matters are conditions which God promises to fulfil from His side. God offers to give these matters to the person who enters into covenant with Him, as has been demonstrated above. If these are conditions which God from His side promises to bestow upon man, they cannot be conditions which man from his side promises to fulfil.

Objection #1: One could be inclined to think that man neither needs to exercise his will, nor believe. All promises are contingent upon believing, and there are threatenings for those who do not believe. If these are conditions which God has promised to fulfil in man from His side, they cannot be conditions which man promises to fulfil from his side.

Answer: First of all, conditional promises and threatenings are motives by which God allures and draws man to enter into this covenant. Secondly, the conditional threatenings and promises have reference to the measure in which the benefits of the covenant are applied to those who are in covenant with God, and are means to stir them up. It cannot be concluded, however, that to will and to believe are conditions of the covenant of grace itself, which in its very essence contains no threatenings but only promises. Thirdly, to will and to believe are acts which are prerequisite qualities in someone who enters into this covenant. Prerequisite qualities are not conditions, however, but only qualify a person to enter into a covenant. The desire of a young man and the granting of his request, as well as the giving of a daughter into the marriage covenant, are not conditions for the marriage, but constitute the marriage itself. Such is also the case here. At best, the act of willing and believing could be called *conditio, sine qua non;* that is, a condition apart from which nothing can occur, which however does not pertain to the essence of the matter itself.

Objection #2: One could furthermore be inclined to think, that since God requires nothing from man in the establishment of this covenant, and promises to do everything for him, only God is under obligation and not man, and he may therefore live as he pleases.

Answer: A poor daughter who promises herself to a rich young man, who in turn promises only those conditions which are for her good, is as obligated to this young man without promising any conditions as he is to her with his conditions. Likewise, a believer who enters the covenant binds himself to the Lord, confirming verbally and in writing, "I am the Lord's." To what does the believer obligate himself? He obligates himself to belong to the Lord, to be the object of all God's goodness, and to be led and governed in all his ways by the Holy Spirit. It was stated above that the fifth article of the blessings of the covenant pertains to *sanctification* in all its particulars. Shall a man enter into this covenant, there must be both a true delight in, and a true love for, this article. He who finds delight[4] in sanctification will be motivated to enter the covenant for the very purpose of attaining to holiness, wishing to live a godly rather than an ungodly life. In addition to many other obligations by which he feels bound to a sanctified life, it is love which obligates him to it. Such a commitment constitutes marriage; however, it is not a condition of the covenant. So much about conditions.

Since the majesty, holiness, righteousness, and truth of God do not permit Him to deal with the sinner as a sinner, it is necessary that a *Surety* and *Mediator* intercede, to remove every obstacle in the way. This Surety is Immanuel, *Jesus Christ,* who is very God and very man, thus representing both parties equally. In Him both natures are united in order to unite God with man. In God's

---

[4] à Brakel frequently uses the word *verliefd* to describe the disposition of heart of the godly. Literally translated this word means to be in love, and thus à Brakel literally states that the godly are in love with sanctification.

presence He represents man, taking all the sins of the elect for His account as if He personally had committed them and guaranteeing the payment of their guilt. He also bore their sins in His own body on the tree (1 Pet. 2:24). He engages Himself to obey the law on behalf of the elect, and has also rendered them righteous by His obedience (Rom. 5:19). Before man, so to speak, He represents God, confirming that God will be true to the promises made in this covenant. In consequence of this He dies as testator, in whose death the testament is unbreakable. "For where a testament is, there must also of necessity be the death of the testator. For a testament is of force after men are dead" (Heb. 9:16-17). Thus, He brings these two parties, God and man, together, bringing the sinner to God in the way of reconciliation and peace (1 Pet. 3:18). How desirable and how firm is this covenant, in which all the weighty conditions are laid upon the Surety, and all blessings come upon those who are partakers of the covenant by the Mediator Jesus Christ, in whom all the promises are yea in Him (2 Cor. 1:20).

The Form and Essential Nature of the Covenant of Grace

We now must consider the form and essential nature of this covenant, which consists of mutual consent or acquiescence. Neither benefits, desirability, nor love constitute a marriage, but rather the mutual declaration of consent before each other. Everyone is familiar with the fact that when both parties acquiesce in the conditions, peace is established between those parties which previously were at war. Such is also the case here. To facilitate a clearer understanding of this, four things should be noted. 1) God's offer to the sinner to bring him into a covenant; 2) the allurement by way of offering numerous advantageous conditions; 3) the consent and acceptance of this offer; 4) the right — granted to the partaker of the covenant by virtue of being in covenant with God — to request, in faith and through prayer, those benefits which God has promised and upon which he now has a claim.

From God's side there is acquiescence, for He is the One who offers and invites. If a man, who now correctly understands the conditions, has a heartfelt desire for them, believes the truth of the offer, turns away from all other things to God alone, and quietly, truthfully, and joyfully declares his acquiescence in this covenant, surrendering himself thereby to God in Christ, then the covenant has thus been made and will eternally endure. Happy is he whose eyes have been opened by God, whose will has been inclined, and who has been brought to this earnest acquiescence! He may be assured of his present and future state of blessedness, even if he comes into much darkness, for his state is only secure in this covenant — not in his feeling, faith, or holiness. Those who merely contemplate these matters, however, considering them to be desirable but nevertheless have not heartily and truthfully had any dealings with God in Christ — never having become partakers of the fundamental fruit of this covenant, namely, renewal of heart — should not imagine this to be their portion. But all those who make Jesus their choice, receive Him, look to Him, and yearn for Him, wait upon Him to receive the forgiveness of sin, peace, comfort, and strength for the way of sanctification — all those are truly entering into this covenant. It may be that, due to lack of clear light and guidance, they do not perceive that in these things they have this covenant in view and are engaged in covenant transaction. The perception of this, however, should serve to the strengthening of the little ones in faith.

The purpose of this covenant must also be carefully noted, for this will yield much liberty to a poor son or daughter of man. Since God alone promises the fulfillment of all conditions, requiring none of man in return, what is His purpose in entering into a covenant with man? This is not to His benefit, for it neither increases His felicity nor renders Him more perfect and glorious. Rather, the purpose as far as He is concerned is the revelation of His grace, goodness, wisdom, righteousness, and power; and concerning man, His purpose is to bring him, motivated by love, to felicity. This is confirmed in the following texts: "Having predestinated us unto the adoption of children by Jesus Christ to Himself, according to the good pleasure of His will, to the praise of the glory of His grace, wherein He hath made us accepted in the beloved" (Eph. 1:5-6); "And that He might make known the riches of His glory on the vessels of mercy, which He had afore prepared unto glory" (Rom. 9:23); "To the intent that now unto the principalities and powers in heavenly places might be known by the church the manifold wisdom of God, according to the eternal purpose which He purposed in Christ Jesus our Lord" (Eph. 3:10-11).

If this is God's purpose in executing this great work of redemption by way of a covenant, who then would not wish to be the recipient of all this? Being unfit for everything, we are nevertheless suited for the manifestation of infinite grace, and divine, invincible goodness. If God wills to be the God of sinners and to lead them as His children to glory, does it not behoove us, and do we not have sufficient ground, to freely enter into this covenant and to turn repeatedly to it? Therefore if it is God's purpose to be gracious, let it be your purpose to focus also upon this grace. In love acquiesce in this covenant, to the glory of God's great and free grace, and be saved for that purpose. Entering the covenant with that perspective glorifies God and yields the soul humility, liberty, and sweet quietude.

A clearer knowledge of the nature of this covenant and its desirability is also acquired by a consideration of its *characteristics*. These are both distinct and exceedingly desirable.

First, this covenant is primarily a *one-sided* covenant, for God conceived it, God alone promises the conditions, God provides the Surety, God makes the initial proposal, and God works knowledge as well as to will and to do. Therefore we generally read in Scripture, "I shall establish My covenant"; "I shall make a covenant"; "I will bring you into the bond of the covenant." However, since the establishment of a covenant requires the consent of both parties as a necessary prerequisite, there must therefore be the acquiescence of man from his side, and from that perspective it is a *two-sided* covenant.

Secondly, this covenant is exclusively a *gracious covenant*. Neither good works, good spiritual frames, good desires, desirability, nor misery which would invoke pity — nothing whatsoever from the side of man moved God to conceive a way of redemption and a covenant. Nothing from man's side first moved God to help him. God desires to be gracious, and in this covenant man is willing to receive everything by grace alone. God comes to the foreground here as a *gracious* God (Exo. 34:6). Of His fullness man receives "grace for grace" (John 1:16).

Thirdly, it is a *holy* covenant. The Lord is holy, the Mediator is holy, the way in which partakers of the covenant receive the promises is holy, all the promises are holy, and also the partakers of the covenant are sanctified. Thus, this covenant is holy from every perspective: "...to remember His holy covenant" (Luke 1:72).

Fourthly, it is a *glorious* covenant. The Lord God possesses all glory, the Mediator is glorious and crowned with glory, and the benefits which are promised are lofty and glorious. It is especially glorious for man to be exalted in such a manner that he may enter into covenant with God; by way of this covenant he is brought unto glory (Heb. 2:10). Thus, it behooves all who are in this covenant to exclaim, "For He that is mighty hath done to me great things" (Luke 1:49).

Fifthly, it is a *well-ordered* covenant. "Although my house be not so with God; yet He hath made with me an everlasting covenant, ordered in all things" (2 Sam. 23:5). Everything — the beginning, middle, and end — fits together. Its orderliness is so precise that from every perspective its manifold wisdom, the purity of its righteousness, its unspeakable goodness, and its irresistible power shine forth. In that covenant we behold that eternal purpose to be magnified by inexpressible grace, the beholding of which would yield the felicity and happiness of angels and men. In consequence of this, God created man perfectly holy, and permitted him, by the exercise of his own will, to break the covenant in the commission of sin, thus concluding them all in sin. Subsequent to this, God proposes another way unto salvation: the covenant of grace. The Lord promised the Surety, depicting Him by means of ceremonies; causing Him to be born at a specific moment and by way of suffering to atone for sin; and then exalting Him at His right hand, committing all things into His hands. The Lord causes the gospel to be proclaimed, and by it draws His elect into this covenant, leading them by many remarkable and wondrous ways to glory. This covenant is thus well-ordered in all things.

Sixthly, it is a covenant of *peace* and *friendship*. "...neither shall the covenant of My peace be removed" (Isa. 54:10). From this proceeds the mutual use of the name *friend*. Yes, by way of comparison it is an *offensive* and *defensive* covenant. God says to Abraham, "And I will bless them that bless thee, and curse him that curseth thee" (Gen. 12:3), and the partaker of the covenant responds, "I am a companion of all them that fear Thee, and of them that keep Thy precepts" (Psa. 119:63); "Do not I hate them, O LORD, that hate Thee?... I hate them with perfect hatred: I count them mine enemies" (Psa. 139:21-22).

Seventhly, it is a *marriage* covenant. As husband and wife are united in love and are one, so intimate is the relationship and unity which comes into existence between God and Christ on the one hand and those who are in covenant with Them on the other hand. "Now when I passed by thee, and looked upon thee, behold, thy time was the time of love; and I spread My skirt over thee, and covered thy nakedness: yea, I sware unto thee, and entered into a covenant with thee...and thou becamest Mine" (Ezek. 16:8); "And I will betroth thee unto Me" (Hosea 2:19); "For thy Maker is thine husband" (Isa. 54:5). From this proceeds the use of the names *Bridegroom* and *Bride,* and the mutual use of the word *my.* "I will say, It is My people: and they shall say, The LORD is my God" (Zec. 13:9); "My Beloved is mine, and I am His" (Song of Sol. 2:16).

Eighthly, it is an *everlasting* covenant. It does not merely last for ten or twenty years, or for the duration of one's life, but is a covenant without end. It is therefore frequently called an *eternal covenant* (Jer. 31:33-34), and thus is *steadfast, sure,* and *unbreakable.* This is evident from

(1) Isaiah 54:10, "Neither shall the covenant of My peace be removed;

(2) its issuing forth from "the purpose of God according to election" which shall stand (Rom. 9:11);

(3) its being founded upon the covenant of redemption and the Counsel of Peace, which is unbreakable: "My covenant will I not break" (Psa. 89:34);

(4) being confirmed by the death of the Testator. "For a testament is of force after men are dead" (Heb. 9:17);

(5) being founded upon the truth and faithfulness of God, "which keepeth truth for ever" (Psa. 146:6);

(6) it being a covenant confirmed by God's oath, "wherein God, willing more abundantly to shew unto the heirs of promise the immutability of His counsel, confirmed it by an oath" (Heb. 6:17). So much for the characteristics of this covenant.

Attentively consider the characteristics and the qualities of this covenant. From whatever perspective we view it, is it not a wondrous and desirable covenant? Who can refrain himself from entering into this covenant with his whole heart? Who being in covenant with God would not leap for joy in view of so great a salvation, and sweetly rest in God by way of this covenant?

To this covenant also belong *seals* for the assurance of its steadfastness unto those who are in covenant with God. They do not seal this covenant, for they make no promise. Since only God promises, however, it is only He who seals this covenant. Under the Old Testament administration, circumcision and the passover were seals, as is true for holy baptism and the Lord's Supper under the New Testament administration. God first wishes to prepare man to become a partaker of eternal salvation out of free grace. He leads him, as He led Israel in the wilderness, in many mysterious ways which appear to lead away from heaven. Therefore the Lord gives him seals so he does not faint in the way. The Lord does so in order that 1) these promised benefits may repeatedly come to mind, he may receive a deep insight therein, and focus on nothing else but these benefits; 2) he may increasingly be strengthened in faith and be assured of the certainty of the promises made to him; 3) he may receive a foretaste of the heavenly benefits and experience something of their efficacy; 4) he may repeatedly be stirred up to be courageous in forsaking the world, to strive against his lusts, take up his cross, and seek honor and glory in well-doing. In this manner one ought to use the sacraments, not resting in the use of the sacraments themselves. One must rather view them on the one hand as a symbol of the suffering and death of the

Mediator Jesus Christ, and on the other side perceive in them the unbreakable nature of all the promises of this covenant.

Reasons why Many Do not Enter into this Covenant

We have presented to you the excellency of the covenant of grace. Who would not be desirous to be a partaker of this covenant? Who would not say "Amen" upon all this and exclaim, "This is the LORD's doing; it is marvelous in our eyes" (Psa. 118:23)? Nevertheless, there are many who do not desire it. The Lord Jesus marvelled because of the unbelief of the Jews, and likewise all who know the glory of this covenant will marvel with me, while on the other hand perceive how many have no desire for it, and do not enter in. One would think, "How is this possible?" and we ask, "What are the reasons for this?"

First, there is *ignorance,* for one will not desire that of which he has no knowledge. Many do not perceive what the purpose of preaching is, nor what is being proclaimed. Although there may be a hearing ear to some degree, they do not meditate upon it, nor make any effort to thoroughly understand the matter, and therefore it remains concealed for them. Others contemplate it for mere intellectual reasons, in order to be able to discuss it, and to acquire esteem as being intelligent. Thus they consider the excellency of the covenant as something foreign to them — as something of no value to them.

Secondly, there is *unbelief.* They take notice of the matters relating to this covenant and esteem them to be good and desirable, but do not know whether this is according to truth. Even though they dare not reject it as untruth, they do not believe that men can become partakers of these matters and enter into such a state. They thus leave these matters alone and turn away from them. The Word does not profit them, not being mixed with faith.

Thirdly, there is *listless laziness.* They perceive something of this matter and are desirous of being partakers thereof. This desire is, however, the desire of a sluggard who does not wish to make an effort. It is the meditation and contemplation of one who is half asleep, who falls asleep with this desire, and at the same time loses his desires and exercises concerning it. Therefore they do not become partakers of it. This will be found in no other way except in the way of seeking. "If thou seekest her as silver, and searchest for her as for hid treasures, then shalt thou understand the fear of the LORD, and find the knowledge of God" (Prov. 2:4-5). For such persons, however, all effort is too much. If this blessing were to come automatically upon them, they would allow themselves to be influenced by it. To be continually engaged, however, in searching, praying, wrestling for faith, and receiving it by faith, is too heavy a task for them, and is not worth the effort.

Fourthly, there are *earthly concerns*. Many are desirous for the covenant and are sometimes inclined to enter in, but tribulations and excessive business, the fear of future want, as well as troubling thoughts and considerations draw the heart away, and cause them to forsake their good intentions with a sigh. These are the thorns which choke the good seed, make the heart heavy, and cause man to remain in his state.

Fifthly, there are the *lusts of the flesh*. These individuals would be desirous for the benefits of the covenant as such. However, when they consider the particulars of having to part with, hate, and strive against all those sins which bring them honor, advantage, and entertainment, the benefits of the covenant are no longer appealing to them. That which they enjoy presently is too sweet, and that which is of the flesh too delightful. Therefore they readily choose sin and forget about that which is spiritual. If they cannot enter heaven in any other way, so be it, for it is certain that, regardless of what happens, they cannot and will not forsake sin.

Sixthly, there are *erroneous views*. Many are knowledgeable concerning the truth, view it as glorious and desirable, and esteem those to be very blessed who are partakers of the covenant. They go to church, are outwardly religious, and refrain themselves from being involved in the gross pollution of the world. Thus they consider themselves partakers of the covenant:

(1) even though they do not know the truth internally, do not perceive the spiritual dimension of these matters, and in their hearts neither esteem the Surety of this covenant as precious, nor have a desire for Him alone;

(2) even though they do not break their alliance and covenant with the world and their flesh, treating them at once as enemies, but inwardly, with their inclinations and love, remain united to them;

(3) even though there are no dealings between them and the Surety of this covenant and the God of this covenant that they might enter this covenant wholeheartedly, they only consider the promises to be desirable.

(4) They are very satisfied, even though they neither possess nor have a feeling for the benefits of this covenant. They consider themselves partakers of the covenant even though they are separated from God, live far from Him, are void of holiness, are of the earth, live for themselves, live in secret sin, and with heart, thoughts, inclinations, and objectives are not focused upon God, but upon

that which pertains to the body and is seen before their eyes. Those very matters which are to be found in all true partakers of the covenant are absent in presumptuous and temporal believers, and therefore such individuals ought to be convinced that until this moment they have deceived themselves with erroneous views.

Exhortation to Enter into the Covenant of Grace

You who are convinced that as yet you have not entered into this covenant, hear me, and let me persuade you to become a true partaker of the covenant by entering into it.

First, outside of this covenant there is nothing but misery. God is a Judge whom you have provoked to wrath; you are not a partaker of the Surety and His fullness, and you have no part in any of the promises. Rather, all threatenings apply to you, and all judgments rest upon you. All that you enjoy in the world increases your sins and makes your judgment all the heavier, and eternal damnation shall be your portion. "Wherefore remember...that at that time ye were without Christ, being aliens from the commonwealth of Israel, and strangers from the covenants of promise, having no hope, and without God in the world" (Eph. 2:11-12). Awaken, come to yourself, be terrified and tremble! Let the terror of the Lord move you to faith and flee the wrath to come by entering into this covenant of peace.

Secondly, in this covenant the fullness of salvation is to be found. Page back a bit and examine all the promises of this covenant stated previously and consider if there is anything which you would desire in addition to this. If not (for nothing is lacking), embrace this covenant and yield yourself unto the Lord. You will forsake nothing but filth, and you will lay down that which is but a heavy burden. It is a hard and cruel taskmaster whose service you will renounce. Contrary to this, it is God with whom you shall live in peace and friendship. This consists of nothing but light, love, joy, and pure holiness, which all partakers of the covenant will enjoy both now and forever. Why do you still hesitate? Come, make a resolution, and enter into this covenant.

Thirdly, it is God Himself who beseeches you. He comes to you and calls out, "Turn unto Me and be ye saved." He sent His only begotten Son, and through Him He speaks to you. Will you then not hear God? Will you turn from Him who is from heaven? The Lord sends His servants, and presently also me, unto you. How they labor, how they beseech you, and what use they make of heart-rending reasons, even of tears, to allure you to enter into this covenant! My dear friend, allow yourself to be persuaded. Be reconciled with God, be conquered by the urgency of love, as well as by all the prayers of ministers sent up to God on your behalf.

Fourthly, the Lord shall turn no one away who in truth comes unto Him through Christ — even if for so many years you have been disobedient to this friendly offer; even if until now your entire life has been nothing but sin; and even if until now you have done abominable things, are a murderer, an adulterer and fornicator, a thief, a slanderer, and a liar. If only you would but acknowledge your sin, have true sorrow, and have a true desire to be a partaker of this covenant in all its ramifications, and of its Surety so that through Him alone you may become a partaker of all these benefits. Be not discouraged, for there is hope concerning this matter. Come, for the Lord will certainly not cast you out, but will receive you, as He has said. You may observe this in all the promises, such as in John 6:37, "Him that cometh to Me I will in no wise cast out."

You who are truly partakers of this covenant (which you may know from that which we have said previously), first of all, rejoice and delight yourself in being a partaker of all these benefits and over the steadfastness of this covenant, even though you do not enjoy as much of this as you desire. One day you shall enjoy all this in full measure.

Secondly, reflect upon God as He presently is in this covenant, and transact with Him as a partaker of this covenant who has been graciously received by Him. With humble boldness come into His presence, pray in faith for the enjoyment of these benefits, expect them with patience, and rely in all things on Him, trusting that He will make all things well.

Thirdly, walk worthy of the gospel, as is fitting for one who is a partaker of this covenant. Do not be influenced by your former friends, the world and all that is to be found in it. Deny your fleshly lusts, be heavenly minded, let your conversation be in heaven, and let your light shine among men in order that they may perceive that a more excellent spirit is in you than in them. Strive for humility and meekness; strive to love your enemies; behave yourself wisely in the pathway of uprightness, and be holy as He is holy who has received you into His covenant.

Fourthly, walk in love and peace with other partakers of the covenant. Let the world observe that you are one in heart and soul, and may your example stir up all other partakers of the covenant, so that the mutual love of many may kindle a fire which may ignite those who are without.

Fifthly, magnify God concerning this great work. Be diligent not merely to enumerate the perfections of God unveiled in this covenant, but seek to plumb their depth, so that your soul may lose itself in amazement, and your tongue may be loosened to "shew forth the praises of Him who hath called you out of darkness into His marvelous light" (1 Pet. 2:9). "Praise the LORD, call upon His Name, declare his doings among the people, make mention that His Name is exalted. Sing unto the LORD; for He hath done excellent things: this is known in all the earth. Cry out and shout, thou inhabitant of Zion: for great is the Holy One of Israel in the midst of thee" (Isa. 12:4-6).

Concerning this covenant two questions need to be answered.

The Covenant of Grace Identical in both Old and New Testaments

Question #1: When was this covenant of grace initiated?

Answer: Due to a misunderstanding concerning the nature of the covenant of grace, the *Socinians* and *Arminians*, who are in this respect like-minded, claim that it did not exist in the Old Testament. Although they admit that it was announced that a Savior would come at a given time, and that a covenant of grace would be established at a given time, they claim that there was no such covenant during the Old Testament dispensation. They claim that those living in that dispensation were not partakers of this covenant, did not receive any promises concerning eternal salvation, and did not receive eternal life by faith and hope in a future Savior. Instead, they received it by grace, that is, on the basis of their virtuousness. To this we respond that, although the administration of the covenant was very different in both testaments, this covenant, as far as essence is concerned, existed as well in the Old Testament — being initiated with Adam — as presently in the New Testament.

Proof #1: This is first of all confirmed by the fact that immediately after the fall this covenant was established in Paradise by way of the promise in Genesis 3:15, "It (the seed of the woman) shall bruise thy head (the serpent)." This Seed of the woman is the Lord Jesus, who without the involvement of a man was born of the Virgin Mary. Such never has been nor ever shall be true for any man. Christ alone, and no one else, has bruised the head of the serpent, that is, the devil. "That through death He might destroy him that had the power of death, that is, the devil" (Heb. 2:14); "For this purpose the Son of God was manifested, that He might destroy the works of the devil" (1 John 3:8). Christ, the Seed of the woman, who would bruise the head of the devil, is promised here, which can be deduced from the threat made to the serpent. This promise was not addressed to Adam and Eve, but only within their hearing. From this it follows that the covenant of grace was not established with Adam and Eve, and in them with all their descendants as was true for the covenant of works. Rather, Adam and Eve, hearing this promise, had to receive the promised Savior for themselves in order to be comforted, as every believer has done subsequent to the giving of this promise, which shall become evident in what follows.

Proof #2: The gospel, which is the offer of this covenant, is proclaimed in the Old Testament as well as in the New Testament. "And the Scripture, foreseeing that God would justify the heathen through faith, preached before the gospel unto Abraham, saying, In thee shall all nations be blessed" (Gal. 3:8). He said "in thee," that is, in thy Seed, which is Christ. "He saith not, And to seeds, as of many; but as of one, And to thy Seed, which is Christ" (Gal. 3:16). Abraham believed this good news, not for the heathen who still would come and believe, but for himself. It was to his personal benefit, it being unto justification, which is an acquittal from guilt and punishment, and a granting of the right unto eternal life. This is confirmed in Genesis 15:6, "And he believed (note: not "the LORD," but) in the LORD; and he counted it to him for righteousness"; "And the Scripture was fulfilled which saith, Abraham believed God, and it was imputed unto him for righteousness: and he was called the friend of God" (James 2:23).

That the gospel was proclaimed to him was not an extraordinary privilege afforded to Abraham alone. The church of the Old Testament had the identical privilege, which is evident from Hebrews 4:2a, "For unto us was the gospel preached, as well as unto them." It is proclaimed to us in order that we would receive it to our benefit, and thus likewise also to their benefit. The reason why many did not profit from this was not to be attributed to the fact that it was not offered unto them, but due to their not receiving it by faith. "But the Word preached did not profit them, not being mixed with faith in them that heard it" (Heb. 4:2b). Thus, in the Old Testament dispensation Christ was proclaimed and offered in the gospel, and everyone was obligated by means of this gospel to believe in Christ unto justification as Abraham did. The covenant of grace therefore existed in the Old Testament.

Observe this also in reference to Moses. "By faith Moses, when he was come to years, refused to be called the son of Pharaoh's daughter, esteeming the reproach of Christ greater riches than the treasures in Egypt: for he had respect unto the recompense of the reward" (Heb. 11:24, 26). Moses knew Christ, believed in Christ, esteemed Christ as being precious, and had the promises in view through Christ. This chapter enumerates an entire register of Old Testament believers, and the benefits of which they became partakers by faith in Christ.

Proof #3: The Surety of the covenant was equally efficacious in the Old Testament as in the New, and thus this covenant existed then as well as now. "Jesus Christ the same yesterday, and to-day, and for ever" (Heb. 13:8). "Today" refers to the present time, "for ever" refers to the future, and "yesterday" refers to the past. The apostle does not merely state that Christ was, is and shall be, but he says that Christ has always been the same; that is, unto reconciliation, comfort, and help. Therefore one ought not to faint under oppression. By "yesterday" we cannot understand the time immediately prior to Paul, that is, the period of Christ's sojourn upon earth. It is very evident that the apostle exhorts the believers to be steadfast, since Christ at all times — that is, as soon as the church came into existence and as long as the church shall exist — is the same faithful Savior. "Yesterday" therefore refers to the time prior to Christ's incarnation, which also is confirmed by the statement that Christ has been slain before the foundation of the world. "Whose names are not written in the book of life of the Lamb slain from the foundation of the world" (Rev. 13:8). The words "from the foundation of the world" may not be made to relate to the words "whose names are not written in the book of life." There is no need to go back to that earlier phrase, and Christ never is said to be slain without any modifying statement. Even if one were to interpret these words as such, namely, "whose names are not written in the book of life of the Lamb before the foundation of the world," it remains an established fact that there was a book from before the foundation of the world in which the names of believers were written. This is the book of the Lamb, that is, of Christ, and thus Christ's death is noted as being efficacious at that time, since no one can be written in that book except it be for the efficacy of His death by being slain. It is very simple and clear, however, that one should join the words as the apostle does: "the Lamb, slain from the foundation of the world."

Question: But in what manner has Christ been slain since that time? The apostle appears to contradict this in Hebrews 9:26, where we read, "For then must He often have suffered since the foundation of the world."

Answer: The apostle shows that the death of Christ had to occur but once, and that this one sacrifice was efficacious from the foundation of the world. He thus forcefully confirms that this one death of Christ already was efficacious then, this being such as if

He both at that time and since that time had actually suffered. He thus confirms that Christ is the same yesterday and today. Christ was not slain in actuality from the foundation of the world, but rather as far as the efficacy of His sacrifice was concerned. From that moment believers believed in Him through the sacrifices, wherein they beheld the death of the Savior to come, and received Him by faith unto justification. This was true of Abel and Enoch, for we read, "By faith Abel offered unto God a more excellent sacrifice than Cain, by which he obtained witness that he was righteous, for before his translation he had this testimony that he pleased God" (Heb. 11:4-5). Abel sacrificed in faith, Abel pleased God, and Abel was righteous. This expresses irrefutably that Abel saw Christ represented in his sacrifice.

Proof #4: Believers in the Old Testament had all the spiritual benefits of the covenant of grace, and thus they, as is true for us in the New Testament, had the covenant itself.

(1) God was their God and their Father. "I am the LORD thy God" (Exo. 20:2); "I am thy God" (Isa. 41:10); "But now, O LORD, thou art our Father" (Isa. 64:8); "Wilt thou not from this time cry unto Me, My Father?" (Jer. 3:4).

(2) They had the forgiveness of sins. "As for our transgressions, Thou shalt purge them away" (Psa. 65:3); "Thou forgavest the iniquity of my sin. Selah" (Psa. 32:5).

(3) They had the spirit of adoption unto children, "to whom pertaineth the adoption" (Rom. 9:4); "We having the same Spirit of faith" (2 Cor. 4:13); "Thy Spirit is good; lead me into the land of uprightness" (Psa. 143:10).

(4) They had peace of conscience with God. "Thou hast put gladness in my heart" (Psa. 4:7); "Truly my soul waiteth upon God" (Psa. 62:1).

(5) They had childlike communion with God. "When I awake, I am still with Thee" (Psa. 139:18); "But it is good for me to draw near to God" (Psa. 73:28).

(6) They were partakers of sanctification. "O how love I Thy law! it is my meditation all the day" (Psa. 119:97).

(7) After death they entered eternal bliss, for which they longed. "For he looked for a city which hath foundations. But now they desire a better country, that is, an heavenly" (Heb. 11:10, 16). They were the recipients of this salvation. "But we believe that through the grace of the Lord Jesus Christ we shall be saved, even as they" (Acts 15:11).

The apostle neither refers here to the heathen, nor does he elevate the salvation of the heathen above the salvation of the Jews, but his reference was to the fathers who could not bear the yoke and nevertheless were saved by faith. From this he affirms that their expectation of salvation was also by faith and not by the works of the ceremonial law. From this he concludes that one must not impose the requirement of circumcision and the keeping of the ceremonial law upon the Gentiles. From all this it is evident that believers under the Old Testament enjoyed the benefits of the covenant of grace, had the covenant itself and were partakers of the same covenant with us, having all eaten the same spiritual meat and having drunk the same spiritual drink (1 Cor. 10:3-4). Therefore the apostle Peter called the Jewish nation, "The children of the prophets, and of the covenant which God made with our fathers, saying unto Abraham, And in thy seed shall all the kindreds of the earth be blessed" (Acts 3:25).

Objection #1: In the Old Testament believers did not receive the promises, "not having received the promises" (Heb. 11:13).

Answer: The promises to which the apostle here refers have reference to the incarnation of Christ, which they saw from afar, believed, and embraced.

Objection #2: "For the law made nothing perfect" (Heb. 7:19).

Answer: The ceremonial laws to which the apostle refers here lacked efficacy of satisfaction, but did point to Christ. They were a stimulus for a better hope. By faith in a Messiah to come they were perfect in Him (Col. 2:13).

Objection #3: In Hebrews 9:8 we read "that the way into the holiest of all was not yet made manifest, while as the first tabernacle was yet standing."

Answer: Christ is the way (John 14:6). Christ consecrated the way to God and to glory through the veil, that is to say, His flesh (cf. Heb. 10:19-20). The text states that as long as the ceremonies were still in effect, Christ had not yet actually paid the ransom, nor merited salvation for His own. When this occurred, however, these ceremonies no longer served a purpose. The apostle does not say that no one entered heaven during that time period, which is something most opposing parties would not dare to deny. Enoch, Elijah, Moses, Abraham, Isaac, and Jacob would rebuke them. Neither does the apostle state that the way to heaven was not known as yet, for whoever possesses faith, hope, and love, also knows the way. He stated rather that Christ Himself — who would accomplish that which the entire tabernacle service could not bring to pass, that is, the salvation of sinners — had not yet come in the flesh.

Objection #4: The apostle stated that Christ "hath abolished death, and hath brought life and immortality to light through the gospel" (2 Tim. 1:10). Thus light and life were not present prior to Christ's incarnation.

Answer: The text indeed states that Christ is He who has brought life and immortality to light. It does not mention, however, that Christ did this only subsequent to His incarnation, and not prior to His coming. We have shown above that Christ, who is the same yesterday and today, was thus engaged in the Old Testament, the gospel having been proclaimed also during that time. This text, however, refers to the measure of revelation, and to the revelation of the gospel unto the Gentiles, which, prior to this, had only occurred in Israel. This is confirmed in verse 11, where we read, "Whereunto I am appointed a preacher, and an apostle, and a teacher of the Gentiles." The apostle states this expressly when he says, "Which in other ages was not made known unto the sons of men, as it is now revealed...that the Gentiles should be fellow heirs.... Unto me, who am less than the least of all saints, is this grace given, that I should preach among the Gentiles the unsearchable riches of Christ" (Eph. 3:5-6, 8). In like manner Acts 16:25-26 is to be understood, where we read, "...according to the revelation of the mystery, which was kept secret since the world began, but now is made manifest, and by the scriptures of the prophets, according to the commandment of the everlasting God, made known to all nations for the obedience of faith." From this it is evident that there is not a distinction between the Old and the New Testament as far as the way of salvation is concerned, but the distinction is between the Jewish nation, which at that time was the only recipient of revelations, and the Gentiles who now have the very same revelation.

Objection #5: Consider the following texts. "And these all, having obtained a good report through faith, received not the promise, God having provided some better thing for us, that they without us should not be made perfect" (Heb. 11:39-40); "Unto whom it was revealed, that not unto themselves, but unto us they did minister the things" (1 Pet. 1:12). It is evident from these texts that they who lived during the Old Testament period did not partake of these benefits.

Answer: These texts expressly refer to the incarnation of Christ, it being evident that these promises were not received while these saints lived. They proclaimed that Christ at one time would come, but that they did not expect Him during their time. In this respect they did not minister unto themselves but unto us who live subsequent to the coming of Christ, and may behold and enjoy the fulfillment of that promise. And thus we enjoy better things than they; that is, they are better since the fulfillment of the promise is better than the promise itself. It thus follows that these texts do not refer to the enjoyment of the benefits of the covenant, for they were partakers of this as much as we are (which has already been shown); the apostle pointed to this in the text itself when he stated, "that they without us should not be made perfect." They thus were made perfect, not by the works of the law, but through Christ, whose coming they had in the promises of which we have the fulfillment. They were therefore not saved on any different basis than we, for we and they are saved by the very same Surety. The New Testament is superior to the Old Testament only as far as administration is concerned.

The Existence of an Additional, External Covenant with Men Denied

Question #2: Did God, either in the Old or New Testament, establish a different, external covenant in addition to the covenant of grace?

Answer: Before we answer this question it is necessary to define what an external covenant is.

(1) An external covenant is a relationship between God and man; it is a friendly covenant, or association.

(2) The parties of this covenant are, on the one side, the holy God who is of purer eyes than to behold evil (Hab. 1:13), who has no pleasure in wickedness, with whom evil shall not dwell, in whose sight the foolish shall not stand, who hates the workers of iniquity, who shall destroy them that speak leasing, and who abhors the bloody and deceitful man (Psa. 5:5-6). The other party is the unregenerate, whose throat is an open sepulchre, whose tongue use deceit, who have the poison of asps under their lips, whose mouth is full of cursing and bitterness, whose feet are swift to shed blood, whose ways are destruction and misery, who do not know the way of peace, and who do not have the fear of God before their eyes (Rom. 3:13-18). As long as they remain in this condition, they are the children of wrath (Eph. 2:3), and vessels of wrath fitted to destruction (Rom. 9:22). These would have to be the parties of this covenant.

(3) The promises of such a covenant merely relate to physical blessings, be it the land of Canaan, or in addition to that, food and clothing, money, delicacies, and the delights of this world.

(4) The condition is external obedience, merely consisting in external observance of the law of the ten commandments and the ceremonies, church attendance, making profession of faith, and using the sacraments, participation being external and without the heart.

(5) Such a covenant would be without a Mediator, being immediately established between God and man.

(6) In the Old Testament this would be the national covenant established only with the seed of Abraham. This covenant would have been an exemplary covenant to typify the spiritual service in the days of the New Testament. In the New Testament it would be a covenant to establish the external church. All of this would constitute an external covenant, it being essentially different in nature than the covenant of works and the covenant of grace.

Upon closer examination of such an external covenant (even though proponents of such a covenant do not perhaps appreciate such a close examination), the question is whether there is such an external covenant? Some deny that such is the case in the New Testament, but claim it existed in the Old Testament. Others maintain that such a covenant also exists in the New Testament. We, however, make a distinction between *external admission* into the covenant of grace, and an *external covenant*. We maintain that there have always been those who externally have entered into the covenant of grace, and who, without faith and conversion but without giving offense, mingle among the true partakers of the covenant. Their external behavior, however, does not constitute an external covenant. God is not satisfied with such an external walk but will punish those in an extraordinary measure who flatter Him with their mouths and lie to Him with their tongue. Thus, there is an *external entrance* into the covenant of grace, but not an *external covenant*. This we shall now demonstrate.

First, the person who joins himself to the church or ever has joined the church never has had such a covenant in view by which he would merely obtain some physical benefits. He has salvation in view. Thus, such an external covenant would be without partakers. This is not to suggest that man does not desire physical benefits, but he does not seek to obtain them by way of such a covenant. Man is neither acquainted with nor believes in such a covenant. There is no such covenant proposed to man, nor is he wooed or enticed to enter it. There is not one text in the entire Word of God supporting such a covenant. Therefore, whatever is neither offered nor pursued does not exist.

Secondly, it is inconsistent with the holiness of God that God, as we have expressly described Him to you, could enter into a covenant of friendship with man, who is as we have just portrayed him. It is inconsistent with God's nature that He would find pleasure in external religion, without the involvement of the heart. God demands the heart, even when He promised Canaan and other external blessings. "And thou shalt love the LORD thy God with all thine heart, and with all thy soul. And it shall be, when the LORD thy God shall have brought thee into the land," etc. (Deu. 6:5, 10). God expresses a dreadful threat to those who serve Him without the heart. "Forasmuch as this people draw near Me with their mouth, and with their lips do honour Me, but have removed their heart far from me...therefore, behold, I will proceed to do a marvelous work among this people, even a marvelous work and a wonder" (Isa. 29:13-14). Thus, it can neither be consistent with God's nature that He be satisfied with external obedience, nor that He by virtue of a covenant of friendship would bestow external blessings upon external obedience. Furthermore, how can it be consistent with the veracity of God to exercise external friendship and yet internally be filled with holy hatred, to bless externally by virtue of a covenant and yet inwardly be truly inclined to condemn the sinner, for the sinner to belong externally to God in a friendly relationship and yet internally be truly a child of His wrath? If men were to interact in this manner among themselves and establish covenants in this manner, would such a practice not be despised by the ungodly? "Far be it from the Almighty that He should commit iniquity" (Job 34:10). And even if it could be consistent with God's nature, which it cannot, it would be a covenant of works and thus be imperfect. Human activity would be the condition, and the promises would relate to the physical. However, God cannot establish a covenant of works with the impotent sinner, which we shall demonstrate at the appropriate time.

Evasive Argument: God bestows external blessings upon many because of correct, external behavior. This can be observed in Ahab, the ungodly king of Israel. "Seest thou how Ahab humbleth himself before Me? because he humbleth himself before Me, I will not bring the evil in his days: but in his son's days will I bring the evil upon his house" (1 Ki. 21:29).

Answer: It is one thing to maintain that God, by His common grace and in certain situations, bestows external blessings upon the ungodly. This we readily admit, for, "The LORD is good to all: and His tender mercies are over all His works" (Psa. 145:9). However, it is another thing to maintain that God does this by virtue of an external covenant, and thus, due to a relationship with the unregenerate and the ungodly, bestows external blessings upon them on the basis of externally good behavior. This we deny vehemently. The example of Ahab is no proof whatsoever, for the blessing bestowed upon him in response to his external manifestation of humility did not proceed from an external covenant (this being the point of contention here which needs to be proven), but by virtue of God's common grace and longsuffering.

Thirdly, if God could establish a covenant of friendship with the unregenerate without a Mediator of reconciliation, as is claimed by some, this necessarily being the proposition, there would be no need for the Surety Jesus Christ and one would be able to be saved without satisfaction of the justice of God. If God is able to establish a covenant of friendship with a sinner for the purpose of bestowing external blessings upon external obedience, doing so apart from a Mediator of reconciliation, God would likewise be able to establish a covenant unto salvation without a Mediator of reconciliation, thus promising eternal life to all the godly by virtue of their sincerity. If that were possible, there would be no need for Christ, for all of this could then transpire without Him. This, however, is impossible, as will be shown in the next chapter, and therefore it is also impossible for such an external covenant to exist. From this it is at once evident that holding to an external covenant undermines Reformed truth and gives opportunity for dissension.

Fourthly, such a covenant either has sacraments or has none. If there are none, then it is not a covenant, for God has never established a covenant without seals. If there are sacraments, which are they? Circumcision and the Passover in the Old Testament and baptism and the Lord's Supper in the New Testament? This cannot be, for then the same sacraments would be of two essentially different covenants, which is an absurdity. Besides, the sacraments of the covenant of grace only have reference to Christ, and are signs and seals of the righteousness of faith (Rom. 4:11). Since this covenant would neither have Christ as its Surety nor spiritual promises and the righteousness of faith, these seals cannot be sacraments of an external covenant. In addition to this, no one has a right to partake of the seals of the covenant of grace unless he is a true believer, since they are seals of the righteousness of faith. This position, however, maintains that the unregenerate are true members of this external covenant, who nevertheless may not partake of the sacraments. Therefore, the sacraments cannot be seals of this external covenant, from which follows that there is no such covenant.

Fifthly, whatever one proposes concerning this external covenant (such as external obedience) is comprehended in the covenant of grace. This obedience, however, proceeds from and is in harmony with an internal, holy spiritual frame. The covenant of grace includes of necessity all the external as well as the spiritual promises requisite unto salvation. Both aspects are confirmed in the following passages. "For ye are bought with a price: therefore glorify God in your body, and in your spirit, which are God's" (1 Cor. 6:20); "I beseech you therefore, brethren, by the mercies of God, that ye present your bodies a living sacrifice, holy, acceptable unto God" (Rom. 12:1); "And I will give unto thee, and to thy seed after thee, the land wherein thou art a stranger, all the land of Canaan, for an everlasting possession; and I will be their God" (Gen. 17:8); "Godliness is profitable unto all things, having promise of the life that now is, and of that which is to come" (1 Tim. 4:8).

Since the covenant of grace also obligates us to external obedience, and also has external promises, there is no need for an external covenant, which would require and promise all matters and benefits already comprehended in the covenant of grace.

Evasive Argument: One may suggest that all these reasons are not compelling since this external covenant presupposes the covenant of grace and coalesces with it.

Answer: (1) This does not confirm the matter, since this covenant must be viewed as being of an entirely different nature. It must therefore be considered independently. Thus, all these reasons remain in full force.

(2) The unregenerate, even though they externally enter into the covenant of grace, are not essentially in the covenant. With an external covenant, however, they would be actual and true members (and thus would be true partakers) of it without any reference to the covenant of grace. Thus they, not being true members of the covenant of grace and therefore without Christ and the promise, would be considered as true members of this external covenant. The covenant of grace is therefore not the issue here at all. Hence, the suggestion that an external covenant, which presupposes the covenant of grace, is established with the unregenerate holds no water. Thus, this evasive argument is without substance and our proof remains in force.

Objection #1: In the Old Testament the entire nation, head for head, the godly and the ungodly, had to enter into the covenant. They were all required to partake of the sacraments, were all in this covenant and used the sacraments, and many broke the covenant. There was thus an external covenant which in its essential nature was entirely different from the covenant of grace. For this covenant has been established with believers only and thus cannot be broken.

Answer: (1) The covenant of grace is an incomprehensible manifestation of the grace and mercy of God. When God offers this covenant to someone, it is an act of utmost wickedness to despise it, and to refuse to enter into it. Therefore everyone to whom the gospel is proclaimed is obligated to accept this offer with great desire and with all his heart, and thus to enter into this covenant. This fact is certain and irrefutable. Thus, the obligation to enter the covenant does not prove it to be an external covenant.

(2) The ungodly, being under obligation to enter into the covenant of grace, were not permitted to remain ungodly, for the promise of this covenant also pertains to sanctification. They were to be desirous for sanctification, and this desire was to motivate them to enter into the covenant. Therefore, if someone remained ungodly, it would prove that his dealings with God were not in truth — as ought to have been the case. It would confirm that he had entered into the covenant in an external sense, as a show before men, and that he was not a true partaker of the covenant.

(3) They were required to use the sacraments in faith. If they did not use them in this way, they would provoke the Lord. Neither in the Old nor New Testament do the ungodly have a right to the use of the sacraments. Unto such God says, "What hast thou to do to declare My statutes, that thou shouldest take My covenant in thy mouth?" (Psa. 50:16).

(4) Just as the ungodly merely enter the covenant under pretext, so they likewise break it again and their faith suffers shipwreck. Thus they manifest by their deeds that they have neither part nor lot in the word of promise. Their breach of covenant was not relative to an external covenant but relative to the covenant of grace into which they entered externally. The manner whereby they entered into this covenant was thus consistent with the breach of this covenant. With all that was within them they destroyed the covenant of grace by changing it into a covenant of works.

(5) In a general sense God established this covenant with the entire nation, but not with every individual. Everyone was to truly enter into this covenant by faith.

Objection #2: In the New Testament the church consists of believers and the unregenerate, the latter being by far the majority. The unregenerate are not in the covenant of grace, and yet they are members of the covenant. Consequently, they are in an external covenant, in view of which there is also an external or visible church. Children of believers, who as they grow older manifest themselves as being ungodly, are thus called *holy* (1 Cor. 7:14). This can only be the holiness of an external covenant. From this it follows that there is such an external covenant.

Answer: (1) The unregenerate are in, but not of the church. They are not true members constituting the church, but are merely parasites. All who are present in someone's home do not necessarily belong to this home and the family members. The unregenerate have externally gained entrance into the church, but the external entrance into the covenant of grace does not constitute an external covenant.

(2) There is only an external church as far as the external congregation in its totality is concerned, but not relative to individual members where the evil intermingle with the good.

(3) The children of believers are called "holy" not in reference to an external covenant, but in reference to the covenant of grace, into which the parents, be it externally or in truth, have entered, and to which they may also entrust their children, doing so by virtue of their baptism. They also have no other covenant in view than a covenant by which they and their children can be saved. Thus, we have presented the covenant of grace in all its ramifications to you, and it is our wish that everyone would be endeared to it and truly enter into it. Amen.

CHAPTER SEVENTEEN

The Necessity of Satisfaction by the Surety Jesus Christ

In the previous chapter we have dealt with the covenant of grace in general. We will now proceed to examine particular aspects of this covenant: 1) the Surety of this covenant; 2) the partakers of this covenant, the church; and 3) the way whereby the Lord translates them into this covenant, directs them in this matter, and leads them to its culmination — glory. We shall first discuss the Surety of this covenant. It is essential that we consider Him more comprehensively, so that in knowing Him we may believe in Him with an understanding heart. It is, however, in vain to consider the Surety and His accomplishment unless we are convinced of the necessity of satisfaction. We shall therefore first of all expound this to you as a matter of utmost importance.

The Nature of Satisfaction Defined

In order to understand the nature of satisfaction correctly, we need to consider the nature of sin, the Judge, and the work of redemption.

(1) *Sin* brings upon man guilt, wrath, and punishment. If the sinner is to be delivered, he must be acquitted and be delivered from guilt. God must be appeased and the punishment must be borne.

(2) God is the *Judge* who appears here not so much as a creditor, nor as Lord and offended party, but as Judge. A creditor may forgive a debt if he so desires, and a lord and offended party may relinquish his rights; such freedom of action has been afforded to man by the supreme Judge. A judge, however, may neither relin-

quish justice nor the punishments due upon crime. However, the manner, time, place, and nature of the punishment, God has left to the discretion of the judge. Since God is the supreme Judge, His justice demands the punishment of the criminal.

(3) The work of satisfaction is contingent upon the diversity of the debt in question. In retiring monetary debts the debtor is not taken into consideration, but only the debt to be paid, which is satisfied with an amount equivalent to the debt. It is immaterial to the creditor whether this debt is paid by the principal debtor or by another who functions as surety. He will be paid with the identical sum of money, which is not a concession at all. With criminal guilt, however, the situation is different. Then the debt cannot be retired by something equivalent in value, but punishment is required for the satisfaction of justice as administered by the judge. Not only the debt or guilt is considered, but also the person who has rendered himself guilty, the criminal. If this satisfaction were to be accomplished by a surety, then, in addition to the surety making satisfaction by bearing the punishment, there must also follow the forgiveness of the criminal. Thus justice would be satisfied; the judge, however, must be willing to admit and accept the surety as well as to punish the incurred guilt in him. Viewing his rights in the absolute sense of the word, the judge would not have to do so. He must thus not impute the punishment to the criminal, but release him from guilt, wrath, and judgment, since all these have been imputed to the surety. Thus mercy and justice, satisfaction and forgiveness meet each other in the atonement, all of which is true in Christ.

Secondly, the word "satisfaction" appears twice in Scripture (Num. 35:31-32), whereas the word "atonement" occurs eighty-one times.[1] Scripture gives further expression to this matter by the use of many related words such as כָּפַר (kipper), that is, *to make atonement* (Exo. 30:10). From this word are derived the words *ransom, day of atonement,* פָּדָה (pada), that is, to redeem by way of restitution. In Exodus 13:13 we have λύτρον (lutron), that is, *ransom;* in Matthew 20:28, αντιλυτρον (antilutron), that is, *ransom;* in 1 Timothy 2:6, απολύτρωσις (apolutrosis), that is, *redemption* by payment of a ran-

---

[1] The Dutch reads as follows: "Het woord voldoening staat wel met zoovele letteren in de Schrift niet, maar de zaak zelve wordt met vele andere woorden klaar in de Schrift uitgedrukt." The Wolters Dutch-English dictionary gives the following translations for voldoening: satisfaction, reparation, atonement, settlement. The choice is clearly between the words satisfaction and atonement. Since both words do occur in the KJV, the sentence had to be reconstructed.

som; in Ephesians 1:7, ἱλασμός *(hilasmos)*, that is, *redemption;* and in Romans 3:25, ἱλοςτήριον *(hilasterion)*, that is, *propitiation* on the basis of satisfaction. All these words, when considered in the original texts, refer to an atonement and a redemption accomplished on the basis of payment and satisfaction.

The Absolute Necessity of Satisfaction

In considering the matter itself we shall show that satisfaction is absolutely necessary. Since man by sin not only became subject to guilt, wrath, and punishment, and by breaking and transgressing the law also lost the right to eternal life, he might by way of satisfaction, that is, only by the bearing of punishment, be delivered from the punishment. In this way he would not receive a right to eternal life, however, since this was promised only upon perfect obedience to the law. Therefore, in addition to bearing the punishment, also a perfect holiness and fulfilling of the law are necessary. The necessity of both we shall demonstrate by considering each aspect individually.

Question: In order to remove the guilt and punishment of the sinner, is the bearing of punishment due upon sin absolutely necessary for the satisfaction of divine justice?

Answer: The *Socinians* deny this. We, however, maintain that it is absolutely necessary for the satisfaction of divine justice that the punishment be borne. Without this satisfaction, no forgiveness of sin is to be expected. This is not only true in reference to the decree and truth of God, but also in reference to the essential nature of the justice of God whereby He cannot let sin go unpunished. This will become evident from the following arguments.

First, natural man knows innately that God exists, that He is Judge, that His avenging justice demands punishment (Rom. 1:32), and that therefore He punishes sin. Pagan literature, which only recognizes that which naturally belongs to God's essence, bears abundant witness to this. Consider the following quotes: "God bears a garment of wrath." "Rarely will the rascal escape his punishment." "Since God is Judge, no guilty person will be acquitted." "Judgment upon the wicked puts me at ease, and excuses God." The inhabitants of Melita said, "No doubt this man is a murderer, whom, though he hath escaped the sea, yet vengeance suffereth not to live" (Acts 28:4). Even though pagans are more in the dark concerning the fact that God cannot forgive sin without satisfaction, they nevertheless manifest such understanding in their deeds. They are always ready to do something to make satisfaction for their sins, be it by torturing themselves, or by sacrificing animals or other objects. Indeed, even people were sacrificed as their substitute; they said, "Since they themselves were guilty, a sacrificed animal could not give satisfaction and the wrath of God can only be appeased by the blood of men." All these statements, together with their deeds, indicate that pagans were cognizant of the avenging justice of God, of the necessity of satisfaction, and of God permitting the substitution of a Surety. This argument is very much reinforced when viewing it in the light of Scripture.

Secondly, it is evident from the attributes of God:

(1) The *justice* of God. The entire Scriptures are permeated with expressions pertaining to God's justice. One should not merely understand God to be just, equitable, and proper in His nature and deeds, but also that He executes justice as a Judge. This is confirmed by the following texts: "Shall not the Judge of all the earth do right?" (Gen. 18:25); "God judgeth the righteous" (Psa. 7:11); "Righteous art Thou, O LORD, and upright are Thy judgments" (Psa. 119:137). It is common knowledge that the justice of a judge is an attribute consisting in giving everyone his just reward: treating each according to his desert whereby the guilty one is condemned and the innocent acquitted. It is an abomination before God if an earthly judge acts contrary to this (cf. Prov. 17:15). However, God being Judge, who will judge all men, cannot but condemn or acquit. Both acts are attributed to God in Scripture. "He that believeth not shall be damned" (Mark 16:16); "It is God that justifieth" (Rom. 8:33). The Hebrew word הצדיק *(hitsdik),* and the Greek δικαιοῦν *(dikaiun)* never convey the meaning of *absolution* or *forgiveness,* but always refer to *acquittal* by a judge. From this we may conclude with certainty that God cannot justify anyone unless they are righteous and free from guilt. Furthermore, since God justifies many, they are most certainly righteous. Now, in order for such persons to become righteous who in themselves most certainly are sinful and condemnable, their sin must first be punished and the law must first have been perfectly obeyed. Only in this manner will they be righteous and be able to stand before the righteous judgment of God. It is thus evident that God's justice cannot permit sin to go unpunished. If one admits God to be Judge, one must admit that God can only condemn the sinner, and must also admit of the absolute necessity of satisfaction for sin for those whom He justifies by bearing the punishment due upon sin.

Evasive Argument #1: God's justice is nothing more than His fairness, His righteousness; that is, the holiness of His nature and His deeds rather than an avenging justice.

Answer: This is a false statement. We have just shown the contrary to be true as far as the execution of His justice as Judge is concerned. If the justice of God consists, however, in His fairness and the righteousness of His nature and His deeds, then this also applies to His execution of judgment as Judge, which implies that He will justify no one but he who is righteous.

Evasive Argument #2: The justice of God is an act of His free will; God may or may not choose to exercise this, and thus may either punish or not punish.

Answer: If the proposition is true that the justice of God consists in fairness and righteousness as far as nature and deeds are concerned, then it would necessarily follow that God who does everything of His own volition could choose either to be or not to be just and fair, to deal or not to deal righteously. Such a proposition is blasphemous! If, however, He is of necessity just and fair in His nature and deeds, this also applies to Him as Judge in the execution of justice.

Evasive Argument #3: Avenging justice is inherent to God's nature rather than being an element of His free will. God, similar to fire which always burns, of necessity must always and at every moment punish.

Answer: God is not just by compulsion, but of His own volition. Here volition and necessity, that is, whatever is consistent with one's nature, are not contradictory. Volition is not a matter of course but it is a necessary consequence issuing forth from His perfect nature and activity. He who functions of necessity and according to his nature, doing so rationally, knows both the time and manner of his actions.

(2) Furthermore, the *holiness* of God confirms that in order for man to be redeemed, the satisfaction for sin by the bearing of punishment is an absolute necessity. God is holy; He is holy in His essential nature and is holiness itself. Since God is holy in the very essence of His being, He, by His very nature, hates sin. Since God is infinitely holy, He also has an infinite hatred for sin — much more so than an angel and the godly, who have but a small droplet of holiness. Since God by His very nature hates sin with an infinite hatred, He cannot unite Himself to nor love a sinful thing or person. Thus, by His very nature, He can only cast away the sinner eternally. This eternal casting away of a sinner is an eternal judgment. "Who shall be punished with everlasting destruction from the presence of the Lord" (2 Th. 1:9). Yes, God's essential, infinite holiness, and His hatred of the sinner proceeding from this, can have no other consequence but the utter damnation of the sinner.

Thus, sin and the sinner cannot remain unpunished but must be punished. This deduction that God hates sin by virtue of His essential holiness, is evident to every man who is able or willing to use reason. It is also confirmed very clearly by Scripture. "Thou art of purer eyes than to behold evil" (Hab. 1:13); "Thou lovest righteousness, and hatest wickedness" (Psa. 45:7); "Ye cannot serve the LORD: for He is an holy God; He is a jealous God; He will not forgive your transgressions nor your sins" (Josh. 24:19); "For Thou art not a God that hath pleasure in wickedness: neither shall evil dwell with Thee. The foolish shall not stand in Thy sight: Thou hatest all workers of iniquity. Thou shalt destroy them that speak leasing: the LORD will abhor the bloody and deceitful man" (Psa. 5:4-6). Consider these texts attentively and you will observe that since God is holy He hates the sinner, and because God is holy and hates sin, He cannot allow sin to go unpunished. Therefore, in order for a sinner to be delivered, it is absolutely necessary that guilt, wrath, and punishment be removed by the bearing of the punishment of sin.

Evasive Argument: God chooses to hate sin merely because He desires to do so.

Answer: Even though God manifests this hatred as an act of His free will — God exists and does everything by an act of His free will — His hatred is not an arbitrary act of volition, as if He were also capable of not hating, but even loving sin itself. Such a proposition is blasphemous! God's hatred issues forth from His holiness; holiness is a manifestation of His character. Thus, by virtue of His nature, He loves holiness. Since unholiness and sin are contrary to His character and His being, it is natural for Him to hate sin. Since God is righteous, holy, and sovereign, and the sinner is subject to Him, His holiness and hatred for sin cannot but result in the rejection and punishment of the sinner.

(3) The *mercy* of God also confirms that God cannot allow sin to go unpunished. It is an indisputable fact that God is infinitely merciful, this being consistent with His character. If it were possible that the justice of God could permit the sinner to remain unpunished, no sinner could or would be punished with temporal, much less, eternal punishment, for the eternal mercy and grace of God would not permit Him to execute His justice and power by way of punishment. It would even be considered cruel among men if someone who had the right and authority to make another person miserable and who had the freedom to execute or not to execute that right, would use this right to gain no other advantage than the opportunity to demonstrate that he had both the right

and the authority to subject another to utmost misery, poverty, pain, and terror; whereas by manifesting mercy he could receive more praise. If this is true among men, it is much more true of Him who is supreme goodness itself, and infinite in grace and mercy. Would He, as an exercise of pure sovereignty, be able to permit His creature, according to body and soul and without any relief, to suffer extreme pain and anxiety to all eternity, being able to do otherwise? Therefore, since God's punishment is both temporal and eternal, and since His punishments are not a manifestation of cruelty (He being goodness itself), it necessarily follows that divine punishment is not merely due to His right and power, but to His perfect justice — which, when considered by itself, is as adorable as His goodness — and therefore He cannot but punish sin. Consequently, there is an absolute necessity that sin be fully punished in order that man might be delivered.

(4) This is also confirmed by the *truth* of God, where it is expressly stated in Scripture, "... and that will by no means clear the guilty" (Exo. 34:7); "God is jealous, and the LORD revengeth; the LORD revengeth, and is furious; the LORD will take vengeance on His adversaries, and He reserveth wrath for His enemies" (Nahum 1:2). In Genesis 2:17 we have the pronouncement upon Adam and all who are comprehended in him and have sinned in him: "For in the day that thou eatest thereof thou shalt surely die" (Gen. 2:17). The following passage does not only contain the pronouncement of a sentence upon the Jews, but upon all that have received the law, either by nature or by way of the Scriptures: "Cursed be he that confirmeth not all the words of this law to do them" (Deu. 27:26). Consider all these and similar passages, "For the wrath of God is revealed from heaven against all ungodliness and unrighteousness of men, who hold the truth in unrighteousness" (Rom. 1:18); "For the wages of sin is death" (Rom. 6:23). It is certain that God can neither lie nor recant what He has said; thus there is no other way to be delivered than in a way of complete satisfaction by bearing the punishment due upon sin.

Evasive Argument: A natural man may readily think: all threatenings and sentences are contingent upon sorrow, faith, and repentance.

Answer: This is not stated at all; they are absolutely unconditional. If one were to say that such threatenings do occur in Scripture, as for example in regard to Nineveh, I respond as follows: 1) By producing a single example, where the circumstances make it evident that a condition was comprehended in the threat, it does not follow that all threatenings and sentences are conditional. 2) If God, upon outward repentance, temporarily postpones temporal punishment, this neither constitutes the removal and forgiveness of sins, nor deliverance from eternal punishment. 3) By referring to the conditions of sorrow, faith, and repentance, one is certainly referring to true sorrow, faith, and repentance; that is, such faith and repentance which are pleasing to God, and not such as man would propose on the basis of his own opinion, contrary to the Word of God. In the exercise of true faith, however, satisfaction by a Surety is considered a certainty for He is received by faith. Furthermore, faith in Christ is an element of every true conversion, and this faith engenders an internal change from death to life and from the world and self to God, from which ensues a manifestation of that spiritual life in all [the believer's] activities. If God upon — and thus not *because of* — such faith and repentance removes sin, it occurs because His justice has been satisfied by the Surety Jesus Christ whose ransom is received by faith. Being a partaker of that ransom manifests itself in conversion. We therefore never read that God removes sin and punishment because of worthiness, faith, or repentance, but always *upon* or *by* faith and repentance. Thus, none of the threatenings of curse, death, and condemnation are conditional, but are certain and unchangeably sure.

It is necessary that the punishment be borne, either personally or by the Surety. He who is not the recipient of the payment made by the Surety will eternally be required to bear the punishment himself. Such a person will experience that outward and natural sorrow, a historical and temporal faith, and an outward conversion will not acquit him from this punishment. If one responds to this by saying that if the Surety pays, the sinner does not make payment himself, and thus the threatening is not absolute, but rather conditional, I reply that the threatening remains absolute and unchangeable. The threatening was made relative to sin and thus sin is punished and the demands of the law are met, even if all this transpires through a Surety. Since the Surety has the same nature as he who has sinned, the sinner and the One making the payment are one and the same in that respect. Therefore the apostle testifies, "But now the righteousness of God without the law is manifested, being witnessed by the law and the prophets, even the righteousness of God which is by faith of Jesus Christ" (Rom. 3:21-22).

Thirdly, the need for satisfaction is evident from the Surety's execution of His work. This demonstrates that satisfaction of the justice of God is an absolute necessity.

(1) Scripture testifies that it pleased God to require the Surety to make payment in order to save sinners. "For it became Him, for

whom are all things, and by whom are all things, in bringing many sons unto glory, to make the captain of their salvation perfect through sufferings" (Heb. 2:10). If God were to forgive sin and save the sinner apart from the sufferings of the Surety, He would do something which would be unbecoming to Him. Far be it from us to attribute this to God. Satisfaction is thus a necessity.

(2) In sending forth the Surety there is a manifestation of most eminent and unfathomable love. "For God so loved the world, that He gave His only begotten Son" (John 3:16). It certainly would not be an act of love but rather the greatest act of cruelty, to let the holy Jesus suffer and die as He did if there were no need for this and if man could be saved without satisfaction. This love is so great and therefore satisfaction is an absolute necessity.

(3) Scripture states plainly that in the Surety Jesus Christ we have a declaration of the righteousness of God. "Whom God hath set forth to be a propitiation through faith in His blood, to declare His righteousness" (Rom. 3:25). This was neither a declaration of His authority nor of His justice which would grant him license to perform His task, but it was a declaration of His *righteousness,* which in this manner was satisfied.

(4) If, from Adam on, we also consider the entire focus of all the prophecies, ceremonies, promises, and desires and hopes, who would be able to think that all of this was merely pretext, was related to something for which there was no need? Does not all of this demonstrate the absolute necessity of satisfaction, and that without it there can neither be forgiveness of sin nor salvation?

Objection #1: Mercy and avenging justice are two opposite attributes, and therefore cannot coexist within one and the same God. Since mercy belongs to the very nature of God, avenging justice cannot be inherent in His nature.

Answer: (1) Earthly judges will answer this question for me. They can be eminently merciful, and yet this does not prevent them from being just in punishing evildoers.

(2) The simultaneous existence of mercy and wrath in God is taught throughout the entire Scriptures and is confirmed by daily experience in man's judgment by way of various ailments. The attributes of mercy and wrath, however, are as opposite as the attributes of mercy and avenging justice from which wrath issues forth.

(3) There is a difference as far as the objects are concerned, but not in the nature of God. This nature remains inherently merciful and just. This was also true prior to creation, when there were no objects for the manifestation of these attributes. However, since there are a variety of such objects after creation — the one sinful

and the other as viewed in the Surety — the same divine nature manifests itself justly to the sinner, and in mercy to the partakers of the covenant. Nevertheless, this mercy is shown neither in consequence of the misery of man nor even as a result of the satisfaction of Christ. These are merely means and presupposed qualities whereby this mercy is bestowed upon partakers of the covenant. However, they are not the causes of divine mercy; mercy has no higher nor previously existing cause than God Himself. God, in His wisdom and without compulsion — and thus not in an arbitrary or compulsory manner, but as a necessary consequence of His nature — at a time, manner, and degree determined by Him, executes His avenging justice upon the ungodly according to the measure of their ungodliness, and manifests His mercy to His elect in Christ. "Therefore hath He mercy on whom He will have mercy, and whom He will He hardeneth" (Rom. 9:18).

Objection #2: Cannot God relinquish His justice without satisfaction as men may and can do by forgiving those debts and crimes committed against them? If this is true, then God can also forgive sin without satisfaction.

Answer: (1) A law has been given to man by which he must govern his behavior. Therefore, one cannot make a determination of God's acts on the basis of man's obligation. "For My thoughts are not your thoughts, neither are your ways My ways, saith the LORD" (Isa. 55:8).

(2) Also, judgment and justice are not one and the same matter.[2] Judgment relates to the exercise of authority, whereas justice is a virtue. Every individual may in many instances relinquish his right to be just, but never the virtue of justice. A government may never give its subjects license to sin.

(3) A judge may never relinquish justice — or else he would be committing an injustice. In this situation God must not be viewed as an offended party, but as the highest Judge of heaven and earth. God and men are not on equal footing.

Objection #3: If, as Scripture states, sins are forgiven and remitted on the basis of grace, satisfaction is not necessary, for satisfaction and forgiveness are contrary to each other. Where the one occurs, the other is excluded.

Answer: It has already been shown how the satisfaction rendered by the Surety and the forgiveness of men harmonize. Relative to man there is nothing but grace and forgiveness. Man has not

_____
[2] Cf. 2 Sam. 8:15

contributed anything himself, for he is miserable, hateful, and impotent. God, however, has chosen certain individuals according to His sovereign good pleasure; has thought out, ordained, and sent the Surety; imputes the merits of the Surety to those who are His; and thus forgives and remits all their sins. It is in this manner that man receives forgiveness. As far as the Surety is concerned, however, there is complete satisfaction. Therefore, the apostle conjoins grace and satisfaction: "Being justified freely by His grace through the redemption that is in Christ Jesus" (Rom. 3:24).

Objection #4: Since God has granted Christ as a gracious gift, the elect already had been loved and accepted in grace prior to that. Satisfaction was therefore not needed.

Answer: God has elected them in Christ (Eph. 1:4). God loved them with the love of *benevolence,* and therefore God ordained the Surety so that by His satisfaction He could remove sin which He hates. Sin would have prevented God from uniting Himself to the sinner with the love of His delight, as well as from blessing them. God thus sent the Surety for them because He loved them and because then they would eternally enjoy felicity with Him.

Perfect Holiness: Essential unto Salvation

Having perceived the necessity of satisfaction to the justice of God by the bearing of punishment, one ought also to know that *a perfect holiness is required* in order for man to be delivered and to be saved.

This is first of all confirmed by the fact that salvation is promised upon no other condition than perfect holiness. "For Moses describeth the righteousness which is of the law, That the man which doeth those things shall live by them" (Rom. 10:5). Transgression merits temporal and eternal death. Assuming that the punishment has been fully borne and death has been conquered, man has then not progressed beyond his original state as far as punishment is concerned. Punishment could not be imposed upon him, and he could not inherit salvation, since the condition of perfect obedience to the law — that is, perfect inward and outward conformity to the law — had not as yet been fulfilled. The law, of necessity, had to justify "from all things, from which ye could not be justified by the law of Moses" (Acts 13:39); "For what the law could not do, in that it was weak through the flesh...that the righteousness of the law might be fulfilled in us" (Rom. 8:3-4). The law cannot justify, however, as long as man has not fulfilled it and does not actually possess righteousness. That is the prerogative of the law. Therefore, man must first be in possession of perfect holiness will he ever be saved.

Secondly, "the judgment of God is according to truth" (Rom. 2:2). Justification does not merely consist of acquittal, but also in granting a right to eternal life. When man will be placed before the bar of divine justice, investigation will not merely be made as to whether he is worthy of punishment, whether the punishment has been borne; but also whether, in addition to this, he possesses holiness and has fulfilled the law. The salvation of man does not consist in an absence of punishment, but rather in perfect communion with God. In order for God to justify man and to grant him the right unto the enjoyment of eternal felicity, he must truly be righteous and holy, for God's judgment is according to truth and His sentence is righteous and just. Here nothing can be overlooked or remitted, for God is Judge, and the task of a judge is either to condemn or to acquit and to grant to a person his right and possessions. Therefore there must be perfect holiness in order for man to be justified and to obtain salvation.

Thirdly, this is also confirmed by the imputation of the perfect holiness of Christ to the elect, which we will consider at the appropriate time. At this time consider the following passages: "So by the obedience of one shall many be made righteous" (Rom. 5:19); "...that we might be made the righteousness of God in Him" (2 Cor. 5:21); "And ye are complete in Him" (Col. 2:10). It is thus evident that sanctification is prerequisite unto the justification and salvation of a sinner.

Having therefore concluded that these two matters are absolutely required for the redemption of man — the satisfaction of divine justice by the bearing of punishment, and perfect holiness — it now must be considered who can and who does accomplish this. Does man himself or another who functions as a Surety accomplish this? If by another as surety, we must consider who can be and is qualified to be surety.

Man can accomplish neither one for himself. He can neither make satisfaction by bearing punishment, nor can he bear this punishment to its full end. "What shall a man give in exchange for his soul?" (Mat. 16:26); that is, he cannot contribute anything. Neither supplication for grace, the forsaking of evil, nor the performance of what man deems to be good are of any value here. Guilt already has been established and man cannot make any payment towards this debt. All his suffering in this world cannot atone for this. Punishment upon sin is eternal and thus without end. Man must bear this punishment eternally. Being a finite creature, man cannot transcend beyond that which is infinite. He also remains a sinner and continually increases his guilt so that also his punishment can never cease. He can neither convert himself, make himself perfect, nor fulfill the law in such a manner that he will not transgress a single commandment, which would render him guilty of violating all the commandments. "...there is no man that sinneth not" (1 Ki. 8:46); "Who can say, I have made my heart clean, I am pure from my sin?" (Prov. 20:9); "For in many things we offend all" (James 3:2); "If we say we have no sin, we deceive ourselves, and the truth is not in us" (1 John 1:8). Thus, man must in himself completely despair of the idea that he can deliver himself.

The Sinner's Absolute Need of a Surety to Make Satisfaction

For a sinner to be saved this work must be accomplished by another person, who functions as a Surety.

Question: Is it possible and just that a Surety makes satisfaction on behalf of the sinner?

Answer: Socinians deny this, but we answer affirmatively. Such satisfaction is possible, just, and also necessary.

This is first of all evident from the fact that among both the heathens and the godly it is customary, as recorded in Scripture, that a surety makes payment for someone else. It is just that he who has obligated himself to be surety also makes payment and that the government may also justly demand satisfaction from him. Heathens are known to have killed those who had obligated themselves for the debt of others when such a person either fled the scene or was not true to his word. They are also known to have killed animals and even persons in the place of others to make satisfaction for their sins before God. There was thus some degree of knowledge that someone else could bring about reconciliation with God on their behalf. In Scripture we have the example of Paul: "Put that on mine account...I will repay it" (Phile. 18-19). Judah offered himself to be surety and was willing to be a slave the remainder of his life on behalf of his brother Benjamin: "For thy servant became surety for the lad.... Now therefore, I pray thee, let thy servant abide instead of the lad a bondman to my lord" (Gen. 44:32-33).

Secondly, Scripture states expressly that the Lord Jesus is a Surety. "By so much was Jesus made a surety of a better testament" (Heb. 7:22); "For Christ also hath once suffered for sins, the just for the unjust" (1 Pet. 3:18); "And the LORD hath laid on Him the iniquity of us all. He was oppressed, and He was afflicted" (Isa. 53:6-7); "The Son of man came...to give His life a ransom for many" (Mat. 20:28). We shall shortly deal more comprehensively with this matter.

Objection #1: Relative to monetary debt, one person may become surety for another simply because it is permissible to share one's resources with someone else. This, however, is not permissible relative to life itself; much less is it permissible that someone should become surety for another by bearing the punishment of eternal condemnation and by fulfilling the law, and thus merit a right to eternal life.

Answer: Relative to monetary debt, one is authorized to become a surety for someone else only because God has authorized man to do so. Man, however, may not become a surety in cases relative to human life on behalf of someone who is worthy of death. Under such circumstances governments are not permitted to accept a suretyship.

(1) This is expressly forbidden by God. "Moreover ye shall take no satisfaction for the life of a murderer" (Num. 35:31).

(2) God has not authorized man to dispose of life at his own discretion. Man is not permitted to give his life as a ransom, and therefore it cannot be accepted as a ransom.

(3) In giving his life as a ransom, man would act beyond his ability. For he cannot make full payment while simultaneously preserving himself, but rather he remains indebted since he cannot quicken himself.

(4) If God had not forbidden this, and if man were capable of quickening himself and remaining alive, there would be no reason why one would not be able to deliver another person from death by dying on his behalf, as well as to deliver another person out of monetary straits.

God is the supreme and sovereign Lord who gives His laws to man. He Himself is above the law, however, and is not bound by the law He has given. God knows what is appropriate and what is able to satisfy His justice. He Himself has appointed a Surety and is satisfied with His Suretyship. "This is My beloved Son, in whom I am well pleased; hear ye Him" (Mat. 17:5). The Surety, Jesus Christ, due to His divinity, 1) is Lord over His own life, 2) has power to lay down His life and to take it again (John 10:18), thus enabling Him to resurrect Himself and transcend the payment itself,[3] 3) voluntarily became Surety (Heb. 10:7), this being His will and His pleasure, and 4) is able, by virtue of His death, to grant eternal life to an exceptionally large multitude. God is thereby satisfied and the elect are reconciled with Him. "For if, when we were enemies, we were reconciled to God by the death of His Son ..." (Rom. 5:10); "For it pleased the Father... having made peace

---

[3] The Dutch reads as follows: "...en de betaling te boven komen."

through the blood of His cross, by Him to reconcile all things unto Himself…" (Col. 1:20).

Thus, we have clearly established that a Surety can make satisfaction for a sinner. How can anyone consider this to be cruel, as this all testifies of willingness and goodness? It would have been cruel if God were to have subjected a holy and innocent Jesus to so much dreadful pain, anxiety, and death if He had not appointed Him to be Surety to deliver others by virtue of His satisfaction but merely had made Him an example of meekness. Those who object thus grapple with and argue against the truth, and accuse God of cruelty.

Objection #2: In Deuteronomy 24:16 we read, "The fathers shall not be put to death for the children, neither shall the children be put to death for the fathers," and in Ezekiel 18:4, "The soul that sinneth, it shall die."

Answer: (1) In these texts there is no reference to a surety or a dying on behalf of someone else in order to deliver this person (this being the issue at hand), but rather to dying due to the sins of someone else, thus relating their sins to this individual's punishment. These texts are therefore not applicable here.

(2) God forbids man to kill a person for the sake of someone else's sin. He, however, remains sovereign and thus punishes parents in their children, which results in much more grief than if one had to bear this punishment himself — "visiting the iniquity of the fathers upon the children" (Exo. 20:5).

(3) Children are as sinful as all other men, and therefore are worthy of temporal and eternal punishment. Thus, no injustice is done by God when He pours out His wrath upon them at the occasion of someone else's sin — whether they be fathers, governments, or whoever else they may be related to. God does declare, however, that in specific cases and at certain occasions He will not do so, especially if the children do not follow in the footsteps of their fathers. When the godly are subject to general judgments upon a nation due to the sins of its inhabitants, such judgments are but fatherly chastisements upon them.

The Necessary Qualifications of a Surety for Sinners

Having concluded that without doing injury to God's justice it is possible for a surety to make satisfaction for another, it must be asked, "Where may such a qualified surety be found?" It is not possible for everyone to become surety for another even as far as monetary debt is concerned, and those who are capable of being surety often are not willing.

If we turn to our fellow man, we must conclude that he is as miserable as everyone else. He cannot even make satisfaction for himself. He, being unable to exhaust eternal punishment, would eternally have to be subject to it. He would not be willing to be eternally damned on behalf of someone else. He neither can fulfil the law on his own behalf nor on behalf of someone else — even if his holiness were to excel that of the other person. Yes, even if he were perfect by virtue of someone else's perfection, this would only be of benefit to himself. Such a surety would also not be acceptable to God. How miserable will be the outcome for those who look to man!

In turning to angels we are confronted with an entirely different nature. The nature which has sinned is punishable and must itself bear the punishment. The human nature was subjected to the law, was threatened with punishment, and has transgressed, so that none other but He who has that same human nature can be surety. Angels are also finite, and therefore cannot overcome infinite punishment. Whatever they are, they are for themselves, and they can neither communicate unto others what belongs to their nature nor clothe others with perfection. There is then no expectation from these quarters.

To be a surety, one must have the following four qualities: He must 1) be very man, having proceeded from man; 2) be a holy man; 3) be very God, and 4) be God and man united in one person.

First, *the Surety must be very man.*

(1) This is due to a) the law having been given to man, which primarily requires that man serve God with body and soul, and love God and his neighbor; b) man having been threatened with death upon disobedience and having been promised felicity upon perfect obedience; and c) man having actually transgressed, thus being subject to death. In order for man to again obtain felicity, someone of necessity had to come forth from the human ranks who would fully bear the punishment due upon sin and perfectly fulfill the law placed upon him.

(2) Scripture states this very clearly. "Forasmuch then as the children are partakers of flesh and blood, He also himself likewise took part of the same; that through death He might destroy him that had the power of death, that is, the devil" (Heb. 2:14). The incarnation and being under the law are joined together, confirming that no one can be under the law unless he is man. "...God sent forth His Son, made of a woman, made under the law" (Gal. 4:4).

These texts as well as the nature of the subject indicate that the Surety not only had to be man, but also *man proceeding from man.* The Surety Jesus Christ is called the seed of the woman, of Abraham, of David, of Mary and thus of "the fathers...as concerning the flesh" (Rom. 9:5). If another human nature had been created anew, either out of the earth or out of nothing, such a man, having merely a similar nature, could not be surety, not having the identical nature. Such a man would not have transgressed, and thus could also not bear the punishment. The surety had to come forth from the human nature which had sinned.

Secondly, *the Surety must be a holy man;* otherwise,

(1) this nature could not have been assumed in union with the Person of the Son of God, for God cannot unite Himself to something which is sinful;

(2) He would be obligated to suffer for Himself, and His suffering could not be of benefit to others;

(3) His sacrifice would be tainted, could neither be pleasing to God nor procure the removal of sin;

(4) He would not be able to clothe others with holiness, He Himself being without it;

(5) He would not be able to approach unto God to intercede for the elect, for God does not hear sinners;

(6) Indeed, all the reasons mentioned above, which give evidence that God's justice must be satisfied by both the bearing of punishment as well as perfect obedience, confirm that the Surety must be a holy man.

(7) Scripture states this very clearly. "For such an high priest became us, who is holy, harmless, undefiled, separate from sinners ...who needeth not daily...to offer up sacrifice, first for His own sins, and then for the people's" (Heb. 7:26-27).

Thirdly, *the Surety must be very God:*

(1) Otherwise, His suffering would not have *infinite efficacy and value.* If eternal punishment had to be suffered in its duration, His suffering could neither be concluded nor be exhaustive, and therefore satisfaction had to be made by such suffering which in efficacy and value was equivalent to eternal duration. This could only be accomplished by one who is infinite Himself. It is true that the divine nature neither did nor could suffer; however, the Person who suffered in His human nature was God and therefore the efficacy and value of His suffering was consistent with His personhood. This is not a partial acceptance, that is, to accept a part as representing the whole, for that would not be true satisfaction but would amount to remittance without payment. This efficacy and value are also not the result of having respect for His Person, so that His suffering as such could be accepted as being sufficient. Rather, it was truly such a Person, such an efficacy, and such a

value. It was an infinite Person who suffered according to His human nature, and thus His suffering was of infinite efficacy and value, "...having obtained eternal redemption for us" (Heb. 9:12).

(2) In order to bear the magnitude of God's wrath, His human nature needed more fortitude than a common man possesses; therefore His divine nature had to support and fortify His human nature so that He would not succumb under this burden. (God's ability to support a creature in such a fashion exceeds our comprehension.) For this reason we read, "...Christ, who through the eternal Spirit offered Himself without spot to God" (Heb. 9:14).

(3) The Surety, by way of perfect obedience to the law to which man is obligated, was not only required to clothe one, but rather all of the elect with His holiness. A finite man, even if he were holy and was himself not subject to the law (which cannot be), could not accomplish this, for at best he could hypothetically fulfil the law for only one person. Since, however, the Surety had to fulfil the law on behalf of all the elect, He of necessity had to be very God. It is true that a human person is himself subject to the law. This is, however, not true for a divine Person who assumed, not a human person, but a human nature. As a divine Person He Himself is not under the law, but as Surety He places Himself under the law. Since He is infinite in His personhood, His fulfillment of the law renders a sufficient and complete satisfaction for all the elect. *Actus sunt sappositorium*, that is, *deeds are the persons who perform them*. If an infinite Person places himself under the law, and an infinite Person fulfills the law as Surety, the fulfillment of that law is perfect and sufficient. For this reason the Surety had to be very God.

(4) The Surety had to actually *deliver* His own from the power of the devil, to set them free and make them children of God. He had to regenerate them, bring them to God, keep them, and give them eternal life — all of this being required unto salvation. No one can accomplish this but He who is very God.

The fourth quality of the Surety is that He had to be *God and man united in one Person*. The reason for this is obvious from the foregoing. God Himself can neither be subject to the law, nor suffer and die. Man in subjecting himself to suffering and dying, could not suffer exhaustively nor resurrect himself. Besides that, his suffering would only benefit one person. In order, therefore, for His suffering and obedience to be of eternal efficacy, and in order that He, by His suffering and death, would conquer without the assistance of anyone else (the suretyship having to be executed as such), the Surety of necessity had to be God and man in one

Person, descending from "...the fathers...of whom as concerning the flesh Christ came, who is over all, God blessed for ever" (Rom. 9:5).

Jesus Christ: the Divinely Appointed Surety

It now remains to show who this Surety is. It is Jesus Christ. In view of His office, the Surety has various names. He is called:

(1) *Surety,* since He gives Himself as substitute for the sinner, removing his guilt and taking it upon Himself as if He Himself had incurred it. He bears the punishment due upon sin, and fulfills the law. We read of this in Hebrews 7:22 and in Jeremiah 30:21, "For who is this that engaged his heart[4] to approach unto me? saith the LORD";

(2) *Mediator,* because He brings together, unites, and satisfies both God and man. He removes from both sides whatever would prevent rapprochement by satisfying God's justice and by changing man from unwilling to willing, making him desirous and prayerful and causing him to come. "For there is...one Mediator between God and men, the man Christ Jesus" (1 Tim. 2:5); "Jesus the Mediator of the new covenant" (Heb. 12:24);

(3) *Deliverer,* because He delivers from whatever makes man miserable. "There shall come out of Sion the Deliverer" (Rom. 11:26);

(4) *Savior,* because He actually imparts to man all that can eternally and perfectly make him happy (cf. Mat. 1:21; Luke 2:11);

(5) *Prophet, Priest, King, Goel, Bridegroom, and Immanuel.* Each name has its own specific purpose.

It is not necessary to prove to Christians that the Lord Jesus is Christ, the promised Messiah, being both Surety and Savior. He was born in Bethlehem of the Virgin Mary. He preached throughout the entire Jewish nation, performed innumerable miracles, was crucified by Pontius Pilate on the hill Golgotha near Jerusalem, arose on the third day, and ascended into heaven after forty days. Every Christian acknowledges this. It is beneficial, however, and it also quickens and strengthens faith to observe how precisely all prophecies and types have been fulfilled in Christ. For this reason we will briefly focus upon some of these.

First, let us consider the *time* frame in which the Messiah had to be born.

(1) It would be when the tribe of Judah would still be fully intact according to its genealogy. "The sceptre shall not depart from Judah, nor a lawgiver from between his feet, until Shiloh come" (Gen. 49:10). The word שֵׁבֶט *(shebet)* means "trunk," "stick," or

---

[4] The Statenvertaling reads as follows, "Wie is hij, die met zijn hart borg worde?"; that is, "Who is He, who has engaged his heart to become Surety?"

"staff." Since kings had a staff — one being more ornate than the other — it thus means (albeit not frequently) "scepter." Its most common meaning is "genealogy," by which one is able to prove his ancestry, and from which noble family (such as Judah, Reuben, or Levi) he has descended. I am of the opinion that the word *schebeth* here means "genealogy" and in this text it therefore means that Judah will continue to have a well-defined genealogy and his tribe will not be mixed with other tribes or nations. His genealogy will be completely maintained until Shiloh, the Messiah, comes. This was needful in order that one would know that the Messiah, who had to come out of Judah, did indeed come out of Judah. If one maintains that other tribes were also still fully preserved, I reply that the ten tribes, to a large extent, had intermingled internally, so that only a few here and there knew to which tribe they belonged. Anna was from the tribe of Aser, and Paul was out of the tribe of Benjamin. However, it does not carry any weight — even if all the tribes at the time of Christ's birth had still been fully preserved. Judah had to be preserved in its entirety and was preserved in its entirety until the coming of Christ. "For it is evident that our Lord sprang out of Judah" (Heb. 7:14).

If one wishes to interpret the word "scepter" as a reference to the royal government of the Messiah, I have difficulty in reconciling this with the text. First of all, such royal government was not associated with the tribe of Judah until the time of David, prior to which Benjamin reigned in the person of Saul. Here we read that the *schebeth* shall not depart from Judah, indicating that the Messiah was already present in Judah as the trunk and in his children who already were as branches in him. However, royal government was not as yet associated with Judah. Whatever does not exist cannot depart.

Secondly, the scepter had departed from Judah long before the coming of the Messiah. At that time they were subject to a foreign sovereign, the emperor. In addition to this, Israel had to be severed from Judah before the Messiah would come. "Remove the diadem, and take off the crown...I will overturn, overturn, overturn, it: and it shall be no more, until He come whose right it is; and I will give it Him" (Ezek. 21:26-27). This being the case, how can one maintain that the *royal government* would not depart from Judah until Shiloh, the Messiah, would come? If one understands the word "scepter" to refer to genealogy, however, the matter is cleared up at once. This genealogy was still intact at the time of the birth of Christ. This is confirmed by the genealogies of Joseph and Mary in Matthew 1 and Luke 3. This genealogy departed from Judah shortly afterwards, a fact which is still true until this day.

(2) The Messiah had to come when the second temple was still standing. "Yet once, it is a little while, and I will shake the heavens, and the earth, and the sea, and the dry land; and I will shake all nations, and the desire of all nations shall come: and I will fill this house with glory" (Hag. 2:6-7); "And the Lord, whom ye seek, shall suddenly come to His temple, even the messenger of the covenant, whom ye delight in" (Mal. 3:1). It cannot be denied that this house, this temple, must be understood to refer to the second rather than the first temple, for both prophets prophesied after the Babylonian captivity, during and after the building of the second temple. The second temple as such was much inferior to the first temple. The old people who had seen the first temple wept when they viewed the foundation of the second, it being so inferior to the first temple (Ezra 3:12). They missed several things in the second temple which made the first so glorious. Nevertheless, this second temple would be filled with glory, and this glory would consist in the fact that the Messiah, as the fulfillment of all the types, would come to this temple. The Lord Jesus, the desire of all nations, came to this temple, as confirmed by all the gospel writers. This second temple was destroyed forty years after His suffering and death. The Lord Jesus is thus the Messiah.

(3) The Messiah had to come after seventy weeks (one week representing seven years), thus four-hundred-ninety years, after the revelation to Daniel. "Seventy weeks are determined upon thy people and upon thy holy city, to finish the transgression...from the going forth of the commandment [that is, the command of Cyrus in Ezra 1:1-2] to restore and to build Jerusalem unto the Messiah the Prince shall be seven weeks, and threescore and two weeks: the street shall be built again, and the wall, even in troublous times" (Dan. 9:24-25). Precisely at that time the Lord Jesus was born.

Secondly, the *location* where the Messiah had to be born was Bethlehem. "But thou, Bethlehem Ephratah, though thou be little among the thousands of Judah, yet out of thee shall He come forth unto Me that is to be ruler in Israel" (Micah 5:2). This has been fulfilled at the birth of Christ (Luke 2:4, 6-7).

Thirdly, the *family* from which the Messiah had to be born was Judah. "The sceptre shall not depart from Judah,...until Shiloh come" (Gen. 49:10). He also had to come forth out of the house of David. "And when thy days be fulfilled, and thou shalt sleep with thy fathers, I will set up thy seed after thee, which shall proceed out of thy bowels, and I will establish His kingdom" (2 Sam. 7:12). For this reason the Messiah is frequently called "David" (cf. Hosea 3:5).

This has been fulfilled in Christ. "For it is evident that our Lord sprang out of Judah" (Heb. 7:14); "...and the Lord God shall give unto Him the throne of His father David" (Luke 1:32). The fact that Mary was a cousin of Elizabeth, the wife of Zacharias the priest, does not negate the fact that Mary was from the tribe of Judah.[5] Levites, having no inheritance, were permitted to take wives from all the tribes; yes, all daughters without an inheritance were permitted to marry into other tribes, so that it is very well possible that Elizabeth hailed from Judah. The law forbidding marriage into other tribes pertained only to those daughters in whose families there was no male seed. Since the inheritance was theirs, they could not marry into another tribe, lest the possessions of the tribes be intermingled.

Fourthly, the Messiah had to be born out of a *virgin.* "Behold, a virgin shall conceive, and bear a son" (Isa. 7:14). He could not be of the seed of a man — in order that He could be born without original sin — but He had to be of the seed of the woman (Gen. 3:15). Our Lord Jesus was the fruit of Mary's womb (cf. Luke 1:42; Matt. 1:18).

Fifthly, the Messiah had to be *God.* "Thy throne, O God, is for ever and ever: ...therefore God, thy God, hath anointed Thee" (Psa. 45:6-7); "...and this is His Name whereby he shall be called, THE LORD OUR RIGHTEOUSNESS" (Jer. 23:6). Our Lord Jesus is very God (1 John 5:20).

Sixthly, the Messiah must be *prophet, priest, and king.* He must be a *prophet.* "The LORD thy God will raise up unto thee a Prophet from the midst of thee" (Deu. 18:15). This is the Lord Jesus, a fact deduced from all the sermons He preached, as well as from statements made by the gospel writers. "...Jesus of Nazareth, which was a prophet mighty in deed and word" (Luke 24:19). He must be a *Priest.* "Thou art a priest for ever after the order of Melchizedek" (Psa. 110:4). This refers to Christ who is "a merciful and faithful high priest" (Heb. 2:17). He must be king. "Yet have I set My king upon My holy hill of Zion" (Psa. 2:6). This also refers to Christ, for He is the "KING OF KINGS" (Rev. 19:16).

Seventhly, the Messiah would perform many *miracles,* as is recorded throughout Isaiah 35. The fulfillment of this prophecy is recorded in all the gospel writers.

---

[5] In Dutch this phrase follows, "want zusters kinderen zijn ook nichten." à Brakel adds this statement since the Dutch word "nicht" has a dual meaning in English. "Nicht" can be translated as "cousin" or "niece." Since the clarification intended by this phrase is not necessary in English, the phrase has been omitted in the translation.

Eighthly, the Messiah would fulfill all types, suffer and die as is recorded in the entire fifty-third chapter of Isaiah. The fulfillment of this prophecy is recorded by all the gospel writers. We also read in 1 Corinthians 5:7, "For even Christ our Passover is sacrificed for us."

Ninthly, the *Gentiles* would believe in the Messiah. "And unto Him shall the gathering of the people be" (Gen. 49:10); "...the desire of all nations" (Hag. 2:7). The Gentiles never believed or followed anyone of the Jewish nation; however, they do believe in the Lord Jesus, the Son of Judah and David. Since His ascension this has occurred with such powerful efficacy that the name of Jesus is glorious and precious throughout the entire world.

Tenthly, the Messiah would cause all *ceremonial worship* to cease. The temple had to be broken down, Jerusalem had to be destroyed, the Jewish nation had to be dispersed and would roam about among the Gentiles in dishonor for a long period of time. "And the people of the prince that shall come shall destroy the city and the sanctuary; and...He (that is, the Messiah) shall cause the sacrifice and the oblation to cease" (Dan. 9:26-27); "For the children of Israel shall abide many days without a king, and without a prince, and without a sacrifice, and without an image, and without an ephod, and without teraphim" (Hosea 3:4). All of this was fulfilled shortly after the days of Christ, and it continues to be fulfilled until this very day. Our hearts are hereby fully established and assured that "...Jesus is the Christ, the Son of God; and that believing ye might have life through His Name" (John 20:31). Nevertheless, the Jews do not perceive this as yet, and will continue to harden their hearts until the Redeemer will come out of Zion to turn away the ungodliness from Jacob.

Exhortation to Focus upon the Sinner's Need for Satisfaction

We have thus held before you the marrow of the gospel, that is, the necessity of satisfaction by the Surety Jesus Christ. Whoever errs here will err unto his eternal condemnation. Therefore, take it to heart. You know that you are sinful and commit sin. However, are you truly conscious of this? Do you have a deep impression that every sin is deserving of death, and if this begins to trouble you somewhat, what emotion does this generate?

(1) Perhaps you are avoiding this conviction, diverting yourself with other thoughts and activities, since such a conviction robs you of your rest. Be aware, however, that you are time and again resisting the Holy Ghost who works such convictions in you, and thus you repeatedly shun heaven itself. It is as if you say, "I do not wish to be saved; the way to heaven is not to my liking, and is of

little value to me. If I cannot be saved in any other way, well, so be it." Poor man; how else will you be saved? How dreadful it will be for you to contemplate this in hell! Then you will say, "How obstinate and evil I was to turn a deaf ear to all the knocks upon my heart, even resisting them. Who did I ensnare but myself? Then I could have been saved, but I would not; now it is eternally too late, and I am eternally damned! Woe, woe is unto me!" Therefore take notice: If ever you are convicted within, if your heart smites you because of your sin, if you are terrified by the wrath of God and the prospect of eternal damnation, consider it to be an inexpressible blessing. Open your heart and exclaim, "Speak, Lord, for I hear! Lord, what wilt Thou have me to do? Neither cease to deal with me nor allow this conviction to pass by. Let it progress within me until I may find grace in Thy eyes and be converted."

(2) Perhaps you go in the wrong direction when you are convinced of sin and judgment. Perhaps you are ignorant of the righteousness of God and of knowing that it is impossible to be saved without perfect satisfaction by the bearing of punishment, and without perfect holiness. Therefore you seek to be saved by the fact that you grieve over your sins and your condition, and think by yourself: "I shall pray to God for mercy; I shall repent and do my utmost to cease from sin; I shall attend church more frequently; I shall go to the Lord's Supper; I shall read God's Word; I shall give alms; I shall do well to my neighbor; I shall live a decent life; I shall no longer get drunk, dance, or gamble; I shall be righteous in my dealings and walk; and then I hope that because of all this God will be gracious to me. More than this I cannot do." Poor man, this is the net in which the devil catches men by the thousands and drags them to hell. This is the way in which a multitude of people deceive themselves so miserably and hasten towards eternal destruction — something which they will not be aware of until it is too late. Here the proverb of Solomon applies: "There is a way that seemeth right unto a man, but the end thereof are the ways of death" (Prov. 16:25).

In God's stead I declare to you that God will not forgive a single sin without punishing it both temporally and eternally, something which we have proved above to be undeniably true. Consider this matter attentively until you perceive and feel it to be the truth. If you then proceed to pray to God, let this truth first of all confront you. Be conscious that God is a consuming fire for the sinner: He closes His ear against you and casts you away. Thus you sink away in despair and think thus, "My sins are a reality, and God neither hears the sinner, nor can the righteous Judge be satisfied with anything else but temporal and eternal punishment upon sin. What must I do? There is absolutely no hope for me. I cannot make satisfaction but will be eternally subject to punishment, for my present suffering will not render satisfaction." Remain in such a state of perplexity until you look outside of yourself and become conscious of a way in the Surety Jesus Christ — until that way becomes precious to you, you flee to that way, and seek salvation in that way. In so doing you will find.

As impossible as it is for you to bear the punishment and to satisfy for your guilt, so impossible is it for you to convert yourself. Man imagines in his heart that he is able to do something himself, and for that reason he is not very concerned about his state. He vainly imagines that the matter is in his hand, and he will one day betake himself to convert himself. In this way he is encouraged and the gnawing of conscience subsides somewhat upon making the resolution that he will convert himself, for now it will take place. This is the reason that he becomes upset with himself when he does not act according to his resolution, thinking there is still so much good to be found in himself which would enable him to be steadfast and to exercise his will in a right manner to convert himself. Even if he cannot make perfect satisfaction, God will be satisfied with it; and even if he cannot earn heaven with it, God will be moved by his efforts and grant him heaven anyway. With these notions such a person, not being upon the right way, travels on to his eternal destruction.

We have already demonstrated above that man is entirely incapable of converting himself. Allow me to make you acquainted with yourself, your inability, as well as that your refraining from evil and doing good is of no value before God. Allow me briefly to convey to you what true conversion is.

Some imagine that conversion consists in refraining from the commission of gross sins and in the performance of some good deeds. Conversion, however, is a complete change of man as far as his spiritual frame, intellect, will, thoughts, words, and deeds are concerned. This change can be compared with a person born blind receiving his sight, a deaf person being enabled to hear, a dumb person being enabled to speak, or a totally paralyzed person being enabled to move about. The Holy Spirit is given to the person who is to be converted, who, having made His residence in the soul, reveals to the soul how polluted it is from every perspective, causing the soul to detest and abhor itself, to be filled with shame, to be humbled, and to be perplexed concerning its condition. In addition to this the Holy Spirit reveals God to the soul as being holy, majestic, just, good, and a God of truth. He reveals to the soul the necessity and the fullness of the Mediator and grants him some understanding as to how he can be reconciled and united to God. He works love and fear for, and obedience towards, God. How precious this becomes to the soul, causing him to betake himself to the Mediator Jesus, to receive these matters out of His fullness! This produces grief and sorrow over the fact that the soul cleaves to all that is before the eyes and cleaves to sin — both the great as well as the small sins, both external and internal sins. Now he perceives and is conscious of all these sins of which previously he took no notice. Such a soul now seeks to exercise communion with God and desires to be near Him. The soul is either joyful or sorrowful in relation to whether he is far from God or close to Him. His disposition is one in which his back is turned the world and sin, even though he is frequently ensnared by them. He lives focused upon God, and even though all is darkness, he looks to Him for light, life, spirituality, comfort, strength to do battle against sin, as well as for holiness. Such a soul is not satisfied with mere performance. He knows that he must perform good works, but wishes to do so by faith, in union with Christ, and through Him unto God, doing so in the presence of the Lord out of love to God, in the fear of God, in obedience to God, and with denial of self. He has much grief over ulterior motives he perceives within himself. He abhors not only sinful company, but also all that pertains merely to civil and natural life. His desires on the contrary are towards godliness and he would rather be despised and oppressed with the godly than to obtain riches and glory with others.

This is just a brief statement about conversion, which will be considered much more comprehensively in chapter 31. What do you think? Are you able to bring this about? Try it once! Examine your conduct of one day by what has just been stated. Do your utmost, and than observe whether you are able to conduct yourself in such a manner. You will most certainly experience that you cannot take even one step in that direction and that it is impossible for you to bring about the very beginning of spiritual life. You will perceive that your conduct is wanting. Focus for some time upon this truth until you lose courage within yourself and feel yourself to be destitute, impotent, and without hope. Furthermore, should you have made some progress, realize that the spirituality you need will still be lacking, so that your conduct cannot be acceptable to God nor move God to look down upon you to save you — all of which has been shown. Such is the misery and hopelessness of your condition. You cannot satisfy the justice of God by your bearing of punishment. Such holiness is not obtainable.

Oh, that you were truly destitute and perplexed! Then there would be hope for your salvation, not because of your perplexity, but because there is a Surety for such perplexed ones — Jesus Christ, whose voice sounds forth, "Come unto Me, all ye that labor and are heavy laden, and I will give you rest" (Mat. 11:28). To you who are perplexed, without hope, destitute, and troubled, I proclaim that there is one Savior — a Savior unknown to the heathen. Although they know that there is a God, they do not know that there is a Savior and Surety who is proclaimed among us. This Surety calls you, invites you, and promises to save you if you come to Him. Therefore rejoice in such a blessed reality. Look outside of yourself, go to Him, receive Him by faith, and be saved.

CHAPTER EIGHTEEN

The Divinity, Incarnation, and Union of Two Natures in the Person of Our Lord Jesus Christ

In the previous chapter we have shown that the Mediator had to fulfil four conditions. He must be 1) very God, 2) very man out of man, 3) a holy man, and 4) God and man in one Person. We also have shown the Lord Jesus Christ to be this Surety and Mediator. It is therefore also essential that these four conditions are fulfilled in Christ Jesus.

We first of all wish to affirm that there is only one God, and not two or three gods. There is neither an inferior nor a superior God. God is superior to all creatures, but this is not true in reference to another god, for there is no other god. "For though there be that are called gods...to us there is but one God" (1 Cor. 8:5-6).

Secondly, we affirm that this one divine Being subsists in three independent Persons: the Father, the Son, and the Holy Ghost. "For there are three that bear record in heaven, the Father, the Word, and the Holy Ghost (1 John 5:7).

Thirdly, we affirm that these three Persons are neither separate from the divine Being, nor from each other. There is but one God. "...and these three are one" (1 John 5:7).

Fourthly, we affirm that these three persons are distinct, so that one Person is not identical with another Person. Each Person is a different Person, and yet not a different God. "Another Comforter (John 14:16) ...whom I will send unto you from the Father" (John 15:26).

Fifthly, we affirm that each Person is the one and only true God.

The Lord Jesus Christ is Very God

It is first of all necessary to show that *the Lord Jesus is very God.*

The *Socinians* and *Anabaptists* deny this. We, however, uphold this as a major tenet of the Christian religion. This is evident from all those proof texts by which we are convinced that *Jehovah* is God. We shall prove that Jehovah is God from the fact that,

(1) He is called *God* everywhere in Scripture. It is without question that whenever *Jehovah* is called *God* the reference is not to angels or authorities, but to the eternal God;

(2) He is eternal, infinite, omniscient, and omnipotent;

(3) He has created heaven and earth and still upholds and governs the same;

(4) He must be honored, worshipped, believed, feared, and served.

There is no one who would dare to cast doubt upon these proofs. These proofs being an absolute certainty, the Lord Jesus is therefore very God, for there is abundant testimony in Scripture that these four matters are stated in reference to Him. It is therefore blasphemous if one would dare to deny that the Lord Jesus is very God, and to suggest that He is merely called God because of His miraculous conception, His mission in this world, God's love towards Him, His miracles, His ministry, His resurrection from the dead, and His glorification. None of these things render one divine. They are the proofs of, rather than the basis for, His divinity.

That Christ is the true, eternal God is therefore evident from the four aforementioned proofs.

First, He is referred to as *God* throughout Scripture, and the context of these references is such that all evasive arguments are silenced.

(1) Only consider these texts: "Therefore God, Thy God, hath anointed Thee with the oil of gladness above Thy fellows" (Psa. 45:7).[1] That this initial reference to *God* relates to the Lord Jesus is evident when we read, "But unto the Son He saith, Thy throne, O God, is for ever and ever:...therefore God, even Thy God, hath anointed Thee" (Heb. 1:8-9).

Without a doubt *thy God* refers to the true, eternal God. How can this be confirmed? The answer is that He is expressly called *God* here. Likewise the Lord Jesus, is also here called God as well as is the Father: therefore He is the eternal, true God.

(2) Add to these the texts in which He is called *Jehovah*. In the entire Scriptures this name is neither attributed nor can be attributed to anyone else but the eternal, true God — a truth which we already have confirmed in chapter three. The fact that the Lord Jesus is called JEHOVAH is confirmed for instance in Jeremiah

---

[1] The Statenvertaling reads as follows: "Daarom heeft U O God! uw God gezalfd," that is, "Therefore Thou, Oh God! hast been anointed by Thy God."

23:5-6, where we read, "I will raise unto David a righteous Branch...
and this is His Name whereby He shall be called, THE LORD (that
is, *Jehovah*) OUR RIGHTEOUSNESS." That the Lord Jesus is here
called *Jehovah* is confirmed by the fact that He is the *Branch*, the
King of Zion, who is here called by this name. Thus, the Lord Jesus
is the true and eternal God.

(3) Add to these from the New Testament, Romans 9:5, where
we read, "Whose are the fathers, and of whom as concerning the
flesh Christ came, who is over all, God blessed for ever." In the
preceding context no mention is made of God the Father, but only
of the Lord Jesus, and He is said to have come from the fathers as
concerning the flesh. It is beyond all controversy that the reference
here is to the Lord Jesus and His human nature. Of the very same
Person it is said immediately (as in one breath) that He is God who
is to be blessed for ever. I repeat, as in one breath, for nothing
separates these two clauses, neither a *period*, nor a *colon*, but only a
comma, upon which follow the words ὁ ὢν (*who is*), which always
refer to the antecedent and relate to whomever had just been
mentioned. The Lord Jesus is therefore the God who is blessed
forever, this expression being a description of the eternal God.
"To whom be glory for ever." (Rom. 11:36); "Thou art worthy, O
Lord, to receive glory," etc. (Rev. 4:11); "God is...to be had in
reverence of all them that are about Him" (Psa. 89:7); "For the
LORD is a great God...above all gods" (Psa. 95:3); "The LORD...is
high above all the people" (Psa. 99:2).

(4) This is also confirmed in 1 John 5:20, where we read, "This
is the true God." It is not written here that He is God, nor merely
that He is truly God, but rather that He is the true God, and thus
the only God. He is also said to be ἐν μορφῇ (*in forma*) Θεοῦ, that
is, *in the form of God* (Phil. 2:6), χαρακτὴρ τῆς ὑποστάσεως αὐτοῦ,
(*the express image of His Father's Person*) (Heb. 1:3), and that the
Name *Jehovah*, that is, the essence of *Jehovah*, is in Him (Exo. 23:20).

Evasive Argument: The use of this name cannot be the basis for
concluding the eternal Godhead of Christ, for governors are also
referred to as gods.

Answer: When they are called "gods," the context is such that
one is able to observe at once that the name is contrasted with
actual existence (cf. 1 Cor. 8:5-6). In such descriptions one can
perceive at a glance that the reference is to creatures to whom
special gifts from God are ascribed, as is true in Psalm 82:6. In
verse 2 of this psalm the reference is to ungodly judges who are
threatened with death in verse 7. When the Lord Jesus is called
"God," however, He is called *Jehovah, God to be praised for ever, the*

true God, the form of God, and *the express image of His Father's Person.* Neither angels nor authorities are referred to as *God* in the *singular.*

The second proof for the Godhead of the Lord Jesus can be deduced from the divine *attributes* which are ascribed to Him. He who is eternal, omniscient, and omnipotent, is the true God. This is undeniably true. Since all this applies to the Lord Jesus, He is thus very God.

(1) Christ's *eternity* is confirmed in the following text: "But thou, Bethlehem Ephratah...out of thee shall He come forth unto Me that is to be ruler in Israel; whose goings forth have been from of old, from everlasting" (Micah 5:2). Matthew 2:6 and John 7:42 confirm that this refers to the Lord Jesus, who, according to the flesh, would come forth out of Bethlehem. This very Person was from eternity. He is consequently also called the "everlasting Father" (Isa. 9:6), the One who existed "before Abraham was" (John 8:58), and the "...Alpha and Omega, the beginning and the ending ...which is, and which was, and which is to come" (Rev. 1:8). This is an express description of eternity, which can only be properly ascribed to the true God. "And Abraham...called there on the name of the LORD, the everlasting God" (Gen. 21:33). Thus, Christ is the true God.

(2) Christ's *omniscience* is confirmed by the following texts: "...I am He which searcheth the reins and hearts" (Rev. 2:23); "And needed not that any should testify of man: for He knew what was in man" (John 2:25). This is a divine attribute: "For Thou, even Thou only, knowest the hearts of all the children of men" (1 Ki. 8:39). Thus, Christ is the true God.

(3) Christ's *omnipotence* is confirmed by the following texts: "... the Almighty" (Rev. 1:8); "...according to the working whereby He is able even to subdue all things unto Himself" (Phil. 3:21). However, only God is omnipotent: "... the Lord God omnipotent reigneth" (Rev. 19:6). Thus, Christ is the true God.

The third proof for the Godhead of the Lord Jesus we deduce from *divine works.* He who has created heaven and earth, upholds and governs everything, of Himself performed miracles, regenerates man, and resurrects the dead — He is the true God. No one denies this (cf. Jer. 10:11-13; Isa. 44:25-28). Since this all applies to Christ, however, He is therefore the true God.

(1) John 1:3 confirms that Christ created the world, for we read, "All things were made by Him (the Word); and without Him was not any thing made that was made." Christ is the Word (vs. 1). Creation here does not refer to regeneration, but to the generation of everything out of nothing. "All things" — therefore noth-

ing is excluded. This is also found in Colossians 1:16-17, where it is written, "For by Him (the image of the invisible God) were all things created, that are in heaven, and that are in earth . . . all things were created by Him, and for Him." Through Him, that is, not as a means or instrument (for even then He would have existed prior to creation), but rather through Him as the energizing cause, since the preposition "through" refers to the initial energizing cause. "Through Him . . . are all things" (Rom. 11:36); ". . . by Jesus Christ, and God the Father . . ." (Gal. 1:1). All things are also *unto* Him, which can be ascribed only to the initial energizing cause and not to the instrument. ". . . to Him, are all things" (Rom. 11:36).

(2) That Christ upholds and governs all things is also evident. "My Father worketh hitherto, and I work . . . for what things soever He doeth, these also doeth the Son likewise" (John 5:17, 19). When it is stated that He cannot do anything of Himself unless He sees the Father do them, this refers to the manner of subsistence and operation of the three Persons in the divine Essence, as well as to His mediatorial office. Consider also the following texts: "By Him all things consist (Col. 1:17) . . . upholding all things by the word of His power" (Heb. 1:3).

(3) That Christ performs miracles by His own power is evident ". . . there went virtue out of Him, and healed them all" (Luke 6:19); ". . . I perceive that virtue is gone out of Me" (Luke 8:46). When the apostles performed miracles, they did not do so by their own power, but by the power of Christ. "Why marvel ye at this? or why look ye so earnestly on us, as though by our own power or holiness we had made this man to walk? And His Name through faith in His Name hath made this man strong" (Acts 3:12, 16); ". . . even by Him doth this man stand here before you whole" (Acts 4:10).

(4) That Christ resurrects the dead is evident, "For as the Father raiseth up the dead, and quickeneth them; even so the Son quickeneth whom He will." "All that are in the graves shall hear His voice, and shall come forth" (John 5:21, 28-29). All of this is the work of God alone, and thus Christ is the true God.

The fourth proof we deduce from His divine *honor*. He who must be honored in like fashion as the Father — in whose Name one must be baptized, whom one must worship, in whose name one must believe and in whom one must trust — is the true God (cf. Isa. 42:8; Matt. 4:10; Jer. 11:5, 7). All of this applies to the Lord Jesus, and thus He is the true God. This is true:

(1) in reference to honor: "That all men should honour the Son, even as they honour the Father" (John 5:23);

(2) in reference to baptism: "...baptizing them in the name of the Father, and of the Son, and of the Holy Ghost" (Mat. 28:19);

(3) in reference to worship: "And let all the angels of God worship Him" (Heb. 1:6); "Blessing, and honour, and glory, and power, be unto him that sitteth upon the throne, and unto the Lamb for ever and ever" (Rev. 5:13);

(4) in reference to faith: "Ye believe in God, believe also in Me" (John 14:1). When we read that Israel believed Moses (Exo. 14:31), this refers to the doctrine of Moses, and that they believed Moses to have been sent from God. When we read that Israel was baptized unto Moses (Exo. 14:22; 1 Cor. 10:2), this means that it was performed by the hand of Moses and by His service;

(5) in reference to trust: "Blessed are all they that put their trust in Him" (Psa. 2:12).

Each of these proofs is sufficiently forceful to believe in the Godhead of the Lord Jesus. When considering all these proofs together, we can only lift up our hearts to the Lord Jesus and exclaim, *"The Lord Jesus is God."*

Objection: The thought could occur that some may not be able to harmonize various expressions in the Word of God with the aforesaid. How ought we to understand that Christ is said to 1) be less than His Father? "For My Father is greater than I?" (John 14:28); 2) not be able to do anything of Himself (John 5:19); 3) receive everything from the Father (2 Pet. 1:17; Mat. 28:18); 4) be God's servant (Isa. 42:1); 5) be sent of the Father (John 10:36); 6) pray to the Father (Heb. 5:7); 7) be distinguished from the Father (John 17:3); 8) be the firstborn of all creatures (Col. 1:15); 9) and the beginning of the creation of God (Rev. 3:14)?

Answer: These difficulties will at once be resolved when one considers:

(1) Christ has two natures, and that some things about His Person are said about His natures.

(2) To consider Christ in His divine nature is an entirely different matter than viewing Him in His mediatorial office and administration. Respecting the latter He is said to be less, to be a servant, to pray, to receive, and to have been sent.

(3) He is distinct from the Father, but not severed from Him as a Person, and thus coessential with the Father. John 17:3 neither denies the Godhead of Christ nor states that the Father alone is God in distinction from Christ, but rather that the Father is the *only* God in distinction from idols. Likewise the Son and the Holy Spirit are the *only* God. In this text Christ is distinguished from His

Father in reference to His mediatorial office, a distinction that must be understood in order to obtain eternal life.

(4) Although He is called the *firstborn* of all creatures, He is never called the *first-created*. He is the firstborn of the Father by eternal generation; in reference to the creature He is the heir of all things, and as Mediator He has the Old Testament right of the firstborn.

(5) When He is called the *beginning* of creation, this must not be understood in a *passive* sense, as if He were first created, but in an *active* sense, having created all things, and all things having their origin in Him. All things must thus end in Him, He being their origin.

The Lord Jesus, being true and eternal God, has assumed the human nature. Neither the divine Essence, nor the Father, nor the Holy Ghost became man, but only the second Person, the Son. According to His Godhead, Christ is the eternal Son of the eternal Father by an eternal and incomprehensible generation, and thus He is called the Son par excellence (Heb. 1:5). "...His own Son" (Rom. 8:32); "...the only begotten Son" (John 1:18); "...the image of the invisible God" (Col. 1:15); "...the express image of His person" (Heb. 1:3). This Son causes all believers to be sons and daughters of God by their betrothal to Him as bride to her Bridegroom, but also by faith as members of Him their Head.

The Lord Jesus Christ is Very Man

The Lord Jesus is not only true and eternal God, but He is also very man — a man out of man. I repeat, He is very *man*. This is not merely so in appearance, but in very truth, having that very nature.

First, He is frequently referred to as a man. "...which is by one man, Jesus Christ" (Rom. 5:15); "...the last Adam..." (1 Cor. 15:45); "...the man Christ Jesus..." (1 Tim. 2:5).

Secondly, He had:

(1) a *true human body;* "Forasmuch then as the children are partakers of flesh and blood, He also Himself likewise took part of the same" (Heb. 2:14); "Behold My hands and My feet, that it is I Myself: handle Me, and see; for a spirit hath not flesh and bones, as ye see Me have" (Luke 24:39);

(2) a *true human soul*; His Godhead was not a substitute to Him for a soul. "Even as the Son of man came not to be ministered unto, but to minister, and to give His life a ransom for many" (Mat. 20:28); "My soul is exceeding sorrowful, even unto death" (Mat. 26:38).

Thirdly, He was subject to various human afflictions and emotions, however, without sin. He was an hungered (Mat. 4:2), thirsted (John 19:28), was sorrowful (Mat. 26:38), wept (John 11:35), was glad (John 11:15), and was wearied (John 4:6). Thus, Christ was very man.

He did not bring this human nature with Him from heaven; it was not created out of nothing, nor from some matter as some Anabaptists insist. He is *man out of man*, in order that He would have the *identical* nature (not merely a *similar* nature) which He would redeem. This is confirmed in the Old Testament by way of prophecy, and in the New Testament by way of fulfillment.

In the Old Testament He is called the *Seed of the woman*. "And I will put enmity between thee and the woman, and between thy seed and her seed; it shall bruise thy head" (Gen. 3:15). "Thee" refers to the serpent, the devil, who beguiled Eve (2 Cor. 11:3). *The seed of the serpent* refers to the ungodly, the children of the devil (1 John 3:10). *The woman* refers to the woman who had sinned, who had been beguiled by the devil and who would have sorrow in carrying and bearing children. This woman was Eve, the wife of Adam, the mother of all living. *The Seed of the woman* does not refer to all mankind descended from her, but to the Lord Jesus Christ. This is confirmed not only by the mere fact that the word *seed* is used in reference to Christ in Galatians 3:16, nor that He is called the fruit of Mary's womb (Luke 1:42), and was made of a woman (Gal. 4:4), but particularly because whatever is written concerning this seed can only be applicable to Christ — that He would bruise the head of the serpent; that is, that He would conquer the devil (Heb. 2:14).

Furthermore, consider those texts in which Christ is called the seed of Abraham, Isaac, and Jacob (Gen. 22:18; 26:4; 28:14). This *seed* should not be understood to refer to Isaac and Jacob, since the very same promise was made to them. Abraham and his godly descendants did not receive the promise (cf. Heb. 11:39). He had, however, already received Isaac. Yet, neither in Isaac nor in Jacob were all nations of the earth blessed, but only in Christ; He is the seed of Abraham. "He saith not, And to seeds, as of many; but as of one, and to thy seed, which is Christ" (Gal. 3:16). The reference is not to a spiritual seed, for Christ was not the spiritual seed of Abraham. Such are the believers who walk in Abraham's steps and do Abraham's works. Christ is called the seed of Abraham because He came forth from His descendants according to the flesh as can be observed in the genealogy of Christ in Matthew 1 and Luke 3. This is also evident in 2 Samuel 7:12, where we read, "And when thy days be fulfilled, and thou shalt sleep with thy fathers, I will set up thy seed after thee, which shall proceed out of thy bowels," etc. It cannot be denied that this text refers to Christ, for in Acts 2:30 we read, "Therefore being a prophet, and knowing that God had sworn with an oath to him, that of the fruit of his (David's) loins, according to the flesh, he would raise up Christ to sit on his throne" (Acts 2:30). Consider also the following text, "Of this man's seed (David's) hath God according to His promise raised unto Israel a Saviour, Jesus" (Acts 13:23). Even though some of these things can be applied to Solomon, they primarily refer to Christ. The following phrases, however, in no wise refer to Solomon but to Christ only:

(1) "I will set up thy seed after thee"; Solomon was already born and sat upon the throne while David was still alive;

(2) "I will stablish the throne of His kingdom forever" (2 Sam. 7:13). Solomon died and his descendants ceased to be kings. Concerning Christ, however, the angel said, "And He shall reign over the house of Jacob for ever" (Luke 1:33). Since this text speaks of Christ, it is clearly confirmed that He was of David's seed, and came forth out of his bowels as far as His flesh was concerned.

The same is also evident in the New Testament, so that there is no need to quote any texts. Nevertheless, consider those texts in which:

(1) Mary is called the mother of our Lord Jesus Christ, and in which Christ is called the Son of man. Both nature and Scripture teach and confirm that no one can be a mother unless she has brought forth a man, and no one can be a son of man unless his existence originates in man.

(2) Add to this, "Blessed is the fruit of thy womb" (Luke 1:42). Whatever fruit trees and animals bring forth, has proceeded from their substance. The children of humanity are the fruits of its womb, and thus proceed from its substance. Christ thus proceeded from the substance of Mary. This is also confirmed by those texts which make mention of Mary's impregnation, as in Luke 1:31. This is also stated concerning other women, such as in Luke 1:36.

(3) Add to this the following texts: "Concerning His Son Jesus Christ our Lord, which was made of the seed of David according to the flesh" (Rom. 1:3); "Whose are the fathers, and of whom as concerning the flesh Christ came" (Rom. 9:5); "...made of a woman" (Gal. 4:4); "For both He that sanctifieth and they who are sanctified are all of one: for which cause He is not ashamed to call them brethren" (Heb. 2:11). Add to this the genealogies of Matthew 1 and Luke 3. These texts ought to fully convince everyone in his own mind that Christ is very man out of man.

Objection #1: "That which is conceived in her is of the Holy Ghost" (Mat. 1:20).

Answer: Since God is a Spirit, this does not refer to the origin of substance but to the original cause of this conception. Mary did not become pregnant spontaneously and as a consequence of her womanhood, but by the creative power of the Holy Spirit. He is nevertheless not a son of the Holy Spirit. Fatherhood and sonship are the result of generation, by which a person comes into existence from the substance of another, and after its own kind. In referring to the Holy Spirit, we cannot speak here of generation, but rather of a creative act in regard to the seed of Mary. For this reason He is said to be without a father as far as His human nature is concerned (Heb. 7:3).

Objection #2: In Romans 8:3 we read, "in the likeness of sinful flesh," and in Philippians 2:8, "And being found in fashion as a man."

Answer: (1) The words "likeness" and "in fashion as" do not refer to external appearance, but to an internal reality, such as man being truly human. "And Adam...begat a son in his own likeness, after his image" (Gen. 5:3). "In the likeness of sinful flesh" refers to the human nature of which all sinful men are partakers. Christ, however, possesses this without sin.

(2) If one wishes to consider "likeness" and "in fashion as" to be references to that which is human-like rather than that which is truly human, then this must refer to man in his *sinfulness.* Christ had neither the form nor the sinful nature of sinful men. Natural men, perceiving all men to be sinful, considered Him as such, as they did not truly know Him. He, being truly human and being known as such, was without sin, however; and by virtue of a wrong conclusion that all men are sinful merely appeared to be sinful to other natural men (Isa. 53:4).

Objection #3: He is said to be "from heaven" (cf. John 6:33; Eph. 4:9; 1 Cor. 15:47).

Answer: Christ has two natures. "To be from heaven" properly refers to His personhood, His divinity, as it likewise properly belongs to His human nature to be "from man."

Objection #4: If Christ is very man of man, should He not of necessity have original sin?

Answer: (1) Those who deny original sin obviously cannot raise this objection.

(2) Original sin is passed on to descendants by way of generation which involves both the man and the woman. This, however, does not apply to Christ, who was neither conceived by the involvement of a man nor by the exercise of a human will, but rather by the creative power of the Holy Spirit, having been formed from the blood and seed of Mary which in itself is not sinful.

Christ, being man out of man, was born out of the *Virgin Mary.* She was a *virgin* when the Lord Jesus was formed within her and remained a virgin throughout her entire pregnancy, during which time Christ's body developed in a normal human manner. She was a *virgin* when, after the normal period of time, she gave birth to Christ in a normal manner, and it is credible that she remained a *virgin* until the day of her death. The prophecy was as follows, "Behold, a virgin shall conceive, and bear a son" (Isa. 7:14), which was fulfilled in Matthew 1, and in Luke 1 and 2.

The Lord has concealed from us the month, day, and hour of the birth of Jesus Christ, in order that there be no occasion for superstition. The approximate time of His birth, however, is given us as being:

(1) during the reign of Caesar Augustus, at his first taxation, which occurred when Cyrenius was governor of Syria (Luke 2:1-2).

(2) when Herod was king at Jerusalem (Mat. 2:1).

(3) during the fifteenth year of the emperor Tiberius.

When Pilate was governor of Judea and Herod was the tetrarch of Galilee, Jesus Christ was baptized, being about thirty years old (Luke 3:1-23). This having been researched in Roman historical documents, His birth appears to have occurred approximately 1700 years ago.

We have thus observed that the Lord Jesus is very God, the Son of God, and that He is very man out of man. It need not be proven that He was a holy man and thus without sin, since He is known as such to all. The angel called Him "that holy thing" (Luke 1:35); Peter and John, that "holy child Jesus" (Acts 4:30); Paul, "holy, harmless, undefiled" (Heb. 7:26); and Peter, "a Lamb without blemish and without spot" (1 Pet. 1:19).

The Lord Jesus Christ: Very God and Very Man in One Person — the Hypostatic Union

It now remains for us to show against *Socinians* and *Anabaptists* that He is *very God and very man in one Person*.

This is first of all confirmed by many texts which speak of the two natures together, making mention of them in reference to the same Person. "Concerning His Son Jesus Christ our Lord, which was made of the seed of David according to the flesh, and declared to be the Son of God with power" (Rom. 1:3-4); "...of whom as concerning the flesh Christ came, who is over all, God blessed for ever. Amen" (Rom. 9:5); "God was manifest in the flesh" (1 Tim. 3:16).

Secondly, in the aforementioned, both divine and human characteristics and activities are attributed to the same Christ. Christ is eternal, omnipotent, omniscient; He created the world, and upholds and governs all things. Christ also had a body and a soul, was born in time, suffered, and died. Jesus Christ is thus God and man in one Person.

The human nature of Christ, consisting in the union of body and soul, did not exist independently, was not for some time on its own, but from its very first moment existed by virtue of the personhood of the Son of God. Thus, the human nature, not being an independent person, from the very beginning has existed by means of and within the divine Person of Christ. It is and remains personally united to His divine nature.

This union was established by way of *assumption*. The divine nature, being a Person, has assumed the human nature (having no independent existence) within the singularity of its personhood. This is according to Scripture: "Who, being in the form of God, thought it not robbery to be equal with God, but made Himself of no reputation, and took upon Him the form of a servant" (Phil. 2:6-7). This is also confirmed by Hebrews 2:16, "For verily He took not on Him the nature of angels; but he took on Him the seed of Abraham." "The seed of Abraham" does not refer here to the natural descendants of Abraham, but seed is mentioned here in the singular, as in Galatians 3:16. "Took" is in the present tense,[2] because "the taking upon him the seed of Abraham," that is, the human nature proceeding from Abraham, is a continuous action resulting in an endless union to all eternity.

The verb "to take" does not mean "to deliver," for then the meaning would be as follows, "For verily He did not deliver the angels, but he delivered the seed of Abraham."

(1) Nowhere in Scripture does this verb have that meaning, but it always means "to take," "to accept," or "to take hold of." Even though deliverance could be the result of "to take hold of," such is not the meaning conveyed by this word. Rather, its meaning is made known from the other words appended to it.

(2) In this text it cannot be understood as such, for Christ does not only deliver the seed of Abraham, but also all believers who lived prior to Abraham, as well as all believing Gentiles. All of these would then have to be contrasted with the angels rather than with the seed of Abraham only. This not being the case, however, it is evident that "to take" does not mean "to deliver" in this text.

(3) In this entire epistle devils are never referred to as angels, and it is nowhere suggested that the devils can also be delivered. Above, mention is made of good angels, however, who are neither

---

[2] The Statenvertaling uses the present tense and reads as follows, "Waarlijk Hij neemt de engelen niet aan, maar Hij neemt het zaad Abrahams aan."

delivered by Christ, nor have need of Him as such. Thus, the act of "taking" cannot refer to the deliverance of angels.

(4) The context reveals that the taking upon Him of Abraham's seed is to have the human nature proceeding from Abraham's seed, this being according to the promises, for in verse nine the apostle declares that Christ has been made a little lower than the good angels in view of Him suffering death for the deliverance of man. Verse eleven demonstrates that for this purpose He had to be one with them — man out of man — and as the children, has partaken of flesh and blood (vs. 14). He continues His argument in verse sixteen by showing that He did not take upon Him the nature of angels, but according to prophecy, assumed the human nature out of the seed of Abraham.

The human nature having no independent existence and from its initial moment having existed by virtue of the existence of the Son of God, (to which it is and remains indivisibly and inseparably united), it is evident that there are two natures in Christ, but not two persons, that is, not a divine and a human person. There is but one divine Person. Therefore Mary did not bring forth a mere nature nor a human person, but rather a human nature existing by virtue of the personhood of the Son of God. She thus brought forth a divine Person into the world. This is not to say that the Godhead was born of her, but rather the divine Person according to His humanity.

The Hypostatic Union: Without Change and Without Mixture

This union, having been established by way of assumption, did not occur by the Godhead changing into man, for God is and remains immutable, invisible, and immortal (cf. Psa. 90:1; 1 Tim. 1:17; Heb. 1:12). When John states, "And the Word was made flesh" (John 1:14), he gives expression to the union of these two natures in one Person, but by no means suggests that the Godhead has changed into man. "To be made" does not always suggest a change, which is confirmed in Galatians 3:13, where we read, "... being made a curse," which cannot mean that He was changed into a curse. In Genesis 1:3 we read, "...and there was light." This did not occur by something changing into something else, but it came into existence by way of creation. In Genesis 2:7 we read, "... and man became a living soul," which neither implies that the body changed into a soul, nor that the soul changed into a body, but rather that a union was established between these two parts. Such examples can be found in many other texts. Thus, to be made flesh is not to be understood as changing into flesh, but it rather refers to the assumption of the flesh, that is, of the human nature, and its personal union with it.

As the divine nature does not change into the human nature, likewise the human nature does not change into the divine nature, for whatever is finite cannot become infinite and eternal. Furthermore, the divine nature cannot be communicated to the creature.

This union also was not established by mixing these two natures, with a third type of person coming forth. Rather, this union was established *without change and without mixture*, each nature retaining its own attributes; each nature contributes its attributes to the Person. Thus, the same Christ has divine as well as human attributes by virtue of the union of these two natures in Him. However, the one nature does not have the attributes of the other nature.

The union of these two natures in one Person has three consequences — *communication of: 1) gifts and honor, 2) attributes,* and *3) activity and office.*

First of all there is *a communication of gifts and honor.* By virtue of this union the human nature of Christ has acquired a value exceeding that of all creatures, including that of the holy angels, for it is the soul and body of the Son of God. This is true for His human nature only. By virtue of this union, this human nature is also the recipient of an extraordinary measure of the Spirit, wisdom, holiness, and other gifts. We read, "And the Spirit of the LORD shall rest upon Him, the Spirit of wisdom and understanding, the Spirit of counsel and might, the Spirit of knowledge and of the fear of the LORD" (Isa. 11:2); "Therefore God, Thy God, hath anointed Thee with the oil of gladness above Thy fellows" (Psa. 45:7); "...full of grace and truth" (John 1:14); "God giveth not the Spirit by measure unto Him" (John 3:34). All these gifts are not infinite, however, for that which is finite cannot comprehend infinity. Rather, the measure of these gifts far exceeds that afforded to all creatures; that is, Adam, the glorified saints in heaven, and all the angels. This does not mean that Christ according to His human nature had these gifts in that measure from His first beginning and prior to His birth, or immediately at His birth. Nor does it mean that He neither could nor did increase in the same, for "Jesus increased in wisdom" (Luke 2:52), and "Yet learned He obedience by the things which He suffered" (Heb. 5:8).

Albeit that Christ in His human nature has received such excellent gifts in which He exceeds all creatures, *He must not therefore be worshipped as man or as Mediator.* It is true that Christ the Mediator, that is, Christ as God and man, must be worshipped, and is the object of worship. The basis for this worship, however, lies neither in His mediatorial office, His human nature, nor in the excellency of His gifts, but solely in His divine nature. His mediatorial office is indeed the motive whereby we are stirred up to worship the Mediator. However, this worship neither terminates in nor is directed toward His mediatorial office or His gifted human nature, for:

(1) We may only worship God (Mat. 4:10). As gifted and glorious as the human nature of Christ is, it is not God, and thus ought not be worshipped.

(2) It is an act of idolatry to worship that which by nature is not God (Gal. 4:8). Christ's human nature is by nature not God, and thus it would be idolatrous to worship it.

(3) All the gifts of His human nature and its glory have been bestowed and are a gift, as can be observed in the aforementioned texts and which also is self-evident. Gifts cannot be the basis for worship.

(4) Even His divine works such as creation, upholding, and government are no basis for worship, but are merely motives for it, since they are not God Himself. Thus, both His mediatorial office and His gifted human nature are not the basis for worship.

Secondly, there is *communication of attributes*. The union of the two natures in Christ occurred without there being *change and mixture*, so that each nature retained its own attributes. Each nature communicates these unique attributes to the Person, so that the Person, being God, is eternal, infinite, omniscient, and omnipotent. At the same time, however, the Person of Christ, due to His humanity, was born in the fullness of time, can only be at one location at one time, does not know all things, had human but sinless emotions, hungered, thirsted, suffered, and died. These various qualities are attributed to Him in Scripture *in a threefold manner*, which we will identify in a moment.

As the human nature did not communicate its attributes to the divine nature, *likewise the divine nature did not communicate any or any part of its attributes to the human nature*. This we prove against the *Lutherans* by the following:

We first of all prove this from the word "attribute" itself, for whatever is imparted to someone is no longer unique but common. If it were true that the divine attributes have been imparted to the human nature, then they are no longer unique to the divine nature, which is as much as to say that God is no longer God.

Secondly, since all the attributes of God are the divine essence itself (which can only be understood by us puny human beings by way of attributes), then all these attributes of necessity would have to be imparted if one or some were to be imparted. Then the human nature would be God; the human nature would be eternal and would thus have existed before Christ was born of Mary, eternity being one of the attributes of God. Then Christ could not have been born as far as the flesh is concerned, since He already existed. He could not have been buried, for He would have been in the grave prior to this. He could not have arisen and exited the grave, for He would have done so prior to this, or He would have to remain in His grave after His resurrection, and whatever other absurdities could be suggested.

Thirdly, not only does Scripture state this nowhere, but it contradicts this expressly, for we read that Christ was not omnipresent according to His human nature:

(1) This is true in the state of His humiliation when He is said to leave one place and to go to another, or to be present in one place and not in the other. "And I am glad...that I was not there..." (John 11:15).

(2) He is also not omnipresent in His exaltation. "He is not here: for He is risen" (Mat. 28:6); "I leave the world" (John 16:28); "For if He were on earth, He should not be a priest" (Heb. 8:4).

To the suggestion that His visible presence is being referred to here, I respond that this is not stated, but it must be understood in its absolute sense. It cannot be understood as such, for it is an inseparable attribute of the human body to be visible. One would then be able to reason likewise in reference to the absurdities which we will be considering further.

Objection #1: Since the human nature has been united to the divine nature, it also has divine attributes.

Answer: (1) Our body is also united to our soul. It then ought to have the attributes of the soul.

(2) By the same argument the divine nature would also have the attributes of the human nature.

(3) On this basis all attributes would have to be imparted, eternity inclusive.

(4) This union necessarily implies that the Person possesses the attributes of both natures, but one nature does not have the attributes of the other nature.

Objection #2: The fullness of the Godhead dwells in Christ bodily (Col. 2:9), and therefore also the divine attributes.

Answer: (1) This argument must then hold true for all the attributes, eternity inclusive.

(2) This text refers to Christ's personhood and not to His human nature. You cannot logically proceed from His Person to His nature.

(3) "Bodily" means to say: evidently, truly, not by way of comparison, and not by way of examples and ceremonies — Christ being the body or substance of these shadows (vs. 17).

Objection #3: If the attributes are not mutually imparted, then the natures must be separate from each other.

Answer: (1) By this argument all human attributes would have to be imparted to the divine nature.

(2) The opposite is true for the union of body and soul.

(3) This union is not local but personal in nature.

Objection #4: It is written: "He that descended is the same also that ascended up far above all heavens, that He might fill all things" (Eph. 4:10).

Answer: No mention is made here of all places being filled with His body, but rather of His church and all her true members being filled with His Spirit and His operations.

Objection #5: It is not by measure (John 3:34).

Answer: The reference here is not to infinity, but that it far excels that of others.

Objection #6: There is written, "All power is given unto Me in heaven and in earth" (Mat. 28:18).

Answer: The reference here is not to His human nature, but to His Person. Also, it does not say δύναμις (*dunamis*), that is, power, but ἐξουσία (*exousia*), that is, authority, power, domain.

Objection #7: God's Word states: "In whom are hid all the treasures of wisdom and knowledge" (Col. 2:3).

Answer: (1) The reference is to His Person and not to the human nature.

(2) Christ can be viewed here as the object of faith, and thus believers may obtain all wisdom and knowledge looking upon Jesus, in whom all the mysteries of the gospel are revealed. It thus remains certain that the human nature did not receive the attributes of the divine nature.

Thirdly, there is *communication of works and official administration.* Both natures having been united in one Person — they do not function independently — all activity is of the Person. Since Christ is but one Person, there is but one principle which is operative. Since there are two natures within this one Person, which in reference to His personhood are *indivisible and inseparable* and in reference to each other are united *without change and without mixture,* the Person of Christ works by means of these two natures. Since each nature functions according to its own properties, there is a twofold operation. As God, the Person of Christ functions according to His divine nature, and as man, according to His human nature. Thus, each nature contributes to the execution of the *one* work of redemption in all its parts.

Christ is therefore Mediator according to both natures; that is, not only according to His human nature but also according to His divine nature.

This is first of all evident from the fact that the divine nature constitutes the personhood of Christ, from which therefore the work of redemption originates. This work of redemption was not accomplished by His incarnation only, nor should it be viewed only in reference to His mediatorial office, placing Himself on the same level as His church, but it should also be considered how He, in His incarnation, made Himself of no reputation by concealing His Godhead, taking upon Him the form of a servant, and becoming obedient to His Father, even unto death (Phil. 2:7-8). This is a work of His Mediatorial office, and *actus sunt suppositorum*; these deeds are attributed to the Person. Christ is thus Mediator also according to His divine nature.

Secondly, as we have shown, the two natures and their particular workings are prerequisite for the office of Mediator. The divine nature had to support the human nature and resurrect it from the dead, render both His suffering and His fulfillment of the law valid and efficacious, and actually apply everything, delivering His own from the greatest evil and making them partakers of the highest good.

Thirdly, Scripture expressly relates the mediatorial office to the divine nature. "…to feed the church of God, which He hath purchased with His own blood" (Acts 20:28); "…they would not have crucified the Lord of glory" (1 Cor. 2:8); "…Christ, who through the eternal Spirit offered Himself without spot to God" (Heb. 9:14).

Due to the union of the two natures in one Person, there are various expressions which relate to the same Christ. First of all, this occurs when, in mentioning the Person, that which properly belongs to one of the two natures is attributed to Him. Such is true when it is said that *Christ is from eternity, and yet came in the fullness of time out of a woman; Christ is omniscient, and not omniscient; Christ is omnipresent and not omnipresent; and Christ had glory with His Father before the world began, and yet has died.* Secondly, this occurs when reference is made to the Person as far as one nature is concerned, while attributing to Him that which properly belongs to the other nature. *God has purchased His Church with His blood* and *the Lord of glory has been crucified.* Thirdly, one nature will be mentioned, while attributing to Him that which belongs to His Person and properly to both natures. "For there is…one Mediator…the man Christ Jesus" (1 Tim. 2:5).

Exhortation to Meditate upon the Preciousness of the All-Sufficient Mediator Jesus Christ

Thus we have shown that the Lord Jesus is very God, very man, a holy man, and God and man in one Person. It is necessary to pause for a moment to consider this Mediator whose Name is Wonderful from every perspective, in order that we might properly be motivated to godliness.

First, this wondrous work shall neither be comprehended nor fathomed by angels or men to all eternity, but will always remain an unfathomable source of adoration. Nevertheless, being yet upon earth, we can and must attempt to gain insight into this work of redemption.

(1) No one could be Surety and bring man to God but He who was God and man in one Person. The Son of God first had to be personally united to the human nature before sinful man could be restored into friendship and union with God. Behold, how great a work it is to save a sinner! What manifold wisdom was required to conceive such a remedy! All the holy angels together could not have conceived such a remedy as God has conceived and revealed. They are desirous to look into this, but they shall never be able to comprehend it. What a blessing it is that none but He was able to do this, that He has sent His own Son for this purpose and caused Him to unite personally with the human nature! What omnipotence is required to execute such a design!

(2) How intimately the elect are united to God, when even their nature has been assumed within the Person of the Son of God! In this they are even exalted above the angels of God, whose nature is not personally united to God. Is it a small matter to be so near to God? If only we would attempt to reflect more upon this wonder of wonders! The angels are desirous to look into this. It is an activity with which they continually occupy themselves since they are not able to satisfy their desire. If we were to be continually exercised with this, we would lose ourselves in holy adoration, joyously approve of this, and before realizing it we would find ourselves wonderfully near to God, being united in communion with Him. We would understand what it means when the Lord Jesus says, "That they all may be one; as Thou, Father, art in Me, and I in Thee, that they also may be one in Us" (John 17:21). This exceeds all comprehension and adoration. This is not only true regarding the matter itself but also relative to the rapturous frame of heart of all those who may occupy themselves in reflecting upon this. This will fill our mouths with praise, and time and again will cause us to conclude with the psalmist, "What is man, that Thou art mindful of him? and the son of man, that Thou visitest him?" (Psa. 8:4); ". . . that Thou shouldest magnify him? and that Thou shouldest set Thine heart upon him?" (Job 7:17)

Secondly, let your consideration not be merely of a general nature, but proceed to meditate both upon His Godhead and His humanity. Let us consider His Godhead. If our Lord Jesus is God, and if according to His Godhead He is also our Mediator, then

(1) we observe that His ransom has eternal and infinite value and efficacy. "How much more shall the blood of Christ, who through the eternal Spirit offered Himself without spot to God, purge your conscience from dead works to serve the living God?" (Heb. 9:14). All the sins of all believers, however great and many they may be, without the least exception, are fully remitted and not the least measure of debt or punishment remains. Yes, this satisfaction is so perfect that it is as if they had no sin but had kept the law perfectly, for He who has made satisfaction is the true and eternal God.

(2) If the Lord Jesus is God, meditation upon Him as such will generate great reverence in our hearts, and cause us to exalt Him far above everything. It will cause us to bow before Him, to worship Him with the angels, to honor Him as the Father, He being one with Him; and we will join all creatures in heaven and upon earth by exclaiming, "Blessing, and honour, and glory, and power, be unto Him that sitteth upon the throne, and unto the Lamb for ever and ever" (Rev. 5:13).

(3) Meditation upon His Godhead will cause us to trust in Him according to His own command, "Let not your heart be troubled: ye believe in God, believe also in Me" (John 14:1). Oh, how confident a person may be who has received Him by faith, and when his entire case and all his circumstances have been given over into His hand! How safely is the soul preserved who has surrendered to Him. Such a soul may put all fear and concern aside and say with an assured and steadfast heart, "Thou shalt guide me with Thy counsel, and afterward receive me to glory" (Psa. 73:24). He is God and therefore supreme goodness Himself. He is omniscient and thus knows the frame, desires, sincerity, and anxieties of the soul. He is almighty to deliver, keep, and comfort the soul, as well as usher him into eternal felicity. How blessed is such a soul which may have the Lord Jesus as his Savior! Let such a soul rejoice in His Name.

Thirdly, let the *incarnation* of the Lord Jesus also be the frequent subject of your meditation, for the manifestation of God in the flesh is a "mystery of godliness" (1 Tim. 3:16). All true godliness proceeds from the knowledge of, and a believing union with, the Lord Jesus. This generates love and all that proceeds from love. Whatever does not proceed from this source cannot be called godliness. Even though nature may give us an impression of God and religion, it does not reveal this mystery. He who has only been illuminated outwardly is also ignorant of the frame of heart which proceeds from knowing Jesus (that is, as both God and man) and being in a believing union with Him. This frame consists in having peace in and with God, resting in Him without fear, loving Him, and being desirous in all things to live in a manner pleasing to the Lord — thus to be lifted up in magnifying God in response to the manifestation of His perfections in the incarnation of the Lord Jesus.

(1) This will confront us with the *dreadfulness* of sin on the one hand, and the pristine *righteousness* of God on the other hand. The one could not be taken away and the other could not be satisfied unless the Son of God would become man, conceal His glory behind the veil of His human nature, and permit Himself to suffer all shame and suffering according to His human nature. Yes, the Lord of glory had to be crucified.

(2) Herein we may observe God's unfathomable *love for humanity*. The elect, rather than being desirable, were hateful in themselves. God, however, loves them for reasons within Himself, purely because He wills to love them. This love moved the Father to send forth His Son in the flesh, concerning which the Lord Jesus exclaims, "For God so loved the world, that He gave His only begotten Son" (John 3:16). Motivated by this love the Son went forth, assumed the human nature, and endured all manner of suffering and death. "...as Christ also loved the church, and gave Himself for it" (Eph. 5:25). If there is anything that stirs up love, then this love of God and of Christ ought to quicken our love and cause it to burn within us.

(3) The incarnation manifests the infallible *veracity* of God. His performance is in agreement with His Word, for here we observe the fulfillment of the promise made in Paradise, "It (the Seed of the woman) shall bruise thy (the serpent's) head" (Gen. 3:15). Here all the promises made to the fathers are fulfilled — something which they so eagerly anticipated. Here we have the fulfillment of all the shadows and sacrifices which functioned as prophecies and descriptions of the Messiah. God thus reveals that He is true and will not allow one promise to go unfulfilled. Mary acknowledged this when she said, "As He spake to our fathers" (Luke 1:55). This was likewise true for Zacharias when he said, "As He spake by the mouth of His holy prophets, which have been since the world began" (Luke 1:70).

(4) The incarnation is that great work of God in which the *wisdom, goodness, power, mercy, and glory of God* shine forth in a most excellent manner. What wisdom, goodness, and power is mani-

fested in bringing a sinner back to a holy God by way of the most sublime manifestation of His justice; by a Person who is both God and man; through such a way of suffering; and by leading the sinner to such a felicity in ways which pass all understanding! All this the holy angels observe, and it is an element of their felicity to perceive the perfections of God in the work of redemption revealed by the incarnation. "To the intent that now unto the principalities and powers in heavenly places might be known by the church the manifold wisdom of God" (Eph. 3:10). Mary perceived all this and said, "For He that is mighty hath done to me great things; and holy is His Name; and His mercy is on them that fear Him from generation to generation. He hath shewed strength with His arm" (Luke 1:49-51).

One ought thus to meditate upon the incarnation, in order to discern clearly these and other attributes of God, approving of them with holy adoration and joyously magnifying God with the holy angels, saying, "Glory to God in the highest, and on earth peace, good will toward men" (Luke 2:14).

Fourthly, the description of the incarnation of Christ also ought to arouse in us a joyous gratitude towards God, and we ought to welcome the fact that the Lord Jesus has assumed our nature. This the angel conveyed in his message to the shepherds when he said, "I bring you good tidings of great joy, which shall be to all people" (Luke 2:10). If our soul should rejoice in anything, it ought to rejoice in this great and wondrous work of God. To this end consider the following:

(1) It was prophesied that men would rejoice upon the Savior's advent into the world. "They joy before Thee according to the joy in harvest, and as men rejoice when they divide the spoil. For unto us a Child is born, unto us a Son is given" (Isa. 9:3, 6); "And it shall be said in that day, Lo, this is our God; we have waited for Him, and He will save us: this is the LORD; we have waited for Him, we will be glad and rejoice in His salvation" (Isa. 25:9); "Rejoice greatly, O daughter of Zion; shout, O daughter of Jerusalem: behold, thy King cometh unto thee: He is just, and having salvation" (Zec. 9:9). Since it has been prophesied as such, and since we are living in the fulfillment of all this, we ought to lift up our souls with joy and thanksgiving.

(2) Consider the longing of the saints for the coming of Christ in the flesh. After Eve had given birth to her first son, it appears that she was of the opinion that the promise had been immediately fulfilled, for she said, "I have gotten a man from the LORD" (Gen. 4:1). The Lord Jesus said concerning Abraham, "Your father Abra-

ham rejoiced to see My day" (John 8:56). David gave expression to his desire when he said, "For this is all my salvation, and all my desire, although He make it not to grow" (2 Sam. 23:5). This desire was also present in the God-fearing kings and prophets. "For I tell you, that many prophets and kings have desired to see those things which ye see" (Luke 10:24). Yes, all the saints of the Old Testament longed for this. "These all died in faith, not having received the promises, but having seen them afar off, and were persuaded of them, and embraced them" (Heb. 11:13). What joy they would have manifested if they had seen the Lord Jesus in the flesh! We may experience the fulfillment of this. Therefore it behooves us to rejoice and to thank the Lord for this most precious gift, for such a dear and precious Savior.

(3) When Christ came into the world, heaven and earth were filled with joy. John the Baptist leaped for joy in his mother's womb (Luke 1:44). Mary sang a doxology, "My soul doth magnify the Lord, and my spirit hath rejoiced in God my Saviour" (Luke 1:46-47). The tongue of a dumb Zacharias broke loose, exclaiming, "Blessed be the Lord God of Israel; for He hath visited and redeemed His people, and hath raised up an horn of salvation for us in the house of his servant David" (Luke 1:68-69). Old Simeon took the child in his arms, praised God, and exclaimed, "Lord, now lettest Thou Thy servant depart in peace, according to Thy word, for mine eyes have seen Thy salvation" (Luke 2:29-30). Come, join and rejoice with them. Will your heart always be heavy-laden? Would you not rejoice for once? And if your heart would rejoice, what could be more motivating than the incarnation of Christ? Therefore, "Rejoice in the Lord alway: and again I say, Rejoice" (Phil. 4:4).

However, someone may possibly say, "My heart remains in bondage; I cannot rejoice in this, for I fear that He was not born for me anyway, and that I am not a partaker of all this." I respond to this by saying that:

(1) This is merely a fear, for you are also not assured that the contrary is true;

(2) This is not the only problem. The reason one does not rejoice in the incarnation is for lack of holy meditation upon the subject, its miraculous nature, the promises, the Person, the fruits, and this great salvation brought about by His suffering and death. What reason for rejoicing would he who does not attentively reflect upon this have?

(3) Since there is such a Savior, however, can it be a matter of indifference to you whether or not there is such a Savior? If you

are not indifferent to this, why do you not rejoice over His coming into the world, even if you still are no partaker of Him?

(4) You who yearn for Jesus, however, in order to be justified and sanctified by Him, even if it is accompanied by much darkness, fear, anxiety, and concern (John 6:40); you, in whose heart Jesus dwells by faith, so that your desires are repeatedly drawn towards Him (Eph. 3:17); you, in whom Jesus has been formed (Gal. 4:19) and in whom Jesus lives (Gal. 2:20), so that He is all your joy and desire, generating within you a hatred towards sin, a desire to walk as He walked, and perceiving within you a battle between spirit and flesh; you, who love Jesus (1 John 4:19) — you have reason to be assured that He has been born for you. Therefore you have double reason to rejoice with delightful and unspeakable joy, and to jubilate concerning the coming of the Lord Jesus in the flesh.

Fifthly, come therefore, and acknowledge Him as your Lord. "Kiss the Son" (Psa. 2:12), "For He is thy Lord; and worship thou Him" (Psa. 45:11). Surrender yourself to Him, seek to please Him, fear Him, serve Him, and hold Him before you as your only and perfect example, and thus follow in His footsteps (1 Pet. 2:21).

As one must consider the Lord Jesus as being very God — and thus interact with Him with awe, reverence, fear, confidence, and in a worshipful frame — one may and must likewise have fellowship with Him as man, as being our brother, "for . . . He is not ashamed to call them brethren" (Heb. 2:11). Such fellowship with Him the bride desired. "O that Thou wert as my brother!" (Song of Sol. 8:1). Since He has become our brother, we may and must have fellowship with Him as such, always viewing Him as being in such a relationship to us, "For both He that sanctifieth and they who are sanctified are all of one" (Heb. 2:11). *He is flesh of our flesh and bone of our bones.* This yields boldness and familiarity to bring all our needs before Him who, being man Himself, understands man's frame of mind when he suffers pain and is troubled in both soul and body. He can and does have compassion with them (Heb. 2:17; 4:15). This familiarity makes the heart tender. It gives boldness to approach unto Him and commune with Him in human fashion as speaking to a man, commending our cause to Him, and on the basis of His Godhead entrusting it to Him. This in turn will stir up the heart in sweet love towards Him.

CHAPTER NINETEEN

Concerning the Three Offices of Christ, and Particularly His Prophetic Office

Having discussed the Person of the Mediator, it now follows that our discussion focuses on His offices. The Savior Jesus generally is also called *Christ*. The Savior had been promised in the Old Testament under the name מָשִׁיחַ *(Meschiach),* "unto the Messiah the Prince" (Dan. 9:25). The Greek have translated this as Χριστός *(Christos).* "We have found the Messias, which is, being interpreted, the Christ" (John 1:41). The meaning in our language is "Anointed One," which is derived from the Old Testament practice of anointing. In those times and places, rather than using a fragrant powder for one's hair as we do, they used fragrant oils which, by way of the apothecary's art, were created as a very choice mixture whereby all its fragrance was derived from mixing a small quantity of ingredients together, creating a *quintam essentium.* This oil would be sprinkled in the hair in small quantities in order to make one's appearance presentable, and by the loveliness of the fragrance to make oneself desirable in the presence of others. The Lord had commanded to make a special oil from various fragrant spices according to the art of the apothecary (Exo. 30:25). No one was permitted either to imitate this or to sprinkle with this ointment, the violation of this injunction resulting in being cut off from his people (Exo. 30:32-33). With this oil Aaron and his sons were anointed to minister in the priest's office (vs. 30). Prophets, as well as kings (1 Sam. 10:1; 16:13), were anointed with this oil (1 Ki. 19:16).

The Anointed One: Foreordained and Qualified

This anointment was expressive of two matters. It first of all conveyed that such persons were *foreordained* and called to this office by God, for one would smell the fragrance of the Lord upon this person. Secondly, it conveyed that the Lord would *qualify* such persons for that office. Thereby they would be desirable to the people, as the fragrance of this oil was most desirable and the anointed one would exude a pleasant scent due to the fragrance of this oil. Therefore they were called the *anointed ones,* and the *anointed of the Lord.* Christ is thus called the *Anointed One*, being expressive of those two matters: *foreordination and qualification.*

We shall first of all consider *foreordination.* Christ did not take the office of Mediator upon Himself by His own initiative. "So also Christ glorified not Himself to be made an High Priest" (Heb. 5:5).

(1) He was ordained to this office by His Father. "Who verily was foreordained before the foundation of the world" (1 Pet. 1:20); "I was set up from everlasting" (Prov. 8:23).

(2) The Father sent Him into the world for that purpose. "...Him, whom the Father hath sanctified, and sent into the world..." (John 10:36). He also called Him. "I the LORD have called Thee in righteousness" (Isa. 42:6). He was inaugurated into this office at His baptism. "And lo a voice from heaven, saying, This is My beloved Son, in whom I am well pleased" (Mat. 3:17). He was thus made "both *Lord and Christ*" (Acts 2:36).

Secondly, His *qualification* consists in:

(1) the union of the two natures in one Person, without which He could not have been Mediator. God by Himself or man by himself would not have been qualified, but God had to be manifested in the flesh (1 Tim. 3:16);

(2) an extraordinary anointing of the Holy Spirit. "For God giveth not the Spirit by measure unto Him" (John 3:34).

Just as three categories of individuals were anointed as types of Christ — prophets, priests, and kings — it was thus necessary that Christ would also have these three offices and minister in them, so that He would be able to remove the threefold misery of man. He removes blindness by His prophetic office, enmity with God by His priestly office, and inability by His kingly office. That Christ is Prophet, Priest, and King, ministering in these three offices on behalf of His elect, is evident throughout the Holy Scriptures. We will consider each office in particular.

The Prophetical Office of Christ

The prophetical office of Christ is confirmed by both prophecy and fulfillment.

(1) He was promised as a prophet in Deuteronomy 18:15, "The

LORD thy God will raise up unto thee a Prophet from the midst of thee, of thy brethren, like unto me; unto Him ye shall hearken." Acts 3:22 confirms that this reference is to Christ; these very words are quoted as relating to Christ. Consider also the following text: "The Spirit of the Lord GOD is upon Me; because the LORD hath anointed me to preach good tidings unto the meek." etc. (Isa. 61:1-2). Having read these words, the Lord Jesus applied them to Himself, saying, "This day is this Scripture fulfilled in your ears" (Luke 4:21), and in verse 24 He refers to Himself as a Prophet.

(2) In His sojourn upon earth the Lord presented Himself as a Prophet. "This is My beloved Son, in whom I am well pleased; hear ye Him" (Mat. 17:5). Everywhere the Lord Jesus conducted Himself as a prophet. "And Jesus went about all the cities and villages, teaching in their synagogues, and preaching the gospel of the kingdom" (Mat. 9:35). He was recognized as such by the people. "A great prophet is risen up among us" (Luke 7:16); "...which was a prophet mighty in deed and word before God and all the people" (Luke 24:19).

The ministry of the prophets consisted in 1) reception of immediate revelation from God concerning divine mysteries which occurred among prophets with an extraordinary calling; 2) the proclamation and exposition of the Word of God; 3) the foretelling of future events; 4) confirmation of revelation by means of miracles.

First, the prophets received divine mysteries by immediate revelation. "If there be a prophet among you, I the LORD will make Myself known unto him in a vision, and will speak unto him in a dream" (Num. 12:6); "...holy men of God spake as they were moved by the Holy Ghost" (2 Pet. 1:21).

The Lord Jesus received all things from the Father in this fashion. "For the Father loveth the Son, and sheweth Him all things that Himself doeth" (John 5:20); "The Revelation of Jesus Christ, which God gave unto Him, to shew unto His servants things which must shortly come to pass" (Rev. 1:1).

This does not mean that Christ was taken up into heaven after His baptism to receive these mysteries. This is a fabrication of the *Socinians* for the purpose of denying the Godhead of Christ all the more effectively, for:

(1) Holy Writ does not mention a word concerning this; when mention is made of Christ's descent, the reference is to the assumption by the divine nature of the human nature, and His descent is mentioned prior to His ascension, which is contrary to their view; they place His ascension before His descent.

(2) It was not necessary for Him to be taken into heaven in order

to receive divine revelations, for as God He was omniscient, and all things had their origin in Him. "I speak that which I have seen with My Father" (John 8:38). According to His human nature He had received the Spirit without measure (John 3:34). "And the spirit of the LORD shall rest upon Him, the Spirit of wisdom and understanding, the Spirit of counsel and might, the spirit of knowledge and of the fear of the LORD" (Isa. 11:2).

Secondly, the ministry of the prophets consisted in exposition and proclamation of the Word of God, which is to be observed in their prophecies. Thus, also the Lord Jesus, as God, as the sole Lawgiver and as the King of His people, gave them the law to be a rule of life for His people, declared this law to them, and purified it of erroneous exposition and distortion (Mat. 5). He rebuked the transgressors (Mat. 23) while exhorting and stirring up everyone to obedience by saying, "Repent ye, and believe the gospel" (Mark 1:15).

However, Christ did not preach a new doctrine, did not issue forth a new law, and did not reveal a new way to heaven — a way which would not have been declared in the Old Testament, and which to the godly would neither have known nor walked in. He merely fulfilled and confirmed that which prior to His coming had been written concerning Him and the way of salvation. "Think not that I am come to destroy the law, or the prophets: I am not come to destroy, but to fulfil" (Mat. 5:17).

Just as Christ conducted Himself in respect to the law, so likewise He proclaimed the gospel as a prophet. Christ is the author of the gospel, "For the law was given by Moses, but grace and truth came by Jesus Christ" (John 1:17). Christ is also the messenger of the gospel. "And came and preached peace to you" (Eph. 2:17). Furthermore, Christ is the object of the gospel. "But we preach Christ crucified" (1 Cor. 1:23). For this reason the gospel is called the *gospel of Christ* (Rom. 1:16).

Thirdly, the ministry of the prophetical office also consists in foretelling future events; the Greek word "prophet" is derived from this fact. Christ did not merely foretell what He Himself would have to encounter in order to merit salvation for His elect, but also what would transpire in the world, the church, and upon the Day of Judgment. This is confirmed by the entire revelation of divine truth, the gospels included.

Fourthly, just as the prophets confirmed their doctrine by means of miracles — as we observe in Elijah and Elisha — the Lord Jesus confirmed His doctrine by miracles. The gospels abundantly bear witness to this, so that the multitude exclaimed, "When Christ cometh, will He do more miracles than these which this man hath done?" (John 7:31). Peter stated, "Jesus of Nazareth, a man approved of God among you by miracles and wonders and signs, which God did by Him in the midst of you, as ye yourselves also know" (Acts 2:22). The other prophets performed miracles by the power of Christ, to which Peter alluded when he said, "Why look ye so earnestly on us, as though by our own power or holiness we had made this man to walk? And His Name through faith in His Name hath made this man strong " (Acts 3:12,16). Christ, however, did miracles by His own power. "And Jesus, immediately knowing in Himself that virtue had gone out of Him..." (Mark 5:30); "For there went virtue out of Him, and healed them all" (Luke 6:19).

Christ's Administration of His Prophetical Office

Christ administered His prophetical office:

(1) by means of His prophets in the Old Testament. "Searching what, or what manner of time the Spirit of Christ which was in them did signify, when it testified beforehand the sufferings of Christ, and the glory that should follow" (1 Pet. 1:11); "By which also He (Christ) went and preached unto the spirits in prison" (1 Pet. 3:19);

(2) during His sojourn upon earth. "God, who at sundry times and in divers manners spake in time past unto the fathers by the prophets, hath in these last days spoken unto us by his Son" (Heb. 1:1-2);

(3) after His ascension. He still administers His prophetical office by means of His apostles, pastors, and teachers. "And He gave some, apostles; and some, prophets; and some, evangelists; and some, pastors and teachers, for the perfecting of the saints, for the work of the ministry, for the edifying of the body of Christ" (Eph. 4:11-12). Since they are His messengers and preach in His Name, the Lord Jesus thus requires that we hear them as if we heard Him. "He that heareth you heareth Me; and he that despiseth you despiseth Me" (Luke 10:16).

There is a twofold administration of this prophetical office: an external and an internal one. They are conjoined in Isaiah 59:21: "My Spirit that is upon thee, and My words which I have put in thy mouth, shall not depart out of thy mouth."

Christ administers His prophetical office *externally* by the written and printed Word, and by the Word preached by His servants. This is no longer limited to the Jewish nation, as was true prior to the coming of Christ (Psa. 147:19-20), but the gospel is now proclaimed to the Gentiles and all who hear the voice of Christ, for His "sound went into all the earth, and their words unto the ends of the world" (Rom. 10:18). Many nations, however, are and remain deprived of the means of salvation unto the present time.

For even though all are not saved who hear the words of Christ, as "the word preached did not profit them, not being mixed with faith in them that heard it" (Heb. 4:2), no one can be saved unless he hears the external preaching of Christ. "How shall they believe in Him of whom they have not heard? and how shall they hear without a preacher? So then faith cometh by hearing, and hearing by the Word of God" (Rom. 10:14-17).

Christ administers His prophetical office *internally* when by His Spirit He illuminates souls by His "marvelous light" (1 Pet. 2:9). He illuminates the heart "to give the light of the knowledge of the glory of God in the face of Jesus Christ" (2 Cor. 4:6), enabling them to understand the truth in its very essence, "as the truth is in Jesus" (Eph. 4:21), and to have the mind of Christ (1 Cor. 2:16). He causes their hearts to burn within them (Luke 24:32), regenerates them (James 1:18), grants them faith (Eph. 5:8), sets them free by the truth (John 8:32), and they walk in the truth (3 John 4). When the Lord Jesus teaches sinners internally, He does not address Himself differently to them than He does to others. The same Word, the same sermons heard simultaneously by many, some only hear with the ear and understand the truth in a natural sense without their hearts being renewed by it. That same Word affects others internally, enlightening and renewing the heart. Thus, this difference is not to be attributed to the Word or person who hears it. It is the applying power of Christ that makes the difference, affecting the one and not the other.

In this we perceive the great distinction between all other prophets and this great Prophet of prophets. They were only ordinary, and above all, sinful men. They did not give authority to the Word, nor did they bring it forth of themselves. They were only able to preach the Word to the external ear.

But "who teacheth like Him?" (Job 36:22).

(1) He preached with divine authority, "For He taught them as one having authority, and not as the scribes" (Mat. 7:29).

(2) He preached with a holy and penetrating zeal, so that the zeal of the Lord's house ate Him up (John 2:17).

(3) His preaching was accompanied by divine power, so that even His enemies said, "Never man spake like this man" (John 7:46).

(4) He preached with a wondrous wisdom, so that no one could resist Him, for "He had put the Sadducees to silence" (Mat. 22:34). He Himself says, "The Lord GOD hath given Me the tongue of the learned, that I should know how to speak a word in season to him that is weary" (Isa. 50:4).

(5) He preached with delightful eloquence, for "...all bare Him

witness, and wondered at the gracious words which proceeded out of His mouth" (Luke 4:22).

(6) He preached internally to the heart — illuminating, warming, converting and sanctifying it. He baptized with the Holy Ghost and with fire (Mat. 3:11). Oh, how blessed is he who may have such a Teacher!

Two matters must be considered more particularly regarding the prophetic office of Jesus Christ. First of all, one must seek to derive personal benefit from this office. Secondly, one must seek to follow His example for the benefit of others, that we also might be prophets, since as Christians we are named after Christ and are thus partakers of His anointing.

Exhortation to Seek Personal Benefit from Christ's Prophetical Office

First, we must make use of this office to our own benefit. If Christ is a Prophet — yes, such a prophet as we have shown Him to be — then come to Him, you who are born blind, ignorant, and strangers of the life of God due to this ignorance within you. You also ought to come, who may perceive some light but are as the man born blind, seeing but a glimmer, who, when he began to see, saw "men as trees, walking" (Mark 8:24). You ought to come who have received more light, which in turn makes you more desirous for additional light. You also ought to come — you who have come into a condition of spiritual stupor and darkness, rendering your knowledge ineffectual and not bringing forth inner warmth, comfort, joy, and godliness. Therefore, all who are desirous for the knowledge of God, come, so that you may grow in the knowledge of the Lord Jesus Christ. Come to this Prophet and beseech Him to instruct you, and attentively heed His instructions.

First of all, you need to do so, considering your ignorance. Solomon says concerning you, "Also, that the soul be without knowledge, it is not good" (Prov. 19:2). You are not suited for godliness or for salvation.

(1) You know that no one can be saved without faith. "He that believeth not shall be damned" (Mark 16:16). But he who has no knowledge of the divine mystery cannot believe. "By His knowledge shall My righteous servant justify many" (Isa. 53:11); "How shall they believe in Him of whom they have not heard?" (Rom. 10:14). Bind this upon your heart, you who boast of having faith, and nevertheless are without knowledge!

(2) You know that without conversion no one shall enter heaven (John 3:5). Without knowledge, however, there can be no conversion. The very first thing that manifests itself in regeneration is

knowledge. The Lord first opened Lydia's heart (Acts 16:14). Therefore conversion is referred to as an act of illumination. "To open their eyes, and to turn them from darkness to light" (Acts 26:18); "Him who hath called you out of darkness into His marvelous light" (1 Pet. 2:9). It is a sure sign that one is unconverted if he has no knowledge of divine mysteries, even if he lives blamelessly according to the law and excels in good works. His ignorance conveys that his works are not of the same nature as true good works. Take this to heart, you who are of the opinion that the knowledge of the truth is of little value, but that our actions are of primary importance. The absence of light and virtue renders our deeds null and void.

(3) You know that he who does not love God and Christ is accursed. "If any man love not the Lord Jesus Christ, let him be Anathema Maranatha" (1 Cor. 16:22). But without knowledge no one can love God and Christ, for no one has any interest or desire for the unknown. Ignorance begets lack of desire. Even if you call God "dear Lord," or if you say "I love God," you nevertheless are not truthful if you do not know Him in Christ.

(4) You know that he who does not serve God cannot be saved. "Where I am, there shall also My servant be" (John 12:26). But without knowledge no one is able to serve, honor, fear, and obey God, for true religion is a reasonable service (Rom. 12:1). Religion without knowledge is a "sacrifice of fools" (Eccl. 5:1), and idolatry (Acts 17:16, 23).

(5) Ignorance is the cause of all sin. Paul persecuted the church of God and, due to ignorance, even compelled its members to blaspheme Christ (1 Tim. 1:13). Through ignorance the Jews crucified Christ (Acts 3:17). The apostle therefore establishes ignorance as the chief of all sins. "For we ourselves also were sometimes foolish, disobedient, deceived, serving divers lusts and pleasures, living in malice and envy, hateful, and hating one another" (Titus 3:3). Therefore do not pacify yourself by asserting that you have done this or that out of ignorance, for you ought to have known it.

(6) In a word, ignorance deprives man of all grace and leads him to eternal damnation. "It is a people of no understanding: therefore He that made them will not have mercy on them, and He that formed them will shew them no favour" (Isa. 27:11); "In flaming fire taking vengeance on them that know not God..." (2 Th. 1:8). Therefore do not soothe your conscience by reasoning that you have done some good, and have not publicly been ungodly, for ignorance alone is a cause for condemnation.

(7) You who have received some light, is it not your experience

that your unbelief, your failure to fear, love, and obey God; your fearfulness, anxiety, and sorrow are all caused by ignorance? Consider all this together and you ought to be frightened by what you perceive about yourself. Let this motivate you to go to this Prophet in order that He may teach you and that, being illuminated, you may walk in the light.

Secondly, if you may perceive the essential nature of this light and of saving knowledge, you will be motivated to be taught by this Prophet, for:

(1) It is an experience of extraordinary joy. "Her ways are ways of pleasantness, and all her paths are peace" (Prov. 3:17); "My son, eat thou honey, because it is good; and the honeycomb, which is sweet to thy taste. So shall the knowledge of wisdom be unto thy soul" (Prov. 24:13-14); "Light is sown for the righteous, and gladness for the upright in heart" (Psa. 97:11); "They shall walk, O LORD, in the light of Thy countenance; in Thy Name shall they rejoice all the day" (Psa. 89:15-16).

(2) Sound knowledge sanctifies powerfully. "And ye shall know the truth, and the truth shall make you free" (John 8:32); "But we all, with open face beholding as in a glass the glory of the Lord, are changed into the same image from glory to glory, even as by the Spirit of the Lord" (2 Cor. 3:18).

(3) Such knowledge yields steadfastness in faith and stability for our entire pathway of life. "And wisdom and knowledge shall be the stability of thy times, and strength of salvation" (Isa. 33:6); "Till we all come in the unity of the faith, and of the knowledge of the Son of God...that we henceforth be no more children, tossed to and fro, and carried about with every wind of doctrine" (Eph. 4:13-14).

(4) This knowledge is the way unto salvation and pertains to the special felicity that shall be enjoyed in heaven. "In Thy presence is fulness of joy" (Psa. 16:11); "I will behold Thy face in righteousness" (Psa. 17:15); "And this is life eternal, that they might know Thee the only true God, and Jesus Christ" (John 17:3). These matters being so desirable, they ought to strongly motivate us to go to this Prophet in order that He might instruct us.

Thirdly, who shall instruct you? You cannot teach yourself, for were you through some effort to increase in a natural knowledge of God, such knowledge would merely be as moonlight and will not save you. Even if by study you were to increase your natural knowledge of the truth to some degree, your knowledge will nevertheless remain natural and shrouded in darkness. Even if you were to understand the entire Bible as to the meaning of the words and their respective context, you would not understand the matter expressed by these words. Even if you imagine to know God, that Christ is the Savior, and that those who believe in Him shall have everlasting life — then what do you know more than the devils? Exert as much effort as you wish, and seek the assistance of wise teachers; together you will not be able to illuminate yourself spiritually. Although you have the notion that you do see, you are nevertheless blind. In order to be delivered from your darkness and to be illuminated with spiritual light, the Lord Jesus, this great Prophet, must take the task in hand to instruct you. He can, will, and does so to all who come to Him for such instruction.

(1) This Prophet is able to teach, for He Himself is the Sun of Righteousness (Mal. 4:2) He is "as the light of the morning, when the sun riseth" (2 Sam. 23:4). He is "a light to lighten the Gentiles, and the glory of thy people Israel" (Luke 2:32).

(2) It is His desire to instruct, for He invites everyone, saying, "Whoso is simple, let him turn in hither: as for him that wanteth understanding, she saith to him, Come" (Prov. 9:4-5). He says, "I counsel thee to buy of Me...and anoint thine eyes with eyesalve, that thou mayest see" (Rev. 3:18).

(3) He does this very thing, not only by giving His Word to this or that nation, by sending them His servants with this commission, "Go ye therefore, and teach all nations" (Mat. 28:19), but also, by His Spirit, illuminating His own. "That the God of our Lord Jesus Christ, the Father of glory, may give unto you the Spirit of wisdom and revelation in the knowledge of Him, the eyes of your understanding being enlightened" (Eph. 1:17-18). He is the One who fills the soul with "the knowledge of His will in all wisdom and spiritual understanding" (Col. 1:9); He shines "in our hearts, to give the light of the knowledge of the glory of God in the face of Jesus Christ" (2 Cor. 4:6).

You who are unconverted, reflect upon your case for a moment. How long has this Prophet already been engaged in instructing you? How many teachers did He already send to you? How many agitations of conscience have you felt? How often has He convinced you of sin, your unconverted state, and eternal condemnation? How frequently has He stirred you up to become a Christian, to repent and enter into covenant with Him? You have not been inclined to do so, however, nor have you had desire for a knowledge of the truth; but you have ignored it as if it were something strange when He held before you the excellency of the gospel. You have permitted all convictions to disappear and have stifled them by turning to other matters. Perhaps you have hardened yourself against His rebukes and thus have made your bands even stronger

(Isa. 28:22). Tell me, would it not be just for this Prophet to turn away from you and allow you to go your own way, since you do not desire to hear Him anyway? Has He not stretched out His hands long enough to you? If He were to cease doing so at this moment, would your condemnation not be just? Yes, would your judgment and condemnation not be more severe and intolerable than others to whom God never caused His gospel to be proclaimed? Consider attentively this one text which I wish would be bound upon your heart: "See that ye refuse not Him that speaketh. For if they escaped not who refused him that spake on earth, much more shall not we escape, if we turn away from Him that speaketh from heaven" (Heb. 12:25).

And you, children of God, consider that prior to your conversion you behaved yourself in like manner towards this Prophet. Consider what a great mercy it is that the Lord nevertheless persisted and by His almighty power opened your heart so that you gave heed to His voice, He shining in your heart to give the light of knowledge. It is only for this reason that you now properly perceive the truth — that it is so desirable to you, quickens your heart, causes you to rejoice, and changes you. Acknowledge this. Perceive it as a wonder and blessing for you. Rejoice over this and give thanks to the Lord whose work alone this is. But consider at the same time how disobediently you still behave with regard to this Prophet. You have but a glimmer of light. Should you be satisfied with that? And even if this lack of light does not grieve you — although it ought to — you should have such esteem for this Prophet that you would not so frequently allow Him to speak in vain.

A Diligent Exhortation to Converted and Unconverted Alike to Give Heed to the Words of this Prophet

Therefore, both converted and unconverted, hear this Prophet with more reverence, attention, and desire.

(1) You must consider that this Person is God Himself. Should God speak and we not give heed? In what a powerful manner Isaiah began his prophecy! Oh, that it would move us! "Hear, O heavens, and give ear, O earth: for the LORD hath spoken" (Isa. 1:2). Consider that the Father has sent Him to you, and that He exhorts you from heaven. Hear ye Him! (Mat. 17:5).

(2) Consider the matters themselves for they are the mysteries of salvation. They pertain to God, Christ, peace, joy, and the way in which a soul finds satisfaction in God. They do not merely point you the way to heaven, but seek to cause you to rejoice in this light already here.

(3) Consider the manner of His instruction. He does so in such a kindhearted, friendly, and quiet way; it is so wise and suitable to your circumstances — counseling you precisely at the right moment, warning you, stirring you up, continually saying, "This is the way."

(4) You who are unconverted, if you do not give heed, know that He will not always speak to you. He will remove either His Word, His Spirit, or you, and then it will be too late. "To-day if ye will hear His voice, harden not your heart" (Psa. 95:7-8). You who are converted, know also that if you are not diligent in listening to Him, in continually beseeching Him, in expecting His answer, nor in following His counsel, He will remain silent, hide Himself more and more, and leave you in darkness. The more attentively and persistently you hear His instruction, however, the more He will reveal His secrets to you, and grant deeper insight into that which you may know already. His voice of instruction will be more enduring and efficacious within you. Therefore, "Hear attentively the noise of His voice, and the sound that goeth out of His mouth" (Job 37:2). The Lord Jesus says, "Hearken diligently unto Me, and eat ye that which is good, and let your soul delight itself in fatness" (Isa. 55:2); "Blessed is the man that heareth me, watching daily at My gates, waiting at the posts of My doors. For whoso findeth Me findeth life, and shall obtain favour of the LORD" (Prov. 8:34-35).

All of you who are conscious of your blindness and are desirous for spiritual light, come to this Prophet who can and will instruct you, in order that by His instruction you may make progress.

(1) Renounce therefore your own intellectual ingenuity and shrewdness and cast yourself at His feet as one who is ignorant and even unfit to be instructed. Follow the advice of Paul, "If any man among you seemeth to be wise in this world, let him become a fool, that he may be wise. For the wisdom of this world is foolishness with God" (1 Cor. 3:18-19); "And if any man think that he knoweth any thing, he knoweth nothing yet as he ought to know" (1 Cor. 8:2).

(2) Come with an obedient heart, being not only desirous to know, but also to do the will of God, saying with Samuel, "Speak; for Thy servant heareth" (1 Sam. 3:10) and with Paul, "Lord, what wilt Thou have me to do?" (Acts 9:6).

(3) Come and hear with an attentive heart, taking note not only of the meaning of the Word, but also of every illumination and motion of the Holy Spirit by and according to the Word. Lydia attended to the words spoken by Paul (Acts 16:14). Habakkuk stood upon his watch to see what God would say unto him (Hab. 2:1). The church confesses, "I will hear what God the LORD will speak" (Psa. 85:8). Cornelius said, "Now therefore are we all here

present before God, to hear all things that are commanded thee of God" (Acts 10:33).

(4) Come to this Prophet, humbly beseeching Him that He will teach and guide you. "Shew me Thy ways, O LORD; teach me Thy paths; Lead me in Thy truth, and teach me" (Psa. 25:4-5); "Open thou mine eyes, that I may behold wondrous things out of Thy law" (Psa. 119:18). Then believe that He shall hear you and grant you wisdom. "If any of you lack wisdom, let him ask of God, that giveth to all men liberally, and upbraideth not; and it shall be given him. *But let him ask in faith, nothing wavering*" (James 1:5-6), that is, doubting neither the power and the willingness of the Lord nor the fact that He will grant any matter at His time, in His manner, and in a measure determined by Him.

(5) In addition to this, be occupied in reading the Word, which is the voice of this Prophet, as well as in hearing sermons and catechism instruction. Meditate upon what you have read and heard. "Search the Scriptures" (John 5:39); "Let the word of Christ dwell in you richly" (Col. 3:16); "In His law doth he meditate day and night" (Psa. 1:2). Do not imagine that you will either acquire or increase in knowledge if your mind is not set on this, if you are not willing to make an effort, and if the ordained means are not used in earnest. "Yea, if thou criest after knowledge, and liftest up thy voice for understanding, if thou seekest her as silver, and searchest for her as for hid treasures, then shalt thou understand the fear of the LORD, and find the knowledge of God" (Prov. 2:3-5).

(6) Be especially careful and diligent to apply at once what you have learned, for you will only understand each truth if you practice it. "If any man will do His will, he shall know of the doctrine, whether it be of God" (John 7:17); "If ye continue in My word, then are ye My disciples indeed; and ye shall know the truth" (John 8:31-32). Give careful consideration to all these matters, and order your conversation accordingly. In so doing you shall be taught of the Lord (Isa. 54:13) and "grow in grace, and in the knowledge of our Lord and Saviour Jesus Christ" (2 Pet. 3:18). It is thus that we are to make use of Christ in His prophetical office to our own benefit.

The Christian's Sacred Duty to Be a Prophet

Secondly, if someone has thus been taught by the Lord Jesus as Prophet, it behooves him, in some measure and in a manner worthy of Him, to be conformed to Him in His prophetic office, since believers are named Christians after Christ, being partakers of His anointing. They were first called by this name in Antioch

(Acts 11:26), although it is not known whether believers called themselves by this name or whether those from without called them such. The use of this name became common. King Agrippa also called them by this name when he stated, "Almost thou persuadest me to be a Christian" (Acts 26:28). The use of this name was authorized by the Holy Spirit when Peter wrote, "Yet if any man suffer as a Christian, let him not be ashamed; but let him glorify God on this behalf" (1 Pet. 4:16). This name, as despised as it is by Jews and Turks, is so precious for Christians, for this name is expressive of their union with Christ and the fellowship with His anointing. This anointing comprises their ordination and qualification for the discharge (in a manner applicable to them) of the three offices: prophet, priest, and king. "But the anointing which ye have received of Him abideth in you, and ye need not that any man teach you: but as the same anointing teacheth you of all things, and is truth, and is no lie, and even as it hath taught you, ye shall abide in Him" (1 John 2:27). They are therefore called *prophets* according to the promise found in Joel 2:28. "Your sons and your daughters shall prophesy" (Acts 2:17). They are also called *kings and priests* (Rev. 5:10), and a *royal priesthood* (1 Pet. 2:9).

That which Moses once desired, "Would God that all the LORD's people were prophets" (Num. 11:29), has come true in a special manner in the New Testament, it being superior to the Old Testament dispensation. For believers are prophets, albeit not to foretell future events. We do believe, however, that the Spirit of prophecy concerning future events has not fully ceased in the church. We believe that the Lord will still reveal to this or that one of His faithful servants such things which relate either to themselves, His judgment upon the enemies of the church, redemption, or the oppression of the church. This agrees with what Christ said, "And He will shew you things to come" (John 16:13).

Nevertheless, such revelations are not regulative for others, either in doctrine or in life; neither ought we to expect these things from others. Man is naturally inclined towards foretelling future events. The devil can transform himself into an angel of light. Since the outcome of events is at times consistent with his predictions, this draws man away from God and inclines him towards superstitious predictions by way of dreams and other incidents, all which may easily lead a person to be ensnared. A Christian should therefore take care and refrain himself from desiring to know future events outside of the context of the Bible. Furthermore, he should refrain from yielding to a desire for revelations and from giving heed to dreams, interpretations, and incidents, as if they had some significance for the future. A Christian, however, resting in God's providence, must be governed in faith and practice by the *law and testimony*. If he walks according to this rule, he will walk safely and have peace. He will cleanse his way if he takes heed thereto according to God's Word. Then he will not be "soon shaken in mind, or be troubled, neither by spirit, nor by word" (2 Th. 2:2). The difference between revelation and imagination I will not discuss here. It is a wise proverb which says that בינה *(bina),* that is, *wisdom or prudence* is better than נביא *(nabi),* which means *a prophet who foretells future events.*

The Prophetical Obligations of the Christian

Believers, however, are prophets, and must strive to function more and more as such. They must do so in a twofold manner: to know the mysteries of the gospel, and to make them known to others.

First of all, believers are prophets for the purpose of acquiring a clearer knowledge of the mysteries of the gospel. Their knowledge is so limited, and they have but glanced at the matters with which they are acquainted. They therefore stand in need of an increasing knowledge, both by a continual searching of God's Word and by the immediate instruction of God's Spirit who discovers to the soul the essential spiritual nature of that which is written. Oh, that they would thus turn unto the Lord, open their hearts for the influence of the Spirit, and give the Holy Spirit opportunity to work! Thus they would keep watch at the door of supreme Wisdom until they are brought into the inner chambers to be taught there of God; there the Lord Jesus would reveal Himself to them according to His promise (John 14:21).

The Lord has also made known in His Word what the church of the New Testament will encounter until the end of the world. This they must search out. They should especially read the Revelation of John frequently, that they may be enabled to strengthen both themselves and others against tribulations which shall come, and to comfort themselves and others with the blessed outcome which has been prophesied.

The second prophetical task of believers is to make known to others the mysteries revealed in God's Word and which would have been sealed to their own soul. They are called to instruct, warn, exhort, and comfort others. Everyone must do so, however, in the position which God has assigned to him. A minister must do so differently from a church member. The latter must give heed that he neither assumes nor imitates the role of a sent servant of God, in order that the mission of the servants of God and the necessity thereof be not overshadowed, as this would be very detrimental to a congregation.

The above is not merely the task of ministers, but each individual member ought to be convinced that this duty has been imposed upon him by God. Attentively consider the following texts, and bind them as a command of God upon your heart, especially since this duty is so greatly neglected. "And these words, which I command thee this day, shall be in thine heart. And thou shalt teach them diligently unto thy children, and shalt talk of them when thou sittest in thine house, and when thou walkest by the way, and when thou liest down, and when thou risest up" (Deu. 6:6-7). This is intended for you, fathers and mothers. Are you thus engaged? In the future, will you not earnestly engage in this task as a task commanded by God? "And many people shall go and say, Come ye, and let us go up to the mountain of the LORD, to the house of the God of Jacob; and he will teach us of His ways, and we will walk in His paths" (Isa. 2:3). In the prophecy of Zechariah we read, "And the inhabitants of one city shall go to another, saying, Let us go speedily to pray before the LORD, and to seek the LORD of hosts: I will go also" (Zec. 8:21). Notice that mention is made here of individuals, not of ministers. Observe how these prophecies relate to the days of the New Testament. Therefore consider the obligation to which the Lord binds you.

Attentively consider also these texts in the New Testament. "Even so ye, forasmuch as ye are zealous of spiritual gifts, seek that ye may excel to the edifying of the church" (1 Cor. 14:12); "Wherefore, brethren, covet to prophesy" (1 Cor. 14:39). The apostle is not writing to ministers, but to the congregation and to saints who are called (1 Cor. 1:2). This exhortation therefore applies to each individual member, and thus also to you, whoever you may be. "Teaching and admonishing one another" (Col. 3:16); "But exhort one another daily, while it is called To day" (Heb. 3:13); "And let us consider one another" (Heb. 10:24). If God's command has any effect upon you at all, observe this duty to which the name of Christian obligates you.

In order to stir you up even more, consider the following:

First, the light, grace, and ability you may possess, you have received for that express purpose and are to give an account of both its receipt and use. "And he called his ten servants, and delivered them ten pounds, and said unto them, Occupy till I come. . . . Then he commanded these servants to be called unto him, to whom he had given the money, that he might know how much every man had gained by trading" (Luke 19:13,15). Do you observe how that you have received gifts and graces to make gain and that you shall have to give an account of what you have gained with them? If a group of beggars were to stand before your door and you were to give a piece of money to one of them, commanding him to share this with the others, would he not be unfaithful if he were to keep it for himself? How did the unfaithful servant in Matthew 25:30 fare?

Secondly, love for the honor of Christ ought to compel you to do so. If you love Christ, you will be desirous to speak of Him, and you will be desirous that He be known, praised, and glorified by everyone. That desire will motivate you to display His beauty and to declare His perfections, saying, "This is my Beloved, and this is my Friend" (Song of Sol. 5:16); "For how great is His goodness, and how great is His beauty! corn shall make the young men cheerful, and new wine the maids" (Zec. 9:17).

Thirdly, love for noble and precious souls ought to compel you to engage in this task. In observing that your children, servants, close friends, neighbors, and acquaintances are ignorant, live in sin, and are travelling to hell, how can you quietly observe this and see them go lost? If a child has fallen into the water and is in danger of drowning, will you not do your best to save it? And if you cannot do so yourself, will you not cry and gather everyone together to help you? Will you be silent when you observe that such and such individuals are going lost? Will you have no compassion for these poor souls, forbearing to warn, exhort, and instruct them? Yes, will you not be held accountable for the damnation of souls which you could have helped as much as is in you?

Fourthly, to be instrumental in the conversion of souls is a very sweet and delightful task. Someone who plants a tree or orchard finds sweet delight in perceiving that the tree begins to show forth new branches, grows, blossoms, and bears fruit. He says to himself, "I have planted this tree with my own hands." However, to be instrumental in the conversion of souls is infinitely more delightful. Yes, this is not only delightful for the person himself, but it brings joy to the angels in heaven and to believers upon earth, for "there is joy in the presence of the angels of God over one sinner that repenteth" (Luke 15:10).

Fifthly, to be engaged as a prophet greatly promotes the upbuilding and growth of the church. If everyone would make this to be his duty, what a blessing would rest upon the church! Knowledge would increase, multitudes would be converted, and everyone would be "sheep that are even shorn, which came up from the washing; whereof everyone bear twins, and none is barren among them" (Song of Sol. 4:2). When the congregation of Jerusalem was scattered, "they that were scattered abroad went every where preaching the Word" (Acts 8:4). This was the means for a wondrous expansion and increase of the congregation. It is remarkable that everyone who helped build the walls of Jerusalem is mentioned individually. Among them also the daughters of Shallum are recorded for an everlasting remembrance (Neh. 3:12). From experience I may know what blessing the Lord imparted by means of six or eight daughters of the congregation of Harlingen (then my congregation), each as prophetess giving herself to the service of the Lord, and wherever finding entrance, exhorted everyone to seek after knowledge and repentance. What a blessing the Lord bestowed through them! If you may be instrumental in the conversion of one soul, consider that this is not merely beneficial for this one soul, but such a soul may be the means whereby others may be converted, and this seed shall remain from generation to generation.

Oh, how sweet and delightful it shall be to be able to say on the last day, "Behold I and the children which God hath given me" (Heb. 2:13)!

The Lord shall multiply His blessing upon such laborers. If someone is unfaithful, lazy, void of desire, and neglectful of the work of a prophet, such a person will generally walk in darkness and be lacking spirituality; his light will become dimmer and dimmer and he will become less and less capable of performing this task. He will complain frequently about this frame, but he knows that his neglect in this duty is the cause of it. If you engage yourself on behalf of others, the promise shall be fulfilled, "Unto every one which hath shall be given" (Luke 19:26). You shall experience that in teaching others you shall receive more light in these matters, and that while rebuking others, the rebuke will bear down upon you. While exhorting others, you yourself will be stirred up; and while comforting, you yourself will receive more faith and comfort and will go on your way rejoicing. All this considered together will undoubtedly touch and move you to be engaged as a prophet.

Our nature, however, will not readily submit to this; it would rather receive than give. For this reason one will think of many excuses and pretend to be confronted with great difficulties, in order, if it were possible, to discontinue this task and yet have a quiet conscience.

Exhortation and Guidelines for Personal Evangelism

One will argue:

(1) "I have no qualifications for it, and if I wish to begin with this task, the words freeze upon my tongue and I do not know what to

say; if I say something, it has no effect." To this I respond, "You learn by doing." If you are not capable of speaking to certain individuals, and about such matters, speak to others. Begin with beggars and children, by whom you are not intimidated, and discuss general and rudimentary principles. You will subsequently acquire more skill.

(2) You may say, "I do not know much myself, and I am in need of being instructed myself." To this I respond that if you are a Christian, you will have some knowledge. If you know three words, then teach others two, even if you were only to say, "We are going to die, which will be followed by eternity." This could be a means to someone's conversion.

(3) "My words have no effect. They neither have authority nor power. None wish to listen to me. They even laugh at it." To this I respond that fruit upon your words does not come forth from you. You will not be held accountable for fruitlessness, but for faithfulness. If any do not wish to hear you, you will be able to find another who will readily hear you. If anyone laughs, another will weep.

(4) "I am sinful and people see my faults; thus I am incapable of edifying even to some degree. Yes, it will be an offense and one shall say, 'At that time he acted and spoke in such a fashion and now acts as a pious one. It is nothing but hypocrisy, which is true for all who are like him.' Yes, I am in such a sinful condition that my lusts have the upper hand, and thus I cannot speak." My response is that if someone were to wait with prophesying until he would be without sin or without obvious errors, there would be silence over the whole world and one would not hear Christ proclaimed. All His messengers are men of like passions as others. Let it be evident that you are conscious of your failures, that you grieve over them, and do battle against them while seeking to improve in these areas. Own your insignificance more frequently. When you address others, include yourself; do not say *you*, but *we*. In doing so you will perceive that while using your talent, you will become more careful and be more watchful against your own sins.

(5) If you are truthful, you will say, "I am ashamed to speak of spiritual matters, even to my children, and to those who are placed under me — yes, even to the poor to whom I wish to give temporal support." How dreadful this is! Ought you to be ashamed of Christ and His words? Ought the Lord Jesus detect shame of Him in you? Where is your love? This is being irresponsible. If you are overcome by a feeling of shame, press on that much more forcefully, and do not yield to such feelings — feelings which Christ will

detect. As you engage in your task, you shall overcome this sense of shame.

(6) Laziness is another obstacle. If one examines the inner recesses of the heart, one will say, "This task is too heavy for me; I look up against it. It is as if I become ill when I decide to proceed with that objective in mind. I postpone it from one time to another, and thus nothing comes of it." Be ashamed, you who are lazy in reference to this great, glorious, and beneficial task. Consider what befell the lazy servant. Therefore be diligent and fervent in spirit.

(7) "I perceive that I seek myself in this work; that I am motivated by my own honor, and a desire to be praised by those who hear me. The fear of not doing well makes me fearful to begin. Therefore I think it best to refrain from saying anything." I respond that it is first of all a desirable fruit to have self-knowledge which gives you much strife and causes you to pray and to struggle while proceeding in this work as well as can be expected. In so doing the purity of your motivation will increase. To refrain from engaging yourself in this task for this reason, however, is but to continue in your impure pursuit of seeking yourself.

Having overcome all obstacles, and having been inclined and made willing to begin this work of evangelism upon due consideration of its obligation, glory, sweetness, and advantage, it is necessary to engage in this task properly. For this purpose one ought to read much in the gospels with the objective of making Christ your example, observing in what manner the Lord Jesus engaged in this task.

(1) It is essential to begin with those individuals by whom you are not intimidated, who are under your command (such as children and servants), or those who depend on your financial support. Such persons will have a hearing ear, or they will at least pretend to be desirous and attentive.

(2) One must conduct himself according to the circumstances. Sometimes it will be wise to speak of civil matters. Thereby we will manifest ourselves as being discreet, and it will prevent antipathy for us or prejudice against us from arising. Upon having inclined their hearts somewhat towards us, however, one should not cease at this point. At that moment or at a future occasion, create an opportunity with your words, be they few or many, and impress upon them the necessity of repentance and faith in Christ. Sometimes you will have set some time aside to speak with this one or that one about nothing else but spiritual matters. This could be when catechizing by way of questions and answers those who are subject to us, or when one seeks to engage in spiritual conversation. If our heart is but determined to be thus engaged, numerous

opportunities will present themselves, and subject matter for discussion will be at hand.

(3) Above all, one ought to be watchful against pride and an air of superiority; otherwise there will be no edification. It must all be done in an amiable, loving and humble manner. Our conduct must be such, however, that we are serious about our intentions, have great reverence for God, and greatly esteem spiritual truths. It will soon be noticed whether we merely *speak* of spiritual matters, and thus it will have no effect.

(4) One must therefore often be engaged in private prayer; there must be prayer before one begins and while one is engaged. There must be prayer for enabling grace, as well as for fruits in others. Having performed the task with humbleness concerning the shortcoming in our own performance, we ought to again lift up our hearts to God with thanksgiving for having received proper motivation and for the fact that we were able to say something. Oh, that the Lord would touch, move, and qualify many to do the work of a prophet! Indeed, the congregation would be blessed and many souls would be converted.

CHAPTER TWENTY

The High-Priestly Office of Christ

Having discussed the prophetic office of Christ, it now follows that we discuss His second office, namely that of *High Priest*.

The Priestly Office Defined

First, we must attentively consider *the high-priestly office* in order that we may know the perfect way in which man is reconciled with God. Sometimes the title "priest" is used for persons who are held in high esteem, such as princes, rulers, and officers. "He leadeth כהנים *(cohanim)* princes away spoiled" (Job 12:19); "...David's sons were chief rulers" (2 Sam. 8:18); "And Ira also the Jairite was a chief ruler about David" (2 Sam. 20:26). They bore the name כהן *(coheen),* that is, priest, because

(1) of the excellent glory manifested by the high priest — for this reason the prophet calls the most excellent ornament a *priestly ornament* (Isa. 61:10);

(2) prior to the tribe of Levi being set apart unto the priestly office, fathers, after them the firstborn, and thereafter the chief and most excellent members of the family ministered in the priest's office.

Secondly, a priest, when considering the essential meaning of the word, is one who "...taken from among men is ordained for men in things pertaining to God, that he may offer both gifts and sacrifices for sins" (Heb. 5:1).

The priestly office consists of two particulars: *sacrifice and prayer,* the pronouncement of a blessing being included in the latter. The duty to sacrifice is described in Leviticus 4. Of the duty of intercession we read, "Speak unto Aaron and his sons, saying, On this wise ye shall bless the children of Israel," etc. (Num. 6:23-26); "Let the priests, the ministers of the LORD, weep between the porch and the altar, and let them say, Spare Thy people, O LORD" (Joel 2:17). Once a year the high priest had to sacrifice a bullock and a goat, enter into the Holy of Holies, sprinkle the blood upon the mercy seat, and burn the incense (Lev. 16), the latter symbolizing intercession. This can be deduced from Psalm 141:2, where we read, "Let my prayer be set forth before Thee as incense"; "And the smoke of the incense, which came with the prayers of the saints, ascended up before God out of the angel's hand" (Rev. 8:4). Christ's high-priestly office likewise consists of sacrifice and prayer. We will first discuss His high-priestly office in general, and afterwards speak in particular of these two parts.

A General Overview of the Priestly Office as Being Distinct from the Kingly Office of Christ

Let us view this office from a *general* perspective. The Lord Jesus is High Priest not only in name, but in very deed; that is, neither figuratively, metaphorically, nor comparatively, but in truth and very essence. He was not a priest in a prestigious sense, so that it would have reference to His kingly office; rather, His being Priest is such that His priestly office is entirely distinct from His kingly office. His being a priest relates simultaneously to the offering of an atoning sacrifice and intercession. He did not first become priest *after* His ascension, solely because of His intercession, but He already was Priest when He was upon earth. There, by His suffering and death, He offered Himself as an atoning sacrifice unto God, and by virtue of His sacrifice has entered heaven, this being the Holy of Holies. There He administers the second part of His priestly office, namely, intercession, executing this on the basis of His sacrifice made upon earth. All such concepts are objected to by the *Socinians* in order to undermine the satisfaction of Christ. We must therefore give extra attention to this.

First of all, we maintain that *the high-priestly office and the kingly office of Christ are not one and the same,* nor does the difference consist only in the fact that in His high-priestly office He would merely be desirous and inclined to assist man, and that His kingly office consists in the execution of this inclination, for:

(1) Scripture teaches this nowhere, but declares that the high-priestly office consists in sacrifice and prayer, which we have shown. The kingly office consists in government and protection, and thus these offices are entirely distinct.

(2) Add to this that the office of High Priest is executed in the presence of God on behalf of man (Heb. 5:1), and the kingly office is executed in the midst of and towards men.

(3) Just as the various ministries were distinguished in the Old Testament, there was likewise a distinction among persons under the Levitical ministry. Whoever was king was not permitted to sacrifice, which was the reason why Saul was punished (1 Sam. 13:13). Whoever hailed from the tribe of Judah, such as the king, was not permitted to be a priest (Heb. 7:14). Since these ministries were typologically distinct, the same is true for the antitype.

Secondly, we maintain that *Christ is not merely a High Priest in name, but also in very deed; that is, neither figuratively, nor abstractly, nor metaphorically, but in truth and very essence.* This is evident:

(1) By expressly being called such, along with specific circumstances which clearly demonstrate that Christ is Priest in the true and essential sense of the word. "The LORD hath sworn, and will not repent, Thou art a priest for ever after the order of Melchizedek" (Psa. 110:4). Hebrews 5:5-6 makes it clear that the reference here is to Christ, for in this text the very same words, taken as a prophecy concerning Him, are applied to Christ. Here He is expressly called a Priest, being designated as such by God and ordained in this office by the swearing of an oath. All this confirms that Christ is a Priest in the true and literal sense of the word. This is also evident from Hebrews 2:17, "Wherefore in all things it behoved Him to be made like unto His brethren, that He might be a merciful and faithful High Priest in things pertaining to God, to make reconciliation for the sins of the people." A matter can hardly be expressed any more precisely. Add to this Hebrews 4:14-15.

(2) All the activities of a true priest are attributed to Him, such as sacrifice and prayer (cf. Heb. 7:26-27; 9:25-26). "By the which will we are sanctified through the offering of the body of Jesus Christ once for all.... For by one offering he hath perfected for ever them that are sanctified" (Heb. 10:10, 14). This is also true for prayer (cf. Hebrews 7:24-25). "We have an advocate with the Father, Jesus Christ the righteous" (1 John 2:1).

(3) Since Christ is the antitype of the priests of the Old Testament, and since these types were priests in the true sense of the word, this is much more true of Christ the antitype, who is the embodiment of the priesthood.

Thirdly, we maintain that *Christ is not merely a Priest in heaven subsequent to His ascension, but He was a Priest and administered His priestly office prior to His ascension while yet upon earth.*

(1) This is evident in Hebrews 7:26-27, "For such an High Priest became us...this He did once, when He offered up Himself." This text does not refer to what He did in heaven, but to what He has done while upon earth. He is said to be a High Priest, and to have

offered Himself once, which irrefutably refers to His suffering and death. He performed this sacrifice as High Priest, His sacrifice by comparison being the antitype of the sacrifices which the priests offered as types. They sacrificed upon earth outside of the Holy of Holies, first for their own sins and then for the sins of the people, after which they would enter the Holy of Holies with the blood of that sacrifice. Likewise Christ, while upon earth, as a High Priest sacrificed Himself, and this sacrifice is said to have been offered up once. This had already been accomplished and was history, whereas His intercession still occurs and continues.

(2) It is also confirmed by such texts in which it is expressly stated that this sacrifice of Christ was performed prior to both His ascension and His sitting at the right hand of the Father. Yes, He has entered heaven by and with His blood sacrificed upon earth. He entered heaven in the same fashion as the high priest entered the Holy of Holies with the blood of animals. "...when He had by Himself purged our sins, sat down on the right hand of the Majesty on high" (Heb. 1:3). The word "when" implies that this purging occurred first. "But Christ being come an High Priest...neither by the blood of goats and calves, but by His own blood He entered in once into the holy place, having obtained eternal redemption for us" (Heb. 9:11-12). First He sacrificed Himself as High Priest; first He brought about eternal redemption, and after this He entered the sanctuary by His own blood. The same is to be observed in Hebrews 10:12, "But this man, after He had offered one sacrifice for sins for ever, sat down on the right hand of God." First, He performed the sacrifice and afterward ascended into heaven.

(3) Christ also performed the second element of His high-priestly office while upon earth: *intercession*. This is to be observed in the high-priestly prayer and in Hebrews 5:7, where it is written, "Who in the days of his flesh, when He had offered up prayers and supplications with strong crying and tears unto Him that was able to save Him from death, and was heard in that he feared."

Objection #1: His suffering and death were merely a preparation, but not the sacrifice itself.

Answer: This is not only unscriptural, but expressly contradicts Scripture which clearly calls it a sacrifice and refers to it as the high-priestly sacrifice of Christ. "For this He did once, when He offered up Himself" (Heb. 7:27); "...the offering of the body of Jesus Christ once for all. By one offering..." (Heb. 10:10, 14).

Objection #2: "For if He were on earth, He should not be a priest" (Heb. 8:4). Does this not suggest that Christ was not a priest upon earth?

Answer: This is not true in the least, but rather confirms it, for he states that in performing the high-priestly office it was not sufficient to sacrifice only, but with that blood He had to enter into the Holy of Holies. If He had remained upon earth, He could not have fully performed His priestly office and thus would not have been a priest. The High Priest in the Old Testament likewise would not have fully performed his office if he had merely sacrificed and remained outside the sanctuary. Such would have been true if Christ were presently upon earth after He had offered Himself, for then He would not have entered the sanctuary. He would thus not have been a priest, not having fully accomplished His task.

Christ, a Priest After the Order of Melchizedek

Thus we have shown that Christ's high-priestly office is distinct from His kingly office, that He is a High Priest in the true sense of the word, and that He is not merely a High Priest in heaven by virtue of intercession, but was also a High Priest upon earth by virtue of sacrifice and prayer. Even though all this pertains to Christ, He greatly exceeds the Aaronic priests in excellence in numerous aspects, as the body exceeds its shadow.

(1) The Levitical priests hailed from the tribe of Levi, and it is evident that Christ came forth out of the tribe of Judah (Heb. 7:14).

(2) They were merely men, but Christ is also God, "who is over all, God blessed for ever" (Rom. 9:5).

(3) They were merely priests, but Christ is also King (Zec. 9:9).

(4) They were sinners having need to offer sacrifices for their own sins; Christ, however, was holy, innocent, undefiled, and sacrificed Himself only for the sins of His elect (Heb. 7:26-27).

(5) They were but shadows and types, but Christ was the embodiment, the antitype (Heb. 8:5).

(6) They were priests by succession and in the place of their deceased fathers. Christ, however, "because He continueth ever, hath an unchangeable priesthood" (Heb. 7:23-24).

(7) They were ordained without the swearing of an oath; Christ, by the swearing of a divine oath (Heb. 7:20-21).

(8) They were inaugurated by being anointed with natural oil; Christ was anointed with the Holy Ghost (Acts 10:38).

(9) They were appointed to minister in the old covenant; Christ is the Mediator of the new (Heb. 9:15) and better covenant (Heb. 8:6).

(10) They sacrificed animals, but Christ offered Himself (Heb. 9:12,26).

(11) Their sacrifices could not remove sin and purge the conscience (Heb. 9:12, 14).

(12) Their sacrifices had to be repeated until the time of reformation, but the one sacrifice of Christ has eternal atoning efficacy (Heb. 9:10; 10:1, 14).

(13) They offered upon the altar in the temple, which was sanctified in order that the sacrifices might be sanctified (Mat. 23:19). Christ, however, "...through the eternal Spirit offered Himself without spot to God" (Heb. 9:14). Thus He was simultaneously the Priest, the altar, and the sacrifice (Heb. 13:10).

(14) They were priests after the order of Aaron, but Christ after the order of Melchizedek (Heb. 6:20). This does not suggest that the Aaronic priests and their sacrifices were not types of Christ, for this we have proven above. A matter can be viewed from different perspectives, one thing harmonizing with one perspective, another thing with another perspective. This priestly order, however, is indicative of Christ's superiority.

Little is recorded for us about *Melchizedek* in the Old Testament. The history is recorded in Genesis 14. In Psalm 110 he is declared to be a type of Christ. Paul, however, deals much more extensively with him in Hebrews 7. In these matters we must not seek to be wiser than what has been recorded. It should suffice us to know in what manner he is a type of the Lord Jesus, and how type and antitype agree with each other.

It can be said of him that he was not the Son of God Himself who in foreshadowing His incarnation was to have appeared to Abraham.

(1) For Moses describes him as a man in the true sense of the word, having the proper name of Melchizedek, whose residence and domain was a well-known city in Canaan, named Salem. This city was later comprehended in Jerusalem, together with the mountain in its vicinity, where Abraham intending to sacrifice his son, said, יהוה יראה (*Jehovah-jireh*), that is, the LORD will provide. For this reason these two words — the word uttered by Abraham, *Jireh*, and the name of this city *Salem* — are brought together and coalesce in the name of the city of Jerusalem. That which first was called *Salem* later was called *Jerusalem* (Joshua 10:1). Moses describes him as being king of *Salem*, and a priest of the most high God, who gave bread and wine to Abraham and his people for refreshment when he returned from his glorious victory. He blessed Abraham, and Abraham acknowledged him as priest, giving him the tenth of the spoils. All of this is recounted as true historical fact so that not the least appearance is created that this must be understood in a figurative sense. Rather, it is clearly indicated that this history must be understood as a literal event — as is true for other histories.

(2) It could not have been said of Melchizedek that he was *like*

unto the Son of God if he had been the Son of God himself. Christ's description as a priest after the order of Melchizedek would not have been so extensive if He Himself had been Melchizedek. To be like someone is not the same as being that person, and He who is according to another's order is someone else.

(3) The offering up of animals and the possession of an earthly territory, all of which was true for Melchizedek, cannot be applicable to the Son of God.

Objection #1: Melchizedek is said to be *without father, without mother, without genealogy, having neither beginning of days nor end of life.* This can be said of the Son of God only.

Answer: This ought not to be understood in the absolute sense of the word, but only with reference to human knowledge; or else one may possibly not have known his genealogy. At least we do not know this, as it has not been made known in Scripture who his father and mother were, when he was born, and when he died. This is also applicable to his priestly office. The Aaronic priests were priests by succession; that is, the son would take the place of the father, and was required to give evidence of his genealogy. Melchizedek, however, was a priest without succession. Prior to him there was no one in his order whose place he had taken, nor was there anyone who succeeded him in this order. Not only is the suggestion that He would have been created in an extraordinary manner and as Enoch taken into heaven without seeing death not recorded in Scripture, but it is also contrary to it (Acts 17:26). Even then he would also have had a beginning of days.

Objection #2: He is said *to be a priest for ever.*

Answer: "For ever" often means "always," "as long as possible," whether "to the end of the world" or for "the duration of one's life" (Deu. 15:17), or till the moment when the antitype comes. "For ever" here means that he — without anyone succeeding him and thus coming between him and the antitype — remained priest of his order until the antitype came. It also means that in his order he, in Christ, for ever remains the antitype.

Objection #3: It is said of Melchizedek that "he liveth" (Heb. 7:8). This cannot be applicable to a man.

Answer: If he were still alive long after the antitype came, he could not be a type, for a type ceases to exist upon the arrival of the antitype. His being alive is therefore no different from what is said to be the case with Abraham, Isaac, and Jacob (Mat. 22:32). He is said to live, however, since no mention is made of his death. He also continues to live in respect to his order — in his antitype Christ. Melchizedek is thus not the Son of God Himself.

Melchizedek was therefore truly a man. Who he was, however, is unknown. It could not have been Shem, for 1) Scripture records the birth, age, and death of Shem; 2) no reasons can be advanced that Moses would have changed his known name; and 3) it is also not credible that Shem lived in Canaan, since Abraham sojourned there. It would then not have been the land in which he was a stranger, since it would have belonged to his ancestors.

From the foregoing and from Hebrews 7 it is evident that Melchizedek was a man of whom we do not know who he was, but that God had called and honored him in an extraordinary manner to be king and priest of Salem. He was most excellent in glory, greatly revered and esteemed, and thus typified in a most excellent manner the eternal duration of the kingly and priestly office of Christ, united in one person.

In Hebrews 7 Paul establishes the resemblance between the two:

(1) They resemble each other in name, for Melchizedek means "king of righteousness," and Christ is likewise "THE LORD OUR RIGHTEOUSNESS" (Jer. 23:6). "The sceptre of Thy kingdom is a right sceptre. Thou lovest righteousness, and hatest wickedness" (Psa. 45:6-7).

(2) His kingdom was Salem, which in our language means "peace." Christ is likewise "the Prince of Peace" (Isa. 9:5), and "our peace" (Eph. 2:14).

(3) Melchizedek is said to be "without father, without mother, without descent, having neither beginning of days, nor end of life" (Heb. 7:3). Christ likewise was without father according to His human nature, without mother according to His divine nature, without descent, and without beginning or end.

(4) Melchizedek was a priest for ever. Likewise Christ "because he continueth ever, hath an unchangeable priesthood" (Heb. 7:24).

(5) Melchizedek was both king and priest, which is also true for Christ (Psa. 110:2, 4).

(6) Melchizedek was more excellent than Abraham, Aaron, and all successive priests, for they gave tithes to Melchizedek. Likewise Christ is more excellent than all, being above His fellows (Psa. 45:7).

Although one or another of these matters may be applicable to others, there is no one to whom all of these things are simultaneously applicable. None of them belonged to such an extraordinary priestly order, and none were types of Christ in that sense.

The resemblance did not consist in the giving of bread and wine, as if he had performed a sacrifice, for he did not sacrifice bread and wine to God, but gave these to Abraham and his people for refreshment. Also in this respect he does not resemble Christ, for

Christ did not offer bread and wine but His own body. In using bread and wine at the institution of the Lord's Supper with His disciples, Christ did not offer a bloodless sacrifice, but instituted it as a symbol of His suffering and death, and as seals of the forgiveness of sins on the basis of His death.

Neither before nor after Christ has there been anyone who was a priest after the order of Melchizedek. This is true for Christ alone, who has no successor in His priestly office since He continues eternally. Thus there are no longer any priests upon earth, neither after the order of Melchizedek nor after the order of Aaron (who had to be out of the tribe of Levi which ceased to function in Christ). If anyone were to be a priest today, he would have to be a priest of Baal, as each idolatrous nation still has its Baal priest. All of this has been stated concerning the office of Priest in general.

The office of High Priest considered in particular, consists of two elements: sacrifice and prayer.

Concerning *sacrificing* we read, "Christ...hath given himself for us an offering and a sacrifice to God" (Eph. 5:2), "to put away sin by the sacrifice of Himself" (Heb. 9:26), "...through the offering of the body of Jesus Christ once for all. For by one offering He hath perfected for ever them that are sanctified" (Heb. 10:10, 14). The nature of this sacrifice, the genuineness of its satisfaction, its perfection, and its limitation to the elect only, will be discussed more comprehensively in chapter 22, which deals with the *humiliation of Christ*. We will therefore pass this by at present.

The Intercessory Ministry of Christ's Priestly Office

Intercessory prayer is the second element of His priestly office, of which we read: "...who also maketh intercession for us" (Rom. 8:34); "...He ever liveth to make intercession for them" (Heb. 7:25); "...to appear in the presence of God for us" (Heb. 9:24); "...we have an advocate with the Father" (1 John 2:1). Concerning His intercession we must consider its necessity, nature, and efficacy.

We will first of all consider its *necessity*. Intercession is a task which belongs to Christ's high-priestly office: "We have such an high priest, who is set on the right hand of the throne of the Majesty in the heavens" (Heb. 8:1). As High Priest He is in heaven, as High Priest He sits at the right hand of God. The task in which He engages Himself as High Priest is to appear before His Father on behalf of His elect, interceding for them. It is thus a task of Christ's high-priestly office to *intercede*.

The matters for which He interceded there are:

(1) All that which His elect are in need of in this life in order to enable them to walk in the way to heaven, namely, the Holy Spirit who illumines, comforts, and sanctifies them. This we observe in John 14:16-17 "And I will pray the Father, and He shall give you another Comforter, that He may abide with you for ever, even the Spirit of truth."

(2) He intercedes for them so that they may perfectly possess salvation after this life. "Father, I will that they also, whom Thou hast given Me, be with Me where I am" (John 17:24). This is also confirmed in Hebrews 7:25: "Wherefore He is able also to save them to the uttermost that come unto God by Him, seeing He ever liveth to make intercession for them."

For men to be saved, it was not sufficient that by His suffering, death, and holiness He *merited* salvation, but it is also necessary that by means of His intercession He would *apply* salvation and make them actual partakers of it. This was typified in the Old Testament by the high priest, who was not finished after offering the sacrifice, but had to enter the Holy of Holies with blood in order to sprinkle it upon the mercy seat and burn incense. The Lord Jesus, being the antitype, likewise had to enter in with His own blood (Lev. 16; Heb. 9:12). This prerequisite was of such necessity that without it He could not be a High Priest. "For if He were on earth, He should not be a priest" (Heb. 8:4). Had He not been a priest, there would be no salvation for the elect, for they must come to God and be saved by way of a priest. For this reason sacrifice and prayer are joined together. "It is Christ that died . . . who also maketh intercession for us" (Rom. 8:34); ". . . we have an advocate with the Father, Jesus Christ the righteous, and He is the propitiation for our sins" (1 John 2:1-2).

This necessity is also evident for the following reasons:

First, it is fitting to God that it be continually acknowledged that He has been despised by man, that His righteousness neither permits man to approach to Him nor He to man, except by an atoning Surety who continually displays His atonement. He therefore "ever liveth to make intercession for them" (Heb. 7:25).

Secondly, since God's majesty had been despised, it could not be tolerated that He would come to man or even to the Surety, but rather that the Surety would come to Him, and that, so to speak, He would bring the ransom home and lay it down before His countenance.

Thirdly, in reference to man as well as to the gift of the Surety, God also wills that His free grace in the salvation of the sinner be displayed and ever be acknowledged. "Being justified freely by His grace through the redemption that is in Christ Jesus" (Rom. 3:24). Therefore, although the sacrifice of Christ is perfect and is of an eternally atoning efficacy, it must nevertheless be applied by way of intercession. "Seeing then that we have a great High Priest...Let us therefore come boldly unto the throne of grace, that we may obtain mercy, and find grace to help in time of need" (Heb. 4:14, 16). Thus even though there is satisfaction, it is grace as far as man is concerned and is acknowledged by him as such.

Fourthly, it was also necessary in reference to the Lord Jesus Himself. He was Surety and could not be released from His Suretyship as long as His elect had not in actuality been made partakers of salvation. In order to prepare a place for the elect, however, and to lead them unto salvation, intercession necessarily had to occur (cf. John 17:24; Heb. 7:25). Thus, the Lord Jesus must continue with His intercession until all His elect will have been gathered into heaven.

Fifthly, the Lord also wills that the Lord Jesus be acknowledged as still being engaged to their advantage, so that they would come to the throne by Him, and in coming would there find Him to be an Advocate who brings their prayers before the Father (Rev. 8:3-4). "That all men should honour the Son, even as they honour the Father" (John 5:23). This continual appearance before the throne on behalf of the elect is also necessary:

(1) In order that there be no remembrance of sin. In the Old Testament there was always a repeated remembrance of sins, because they had not actually been atoned for and because the blood of animals could not purge the conscience. The high priest time and again would return from the Holy of Holies, and every year would once again return (Heb. 10:3). In order that there be no remembrance, however, the high priest would always have to be before the throne and forever sit down "...on the right hand of God" (Heb. 10:12), "and thus God would no more remember their sins and iniquities" (Heb. 10:17), since the high priest would remain in the sanctuary and before the throne.

(2) Also in order that the wrath of God would not be aroused by daily sin, it is necessary that the Surety continually display the atonement before the throne. Paul pointed to this in Romans 5:10, "For if, when we were enemies, we were reconciled to God by the death of His Son, much more, being reconciled, we shall be saved by His life." And why are we saved by His life? "...seeing He ever liveth to make intercession for them" (Heb. 7:25).

The second thing that must be considered in reference to intercession is *the manner in which He prays.*

First, even as Christ executed the first element of His high-priestly office as Surety, that is, the sacrifice of His body, He likewise administers the second element of His office, that is, intercession, as Surety. He does not merely stand before the throne as a friend who speaks well on behalf of His people but stands there as Surety, who has taken upon Himself to fully execute the salvation of His own. This is evident from Hebrews 7:22-25. In verse 22 the apostle expressly calls Him "Surety." He also speaks of Him as such in the subsequent verses, that "He continueth ever, hath an unchangeable priesthood" (Heb. 7:24), and "ever liveth to make intercession for them" (Heb. 7:25). Furthermore, since He executed the first aspect of His priestly office as God and man, the efficacy of His sacrifice being derived from His divine nature — from the divine Person — Christ must likewise be viewed as God and man in the second element of His priestly ministry. That the efficacy of His intercession is also derived from His Person, that is, from His divine nature, is demonstrated by the apostle in Hebrews 4:14, "Seeing then that we have a great High Priest, that is passed into the heavens, Jesus the Son of God." He is great, for He, being the Son of God, is equal to the Father. That is the critical point, and it is that which yields comfort and boldness. Therefore the apostle adds, "Let us hold fast our profession," and in verse 16, "Let us therefore come boldly unto the throne of grace."

Secondly, one must not think that Christ falls upon His knees there and prays with strong crying and tears (Heb. 5:7); no, that was His engagement in His humiliation. His intercession, however, consists in His appearance in the sanctuary before the countenance of His Father with His blood, "that speaketh better things than that of Abel" (Heb. 12:24). It consists in the demonstration of the efficacy of His suffering and death.

Thirdly, it consists in His efficacious will whereby, on the basis of the covenant, He demands the fulfillment of all the promises for His elect both in this life (John 17:15-17) and in the life to come. "Father, I will that they also, whom Thou hast given Me, be with Me where I am" (John 17:24). The Father gives Him license to make such demands by saying, "Ask of me, and I shall give Thee the heathen for Thine inheritance, and the uttermost parts of the earth for Thy possession" (Psa. 2:8). The Father has promised Him this. "When Thou shalt make His soul an offering for sin, He shall see His seed, He shall prolong His days, and the pleasure of the LORD shall prosper in His hand" (Isa. 53:10). This the Son demands.

Fourthly, His intercession consists in advocating and pleading the cause of His elect against all accusations made against them. The apostle John therefore calls Him an Advocate (1 John 2:1). This is confirmed by the apostle, who says, "Who shall lay any thing to the charge of God's elect? It is Christ...who also maketh intercession for us" (Rom. 8:33-34). Since He is able to demonstrate that He has fully paid for each and every sin, and has fulfilled the law on their behalf by placing Himself under and being obedient to the law, He concludes that there is no condemnation for His elect, but that they have a right to eternal felicity.

Fifthly, it consists in presenting the prayers of His children which, through the Spirit of grace and supplication, have been offered in His Name. Since they have been offered in His Name, His merits must have such efficacy that their prayers are heard. This is confirmed in Revelation 8:3-4: "...that he should offer it with the prayers of all saints upon the golden altar which was before the throne. And the smoke of the incense, which came with the prayers of the saints, ascended up before God out of the angel's hand."

The third matter that must be considered in reference to intercession is *its efficacy*. Such is evident for three reasons.

First, there is the righteousness of the cause. Here, neither favoritism comes into play, nor is there a looking the other way, nor does Christ merely make a request. Rather, the matter which Christ pleads as Advocate is entirely just and is confirmed by superlative documentation. He appears on behalf of His elect with His paid ransom, which is so perfect that not one penny is lacking. "...He had by Himself purged our sins" (Heb. 1:3), "by His own blood He entered in once into the holy place, having obtained eternal redemption for us" (Heb. 9:12). He has so completely fulfilled the law on behalf of the elect that they are "the righteousness of God in Him" (2 Cor. 5:21). The righteousness of the law is fulfilled in us (Rom. 8:4). This he demonstrates to His Father, and therefore this can only be followed by actual justification, and the bestowal of the right to possess eternal felicity.

Secondly, the efficacy of His intercession is also evident from the relationship between God and the elect, which is as between a father and his children. The Lord Jesus prays for those whom the Father has loved with an everlasting love, accepted as His children, designated to be the objects of His grace and benevolence, and towards whom His heart is tenderly inclined. The Father is therefore desirous that someone would speak to Him on their behalf. How can this Advocate then possibly be rejected?

Thirdly, this efficacy is also evident from the Person Himself who is the Advocate. He is the *great* High Priest (cf. Heb. 4:14; 10:21). He is great in His Person, being coessential with the Father, and great is the friendship between Him and His Father. "For the Father loveth the Son" (John 5:20). With full acquiescence and total delight He has become Surety. By an oath He has been consecrated to His priestly office, and has been obedient to His Father in all things, even unto the death upon the cross. The Father Himself says to Him, "Ask of Me, and I shall give Thee." How can such an Intercessor possibly be rejected? Now consider all of these things together. As such a High Priest — the very Son of God who as the one party in the covenant of redemption has submitted Himself willingly and obediently to everything — He represents the most righteous cause, which He can confirm by way of His passion and death and prove from His obedience to the law. With all of this He pleads the cause of His elect, doing so before a gracious and benevolent Father on behalf of His beloved children and heirs. For these reasons His intercession is efficacious to the superlative degree. It is thus most certain that it will prevail and the matter be given to His children. Yes, if Christ, while upon earth, was always heard (John 11:41-42), much more will He, now being in heaven, receive everything at His request.

The fourth aspect of intercession to be considered is its *all-sufficiency*. This Intercessor alone is sufficient. No intercessors need to be added, nor are others able to be intercessors. The saints in heaven are not intercessors for specific individuals upon earth. One is not permitted to approach God or Christ through them. This, first of all, originates with pagans who wish to come to God by way of inferior gods.

Secondly, this is an insult to Christ, as if He were neither fully adequate, nor sufficiently compassionate, nor sufficiently familiar with His elect: His bride, the members of His own body. This would imply that there must be other intercessors through which one could come to God or to Christ, but such are never found in Scripture. There is neither a command for nor an example of this in Scripture.

Thirdly, this is directly contrary to Scripture, which teaches us that Christ alone is Intercessor, and that there can be none other:

(1) The fact that Christ alone is Intercessor is confirmed by 1 Timothy 2:5, "For there is one God, and one Mediator between God and men, the man Christ Jesus." In the original text we read εἷς (*heis*), that is, *one* or *only*. It is mentioned in conjunction with the Godhead, and since there is only one God, there is likewise only one Mediator. This is also confirmed by 1 John 2:1, "We have an

Advocate with the Father, Jesus Christ the righteous." Scripture states that there is but one, and therefore whoever wishes to be scriptural may not fabricate additional intercessors.

(2) The Bible also teaches that there can be no other intercessors except the High Priest Jesus, since no one is qualified to be an intercessor except He who can intercede on the basis of atonement. "By His own blood He entered in once into the holy place, having obtained eternal redemption for us" (Heb. 9:12). Add to this those texts in which atonement and intercession are joined together: "It is Christ that died ... who also maketh intercession for us" (Rom. 8:34); "For there is ... one Mediator ... who gave himself a ransom for all" (1 Tim. 2:5-6); "We have an Advocate with the Father ... and He is the propitiation for our sins" (1 John 2:1-2). Deceased saints cannot be intercessors, for they are not mediators of reconciliation. They are also not able to go to God on the basis of a ransom paid by them on behalf of others, nor can they demand and request on the basis of such a ransom. The two aspects of the priestly office cannot be separated. It is thus a futile deception to make a distinction between a Mediator of reconciliation and a Mediator of intercession. For if the first is not a fact, the second can also not occur.

Fourthly, deceased saints do not have any special knowledge of the needs, desires, and sincerity of those who seek them out as intercessors. It is contrary to the nature of man to be able to perceive with one glance and to be aware in one moment of what transpires upon the entire earth — to know the needs of every human being. How can intercession take place without this being true? Yes, even if the saints were aware of everyone's needs — which is not the case — this is no reason why they should be intercessors, intercession having a different foundation.

Objection: Believers upon earth pray for each other. Why do saints in heaven not pray for those who are upon earth?

Answer: Using the same argument one could conclude that the godly upon earth pray for the saints in heaven, for if there is mutual communion, there is also mutual activity. Besides one may not establish a relationship between the activity of man upon earth and of the saints in heaven. They each exist in an entirely different state. Intercession upon earth is commanded, but not a single word is written about the other. Those on earth may be aware of each other's needs. Those in heaven are not aware of those on earth. Those who are on earth intercede for each other as equals, not on the basis of their own worthiness or merits, but in the name of Christ. To maintain the intercession of saints in heaven one must attribute to them majesty, worthiness, merit, and the ability to hear prayer. It thus is very evident that the intercession of saints is nothing but a fabrication, and it is idolatry to expect such intercession from them and to place your trust in this.

The priestly office of Christ obligates us to be exercised in a twofold manner. First of all we must make use of Him as Priest, and secondly, as partakers of His anointing and consistent with our name "Christian," be spiritual priests in a manner becoming to us.

The Believer's Use of Christ as High Priest

One must first of all make use of Christ as High Priest in reference to both His sacrifice and His intercession.

In order to do so, one must first know his sins and feel them to be a heavy burden; one must abhor himself due to his polluted and abominable condition; one must have a lively impression of and acknowledge the hatred and wrath of God against the sinner, which can only be removed by perfectly bearing the punishment due upon sin: the curse in this life and eternal condemnation. It must be acknowledged that the sinner neither knows how nor is able to deliver himself. Meditate upon these matters until you sink away entirely in your misery, perceiving yourself as completely destitute and desperate. Present yourself as such to the Lord, declaring and confessing that you are in such a condition.

Everyone who had sinned in the Old Testament came to the Lord in this manner when bringing a sacrifice (Lev. 4). The sinner who was desirous for reconciliation had to go to the priest with a sacrifice, and before the countenance of God had to lay his hand upon the head of the animal to be sacrificed in his place. In this manner he indicated that he cast his sin upon the sacrifice, and thus, by faith, upon the typified Messiah yet to come. Likewise, everyone who is exercised with his sin as described above, must come to Christ, acknowledging Him to be the perfect ransom, the only sin-offering, and perfect High Priest who sacrificed Himself for sin. He must acknowledge Him to be the compassionate and merciful High Priest who calls all apprehensive and timid[1] sinners to come to Him, annexing to this the promise that He will in no wise cast them out, but will reconcile them with God and grant them rest, peace, and salvation. In coming to Him, while acknowledging all this, one must lay his sin upon the Lamb of God which

---

[1] The Dutch word use is "verlegen." This word is pregnant with meaning here, as it expresses the emotion of the sinner who, overwhelmed with the sense of his sinfulness, dares not believe he is welcome with Christ.

taketh away the sins of the world (John 1:29). As the sinner in the Old Testament would stay near the sacrifice to witness the sacrifice of that animal on his behalf, such a sinner must likewise focus upon Christ and behold Him in His suffering and death, considering His sacrifice to have been offered on his behalf. As the sinner in the Old Testament on the basis of the sacrifice obtained ceremonial reconciliation, and true reconciliation if he believed in the Messiah, one must likewise apply Christ to himself as his atoning sacrifice for reconciliation and peace.

Secondly, since the Lord Jesus is High Priest, one must (as was done by way of the priest in the Old Testament), go to God by Him. "Wherefore He is able also to save them to the uttermost that come unto God by Him" (Heb. 7:25). One must not end in the Lord Jesus as Mediator, but through Him must go to the Father.

Question: How does one go to God through Christ?

Answer: (1) By receiving this offered ransom as his own sufficient and perfect satisfaction, as well as His perfect fulfillment of the law as his own righteousness.

(2) By presenting this to the Father, asking Him, "'By the resurrection of Jesus Christ' (1 Pet. 3:21) have not all my sins been paid for by His suffering and death? Has not Thy justice been satisfied? Am not I reconciled with Thee? Am not I at peace with Thee?"

(3) On the basis of that sacrifice one receives all the promises which in Christ are yea and amen, as being made to himself, so that God is therefore our Father and we His children, by faith thus calling God, "Abba Father!"

(4) Thus one proceeds, requesting in the name of Christ all that which the soul desires: illumination, comfort, sanctification, and preservation — as well as that which one desires for the body such as deliverance from crosses, health, and prosperity. We do so, believing that God, our merciful Father, hears us and will give us as much as is commensurate with our need. Here we rest and are satisfied, thanking God for everything, as all this does and will proceed from our Father in love and to our advantage.

Thirdly, the intercession of Christ renders much support in prayer. If one considers and believes that every prayer, every sigh, and the lifting up of the soul heavenward for God's Spirit and grace is a fruit of His intercession, whereby each believer receives the Holy Spirit (John 14:16); that He brings every motion of the soul and the expression of one's desires before the throne, presents it to His Father, and that all this transpires in His Name, in reference to His merits and by His Spirit; that on the basis of His merits these prayers can rightfully be heard, and furthermore that

He makes their desires His own, adding His incense to them, thus making their prayer pleasing to Him; if all this is considered and believed, this will greatly stimulate prayer. It will cause us to pray attentively, fervently, and boldly. It yields confidence that our prayer, however feeble, is pleasing, is received, and will be heard. Yes, when we are not able to pray, be it due to a negative spiritual frame, or in the hour of death, and contemplate and believe that the Lord Jesus prays for us even then and remains active as the faithful Intercessor who will not neglect our affairs, but will bring them to a certain conclusion, not resting until He has brought us to Himself — this yields much strength, causing us to surrender ourselves in quiet confidence into His hands. Due to His intercession we will be able to say calmly and confidently, "The LORD will perfect that which concerneth me" (Psa. 138:8).

Fourthly, great comfort may be extracted from this for all bodily as well as spiritual miseries. Do your sins weigh you down and do you go bowed down because of them? "He is the propitiation for our sins" (1 John 2:2). Is the soul ashamed because of its nakedness? He is "THE LORD OUR RIGHTEOUSNESS" (Jer. 23:6). He will clothe them with the garments of salvation, and will cover them with the robe of righteousness (Isa. 61:10). Is the soul troubled by the wrath of God? He delivers him "from the wrath to come" (1 Th. 1:10). Do you fear eternal condemnation? "There is...no condemnation to them which are in Christ Jesus" (Rom. 8:1). Does the soul long for communion with God? He will bring him to God (1 Pet. 3:18). Is the soul experiencing desertion, sorrow, and grieving as a lonely sparrow? Is it discouraged and at wit's end? Do bodily troubles afflict such a soul — being numerous, heavy, and of long duration? In all these things great comfort is to be obtained from this High Priest. He is a Priest in name and in deed. He is the great High Priest, who is moreover a faithful and a merciful High Priest. Consider this attentively in these two texts: "Wherefore in all things it behoved Him to be made like unto His brethren, that He might be a merciful and faithful High Priest in things pertaining to God, to make reconciliation for the sins of the people. For in that He Himself hath suffered being tempted, He is able to succour them that are tempted" (Heb. 2:17-18); "For we have not an High Priest which cannot be touched with the feeling of our infirmities; but was in all points tempted like as we are, yet without sin" (Heb. 4:15).

If one believes Christ to be such as He is, why would we not take refuge with Him, and in taking refuge, not believe that He can be touched with our infirmities, will receive us, and will grant us the desire of our hearts?

Many who are weak in faith are of the opinion that the Lord Jesus is not as easily moved as when He sojourned upon earth. They reason that if they could but interact with Him as the disciples and the women did, enter a home in which He was present, converse with Him as familiarly as Mary and Martha did, or be in His company, then they would touch the hem of His garment, would wet His feet with tears, make their needs known to Him and beseech Him to have mercy upon them, to take away their sins, to give them another heart, and to cause them to feel His love. Then they would have hope that He would have compassion upon them and help them. But now He is so far away, so high in the heavens, and in such great glory, that they cannot address Him as it were in immediate proximity, nor will He allow Himself to be moved by the prayer of such insignificant persons as they are. Know, however, that such thoughts are earthly, proceeding from ignorance and a feeble faith. I assure you out of the Word of God that the Lord Jesus is as compassionate now as He was then, taking note of the misery and desires of man as carefully now as He did then. Therefore, also now one may speak to Him as freely and familiarly as then. It grieves me that one impugns the compassion of the Lord Jesus. Oh, that one would know Him as He is! How many a weak believer would then have bold access, pour out his heart with tears and supplications, and have confidence that He would help!

Take note therefore that the Lord Jesus, now being in heaven, is not only compassionate as God — that is, in a manner which is natural to His divinity, proceeding from eternal and infinite love, by which He observes and takes to heart the grievous and sinful miseries of His children and is willing and ready to help them — but He is also compassionate as man. In order to be able to be compassionate, He had to assume the human nature, which is evident from Hebrews 2:14-17ff. For this reason He was tempted with many tribulations and was subject to anxiety and suffering, in order that He would know by experience how grievous suffering is and understand the frame of mind of the one who is in misery. He would thus be all the more able to have compassion on them (Heb. 4:15). Now consider both natures together, and view Him as God and man, as Mediator and as high priest. This high-priestly office requires compassion of the most sensitive sort. "For every high priest taken from among men is ordained for men in things pertaining to God . . . who can have compassion on the ignorant, and on them that are out of the way; for that he himself also is compassed with infirmity" (Heb. 5:1-2). Since Christ is High Priest, He has the special quality which belongs to this office: *compassion*.

How compassionate He was when He was upon earth! Repeatedly we read, "And Jesus was moved with compassion." Not only does the Lord Jesus have this same compassionate nature in heaven (for if a perfect nature can be compassionate, this is likewise true for a glorified nature), but since there is perfection in a larger measure, the quality of compassion must be even more excellent since it flows forth out of love. The Lord Jesus being also High Priest in heaven, now ministers in this office with superlative excellence. Consequently, He possesses the quality of the High Priest, that is, compassion of the highest excellence.

Take note also of how intimately the Lord Jesus is united to His elect. They have been given to Him by the Father, in order that, as His children, He would deliver, preserve, and lead them to felicity. Would He then not exercise tender care over them, and be compassionate towards them when they are in distress? They are His bride, children, and members. He has their very own nature — "for which cause He is not ashamed to call them brethren" (Heb. 2:11). When they are in misery and sorrow, they weep and long for Him, and cry out to Him for help and comfort. How can it be any different but that the Lord Jesus is greatly moved to compassion, especially since He is experientially acquainted with the feeling of their suffering?

Perhaps you say, "I grieve over sin. This is a grief which the Lord Jesus has never experienced, and thus sin cannot move Him to compassion, but will rather provoke Him to anger."

I respond to this that it is true that Jesus was holy, and neither knew sin nor committed it. He tasted, however, all the bitter fruits of sin in such a manner as if He Himself had committed them. He experienced the hiding of God's countenance, the wrath of God, sorrow unto death, curse and condemnation. He suffered all of this in a measure which exceeds our comprehension. He knows the soul's disposition toward the commission of sin, and thus is able to and does have compassion by virtue of experience. It is true that sin itself is hateful, but He already has fully atoned for it, so that instead of wrath, only compassion remains. Consider all this together, believing that the Lord Jesus has such compassion for you, and seek to have a lively impression of Him as such. Would not this strengthen you in all your distress? Lament about your sorrow to Him in a filial manner, and comfort yourself in His compassion, knowing that He has been afflicted in all your affliction (Isa. 63:9). You may say, "Why then does He not help, considering He is able?" My answer is, "It is not the time, and this is to your benefit. He is preparing you to be the recipient of additional grace, because it will be to the honor of God. Even if you have not been delivered as yet, the compassion of a Friend — of such a beloved Lord, High Priest, and Friend — nevertheless comforts. Therefore, await your deliverance with anticipation and in quietness.

The Christian's Obligation to be a Spiritual Priest

Having considered how one ought to make use of Christ as Priest, it is necessary in the second place that we be exhorted to be spiritual priests, in harmony with our name *Christian*. God has given the name priest to believers. "But ye shall be named the priests of the LORD" (Isa. 61:6);

"And hast made us unto our God...priests" (Rev. 5:10). They are priests, but not to sacrifice for their sins or the sins of others, for such is attributed to the Lord Jesus alone. "By one offering He hath perfected for ever them that are sanctified" (Heb. 10:14). Rather, they are "an holy priesthood, to offer up spiritual sacrifices, acceptable to God by Jesus Christ" (1 Pet. 2:5).

Their work as priest is first of all to approach unto God, to enter the Holy Place, and to be continually engaged there in the service of God. "Having therefore, brethren, boldness to enter into the holiest by the blood of Jesus, let us draw near with a true heart" (Heb. 10:19, 22). Thus our conversation must be in heaven (Phil. 3:20).

Secondly, the priests had no inheritance in Canaan, but God was their portion. They must likewise also turn away from all that is of the earth, leaving this for the men of this world, and look not at the things which are seen (2 Cor. 4:18), but rather delight themselves in the Lord who is their portion (Lam. 3:24).

Thirdly, they must be engaged in sacrifice:

(1) They must mortify the old man. "Mortify therefore your members which are upon the earth" (Col. 3:5); "And they that are Christ's have crucified the flesh with the affections and lusts" (Gal. 5:24).

(2) Their prayers must be sacrificed upon the golden altar which is before the throne (Rev. 8:3). They must do so for themselves: "In every thing by prayer and supplication with thanksgiving let your requests be made known unto God" (Phil. 4:6); as well as for others: "Pray one for another" (James 5:16).

(3) They must sacrifice their goods to the Lord by being generous to the poor, "for with such sacrifices God is well pleased" (Heb. 13:16).

(4) We must sacrifice ourselves to God with heart, tongue, and deeds, confessing, "Lord, here am I. I surrender myself entirely to Thy service. I am Thine, and whatever I am, I shall be for Thee. I offer myself to Thee as a thankoffering." The apostle exhorts us to do so in Romans 12:1, "I beseech you therefore, brethren, by the

mercies of God, that ye present your bodies a living sacrifice, holy, acceptable unto God, which is your reasonable service."

(5) If therefore the Lord leads us in difficult ways, and brings us in a situation where we must lose our life for the truth's sake, may we then not love our life and deem it precious, but offer it willingly to the Lord as a sacrifice. Paul said, "For I am now ready to be offered, and the time of my departure is at hand" (2 Tim. 4:6). There is no more glorious death imaginable than to die as a martyr for Christ. Oh, how blessed is he who may thus use Christ as Priest, and who himself may be a spiritual priest!

CHAPTER TWENTY-ONE

The Kingly Office of Jesus Christ

The kingly office is the third office of Christ. A king is a person in whom alone the supreme authority over a nation is vested. Thus, the Lord Jesus is King, and none but Him. This is true in a threefold manner:

(1) as God (being coessential with the Father and the Holy Spirit), He rules over the *kingdom of power*, to which all creatures belong;

(2) as Mediator He rules over the *kingdom of grace* upon earth; and

(3) as Ruler over the *kingdom of glory* in heaven, of which both angels and all the elect are subjects.

Christ, the King of Creation

First, as God, the Lord Jesus has within Himself all majesty, worthiness, honor, glory, and power, even if there were no creatures. Having created creatures, however, He, due to the majesty, ruling power, and actual governing implicit in His Being, is the great and sole King over everything. "Thine, O LORD, is the greatness, and the power, and the glory, and the victory, and the majesty: for all that is in the heaven and in the earth is Thine; Thine is the kingdom, O LORD, and Thou art exalted as head above all" (1 Chr. 29:11); "The LORD hath prepared His throne in the heavens; and His kingdom ruleth over all" (Psa. 103:19). The Lord has no need of servants or of viceregents; however, it is the Lord's wisdom and goodness to govern all things mediately, and thus to govern one man by means of another. For this purpose the Lord has instituted governments which vary in structure and dignity. Such governments are neither sovereign nor independent, even though they may often imagine themselves to be. They are but insignificant viceregents (assuming that I may give them such a title, and that such a title is not too high for them) who, on God's behalf and by His power, must govern according to His laws. This dignity is not acquired by skill, power, or friends, nor does anyone remain in government because of these things. It is the Lord who establishes and deposes kings; He exalts and He humbles.

Christ, the King of His Church

Secondly, God has a special and peculiar people among men whom He gathers by His Word and Spirit and who are referred to by the name, *"kingdom of grace."* The Lord has established a special King to rule over this people: the Lord Jesus Christ as Mediator. The church is neither a community without a Head, nor a flock without a Shepherd, nor a nation without a Ruler. Such can certainly not be true, even though it presently pleases Him not to demonstrate His glory and majesty as visibly as He has at other times. Even if it seems that no one is held accountable for misdeeds towards the church — that one can trample upon, extinguish, and destroy the church without retribution — and that the church has neither a Keeper nor a King, *Jesus is nevertheless King over His church.* He is not a King in heaven only, nor in a distant land, nor in the hearts of His elect only, but He is a King who dwells near and in His church: His own people, that gathered congregation, that visible multitude in the world who have accepted Him to be their Head and King, having sworn to be subject and obedient to Him and to live according to His laws.

Believers, hear this and rejoice; hear this, oh world, and be filled with terror! God "hath put all things under His feet, and gave Him to be the Head over all things to the church" (Eph. 1:22); "Therefore let all the house of Israel know assuredly, that God hath made that same Jesus, whom ye have crucified, both Lord and Christ" (Acts 2:36); "Him hath God exalted with His right hand to be a Prince and a Saviour" (Acts 5:31); "Yet have I set My king upon My holy hill of Zion" (Psa. 2:6); "Behold, the days come, saith the LORD, that I will raise unto David a righteous Branch, and a King shall reign and prosper, and shall execute judgment and justice in the earth. In His days Judah shall be saved, and Israel shall dwell safely: and this is His Name whereby He shall be called, THE LORD OUR RIGHTEOUSNESS" (Jer. 23:5-6).

God has established Him in His kingdom and has consecrated Him by anointing (Psa. 2:6). As He did not exalt Himself to be High Priest, He likewise did not exalt Himself to be King. Rather, the Father has appointed and consecrated Him to this office by way of anointing (which signifies ordination and qualification), by uniting the two natures in one Person, and by the extraordinary outpouring of the Holy Spirit.

The ministry of His kingly office consists 1) in the gathering of His church, drawing her from the power of darkness and translating her into His kingdom (Col. 1:13); 2) in protecting her against her enemies (cf. Psa. 72; Jer. 23:6); and 3) in governing her by His Word and Spirit. "For the LORD is our judge, the LORD is our lawgiver, the LORD is our king" (Isa. 33:22).

The Excellency of King Jesus

Even if there are individuals upon earth who are kings, the excellency of this King is nevertheless incomparably greater than the excellence of them all.

(1) All kings have nothing within themselves, nor much wherein they excel other men. This King, however, is glory and majesty personified (Heb. 2:9). He had glory with the Father before the world was (John 17:5), is "sat down on the right hand of the Majesty on high" (Heb. 1:3), and is crowned with glory and honor (Heb. 2:7).

(2) Other kings govern but a small country and have but few subjects consisting of men, and their subjection is only physical in nature. This King, however, has "dominion also from sea to sea, and from the river unto the ends of the earth" (Psa. 72:8), "Wherefore God also hath highly exalted Him, and given Him a Name which is above every name, that at the name of Jesus every knee should bow" (Phil. 2:10). He is the "KING OF KINGS, AND LORD OF LORDS" (Rev. 19:16), of whom it is written, "let all the angels of God worship Him" (Heb. 1:6). He is the Shepherd and Bishop of souls (1 Pet. 2:25).

(3) Other kings have but little power, are fully occupied in protecting themselves and their subjects, and are even conquered by others, but our King is "the Almighty" (Rev. 1:8). To Him is given "all power...in heaven and in earth" (Mat. 28:18); He is the "LORD strong and mighty, the LORD mighty in battle" (Psa. 24:8).

(4) Other kings are often harsh and cruel towards their subjects. This King, however, is very gracious, gentle, faithful, and benevolent. He is a Savior (Zec. 9:9). "He shall deliver the needy when he crieth; the poor also, and him that hath no helper. He shall spare the poor and needy, and shall save the souls of the needy. He shall redeem their soul from deceit and violence: and precious shall their blood be in His sight" (Psa. 72:12-14).

(5) Other kings die, are deposed, exiled, and cease to be kings. This King, however, "shall be great, and shall be called the Son of

the Highest: and the Lord God shall give unto Him the throne of His father David. And He shall reign over the house of Jacob for ever; and of His kingdom there shall be no end" (Luke 1:32-33). Our Lord Jesus is indeed such a glorious and eminent King.

Christ's Kingship in the Old Testament

The Lord Jesus is not only King by virtue of His presence in heaven, but was already King of His church in the Old Testament and when He was upon earth. This is evident from Psalm 2:6. As King He entered Jerusalem (Mat. 21:9) according to the prophecy. "Behold, thy King cometh unto thee ... riding upon an ass, and upon a colt the foal of an ass" (Zec. 9:9). And even though He is now in heaven, He continues to govern upon earth in His church until the end of the world. "And He shall reign over the house of Jacob for ever; and of His kingdom there shall be no end" (Luke 1:33). Yes, after the end of this world, He will eternally remain King over the *kingdom of glory*, even though, as far as administration is concerned, He will give the kingdom to His Father and He Himself will be subject to the Father. God will then be all in all (1 Cor. 15:24, 28).

Throughout history earthly kings have had an evil eye towards the church. They were of the opinion that their government was limited if they could not rule over the church. They have feared that the church would be detrimental to them, since they neither knew the glory of King Jesus nor understood the nature of the kingdom of Christ in the church. The kingdom of Christ is of an entirely different nature, as it is not of this world, but heavenly. "My kingdom is not of this world: if My kingdom were of this world, then would My servants fight, that I should not be delivered to the Jews: but now is My kingdom not from hence" (John 18:36). It is therefore called the *kingdom of heaven* (Mat. 3:2), which "cometh not with observation" (Luke 17:20). The subjects of this kingdom, even though they are men, are *spiritual* in nature (1 Cor. 2:15). "And they that are with Him are called, and chosen, and faithful" (Rev. 17:14). The blessings of this kingdom do not consist in the things of this world, but are spiritual, "for the kingdom of God is not meat and drink; but righteousness, and peace, and joy in the Holy Ghost" (Rom. 14:17). Its weapons are not carnal, but spiritual, the Word of God being the sword (Eph. 6:17). "For the weapons of our warfare are not carnal, but mighty through God" (2 Cor. 10:4). Thus, earthly kings need not fear this kingdom. If, however, their lust to govern is of such a nature that they do not desire Christ to be King, but instead wish to include the church itself in their domain; if they desire to determine what shall or shall not be preached, what must or must not be believed unto salvation, when or when not discipline will be administered; and if they themselves wish to either appoint or dismiss ministers and consistories; and whatever more they may desire, then we submit the following words for meditation: "But those mine enemies, which would not that I should reign over them, bring hither, and slay them before Me" (Luke 19:27). If the government does not desire to be judged, exhorted, nor rebuked by the church, she must remain outside the church; the church will then leave her alone and not involve herself with her. If government officials wish to be members of the church, however, they must bow under the scepter of Christ and should not oppose this King to whom they have subjected themselves; else they will experience that this King is too powerful for them.

The Separation Between Church and State

Since the Lord Jesus alone is King, it is undeniably true that He alone legislates in His church and is vested with authority. Nobody may therefore be emboldened to interfere with doctrine, life, or government of the church and act according to his own will. Everything must transpire in strict conformity with Christ's rule. He wills that the church shall always be separate from the state, and that the church will be governed by ecclesiastical authorities as the state is governed by civil authorities.

The church is not to rule over the state and the state may not rule over the church, but each must limit itself to its own domain. Not the least dominion may be exercised in the church by either ecclesiastical or civil authorities, but whatever transpires in the church must be by way of servanthood according to the rule and on behalf of the King. Whatever transpires in the state takes place authoritatively — as a reflection of the sovereignty of God. The lording of men over the church is the work of the antichrist (2 Th. 2:4). As men, the members of the church are subject to civil governments. He who does not obediently subject himself to the government, and rejects and opposes the government, opposes the ordinance of God (Rom. 13:1-5).

Thus church and state are fully separate from each other. The one is heavenly and the other earthly. The one pertains to souls and the other to the body. The one is characterized by servanthood, allowing no room for the least exercising of dominion; the other is characterized by authority and dominion. The one is not to meddle in the affairs of the other. The church labors to uphold the state, urging obedience to the government. Government must protect the church from all oppression in order that her members may safely conduct themselves according to the laws of their King. Happy is the land where this is true. 2 Chronicles 19:11 is a significant text in this regard: "And, behold, Amariah the chief priest is over you in all matters of the LORD; and Zebadiah the son of Ishmael, the ruler of the house of Judah, for all the king's matters: also the Levites shall be officers before you."

Thus must everyone function within his own sphere. Let the church refrain from bringing the state under her dominion, but see to it that governments are honored, feared, and obeyed. Likewise, let all ecclesiastical authorities refrain themselves from "being lords over God's heritage" (1 Pet. 5:3).

Governments are to refrain themselves from touching the crown and scepter of Jesus by imposing her authority upon the church as far as doctrine, life, discipline, and the appointment and/or removal of ministers and consistories are concerned. This must be so since 1) the Lord Jesus, who is also King over them, did not vest them with such authority; 2) the Lord Jesus has forbidden every form of dominion in the church; 3) He Himself has issued regulations for doctrine, life, and discipline; and 4) He has decreed in His Word the method by which He wills that ministers and elders of the church are to be called (cf. Eph. 4:11-12; Acts 6:2-4; 13:2; 14:23).

As we have considered how we must make use of and imitate the other offices, so it is also necessary that we do this in reference to the kingly office. In view of the *first* duty there are several matters which must be practiced in reference to the kingship of the Lord Jesus.

The Rejection of and Opposition Towards the Kingship of Christ

They who know the Lord Jesus in His royal glory and love Him in truth ought to have a heartfelt sorrow that the sovereign majesty of this great King is not known, feared, or obeyed. David said, "The transgression of the wicked saith within my heart, that there is no fear of God before his eyes" (Psa. 36:1). Thus a godly person endowed with wisdom must likewise say with sorrow, "All the activity of man, the behavior of great and small, the entire life, even of church members (with few exceptions), tells me that Jesus is neither known nor acknowledged as King. It seems as though there are not two kingdoms nor two kings on earth who are continually at war with each other: the Lord Jesus and the devil, but rather as if there is but one domain. Externally it almost appears as if everyone has the same nature and the same objectives, and is subject to the same rule. It seems as if church and society are of one opinion, differing but little in fundamental principles. Who can perceive that the church has a King, such a great King, and is actually controlled and governed by Him?

One will probably admit that Jesus is King, but then only as a King in a distant land, with whom he has no association and whose only acquaintance with Him is by hearsay. One may say, "He is King, but let Him secretly and invisibly be King in the hearts of certain specific individuals." But who believes that the church is His kingdom and that He Himself actually rules there? Who views Him as sitting upon the throne? It appears as if it is a people governed by no one, being without shepherd, protector, and governor. There is no longer a fear to oppress and destroy the church, nor to torment, torture, and kill professors of the truth. They only deliberate how sufficient power can be amassed to utterly destroy and eradicate the church.

If but a few who bear the image and garments of this King manifest themselves, the nature of the devil and the enmity of the seed of the serpent towards the seed of the woman immediately reveal themselves. Men oppose them with all their power. The godly are the objects of entertainment, mockery, and various forms of slander, as well as nicknames such as "speckled birds" and "despicable wretches." They are considered to be a people which men can freely abuse and treat unfairly in all respects without fear of retribution. The one does this ignorantly, another recklessly, a third with evil intent, this person with delight, and someone else does so in order to please others. With full hatred and wrath men oppose the keys of the kingdom of heaven. The scepter of this King and the discipline of the church are viewed as tyrannical repression. All other organizations are permitted to exclude whomever they wish, and other sects may treat their members according to their rules, but the true church is not permitted to do so. Jesus ought to be silent and not stir Himself. Tares ought to be permitted to grow in this kingdom, and woe be to those who determine to remove them.

Men do not acknowledge Him as King in the sending forth of ministers, not acknowledging them to be ambassadors of Christ; and the King's wrath is not feared when injury and sorrow are inflicted upon His ambassadors. They merely view them as hired school teachers, yes, as an unprofitable element of the republic. Men view the consistory with resentment, as if it were a government within a government, desiring to undercut and assume the authority of the civil government. In one word, the Lord Jesus is not perceived and acknowledged as King over His church. Instead, it is as Pharaoh once said, "Who is the LORD, that I should obey His voice to let Israel go? I know not the LORD" (Exo. 5:2). Men speak and think likewise also today. "Who is the King of the church? I know Him not."

Even those who have received some measure of light, stand and observe this from afar and do not concern themselves with it, since it only pertains to Zion. They only shrug the shoulder when perceiving that the royal glory of Jesus is suppressed. Some may secretly complain of this to a friend, but lacking either insight or boldness to deal with it, this evil progresses continually.

The Lord Jesus observes all this from the lofty heavens, but conceals His glory and restrains His governing might. He considers the inhabitants of the earth to be not worthy of a public revelation of Himself as the King of His church, yet keeps His church as the apple of His eye and is a fiery wall round about her, protecting her against the attacks of the enemy and reproving her enemies, as He formerly reproved kings for her sake (Psa. 105:14).

Oh, all you who know and delight in this King, observe all this. Let it wound your heart; let your soul bleed; and for sorrow let your eyes cry rivers of tears by reason of the fact that this glorious King of His church is thus despised and scorned.

Pray continually for Him (Psa. 72:15) and to Him, that He would reveal Himself to His church as King before the eyes of the entire world. "Give ear, O Shepherd of Israel, Thou that leadest Joseph like a flock; Thou that dwellest between the cherubims, shine forth. Before Ephraim and Benjamin and Manasseh stir up thy strength, and come and save us" (Psa. 80:1-2).

Let the enemies of God's church tremble and let those who are angry with Zion fear, for you are first of all at war with this lofty King, who sits on the throne of God at God's right hand in the lofty heavens, who is the "KING OF KINGS," and "LORD OF LORDS," who in righteousness "doth judge and make war" (Rev. 19:16, 11).

Secondly, you are opposing a most benevolent King, who offers all His graces and blessings, and who commissions His ambassadors to beseech sinners in His stead to be reconciled with God through Him. It is therefore the ultimate wickedness to despise and oppose such a good and benevolent King.

Thirdly, what will be the end of those who do not desire Him as King? Of this we read in Luke 19:27, "But those Mine enemies, which would not that I should reign over them, bring hither, and slay them before Me."

Exhortation to Know and Acknowledge Christ as King

Since Jesus is King, He must be *known and acknowledged* as such by every one of His subjects. For this purpose it is needful to consider Him in accordance with the description given of Him in the Holy Scriptures. Here we read that He is "the true God" (1 John 5:20); "...over all, God blessed for ever" (Rom. 9:5); "the form of God" (Phil. 2:6); and "the brightness of His (Father's) glory, and the express image of His Person" (Heb. 1:3). He, in order to be a qualified Savior, has assumed our human nature, being man out of man, of "the fathers...as concerning the flesh" (Rom. 9:5), "made of a woman" (Gal. 4:4), and "in all things...like unto his brethren" (Heb. 2:17). He is the Branch with whom the Lord established the Counsel of Peace (Zec. 6:12-13) and the covenant of redemption (Psa. 89:28). By virtue of this He is the Surety of the covenant of grace (Heb. 7:22). "The Son of man came...to give His life a ransom for many" (Mat. 20:28); "by one offering...perfected for ever them that are sanctified" (Heb. 10:14); and "when He had by Himself purged our sins, sat down on the right hand of the Majesty on high" (Heb. 1:3). He, though in heaven, nevertheless rules as King in His church upon earth and takes careful note what transpires there and what everyone does. He chastises the unruly, and comforts the obedient.

Thus everyone ought to know and acknowledge Him as King and have such an impression of Him in their hearts that it causes such motions within as are requisite for such attributes.

Since Jesus is King, everyone ought to honor Him as such. "That all men should honour the Son, even as they honour the Father" (John 5:23), for He is the King of glory (Psa. 24:10). In heaven all the angels worship Him (Heb. 1:6). All His subjects on earth must likewise worship Him. Such worship consists in considering His various attributes, the approval of them with sweet delight, a rejoicing that He is such a King, a losing oneself in holy adoration when viewing Him as such, and a bowing before Him in worship, "for He is thy Lord; and worship thou Him" (Psa. 45:11). It is to kiss Him in subjection and adoration (Psa. 2:12), and to cast yourself before the throne, exclaiming, "Blessing, and honour, and glory, and power, be unto Him that sitteth upon the throne, and unto the Lamb for ever and ever" (Rev. 5:13).

Since Jesus is King, all and everyone of His subjects must delight in Him as such. God has instilled in the nature of these subjects that they delight in their King because of the majesty and eminence to be found in Him. Therefore Jesus must also be loved by all His subjects — indeed, love is a constituent element of their regenerated nature. "Thy Name is as ointment poured forth, therefore do the virgins love Thee" (Song of Sol. 1:3). The words "Beloved" and "my Beloved" are as it were on the tip of the bride's tongue throughout the entire Song of Solomon. The Lord Jesus Himself gives this testimony of His disciples, "For the Father Himself loveth you, because ye have loved Me" (John 16:27). Upon the question of Christ, "Lovest thou me?" Peter answered resolutely, "Yea, Lord; thou knowest that I love Thee" (John 21:16). Paul was so filled with love towards the Lord Jesus, that, due to the impulse of love, he did not act wisely in the opinion of some: "For whether we be beside ourselves, it is to God: or whether we be sober, it is for your cause, for the love of Christ constraineth us" (2 Cor. 5:1-3, 14). This love moved him to pronounce a curse upon those who do not love that Jesus. "If any man love not the Lord Jesus Christ, let him be Anathema Maranatha" (1 Cor. 16:22)!

Wherever love for this King is active, there will be exceptional light, clarity, and delight within the soul. The soul looks to Him, beholds Him, and meditates and reflects upon His glory and preciousness, rejoicing that Jesus is so highly exalted and is crowned with honor and glory. Such a soul wholeheartedly desires this to be so, and delights to see how all the angels bow before Him and worship Him; how all the godly in radiating their love end in Him as their focal point; how the devils tremble before Him; and how all things are in His hand and must be subservient to Him. Of such reflection the soul can never have enough, and it grieves him that so often it is dark within, and that he must stand so far away. How he wishes to behold Him with more clarity and in closer proximity, and to be satiated with the brilliance of His glory! Such a soul exalts Him above all and has a high esteem for His majesty, which is delightful and awe-inspiring, and stirs up in him extraordinary reverence. It causes him to fall down before Him, kissing, as it were, the earth as an expression of this reverence. This love cannot tolerate separation or estrangement, for then the soul grieves. He hates all whom Jesus hates and delights in all in whom He delights. Such a soul, repulsed by all that is not in conformity to Him, finds a delight in all that resembles Him. How blessed are the footsteps of this King to such a soul! How it draws his heart in love to Him! His will is the soul's will, and it is the greatest delight of such to do and refrain from doing as pleases Him. Oh, how the soul longs for immediate communion with Him, to behold Him face to face, and to sink away eternally in this mutual and perfect love! Already on this side of the grave, the name of Jesus is written with golden letters in his heart. For His sake the soul would readily part with his honor, belongings, friends, husband, wife, parents, and children. His life is precious; yet he would readily surrender it for Him. "Love is strong as death; jealousy is cruel as the grave: the coals thereof are coals of fire, which hath a most vehement flame. Many waters cannot quench love, neither can the floods drown it: if a man would give all the substance of his house for love, it would utterly be contemned" (Song of Sol. 8:6-7).

Since the Lord Jesus is King, one must confess Him as such and not be ashamed of Him. "Whosoever therefore shall confess Me before men, him will I confess also before My Father which is in heaven. But whosoever shall deny Me before men, him will I also deny before My Father which is in heaven" (Mat. 10:32-33). This must be practiced with discretion, and yet at the same time boldly, willingly, manifestly (and thus without disguise), and in dependency upon the Lord Jesus, persevering therein until death.

Since the Lord Jesus is King, you ought to *obey* Him. "Hear ye Him" (Mat. 17:5); "Beware of Him, and obey His voice" (Exo. 23:21). He is the high and lofty One. "Who would not fear Thee, O King of nations? for to Thee doth it appertain" (Jer. 10:7). We are placed in subjection to Him. "O LORD, truly I am Thy servant; I am Thy servant" (Psa. 116:16). Know Him in His glory, submit yourself at once to Him, approve with delight your obligation to be subject to Him, and offer yourself. Seek to know His will, listen to His answer, and be zealous in your performance.

Since the Lord Jesus is King, you must *trust* Him, and with confidence consider yourself safe under His protection. Seek no protection apart from Him. "He that dwelleth in the secret place of the Most High shall abide under the shadow of the Almighty. I will say of the LORD, He is my refuge and my fortress: my God; in Him will I trust" (Psa. 91:1-2); "Blessed are all they that put their trust in Him" (Psa. 2:12). In the Lord Jesus everything is to be found which can bring about rest. He is all-sufficient, omnipotent, good, faithful, and true. To trust in Him is to magnify Jesus in all His perfections. For such there are glorious promises. "They that trust in the LORD shall be as mount Zion, which cannot be removed, but abideth for ever" (Psa. 125:1); "Commit thy way unto the LORD; trust also in Him; and He shall bring it to pass" (Psa. 37:5).

The Duty of the Christian to Imitate Christ in His Kingship

Having considered how we must make use of the Lord Jesus as King, we will now proceed with the second point. In a fitting manner we must take note of Christ in order that we, being partakers of His anointing, may imitate Him, since He has deemed us worthy to be called Christians after His name.

The Lord Jesus, by means of His merits, has made His elect kings, and honors them with this title. "And hath made us kings"

(Rev. 1:6); "And hast made us unto our God kings...and we shall reign on the earth" (Rev. 5:10); "But ye are ... a royal priesthood..." (1 Pet. 2:9). They are kings, for they have a royal heart, are in a royal state, enjoy royal dignity, have royal goods, and exercise royal dominion. All of this they possess in principle, and it is their duty to earnestly conduct and manifest themselves as such.

First, they have *a royal heart.* There was an excellent spirit in Daniel (Dan. 5:12). They have a courageous heart, and therefore they are compared to "a company of horses in Pharaoh's chariots" (Song of Sol. 1:9). They are called "his goodly horse in the battle" (Zec. 10:3). They have a prince-like and free spirit (Psa. 51:12). They have a wise heart, for the Son of God "hath given us an understanding, that we may know him that is true" (1 John 5:20); "I speak as to wise men" (1 Cor. 10:15). They also have a strong heart. "His heart is fixed, trusting in the LORD" (Psa. 112:7). They consider earthly possessions to be insignificant, yes, as dung (Phil. 3:7-8), and have great and lofty things in view. "While we look not at the things which are seen, but at the things which are not seen" (2 Cor. 4:18). Thus, they persevere in all circumstances without fear. "Though an host should encamp against me, my heart shall not fear" (Psa. 27:3). Let hell and the entire earth freely conspire — the least of the subjects of this King will neither yield nor subject themselves to them. Rather, in all things they will be more than conquerors, and will always be of good courage (2 Cor. 5:6, 8). Manifest yourself as such, Christians!

Secondly, they, *as kings, are in a state of freedom.* They are not subject to anyone as far as the state of their soul is concerned, except to the King of kings. They are "of the freewoman" (Gal. 4:23), "as free..." (1 Pet. 2:16), and the Lord's freeman (1 Cor. 7:22). They have the Spirit, and "where the Spirit of the Lord is, there is liberty" (2 Cor. 3:17). They "have been called unto liberty" (Gal. 5:13); the Son has made them free (John 8:36), and the truth has made them free (John 8:32). They have thus been placed "into the glorious liberty of the children of God" (Rom. 8:21). Therefore, Christians, "Stand fast therefore in the liberty wherewith Christ hath made us free" (Gal. 5:1), "be ye not the servants of men" (1 Cor. 7:23), and be not "brought under the power of any" (1 Cor. 6:12). I am not suggesting at all that one ought not to subject himself to the rule of those who have been placed over us in the domestic, civil, and other spheres. Even a pagan has said that *true freedom is to be obedient to governments and laws.* Every soul ought to be subject to the higher powers, since they are ordained of God (Rom. 13:1). They are, however, not to be servants of men. They are not to allow anyone to control them by either favor or disfavor, or out of love or fear for them, and thus be drawn away from obedience to our sovereign King. They are to refrain from activity or neglect of that which in any degree would be contrary to the conscience, robbing them of their peace and hindering them in their walk with God, and thus be detrimental to their inner freedom. The Christian's objective is not to be subject in a slavish manner, but only because he has the Lord in view and serves Him in this manner, that is, in doctrine and life. Rather, his objective is above all to live in and with God in the enjoyment of peace and freedom.

Thirdly, they also have *royal glory*. When examining believers closely, one will detect the radiance of the image of God, which they may possess in principle and wherein majesty and glory are displayed (1 Chr. 29:25). God says of His people, "And thy renown went forth among the heathen for thy beauty: for it was perfect through My comeliness, which I had put upon thee, saith the Lord GOD" (Ezek. 16:14). Peter says of them, "The Spirit of glory and of God resteth upon you" (1 Pet. 4:14). They are recognizable due to this glory within them; the godly honor them and delight in them. "But to the saints that are in the earth, and to the excellent, in whom is all My delight" (Psa. 16:3). They are also known and revered by the unconverted due to the excellency within them. "And their seed shall be known among the Gentiles, and their offspring among the people: all that see them shall acknowledge them, that they are the seed which the LORD hath blessed" (Isa. 61:9). By their behavior the council knew that Peter and John "had been with Jesus" (Acts 4:13). The godly fill the unconverted with awe, for it is remarkable what is recorded in Acts 5:13, "And of the rest durst no man join himself to them: but the people magnified them." Consider also Mark 6:20 "For Herod feared John, knowing that He was a just man and an holy, and observed him." An ungodly master has more respect for his godly maid than for ten prominent but unconverted people.

One might think, "Why are they then despised in the eyes of the world, and why does the world persecute them?"

My answer is: the world will first resist and suppress the esteem and respect they have for the godly, and then proceed to oppose them. Generally, however, the worldly have not observed the godly in close proximity, and have entertained erroneous prejudices towards them. This moves them to despise and persecute them.

Children of God, if there is such royal glory in you, manifest this glory by an increase in all holiness, humility, meekness, wisdom, and dignity. Keep from soiling this glory by your sins, a seeking of self, or by hypocrisy; for this will promote the honor of King Jesus.

Fourthly, the godly have *royal benefits*. All that is in the world is rightfully theirs. "For all things are yours, whether . . . the world . . ." (1 Cor. 3:21-22). The least thing they possess is better than a thousand worlds. "For the kingdom of God is not meat and drink; but righteousness, and peace, and joy in the Holy Ghost" (Rom. 14:17). Therefore, leave the earth to the men of this world who choose earthly things as their portion, and who as swine despise the unknown pearls of the kingdom. You, however, delight and rejoice in these spiritual benefits, knowing that you are "heirs of God, and joint-heirs with Christ" (Rom. 8:17).

Fifthly, as spiritual kings, God's children also have *royal territory and dominion*. They are exalted high above the world and have conquered it. "For whatsoever is born of God overcometh the world" (1 John 5:4). They triumph over the devil and his kingdom. "Ye have overcome the wicked one" (1 John 2:13). "And they overcame him by the blood of the Lamb, and by the word of their testimony" (Rev. 12:11). They rule their spirit (Prov. 16:32), sin has no dominion over them (Rom. 6:14), "and they that are Christ's have crucified the flesh with the affections and lusts" (Gal. 5:24). It is true that they still must do battle, but this does not remove the dominion afforded them. A king who is at war still rules. However, the enemies will not be victorious; these kings will most certainly prevail.

Therefore, children of God, as you possess all these things in principle (the one more and the other less), stir up this principle, use it with royal magnanimity, freedom, glory, and dominion, and manifest all this to the honor of the Lord Jesus, and as an ornament to the church.

CHAPTER TWENTY-TWO

The State of Christ's Humiliation by Which He made Satisfaction for the Sins of the Elect

Having discussed the offices of the Lord Jesus Christ, we will now proceed to consider the *states* wherein the Lord Jesus has administered these offices. We will do so particularly in regard to the high-priestly office which He administered in the state of humiliation by way of sacrifice, and thus *meritoriously*, and in the state of His exaltation by way of intercession, and thus by way of application.

There are two states: the state of humiliation and the state of exaltation. Both are joined together in the Old Testament. "He shall drink of the brook in the way: therefore shall He lift up the head" (Psa. 110:7); "When thou shalt make His soul an offering for sin, He shall see His seed, He shall prolong His days, and the pleasure of the LORD shall prosper in His hand" (Isa. 53:10). This is also true in the New Testament. "Ought not Christ to have suffered these things, and to enter into His glory?" (Luke 24:26); "But made Himself of no reputation, and took upon Him the form of a servant . . . wherefore God also hath highly exalted Him, and given Him a Name which is above every name" (Phil. 2:7-9).

The Incarnation of Christ: Not a Step of His Humiliation

The act of *humiliation* relates to the person of the Lord Jesus and not to one of His natures. Being a divine Person, His entire suffering was therefore a work of divine efficacy and value. The Person of the *God-man* as such did not humble Himself according to His divine nature. This is impossible, since His divine nature is immutable and incorruptible. He has, however, concealed His divine glory behind His assumed humanity, so that men did not perceive Him as He was, namely, as God; and thus they had the audacity to kill Him. Therefore the assumption of the human nature as such was not a humiliation in and of itself, but rather qualified His Person to be Mediator.

The *God-man* Christ was born in poverty, had no reputation or beauty, but had the form of a servant, that is, of the most insignificant of men, yes, of all men. Due to the sinfulness of all humanity, He was likewise viewed as a sinner and considered to be one of them. All of this truly constituted a step of the humiliation of the *God-man* Christ. The assumption of the human nature itself, however, considered apart from those humbling circumstances, neither did nor can constitute the essential nature of His humiliation, for:

(1) Christ, prior to His incarnation, was not yet *God-man;* therefore He could not be humbled as such. According to His divine nature this humiliation, properly speaking, could not take place.

(2) Furthermore, the union of the divine and human natures will continue in His state of glory — yes, to all eternity. Thus, the incarnation itself, without these humiliating circumstances (which should not be considered here at all), was not a humiliation. It was rather a qualifying of His Person, enabling Him to be Mediator.

In 2 Corinthians 8:9 we read, "Though He was rich, yet for your sakes He became poor." The reference here is not to the fact of the incarnation, but to the humbling circumstance of *poverty:* "...made of a woman, made under the law" (Gal. 4:4). Here is no mention of humiliation, even though being made under the law is humiliating. This does not imply that being made of a woman is an act of humiliation. "But made Himself of no reputation, and took upon Him the form of a servant" (Phil. 2:7). Here His humiliation is defined, not as the assumption of the human nature, but as consisting of humble circumstances: to be in the form of a *servant,* and to be obedient to the Father to the very *death on the cross.*

The State of Humiliation: His Suffering and Submission to the Law

The humiliation of Christ has two elements: His suffering for the purpose of making satisfaction, and the placing of Himself under the law in order to merit salvation for His elect. His suffering can further be subdivided into His suffering of soul and His suffering in body — to which the suffering of the soul was conjoined. According to His divine nature He neither can suffer nor has suffered.

Christ did not only suffer in His body, but especially in His soul. He did so rationally, and thus not merely by identifying and sympathizing with the suffering of the body. He who considers the suffering of the soul to be no more than a sympathizing with the suffering of the body is exceedingly ignorant. The sense of God's wrath in the soul is the soul of suffering, even when the body does not suffer.

The fact that Christ had to suffer in soul, and indeed has done so, is evident for the following reasons:

First, this is so typologically. The sacrifices typified the suffering which had to come upon Christ. In the sacrifices the blood of animals had to be offered. Why the blood? The blood constitutes the soul of the animal, typifying that atonement could not be made for the souls of men except by the soul-suffering of the Surety. "For the blood is the life" (Deu. 12:23); "For the life of the flesh is in the blood: and I have given it to you upon the altar to make an atonement for your souls: for it is the blood that maketh an atonement for the soul" (Lev. 17:11).

Secondly, this is confirmed by the prophecies. "When Thou shalt make His soul an offering for sin... He shall see of the travail of His soul... because He hath poured out His soul unto death" (Isa. 53:10-12).

Thirdly, this is confirmed by the righteousness of God. The soul of man commits sin and therefore the soul also must be punished. Such a sin requires punishment commensurate to it (cf. Rom. 1:27). "The soul that sinneth, it shall die" (Ezek. 18:4). The curse — separation from God and the wrath of God — was threatened upon men and is due upon sin. "...indignation and wrath, tribulation and anguish, upon every soul of man that doeth evil" (Rom. 2:8-9). The soul is the subject of this suffering. In order to remove all this, the Surety had to be punished in His soul and endure soul's distress.

Fourthly, this is confirmed by clear passages of Scripture. In Matthew 26:37-38, we read that "He began λυπεῖσθαι καὶ ἀδημονεῖν to be sorrowful and very heavy. Then saith He unto them, My soul is περίλυπος *exceeding* (that is, fully surrounded by, through and through) sorrowful, even unto death." "And he...began ἐκθαμβεῖσθαι to be sore amazed, and to be very heavy" (Mark 14:33); "And being in an ἀγωνία agony..." (Luke 22:44); "Now is my soul τετάρακται troubled" (John 12:27); and He "was heard in that He εὐλαβείας feared" (Heb. 5:7). As is true for our English words, which are expressive of the highest degree of sorrow, the Greek words are exceptionally emphatic in order to convey this sorrow as being the exertion of effort of the highest degree.

Fifthly, in order to gain a deeper insight into His soul's suffering, consider, in addition to these expressions of grief, the results of this sorrow.

(1) "My soul is exceeding sorrowful *even unto death*." Although His human nature was supported in a superhuman and extraordinary manner, enabling Him to endure suffering of an infinite magnitude, the human nature could not have endured a higher degree of sorrow without having succumbed and died. Not only was the body unable to endure a greater degree of sorrow, but the soul was also not able to endure any more, or, if this were possible, it would so to speak have succumbed and been destroyed.

(2) "And His sweat was as it were great drops of blood falling down to the ground" (Luke 22:44). This is neither an indisposition or weakness of nature in that perfect body, nor a physical labor which exceeded human strength. Rather, the anguish of soul so afflicted and troubled the heart that it forced blood out of the sweat pores. This did not merely consist in a bloody sweat, but great drops of blood fell from His body upon the earth.

(3) Take note here of the prayer of Christ. "If it be possible, let this cup pass from Me" (Mat. 26:39). One ought not to entertain the thought that Christ wished to be released from His mediatorship and was not willing to die for the elect. Indeed not! He did not regret the fact that He had entered into the covenant of redemption with the Father; He would rather have suffered a thousand times more. His will was not opposed to His Father's. Nothing of the sort is true, for He surrendered His will to the will of His Father. We insignificant human beings take no delight in suffering, it being painful. We are inclined not to suffer when we consider suffering in and of itself. It may nevertheless be true that we are willing to suffer because it is the will of God, albeit with tears in our eyes. Such is much more true of the perfect human nature of Christ. He did not know in advance how bitter this cup was. He presently felt it, and His natural inclination could have no pleasure but only be repulsed by suffering as such. He presented this holy inclination to His Father and prayed for deliverance, if it were possible. He knew quite well that He had to suffer. He neither refused nor tried to avert this, for He voluntarily wished to surrender Himself to this suffering. However, according to His human nature He did not know the extent of His suffering. Therefore He prayed, if it were possible, that sin could be atoned for by less suffering, that is, by some decrease of the anguish He suffered, or by bringing it to an end, and that He would not need to die in such darkness, desertion, and with such a sense of anger and wrath, for this would be the severest degree of suffering possible. He requested that He might be delivered from such a degree of suffering, but if not, He would be satisfied that the will of God be done.

(4) The greatness of His distress is also evident from the appearance of and the comfort afforded by an angel (Luke 22:43). His divine nature did support Him, albeit in a secret manner. The Father withdrew all sense of light and favor, and fully poured out His wrath upon Him; thus He found Himself alone, being in a condition of extreme sorrow. The angel did not come to help Him endure His suffering, for he did not suffer along with Him. Rather, the angel came to encourage Him, possibly by speaking to Him about Old Testament shadows, the prophets, the glory which He would subsequently receive, the impending redemption of so many souls — all of whom He loved — and the glory of His Father in all this, thereby strengthening and encouraging Him. It all came to such a climax that an angel came to comfort Him!

(5) The magnitude of His soul's suffering is also evident from His complaint upon the cross. "My God, My God, why hast Thou forsaken Me?" (Mat. 27:46). He was not forsaken by His divine nature, for the hypostatic union could not be dissolved. He was also not forsaken by the love of His Father, which remained immutable. Neither was He forsaken by the Holy Spirit, with whom He had been anointed in abundant measure; nor did He complain of being forsaken into the hands of men. Rather, He complained about the withdrawal of all light, love, help, and comfort during the specific moment when His distress was at its highest and when He needed them to the utmost. When Christ uttered the word "Why?," He was not asking to know the cause, but it was instead an emotional expression of sorrow. It was not an expression of despair, for He said, "My God," "Father." It was rather indicative of a most comfortless, helpless, and distressful condition.

Question: What caused this extreme distress in Christ?

Answer: His suffering in Gethsemane which we have just discussed was not due to the sins of the Jews, their rejection, His pity with all the ungodly who perish, the betrayal of Judas, and the offense and contempt which would result from His suffering. He had foreknowledge of all this. It also was not due to fear of the violent and ignominious death before Him, for then He would have been weaker than many martyrs who with joy faced death and courageously endured it.

Instead, the true cause of all His soul's suffering was first of all that He felt the full extent of what sin is, as well as what it means to be a sinner. He Himself had neither committed sin nor had known sin, for He was holy, undefiled and separate from sinners. But He had removed all sins from the elect by taking their sins upon Himself as if He Himself had committed them, thus standing in their place. He now felt what it meant to break the relationship and the covenant with God, to forsake God, to be disobedient to God, to oppose God, to sin against His law and will, and to be conscious of being a partaker of sin. To behold sin as sin, and to feel it to be such, is unbearable, even if there were no punishment upon sin. This caused David to exclaim, "Against Thee, Thee only, have I sinned, and done this evil in Thy sight" (Psa. 51:4). The Lord Jesus, who was made to be sin for us (2 Cor. 5:21), experienced sin as sin. This was an unbearable condition in Him who loved God perfectly.

Secondly, Christ felt the full force of being separated from God due to sin. It is neither imaginable, nor can it be expressed what terror, unrest, darkness, and misery are experienced, and what a sorrowful condition it is when God in indignation fully separates Himself from a sinner, withdrawing all favor, grace, and light; forsaking, rejecting, and casting him out; leaving him over to himself — man not being able to live without finding relief for his soul somewhere. For a man to have a soul — a soul which cannot satisfy itself and can only be satisfied by something external to itself — and then to have nothing and be unable to find anything for fulfilment; to miss God, who alone is the satisfaction of a rational creature; and to be empty within while weeping in total separation from God, is both unbearable and intolerable. Such will be the eternal punishment of the ungodly, "who will be punished with everlasting destruction from the presence of the Lord, and from the glory of His power" (2 Th. 1:9). The elect were deserving of all this, but the Lord Jesus bore this in their place. Such sorrow of soul exceeds our comprehension.

Thirdly, Christ experienced the full force of the curse, the execution of what it is to be cursed (Gal. 3:10, 13), the just manifestation of *divine wrath*, the Lord's *anger* towards the sinner (Nahum 1:2), the *terribleness* of falling into the hands of the living God (Heb. 10:31), and the experience of God being a terror (Jer. 17:17). As this cannot be understood by anyone who has not experienced it, so it can only be understood in a small measure by someone who has felt this in principle or by approximation, and cannot be fully understood and expressed by anyone. Let us take the most extreme conception of it as deduced from all the expressions of Scripture, and then consider our perception to be almost nil in comparison to what the Lord Jesus experienced in this respect. Christ was the Son of love, and as such God was not angry with Him. God was wrathful towards sin, however, and in righteously executing justice as Judge, caused Him who had taken sin upon Himself to feel this wrath.

Fourthly, Christ experienced the terror of the devil in full force (Luke 22:53). Due to sin, man has become the property of the devil (2 Tim. 2:26), and therefore the Surety had to endure all the attacks of the devil on behalf of His elect. The tempter tempted Him with subtlety (Mat. 4), departed from Him for a season (Luke 4:13), but came with his greatest power and severest attacks at the very end ... at the time and hour of his power. Imagine your feeling sin in all its abominableness, utterly forsaken of divine favor, sensibly experiencing the highest degree of the divine wrath and anger of God as just Judge — and at such a moment being attacked and assaulted in the most subtle and horrible manner by the powers of hell. What an extreme state of unspeakable distress this must have been!

Such was Christ's suffering according to His soul. Let us now also consider Christ's physical suffering. In considering this we must understand that all of this came upon Him due to the righteous wrath of God, and that this suffering was at the same time a suffering of the soul, not merely as having sympathy, but in an immediate sense. The suffering of His body was added to increase the suffering of His soul. The elect had used their members as instruments of unrighteousness and had engaged in sin with their bodies, and thus they were worthy to also eternally suffer all manner of physical pain. In this suffering we can distinguish several steps.

The Steps of Christ's Humiliation

The first step consists of His suffering prior to His baptism and entering upon His public ministry. He was born in poverty and under contemptible circumstances. He endured the painful act of circumcision upon the eighth day; He had to flee His fatherland, and as an outcast and stranger sought refuge in Egypt. He most likely labored as a carpenter (cf. Mat. 13:55; Mark 6:3), thereby submitting Himself to the sentence, "In the sweat of thy face thou shalt eat bread" (Gen. 3:19), to earn His bread.

The second step covers the period from His baptism to Gethsemane. He was tempted and assaulted by His archenemy, the devil, who to the utmost of his ability did not cease to stir up everyone against Him. He was hated and despised by the Pharisees, scribes, and rulers. They deliberately sought to trap Him in His speech, hoping to find something against Him. They forbade anyone to provide lodging for Him, while commanding everyone who knew His whereabouts to report Him. Everywhere He was despised, held in contempt, contradicted, reviled, and cursed. At one time they wanted to cast Him from a steep incline, and then again they took up stones to kill Him. He lived in poverty, suffering hunger and thirst, and had no place where He could lay His head.

The third step consists of the last segment of His suffering in Gethsemane; being in the hall of Caiaphas and the judgment hall of Pilate; standing before Herod; and being on the way to and upon Golgotha. In *Gethsemane* He was immersed in the suffering of soul related earlier. He fell on His face, prayed, sweat blood, and was betrayed by His own disciple which was an unbearable shame and defamation! He was forsaken by all His disciples, captured by enemies and officers, bound roughly, and led as a murderer to the judge. As a criminal He was brought before the ecclesiastical tribunal in the *hall of Caiaphas*, accused by false witnesses, struck upon the mouth by a servant, condemned to death as a blasphemer, mocked by wicked servants, and spit upon and hit in the face. Then He was delivered to the Gentile, *Pontius Pilate*, vehemently accused, sent to *Herod*, clothed in a garment for which He was ridiculed, led along the streets of Jerusalem as a fool, and delivered again to Pilate. He was put on par with a murderer; His death was demanded by the people; He was scourged mercilessly, crowned with thorns, and delivered to be crucified. As a condemned one, He was led out of the city bearing His cross. Upon *Golgotha*, the place of gallows, He was nailed to the cross and as a cursed one He was lifted up between heaven and earth, and placed between two murderers before the eyes of thousands of people. In His thirst He received vinegar mingled with gall to drink. In this state of misery He was ridiculed; stinging words penetrated His very heart and even the light of the sun was taken from Him. For three hours He hung in darkness; He died while experiencing the oppressing wrath of God. Behold the Man of sorrows! Can any manner of sorrow, contempt, and ridicule be imagined, with which the Lord Jesus was not afflicted? In this manner the Prince of life was killed, and the Lord of glory was crucified.

The fourth step pertains to His burial. After the Lord Jesus had given up the ghost, a servant pierced His side and with his spear penetrated His very heart, resulting in blood and water flowing out of this wound. Joseph of Arimathea — a rich, good, and righteous man, as well as an honorable counselor — and Nicodemus, having requested and received permission from Pilate, took the body of Jesus. After wrapping it in fine linen with one hundred pounds of spices, they laid the body in a new grave which was hewn in a rock and closed it off with a large stone. He, who prior to this had been mocked and despised of men, was now removed from their view as one unfit to be viewed by them.

Christ's Descent into Hell

In the twelve Articles of Faith it is written that *He was buried and descended into hell.* Even though the articles of faith agree with the Word of God in every detail and are the truth, this wording is nevertheless not recorded in Scripture in this context, but has been composed by men and accepted by the church as such. Therefore we need not regard the wording as if it were inspired by the Holy Spirit. But it does raise the question: *Must these phrases be considered as referring to one and the same matter, or must each be understood as pertaining to a different matter?*

We deem them to be essentially one in meaning, since:

(1) These two expressions were not placed together in the original Articles of Faith; some used either one or the other. At the council of Nicea, held in 325, it was only stated, "buried" or "laid in the grave." In the Athanasian Creed it only reads, "descended into hell."

(2) The two phrases have one and the same meaning, for the Hebrew word שאל (*sheol*), and the Greek word ᾅδης (*hades*), refer either to places deep under the surface of the earth, the grave, or the domain of the dead. The latter means "being put beneath the surface of the earth in a pit or a grave." Since the place of the damned and the devils is below and the place of those who are glorified is above, this location is thus denominated as such. This agrees with the fact that our word "hell" originates from the word "hollow." For the same reason mentioned above we call the place of the damned "hell," for "hell" is still called "hol" in the Frisian dialect. Thus, even though the place of the damned is called *sheol* (hades), it nevertheless in its original meaning referred to a pit, grave, or hollow cavity. For this reason we deem "being buried" and "descending into hell" to mean one and the same thing.

Although only one of these phrases was used originally, they have been conjoined at a later date and are interpreted as each having a different meaning. It is fitting that one understand "was buried" to refer to His lying in the grave, and "descended into hell" to refer to the suffering of Christ's soul.

Roman Catholics are obviously in error when they consider the descent into hell as a step of Christ's exaltation. They also understand by this that Christ, having died, went with respect to His soul, either to the place of the damned or to an ornate dwelling place for the deceased saints of the Old Testament in order to deliver their souls from this place. Instead, Christ's soul went immediately to heaven. He commended it into the hands of His Father (Luke 23:46) and said to the murderer, "Today thou shalt be with Me in Paradise" (Luke 23:43). The texts which are produced to support this error do not prove anything. "...His soul was not left in hell, neither His flesh did see corruption" (Acts 2:31). The word *sheol* which is found in Psalm 16:10, and the word *hades* found in this text, both signify "the grave" in their primary meaning. This is the case here and is also evident from what follows: it saw no corruption, that is, it did not decay as a body normally would in the grave. The word "soul" is here used figuratively, referring to the person, and more particularly to that part which is naturally inclined to decay, namely, the body; the soul does not enter the grave. If one understands this hell to be the place of the damned, the souls of the forefathers were not there, but were in heaven. According to their own view they would not be in the place of the damned, but in a purgatory.

Also 1 Peter 3:19 does not afford proof. "By which also He went and preached unto the spirits in prison." The words "by which" refer to the antecedent, "quickened by the spirit." The word *"Spirit"* does not refer to the *soul* of Christ, for He was not resurrected by His soul. Thus, this text yields no proof. The Spirit by which He came and went is His divine nature, by which he made Himself alive. In this nature He spoke with Abraham, Isaac, Jacob, Noah, and the other prophets, it being stated in 1 Peter 1:11 that the Spirit of Christ was in them. By the prophets He caused men to be exhorted, rebuked, and warned, so that He preached by means of those prophets who spoke by His Spirit. Mention is made in this chapter of Noah and the flood, and of people who then were disobedient and did not repent upon Noah's preaching by the Spirit of Christ (1 Pet. 3:20). The ungodly who died were cast — not in body but in soul — into this prison, that is, into hell, the place of the damned, being condemned and rejected not according to body but to the soul, which is a spirit. The soul, being the rational spirit of man, is the object towards which preaching is directed, and is the primary and immediate subject of sin and disobedience. The soul, being immortal, is destroyed in hell (Mat. 10:28). The meaning of the text cited is that Christ, by His Spirit, preached through Noah unto the people who were then disobedient, and who, according to the body, were killed in the flood, and according to their soul or spirit were cast into hell where they still are in prison.

All the Suffering of Christ Atoning in Nature

Christ had to endure all the aforementioned suffering in fulfillment of the ceremonies and prophecies. This suffering in its entirety atoned for the sins of the elect — not merely His suffering on the cross during the three hours of darkness. Such a limitation is not found in the Word of God. This is evident for the following reasons:

First, whenever Scripture speaks of the satisfaction of Christ, it refers to His suffering in general without any exceptions and limitations as far as time or substance is concerned. "For Christ also hath once suffered for sins, the just for the unjust, that He might bring us to God" (1 Pet. 3:18). Who would be so bold that he would dare to selectively place a limitation on His suffering?

Secondly, Christ did not only suffer during the three hours of darkness, but also prior to this. His suffering according to soul and body in Gethsemane was thus also of an atoning nature. "And with His stripes we are healed" (Isa. 53:5). He already hung on the cross prior to this darkness. Is not the crucifixion of the Lord of glory also of a satisfying nature? (1 Cor. 2:8). This is also true for His poverty. "Yet for your sakes He became poor, that ye through His poverty might be rich" (2 Cor. 8:9). Since His suffering prior to this darkness renders satisfaction, it cannot be limited to the three hours of suffering.

Thirdly, from the very beginning Christ was already the *Lord's Christ* (Luke 2:26), High Priest, King (Isa. 9:6), and Savior (Luke 2:11). At the age of twelve He was doing *His Father's business* (Luke 2:42, 49). From the very beginning He already was "the Lamb of God, which taketh away the sin of the world" (John 1:29), "despised and rejected of men; a man of sorrows, and acquainted with grief" (Isa. 53:3). He was all of these on behalf of His elect. From all this it is evident that He did not only make satisfaction during His three hours of suffering, but during His entire lifetime.

Objection #1: It is written, "I will remove the iniquity of that land in one day" (Zec. 3:9).

Answer: (1) One ought then at least to include all that Christ suffered on that last day and not limit it to three hours.

(2) On one day He accomplished everything that was subservient to the elimination of sin. All this had to be finished before He had fully satisfied and paid to the very last penny.

Objection #2: Frequently reference is only made to the crucifixion of Christ.

Answer: (1) There is also frequent reference to other elements of His suffering.

(2) The crucifixion of Christ is most frequently mentioned since it is the greatest, final, and most public element of His suffering.

(3) On the cross He suffered both prior and subsequent to the darkness, and thus one cannot limit His suffering to three hours.

Concerning this suffering, three matters need to be considered in more detail: This suffering truly satisfies, perfectly satisfies, and satisfies for the sins of all the elect and for them only.

The Veracity of Christ's Satisfaction

First of all we state that *Christ by His suffering has in essence and truth on behalf of God's children satisfied the justice of God relative to their sins.*

The Socinians deny this. We maintain that Christ is not only a Savior because He revealed the truth and the way of salvation, confirmed this by His miracles and His death, was an example for us in His holy life, etc. and thus suffered and died to the benefit of man. Instead, we maintain that Christ as Surety has taken the place of His elect, taking upon Himself all their sins; that is, original as well as actual sins committed both prior to baptism and conversion and to the very last moment of their lives. On their behalf He Himself has borne the punishments which they deserved, and thus has completely, essentially, and truly satisfied the justice of God without overlooking any sin or by accepting a part as being equivalent to the whole. On the basis of this satisfaction and His merits, He delivers them from all punishment, temporal and eternal. This is the cardinal point and distinctive of Christianity. He who errs here and denies this truth cannot be saved. This truth is confirmed by the following proofs.

First, this is proven by the necessity of satisfaction. God, due to His majesty, holiness, justice, and veracity, cannot allow sin to remain unpunished. He cannot receive the sinner in grace, nor grant salvation unto him, without perfect satisfaction of His justice by the bearing of deserved punishment. Man cannot make satisfaction. It is consistent with the justice of God, however, that this can be accomplished by a qualified Surety; and since the Lord Jesus is such a Surety, Christ has truly, essentially, and perfectly made atonement by His suffering and death. The first is true as has been proven in chapter 17, and it thus follows that the second is also certain and true.

Secondly, this is proven by the Suretyship of the Lord Jesus.

(1) It has previously been proven that the Lord Jesus is Surety, which is evident from the following texts: "By so much was Jesus made a Surety of a better testament" (Heb. 7:22); "The LORD hath laid on Him the iniquity of us all. He was oppressed, and He was afflicted" (Isa. 53:6-7). It is a known fact that a surety takes the

place of another, be it that he is a *fidejussor,* one who is obligated to pay when a debtor cannot pay, (which in this case no sinner is capable of doing); or be it that he is *expromissor,* who first of all takes the debt upon himself, makes payment as if it were his own, and releases the debtor from all obligations. Paul made himself such a surety on behalf of Onesimus towards Philemon (Phile. 18-19). Jesus, being Surety, has taken their place, however, and paid the debt on their behalf.

(2) This is also confirmed by such texts in which the words ἀντὶ (*anti*) and ὑπὲρ (*huper*) are to be found. "Even as the Son of man came...to give his life a ransom ἀντὶ (*anti*) for many" (Mat. 20:28); "Who gave himself a ἀντιλυτρον (*antilutron*), that is, ransom for all" (1 Tim. 2:6). It is undeniably true that the word ἀντὶ (*anti*) means "to take someone's place." "Archelaus did reign in Judaea *anti*, in the room of his father Herod" (Mat. 2:22); "An eye *anti* for an eye" (Mat. 5:38); "For her hair is given her *anti* for a covering" (1 Cor. 11:15); "Will he *anti* for a fish give him a serpent?" (Luke 11:11). Also the word ὑπὲρ (*huper*) means "in someone's stead." "For scarcely *huper* for (*that is, in stead of*) a righteous man will one die" (Rom. 5:7). Thus, Christ died for, and on behalf of, the sinner. "...but delivered Him up for us all" (Rom. 8:32); "Who gave Himself for us, that He might redeem us from all iniquity" (Titus 2:14); "...that He by the grace of God should taste death for every man" (Heb. 2:9); "For Christ also hath once suffered for sins, the just for the unjust" (1 Pet. 3:18).

In these texts the word *huper* is found. It is thus very clear that Christ, as Surety, has suffered on behalf of sinners and has made satisfaction for their sins. This is also confirmed in Isaiah 53:4, "Surely He hath borne our griefs, and סבלם (*sebalaam*) carried our sorrows." This word means "to carry with great difficulty," "to bear a burden upon one's shoulders."

Thirdly, this is evident from the high-priestly office of the Lord Jesus discussed in chapter 20. According to Scripture, Christ is High Priest (cf. Heb. 2:17; 4:14-16; 5:10). It was the task of a priest to sacrifice, and Christ, as Priest, did indeed sacrifice — sacrificing Himself (cf. Eph. 5:2; Heb. 9:14, 26, 28). The sacrifices, that is, the animals which were sacrificed, were killed on behalf of the sinner. "For the life of the flesh is in the blood: and I have given it to you upon the altar to make an atonement for your souls" (Lev. 17:11); "And Abraham went and took the ram, and offered him up for a burnt offering in the stead of his son" (Gen. 22:13). The death of the sacrificial animal was imputed to the account of the sinner who placed his hand upon the head of the sacrificial animal, and by this the sinner was declared innocent as if he himself had made satisfaction for his sins (cf. Lev. 4:4, 15, 20). This typified that the Messiah who was to come would likewise put Himself in the place of the sinner, would sacrifice Himself on their behalf, and His suffering would be imputed to all believers as if they themselves had made payment for their sins. Consider 2 Corinthians 5:21, "For He hath made Him to be sin for us, who knew no sin; that we might be made the righteousness of God in Him." Christ has been made sin for us by the imputation of all the sins of the elect to Himself as Surety, as a sacrifice for sin. Thus, "the LORD hath laid on Him the iniquity of us all" (Isa. 53:6). Since Christ has been made sin for us, we by virtue of His merits are made the righteousness of God in Him. This is also evident in the following texts: "Who His own self bare our sins in His own body on the tree" (1 Pet. 2:24); "He is the ἱλασμος (hilasmos) propitiation (an atoning sacrifice) for our sins" (1 John 2:2). Since the Lord Jesus as High Priest and the Sacrifice has sacrificed Himself for the sins of the elect, He has thus essentially and truly made atonement on behalf of the sinner by His suffering and death.

Fourthly, this is evident from the price that was paid. The suffering of Christ is referred to as a ransom: "...to give his life a λύτρον (lutron) ransom for many" (Mat. 20:28); "Who gave himself a ἀντιλυτρον (antilutron) ransom for all" (1 Tim. 2:6). He is called "redemption," that is, a sacrifice unto redemption. "In whom we have απολύτρωσιν (apolutrosin) redemption through His blood, the forgiveness of sins" (Eph. 1:7). He is called a "propitiation." "Whom God hath set forth to be a hilasterion propitiation through faith in his blood" (Rom. 3:25); "He is the ἱλασμός (hilasmos) propitiation for our sins" (1 John 2:2). These words have a strong emphasis, and signify a redemption, an atonement — the manner of accomplishment not being a matter of indifference but referring to that which must occur by payment for someone's redemption. If the suffering of Christ is such a price and ransom, it is truly sufficient and thus also atones. Add to this the texts in which the Greek words have special emphasis, as well as those which state plainly that the redemption of man occurs by the blood of Christ, it being the price paid: "Forasmuch as ye know that you are redeemed with the precious blood of Christ" (1 Pet. 1:19); "For ye are bought with a price" (1 Cor. 6:20); "For Thou wast slain, and hast redeemed us to God by Thy blood" (Rev. 5:9). Thus, we are redeemed, not by a mere release as a lord grants freedom to his slave or as prisoners of war are exchanged or released, but by a transaction in which payment is made of proper value. Such is true for the suffering of Christ.

Fifthly, it is evident from the fruits of the suffering and death of Christ. By the suffering and death of Jesus Christ real satisfaction has been made and peace has been established between God — whose justice has been satisfied — and the sinner. Scripture states this emphatically and clearly: "When we were enemies, we were reconciled to God by the death of his Son" (Rom. 5:10); "Who hath reconciled us to Himself by Jesus Christ... to wit, that God was in Christ, reconciling the world unto Himself, not imputing their trespasses unto them" (2 Cor. 5:18-19); "And that He might reconcile both unto God in one body by the cross, having slain the enmity thereby" (Eph. 2:16). Not only did Christ make those two — Jews and Gentiles — one, and thus reconcile them to each other, but He has reconciled both with God. "And, having made peace through the blood of His cross, by Him to reconcile all things unto Himself; by Him, I say, whether they be things in earth, or things in heaven. And you, that were sometime alienated and enemies in your mind by wicked works, yet now hath He reconciled" (Col. 1:20-21). He not only has brought about reconciliation between all His elect, that is, those who are in heaven and upon earth, but He has also reconciled them to Himself, and thus they all have peace with God through the blood of Christ. There was enmity between God and man. God hates the sinner (Psa. 5:5); men are children of wrath (Eph. 2:3); Christ removes this enmity (Eph. 2:15); He delivers men from the wrath of God (1 Th. 1:10); He reconciles them with God (Rom. 5:10); and He brings them to God (1 Pet. 3:18). He does not do this by merely pointing out the way of conversion to them, but through His blood as the ransom. Thus, Christ has essentially, truly, on behalf of sinners and by His suffering and death satisfied the justice of God.

Even though the proofs mentioned above are very convincing, we shall seek to remove some objections in order that there be no reason that anyone should be hindered from receiving this truth.

Objection #1: God was not angry towards men, but rather loved them (cf. John 3:16; Titus 3:4). *God* is also not said to be reconciled, but rather that *man* is reconciled, which is the result of 1) man's conversion to God, 2) gracious acquittal, and 3) the intervention of a Mediator — and thus not due to the bearing of punishment, satisfaction of divine justice, and removal of wrath.

Answer: (1) It is clearly contrary to the Word of God to say that He is not angry with sin. "For thou art not a God that hath pleasure in wickedness... Thou hatest all workers of iniquity...the LORD will abhor the bloody and deceitful man" (Psa. 5:4-6). "God is angry with the wicked every day" (Psa. 7:11); "For the wrath of God is revealed from heaven against all ungodliness" (Rom. 1:18); "We...were by nature the children of wrath, even as others" (Eph. 2:3).

(2) God loves humanity, but not with a love of *delight*, for in men there is nothing but sin, and they are the enemies of God (Rom. 5:10). Rather He loves men with a love of *benevolence* which He manifested in the giving of the Mediator. As sinners, His elect were children of wrath; but as His elect, God loved them with benevolent love.

(3) It is contrary to God's Word to maintain that not God but man was reconciled. Did man receive something from God so that man in turn could have God be reconciled with him? Is man the one who has been satisfied? Instead, God was provoked to anger (man being the cause of this), God's wrath was appeased, God received the ransom, and the appeasement of God's wrath was to the benefit of the elect, who due to this paid ransom are received in reconciliation.

(4) It is nowhere recorded in Scripture that this reconciliation comes about by way of conversion. It is self-evident that conversion is not the same as atonement. Everywhere in Scripture reconciliation is attributed to the passion of Christ, as we have abundantly shown above. Acquittal does not occur apart from the satisfaction of divine justice, but on the basis of satisfaction. This acquittal and manifestation of grace take place toward men who have contributed nothing towards this satisfaction.

(5) Reconciliation does not come about by mere intercession and intervention, since the satisfaction made by the bearing of punishment is the basis for intercession. In order for Christ to enter into the sanctuary, He had to do so by His own blood (Heb. 9:12). John therefore joins these two principles together. "We have an Advocate with the Father,...and He is the propitiation for our sins" (1 John 2:1-2).

Objection #2: The word "satisfy" does not occur in Scripture (in regard to Christ's work), and therefore one cannot prove that satisfaction has been made.

Answer: Even if the letters of that word do not occur, for a rational person it will be sufficient if the matter itself is expressed clearly and transparently. Scripture states that Christ has restored that which He took not away (Psa. 69:4), that He has given His soul as a ransom for many (Mat. 20:28), for all (1 Tim. 2:6), that in Him we have redemption (or a sacrifice unto redemption) (Eph. 1:7), and that He is a propitiation for our sins (1 John 2:2), etc. Is not this the equivalent of making satisfaction? It does not matter whether one uses these words or the word "satisfy."

Objection #3: If Christ has made satisfaction for us, He has also made atonement for Himself, which is an absurdity.

Answer: Even though making payment on one's own behalf cannot really be associated with a transaction in which righteousness is acquired by way of exchange, this can very well be true of avenging righteousness. Why would a judge, who himself has done wrong, not be able to condemn himself and bring judgment upon himself? Would it be against all rhyme and reason if a judge, whose son has committed a crime and forfeited the right to both of his eyes, would cause one eye of his son and one of his own eyes to be put out? What I have just stated applies to human justice. Here the matter is both clear and transparent, however, for it is God who says that Christ by His suffering and death has removed the enmity between God and man, and reconciled man to God (Rom. 5:10), has made peace (Col. 1:20), and has brought man to God (1 Pet. 3:18). This is therefore the end of all argument. He who wishes to understand this clearly should recognize that Christ as God-man and as Surety, did not make satisfaction to Himself but to His Father. When we consider Him as being coessential with the Father, as being of divine essence, then He indeed, as Surety, has made payment to God and thus to Himself, being both God and man. You must make a distinction between essence and personhood: the Father is one Person, and the Son is another Person. In doing so the difficulty will be cleared up.

Objection #4: In order for Christ to make satisfaction He had to suffer all that the sinner deserves. This means that He would have to suffer eternal damnation, be eternally in hell, and be in a state of despair. Christ did not suffer all this, however, and thus He has not made satisfaction.

Answer: (1) Christ did indeed suffer eternal damnation, for eternal damnation, death, and pain consist in total separation from God, in the total manifestation of divine wrath, and all of this for such a duration until the punishment upon sin was perfectly and satisfactorily born. However, Christ has suffered all this to the fullest extent, as has been demonstrated earlier. He suffered as long and in such a measure until He could say, "It is finished" (John 19:30), and "I have finished the work which Thou gavest Me to do" (John 17:4).

(2) Christ did not need to be locally in hell, for this does not belong to the essence of eternal damnation.

(3) His suffering did not have to be endless or eternal in duration. Man is subject to this due to his inability to endure punishment exhaustively and at the same time restore himself into a state of perfection. Consequently man would have to remain subject to

it until he would make full satisfaction, which could not occur to all eternity. Since, however, the Surety has suffered everything to the most perfect degree and with utmost exertion, that is, as much as was necessary to satisfy divine justice, and since He fulfilled the demands of the law by His perfect obedience, it was neither possible to extend His suffering any further, nor "that He should be holden of" death (Acts 2:24).

Additional Objection: Christ's human nature, in which He suffered, was finite and thus was not capable of bearing infinite wrath. Consequently His suffering was not sufficient to atone for sin which merits eternal punishment.

Answer: We cannot determine to what degree Christ's human nature was fortified, but it always remained finite. In this nature Christ endured a total being forsaken by, and the full wrath of, the infinite God against whom the elect had sinned. One should note, however, that it was not the human nature which suffered, but the Person according to this nature, and since the Person is infinite, all that He suffered was of infinite efficacy and value.

Additional Objection: If the suffering of Christ was of infinite efficacy because He who suffered is infinite, then such would be true by virtue of having respect for His Person. This God will not do according to Romans 2:11. Thus, the atonement was sufficient by accepting a part as being equivalent to the whole — this in view of the Person, but not because the nature of the punishment was such that it could match the deserts of sin.

Answer: To respect a person is to be moved to bestow upon that person some favor in response to some external circumstances or qualities. In this case, however, the word "person" does not refer to man himself as the object of activity. Such an argument does not hold here since the reference is to the Person Himself, rather than to the qualities which would motivate to respect or not to respect. This is also not a case where part is accepted as being equivalent to the whole, since the punishment is such that it deals fully with sin. Neither esteem nor consideration for His Person rendered the suffering of Christ sufficient; rather the suffering of this infinite Person was sufficient and infinitely efficacious due to its intrinsic, true efficacy and value. The rank of the person against whom a crime is committed proportionally aggravates the crime and determines the severity of the punishment. For why is it that he who hits the king in the face is worthy of death, and he who hits a beggar is not worthy of this? Is it not due to the rank and worthiness of the person? Likewise the suffering of punishment for the crime endured by a king is of greater worth and satisfaction, even if he suffers less, than that of a beggar who has committed the same crime and physically suffers more pain and shame. Such is the case here. Since the Person against whom men have sinned is infinite, sin indeed demands infinite punishment, and since the Person who bears the punishment is infinite, the satisfaction is indeed infinite as well, that is, fully sufficient.

(4) Christ also did not need to despair. He could not suffer this since despair is sin, and is not the essence of eternal punishment, but is due both to the unbearable suffering of a miserable creature and a being deprived of all means to ever be delivered. All this does not apply to Christ, since He was able both to bear the punishment and overcome His suffering.

Objection #5: Even if Christ had made satisfaction, it could only be of value for one person and not for all.

Answer: Scripture states that this one Christ has made satisfaction for all (cf. Rom. 5:18; 1 Tim. 2:6; Heb. 2:9). One rich man can deliver many slaves. A king can take the place of many prisoners and deliver them as such. Thus, an infinite Person can make satisfaction for many.

Objection #6: If Christ has made satisfaction for us, we must thank Christ more for our salvation than God the Father.

Answer: This is incorrect logic, for everything proceeds from the Father who has ordained and given the Son.

Additional Objection: Then we need neither to keep ourselves from sin nor practice virtue, since all sin has been paid for and salvation has already been merited.

Answer: This objection reveals total ignorance concerning both the nature of a redeemed person and the nature of grace. "And every man that hath this hope in Him purifieth himself, even as He is pure" (1 John 3:3). Sin is impurity, and therefore those that have been purified hate and flee from it as it is contrary to the regenerated nature. Holiness is their life and joy, and therefore they pursue it. They do not practice virtue to merit heaven, but to thank, serve, and magnify the Lord and to follow in this delightful and plain way until they may possess this merited salvation.

Additional Objection: It is inconsistent with the mercy and power of God to insist upon the satisfaction of Christ. God was either not willing to save the sinner without satisfaction — which would be contrary to His mercy — or He was unable, which would be contrary to His power.

Answer: If God could have saved the sinner without the satisfaction of Christ, it would have been inconceivably merciless of God to cause the holy Christ to suffer so much and so severely. Nevertheless, if God does not save the most abominable and stiffnecked sinner who dies in his sin without the least manifestation of sorrow, then this would be either because He is not willing, which would be contrary to His infinite mercy, or because He is not able, which would be contrary to His omnipotence. Coming to the point, power is not the issue here, but justice and holiness which cannot tolerate that sin should go unpunished. Since His justice will not tolerate unpunished sin, He is also not willing to do so, for His will is in harmony with His nature. It is not an act of mercy to violate justice; instead, His power and mercy are exceedingly magnified by saving the sinner on the basis of Christ's satisfaction. "To the praise of the glory of His grace, wherein He hath made us accepted in the Beloved" (Eph. 1:6); "He hath shewed strength with His arm" (Luke 1:51).

Thus we have confirmed the veracity of the satisfaction rendered.

The Perfection of Christ's Satisfaction

The second thing we must consider concerning the suffering and death of Christ is *the perfection of the satisfaction of Christ*. We must do so especially in defense against *Roman Catholics* and *Socinians*. Four things must be noted here:

(1) that Christ's satisfaction is so perfect that the notion that a part was accepted as being equivalent to the whole or that some sins were overlooked is unacceptable;

(2) that other satisfaction is neither to be added to this nor can be added;

(3) that the satisfaction does not only pertain to sins committed prior to baptism, but rather that satisfaction has been made for all sins, great and small;

(4) that satisfaction was not only made for all incurred guilt, but also for all punishment due. All these matters are clearly evident from what we have stated concerning the doctrine of satisfaction, so that proof is no longer needed.

In order that no hiding-place be left unsearched, however, we shall consider each point individually.

The suffering of Christ itself, when considered in its essential nature, is such a perfect suffering that the notion of a gracious evaluation, that is, acceptance of a part as being equivalent to the whole, is nonexistent and cannot be entertained. This is evident for the following reasons:

First, if the avenging justice of God as Judge is so impeccable that it cannot be satisfied except by the exhaustive bearing of deserved punishment, and if the Lord Jesus has satisfied this impeccable justice, then His satisfaction is so perfect that the very last penny has been paid. In no wise was any sin overlooked, nor did a gracious acceptance of a part as being equivalent to the whole occur. The first proposition has been proven to be true in chapter 18, as well as earlier in this chapter, and therefore the second proposition is also true.

Secondly, the Surety who has made the atonement is infinite in His being, majesty, holiness, and righteousness. Would such a Person become a Surety and leave something undone which He neither could nor was willing to pay? Since He is infinite, His entire suffering is consistent with His nature and therefore is of infinite (that is, of perfectly sufficient) efficacy. This we have briefly demonstrated above.

Thirdly, this is also confirmed by Hebrews 10:14, "For by one offering He hath perfected for ever them that are sanctified." What has been left undone? What has been overlooked? Nothing!

The suffering of Christ is so perfectly sufficient that the notion that satisfaction by men by way of suffering (either in this life or hereafter in a fabricated purgatory) is necessary, neither can nor may be entertained.

First, satisfaction made for men by way of personal suffering is either necessary or not. If it is necessary, then Christ is not a perfect Savior, which He most certainly is. "Wherefore He is able also to save them to the uttermost that come unto God by Him" (Heb. 7:25). If such suffering is not necessary, it also is insufficient, for Scripture makes no mention of this at all, and Christ has made atonement with one sacrifice (Heb. 10:14); therefore nothing can be added to this.

Secondly, the suffering of Christ is so efficacious that it results in the complete removal of sin, complete forgiveness, and complete perfection.

(1) It completely removes all sin: "...He had by Himself purged our sins" (Heb. 1:3); "How much more shall the blood of Christ... purge your conscience from dead works to serve the living God?" (Heb. 9:14).

(2) It results in complete forgiveness: "In whom we have redemption through his blood, the forgiveness of sins" (Eph. 1:7); "...through His Name whosoever believeth in Him shall receive remission of sins" (Acts 10:43); "For I will forgive their iniquity, and I will remember their sin no more" (Jer. 31:34).

(3) It results in the complete restoration of the elect: "...so by the obedience of one shall many be made righteous" (Rom. 5:19); "...that we might be made the righteousness of God in Him" (2 Cor. 5:21). If Christ's suffering is so perfect, what remains to be added? What could be fabricated as a supplement to it?

Objection: The suffering of Christ is applied to us through our suffering, and thus it is necessary for application.

Answer: Our suffering would then not be a satisfaction, which is nowhere to be found in Scripture. Application occurs through faith (Rom. 5:1). He who maintains that Christ has merited so that we can merit ourselves, should know that Scripture makes no mention of this whatsoever, and thus this is a fabrication and invention of men. What would men have to merit if Christ has merited all that is to be merited? Man, by meriting it again would fully undo His merits. This would be tantamount to accusing God of unrighteousness, who would then demand a twofold punishment for the guilt of sin.

The suffering of Christ is so perfect that He not only made satisfaction for sins committed prior to baptism, but also for original and all other actual sins — great and small, from the most extensive sin to the least, and from sins committed from the beginning to the end of life: "The blood of Jesus Christ His Son cleanseth us from all sin" (1 John 1:7); "Who forgiveth all thine iniquities" (Psa. 103:3); "...having forgiven you all trespasses" (Col. 2:13). Which sin then remains? For which sin will man make payment? "All sin" is an all-inclusive statement.

Christ's suffering is so perfect, that He not only made satisfaction for eternal but also for temporal guilt and punishment; thus He not only has removed temporal guilt, but also temporal punishment.

First, it is contrary to justice and reason that punishment should remain after removal of guilt. *Sublata causa tollitur effectus:* If the cause is removed, the effects are removed; these two are inseparable. What benefit would be derived from deliverance of guilt if the punishment remains? If a field commander forgave a soldier his guilt, and then hanged him, what good did this forgiveness do him? Such a view makes a mockery of the satisfaction of Christ, for then He would have made satisfaction for guilt without purpose.

Secondly, Christ would then not be a perfect Savior, for there would be something for which He would not have made satisfaction.

Thirdly, it is contrary to the justice and mercy of God to punish after guilt has been removed, and this would be equivalent to punishing a perfect person who was not deserving of this.

Fourthly, Scripture states very clearly that punishment ceases upon forgiveness of guilt. "Be of good cheer; thy sins be forgiven thee. For whether is easier, to say, Thy sins be forgiven thee; or to say, Arise, and walk? But that ye may know that the Son of man hath power on earth to forgive sins, (then saith He to the sick of the palsy,) Arise, take up thy bed, and go unto thine house" (Mat. 9:2, 5-6). Here we see that the two are inseparable. To forgive sin is to say, "arise." Upon removal of sin, the punishment is removed. "For if ye forgive men their trespasses, your heavenly Father will also forgive you" (Mat. 6:14); "...forgiving one another" (Eph. 4:32). Suppose one were to acquit someone of guilt, while at the same time taking vengeance upon this person, retaliating for the evil committed. Would this be considered forgiveness? Who would not despise such a forgiveness? Therefore when God forgives sin He also removes punishment. In making satisfaction for the guilt of sin, Christ has also made satisfaction for the punishment of sin.

Objection: A murderer, converted in jail, has the forgiveness of sin, but is punished with death. Thus, the punishment remains even if guilt has been forgiven.

Answer: As far as God is concerned this is not a punishment, that is, for the making satisfaction for sin, but rather as far as men are concerned who must act according to established law. Various objections are made to this truth which need to be answered.

Objection #1: "Thou answeredst them, O LORD our God: Thou wast a God that forgavest them, though Thou tookest vengeance of their inventions" (Psa. 99:8). Behold, there was forgiveness, while yet vengeance was taken of the inventions of Moses and Aaron.

Answer: The reference concerning forgiveness and punishment here does not relate to Moses and Aaron. The word "their" refers to the people of Israel. In this psalm Moses and Aaron are presented as priests and intercessors (vs. 6). God gave testimony concerning them that they had kept His ordinances (vs. 7). They did not pray here for the forgiveness of their own sins, but God here indicates the efficacy of their intercession for Israel, as He had threatened several times to destroy Israel due to its wickedness (cf. Exo. 30:10). The *answer* was a fruit upon their prayer. To *forgive* was not to destroy Israel (as God had threatened to do), but to preserve them as His people. To nevertheless take vengeance was to visit them with plagues, not holding them entirely guiltless. God thus revealed His righteousness by causing many tribulations to come upon that people, in the majority of whom God found no pleasure. Thus, the reference here is not to the forgiveness of guilt while maintaining punishment, but to the degree in which punishment was meted out.

Additional Objection: "Thus saith the LORD, Behold, I will raise up evil against thee...the LORD also hath put away thy sin" (2 Sam. 12:11, 13). Here is an example of sin being forgiven while yet raising up evil.

Answer: This evil was not a punishment, but a chastisement.

Objection #2: "...and fill up that which is behind of the afflictions of Christ in my flesh" (Col. 1:24). Behold, here we have that which is left behind of the afflictions of Christ. Thus, Christ did not satisfy for these, but left them for others. Paul suffered and fulfilled these for the benefit of the congregation.

Answer (1) Christ has left nothing undone, but has completely finished everything as is evident from John 17:4 and John 19:30.

(2) The "afflictions of Christ" do not refer to Christ's suffering, but to the afflictions Paul had to endure as a result of preaching and confessing Christ, here referred to as the *cross of Christ* (Phil. 3:18). Paul never used the word "affliction" to refer to the suffering of Christ.

(3) The residual effects of the afflictions of Christ do not constitute a suffering of the same sort, as they are not atoning in nature. Rather, these are the tribulations which Christ had foretold would come upon them for His Name's sake, and would remain the portion of the church. Paul "filled them up," that is, he bore them on behalf of the congregation. He did not do this to make satisfaction on her behalf, for if there were something remaining for which satisfaction was to be made, then he and each member of the church would have had to do so for himself. "None of them can by any means redeem his brother, nor give to God a ransom for him" (Psa. 49:7). However, in this respect nothing had been left undone. Paul, however, suffered for the congregation in order to establish them in the truth by his steadfastness during suffering, and to exhort them also to follow his example to endure all suffering for Christ's sake. "And many of the brethren in the Lord, waxing confident by my bonds, are much more bold to speak the Word without fear" (Phil. 1:14).

Objection #3: "Break off thy sins by righteousness, and thine iniquities by shewing mercy to the poor" (Dan. 4:27).

Answer: (1) This text does not speak of suffering, and therefore is not applicable here.

(2) The reference here is to an unbelieving heathen, while the point in question relates to the temporal punishments inflicted upon believers.

(3) It is stated here that sins must be broken off, that is, they must be refrained from, and opposite virtues are to be practiced. This is therefore an exhortation to repentance rather than to pay for sin and thus satisfy for them. It thus remains certain that the suffering of Christ is efficacious, not only for the payment of guilt but also for eternal and temporal punishments.

The Extent of Christ's Satisfaction: Particular or Limited

We now must consider the third aspect of Christ's suffering: *the limitation of the satisfaction of Christ for the elect only.* Here we must do battle against *Roman Catholics, Arminians,* and *Amyraldians.* The question is not whether all men will be saved, nor whether Christ's death could have been efficient for all if He had so willed it. The question is also not whether Christ became substitute for all men, taking upon Him all their original and actual sins and thus satisfying the justice of God for them all, thereby bringing them all into a reconciled state, granting them the right and possession of eternal felicity.

Rather, the question is:

(1) Whether Christ by His suffering and death has atoned for original sin, and thus has brought the entire human race into a reconciled state.

(2) Whether Christ made satisfaction for original sin and for all actual sin committed prior to baptism, which is the view of the *Roman Catholics.*

(3) Whether it might be proposed that Christ had the salvation of men in view, to make them partakers of it — His objective being only to satisfy the justice of God in order to enable God to transact with men concerning their salvation in a manner pleasing to Him. This would then either be by way of a new covenant of works, or by grace, replacing the law with faith, so that Christ would achieve His goal even if not one person were saved. Christ would thus have died for everyone, that is, for the entire human race, and would have merited restoration in the state of grace, thus acquitting them from guilt and punishment due to original sin. This means that Christ's death would be sufficient for this, not only due to its inherent efficacy, but also due to it being sufficient indeed. Christ would thus have merited salvation, but He would not have applied all of it. Since God has determined that faith, conversion, and good works are to be the cause of man's salvation, and since man has the power to fulfil these conditions but does not do so, salvation is not applied to all men. Such are the sentiments of the *Arminians.*

(4) Whether Christ has died for all men upon condition of faith and repentance; and since man is unable to fulfil these conditions, God by a different decree has determined to grant faith and conversion to some and thus save them through Christ. These are the sentiments of the *Amyraldians.* Such is the variety of sentiments and therefore we have presented them individually.

We maintain, however, that Christ, in conformity to His Father's and His own objective, has become the Substitute only of some — the elect, and not for others. He has truly taken upon Himself as Surety all their sins (original as well as actual) which have been committed from the beginning to the end of their lives, and by His suffering has made satisfaction for both temporal and eternal guilt and punishment. He has so perfectly delivered all the elect, and them only (to the exclusion of all others), granting them in actuality the right and possession of eternal felicity, as if they themselves had perfectly satisfied the justice of God for their sins and had perfectly fulfilled all righteousness. Thus, Christ will most certainly apply to them the salvation which He has merited only for them.

We therefore reject the first propositions mentioned above as errors which reverse the very nature of the work of redemption. However, that which is comprehended in the last paragraph above we embrace as divine truth, deeming it to be full of comfort and to the glory of God. This is evidenced by the following considerations:

First, Christ has suffered as Surety, becoming the Substitute for those for whom He suffered, taking upon Himself all their sins; that is, original sin and the actual sins committed from the beginning to the very end of their lives. Thus, by His suffering and death, He satisfied the righteousness of God on their behalf, removed all temporal and eternal guilt and punishment, merited eternal life for them, and made them heirs of eternal salvation. The others do not perceive it as such; otherwise they would not promote universal redemption. They understand the suffering of Christ to have an entirely different meaning, one being of this opinion, and the other having that opinion, as we have expressed in the questions previously proposed. If, however, the suffering of Christ is to be understood in the manner we have just stated, others will readily have to admit that Christ did not make satisfaction for all men. It is, however, in harmony with divine truth that Christ's satisfaction is such. This we have clearly and lucidly demonstrated a bit earlier in this chapter. This being infallibly true, it follows that Christ did not make satisfaction and die for all men. All men, never having been in such a state of felicity, will not attain to it. They will not all be saved, but many will suffer eternal damnation, which could not be true if all guilt and punishment temporally and eternally had been atoned for and if they had been made heirs of eternal salvation by the meritorious suffering of Christ. God is just and will neither punish where guilt is absent nor refuse what has been merited.

Secondly, Christ's high-priestly office consists of sacrifice and prayer. These two elements are inseparable. It was not sufficient for the High Priest to sacrifice only, but he had to proceed into the sanctuary, and he could only enter this sanctuary with the blood of the sacrifice. This is true for the entire priestly ministry in the Old

Testament, and can also clearly be observed in the high-priestly ministry of Christ (cf. Rom. 8:34; Hebr. 7:25, 27; 9:12; 1 John 2:1-2; chapter 21 above). From this we conclude that for those whom Christ is High Priest He performs the two parts of this office: sacrifice and prayer. It is now evident that Christ excludes many — yes, the majority of men — from His intercession, limiting it to some only. "I pray for them: I pray not for the world, but for them which Thou hast given Me" (John 17:9). Consequently, His sacrifice, suffering, and death are not for all men, but are limited to those whom the Father has given Him, to the exclusion of all others in the world.

Evasive Argument: There is a twofold intercession of Christ, one being general and the other particular. This general intercession is for all men and is based upon the universal satisfaction whereby Christ prays for transgressors and for those who have crucified Him. "He...made intercession for the transgressors" (Isa. 53:12); "Father, forgive them; for they know not what they do" (Luke 23:34). His particular intercession is for believers only.

Answer: (1) It is not true that there is a twofold intercession, for then there would also have to be a twofold sacrifice, one for everyone, and another for those given by the Father. There is but one sacrifice (Heb. 10:14), and since there is but one sacrifice, there is also but one intercession.

(2) Christ's prayer is always heard and cannot be rejected. "And I knew that Thou hearest Me always" (John 11:42). His prayer for transgressors is meant for those who *were* transgressors, which is true for all the elect, but this is not true for all who *are* transgressors. He prayed for those who crucified Him, to whom He, who is always heard, also granted salvation; such was true for the murderer. It thus remains certain that if Christ limits His intercession to the one and not the other, His suffering and death are likewise limited.

Thirdly, it is also evident from the fact that the merits of Christ and their application are inseparable. It is impossible that Christ would not make those partakers of salvation for whom He had merited it, for:

(1) It was the entire objective of both the Father and Christ to bring them to salvation. "For it became Him — in bringing many sons unto glory, to make the Captain of their salvation perfect through sufferings" (Heb. 2:10); "And this is the Father's will which hath sent Me, that of all which He hath given me I should lose nothing" (John 6:39); "And for their sakes I sanctify Myself, that they also might be sanctified through the truth" (John 17:19); "Who gave himself for us, that He might redeem us" (Titus 2:14); "For Christ also hath once suffered for sins...that he might bring

us to God" (1 Pet. 3:18). Thus, the objective is obvious. Since God and Christ cannot be kept from accomplishing their objective, it is therefore certain that salvation is also applied to those for whom it is merited.

(2) The application and meriting of salvation belong together. "I lay down My life for the sheep, and I give unto them eternal life" (John 10:15, 28); "God was in Christ, reconciling the world unto Himself, not imputing their trespasses unto them" (2 Cor. 5:19); "For if, when we were enemies, we were reconciled to God by the death of His Son, much more, being reconciled, we shall be saved by His life" (Rom. 5:10). Notice how inseparably the meriting and application of salvation are joined together.

Evasive argument #1: Christ's objective was only to remove the obstacle from God's side in order to enable Him to transact with men.

Answer: (1) We adamantly deny this, and the contrary has been proven earlier.

(2) The removal of the obstacle from God's side is neither a meriting of salvation for man nor is it the application and impartation of salvation.

Evasive Argument #2: All the abovementioned texts refer to the application of what has been merited upon condition of faith.

Answer: This is not true. Believers do not obtain salvation because they believe, but because Christ has merited it for them. He applies it to them through the instrumentality of faith. Faith is a fruit of the suffering of Christ; it is not the cause of Christ's suffering for them. Christ is the cause of all blessings (Eph. 1:3), as well as of faith. He is "the author and finisher of our faith" (Heb. 12:2). Since the benefits of Christ are not applied to all men — yes, are not even offered to most men* — but are only applied to those for whom He has merited them, it follows that Christ has not died for all men, but only for those who were given to Him.

Fourthly, Scripture expressly limits the death and merits of Christ to some:

(1) "He shall save His people from their sins" (Mat. 1:21). All men, however, are not the people of Christ. "The Lord knoweth them that are His" (2 Tim. 2:19); "I know my sheep, and am known of mine" (John 10:14); "Thou hast redeemed us to God by Thy blood *out of* every kindred, and tongue, and people, and nation" (Rev. 5:9) — and thus not *all* kindreds, tongues, peoples, and nations.

(2) "I lay down My life for the sheep" (John 10:15); however, all

---

*Most men never have an opportunity to hear the gospel — Ed.

men are not Jesus' sheep. "But ye believe not, because ye are not of My sheep" (John 10:26).

(3) "Jesus should die for that nation, and not for that nation only, but that also He should gather together in one the children of God that were scattered abroad" (John 11:51-52). All men are not God's children, however, for many are children of Belial, cursed children.

(4) "Christ also loved the church, and gave Himself for it" (Eph. 5:25). All men do not belong to His church. "And the Lord added to the church daily such as should be saved" (Acts 2:47).

(5) "I pray...for them which Thou hast given Me" (John 17:9). However, all have not been given to Christ, for those who are given to Him are contrasted with the world. He prayed not for the world, but for those who were given to Him.

Evasive Argument #1: These texts make mention of application, and it is true that this does not occur to all; however, they make no mention of the meriting of salvation.

Answer: 1) As we have stated above, Scripture knows of no such distinction. 2) These texts clearly also make mention of the meriting of salvation. They make reference to "laying down His life," "dying," and "giving Himself."

Evasive Argument #2: It is not stated that it is *only* for them. These texts include them, but do not exclude others.

Answer: All others are excluded, as we have demonstrated with each text by way of contrast.

Objections Answered Relative to the Word "All"

Objection #1: Scripture states that Christ has died for all. For example: "Therefore as by the offence of one *judgment came upon all men* to condemnation; even so by the righteousness of one *the free gift came* upon all men unto justification of life" (Rom. 5:18).

Answer: The limitation is clearly stated in the text, since it refers to *all who have been made partakers of this justification unto life.* However, all do not become partakers of the justification unto life, but only the elect. Thus, "all" must not be understood as referring to all men, but only to the elect. Adam is designated as the source of the misery of all who are comprehended in him as all men were comprehended in him, and have fallen in him. In contrast, Christ is presented as the cause of grace for all who are in Him, and all they — and only they — are in Him; that is, all who become partakers of justification unto life.

Additional Objection: "Because we thus judge, that if one died for all, then were all dead: and that He died for all, that they which live should not henceforth live unto themselves, but unto Him which died for them, and rose again" (2 Cor. 5:14b-15).

Answer: It is not stated as "all men." The word "all" refers to all those of whom is spoken here. The reference is clearly to *all who have died to sin, and who are alive through regeneration.* All men have not died to sin, however, and are not partakers of spiritual life. Christ therefore did not die for all men, but for all who, through Christ's death, have died to sin and by virtue of His resurrection have received spiritual life. They are exhorted to manifest this death and this life to the honor of Christ.

Additional Objection: "For as in Adam all die, even so in Christ shall all be made alive" (1 Cor. 15:22).

Answer (1) The text says the opposite of what many have in view here, for it is certain that all men are not made alive in Christ, nor will be made alive in Him. Mention is here made of all who are made alive in Christ, to the exclusion of all others. The text, however, does not speak of Christ's satisfaction, but of the elect being made alive. Here two heads, Adam and Christ, are contrasted, along with the consequences of this. Adam brought death upon all who are in him, and Christ has given life unto all who are in Him.

(2) He speaks of all those to whom he writes, generally addressing them with the pronouns "we" and "our." These are "the church of God which is at Corinth, with all the saints which are in all Achaia" (2 Cor. 1:11). This therefore does not pertain to all men in the world, but is limited to those mentioned.

Additional Objection: "God hath concluded them all in unbelief, that He might have mercy upon all" (Rom. 11:32).

Answer: This text speaks of the hardening and the conversion of the Jews, which is indicated throughout the entire chapter. Thus, this text neither speaks of the satisfaction of Christ, nor of all men upon the face of the earth.

Additional Objection: "Who will have all men to be saved, and to come unto the knowledge of the truth. For there is one God, and one Mediator between God and men, the man Christ Jesus, who gave Himself a ransom for all" (1 Tim. 2:4-6).

Answer: The text itself indicates that the word "all" does not refer to all men, head for head, but refers only to the elect from all nations, and all social ranks.

(1) It is impossible to pray for every man, head for head, for one need not pray for someone who has sinned against the Holy Ghost (1 John 5:16), knowing that God will not be merciful to them. Christ did not pray for all (John 17:9), nor did Paul (cf. 2 Tim. 4:14; Gal. 5:12).

(2) The mention of kings and those who are placed in authority confirms that "all" means "various" (cf. Mat. 4:23; Luke 11:42; Eph. 1:3; 1 Cor. 10:25). It is the apostle's wish that as far as someone's salvation is concerned we ought not to entertain any prejudice.

(3) The text does say that God will have all men to be saved. If, however, all men are to be understood by this, then all of necessity should also be saved, for no one can resist God's will as He always accomplishes it and no one is able to resist His hand. If one maintains that God wills when men are willing, we reply that this is not written anywhere, for salvation does not originate in the exercise of man's will. God knew indeed that only a small minority would be willing, and thus it is not possible that He willed the salvation of all.

(4) The apostle joins together salvation and the knowledge of the truth, and experience teaches that God is not willing that all men should come to the knowledge of the truth, for it is not revealed to all.

(5) Christ gave Himself as a ransom ἀντίλυτρον (*antilutron*), that is, to put Himself in the place of another, to pay the debt, to bear the punishment, to set others free, and to make them partakers of this freedom. Christ, however, does not do this for all men, but only for those who believe in Him. From this it is evident that the word "all" does not refer to all men, head for head, but only to believers from every nation and every social rank.

Objections Answered Relative to the Use of "World" in Scripture

Objection #2: To contradict the truth presented above, also such texts are produced in which Christ is said to have suffered *for the world*. "For God so loved the world, that He gave His only begotten Son, that whosoever believeth in Him should not perish, but have everlasting life" (John 3:16).

Answer: It is not stated here that Christ died for the world nor that God has loved all men in the world, but that He loved the world. Love for the world is the same as love for humanity (cf. Titus 3:4). He did not manifest His love to the angels who sinned, but to the human race, so that love for the world is not love for every single person in the world, but a love for men in general. God has manifested this love in the giving of His Son, which, however, is not to the benefit of all, it being restricted to believers only. This does not imply that the Son would only remove the obstacle from God's side and thus translate the entire human race into a state of reconciliation without making them partakers of salvation. Rather Christ delivers believers from condemnation and gives them *eternal life* (John 3:17). It is stated "to save the world." This does not only imply a meriting of salvation — which those who use this text for rebuttal wish to maintain — but also its application and impartation. It is undeniably true, however, that this does not occur with every single person, but is only true for believers, as is stated in the text. Therefore the word "world" refers to the human race in general, and not to each person in particular. There also is no mention of the meriting of salvation, but of the application and impartation of eternal salvation. Only believers are partakers of this and no one else.

Additional objection: "...which I will give for the life of the world" (John 6:51).

Answer: I repeat that the word "world" refers to the human race. This is in contrast to the fallen angels, as Scripture itself makes this contradistinction, albeit in a different context. "For verily He took not on Him the nature of angels; but He took on Him the seed of Abraham" (Heb. 2:16). Whatever is said of the world in general may not be applied to every individual person. The first world perished in the flood (Luke 17:27). This is not applicable to every person, for Noah and his family remained alive. This is frequently to be observed in other texts of Scripture as well; as is in this text, for Christ gives life to the world, according to Luke 17:33. He does not, however, give spiritual life to every person but only to His elect. It should be very clear that the reference here is not to the meriting of salvation, but to the application of the merits of Christ. No one will propose that this is true for all men, for experience demonstrates the contrary.

Additional Objection: "God was in Christ, reconciling the world unto Himself, not imputing their trespasses unto them" (2 Cor. 5:19).

Answer: The "world" refers to the human race. From a general truth one may not make a deduction for each individual situation, for then we would have to reason as follows: The first world perished, the flood eliminated all men, and thus also Noah and his family. The world has not known Christ (John 1:10) and thus this would also be true for believers. The world hates Christ (John 7:7), and if this excludes no one, this would also be true for the converted who, however, love Christ. The old serpent deceives the entire world (Rev. 12:9) and thus also the elect. The whole world lies in wickedness (1 John 5:19) and thus also the saints without exception, for it is stated to be true for the whole world. Who cannot perceive that these deductions are flawed? Thus we can see that whatever is said of the world in general is not applicable to every individual person. Sometimes evil is pronounced upon the world, which is only applicable to those who are evil; at times something good is said of the world, which is applicable to another group. Therefore, when the word "world" is used, one may not conclude from this word that this is true for every person, but from the context it must be deduced who are to be understood. The text here conveys that "world" must be understood of those who are reconciled with God, whose trespasses are not imputed to them. It is clear that the wrath of God abides upon the disobedient, indicating that this wrath was never removed, that all men are not in a state wherein their sins are forgiven, not being imputed to them — which is to be blessed indeed (Psa. 32:1-2). Thus, it is obvious that the word "world" is not inclusive of every person without exception, but only refers to those whose transgressions have not been imputed to them. This text demonstrates at once that "reconciliation" and "not imputing transgressions" are parallel concepts. Since all do not experience the application of salvation, all also do not experience reconciliation.

Additional Objection: "And He is the propitiation for our sins: and not for ours only, but also for the sins of the whole world" (1 John 2:2).

Answer: (1) One may no less make the deduction that the phrase, "the whole world," is applicable to every individual person than we may from the word "world," for of the first world it is written that the flood destroyed all its inhabitants (Luke 17:27). It is also written that the devil deceived the whole world (Rev. 12:9), and that the whole world lies in wickedness (1 John 5:19).

(2) The words "not ... only, but" indicate that there is a contrast between *Jews* (which John and the believers of that nation were), and *Gentiles,* who by way of contrast are referred to as *world,* not only here but also in Romans 11:12, 15. As one may not conclude that the word "world," being a general reference to the human race, refers to every individual person, one may also not do so in this contrast. Sometimes this refers to the ungodly, and at other times to the godly in a given nation, which is evident from Romans 11:12, 15, "Now if the fall of them be the riches of the world ... for if the casting away of them be the reconciling of the world ..." Not every Gentile will be the recipient of the spiritual riches of Christ as a result of the fall of the Jews, nor will every Gentile without exception receive reconciliation, but only the converted, that is, the believers among the heathen. Everyone will have to admit to this. If therefore it is written that Christ is the propitiation of the sins of the whole world, one cannot understand this to refer to every individual person, but only to believers among the Gentiles.

(3) John here joins the two elements of Christ's high priestly office: He is an Advocate and a propitiation. We have demonstrated above that these two cannot be separated, and that for those for whom He is the one, He is also the other. Since Christ does not intercede for the reprobate world (John 17:9), He is also not the propitiation for them, but only for the elect world which receives reconciliation by virtue of the fall of the Jews. It is thus evident that Christ did not die for each individual person in the world.

Texts Examined Which Seem to Imply that
Christ has Redeemed All Men

Objection #3: As a rebuttal against the truth presented above, men produce those texts in which it is stated that Christ has also sanctified and purchased ungodly men, such as in Hebrews 10:29, "who hath trodden under foot the Son of God, and hath counted the blood of the covenant, wherewith he was sanctified, an unholy thing, and hath done despite unto the Spirit of grace."

Answer: This text does not speak of Christ's death for all men, for all men do not come to that state which is described here. Even if Christ were to have died for some ungodly men (which is not the case), one could not yet conclude that Christ died for all the ungodly. Mention is not made here of reconciliation by the death of Christ. The word "sanctified" refers to an actual state, so the reference here would be to application and not to the meriting of salvation, which is the point of contention. The phrase, "to be sanctified," does not refer here to a change of heart by regeneration, but to a separation from the common populace by virtue of being called to the fellowship of the church. The verb, "to sanctify," frequently makes reference to being set apart for a holy purpose, as is stated concerning all ceremonial objects and the people of Israel. "For thou art an holy people...the LORD thy God hath chosen thee to be a special people unto Himself, above all people" (Deu. 7:6). Thus, to sanctify means "to set apart"; "...the accomplishment of the days of purification" (Acts 21:26). We deny emphatically that "to sanctify" here refers to a holy state of the heart, but maintain that it refers to being set apart from the general populace in order to be included in the fellowship of the church. True saints cannot fall away, which we will prove at the appropriate place. If one were to suggest that this sanctification occurred by virtue of the death of Christ, I reply that by virtue of His death Christ has received power over everything in heaven and upon earth, that He might use it to bring about the salvation of the elect. Thus, the death of Christ also has objectives other than reconciliation only.

Additional Objection: "...even denying the Lord that bought them" (2 Pet. 2:1). Here we perceive that even deniers of the truth are bought by the Lord Jesus.

Answer: This text does not speak of all men, for all do not come into such a situation. The word "buy" does not afford any proof that there is a universal redemption by virtue of Christ's death, for one may buy things for various purposes. One buys vessels for contemptible purposes and also to be used as ornaments. One can buy slaves in order to set them free or to perform the most menial task. One can also buy donkeys to bear burdens. In like manner, these false prophets were bought by the Lord, who here is not called Κυριος (*Kurios*), that is, Lord or Master, but δεσπότης (*despotes*), that is, Master of the house. They were called to perform a task in His house, that is, to be teachers in His church, which was an office they abused and thus became false prophets. By virtue of His death the Lord Jesus has received a claim upon everything and has been appointed heir of all things (Heb. 1:2). The Lord has subdued all things under His feet (1 Cor. 15:28) and at His Name all knees must bow (Phil. 2:10). Thus, also these teachers were under His jurisdiction. He bought them in order to use them to the benefit of the elect, buying them, however, as slaves or donkeys, but not to be His children.

Rebuttal to the Argument that All Men are Commanded to Believe in Christ, and thus Christ Died for All

Objection #4: In an effort to rebut the truth presented above, one will also use this syllogism: Whatever one is obligated to believe is true. Since all men are obligated to believe that Christ died for them, such is of necessity true.

Answer: The first proposition is correct, for faith has nothing but truth as its object; however, the second proposition is nothing but untruth, for:

(1) The gospel is neither proclaimed to the majority of men, nor have they ever heard a word about Christ, and therefore they are not guilty of the sin of not believing in Christ.

(2) All who are called are not obligated to believe that Christ has died for them. The contrary is true. They must believe that as long as they remain unconverted, they are outside of Christ.

(3) It is true, however, that all who are called must receive Christ by faith, and refusing to do so, they will make their condemnation all the heavier. It is one thing to believe in Christ, that is, receive

Christ unto justification and sanctification, and another thing to believe that Christ is my Savior and has died for me. To this end one must perceive the evidences of truly having received Christ, and of being truly converted.

The Second Element of Christ's Humiliation: His Active Obedience

Thus far we have discussed the first aspect of Christ's humiliation, being the suffering of the Lord Jesus Christ whereby He completely satisfied for the sins of the elect. The second aspect of His humiliation consists of subjecting Himself under the law. This raises the following question: *Is the active and actual obedience of Christ, that is, His subjection under the law and the perfect accomplishment thereof, imputed to the elect unto justification and salvation?* We answer in the affirmative. The active obedience of Christ in subjecting Himself under, and fulfilling, the law is not only a necessary requisite for Him who would be Mediator (all of which is true for Christ), but this active righteousness of Christ is a part of His satisfaction for His own. As He delivered them from all guilt and punishment by His passion, by His active obedience, fulfilling the law on their behalf, He has also merited a right unto eternal life for them. These two aspects coalesce in Christ and neither may nor can be separated from each other. Christ has merited salvation atoningly and has made atonement meritoriously. Likewise the elect, in being delivered from guilt and punishment, receive a right to eternal life, and in receiving that right are delivered from guilt and punishment. Nevertheless these two aspects of His humiliation — the atonement for guilt and punishment, and the meriting of eternal life — are not identical, but essentially differ from each other. The active and passive obedience of Christ are equally beneficial to the elect.

This is first of all evident from the necessity that the Surety had to subject Himself to the law on behalf of sinners to perfectly fulfil the law on their behalf. This has been demonstrated previously. Since this was required of the Surety, Christ has performed it in order to perfectly execute His Suretyship.

Secondly, we read in Romans 5:19, "For as by one man's disobedience (that is, Adam's) many were made sinners, so by the obedience of one (that is, Christ) shall many be made righteous." The law demands perfect conformity to itself. A man's transgression of the law results in nonconformity to the law, even if by the bearing of punishment he is free from guilt. One can only be conformed to the law by fulfilling its demands — by perfect internal and external holiness. The law does not demand *either* punishment or holiness, but *both*. Therefore by removal of guilt the Surety cannot make anyone righteous unless the law has also actually been fulfilled. "He that doeth righteousness is righteous" (1 John 3:7). Since Christ makes His elect *righteous*, He of necessity must subject Himself to the law on their behalf, fulfilling it in *obedience*. Thus, by His obedience He makes His elect righteous.

Thirdly, we read in Romans 8:3-4, "For what the law could not do, in that it was weak through the flesh, God sending His own Son in the likeness of sinful flesh, and for sin, condemned sin in the flesh, that the righteousness of the law might be fulfilled in us." The law was weak, not in and of itself since it is and remains a perfect rule, but due to sin. The law was weak, not to sentence the transgressor to punishment, which it is always authorized to do, but to justify the sinner and to declare him an heir of eternal life, which had been promised upon perfect obedience. "The man which doeth those things shall live by them" (Rom. 10:5). The demand of the law was not to bear punishment upon transgression, but obedience to it. Whereas Christ fulfilled the demand of the law for us, He did not do so by the suffering by which He made satisfaction for the threat of the law, but by subjecting Himself to the law, performing it on behalf of God's children. This is stated by the apostle in Galatians 4:4, "God sent forth His Son, made of a woman, made under the law."

Fourthly, Christ's righteousness is imputed to His elect and He clothes them with it; thus in Him they are perfect and are the righteousness of God. Observe this in the following texts: "But now the righteousness of God without the law (that is, the righteousness of Christ) is manifested, being witnessed (that is, being approved of) by the law and the prophets" (Rom. 3:21); "...not having mine own righteousness, which is of the law, but that which is through the faith of Christ, the righteousness which is of God by faith" (Phil. 3:9); "And ye are complete in Him" (Col. 2:10); "...that we might be made the righteousness of God in Him" (2 Cor. 5:21); "He hath covered me with the robe of righteousness" (Isa. 61:10). Suffering is not righteousness. Christ's suffering was not His righteousness (that is, when considering the definition of suffering), but His righteousness is His perfect fulfillment and performance of the law. If therefore Christ's righteousness is imputed to us and we are the righteousness of God in Him, then His being subject to and His performance of the law is imputed to us.

Objection #1: Christ was obligated to be subject to and perform the law on His own behalf, since He, according to His human nature, was a rational creature. Whatever one is personally obligated to do cannot be done on behalf of another. Therefore the righteousness of Christ cannot be our righteousness.

Answer: (1) Whatever Christ was, He was on behalf of His elect. If it had not been on behalf of His elect, He would not have become man. He has become man on behalf of His elect: "For unto us a Child is born, unto us a Son is given" (Isa. 9:6). Consequently all was to the benefit of His children; that is, whatever He was, whatever He suffered, and whatever He performed.

(2) Every human person is *subject to the law* by and for himself, and is obligated to fulfill it. However, Christ's personhood is not human but divine, and thus He was not subject to the law on His own behalf; He was above the law. As Surety, however, this divine Person, which was above the law, subjected Himself under the law according to His human nature, and thus His righteousness is ours.

Objection #2: Salvation has been merited by Christ's suffering (1 Pet. 3:18). Therefore He did not merit the right to eternal life for His elect by His active obedience.

Answer: (1) We have stated above that these two cannot be separated from each other, and that both are essential. When the one aspect is mentioned, the other is not excluded but included.

(2) "To bring to God" is equivalent to being "reconciled with God."

Objection #3: If Christ has fulfilled the law for His elect, they are relieved from the obligation to obey the law, as well as of the bearing of punishment. Thus, their transgressions can no longer be viewed as sin.

Answer: (1) It is true that they are not obligated to the law as a condition of the covenant of works in order to thus obtain a right to eternal life. There is another relationship and another purpose which obliges them to obey the law of love. Obedience to the law is their life, joy, and felicity. Even if they were not obligated to it, it would be their desire; their whole heart would yearn to keep the law, for the demand of the law is perfect love.

(2) Their transgressions must still be viewed as sin, and as such are worthy of eternal death. However, satisfaction has already been made for them by Christ.

We have thus considered the humiliation of Christ from every perspective.

Exhortation to Meditate Believingly upon, and to Make Improvement of the Suffering of Christ

As necessary as it is to know the truth and perfection of Christ's satisfaction in the state of His humiliation, as well as its restriction to God's children only, so beneficial and soul-stirring it is also to make application of it by faith. To consider this truth by way of holy meditation, to persevere in obtaining a proper frame of heart, and to grow by virtue of this frame, are exercises which are hidden for many, even for believers. Truly if a person had more faith to clearly perceive these truths and were to be more occupied with a quiet and sweet meditation upon the suffering of Christ, the severity of that suffering would be better perceived. He would have a deeper insight into the abominable nature of sin and the sublime nature of God's righteousness. He would rejoice more in the truth and perfection of the satisfaction accomplished by that suffering. He would love Christ more, hate sin more, have a heart more steadfast in the practice of godliness, and proceed with more courage, comfort, and peace. Therefore actively and increasingly engage yourselves in these considerations.

(1) This is even the work of angels, who for this reason were positioned with their faces towards the mercy seat in the temple. Of them Peter says, "...which things the angels desire to look into" (1 Pet. 1:12). If angels do this and find felicity in so doing, we ought to do so all the more.

(2) Such observance was depicted in the erection of the brazen serpent in the wilderness, the observance of which healed those who were bitten by the serpents. This practice has also been prophesied. "And I will pour upon the house of David, and upon the inhabitants of Jerusalem, the Spirit of grace and of supplications: and they shall look upon Me whom they have pierced, and they shall mourn for Him" (Zec. 12:10). Such examples and prophecies which have preceded us ought to readily stir us up to be engaged in this practice.

(3) This has been the practice of the godly. The bride of Christ says, "A bundle of myrrh is my wellbeloved unto me; He shall lie all night betwixt my breasts" (Song of Sol. 1:13). What else is this bundle of myrrh but the suffering of Christ, which is bitter but wholesome, protects against corruption, refreshes, strengthens, and is of a sweet savor? The bride not only carried this by day between her breasts as an ornamental bouquet, but even by night it lay upon her heart. In meditating upon this, she would fall asleep; and upon awaking, she would still be occupied with this. The prophets were likewise engaged, "Searching what, or what manner of time the Spirit of Christ which was in them did signify, when it testified beforehand the sufferings of Christ, and the glory that should follow" (1 Pet. 1:11). Paul frequently engaged in such meditation. "That I may know Him, and the power of His resurrection, and the fellowship of His sufferings, being made conformable

unto His death" (Phil. 3:10). The frequency with which the godly have occupied themselves with this (not only at the beginning of the New Testament dispensation but also since the Reformation), is confirmed by their writings. If they fared so well in doing so, if it was a blessed practice which became increasingly sweet and precious, how this ought to stir us up to exercise ourselves in such meditations, for this sweetness will not be tasted without some diligence.

(4) It is a most advantageous exercise. By way of reading and hearing one will readily understand and retain the history itself, but the efficacy and warmth of this history will only be experienced by much meditation, and by applying it.

In doing so we will, first of all, extract the most excellent instruction:

(1) Only then will one truly learn the horrendous nature of sin. Then one will neither focus on sinful deeds alone, nor view sin from a natural perspective, but everyone will perceive the abominableness, filthiness, and hatefulness to be found in every sin, viewing it as it is: an act of denial of God, contempt towards God, and desertion of God. Thus man, due to his sinfulness, will abhor himself and be ashamed that he is such a horrible, hateful, and intolerable creature.

(2) You will thus perceive the essential holiness of God's justice, who can only forgive sin by punishing it fully in the Surety. In doing so you will not only perceive that you cannot entertain a quiet hope upon your supplication for forgiveness — as if that might be acceptable with God (an argument by which thousands deceive themselves, and subsequently perish) — but out of love for the justice of God you will desire to be saved only on the basis of the satisfaction of divine justice.

(3) You will thus perceive the infinity and unsearchableness of God's love, mercy, wisdom, and power, so that in the satisfaction of Christ you will detect much more than deliverance from guilt and punishment, but the soul will find wonderful delight in adoring the perfections of God and will be sweetly stirred up in love, praise, and thanksgiving.

Secondly, meditation upon Christ's suffering will yield strong consolations:

(1) You will perceive the perfect satisfaction of divine justice and how perfect the sinner is before God in Christ in spite of the fact that he remains sinful in himself.

(2) You will perceive how certainly and truly salvation has been merited, how certainly a beneficiary of this suffering is appointed an heir of eternal life, and how infallibly sure it is that he will become a partaker of it.

(3) In meditating upon His suffering you will find peace of conscience in God and free access to the Father.

(4) When considering His passion, all the suffering of this life becomes light and one perceives that "our light affliction, which is but for a moment, worketh for us a far more exceeding and eternal weight of glory" (2 Cor. 4:17). Thus, the soul may find eternal comfort in all this.

Thirdly, meditation upon Christ's suffering will yield heavenly instruction and direction:

(1) Here is an example of how we must die to the world and sin. "Therefore we are buried with Him by baptism into death: that like as Christ was raised up from the dead by the glory of the Father, even so we also should walk in newness of life" (Rom. 6:4).

(2) It yields the most powerful motives to mortify sin and live holily. To perceive that Jesus underwent such bitter suffering out of love for us will quicken our love for Him, causing us to hate and flee sin and to walk in a manner pleasing to Him.

(3) Yes, you will become aware that meditation upon His sufferings will presently yield strength and fortitude to mortify sin. Thus, here we have the fountain of true spiritual life, of true progress, and of the exercise of virtue, all of which will have the proper form and nature of spirituality.

(4) Such meditation will strengthen us in a wonderful way, if and when Christ calls us to suffer and to be martyrs for His Name and cause. Therefore, you who bear the name of Christian and desire to be true Christians indeed, engage frequently in meditating upon the humiliation of Christ, for there is much more to be found in it than you are aware of.

Come, children of God, meditate upon the suffering Jesus. Do not do so by viewing it as merely a history, nor as the suffering of a martyr, but as the suffering of your Surety who took your place and paid for your sins.

First, meditate attentively upon the Person who suffered. He was not a wicked, insignificant, and contemptible man, nor merely a martyr whose death is precious in God's sight and is held in great esteem by the godly.

(1) Rather, this person is God and man, who is over all, God blessed forever, very God, and the Lord of glory. He, in order that He would be able to suffer and die, assumed our human nature from a human being within the context of His Personhood, and became like unto us, sin excepted. This is a miracle in the highest sense of the word, exceeding the creation of heaven and earth. Pause and reflect upon this until the greatness and magnificence

of this Person may become evident to your heart, and you in all humility acknowledge Him as such. Then adoration will ravish your soul and you will exclaim, "Has *such* a Person suffered and made atonement?"

(2) Consider Him also in His relationship towards you, and you in your relationship towards Him. Believers, do you not know Him? He it is who appeared to you when you were dead, blind, and immersed in sin and darkness. He illuminated you with His light, made you alive, and still continually draws you to Himself, causing you to look, long, cry out, and wait for Him. He it is who supports you as you stumble along, who secretly supports you in your cross-bearing, gives you courage, strengthens you, and gives you hope. He it is who at times revealed Himself to you, who at times kissed you with the kisses of His mouth, and caused you to feel His love. He it is who has said to you, "Thy sins are forgiven thee." He it is towards whom all your desire is, your Lord, your Head, your Bridegroom. It is He who out of love — I repeat, out of love — took your place as Surety, who took all your sins from you and took them upon Himself, taking them upon His account. He has received the stripes which you deserved, and the chastisement of your peace was upon Him. Reflect upon this and may your love be stirred up in the acknowledgement of His love for you. Hear your Beloved as it were speak to you, "My friend, I love you so dearly. Consider the evidence of My love. I suffered to make atonement for your sins. This suffering which is so bitter and so heavy a burden to bear caused Me to be covered with blood from head to toe; as well as the fact that I was so distressed within due to God's wrath pressing me down — all of this I suffered willingly. I would rather suffer all this thousands of times than to see you go lost and tolerate the thought that you would not be with Me in eternal glory." Would this not soften your heart and generate love in return? Would this not cause you to melt sweetly in tears of love? The acknowledgement that Jesus is so lofty a Person, who yet is so near to you and who does all this out of love for you, will stir within and render your meditation upon the suffering of Christ efficacious. Do not remain in your unbelief, nor give in to it, for this will render your meditation fruitless. Lift yourself up in faith and behold the suffering Jesus making atonement from such a perspective. It will certainly cause you to rejoice and cause your heart to be warm with love.

Secondly, who are you for whom Christ has suffered all this? In yourself you are nothing but sin within and without, and therefore your nature is so hateful, abominable, intolerable, and damnable.

What incompatibility there is between Jesus and you! Sink away in your wretched condition and acknowledge yourself to be unworthy that anyone, let alone God and the Son of God would look after you and think upon you. Above all, consider that everything is to be found in you which would cause the Lord Jesus to be repulsed by you and refrain from doing good to you. Focus on your wretched condition until you perceive yourself to be entirely as we have just described you to be, and then betake yourself in faith to the Lord Jesus. Be humbled, but be not unbelieving, by this view which passes all understanding; namely, that Jesus should love you, and that He would love you to such an extent that out of love for you He would suffer and die. Believe, however, that such is the case, and confess, "This is the LORD's doing; and it is marvelous in my eyes."

Yes, proceed further, and consider the small number of men for whom the Lord Jesus has become Surety, in comparison to the great multitude of men whom He neither loves nor looks upon, and for whom He was not willing to be a Surety. Then consider, "Why me? Why me in comparison to others — who am the most despicable, evil, foolish and intolerable sinner of them all? Why does the Lord love me out of so many thousands? Why do I belong to those few, to the elect? Why is Jesus my Surety? Why does Jesus love me with an everlasting love, considering that so many millions go to hell? Why, why do I belong to the favored ones who are led to heaven? This is too great, too high for me! Here I must stand still until, in the state of perfection, I shall be able to comprehend more, be more capable of adoration, and be more able to love in return and to give thanks. Since you give evidence of possessing the principal fruits of grace, beware that the greatness of this matter and your own insignificance do not draw you away towards unbelief. This would offend the love of God, and exalt man too highly, as if his lovableness was the primary cause of the love of God. This would turn the entire work of grace upside down and would prevent Him from receiving the praise for His magnificent grace. Therefore, remain steadfast in the faith.

Thirdly, in this frame proceed from the cradle to the cross; focus upon every aspect of suffering particularly and reflect upon them. Christ's suffering has not been described for us in such detail without reason. It should therefore not weary us to consider it from step to step. Each element of His suffering contains something special; each element reveals a particular sin, a particular punishment consistent with this sin, and its removal. This will cause you to perceive the comprehensive nature of His suffering, that your sins are the cause, and that with your sins you have brought this suffering upon Him. There would not have been a need for Jesus' suffering if you had not sinned. Oh, how sweet it is to be sensibly ashamed over our sins as being the cause of Christ's suffering and to say, "Oh dear Jesus, it grieves me that I have been the cause of Thy suffering. Why do I not rather suffer myself? If it were possible, and if I could prevail in it, I could not tolerate that Thou wouldest thus have to suffer for me; I would bear the punishment myself. I can neither endure nor prevail in it, however, and would have to endure it eternally. I therefore acknowledge Thy love and value Thy grief. I truly rejoice that Thou hast taken my place, hast satisfied for my sins, and hast merited eternal life for me. To all eternity I desire to acknowledge this, and to love and thank Thee."

It is remarkable that one is so seldom moved and stirred within about the suffering of Christ. Everyone is conscious of this within himself and complains over the hardness of his heart. Do you ask what the cause of this is? I answer:

(1) In some it is due to ignorance, they having only general thoughts about the fact that Christ died for sin. They are neither acquainted with the dreadfulness of sin, nor with the severity of God's wrath, and therefore cannot properly value His suffering.

(2) In some this is due to familiarity, they having heard this so frequently, and therefore inner workings concerning this have disappeared.

(3) In some this is due to a lack of familiarity, as they are not accustomed to focus upon this suffering.

(4) In some this is due to unbelief — not historical unbelief, but at least unbelief due to lack of application. Since it is not for them, they have neither desire nor interest within their heart to consider this matter, or to make an effort to reflect upon it.

(5) It is due to a lack of spirituality, laziness, and a disparaging of this suffering. Be ashamed of this and be diligent, for the more you engage in such reflection, the easier and sweeter this practice will be to you.

Fourthly, while persevering in this frame, consider the suffering of Christ to your comfort by applying the same as a remedy against guilt, as well as for occasions when you must suffer in likeness to Him.

Believing Reflection upon the Suffering of Christ:
A Remedy Against Guilt

(1) Consider it as a remedy *against guilt*. If the soul finds itself beset with great and small sins, sins against God and against his

neighbor, sins against every commandment, sins that press down heavily as a burden too heavy to bear; and if the soul becomes aware that God hides His countenance, that the way of approach to Him is closed, feeling the wrath of God, having a terrified conscience, and being fearful of yet going lost — then the soul must especially strive not to yield to this ill frame. This would be injurious. Rather, engage yourself in meditating upon the suffering of Christ. Consciously consider the truth of Christ's satisfaction on behalf of the sinner, the perfection of this satisfaction for great, small, and multiple sins — yes, for all original and actual sins, which have been committed by us from our first moment until the time of our death. Meditate long upon this until you perceive from God's Word that this is truth, and until this may become truth within and you may be fully assured that Christ as Surety has made a perfect satisfaction.

Consider how unspeakably happy a man is for whom Christ has made satisfaction. There is not one sin in him which is not atoned for, and therefore God is the reconciled Father of such a sinner and he most certainly is an heir of eternal life. He will indeed become a partaker of this, be the way along which he is led to it ever so dark and undesirable. Having come to a general conclusion that this is an infallible divine truth, then turn to yourself and consider whether the Lord has wrought grace in the least degree in you. Consider whether your soul has not found, or still finds, itself under conviction of sin, damnation, and impotence; whether the Lord has not given you a different heart than before, so that you now love what you hated before, and hate what you loved before; whether the world and sin cause you sorrow rather than joy; whether a living afar from God now causes you bitter grief, and it would be all your desire to walk in the light of God's countenance in truth, uprightness, obedience, and with singularity of heart. Consider whether you do not know Jesus as Surety, yearning, desiring, praying, and crying out for Him; whether you have not frequently presented yourself to Him, surrendering to Him to be both justified and sanctified; whether you have not frequently received Him as Surety, to be reconciled to God by the ransom of His suffering and death. Consider whether it is now your desire and objective not to live in sin and in the world, but rather a life pleasing to God; and whether the Lord upon your frequent seeking, praying, supplicating, believing, and surrendering yourself to Him has not at times granted peace, quietness, and hope in your soul, or also at times granted you assurance and joy.

In considering all this together, this ought not only to cause you to conclude that Christ is your Surety, since such graces are only wrought in those who are partakers of the suffering and death of Christ, but this must also cause you to apply the suffering of Christ. For it is my objective to apply this truth to your soul, so you might view this suffering as atoning for you, as having been suffered in your stead; and that therefore your sins have been fully paid for, God is satisfied with you, and you are designated as a child and heir of God. Unto this end the wrestling of faith is necessary; that is, the actual receiving and true believing until the soul can say in faith, "Who loved me, and gave Himself for me" (Gal. 2:20). Then you will properly value the suffering of Christ and glorify the Father and the Son. Therefore be engaged in such reflection and rest not until you can rejoice in it.

Believing Reflection upon the Suffering of Christ: A Comfort when We Must Suffer in Likeness to Him

(2) Reflect upon the suffering of Christ in order that you may be comforted when suffering in likeness to Him. I need not convince you that a similar suffering according to soul and body will be your portion in this world. You are sufficiently aware of this by experience, and perhaps you are currently tasting it. You will frequently have to experience the bitterness of sin, God's displeasure concerning it, the hiding of God's countenance, an unrestrained and troubled conscience, fear for death, distress pertaining to damnation, the assaults of Satan, poverty, contempt and scorn (which will either be your fault or in response to godliness and the name of Christ), and oppression for the sake of the Word, even though you may not perceive it as such. You may possibly also be called to martyrdom and thus seal the truth with your blood. You may also be called to suffer physical pain and sorrow, albeit the one more and the other less — yes, all manner of Christ's sufferings.

Believers, you may, however, not view this suffering as a manifestation of God's wrath towards you, for Christ has made satisfaction for all guilt and punishment. God is just and does not require punishment for sin twice. The Surety has made satisfaction and therefore you are free. They are not punishments in the true sense of the word nor manifestations of wrath towards the believer. The sting and the curse have been removed from them. They are fatherly chastisements upon you which proceed from love and are for your welfare. It is the way which the Lord has ordained to lead His children to heaven. Therefore in all your tribulations fix your eye upon the suffering of Jesus Christ and apply this to yourself by a living faith until you have the lively assurance that He has removed guilt and curse from you, and that these sorrows are assigned to you in love. Remain near this suffering Jesus, and let it suffice you that you are conformed to your Lord. Take up your cross and follow Him; He has compassion upon you, will support you, and will time and again deliver you. Keep your eye fixed upon future felicity and look away from this world, for this is not the land of your rest. Rejoice in the hope of glory. "Humble yourselves therefore under the mighty hand of God, that He may exalt you in due time" (1 Pet. 5:6); "Wait on the LORD: be of good courage, and He shall strengthen thine heart: wait, I say, on the LORD" (Psa. 27:14).

Christ's Suffering: An Example to Be Followed by the Christian

Fifthly, reflect upon the suffering of Christ in order that you may imitate Him, and thus behave yourself in your suffering as He behaved Himself. Let Christ's suffering also be an example; deal with the old man as Christ was dealt with due to your sins.

First of all, behave yourself in suffering as Christ behaved Himself:

(1) Christ was not without feeling, and therefore you also are permitted to feel the least discomfort.

(2) Christ complained to God and to man about His anxiety inflicted upon Him from within and without, and yet remained with them. You, too, may complain to God and man. To complain due to grief or sorrow is neither an expression of impatience nor of sorrow. Do not forsake the company of people, for woe to the person who is alone! Christ occupied Himself with prayer, and thus you must be engaged likewise. "Is any among you afflicted? let him pray" (James 5:13).

(3) Christ considered all suffering as coming from God. "The cup which My Father hath given Me, shall I not drink it?" (John 18:11). Therefore you also ought to exercise faith in the providence of God and at all times learn to perceive it as the hand of God. To be assured of this requires diligent effort.

(4) Christ persevered in faith and exercised it in His greatest darkness and desertion, saying even then, "My Father, My God." Therefore you likewise ought not to cast away your faith and liberty; the proper bearing of your cross must issue forth from them. If you succumb in faith, you will bear a double cross.

(5) Christ persevered in the endurance of His suffering. He did not wish to resign until all had been finished. May patience also do its perfect work in you. As you should not ask God for a reason why He deals thus with you, but should rather be satisfied with the will of God, lest you be judging whether or not God's dealings with

you are right, so you may likewise not limit the Lord as to the time and duration of your suffering.

(6) Christ comforted Himself with the promise of a good outcome, keeping glory in view. For the joy set before Him, He despised the shame and endured the cross. Therefore you ought also to focus upon the promises, which are yea and amen. Enliven yourself with this; consider the state of glory, reflect upon eternal rest, joy, and felicity, for then the bearing of your afflictions will be easier, your conduct will be holier, and you will experience that they are but light afflictions which will pass very shortly.

Secondly, hold the suffering of Christ before you as an example to deal with the "old man" and to mortify sin. View the world and all sin with scorn and contempt; view them as hanging on the gallows and as being crucified. Crucify the flesh with the lusts thereof. How can you still engage in that for which Christ had to pay so bitterly? Will the love of Christ and the esteem for His suffering not arouse in you a holy vengeance in return, to afflict and put to death that which has caused Christ so much sorrow and put Him to death? While thus holding Christ before you as an example and as a powerful motivation to mortify sin, virtue and strength will go out from Him due to union with the suffering Jesus by faith, which will enable you to proceed with the work of crucifying the flesh and mortifying sin, causing you to increase in strength for that task. Therefore, "Likewise reckon ye also yourselves to be dead indeed unto sin, but alive unto God through Jesus Christ our Lord" (Rom. 6:11); "Judge, that if one died for all, then were all dead...that they which live should not henceforth live unto themselves, but unto Him which died for them, and rose again" (2 Cor. 5:14-15).

An Exhortation to the Unconverted to Reflect upon the Suffering of Christ

Unconverted friends, you also must come and attentively reflect upon the suffering of Christ in order to perceive as in a mirror what will befall you temporally as well as eternally if you do not repent. May this reflection be a means to work repentance and faith in you.

(1) I therefore address myself to you who as yet are ignorant of sin in its abominable and bitter nature and do not perceive and feel your misery, but live in sin with delight, esteeming the same as long as it is delightful and does no harm, while having no regard for whether or not this is sin.

(2) I address myself to you who burrow in the earth as a mole — the one to make a living, the other for riches, another for honor, respect, or status, doing so as if all depended on this. Your thoughts

only focus upon this; all your concerns and desires relate to this, you have nothing else in view and you labor for nothing but this.

(3) I address myself to you who as yet do not feel what a dreadful condition it is to miss God, to be separated from Him, to live forgetful of Him, not realizing how blessed a state it is to be reconciled with God and to have communion with Him. As a result of this you are neither troubled by the one nor desire the other.

(4) I address myself to you who as yet are ignorant of the necessity of satisfaction of divine justice; and are of the opinion that if you but feel remorse over the commission of grievous sins and if you but pray for forgiveness, all will be well.

(5) I address myself to you who as yet do not know Christ as Surety who satisfied for the sins of those who will be saved; to you who are ignorant of the manner in which one receives Christ by faith, and have neither wrestlings nor exercises of faith.

(6) I address myself to you who live civil lives, frequently attend church, are baptized, partake of the Lord's Supper, and live in such a fashion that no one will be able to say anything against you, and who on this basis build your confidence that you will be saved.

Poor people! You are still dead in sins and trespasses, blind, without Christ, and stand without as far as salvation is concerned.

Come, therefore, and consider each detail of the suffering of Christ; search for the reason why Christ had to suffer thus. Consider that this is only the portion of those who are converted, that is, for believers. Be sensibly convinced that you have no part in this, but that if you remain thus and die in this state, you will suffer the same to all eternity. For if the righteousness of God is so provoked to wrath towards the Surety, due to the sins of the elect whom He has loved with an everlasting love, how can you be of the opinion that you will go free? Oh no, "for if they do these things in a green tree, what shall be done in the dry?" (Luke 23:31). Conclude therefore with a lively impression that you are neither a partaker of Christ nor of all He has merited, but that you, as you now are, must eternally endure the absence of God and be subject to the dreadful and unbearable wrath of God. May God apply it to your heart and cause you to tremble and shudder. Knowing therefore the terror of the Lord, betake yourself to this Jesus, seek Him, and endeavor to believe in Him in order to come to God through Him and thus be saved. If you will not heed this, considering such fears to be the anxiety of a coward; and if you turn your heart away from this, you who hear this read or read it yourself, proceed if you wish, but know that you have been warned, and that your condemnation will be the heavier.

CHAPTER TWENTY-THREE

The State of Christ's Exaltation

Having considered the state of Christ's humiliation in which He merited salvation for the elect, we shall now proceed to discuss the state of exaltation in which He applies salvation to His elect, making them partakers of it.

This state is referred to either as a state of *exaltation,* as we read in Philippians 2:9, "Wherefore God also hath highly exalted him," or a state of *glory* as in Luke 24:26, "Ought not Christ...to enter into His glory?" Since Christ, being a divine Person, did not suffer according to His divine nature but according to His human nature, exaltation as such did not occur according to His divine nature. In this nature He remained the Most High, the most glorious One, and the unchangeable One. This divine nature, however, which was generally concealed in the state of His humiliation, manifested itself very clearly in His exaltation. He is nevertheless exalted according to His human nature. As Christ performed and suffered everything as Surety and Mediator in the state of His humiliation, He was also exalted as Surety and Mediator. Though He had merited glory for Himself according to the covenant of redemption, it was all to the benefit of the elect and all of this descended from Him upon them.

Four steps are generally distinguished in Christ's state of exaltation: His resurrection from the dead, His ascension, His sitting at the right hand of God, and His return to judgment.

The Resurrection from the Dead

The first step is the resurrection *of Christ from the dead.* This is the cardinal doctrine of our Christian religion, as salvation hinges upon faith in and confession of this truth. "And if Christ be not risen, then is our preaching vain, and your faith is also vain" (1 Cor. 15:14); "That if thou shalt confess with thy mouth the Lord Jesus, and shalt believe in thine heart that God hath raised Him from the dead, thou shalt be saved" (Rom. 10:9).

This truth is therefore abundantly and clearly presented in God's Word. It is referred to as *rising* (Mat. 28:6), *being raised* (Rom. 4:24); and *to be alive* (Rev. 2:8). We must take note of the veracity, necessity, and benefit of it.

The Veracity of Christ's Resurrection

The *veracity* of Christ's resurrection from the dead is first of all evident from the history of the resurrection recorded in Matthew 28, Mark 16, Luke 24, and John 20.

Secondly, it is confirmed by the testimony (1) of the angels (Mat. 28:5-7; Luke 24:7), (2) of the enemies who guarded the grave (Mat. 28:11), and (3) of the apostles, "This Jesus hath God raised up, whereof we all are witnesses" (Acts 2:32); "And with great power gave the apostles witness of the resurrection of the Lord Jesus" (Acts 4:33); "Remember that Jesus Christ of the seed of David was raised from the dead" (2 Tim. 2:8).

Thirdly, it is confirmed by the appearances of Christ to believers after His resurrection. "To whom also He showed himself alive after His passion by many infallible proofs, being seen of them forty days, and speaking of the things pertaining to the kingdom of God" (Acts 1:3). He appeared to:

(1) Mary Magdalene (John 20:14, 18),

(2) the women who came to the grave (Mat. 28:2, 10),

(3) Peter (Luke 24:34),

(4) the two disciples on the way to Emmaus (Luke 24:13-31),

(5) the eleven in the absence of Thomas (John 20:19),

(6) the eleven in the presence of Thomas — eight days later (John 20:26),

(7) seven disciples who went fishing (John 21:1),

(8) eleven disciples in Galilee where Christ had summoned them to be (Mat. 28:16),

(9) more than five-hundred brethren at once (1 Cor. 15:6),

(10) James (1 Cor. 15:7),

(11) the apostles when He ascended to heaven (Acts 1:9),

(12) Stephen after His ascension (Acts 7:55),

(13) Paul (Acts 9:17, 1 Cor. 15:8),

(14) and John, to whom He gave the Revelation. Christ thus appeared to His people, deeming the ungodly who had so contemptuously rejected Him unworthy of His appearance to them.

Concerning Christ's resurrection, several matters need to be noted:

(1) Christ's resurrection was accompanied by an earthquake. When He died, the earth shook and the veil of the temple was rent. The earth shook again at His resurrection, which was not only a proof of His divinity, but also of the wrath of God against the Jews and their land which would be destroyed and left destitute. The inhabitants would perish miserably and their religion would be taken from them and be transferred to the Gentiles. It also indicated that all temporal ceremonies were now terminated and that an unchangeable religion had taken their place.

(2) Christ's resurrection was also magnified by the descent of an angel in heavenly glory, whose countenance was like lightning and his raiment white as snow. This angel removed the stone from the door of the grave in view of the watchmen, who were terrified and became as dead men. But to the women he said, "Fear not ye...Jesus ...is not here: for he is risen, as he said," which was subsequently confirmed by two angels in white, this being indicative not only of their holiness but also of the joy and triumph of Christ's resurrection.

(3) As far as the time of year is concerned, Christ's resurrection occurred during the spring, at the time when day and night were of equal length. As far as the day is concerned, His resurrection occurred on the third day after His death. He did not spend three twenty-four-hour periods in the grave, for then He would have arisen on the fourth day. Instead, He was in the grave on three successive days: on Friday before sundown (which terminates the Jewish day), from sundown on Friday to sundown on Saturday, which was the second day, and from sundown on Saturday to sunrise on Sunday, which was the third day. In deeming part of the day to be the whole, Christ was thus three days in the grave and arose at sunrise on the third day. Therefore in order to find three days, one need not begin with the suffering of Christ in the garden nor with the three hours of darkness at the cross. He who is the Morning Star (Rev. 22:16), the Sun of Righteousness (Mal. 4:2), the dayspring from on high (Luke 1:78), and the Light to lighten the Gentiles, became alive again at the breaking of the day. Christ arose no sooner, so that men would be fully convinced that he had truly died; He did not arise any later so that His body would not be subject to corruption, according to Psalm 16:10. His entire body would thus remain fit to receive the soul again:

Christ was in the grave during the Jewish Sabbath. The Sabbath, however, did not typify Christ's lying in the grave.

[1] This is nowhere to be found in Scripture.

[2] Christ was also in the grave on Friday and on Sunday.

[3] The Sabbath was a day of joy, and Christ's residing in the grave was a matter of utmost sorrow.

[4] The burial was a step of Christ's humiliation and not of His exaltation. It belonged to the suffering of Christ, soul and body being separated from each other, and thus His residing in the grave was not a time of rest for Christ. When His flesh is said to rest in hope in Acts 2:26, this does not imply that Christ was at rest in this state, finding His delight in it, but rather that He rested in the hope of His resurrection of which He was assured.

[5] If the Sabbath were typical of Christ's burial, we no longer would have a Sabbath, as it would then have been terminated along with all the ceremonies. The commandment concerning the Sabbath, however, is of eternal duration; this will be demonstrated comprehensively in a subsequent chapter. It therefore was not typical. Christ arose on the first day of the week, and since the entire ceremonial worship was terminated, it was necessary that the day on which the ministry of shadows and types was especially performed would be changed and that from that moment on the Sabbath be observed on the day of Christ's resurrection — which John called *the Lord's Day* (Rev. 1:10), and since that time it has been observed on this day.

(4) Christ arose quietly and with wise design. As someone who awakens from sleep, removes his night clothing, and dresses himself, so Christ left His burial garment in the grave, and the napkin which covered His face. They were wrapped together and put in a specific place (John 20:7).

Christ Himself is the cause of His resurrection. The human nature consists of body and soul. These were separated by death, but both elements remained united to the divine nature. They were and remained the soul and body of the Son of God. At His resurrection the divine Person sent forth His soul again from Paradise, the third heaven, and by renewal united it with His body. He thus made His own assumed humanity alive again by His divine power, so that Christ was not resurrected by the power of another, such as is true for ordinary men. Christ, however, *actively* and truly arose and was made alive by His own power. The divine nature resurrected the human nature. This is evident from the following texts:

First, we read in John 2:19, "Destroy this temple, and in three days I will raise it up." The temple of which Christ spoke was His body (vs. 21). This temple, that is, His body, the Jews would destroy, that is, kill, and then the Lord Jesus Himself, and not someone else, would raise it up again. "I will raise it up."

Secondly, we read in John 10:17-18, "I lay down My life, that I might take it again. No man taketh it from Me, but I lay it down of Myself. I have power to lay it down, and I have power to take it again." By the same power which enabled Him to lay His life down, He would be able to take it again. By this power He did the one as well as the other.

Thirdly, we read in Romans 1:4, "And declared to be the Son of God with power, according to the Spirit of holiness, by the resurrection from the dead." The apostle presents the resurrection as a powerful proof that Christ is truly God. However, to be merely made alive and to arise from the dead is no proof of divinity, for this has occurred with others and will occur with all men. Thus, His resurrection, which proves Him to be the Son of God, occurred by His own power; no one can resurrect the dead, much less man himself. Only God can do so. It is also evident from the fact that the natures of Christ are contrasted in Romans 1:3-4 and are clearly distinguished from each other. Christ is presented there according to the flesh, and κατὰ σάρκα (*kata sarka*) according to the Spirit, that is, according to His divinity (Heb. 9:14). As He died according to His flesh, that is, according to His human nature, He was made alive by His eternal Spirit, that is, His divinity. It is thus evident that He resurrected Himself.

Fourthly, it was necessary that He would resurrect Himself, for the Surety who took this suffering upon Himself would also have to triumph over it. If someone else had resurrected Him, He would neither have triumphed over death, nor delivered Himself, and consequently would also not be able to deliver others.

Objection: The Father is frequently said to have raised up Christ, and thus He did not resurrect Himself.

Answer: Since Father and Son are one and the same God, their power is likewise one and the same. Whatever the Father does, the Son does also (John 5:19). When the resurrection is ascribed to the Father, this indicates that He was satisfied with and took delight in the resurrection of the Surety.

Since Christ by His own power has truly arisen under extraordinary and illustrious circumstances, He arose with *the identical body* which was put to death on the cross. It was identical in every detail and retained all characteristics of a body. It remained visible, tangible, and local. It retained the scars of the nails in His hands and feet as well as of the spear in His side. "Behold My hands and My feet, that it is I Myself: handle Me" (Luke 24:39); "Reach hither thy finger, and behold My hands; and reach hither thy hand, and thrust it into My side" (John 20:27) — this in response to the condition stated by Thomas in verse 25.

Upon His resurrection, this same body, while retaining all bodily characteristics, is *immortal*. "Now no more to return to corruption" (Acts 13:34); "Knowing that Christ being raised from the dead dieth no more;" (Rom. 6:9); "I am alive for evermore" (Rev. 1:18). It is also a *glorified* body, "...like unto His glorious body" (Phil. 3:21). It has not been recorded, and thus is unknown, to what degree He was glorified; that is, whether at His ascension His body was glorified internally to a greater degree than during the previous forty days. He may possibly have held back His full glory while interacting with His disciples. He ate with His disciples (Luke 24:43) to further assure them of His resurrection, not because He was in need of nourishment. His stomach also did not digest this nourishment, since this would be inconsistent with a glorified body. Rather, by His omnipotence He caused the food to disappear. So much concerning the veracity of His resurrection.

The Necessity of Christ's Resurrection

Secondly, we need to consider the *necessity* of Christ's resurrection. We do so for the following reasons:

First, it was necessary in order that the prophecies be fulfilled, as Christ Himself states, "Ought not Christ...to enter into His glory? And beginning at Moses and all the prophets, He expounded unto them in all the Scriptures the things concerning Himself" (Luke 24:26-27). Paul speaks likewise, "And that He rose again the third day according to the Scriptures" (1 Cor. 15:4). It is certain that the Old Testament contains more prophecies concerning the resurrection than we can discern. Those texts concerning which we have little light we cannot use as infallible proof. The following texts are clear, however. "For Thou wilt not leave My soul in hell; neither wilt Thou suffer Thine Holy One to see corruption" (Psa. 16:10). According to Peter these words are a prophecy concerning Christ's resurrection (Acts 2:31). "He shall drink of the brook in the way (a reference to Christ's humiliation): therefore shall He lift up the head" (a reference to Christ's exaltation) (Psa. 110:7). Hebrews 1:13 confirms that this psalm speaks of Christ. In Isaiah 53:8-12 we find the following expressions concerning His humiliation: grief, judgment, to be bruised, to make His soul an offering for sin, and to pour out His soul unto death. Concerning His resurrection we find the following expressions: Who shall declare His generation; He shall see His seed; He shall prolong His days; He shall be satisfied; a portion shall be divided to Him with the great, and He shall divide the spoil with the strong. Acts 8:32, 35 and the New Testament in general confirm that this chapter speaks of Christ.

Secondly, the *types* had to be fulfilled. Many things can be presented which in some way are congruent with the resurrection of Christ and which can be applied to it.

(1) Such is the case with *Isaac,* concerning whom Paul states that he was received "even from the dead; from whence also he received him in a figure" (Heb. 11:19).

(2) Consider also *Joseph,* who was delivered from the pit, after this from prison, and subsequently was highly exalted (Gen. 41).

(3) Consider *Samson* who carried away the gates of Gaza, and delivered himself out of the hands of his enemies (Judg. 16).

(4) Consider the scapegoat *Azazel* (Lev. 16), and (5) *the two birds,* one of which was killed above running water, and the other flew away after having been dipped in the blood of the dead bird (Lev. 14:4-7).

(6) Consider also *Daniel* who was delivered from the lions' den, and his companions who came out of the fiery oven unharmed (Dan. 6:23; 3:26). All these examples have something in common; they are applicable to the resurrection of Christ. However, whether they truly typify Christ's resurrection is not certain.

The following two examples are more probable types, but even this is not certain. The first is the *rod of Aaron* (Num. 17). This rod, dead and barren, was placed in the tabernacle of witness, hidden from human vision. "It came to pass that on the morrow, behold, the rod of Aaron was budded" (vs. 8). It is beyond dispute that Aaron and the Levitical priesthood typified the High Priest Jesus Christ, of which frequent reference is made in the letter to the Hebrews. Christ died as High Priest, in death was placed in the earth (and thus concealed from human vision), and as such He again appeared alive and brings forth glorious fruits. Aaron's staff, however, was not placed in the earth.

The second example of *Jonah,* even if not entirely applicable, is presented by the Lord Jesus Himself (Mat. 12:39). His stay in the belly of the whale would typify Christ's residing in the grave. The duration of three days and no longer, as well as his coming on shore again, would typify Christ's resurrection from the dead upon the third day.

Thirdly, the necessity of His resurrection is also evident from the office of the Mediator itself. The Mediator (1) had to conquer death (Hosea 13:14), (2) had to be an eternal King (Psa. 45:6), (3) as High priest had to enter into the Holy of Holies (Heb. 9:24), and (4) had to send forth the Holy Spirit from heaven to His elect (John 16:7). All this He could not do unless He had arisen from the dead. So much for the necessity of His resurrection.

The Efficacy and Benefit of Christ's Resurrection

In the third place we must consider the *efficacy* and *benefits* of the resurrection of Christ. This is most extraordinary, and therefore Paul was so desirous and continually occupied in reflecting upon the resurrection of Christ. "That I may know Him, and the power of His resurrection" (Phil. 3:10).

The first fruit is *justification*. "But for us also, to whom it shall be imputed, if we believe on Him that raised up Jesus our Lord from the dead, who was delivered for our offences, and was raised again for our justification" (Rom. 4:24-25). As long as the Surety still suffered and death had power over Him, the final penny had not as yet been paid. His conquering of the last enemy, death, and His triumphant appearance as being alive, were evidences that sin had been fully atoned for, the ransom had been paid, God's justice had been satisfied (being satisfied with this atonement), and that thus the Surety was justified (1 Tim. 3:16). Consequently all God's children have been reconciled in Him. There is not one sin, not even the least part thereof, for which satisfaction has not been made, and therefore they are free from all guilt and punishment. If someone senses the dreadfulness of guilt and punishment, views God as being provoked by sin so that there is no peace but only terror within the conscience (to such justification is most desirable), let him then turn about and by faith behold this Surety as having risen from the dead, which is the evidence of perfect satisfaction. Receive Him by faith who calls you and offers His fullness without price. Let such a person go to God and ask the Lord, while pleading upon the resurrection of Christ from the dead (1 Pet. 3:21), "Are not my sins punished? Has not my guilt been atoned for? Has not my Surety risen from the dead and thus entered into rest? Art not Thou my reconciled God and Father? Am I not at peace with Thee?" May such a person thus wrestle to apply all this to himself on the basis of the promises made to all who receive Christ by faith, until he experiences the power of Christ's resurrection unto his justification and being at peace with God.

The second fruit is *sanctification*. The apostle demonstrates this in Romans 6:4-5, "Therefore we are buried with Him by baptism into death: that like as Christ was raised up from the dead by the glory of the Father, even so we also should walk in newness of life, for if we have been planted together in the likeness of His death, we shall be also in the likeness of His resurrection" (Rom. 6:5). The apostle emphasizes this also when he states, "And you, being dead in your sins and the uncircumcision of your flesh, hath He quickened together with Him, having forgiven you all trespasses" (Col. 2:13); "If ye then be risen with Christ, seek those things which are above" (Col. 3:1). Even if believers may know themselves to be justified, they cannot find satisfaction in this. Their whole desire and life is to discern the image of God within themselves, to be conformed to that image, to thus be united to Him and to live in Him — that is their salvation. They cannot but find delight in knowing God, in loving Him, in fearing Him, in being subject to Him, and thus in thoughts, words, and deeds be in a spiritual frame which is fully and entirely in agreement with His will. Sin is therefore despicable to them: they abhor themselves: they are ashamed before God and inwardly sorrow over their deeds. How it would be their delight to be delivered from the sins which so grieve them! How this causes them to long for heaven, knowing that they will there behold God's face in righteousness, being satisfied with His likeness when they awake (Psa. 17:15)! Oh, yield to this heartfelt desire and let it motivate you to be engaged in the way of holiness, for it is the Lord's way to cause His children, while thus engaged in battle, to increase and proceed with joy in sanctification.

(1) View Christ's resurrection as an example and a pattern. Christ arose in the *morning*. Accustom yourself to meditate upon Christ's resurrection as you awake. Let every occurrence of waking up and arising out of bed stir you up to arise with Christ. Christ arose *on the first day of the week*. Therefore commemorate the resurrection of Christ on each Sabbath day and, uniting yourself with Him in the resurrection, let it be a renewed revival of your spiritual life. Christ *departed from the grave*, the place of the dead. You likewise must avoid (as much as your profession will suffer you to do so) familiar interaction with worldly and ungodly men. They are dead, they stink, and their stench is contagious. Christ *left His burial garment behind in the grave*. You likewise ought to hate the garment which has been polluted by the flesh. Leave all that is sinful behind in Sodom and Egypt, that is, in the grave, and depart from honor, goods, entertainment, and whatever belongs to the world. Christ appeared *alive*. Let your light therefore also shine and let everyone perceive that there is much distance between you and sinners. Show by your actions that you denounce whatever the world cleaves to. Manifest your love, humility, and heavenly-minded[1] life in the love and fear of God. Let the image of God and the likeness of Christ within you be manifested, doing all this not to be perceived by others as such, but to the glory of Christ, the conviction of the world, and the encouragement of the godly. The purpose of Christ's *association with men* was only to convince His own of the

---

[1] Dutch: "Uw verheven leven," that is, "your elevated life."

veracity of His resurrection and to strengthen them. He also did so to the benefit of His church unto the end of the world, even though this lasted but forty days, after which He ascended into heaven. Let it likewise be the objective of your life to walk godly upon the earth in order that those who are acquainted with you may be convinced and encouraged. Let it also be a preparation for going to heaven itself.

(2) Let Christ's resurrection *motivate* you to live a holy life. This is taught by the apostle, "Likewise reckon ye also yourselves to be dead indeed unto sin, but alive unto God through Jesus Christ our Lord, for if we have been planted together in the likeness of His death, we shall be also in the likeness of His resurrection" (Rom. 6:11, 5); "Because we thus judge, that if one died for all, then were all dead:...that they which live should not henceforth live unto themselves, but unto Him which died for them, and rose again" (2 Cor. 5:14-15). Follow the example of the apostle and thus arrive at the following conclusion: Since the Lord Jesus as my Surety has removed all my sin by His death, and as evidence of this has arisen from the dead, should I then yet live in sin? Should not I then arise with Him from the death of sin and live with Him in all holiness?

The power needed for our spiritual resurrection is inherent in the resurrection of Christ, "which according to his abundant mercy hath begotten us again unto a lively hope by the resurrection of Jesus Christ from the dead" (1 Pet. 1:3); "That I may know Him, and the power of His resurrection" (Phil. 3:10). Every believer is a member of the Lord Jesus. The same Spirit which is in Christ is also in them, and they live by that selfsame Spirit. Whatever the Head experiences, the members must also experience. Since Christ the Head has arisen, life-giving power flows into all His members. Believers are ingrafted into Him as the trunk, for as a graft becomes the recipient of sap and life-giving power, it likewise cannot but be that all believers receive the life-giving power of Christ. If one then unites himself with the risen Christ by faith, one will also become aware of the life-giving power which proceeds from Christ to quicken our souls.

The third fruit of Christ's resurrection is the *blessed resurrection of believers*. It is God's way to lead His children to heaven by way of many crosses. Temporal death also belongs to this. This is not a punishment upon sin as such, but is nevertheless a difficult and painful way which they must traverse together with all men. Their death, however, by virtue of the death of Christ, is without sting and curse, and thus is but a departing in peace. In consequence of Christ's resurrection, they will be resurrected unto salvation. "But if the Spirit of Him that raised up Jesus from the dead dwell in you, He (the Father) that raised up Christ from the dead shall also quicken your mortal bodies by His Spirit that dwelleth in you" (Rom. 8:11). The resurrection is attributed to the Father here; however, the reason that Christ's resurrection is mentioned together with ours is to demonstrate that His resurrection is the meriting cause of ours. "For if we be dead with Him, we shall also live with Him" (2 Tim. 2:11); "But now is Christ...become the firstfruits" (1 Cor. 15:20); "And He is...the firstborn from the dead; that in all things He might have the preeminence" (Col. 1:18). This will therefore transpire with the entire harvest, that is, with all believers after Him, since the church is the fullness of Him that filleth all in all, that is, Christ (Eph. 1:23). The entire congregation of Christ, being members of His body, must therefore arise so that the entire mystical body of Christ may live. Believers may and must apply this to themselves and rejoice in the hope of glory, saying, "For we know that if our earthly house of this tabernacle were dissolved, we have a building of God, an house not made with hands, eternal in the heavens" (2 Cor. 5:1). They may also say with Job, "For I know that my Redeemer liveth, and that He shall stand at the latter day upon the earth: and though after my skin worms destroy this body, yet in my flesh shall I see God: whom I shall see for myself, and mine eyes shall behold, and not another; though my reins be consumed within me" (Job 19:25-27). So much concerning the first step of the exaltation of Christ, the resurrection.

The Ascension of Christ

The second step of Christ's exaltation is His Ascension. As with the resurrection, we must again observe its veracity, necessity, and benefit.

The Veracity of Christ's Ascension

First of all we will consider the veracity of the ascension. Sometimes it is expressed in the active voice, as being the work of Christ Himself. Such is true for the verb "ascend." "I ascend unto My Father" (John 20:17). The following words are also used:

(1) *go*, "And if I go" (John 14:3);

(2) *go away*, "Nevertheless I tell you the truth; it is expedient for you that I go away" (John 16:7);

(3) *enter*, "Whither the forerunner is for us entered" (Heb. 6:20);

(4) *pass into the heavens*, "... that is passed into the heavens" (Hebr. 4:14).

Sometimes it is expressed in the passive voice, as the work of the Father towards Him. It is referred to as being:

(1) *carried up*, or *taken up*, "...carried up into heaven" (Luke 24:51); "...this same Jesus, which is taken up from you into heaven" (Acts 1:11);

(2) as being *exalted*, "Therefore being by the right hand of God exalted" (Acts 2:33);

(3) the pleasure of the Father in giving Him His promised glory, "Wherefore God also hath highly exalted Him" (Phil. 2:9).

In reference to all this we must say something about the Person, the act, the time, the location, and the manner of occurrence.

Concerning the *Person*, the same Person — being God and man, who has suffered, died, and has risen from the dead as a Mediator — also ascended to heaven as Mediator. This act is the work of the Person, but does not properly belong to the divine nature. Prior to this moment He was already in heaven in His divine nature (John 6:62), and had glory with the Father before the world was (John 17:5). As He concealed His divine nature behind His humanity in His descension, He revealed it all the more clearly at His ascension. Since this nature is infinite and without dimensions, however, it can neither change location nor in actuality descend or ascend. Rather, this properly relates to the Person according to His human nature, in which He also suffered. It was not an act of His human nature, it not being a Person but rather the work of the Person according to His human nature. "Now that He ascended, what is it but that He also descended first into the lower parts of the earth? He that descended is the same also that ascended up far above all heavens" (Eph. 4:9-10). The Person is named here, and to Him the work is attributed, this properly belonging to one or the other nature.

The *act* itself is the act of ascending. This word is indicative of a change of location. When a body changes location, it departs from the place where it was, and in traversing through either space or other localities arrives at a locality at which it was previously not present. Likewise Christ, ascending according to the body, left the lower parts of the earth where He had resided for such a long time. He traversed through the atmosphere and the universe until He arrived in the third heaven, the paradise of God and the house of His Father.

The *time* of its occurrence was forty days after His resurrection. The number "forty" frequently occurs in God's Word. Moses was forty days upon the mountain with God (Exo. 34:28); Israel was forty years in the wilderness (Deu. 8:2); Elijah went forty days without food until he came to Horeb, the mountain of God (1 Ki. 19:5-8); after forty days a man-child had to be presented to the Lord (Lev. 12:2-4); on the fortieth day the child Jesus was brought to the temple and presented before the face of the Lord (Luke 2:22);

after forty days of fasting in the wilderness, the Lord Jesus began His public ministry (Mat. 4); after having had communication with His disciples, He ascended to heaven forty days after His resurrection (Acts 1). *His ascent did not take place earlier* so that His disciples would be fully assured of His resurrection, being instructed concerning the things of the kingdom of heaven. Prior to this they could not have endured this event due to their weakness (John 16:12). *His ascent was not at a later date.* They were thus kept from cleaving too much to His bodily presence while being delivered from the notion that the kingdom of Israel would be established at that time.

The general *location* from which He departed was the earth. "Again, I leave the world" (John 16:28), and particularly the Mount of Olives (Acts 1:12); it was Bethany, a place on the mountain (Luke 24:50). The space through which he traversed consisted of *the visible heavens, the atmosphere, and the universe*: "... that is passed into the heavens" (Heb. 4:14). His *destiny* was the third heaven, the place where the holy angels reside together with the elect who are presently rejoicing in eternal bliss. Heaven here must neither be understood as God Himself nor as familiar communion with God or heavenly joy. Rather, it is a location above the visible heavens (Heb. 7:26), far above all the heavens (Eph. 4:10), which is the third heaven, the paradise of God (2 Cor. 12:2, 4), and the house of His Father (John 14:2). Thus, Christ's ascension did not occur figuratively. It did not merely consist in the body disappearing or becoming invisible, thus being glorified and becoming bodily omnipresent, for this would be a change of state rather than a change of location. Indeed, Christ's ascension was a true change of location.

The manner of Christ's ascension is most remarkable:

(1) Christ ascended into heaven while He was blessing (Luke 24:50). He spoke with them, and in a familiar and friendly manner bade them farewell. He pronounced blessings upon them which He immediately applied, for they "returned to Jerusalem with great joy" (Luke 24:52).

(2) He ascended to heaven *visibly*. The apostles were in His presence, spoke with Him and He with them and "while they beheld, He was taken up" (Acts 1:9). Just as Elisha gazed upon Elijah upon his ascent into heaven, the apostles also gazed upon the ascending Jesus until a cloud came between the ascending Jesus and the standing apostles, thus removing Him from their sight. This does not mean that the cloud ascended straight up towards heaven, carrying Christ heavenward as in a chariot. The glorified body of Christ had no need of this, and it also would be

contrary to the text which states that the cloud received Him away out of their sight, so that they could no longer gaze upon Him.

(3) He ascended into heaven in a glorious manner, triumphing over death, devil, and hell, being accompanied by many thousands of holy angels; and thus He entered into the third heaven before the throne of God. "God is gone up with a shout, the LORD with the sound of a trumpet" (Psa. 47:5).

From all this it is evident that *Christ essentially, truly, locally, and visibly ascended into heaven.* This we wish to prove more extensively against the Lutherans with the following proofs:

First, as Christ was not omnipresent in His human nature prior to His ascension, He likewise was not so afterwards. When He was at one location, He was not elsewhere. "And I am glad for your sakes that I was not there" (John 11:15). It is therefore clearly stated about Him that after His ascension He was neither upon earth nor in the world. "...again, I leave the world" (John 16:28); "For ye have the poor always with you; but Me ye have not always" (Mat. 26:11).

Objection: Such texts are applicable to His visible presence, but not to His bodily presence.

Answer: Such an argument is without foundation. God's Word knows of no such distinction and it is contrary to nature, as all bodies are visible. Elijah, in speaking with Christ upon the mountain, was visible even though he had a glorified body.

Secondly, the angels confirm this. "While they beheld, He was taken up" (Acts 1:9). The fact that they could no longer see Christ was not due to Him becoming invisible, but the result of a cloud coming between them which received Him out of their sight. In response to this the angels said, "This same Jesus, which is taken up from you into heaven, shall so come in like manner as ye have seen Him go into heaven" (Acts 1:11). Visibly He ascended into heaven, and on the day of judgment He will come again upon the clouds of heaven and will be seen of all men (Mat. 24:30). Whenever the reference is to a body, the words "taken up" and "ascend" are always indicative of a change of locality. The apostles give abundant witness to this (cf. Mark 16:19; Luke 24:50-51; 1 Tim. 3:16). If one were to use such expressions as "to ascend," "to go away," "to leave the world," and "to be taken up," in reference to a person, and yet insist that he was nevertheless at the same place where he had just been seen, such a person would rightfully be laughed at by both children and fools. If this manner of speech is indicative of a change of locality as far as men are concerned, this is likewise true for Christ, since He also is very man and has a true body as others.

Thirdly, it is also confirmed by those texts in which Christ is said to have been seen in heaven. Stephen saw Jesus "standing on the right hand of God" (Acts 7:55); "And last of all he was seen of me also" (1 Cor. 15:8). Thus Christ remained visible while being in heaven.

Fourthly, as the earth is a place below, heaven is a place above. Enoch and Elijah are locally in heaven, which is also true for the souls of believers, as well as for any who are there bodily; they are locally in heaven, that is, at a specific location. After the resurrection all the elect will be in heaven, a specific place; thus heaven is a place. Christ refers to heaven as "Paradise" (Luke 23:43); Paul called it the third heaven (2 Cor. 12:2); Christ calls it His Father's house (John 14:2-3) where He prepares a place for His elect, where He will take them to Himself to be where He is, and where they will always be with the Lord (1 Th. 4:17). It is certain that Christ at His ascension has entered into this place (Heb. 6:20). Thus, Christ has essentially, truly, visibly, and locally ascended into heaven, and His ascension is neither a disappearance nor a transformation to omnipresence.

Fifthly, it is contrary to the nature of a true body. This we will demonstrate extensively when we deal with the *papal mass* in chapter 40.

Objection #1: Christ's human nature is united to His divine nature, and therefore His human nature is present wherever the divine nature is, and thus is omnipresent.

Answer: (1) This argument refutes itself, for it is as if one said that the sun is united with the universe and therefore the sun must be where the universe is; that is, at the same hour, and thus always surrounding the atmosphere and the globe.

(2) Then Christ, having been conceived within the body, would already have been omnipresent prior to His birth, and the body lying in the crib would not only have been there but everywhere in heaven and upon earth. This reasoning contradicts Scripture as well as nature, for it is evident that one body cannot be at the same location where another body is. Otherwise, all men would exist within the body of Christ and all bodies would be in the same place where His body is.

Objection #2: The following argument has a similar thrust: Christ sits at the right hand of God; since the right hand of God is everywhere, the body of Christ is also everywhere.

Answer: (1) It is never written that the body of Christ is at the right hand of God.

(2) This is stated concerning the Person according to His human nature. Even if this were so, the sitting at the right hand does not occur locally, for God is a Spirit and therefore neither local nor

corporal. It rather refers to being exalted to a position of honor and glory.

(3) If Christ is omnipresent according to the body, being at the right hand of the omnipresent One, then also all believers will be omnipresent in the day of judgment; for they will stand at the right hand of Christ who is omnipresent according to His Godhead. If the conclusion by way of such reasoning were correct, they would also be omnipresent according to the body, since He is at the right hand of God and they are at His. Since the latter statement is clearly false, the first statement is likewise false.

(4) The syllogism is incorrect *in forma*.

Objection #3: "He that descended is the same also that ascended up far above all heavens, that He might fill all things" (Eph. 4:10). Since being "far above all heavens" (which includes the third heaven), is not a location, Christ's ascension is therefore not a change in location, but rather results in being omnipresent. Since He fills all things, He is therefore omnipresent.

Answer: (1) "All heavens" refers to the visible heavens, the atmosphere, and the universe with all its galaxies — beyond which is the third heaven. Christ in going into the heavens (Heb. 4:14) has entered the third heaven, of which the Word frequently states that He resides there where His children will be with Him.

(2) To fill all things is not the same as filling all places corporally, for then several bodies would have to occupy the same place simultaneously. Furthermore, neither in Scripture nor in secular writers does the word "things" refer to places. Rather, the filling of all things refers to the pouring out of the Holy Spirit whom He has poured out upon His church by virtue of the efficacy of His ascension (John 16:7). This is pointed out in Ephesians 4:11, "And He gave some, apostles; and some, prophets; and some, evangelists; and some, pastors and teachers."

(3) The reference here is to the Personhood of Christ, and that which properly belongs to His divine nature. He did not descend from heaven in His human nature, but rather in His Godhead. Thus "He that descended is the same also that ascended."

Objection #4: The descent into hell cannot be taken literally; therefore His ascension into heaven cannot be taken literally.

Answer: (1) One cannot argue that because one thing is stated figuratively concerning Christ that therefore all things stated concerning Him must be viewed figuratively.

(2) The statement "descended into hell," found in the articles of faith, is meant to be understood literally, for it means as much as being laid in a "hollow," that is, to be buried in the grave.

(3) If Christ is said to have descended from heaven according to His divine nature, this is a metaphor, not as far as location is concerned but as far as the act itself. Thus, when He is said to have ascended, this is figuratively true for His divine nature. One cannot, however, draw the conclusion from the Godhead that this is likewise true for His human nature and His body, for a body can literally descend and ascend.

Objection #5: While being in heaven, Christ is nevertheless present with His own upon earth, and thus He is omnipresent. "And, lo, I am with you alway, even unto the end of the world" (Mat. 28:20); "For where two or three are gathered together in My Name, there am I in the midst of them" (Mat. 18:20).

Answer: Christ is both God and man, and therefore whatever can be said of the one nature cannot be said of the other nature, and whatever can be said of the Person, cannot be said of both natures. It is said for example that Christ is from eternity, and that Christ died; Christ is infinite, and Christ is locally in heaven; Christ is always present with His own, and Christ is not always with His own (Mat. 16:11). When Christ promises His presence to His own, this is stated of His Person according to His divine nature and not according to His human nature. The cited texts do not speak so much of the presence of His Person, however, but rather of His assistance, help, comfort, and blessings for all who seek Him, as well as of the power which would accompany His Word. So much as far as the veracity of His ascension is concerned.

The Necessity of Christ's Ascension

There was also a *necessity* for Christ's ascension into heaven. "Ought not Christ...to enter into His glory?" (Luke 24:26).

First, it was necessary in order that the prophecies and the types would be fulfilled:

(1) It was prophesied, "Lift up your heads, O ye gates; even lift them up, ye everlasting doors; and the King of glory shall come in" (Psa. 24:9); "Thou hast ascended on high" (Psa. 68:18-19). The apostle clearly applies this to Christ's ascension (Eph. 4:8).

(2) It was also typified for instance in the ascension of Enoch (Gen. 5:24) and Elijah (2 Ki. 2:11). The bringing of the ark of the covenant to Mount Zion also applies to this, of which David said, "God is gone up with a shout, the LORD with the sound of a trumpet" (Psa. 47:5). The most eminent type of Christ's ascension is to be observed in the entering of the High Priest into the Holy of Holies (Lev. 16), which the apostle applies to the ascension of Christ (Heb. 9:24; 6:19-20).

Secondly, the high-priestly office of Christ also demanded His ascension. In the Old Testament it was not sufficient for the High Priest to kill the animal. His office required that he would enter into the Holy of Holies with the blood. It was likewise not sufficient that Christ suffered and died without the gate and that He died to atone for the sins of the people, but with His blood, that is, with the efficacy of His suffering, "Christ...entered...into heaven itself, now to appear in the presence of God for us" (Heb. 9:24). These two elements of His high-priestly ministry cannot be separated, "for if He were on earth (that is, if Christ had not entered) He should not be a priest" (Heb. 8:4).

The Benefits of Christ's Ascension

The *benefits* of Christ's ascension are exceedingly great and many.

First, in reference to Christ, this event is a cause of extraordinary joy for believers. He who for our sake became poor, was a man of sorrows, and endured the contempt of men, has conquered all and triumphantly ascended into heaven. It was a day of extraordinary joy for all of Israel when David, accompanied by all his people, removed the ark from the house of Obed-edom and brought it to Mount Zion; all Israel rejoiced, and David, being filled with the Holy Ghost, danced before the ark (1 Chr. 15). The psalmist sings of this, "They have seen Thy goings, O God; even the goings of my God, my King, in the sanctuary. The singers went before, the players on instruments followed after; among them were the damsels playing with timbrels. Bless ye God in the congregations, even the Lord, from the fountain of Israel" (Psa. 68:24-26). When Solomon was anointed to be king, and was placed upon the throne of Israel, the whole nation came behind Solomon with such rejoicing that the earth shook and rent (1 Ki. 1:40). With how much more glory and joy the Lord Jesus made His entry into heaven! With what joy the heavenly legions must have accompanied Him upon His entry! With what joy the glorified saints must have beheld Him! With what delight the Father must have received Him! How fitting it therefore is that we also would follow Him and exclaim with joy, "Worthy is the Lamb that was slain to receive power, and riches, and wisdom, and strength, and honour, and glory, and blessing!" (Rev. 5:12).

Secondly, the ascension of Christ is also of great benefit to believers as far as they themselves are concerned. By His ascension all that He has merited for them by His suffering and death is to them. Particularly David (Psa. 68:18) and Paul (Eph. 4:8) conjoin these two matters to the ascension of Christ: He has led captivity captive, and He has received gifts for men.

(1) *He has led captivity captive.* The elect, and also you who may read or hear this, were by nature captive to the devil, and consequently to the world and the lusts of the flesh. Christ, however, having conquered these enemies by His death, triumphed openly over them in His ascension. The Romans, after conquering their enemies, made a triumphant entry into Rome, at which time they triumphantly led their captives with them. Christ did likewise in His ascension; those who held His children captive have been taken captive themselves by Him, manifesting this in His ascension. You therefore, who are partakers of the Lord Jesus, view the devil, the world, and your flesh as captured and shackled enemies, and yourselves as having been delivered from their violence and dominion. Rejoice over this in faith and jubilate, "O death, where is thy sting? O grave, where is thy victory?" (1 Cor. 15:55). They will no longer have dominion over you. It is true that they often assault you fiercely, inflict many wounds, and cause you much grief. They can only go as far as the Conqueror allows the chain with which they are bound to extend; and He knows how far He can let this chain go without incurring danger. He wishes to demonstrate to His children from what dreadful lions and bears He has delivered them, so that they would be all the more thankful. He wishes to exercise them in this battle and make them conquerors over their enemies, that they may triumph with Him. Be therefore encouraged in this battle, knowing that the enemies of Christ will not rob one sheep, but that he who has the least strength will yet overcome and be crowned as conqueror.

(2) From the ascension of Christ also proceed *gifts for men.* One who loves Christ will be very desirous to honor His Lord and to bring others to Christ. For this they are in need of various gifts, such as knowledge, wisdom, boldness, aptness to teach, etc. The Lord Jesus has merited these by His death, and by virtue of His ascension He has received power to give them to His elect, giving them to everyone as they have need of them in his task, and as their desire for these gifts is directed unto Him. If anyone therefore desires with heartfelt love to make Christ known in His beauty and to be instrumental in bringing others into fellowship with Christ, he ought to believe that Christ, who now is in heaven, has received gifts for the purpose of distribution, and that these will be given to him who humbly requests them to this end. "If any of you lack wisdom, let him ask of God, that giveth to all men liberally, and upbraideth not; and it shall be given him" (James 1:5).

Thirdly, *the outpouring of the Holy Spirit* is also a fruit of Christ's ascension. Also prior to Christ's ascension believers received the Holy Spirit by virtue of His future ascension. They would otherwise neither have been Christ's property, nor could have been regenerated, have lived, believed, or prayed. They prayed for this Spirit. "Take not Thy Holy Spirit from me" (Psa. 51:11); "Thy spirit is good; lead me into the land of uprightness" (Psa. 143:10); "The Spirit of Christ which was in them" (1 Pet. 1:11). His presence, however, as far as both His Person and the measure are concerned, was not as abundant and evident. After Christ was glorified, however, He poured out the Holy Spirit in abundant measure, which was according to prophecy. "I will pour My Spirit upon thy seed" (Isa. 44:3); "... for I have poured out My Spirit upon the house of Israel" (Ezek. 39:29); "And it shall come to pass afterward, that I will pour out My Spirit upon all flesh" (Joel 2:28). The fulfillment of this can be observed in Acts 2:16-18. The Lord Jesus promised this on several occasions. "But this spake He of the Spirit, which they that believe on Him should receive: for the Holy Ghost was not yet given; because that Jesus was not yet glorified." (John 7:39). Consider also John 16:7, "For if I go not away, the Comforter will not come unto you; but if I depart, I will send Him unto you."

Believers know that inner spiritual motions must be wrought in them by the Holy Ghost. They are very desirous for communion with the Spirit as well as for His indwelling in them. They continually pray for this and are grieved if they neither perceive Him, nor sense His efficacious operation. They must always hold on to the truth, however, that He Himself remains within them and will remain within them to all eternity. As certainly as they know that Christ has ascended into heaven, so certain is this fruit: they will enjoy the indwelling of the Holy Spirit. Therefore always consider the ascension as a basis of perseverance in prayer for the increase of the operation of this indwelling Spirit.

A fourth fruit of Christ's ascension is His administration of the second element of His high-priestly office, namely, *intercession,* which we have discussed in the previous chapter. Hereby He *prepares a place for them* (John 14:3). There He functions as their Head and there they sit together with Christ in heavenly places (Eph. 2:6). He is there as a *forerunner* (Heb. 6:20), having paved the way whereby believers may continually approach unto the throne of God. The apostle urgently exhorts us to do so. "Having therefore, brethren, boldness to enter into the holiest by the blood of Jesus, by a new and living way, which he hath consecrated for us, through the veil, that is to say, his flesh; and having an high priest over the house of God; let us draw near with a true heart in full assurance of faith" (Heb. 10:19-22). Therefore, exercise your faith and come to the throne by way of Christ's ascension, where you will find and see your Jesus, and then request whatever your soul desires, as if you were there yourself. Rejoice over the fact that Jesus is there on your behalf, prepares a place for you, and at last will take you to Himself to be there eternally.

The ascension of Christ is also efficacious unto *sanctification.* Since the Head is already in heaven, all His members must also become heavenlyminded, and by way of the ascension must continually stir themselves up to holiness of life. This the apostle urges us to do when he says, "If ye then be risen with Christ, seek those things which are above, where Christ sitteth on the right hand of God. Set your affection on things above, not on things on the earth" (Col. 3:1-2).

Children of God, what is there upon earth that would keep you there?

(1) Christ is not there, for He left the earth and has ascended into heaven.

(2) In addition to this, you know by much experience that all is vanity and cannot satisfy; or else you do not obtain that which you desire, as it eludes you as quickly as you pursue it. Thus, this vain desire and unrest makes you tired and worn-out. Even if you obtain what you desire, you experience that it is not what you had in mind. It is often nothing more than a thorny bush, and by embracing it, you find that you have harmed yourself. Yes, it was nothing but pollution by which you defiled yourself. How frequently you have discovered that it has dismayed the soul, affected your peace of conscience, taken away your spiritual liberty, disturbed your fellowship with God, caused you to continually live in unrest, and pricked your conscience! Oh, how the soul is anesthetized by earthly things! How lethargically, restlessly, and without freedom one engages in prayer! How it prevents the familiar enlargement and perseverance in prayer, causing one to come away empty from the exercise of prayer!

(3) Moreover, how readily the desire for tangible things will increase in strength, and how quickly spiritual life is ill-affected by this. Oh, how long it sometimes lasts before one is freed from these snares and before the head is brought above water again!

(4) Since you also have been called out of the world as Abraham was called out of Ur of the Chaldees and as Israel was called out of Egypt, you ought neither to remain in it any longer, return to it, nor look back to Sodom as did Lot's wife. Rather, lift yourself above the

things of time and sense, and let your walk henceforth be in heaven as Paul said concerning himself and believers (Phil. 3:20).

First of all, Christ is there. Does your heart not will to be where your treasure is? Is not Christ your treasure, desire, life, and love? He is in heaven and it is the comfort of believers in this world that they will once be with the Lord (1 Th. 4:17-18). Therefore let your thoughts, conversation, and exercise of love be such as is consistent with your citizenship, and let them thus be where Jesus is.

Secondly, heaven is truly your native country. Acknowledge yourself then to be but guests and "strangers and pilgrims on the earth," and seek this country looking "for a city which hath foundations, whose Builder and Maker is God" (Heb. 11:13-16, 10). Thence is the origin of your spiritual birth, for "Jerusalem which is above is free, which is the mother of us all" (Gal. 4:26). It is your Father's house (John 14:2) and your house, "For we know that if our earthly house of this tabernacle were dissolved, we have a building of God, an house not made with hands, eternal in the heavens" (2 Cor. 5:1). This is where your brothers and sisters reside as well as the angels with whom we are in partnership (Heb. 12:22-23). This is your inheritance, "incorruptible, and undefiled, and that fadeth not away, reserved in heaven for you" (1 Pet. 1:4). As a man's heart, thoughts, and desires are all drawn towards an earthly inheritance, this ought to be much more true for this heavenly inheritance.

Thirdly, heaven alone is truly delightful. The small rays which may be enjoyed upon earth yield unspeakable joy to the soul. How Jacob rejoiced when something of this was revealed to him! He said, "Surely the LORD is in this place...how dreadful is this place! this is none other but the house of God, and this is the gate of heaven" (Gen. 28:16-17). Moses' desire was, "Show me Thy glory" (Exo. 33:18); David's comfort was, "As for me, I will behold Thy face in righteousness: I shall be satisfied, when I awake, with Thy likeness" (Psa. 17:14); Asaph's delight was: "It is good for me to draw near to God" (Psa. 73:28). Since we are permitted not only to seek this in some degree and measure, but also to enjoy it as our delight, let us engage ourselves to seek this delight and to continually rejoice in it.

Fourthly, by maintaining our walk in heaven with Christ, our soul without being conscious of it will also shine as Moses' face shone after he communed with God for forty days upon the mountain. "But we all, with open face beholding as in a glass the glory of the Lord, are changed into the same image from glory to glory, even as by the Spirit of the Lord" (2 Cor. 3:18).

Fifthly, take note of the drawing power of the Lord Jesus. He is now in heaven, and He foretold that when He would be lifted up on the cross, on the basis of which He would enter heaven, that He would draw all men to Himself (John 12:32). Believer, you experience this drawing whenever you lift your heart heavenward, looking for light, life, and communion, and praying, "Draw me, we will run after Thee" (Song of Sol. 1:4). Therefore do not allow Christ to draw in vain. As you perceive this drawing, yield to it willingly and you will experience that you will more readily have your conversation in heaven.

To that end continually reflect upon what is recorded in God's Word concerning heaven. Take special notice of the accounts of others who have been led into the Lord's inner chambers and have received foretastes of heaven. Frequently seek to recall what the Lord has revealed to your own soul, and how sweet this frame was. Be much engaged in prayer and as you pray, reflect upon Christ as being in heaven, and upon the joy of the angels and of the glorified saints. Consider how they bow before the Lord Jesus, the nature of the light with which they are illuminated, the love with which they look upon Jesus, and how they jubilate, "Blessing, and honour, and glory, and power, be unto Him that sitteth upon the throne, and unto the Lamb forever" (Rev. 5:13).

Christ's Session at the Right Hand of God

The third step of Christ's exaltation is *His session at the right hand of God*. We will consider both the veracity and benefit of this step.

The Veracity of Christ's Session at the Right Hand of God

Let us first of all consider its veracity. The session at the right hand of God is frequently confirmed in God's Word. This was promised in the Old Testament. "The LORD said unto my Lord, Sit thou at My right hand" (Psa. 110:1). Acts 2:34 and Hebrews 1:13 confirm that this is said concerning Christ. In the New Testament it is stated that this has actually occurred. "He was received up into heaven, and sat on the right hand of God" (Mark 16:19); "...where Christ sitteth on the right hand of God" (Col. 3:1); "sat down on the right hand of the Majesty on high" (Heb. 1:3).

This is a figure of speech, for God is a Spirit and has nothing in common with a body nor with anything resembling it. Thus God has no right hand, but it is a figure of speech derived from human language. Men are generally strongest in their right hand, and primarily carry out their tasks with this hand. Therefore God's right hand is symbolic of strength and powerful execution. "And the vineyard which Thy right hand hath planted" (Psa. 80:15); "The Son of man sitting on the right hand of power" (Mat. 26:64). Since men consider their right hand to be the most worthy, they will place those whom they wish to honor at their right hand. Solomon did this with his mother (1 Ki. 2:19). Therefore Christ's session at the right hand of God conveys that He is exalted to the highest degree of glory. "He...sat down on the right hand of the Majesty on high" (Heb. 1:3); "...on the right hand of the throne of the Majesty in the heavens" (Heb. 8:1). In view of this Christ is said to be crowned with glory and honor (Heb. 2:9).

The sitting at the right hand is not indicative of superiority over him at whose right hand one is, for the bride, the church of Christ, is also presented as standing at Christ's right hand. "Upon thy right hand did stand the queen in gold of Ophir" (Psa. 45:9). Nevertheless she is and remains subordinate to Christ. Such is also the case here. It only conveys the supreme glory of Christ, and thus it is without any reference to the glory of the Father in regard to greater or lesser. Without controversy, God is and remains the Most High, and no one can be above Him. It is senseless to imagine His having a right, middle, and left hand.

His *sitting* at the right hand is of no special significance, for sometimes Christ is said to stand at the right hand (Acts 7:55), and sometimes that He is there (Rom. 8:34). One may, however, distill sweet meditations from this "sitting":

(1) it renders Him more honor, since it is proper for servants to stand;

(2) it conveys the actual engagement and execution of His mediatorial office, for kings who are seated upon their throne or judgment seat are engaged in the execution of their government;

(3) it conveys the sweet rest which Christ enjoys after His labors;

(4) it is indicative of His permanent residence in glory. Such considerations are both true and sweet, but whether this is implied by the "sitting" is not so certain.

However, the sitting, standing, and being at God's right hand are indicative of the very greatest glory which can be bestowed upon a creature. To this glory only the Mediator, Christ, according to His human nature, has been exalted, far above the holy angels. Concerning this the apostle states, "But to which of the angels said He at any time, Sit on my right hand?" (Heb. 1:13). It is something different when God is said to be at someone's right hand, that is, when one may experience His mighty help; and it is another thing to be at God's right hand, which is indicative of the highest honor and glory, and thus properly belongs to Christ alone. Believers are indeed promised that they will sit with Christ upon His throne (Rev. 3:21), which refers to the communication of His benefits and glory which Christ has merited for them in His humiliation and exaltation; however, they are never said to sit at the right hand of God.

The Lord Jesus, *as Mediator*, sat down at the right hand of the Father. According to His Godhead, He is coessential with the Father and eternally coequal with Him, so in this respect He cannot receive more glory. His session at the right hand reveals, however, that He, the Mediator, is the only glorious God, a fact which in His humiliation He nearly always concealed behind His humanity. He refers to this when He says, "And now, O Father, glorify Thou Me with Thine own self with the glory which I had with Thee before the world was" (John 17:5). In His human nature He is glorified far beyond our comprehension, and the measure of light, love, and enjoyment of God He receives according to His soul are the ultimate of what a creature can absorb. In His bodily glory, He excels all who are roundabout Him. Paul, speaking of this, says, "Who shall change our vile body, that it may be fashioned like unto His glorious body" (Phil. 3:21).

Christ's Execution of His Offices at the Right Hand of God

His session at the right hand of God as Mediator pertains to His three offices. First of all it pertains to His office as *High Priest*. His priestly office is foundational to the execution of His kingly and prophetical office. It had been promised that, upon execution of the established conditions which He had to perform as High Priest (Isa. 53:10), He would be King and Prophet for the protection and instruction of His people. His session as High Priest at the right hand of the Father is evident from Hebrews 1:3, "... when He had by Himself purged our sins, sat down on the right hand of the Majesty on high." The act of purging sin belongs to the priestly office, and is here conjoined to sitting at the right hand, and thus to the high-priestly office itself. Therefore it is as Priest that He is at the right hand of God. This same combination is also demonstrated in Hebrews 10:12, "But this man, after He had offered one sacrifice for sins for ever, sat down on the right hand of God." Add to this the following clear text, "We have such an High Priest, who is set on the right hand of the throne of the Majesty in the heavens" (Heb. 8:1).

Secondly, He also sits at God's right hand as *Prophet*, He being said to send forth His Holy Spirit from there in order to instruct His people. "Therefore being by the right hand of God exalted... He hath shed forth this, which ye now see and hear.... He saith Himself, The LORD said unto My Lord, Sit thou on My right hand" (Acts 2:33-34).

Thirdly, He also sits as *King* at the right hand of God: "...and hath set Him at His own right hand in the heavenly places, far above all principality, and power, and might, and dominion" (Eph. 1:20-21); "Who is gone into heaven, and is on the right hand of God; angels and authorities and powers being made subject unto Him" (1 Pet. 3:22). Sometimes this session at the right hand is called a work of Christ, "...He was received up into heaven, and sat on the right hand of God" (Mark 16:19; cf. Heb. 8:1). He had accomplished all His work upon earth, but still had to accomplish much work in heaven; however, not in a state of humiliation as upon earth, but in glory. After having merited this glory for Himself and for the benefit of His children, He took possession of this, consistent with the covenant established with Him. This session at the right hand is also frequently attributed to the Father. "Therefore being by the right hand of God exalted..." (Acts 2:33); "Thou crownedst Him with glory and honour" (Heb. 2:7). Since He had fulfilled the condition, the Father justly granted Him that glory in accordance with the covenant. "Therefore will I divide Him a portion with the great...because He hath poured out His soul unto death" (Isa. 53:12). When it is said in Philippians 2:9 that the Father has given Him a Name *in His favor* (the Greek rendering), this does not have Christ in view as if He had not merited this, but rather it is mentioned in reference to the Father who, upon His requirements having been fulfilled, in full favor and love has given Christ this Name above every name. It can also be understood as a reference to the elect, to whom and for whose sake Christ has been given in divine favor, in order to execute everything that was needful for their salvation. So much concerning the veracity of this doctrine.

The Benefits of Christ's Session at the Right Hand of God

In a general sense, the *benefit* of Christ's session at the right hand of God, is the efficacious execution of His offices.

First, since He is seated as High Priest at the right hand of the throne of Majesty, how efficacious His intercession is! How could the Father deny Him anything when He Himself said to Him, "Ask of Me, and I shall give Thee" (Psa. 2:8)? How efficacious is the intercession of Him who stands at the right hand of the Father and pleads such a righteous cause!

Secondly, since He is Prophet at the right hand of His Father, He will provide His church and children with sufficient gifts and graces. "Therefore being by the right hand of God exalted, and having received of the Father the promise of the Holy Ghost, He hath shed forth this, which ye now see and hear" (Acts 2:33).

Thirdly, since Christ is King at the right hand of God, He will efficaciously gather His elect together as one Church. "Him hath God exalted with His right hand to be a Prince and a Saviour, for to give repentance to Israel" (Acts 5:31). He will thus powerfully preserve His church, so that not a single one of His elect will perish, nor will the gates of hell prevail over them (Mat. 16:18). He will therefore punish and destroy the enemies of the church. "Sit Thou at My right hand, until I make Thine enemies Thy footstool" (Psa. 110:1). The Lord at thy right hand shall strike through kings in the day of his wrath. He shall wound the heads over many countries" (Psa. 110:5-6).

Christ's Return to Judgment

The last step of Christ's exaltation is *His return to judgment.* The previous steps of Christ's exaltation were invisible to the world; believers only can behold them by faith. This step, however, even though it is embraced by faith as a certain future event, will be visible to the eyes of all men, none excepted. The certainty that Christ as Judge will come to judgment and that this is a step of Christ's exaltation are evident in the following texts: "And then shall all the tribes of the earth...see the Son of man coming in the clouds of heaven with power and great glory" (Mat. 24:30); "When the Son of man shall come in His glory, and all the holy angels with Him, then shall He sit upon the throne of His glory" (Mat. 25:31); "And (the Father) hath given Him authority to execute judgment also, because He is the Son of man" (John 5:27). The word "because" has reference to His suffering and death as a fulfillment of the condition of the covenant of redemption by which He is authorized and empowered to be Judge. More we shall not say at this time, since we shall discuss this in volume three.

Christ's Exaltation Applied

Having concluded the state of Christ's humiliation by way of general application, we shall likewise consider the steps of Christ's exaltation all together, and make application.

May faith make the previously discussed matters a present reality. Frequently join Mary Magdalene in visiting the grave and remain there in quiet meditation. Behold, as it were, Jesus dead in the grave, the glorious descent of the angel who removes the stone from the grave, and the glorious and triumphant manner in which the Lord Jesus, being alive again, exited from the grave. Focus upon the appearance of the angels and all the appearances of Christ. Listen to all His conversations with the women and the disciples, and thus allow yourself to be quietly led into the truth

652 The Christian's Reasonable Service

and glory of Christ's resurrection, considering how all has been finished and conquered by Him. Accompany the disciples to the Mount of Olives; listen to the last blessings of Christ and behold Him ascending into heaven, taking His place upon His Father's command at the right hand of God, surrounded with incomprehensible glory. Hearken to the jubilation of the inhabitants of heaven, "God is gone up with a shout, the LORD with the sound of a trumpet" (Psa. 47:5). How the glorious angels did rejoice, who also rejoiced when the Lord founded the earth (Job 38:7), and who magnified the Lord when the Messiah was born, exclaiming, "Glory to God in the highest, and on earth peace, good will toward men" (Luke 2:14)! How innumerable must have been the multitude which in orderly arrangement reached from earth to heaven! How large was the multitude which preceded Him and followed Him! How they must have rejoiced and bowed themselves before the King of glory at His triumphant entry! And how they must have trumpeted forth His honor and glory! How the glorified saints must have yearned to see Him! How they rejoiced in beholding Him, bidding their Surety and Lord welcome, and bowing down before Him jubilating, *Hallelujah!* Therefore fix your eye at once upon this King of glory and behold this King in His beauty. As He with deep-felt sorrow truly tasted all bitterness, anxiety and shame in His human nature, He has likewise, as man, truly rejoiced; this day was for Him a "day of the gladness of His heart" (Song of Sol. 3:11). How He must have rejoiced over the glory which God His Father received, by bringing to Himself His Son whom He had sent forth to perform so great a task which He had so faithfully performed! How He must have rejoiced in the redemption of His brethren, and in the fact that He would now prepare a place for them! With what delight the Father has received Him and placed Him at His right hand, crowning Him with glory and honor! In one word, all of heaven was filled with joy, and all its inhabitants would sing in turn, "Lift up your heads, O ye gates; and be ye lift up, ye everlasting doors; and the King of glory shall come in. Who is this King of glory? The LORD strong and mighty, the LORD mighty in battle. Who is this King of glory? The LORD of hosts, He is the King of glory" (Psa. 24:7-8, 10).

Exhortation to Meditate upon a Glorified Christ

Even though we are not permitted to see the heavens opened in such an extraordinary manner as Stephen, and thus behold the Son of Man standing at the right hand of God (Acts 7:56), and are not permitted with Paul to enter the third heaven to behold Him there in close proximity (which, however, we shall be permitted to do after death), we may and must by faith behold "Jesus...crowned with glory and honour" (Heb. 2:9). Let faith therefore be for you the substance of things hoped for, the evidence of things not seen; and occupy yourself in beholding the glorified Jesus. It is not sufficient merely to observe the truths which are presented in Scripture by considering the letter of the Word, but one must penetratingly reflect upon the matters themselves. To only focus upon oneself, surrender by faith to God, do battle against sin, mortify the flesh, deny yourself, and seek for a quiet and peaceful conscience in the blood of Christ, are not sufficient in and of themselves. It is not sufficient to reflect only upon Christ's humiliation, seeking and beholding in His humiliation the atonement. To reflect only on these matters is the cause of much deadness, unbelief, and instability, and it also prevents spiritual growth as well as the proper glorification of Jesus. However, the consideration of Christ's humiliation in conjunction with His exaltation will yield much growth, comfort, and strength. That is the beginning of heaven, where the beholding of Christ in His glory will be the eternal joy and occupation of the elect according to the prayer of Christ, "Father, I will that they also, whom Thou hast given Me, be with Me where I am; that they may behold My glory, which Thou hast given Me" (John 17:24). To facilitate our engagement in this here below, He also reveals Himself as such here upon earth, according to His promise, to those who love Him. "He that loveth Me shall be loved of My Father, and I will love him, and will manifest Myself to him" (John 14:21). The promise will motivate one to seek; such revelations will stir up love; love will cause one to think upon Him; and meditation upon Him is rewarded by ever clearer revelations. Thus the one brings forth the other. Accustom yourselves to reflect upon this glorified Jesus, and let your meditation upon Him be enlarged in various respects.

First, view the glorified Jesus as God. Jesus our Mediator is not only a glorious and eminent man, but He is, "over all, God blessed for ever" (Rom. 9:5), "the true God" (1 John 5:20), "the brightness of His glory, and the express image of His person" (Heb. 1:3), "in the form of God," and "...equal with God" (Phil. 2:6). This presents an infinite dimension for reflection. When the soul is permitted to behold Jesus as the only and eternal God and may behold Him in His perfections, doing so one by one, becoming aware of His all-sufficiency, sovereign majesty, omnipotence, righteousness, glory, love, and mercy, beholding in each of them an infinity which cannot be perceived, much less comprehended by the insignificant intellect of a creature, the soul will lose itself. If one may do so, not by mere intellectual reflection, nor gathering it from hearsay, but rather with experiential vision, presently experiencing and tasting the efficacy and sweetness of these incomprehensible perfections; if one considers Him as Mediator in all this and that He manifests Himself as such, considering that "in Him dwelleth all the fullness of the Godhead bodily" (Col. 2:9), that is, truly and evidently; and if one may behold "His glory, the glory as of the only begotten of the Father" (John 1:14); then, I repeat, the soul will lose itself. Then, then is the soul fit and wholeheartedly inclined to give Him honor and glory and, while bowing before Him, to "speak of the glorious honour of His majesty" (Psa. 145:5).

Secondly, proceed and behold Jesus, crowned with honor and majesty, as Mediator amidst the glory bestowed upon Him. Paul speaks of this when he writes, "Wherefore God also hath highly exalted Him, and given Him a name which is above every name: that at the name of Jesus every knee should bow, of things in heaven, and things in earth, and things under the earth; and that every tongue should confess that Jesus Christ is Lord, to the glory of God the Father" (Phil. 2:9-11); "Being made so much better than the angels, as He hath by inheritance obtained a more excellent name than they" (Heb. 1:4). Of this glory Peter, James, and John saw but a small glimpse upon the holy mount, as is to be observed in Matthew 17:2-5. How much more glory has He now received, having conquered all, and being set down with His Father in His throne (Rev. 3:21)! There He is as conqueror, honored as the Savior of all His elect as being the One by whom the manifold wisdom, grace, righteousness, truth, etc., is revealed to angels and men. There He is declared to be and is "appointed heir of all things" (Heb. 1:2). Without exception He is heir of all things in heaven and upon earth, thus also of sun, moon, and stars, of rain, wind, hail, and snow, and of all animals upon earth, from the greatest animal to the very smallest ant. Yes, He is heir of all the ungodly and even of the devils, using them according to His will to the benefit of His fellowheirs and to the glory of His Father. He does not merely bear the title of heir, but is heir in very deed. He has been appointed to possess, use, and govern this His inheritance. "All power is given unto Me in heaven and in earth" (Mat. 28:18); "I shall give Thee the heathen for Thine inheritance, and the uttermost parts of the earth for Thy possession" (Psa. 2:8); "He shall have dominion also from sea to sea, and from the river unto the ends of the earth" (Psa. 72:8); "For He must reign, till He hath put all enemies under His feet" (1 Cor. 15:25); He is the great High Priest at the throne of grace (Heb. 4:14-16); He, as the only great Prophet "gave some, apostles; and some, prophets; and some, evangelists; and some, pastors and teachers; for the perfecting of the saints, for the work of the ministry, for the edifying of the body of Christ" (Eph. 4:11-12). Acknowledge Him to be such and give Him glory.

Thirdly, proceed by considering how all behave themselves towards Him. "All the angels of God worship Him" (Heb. 1:6). They are ready at His bidding, and He sends them forth to execute His commands (Rev. 1:1). Upon receiving a singular command from Him, they execute it as "a flaming fire" (Psa. 104:4). Take note also how the devils tremble before His glory. He has conquered them, having bruised their head, and in their opposition they are so under His control that they cannot even enter into the swine without His permission. Reflect upon the fact that all believers throughout the world look to Him only and meet in Him as the focal point in whom their view of faith culminates. Consider how they all flee to Him as their salvation, how they trust under His wings and humbly bow themselves before Him, exclaiming, "Glory and honor, and blessing, and power, be with the Lamb for ever and ever." When a believer may attentively reflect upon all these matters, how frequently His heart will then be ignited in love! He will rejoice over Christ's glory, and as it were hear the doxologies of the angels, the glorified saints, and believers upon earth. He will find his heart ready to join this singing multitude, jubilating with them, "Sing praises to God, sing praises: sing praises unto our King, sing praises. For God is the King of all the earth: sing ye praises with understanding. God reigneth over the heathen: God sitteth upon the throne of His holiness. The princes of the people are gathered together, even the people of the God of Abraham: for the shields of the earth belong unto God: He is greatly exalted" (Psa. 47:6-9).

In order to further stir up our souls to engage in this holy reflection, consider the following motives:

First, your mind cannot be void of thoughts, and the more glorious the object is upon which it reflects, the more the mind will delight itself in this and increase in perfection. Our understanding cannot focus on a more glorious object, however, than the glorified Jesus, "in whom are hid all the treasures of wisdom and knowledge" (Col. 2:3). That which is of the world is too base, unrefined, and defiled for your mind to be occupied with. Why would you focus your eye upon that which is nothing, that is, upon that which, if God is not to be observed in it, is not more than a shadow and a transitory vanity that harms, oppresses, and corrupts your soul? This glorified Jesus is beyond the reach of the children of this world, and therefore they gravitate towards occupying their minds with earthly objects and find some delight in doing so, there being nothing else for them. But believers, you who know and love Jesus, with what else should the eye of your understanding be occupied than in beholding the King in His beauty (Isa. 33:17)? If one begins to get a view of Him, all that is here below will of itself lose its luster and glory and it will be a light task to withdraw your love and attachment from the earth. Be ashamed that your eye so frequently turns away from Jesus. You will experience daily that this prevents your soul from being joyful and in a heavenlyminded frame, and that it will cause much darkness. It will cause the soul gradually to gravitate towards earthly things. Frequently much time and labor are required to be loosened once again from all these earthly affairs in order to have fellowship with Jesus in solitude and detachment from the world, and to view Him with the eyes of a dove.

Secondly, there is nothing more delightful for a child of God than to behold Jesus. It is God's desire that His children be joyful, for He frequently exhorts them to this, promising that He will meet "him that rejoiceth" (Isa. 64:5). There is nothing in which they find more inward and consistent joy, than in beholding the glorified Jesus. Therefore let your meditations of Him be sweet. After having sweet communion with the Lord, Moses had liberty to express the desire found in His soul, saying, "I beseech thee, show me Thy glory" (Exo. 33:18). The Lord was so good that He did not entirely deny him this request. He said to Moses that he was too weak to endure the luster of His glory. He would nevertheless show him His glory by causing His Name to pass by his countenance and by proclaiming that Name — which indeed occurred (Exo. 34:6).

Reflect upon this and judge whether there be anything more desirable and delightful for you than the following: Suppose that the Lord Jesus were to take you by the hand and lead you into His inner chamber, revealing to you all the heavenly mysteries pertaining to the work of redemption, revealing Himself to you in His divine perfections and in all the glory He has received as Mediator. Let us suppose furthermore that He would assure you with love that all His glory and fullness is for you and to your benefit, that the Father, Son, and Holy Spirit have been mutually engaged to exalt you to incomprehensible and unspeakable felicity, and to satisfy and encompass you both now and hereafter in eternity with His love and all-sufficiency. In your opinion, can there be anything more delightful than this? It was with this promise that the Lord

Jesus comforted and gladdened His disciples. "I will love him, and will manifest Myself to him. We will come unto him, and make Our abode with him" (John 14:21, 23). Add to this all the expressions you have read about this in God's Word, all the delightful accounts of the godly who have ever beheld the Lord, also what you have ever been privileged to experience yourself. I am certain that your heart will long for this with much desire and that you will grieve over having ever turned your eye from this delightful view, this being the reason why He has withdrawn Himself from your vision. May this therefore stir you up to look unto and focus on Him continually in His glory until you may have a clearer and closer view of Him and delight yourself in that view.

Thirdly, it is not only wonderful and delightful to behold Jesus crowned with honor and glory, but such beholding also has a sanctifying and soul-transforming effect. "But we all, with open face beholding as in a glass the glory of the Lord, are changed into the same image from glory to glory, even as by the Spirit of the Lord" (2 Cor. 3:18). As Moses' countenance shone after forty days of fellowship with the Lord on the mountain, those who may behold the glory of Christ will likewise shine forth with such a holy luster. This is indeed that which you long, pray, and sigh for. This you may attain to, however, by beholding Jesus' glory, for:

(1) The soul which is privileged to behold Him as such, will be so filled with sanctification and joy, that it neither desires nor thinks of any other delight. Therefore all that is desirous to the eye, all earthly beauty, and all that is sweet and delightful does not affect such a soul. These things have lost all their glory, effect, and sweetness, and there is no longer any love for them. The soul only delights in being near to the Lord.

(2) The soul, finding such delight and felicity in this beholding of Jesus, would not willingly lose this view. Since he knows that sin would cause this view to be obscured as by a cloud, he will be most careful to refrain from sin. In view of the promise, "Blessed are the pure in heart: for they shall see God" (Mat. 5:8), he will painstakingly take heed of his heart, seeking to keep it pure and undefiled, and thus always be in a frame in which to see God.

(3) He who beholds Jesus in His glory will behold in Him a worthiness of honor, service, and obedience. Such a view will cause the soul, without much argument or contemplation, to oblige itself with all willingness and readiness to be all for Him, and to do whatever is pleasing to Him.

(4) In viewing the perfections of the glorified Jesus, the soul will behold His holiness in all its eminence; not as at Horeb, where it

instilled fear and pronounced a curse upon transgressors, but in its essential nature and delightful beauty. Such a view will at once stir up all the affections of a lover of Jesus, causing a desire to be holy as He is holy.

(5) The soul who may behold the glorified Jesus will become aware of the eternal and perfect love of Jesus towards him, as well as of the preciousness of Jesus Himself. It cannot be otherwise but that the soul will thereby be excited to love Him in return. "We love Him, because He first loved us" (1 John 4:19). The nature of love is such that it will do all in its power to please the one who is loved, while at the same time attempting to be conformed to this beloved one. Behold, thus the one who may behold Jesus in His glory will be set aflame with love, which is the fountain, heart, and very essence of holiness.

(6) Beholding Him as such will cause the soul to be more intimately united with Jesus; and hence, the more virtue will go out from Him. The more the soul may receive the strength and influence of the Spirit, the less strength sin will have within him, and the more zealous he will be to be pleasing unto the Lord. From all this it may therefore convincingly be concluded that beholding the glorified Jesus has a sanctifying influence.

I know quite well that not everyone of the godly is privileged, with the three disciples, to behold Jesus in His glory on the mount, or with Paul, to be drawn into the third heaven. I also know that some who read this will become distressed, and sink down in discouragement, thinking, "How dark it is within me, how inferior is my spiritual life; never during my lifetime shall I attain to such a view of Jesus in His glory!" Know, however, that to be acquainted with these matters mentioned, to perceive a stirring of love, a desire, and a yearning for these things within as you hear or read concerning them, and to be distressed and sorrowful because you are so far from all this, are evidences of the principles of grace. Therefore such motions ought to stir us up to actively strive for this. If we persevere in prayer, waiting, hoping, and believing, we shall discover that the Lord will reveal Himself to such. Therefore, "Be of good courage, and He shall strengthen your heart" (Psa. 31:24).